STR▮▮▮▮S

Buckinghamshire
and Milton Keynes

First published in 1993 by

Philip's, a division of
Octopus Publishing Group Ltd
2-4 Heron Quays, London E14 4JP

Third colour edition 2005
First impression 2005

ISBN-10   0-540-08671-1 (pocket)
ISBN-13   978-0-540-08671-9 (pocket)

© Philip's 2005

This product includes mapping data licensed from
Ordnance Survey® with the permission of the
Controller of Her Majesty's Stationery Office.
© Crown copyright 2005. All rights reserved.
Licence number 100011710.

Printed and bound in Spain by
Cayfosa-Quebecor

Contents

III **Key to map symbols**

IV **Key to map pages**

VI **Route planning**

VIII **Administrative and Postcode boundaries**

1 **Street maps** at 2⅔ inches to 1 mile

214 **Index** of towns and villages

217 **Index** of streets, hospitals, industrial estates, railway
stations, schools, shopping centres and universities
and places of interest

Digital Data

The exceptionally high-quality mapping found in this atlas is available as digital data in TIFF
format, which is easily convertible to other bitmapped (raster) image formats.

The index is also available in digital form as a standard database table. It contains all the details
found in the printed index together with the National Grid reference for the map square in which
each entry is named.

For further information and to discuss your requirements, please contact Philip's on
020 7644 6932 or james.mann@philips-maps.co.uk

Key to map symbols

III

	Motorway with junction number (22a)
	Primary route – dual/single carriageway
	A road – dual/single carriageway
	B road – dual/single carriageway
	Minor road – dual/single carriageway
	Other minor road – dual/single carriageway
	Road under construction
	Tunnel, covered road
	Rural track, private road or narrow road in urban area
	Gate or obstruction to traffic (restrictions may not apply at all times or to all vehicles)
	Path, bridleway, byway open to all traffic, road used as a public path
	Pedestrianised area
DY7	**Postcode boundaries**
	County and unitary authority boundaries
	Railway, tunnel, railway under construction
	Tramway, tramway under construction
	Miniature railway
Walsall	**Railway station**
	Private railway station
	London Underground station
	Tram stop, tram stop under construction
	Bus, coach station

◆	**Ambulance station**
◆	**Coastguard station**
◆	**Fire station**
◆	**Police station**
✚	**Accident and Emergency entrance to hospital**
H	**Hospital**
✛	**Place of worship**
i	**Information Centre** (open all year)
	Shopping Centre
P P&R	**Parking, Park and Ride**
PO	**Post Office**
Ⅹ	**Camping site**
	Caravan site
►	**Golf course**
✕	**Picnic site**
Prim Sch	**Important buildings, schools, colleges, universities and hospitals**
	Built up area
	Woods
River Medway	**Water name**
	River, weir, stream
	Canal, lock, tunnel
	Water
	Tidal water
Church	**Non-Roman antiquity**
ROMAN FORT	**Roman antiquity**
87 24	**Adjoining page indicators and overlap bands**

Abbr	Full	Abbr	Full	Abbr	Full
Acad	**Academy**	Inst	**Institute**	Recn Gd	**Recreation Ground**
Allot Gdns	**Allotments**	Ct	**Law Court**		
Cemy	**Cemetery**	L Ctr	**Leisure Centre**	Resr	**Reservoir**
C Ctr	**Civic Centre**	LC	**Level Crossing**	Ret Pk	**Retail Park**
CH	**Club House**	Liby	**Library**	Sch	**School**
Coll	**College**	Mkt	**Market**	Sh Ctr	**Shopping Centre**
Crem	**Crematorium**	Meml	**Memorial**	TH	**Town Hall/House**
Ent	**Enterprise**	Mon	**Monument**	Trad Est	**Trading Estate**
Ex H	**Exhibition Hall**	Mus	**Museum**	Univ	**University**
Ind Est	**Industrial Estate**	Obsy	**Observatory**	W Twr	**Water Tower**
IRB Sta	**Inshore Rescue Boat Station**	Pal	**Royal Palace**	Wks	**Works**
		PH	**Public House**	YH	**Youth Hostel**

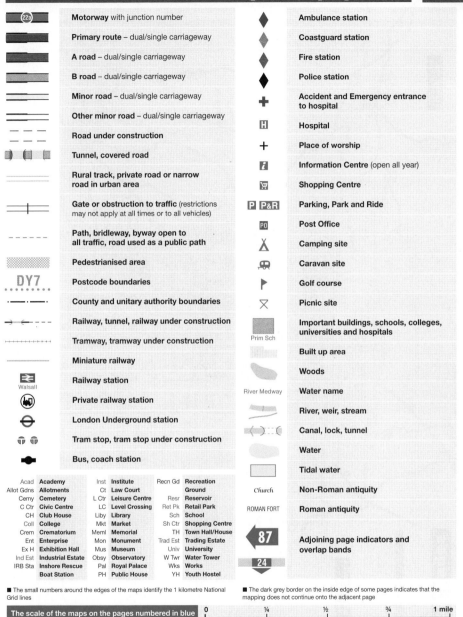

■ The small numbers around the edges of the maps identify the 1 kilometre National Grid lines

■ The dark grey border on the inside edge of some pages indicates that mapping does not continue onto the adjacent page

The scale of the maps on the pages numbered in blue is 4.2 cm to 1 km • 2⅔ inches to 1 mile • 1: 23810

0	¼	½	¾	1 mile
0	250 m	500 m	750 m	1 kilometre

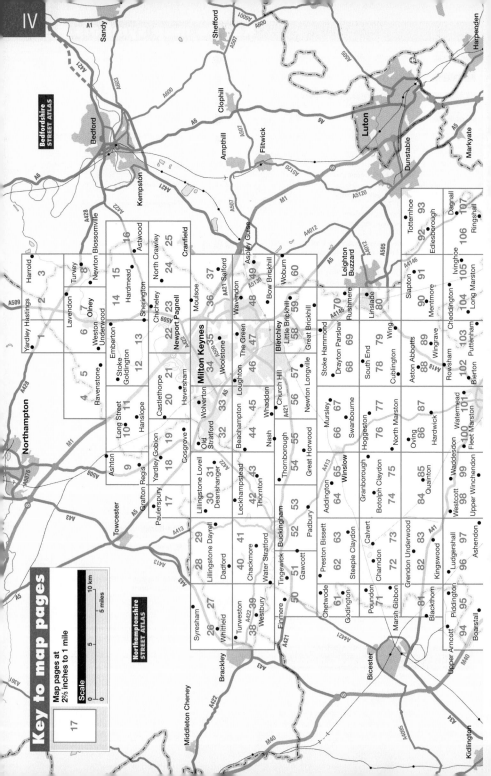

IV

Key to map pages

Map pages at
2½ inches to 1 mile

Scale

| 0 | 5 | 10 km |
| 0 | 5 miles |

17

Bedfordshire
STREET ATLAS

Northamptonshire
STREET ATLAS

Hertfordshire STREET ATLAS

London STREET ATLAS

Surrey STREET ATLAS

Oxfordshire STREET ATLAS

Berkshire STREET ATLAS

St Albans
Redbourn
Hemel Hempstead
Watford
Radlett
Bushey
Harrow
Ruislip
Southall
Hounslow
Hayes
West Drayton
Harmondsworth
Feltham
Ashford
Staines
Egham
Kings Langley
Abbots Langley
Rickmansworth
Brentford
Ealing

Felden 146
Bovingdon
Flaunden 156
Cheries
Chorleywood 167
Maple Cross 178
South Harefield 190
Uxbridge 201
Yiewsley 208
West Drayton 213
Stanwell

Aldbury 120
Little Gaddesden 121
Northchurch 134
Berkhamsted 135
Ashley Green 144
Botley 145
Chesham 154
Latimer 155
Amersham
Amersham Old Town 164
Winchmore Hill 165
Chalfont St Giles 166
Seer Green 176
Chalfont St Peter 177
Gerrards Cross 188
Higher Denham 189
Iver Heath 199
Iver 200
Slough 205
Windsor 206
Old Windsor 207
Datchet 211
Colnbrook 212
Boveney 209

Wilstone Green 118
Tring 119
Wigginton
Hastoe 132
Cholesbury 133
St Leonards
Lee Common 142
Chartridge 143
Great Missenden 152
Little Missenden 153
Cryers Hill 162
Hazlemere 163
Loudwater 174
Beaconsfield 175
Flackwell Heath 185
Farnham Common 187
Hedgerley 186
Wooburn Common 197
Burnham 198
Eton Wick 204
Maidenhead 203
Clewer Green

Aston Clinton 116
Weston Turville 117
Wendover 130
Ellesborough 131
Wendover Dean 140
Little Hampden 141
Prestwood 150
Speen 151
Naphill 160
West Wycombe 161
High Wycombe 172
Booker 173
Marlow 183
Little Marlow 184
Cookham 196
Cookham Rise 195
Taplow 194
Bray 202

Aylesbury 115
Stone 114
Bishopstone
Ford 128
Little Kimble 129
Longwick 138
Princes Risborough 139
Lacey Green 149
Rout's Green 148
Bledlow Ridge 159
Stokenchurch 158
Lane End 171
Frieth 170
Marlow Bottom 182
Lower Woodend
Bisham 193
Hurley 193
Mill End 192
Henley-on-Thames

Brill 110
Upper Pollicott 111
Chilton
Chearsley
Cuddington
Westlington 112 113
Haddenham 126 127
Kingsey
Thame
Henton 137
Chinnor 147
Crowell
Lewknor 157
Christmas Common 168 169
Turville
Fawley 180
Maidensgrove 179
Hambleden 181
Lower Assendon 191
Sonning Common

Horton-cum-Studley 108 109
Oakley
Worminghall 122 123
Ickford
Shabbington
Tiddington
Milton Common 136
Wheatley
Long Crendon 124 125

Oxford
Abingdon
Didcot
Wallingford
Goring
Reading
Twyford
Wokingham
Binfield
Bracknell

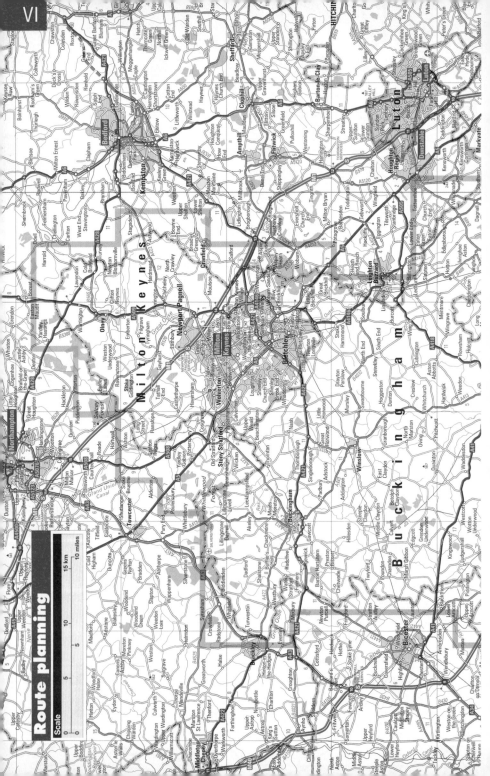

Route planning

Scale

15 km

10 miles

5

10

5

0

0

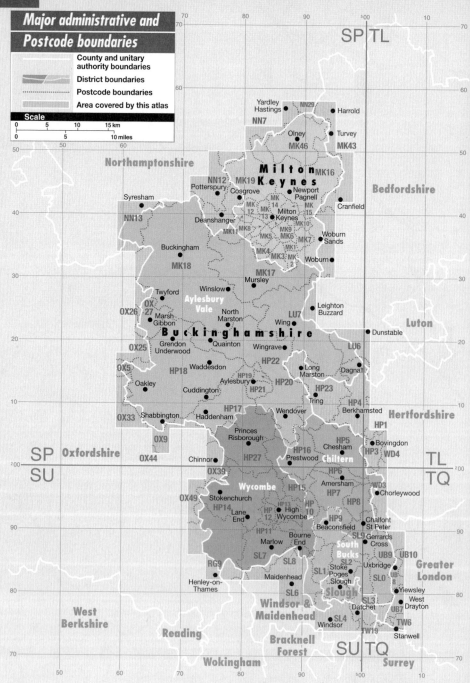

VIII

Major administrative and Postcode boundaries

County and unitary authority boundaries
District boundaries
Postcode boundaries
Area covered by this atlas

Scale
0   5   10   15 km
0   5   10 miles

SP TL

Northamptonshire

Bedfordshire

Yardley Hastings
NN29
Harrold
NN7
Olney
Turvey
MK46
MK43

Syresham

NN12
Potterspury
MK19
Cosgrove
Milton Keynes
MK16
Cranfield

NN13
MK14
MK13
Newport Pagnell
MK
12
MK8
MK11
Deanshanger
Milton Keynes
MK15

Woburn Sands

MK5
MK9
MK6
MK7
MK10
MK1

Buckingham
MK4
MK3
MK2
Woburn

MK18
MK17
Mursley

Twyford
Winslow
Leighton Buzzard

OX 27
Aylesbury Vale
North Marston
LU7
Wing

OX26
Marsh Gibbon
Dunstable

Buckinghamshire
Quainton
Wingrave
LU6

OX25
Grendon Underwood
HP22
Long Marston
Dagnall

OX5
Waddesdon
HP19
HP20
HP23
HP4

Oakley
Aylesbury
Tring
Berkhamsted
Hertfordshire

OX33
Shabbington
Haddenham
HP17
Wendover
HP1

OX9
Princes Risborough
HP5
Chesham
Bovingdon

SP
Oxfordshire
OX44
Chinnor
HP27
HP16
Prestwood
Chiltern
HP3
WD4

SU
OX39
HP6
TL

OX49
Stokenchurch
Wycombe
HP15
Amersham
WD3
Chorleywood
TQ

HP14
Lane End
HP13
HP10
High Wycombe
HP7
HP8

HP12
HP9
Chalfont St Peter

Beaconsfield
SL9
Gerrards Cross

HP11
Bourne End
South Bucks
UB9
UB10

Marlow
SL7
SL8
SL2
Uxbridge
Greater London

RG9
Stoke Poges
SL1
SL0
UB7
UB8

Henley-on-Thames
Maidenhead
Slough
SL3
Yiewsley
West Drayton

SL6
Windsor & Maidenhead
Datchet
UB7
TW6

Windsor & Maidenhead
SL4
Windsor
TW19
Stanwell

West Berkshire

Reading

Bracknell Forest

SU TQ

Wokingham

Surrey

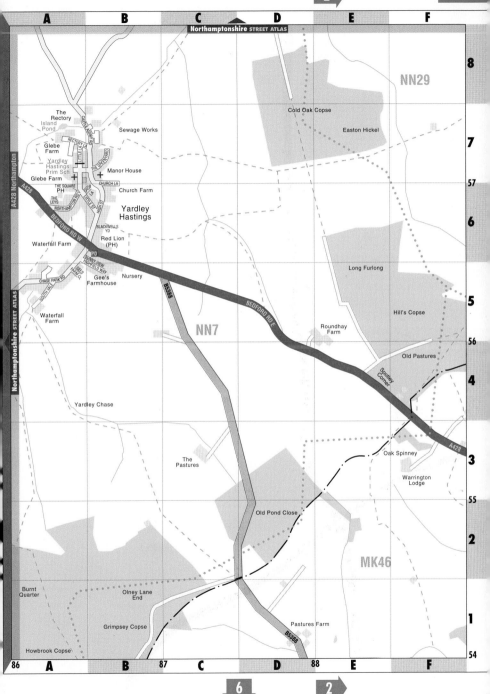

Northamptonshire STREET ATLAS

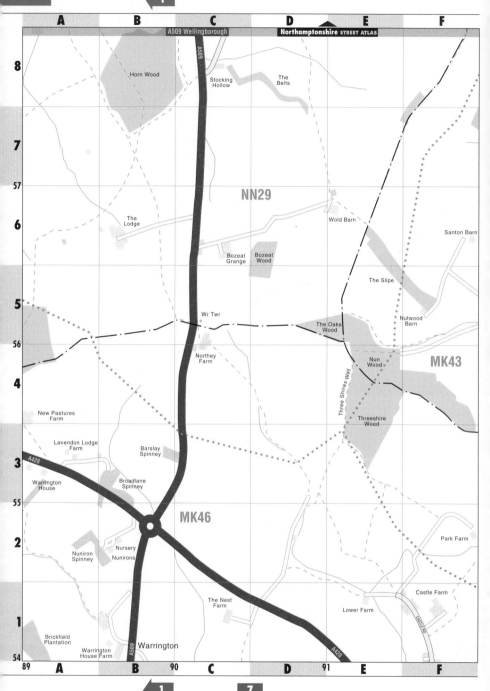

A509 Wellingborough

Northamptonshire STREET ATLAS

Horn Wood

Stocking
Hollow

The
Belts

NN29

The
Lodge

Wold Barn

Santon Barn

Bozeat
Grange

Bozeat
Wood

The Slipe

Nutwood
Barn

Wr Twr

The Oaks
Wood

Nun
Wood

MK43

Northey
Farm

New Pastures
Farm

Three Shires Way

Threeshire
Wood

Lavendon Lodge
Farm

Barslay
Spinney

A428

Broadlane
Spinney

Warrington
House

MK46

Park Farm

Nuniron
Spinney

Nursery

Nunirons

Castle Farm

The Nest
Farm

Lower Farm

CASTLE RD

Brickfield
Plantation

Warrington
House Farm

A509

Warrington

A428

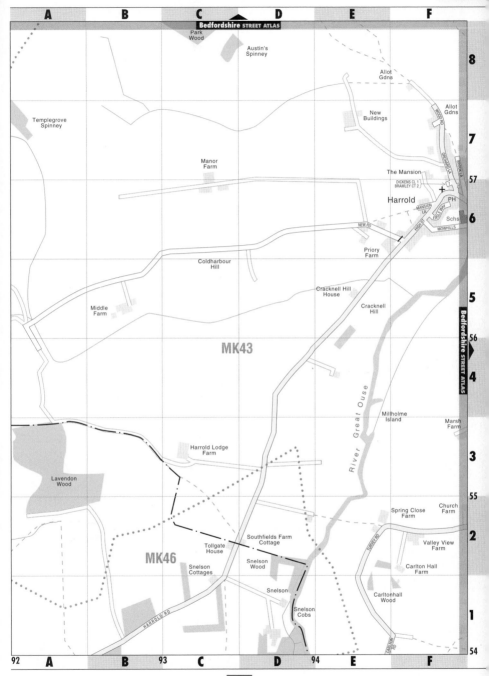

Bedfordshire STREET ATLAS

8

Park
Wood

Austin's
Spinney

Allot
Gdns

7

Templegrove
Spinney

New
Buildings

Allot
Gdns

WOOD RD

ORCHARD LA

PARK LA

Manor
Farm

The Mansion

57

DICKENS CL 1
BRAMLEY CT 2

Harrold

PH

MANSION
LA

HIGH ST

HOYT WAY

NEW RD

Schs

6

Coldharbour
Hill

Priory
Farm

MOWHILLS

Cracknell Hill
House

Cracknell
Hill

5

Middle
Farm

MK43

56

River Great Ouse

4

Millholme
Island

Marsh
Farm

Harrold Lodge
Farm

3

Lavendon
Wood

55

Spring Close
Farm

Church
Farm

Tollgate
House

Southfields Farm
Cottage

Valley View
Farm

2

MK46

Snelson
Cottages

Snelson
Wood

Carlton Hall
Farm

TURVEY RD

Snelson

Carltonhall
Wood

HARROLD RD

Snelson
Cobs

1

CARLTON RD

92   A   B   93   C   D   94   E   F   54

Bedfordshire STREET ATLAS

8

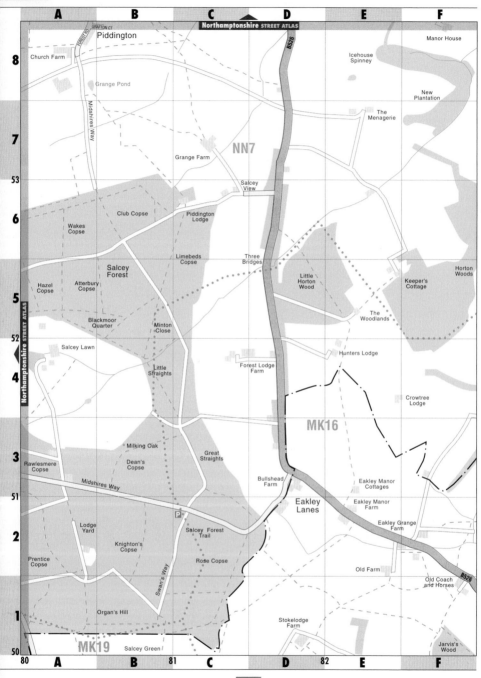

GRAFTON CT

Piddington

Church Farm

FOREST RD

Manor House

Icehouse
Spinney

New
Plantation

Grange Pond

Midshires Way

The
Menagerie

Grange Farm

NN7

Salcey
View

Club Copse

Wakes
Copse

Piddington
Lodge

Limebeds
Copse

Three
Bridges

Horton
Woods

Salcey
Forest

Little
Horton
Wood

Keeper's
Cottage

Hazel
Copse

Atterbury
Copse

Blackmoor
Quarter

Minton
Close

The
Woodlands

Salcey Lawn

Little
Sfraights

Hunters Lodge

Forest Lodge
Farm

Crowtree
Lodge

MK16

Milking Oak

Great
Straights

Rawlesmere
Copse

Dean's
Copse

Midshires Way

Bullshead
Farm

Eakley Manor
Cottages

Eakley
Lanes

Eakley Manor
Farm

Lodge
Yard

P

Salcey Forest
Trail

Eakley Grange
Farm

Knighton's
Copse

Rose Copse

Prentice
Copse

Swan's Way

Old Farm

Old Coach
and Horses

B526

Organ's Hill

Stokelodge
Farm

MK19

Salcey Green

Jarvis's
Wood

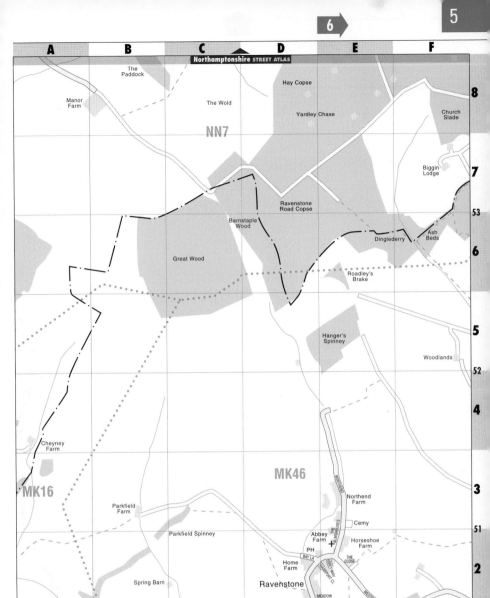

The Paddock

Manor Farm

The Wold

Hay Copse

Yardley Chase

Church Slade

NN7

Biggin Lodge

Ravenstone Road Copse

53

Barnstaple Wood

Dinglederry

Ash Beds

Great Wood

Roadley's Brake

Hanger's Spinney

Woodlands

52

Cheyney Farm

MK46

MK16

Parkfield Farm

Northend Farm

Cemy

Parkfield Spinney

Abbey Farm

Horseshoe Farm

51

PH

THE CLOSE

BAY LA

Home Farm

MEADOW CT

Spring Barn

Ravenstone

WESTON RD

Yew Tree Farm

Mannings Farm

Lower Farm House

Sheep Dip

B526

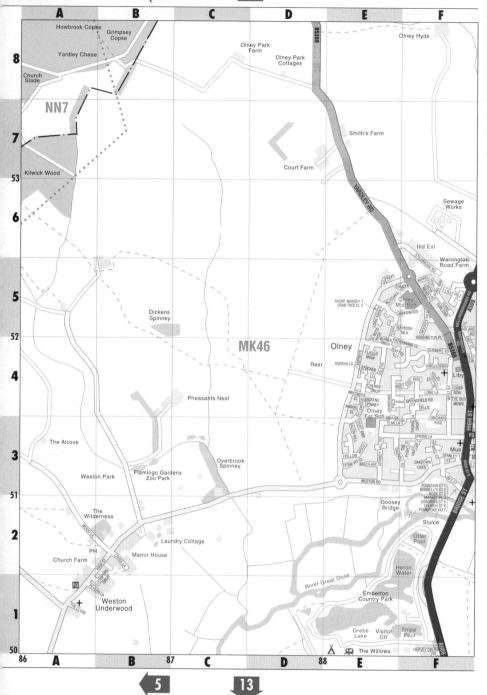

8

Howbrook Copse
Grimpsey Copse
Yardley Chase

Olney Park Farm
Olney Park Cottages

Olney Hyde

Church Slade

NN7

7

Smith's Farm

Kilwick Wood

53

Court Farm

6

Sewage Works

Ind Est

Warrington Road Farm

YARDLEY RD

B5388

A509

5

SHORT MASSEY 1
CRAB TREE CL 2

Olney Mid Sch

Dickens Spinney

52

MK46

Olney

Resr

OVERHILLS

Liby

4

Pheasants Nest

Olney Fst Sch

The Alcove

3

Overbrook Spinney

Mus

Weston Park

Flamingo Gardens Zoo Park

WESTON RD

51

Goosey Bridge

HIGH ST

PO

The Wilderness

Sluice

2

Laundry Cottage

Otter Pool

PH

Manor House

BRIDGE ST

Church Farm

Heron Water

PO

River Great Ouse

Weston Underwood

Emberton Country Park

1

Grebe Lake

Visitor Ctr

Snipe Pool

A509

50

The Willows

HARVEY DR

86 A B 87 C D 88 E F

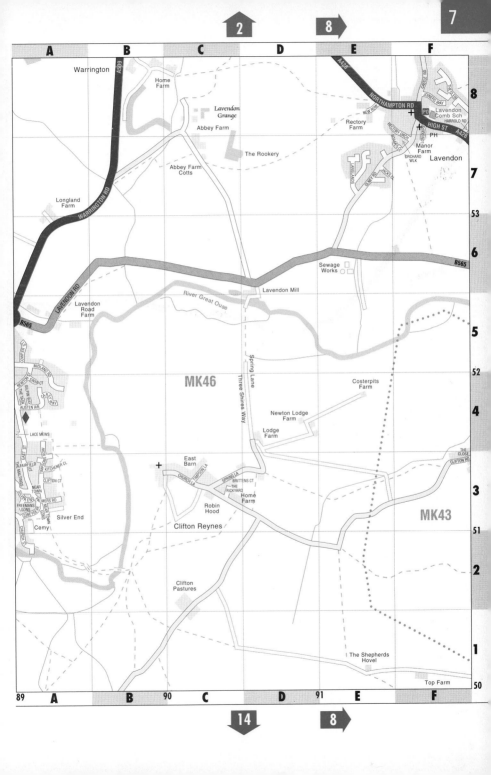

7
3

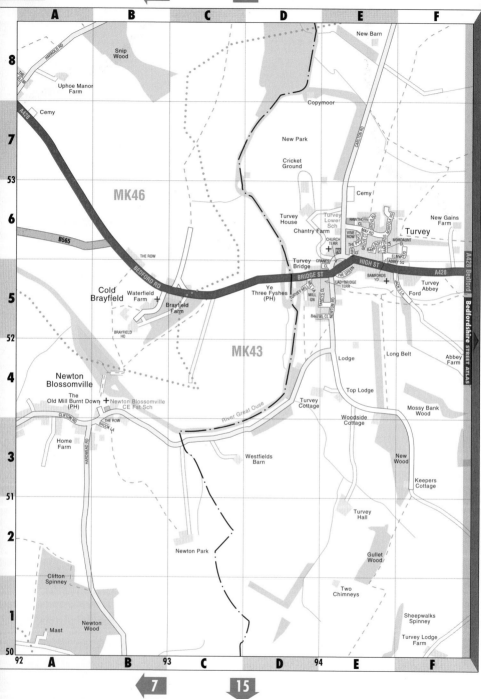

A428 Bedford **Bedfordshire STREET ATLAS**

8

New Barn

Snip Wood

THE CLEAR

HARROLD RD

Uphoe Manor Farm

Copymoor

7

A428

Cemy

New Park

CARLTON RD

53

Cricket Ground

Cemy

New Gains Farm

MK46

6

Turvey House

Turvey Lower Sch

Chantry Farm

HAWTHORN CL

Turvey

VINE ROW

MAY RD

CHURCH RD

MORDAUNT

CHURCH TERR

THE

B565

BEDFORD RD

THE ROW

Turvey Bridge

CRANES CL

ELMWS

ABBEY SQ

BRIDGE ST

THE GREEN

HIGH ST

A428

5

Cold Brayfield

Waterfield Farm

Brayfield Farm

Ye Three Fyshes (PH)

TURVEY MILL

MILL GN

LADYBRIDGE TERR

BAMFORDS YD

JACKS CL

Turvey Abbey

Ford

BAKERS CL

52

BRAYFIELD HO

MK43

Lodge

Long Belt

Abbey Farm

4

Newton Blossomville

The Old Mill Burnt Down (PH)

Newton Blossomville CE Fst Sch

Top Lodge

Turvey Cottage

Woodside Cottage

Mossy Bank Wood

CLIFTON RD

HARDMEAD RD

THE ROW

BROOM LA

River Great Ouse

New Wood

3

Home Farm

Westfields Barn

Keepers Cottage

51

Turvey Hall

2

Newton Park

Gullet Wood

Clifton Spinney

Two Chimneys

Sheepwalks Spinney

1

Mast

Newton Wood

Turvey Lodge Farm

50

7
15

A508 Northampton **Northamptonshire** STREET ATLAS

A B C D E F

CHAPEL LA
Mus P
CANALSIDE
SHUTLANGER RD
CHURCH LA
BAKERS LEAS RD
Sch
Stoke Bruerne
Rookery Farm
Sewage Works
Lock

Ashton Rd
Stoke Rd
St Michael's
Vale Farm
The Old Crown (PH)
Ashton
HARTWILL RD
COSS MILL

8

Towing Path
Locks

7

Park Farm
Rectory Farm
49

Lock
Lower Lock Barn
Grand Union Canal Wlk
Stoke Park Pavilions
NN7
Sewage Works
6

Weir
Weir
Grand Union Canal
Stoke Bruerne Park
Bozenham Cottage
Mill Farm
BOZENHAM
5

River Tove
Towing Path
48

NN12
4

MK19
Brick Kiln Farm
River Tove
3

47

CHURCH LA
Glebe Farm
Alderton
The Manor
SPRING LA
Manor Farm
NORTHAMPTON RD
THE LANE
CHURCH LA
Grafton Regis
2

White Hart (PH)
Paddocks Farm
Grafton Lodge
Towing Path
1

A508
Fiery Furze
46

74 A 75 B C 76 D E F

Northamptonshire STREET ATLAS

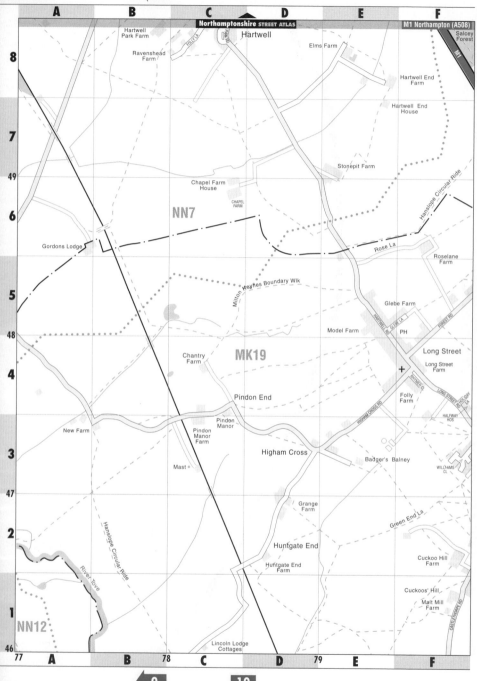

Salcey Forest

Hartwell Park Farm

Hartwell

Ravenshead Farm

Elms Farm

Hartwell End Farm

Hartwell End House

Stonepit Farm

Chapel Farm House

NN7

CHAPEL FARM

Hanslope Circular Ride

Gordons Lodge

Rose La

Roselane Farm

Milton Keynes Boundary Wlk

Glebe Farm

Model Farm

PH

Long Street

Chantry Farm

MK19

Long Street Farm

Pindon End

Folly Farm

HALFWAY HOS

New Farm

Pindon Manor Farm

Pindon Manor

Higham Cross

Badger's Balney

WILLIAMS CL

Mast

Grange Farm

Green End La

Hanslope Circular Ride

Huntgate End

Cuckoo Hill Farm

River Tove

Huntgate End Farm

Cuckoos' Hill

Malt Mill Farm

NN12

Lincoln Lodge Cottages

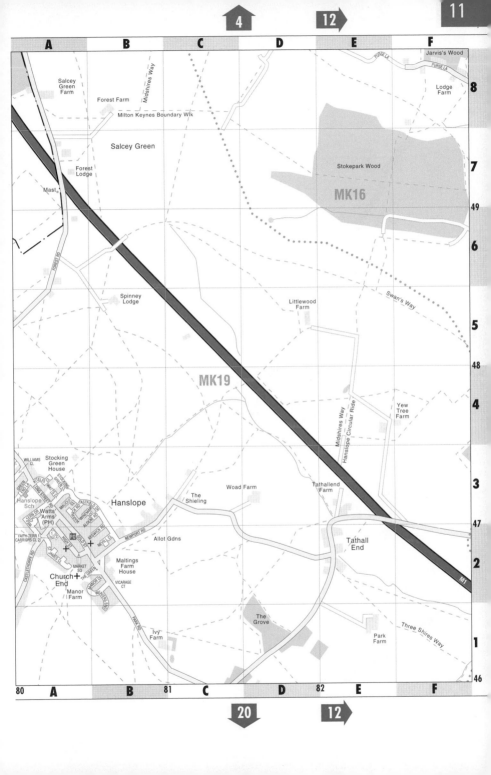

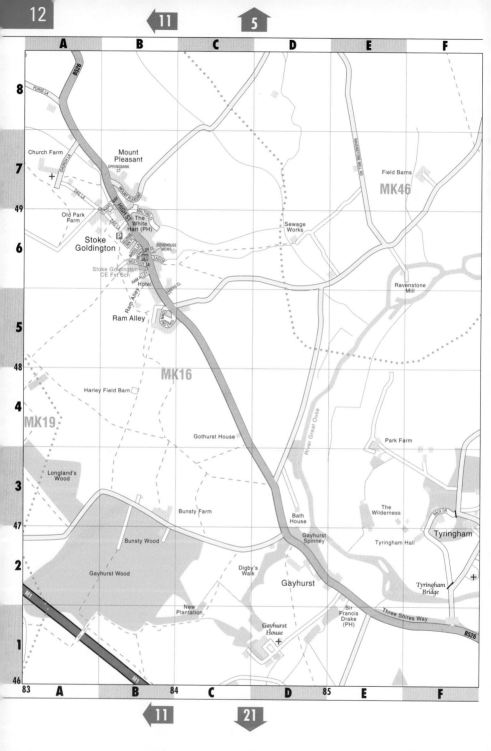

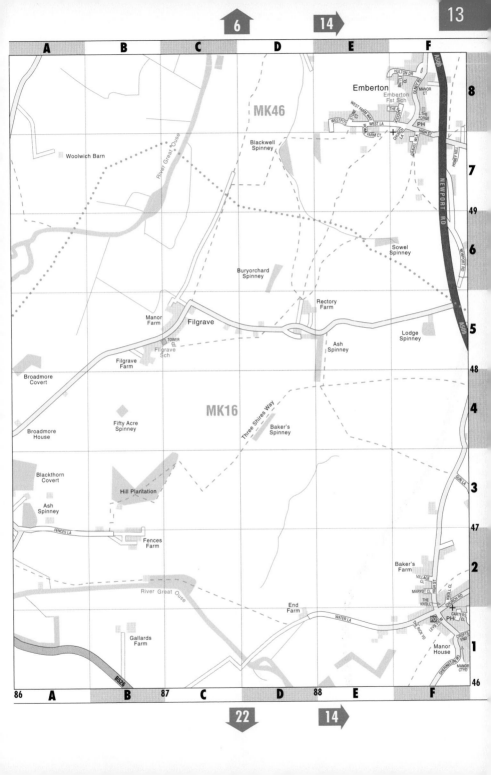

A B C D E F

8

7

49

6

5

48

4

47

3

2

1

46

86 A B 87 C D 88 E F

MK46

MK16

Emberton

Emberton
Fst Sch

Woolwich Barn

Blackwell
Spinney

HULTON DR
BATTLE CL
OLIVER RD
MANOR
CT
THE
FORGE
WEST FARM DR
WEST CL
THE
WESTFIELD
WESTPITS
WEST LA
HOME
FARM CT
DRAKE WY
HIGH ST
CHURCH
LA
PH

Sowel
Spinney

Buryorchard
Spinney

Rectory
Farm

Manor
Farm

Filgrave

TOWER
CL

Filgrave
Sch

Filgrave
Farm

Ash
Spinney

Lodge
Spinney

Broadmore
Covert

Fifty Acre
Spinney

Three Shires Way

Baker's
Spinney

Broadmore
House

Blackthorn
Covert

Hill Plantation

Ash
Spinney

FENCES LA

Fences
Farm

Baker's
Farm

VILLAGE
CL
MARYOT CL
THE
KNOLL
CARTERS
CL
PH
PO
THE HOLT RD
LEYS RD
OLD HIGH RD
CROFTS
END
MANOR
CTYD
SHERINGTON RD

End
Farm

WATER LA

Gallards
Farm

Manor
House

River Great Ouse

River Great Ouse

B526

NEWPORT RD

A509

A509

NEWPORT RD

TILLBROOK

DUN LA

13
7

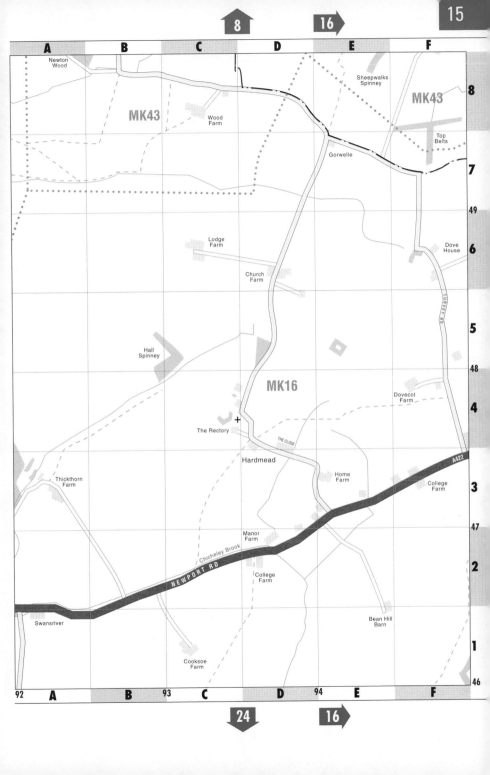

8
16

A   B   C   D   E   F

Newton
Wood

MK43

8

MK43

Sheepwalks
Spinney

Wood
Farm

Top
Belts

Gorwelle

7

49

Lodge
Farm

Dove
House

6

Church
Farm

TURVEY RD

5

Hall
Spinney

48

MK16

Dovecot
Farm

4

The Rectory

THE CLOSE

Hardmead

A422

Home
Farm

College
Farm

3

Thickthorn
Farm

47

Manor
Farm

Chicheley Brook

2

College
Farm

NEWPORT RD

Swansriver

Bean Hill
Barn

1

Cooksoe
Farm

46

92   A   B   93   C   D   94   E   F

24
16

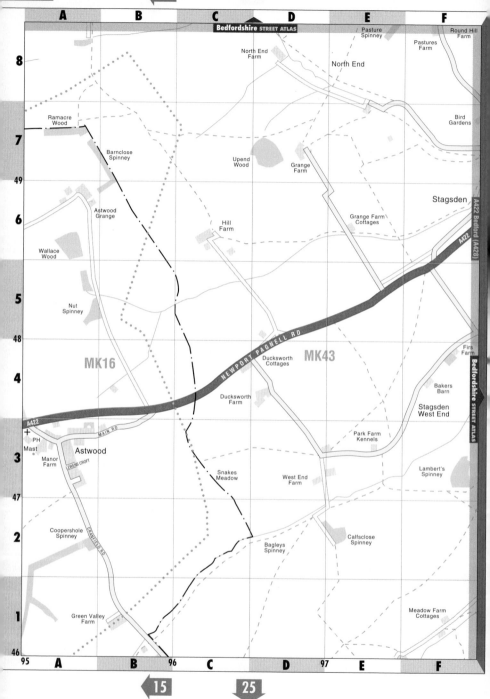

Bedfordshire STREET ATLAS

Pasture Spinney

Round Hill Farm

North End Farm

Pastures Farm

North End

Ramacre Wood

Bird Gardens

Barnclose Spinney

Upend Wood

Grange Farm

Stagsden

Astwood Grange

Hill Farm

Grange Farm Cottages

A422 Bedford (A428)

Wallace Wood

Nut Spinney

NEWPORT PAGNELL RD

MK43

Firs Farm

MK16

Ducksworth Cottages

Bakers Barn

A422

Ducksworth Farm

Stagsden West End

PH

Mast

MAIN RD

Astwood

Park Farm Kennels

Lambert's Spinney

Manor Farm

LEVENS CROFT

Snakes Meadow

West End Farm

Coopershole Spinney

CRANFIELD RD

Calfsclose Spinney

Bagleys Spinney

Meadow Farm Cottages

Green Valley Farm

Bedfordshire STREET ATLAS

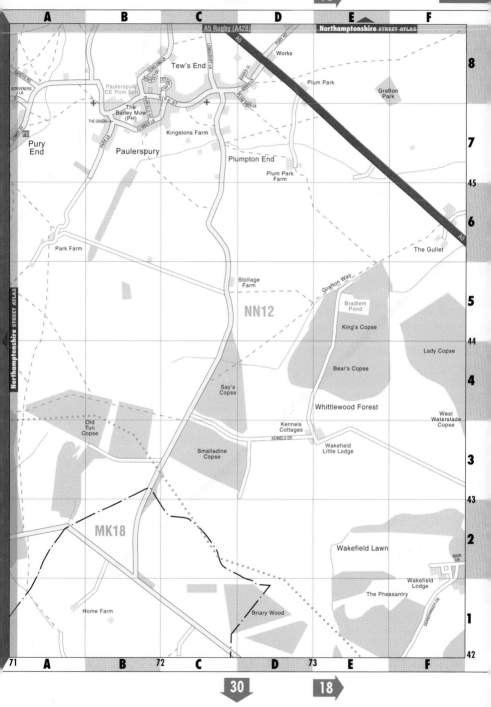

A5 Rugby (A428)

Northamptonshire STREET ATLAS

A B C D E F

8

Works

Tew's End

Plum Park

Grafton Park

Paulerspury CE Prim Sch

Kingstons Farm

The Barley Mow (PH)

THE GREEN

7

Pury End

Paulerspury

Plumpton End

45

Plum Park Farm

6

The Gullet

Park Farm

Grafton Way

Stollage Farm

Bradlem Pond

5

NN12

King's Copse

Lady Copse

44

Bear's Copse

4

Say's Copse

Whittlewood Forest

West Waterslade Copse

Old Tun Copse

Kennels Cottages

KENNELS DR

Smalladine Copse

Wakefield Little Lodge

3

43

MK18

Wakefield Lawn

2

MAIN DR

Wakefield Lodge

Home Farm

The Pheasantry

Briary Wood

1

42

71 A B 72 C D 73 E F

Northamptonshire STREET ATLAS

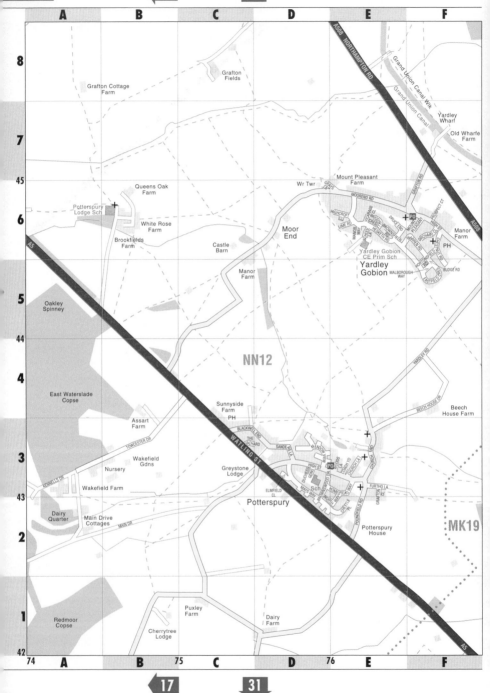

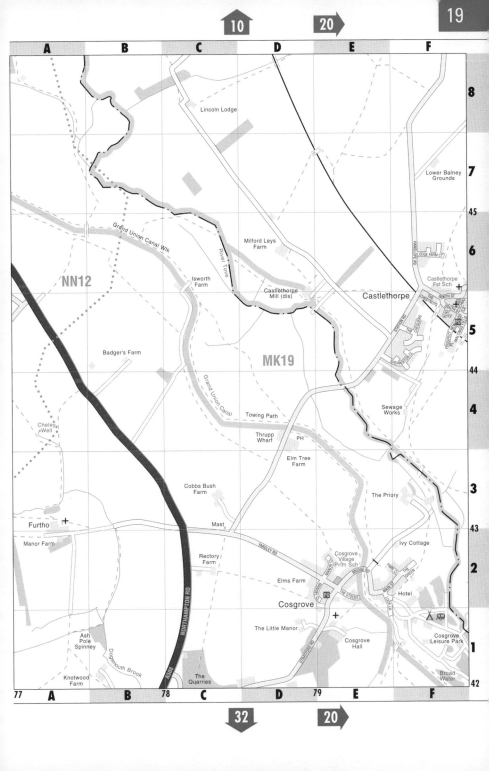

19
11

	A	B	C	D	E	F

8

Manor Farm

Mast

Park House

Long Plantation

Narrow Leys

Swan's Way
Midshires Way

MK16

Hanger Quarter

7

Hanslope Park

Bullington End

45

Hanslope Lodge

Glenmore Farm

New Buildings

6

THRUSH CL

Castlethorpe

Leamington Farm

NORTH ST

COULAR ST

5

Maltings Farm

WOLVERTON RD

Pineham Farm

Swan's Way
Midshires Way

44

MK19

Pikes Farm

Field House Farm

4

Water Tower

Fox Covert

Otley Farm

3

Lodge Farm
Bsns Ctr

Haythorn Spinney

Crossroads Farm

43

THE STABLES

Haversham

The Greyhound (PH)

HIGH ST

2

COLLARD'S TRDE

TITHAM DR

APPELL AVE

BROOKFIELD RD

MANOR DR

THE CRESCENT

Haversham Fst Sch

Haversham Manor

BEECH TREE CL

HAVERSHAM RD

1

River Great Ouse

MK12

P

Cosgrove Leisure Park

42

MK13

80	A	B	81	C	D	82	E	F

19
33

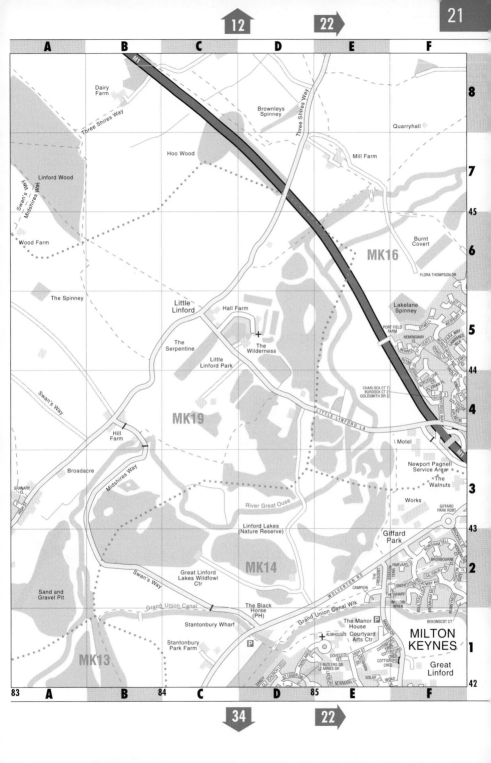

21
13

	A	B	C	D	E	F

8

Quarryhall Farm

B526

Ash Spinney

Chicheley Hill

7

Inn Farm

Lathbury

Bridge House

Sherington Bridge

SHERINGTON RD

45

THE CLOSE

INN FARM

CHURCH LA

NORTHAMPTON RD

Lathbury Park

New Wood Farm

Works

6

Kickles Farm

FLORA THOMPSON DR

THOMAS DR

Bury Field

River Great Ouse

Woad Farm

5

Lakes Lane Farm

SHAKESPEARE CL

LEWIS CL

Portfields Sch

LAKES LA

NEWPORT PAGNELL

MK16

NORTH SQ

MILL ST

Cemy

1 POLLYS YD
2 OUSEBANK ST

Tickford Abbey

44

CHARLES WAY

QUEENS AVE

COOPERS CT

WINDSOR AVE

HIGH ST

ST JOHN ST

CHURCH PAS

Liby

CASTLE ST

LAGONDA

4

1 MORRIS WLK
2 COLLINS WLK

CARLYLE CL

KIPLING DR

PORTFIELDS RD

WOLVERTON RD

COURTHOUSE MEWS

TH

Sch

BURY ST

LOVAT ST

CHURCHHOUSE

CHURCH VIEW

Works

Tickford End

TICKFORD ST

CHICHELEY ST

BUCKINGHAM

ALMOND CL

CALDECOTE

ST PAULS YD

1 STATION RD
2 BEACONSFIELD PL

DERWENT

RIBBLE

MEDWAY

NORTH CRAWLEY RD

BRIDGE CT

3

HILL VIEW

WHITETHORN

SHIPLEY RD

GROVE

HIGHWOOD CL

FRADERICA COTTS

BARNSBURY GDNS

The Green

WELTON RD

TEIGN CL

THAMES

DEBEN

THORNE CL

Lovat Mid Sch

Riverside Fst Sch

Cemy

L Ctr

SAMUEL CL

Ind Est

43

CARRINGTON RD
1 SANDRINGHAM CT
2 BALMORAL CT

Ousedale Sch

Sch

The Kingfisher Ctr

GLADSTONE

River Ouzel or Lovat

B526 LONDON RD

A509

2

MK14

Ind Est

SYCAMORE GDNS

TONGWELL LA

Sewage Works

A422

CALDECOTE LA

Caldecotemill Bridge

Newport Stables

1

Giffard Park Comb Sch

Giffard Park

WEDGWOOD

Blakelands

Tongwell Lake

TA Ctr

KNEBWORTH GATE

Ind Est

MONKS WAY

Ind Est

A422

M1

Caldecote

Caldecote Farm

Caldecote Mill

Weirs

42

MARLE STONE CT

OVERSLEY CT

DELAWARE DR

MICHIGAN DR

MK15

	A	B	C	D	E	F

86 · 87 · 88

21
35

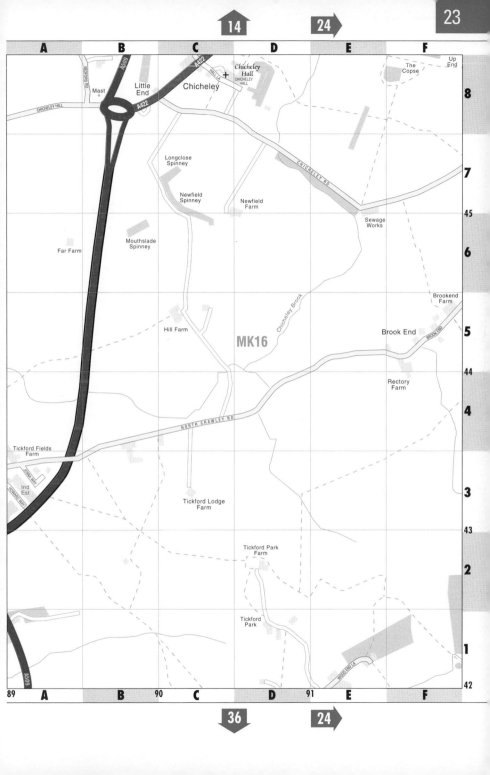

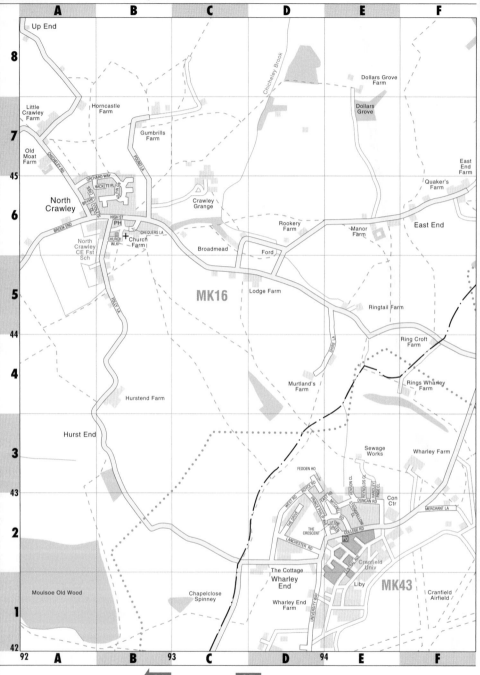

Up End

Little Crawley Farm

Old Moat Farm

Horncastle Farm

Gumbrills Farm

Chicheley Brook

Dollars Grove Farm

Dollars Grove

ORCHARD WAY

HACKETT PL

POUND LA

North Crawley

HIGH ST
PH

CHEQUERS LA

CHURCH WLK

Church Farm

North Crawley CE Fst Sch

BROOK END

Crawley Grange

Broadmead

Ford

Rookery Farm

Manor Farm

East End

Quaker's Farm

East End Farm

MK16

Lodge Farm

Ringtail Farm

Ring Croft Farm

FOLLY LA

SHIRE LA

Murtland's Farm

Rings Wharley Farm

Hurstend Farm

Hurst End

Moulsoe Old Wood

Chapelclose Spinney

Sewage Works

FEDDEN HO

WEST RD

ROPER RD

EAST RD

THE GROVE

LANCHESTER RD

THE CRESCENT

PRINCE RD

MITRE RD

PLOT RD

STENSON CL

STEVENS CL

DUNCAN RD

HANDLEY

PAIGE CL

COLLEGE RD

PO

Con Ctr

MERCHANT LA

Wharley Farm

The Cottage

Wharley End

Wharley End Farm

UNIVERSITY WAY

COLLEGE RD

Cranfield Univ

Liby

MK43

Cranfield Airfield

45

7

6

5

44

4

43

3

2

42

1

8

A B C D E F

92 A 93 B C D 94 E F

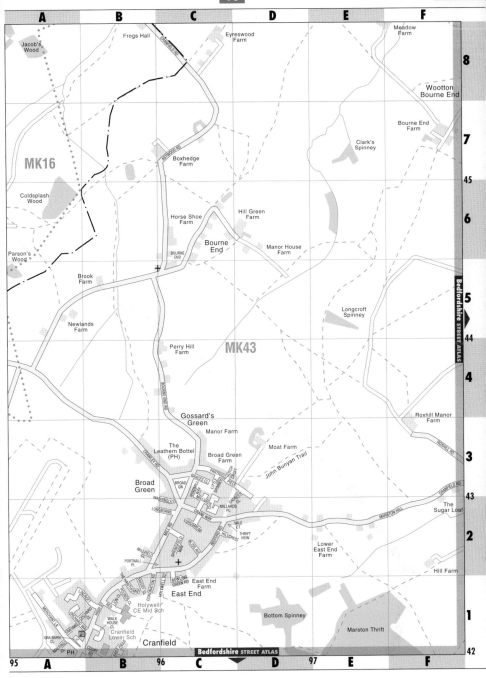

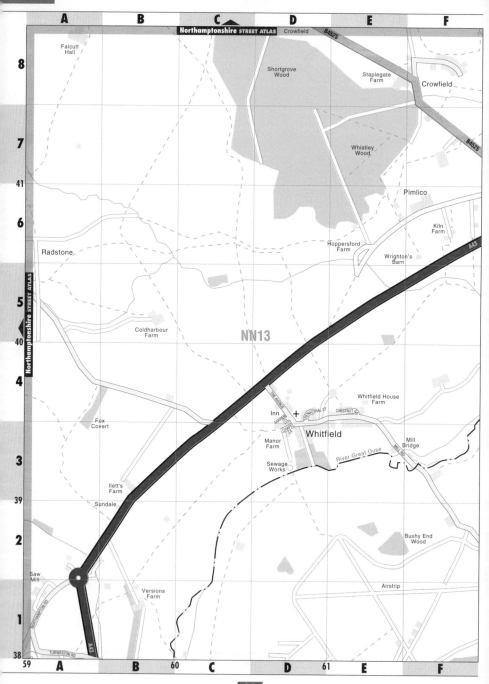

Crowfield

B4525

Falcutt Hall

Shortgrove Wood

Staplegate Farm

Crowfield

B4525

Whistley Wood

Pimlico

Kiln Farm

Radstone

Hoppersford Farm

Wrighton's Barn

A43

Coldharbour Farm

NN13

Fox Covert

Whitfield House Farm

CHESTNUT ST

THE AVENUE

Inn

BARNBROOK

CHAPEL LA

GREENOTHAL ST

Whitfield

Mill Bridge

MILL RD

Manor Farm

River Great Ouse

Ilett's Farm

Sewage Works

Bushy End Wood

Sundale

Saw Mill

Airstrip

Versions Farm

A43

TOWCESTER RD

TURWESTON RD

59   60   61

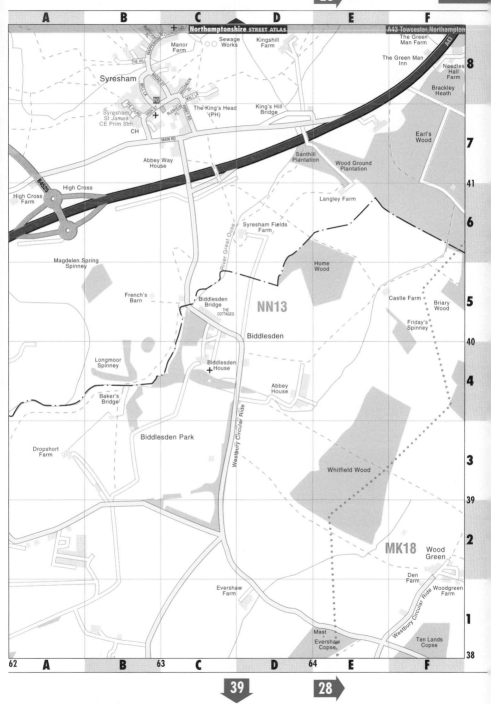

Northamptonshire STREET ATLAS

A43 Towcester Northampton

The Green Man Farm

The Green Man Inn

Needles Hall Farm

Manor Farm

Sewage Works

Kingshill Farm

Brackley Heath

THE HILL

BROAD ST

BELL LA

MAGDALEN

MATT LA

Syresham

Earl's Wood

8

King's Hill Bridge

The King's Head (PH)

King's Hill Bridge

THE POUND

HIGH ST

BLENHEIM

HENLEY RD

Syresham St James CE Prim Sch

CH

PO

MAIN RD

7

Abbey Way House

Santhill Plantation

Wood Ground Plantation

41

High Cross

B4525

High Cross Farm

Langley Farm

6

Syresham Fields Farm

Home Wood

River Great Ouse

Magdelen Spring Spinney

NN13

Castle Farm

Briary Wood

5

French's Barn

Biddlesden Bridge

THE COTTAGES

Friday's Spinney

Biddlesden

40

Longmoor Spinney

Biddlesden House

Westbury Circular Ride

Abbey House

4

Baker's Bridge

Biddlesden Park

3

Dropshort Farm

Whitfield Wood

39

MK18

Wood Green

2

Den Farm

Woodgreen Farm

Evershaw Farm

Westbury Circular Ride

1

Mast

Evershaw Copse

Ten Lands Copse

38

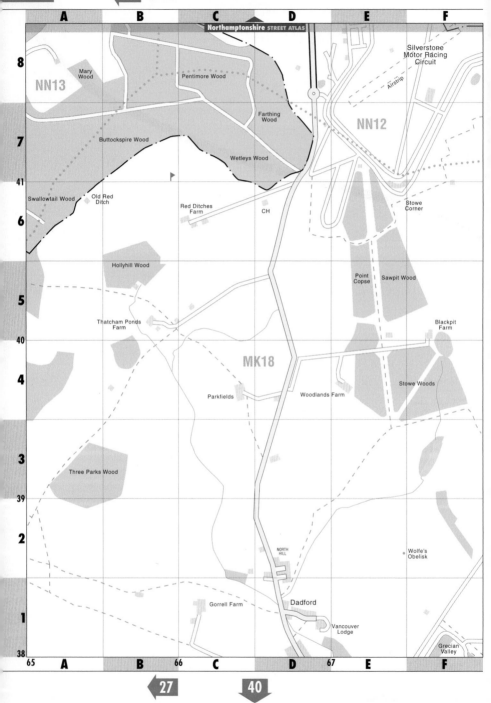

Northamptonshire STREET ATLAS

A   B   C   D   E   F

8

NN13

Mary Wood

Pentimore Wood

Silverstone Motor Racing Circuit

Airstrip

Farthing Wood

NN12

7

Buttockspire Wood

Wetleys Wood

41

Swallowtail Wood

Old Red Ditch

Red Ditches Farm

CH

Stowe Corner

6

Hollyhill Wood

Point Copse

Sawpit Wood

5

Thatcham Ponds Farm

40

Blackpit Farm

MK18

4

Parkfields

Woodlands Farm

Stowe Woods

3

Three Parks Wood

39

2

NORTH HILL

Wolfe's Obelisk

1

Gorrell Farm

Dadford

Vancouver Lodge

Grecian Valley

38

65   A   B   66   C   D   67   E   F

30

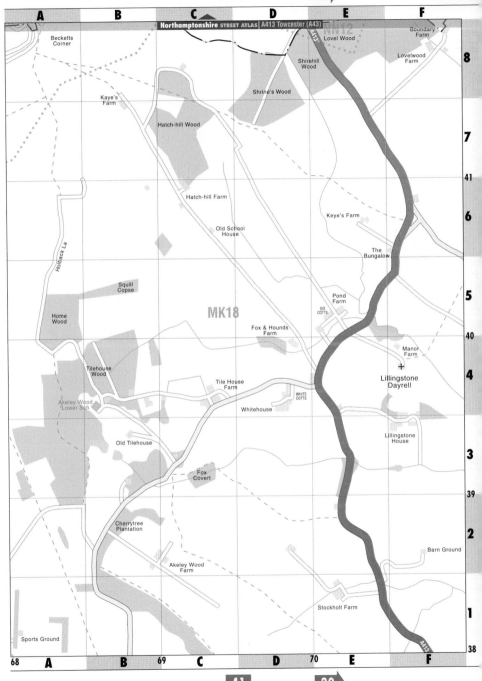

NN12

Boundary
Farm

8

Becketts
Corner

Lovel Wood

Lovelwood
Farm

Shirehill
Wood

Kaye's
Farm

Shrine's Wood

Hatch-hill Wood

7

41

Hatch-hill Farm

Keye's Farm

6

Old School
House

The
Bungalow

Squill
Copse

MK18

Pond
Farm

5

Holback La

SIX
COTTS

Home
Wood

Fox & Hounds
Farm

40

Manor
Farm

Tilehouse
Wood

Lillingstone
Dayrell

4

Tile House
Farm

Akeley Wood
Lower Sch

WHITE
COTTS

Whitehouse

Lillingstone
House

Old Tilehouse

3

Fox
Covert

39

Cherrytree
Plantation

2

Barn Ground

Akeley Wood
Farm

Stockholt Farm

1

A413

Sports Ground

38

68   A   B   69   C   D   70   E   F

41

30

29
17

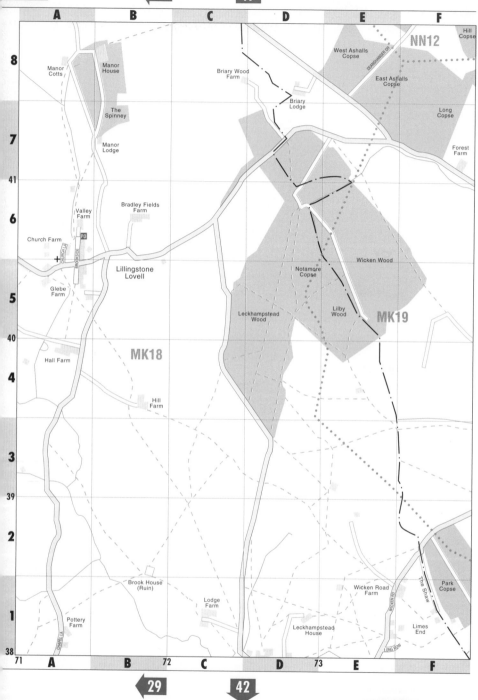

29
42

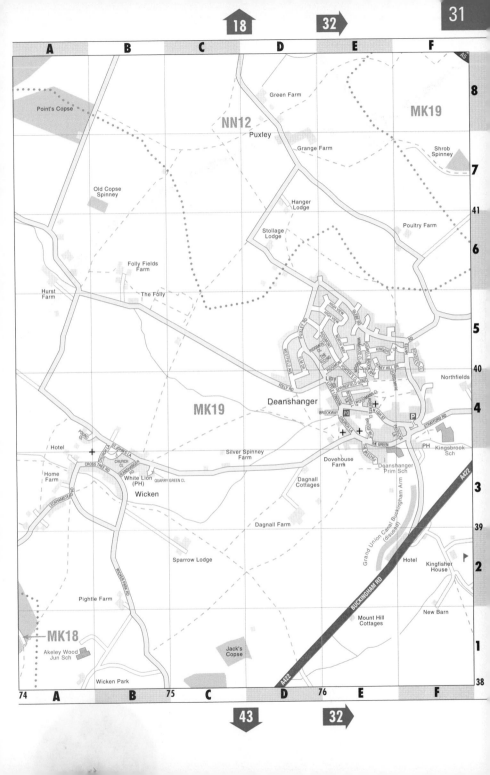

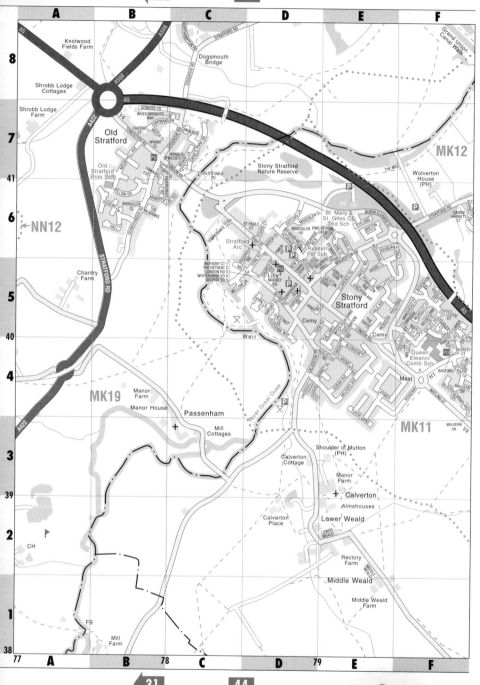

Labels visible on the map:

Knotwood Fields Farm

Shrobb Lodge Cottages

Shrobb Lodge Farm

Old Stratford

Old Stratford Prim Sch

NN12

Chantry Farm

STRATFORD RD

Dogsmouth Bridge

Stony Stratford Nature Reserve

Grand Union Canal Walk

MK12

Wolverton House (PH)

St Mary & St Giles CE Mid Sch

Russell Fst Sch

Stratford Arc

Stony Stratford

Liby MARKET SQ

Cemy

Cemy

Queen Eleanor Comb Sch

Mast

Weir

River Great Ouse

MK19

Manor Farm

Manor House

Passenham

Mill Cottages

Calverton Cottage

Shoulder of Mutton (PH)

Manor Farm

Calverton

Almshouses

Calverton Place

Lower Weald

LOWER WEALD

Rectory Farm

Middle Weald

Middle Weald Farm

MK11

MALVERN DR

CH

FB

Mill Farm

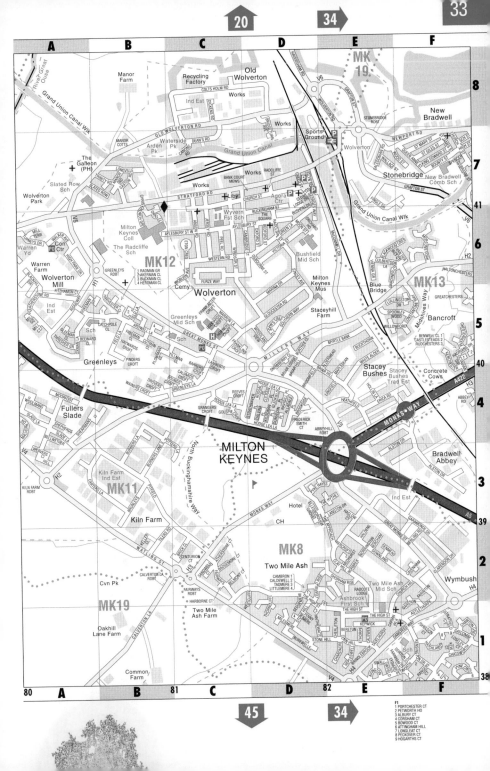

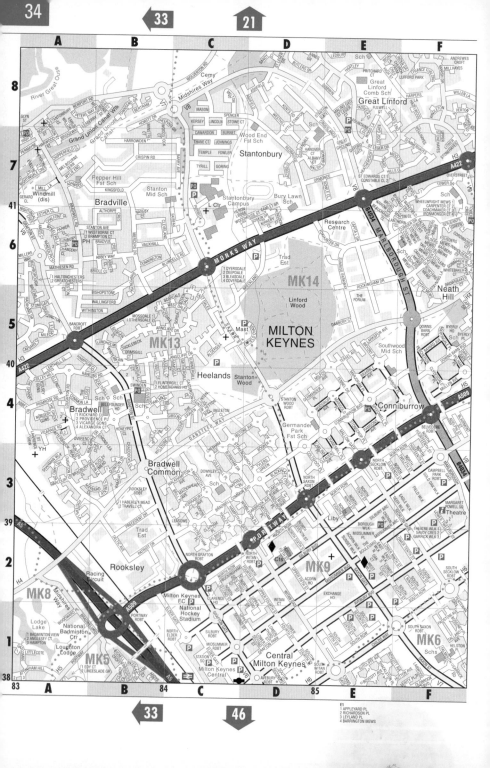

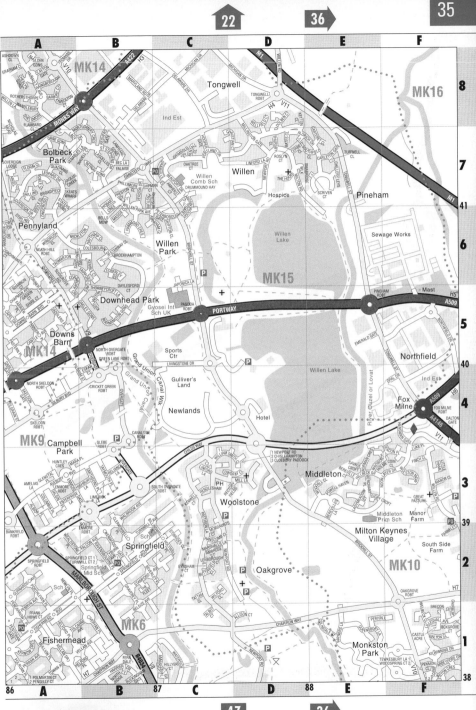

A B C D E F

8

Hotel

COMPTON CT   Moulsoe

Glebe Farm

Church Farm

NEWPORT RD

7

MK16

41

M1

14

Broughton Grounds Com Woodlands Nature Reserve

6

P

Broughton Barn

Old Covert

PORTWAY

A5130

Broughton Barns Cotts

NORTHFIELD RDBT

The Manor House

Roundhill Spinney

5

H5

H6

The Old Rectory

Mast

40

AMBERGATE

Brooklands Farm

New Covert

4

Atterbury

Hotel

Broughton Fields Comb Sch

Ravenstone House

Broughton Manor Bsns Pk

3

MEADOW LA

Broughton

TONGWELL ST

MILTON

WORRELL LA

39

Kingston Bridge

MK17

MILTON KEYNES

2

MK10

MONKSTON RDBT

MAIDSTONE RD

Kingston

Fen Farm

NEWMARKET CT

Europa Bsns Pk

CHIPPENHAM DR

H7

1

MAIDSTONE

Monkston

L Ctr

NEWPORT RD

A5130

BRINKLOW RDBT

BRANSWORTH AVE

KINGSTON RDBT

H8

A421

38

A421

MK7

STANDING WAY

ETHERIDGE AVE

89

A B 90 C D 91 E F

A1
1 PERSHORE CROFT
2 STAVORDALE
3 TYNEMOUTH RISE
4 LEOMINSTER GATE

B1
1 LAUNDE
2 ST BOTOLPHS

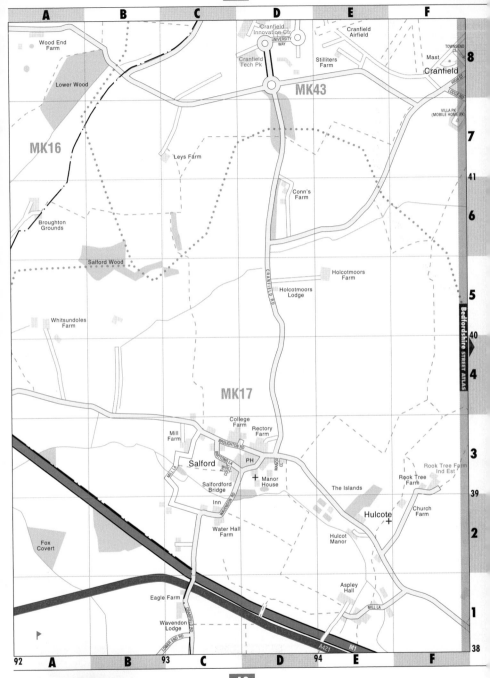

A   B   C   D   E   F

Wood End Farm

Cranfield Innovation Ctr

Cranfield Airfield

Mast
TOWNSEND

8

Lower Wood

Cranfield Tech Pk

UNIVERSITY WAY

Stilliters Farm

Cranfield

HIGH ST
LODGE RD

MK43

VILLA PK
(MOBILE HOME PK)

MK16

7

41

Leys Farm

Conn's Farm

6

Broughton Grounds

Salford Wood

Holcotmoors Farm

5

CRANFIELD RD

Holcotmoors Lodge

Whitsundoles Farm

40

4

MK17

College Farm

Rectory Farm

Mill Farm

Rook Tree Farm Ind Est

3

BROUGHTON RD

PH

MANOR CT

Rook Tree Farm

Salford

COURT LA

The Islands

39

Manor House

Salfordford Bridge

MILL LA

WAVENDON RD

Church Farm

Inn

Hulcote

2

Water Hall Farm

Hulcot Manor

Fox Covert

Aspley Hall

1

Eagle Farm

MILL LA

CRANFIELD RD

Wavendon Lodge

LOWER END RD

A421   M1

38

92   A   B   93   C   D   94   E   F

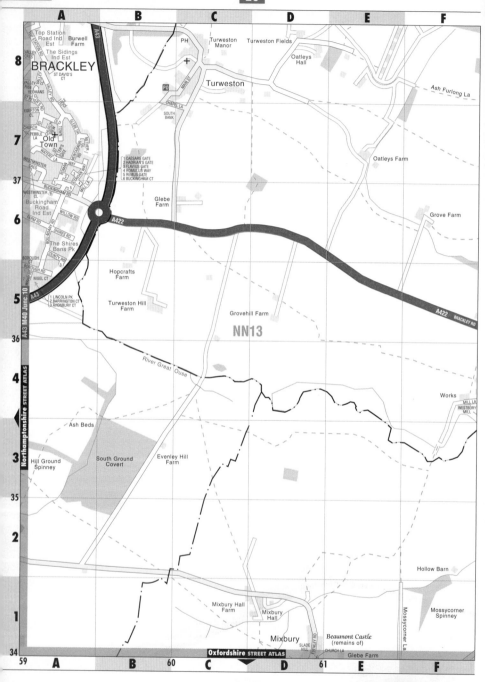

A B C D E F

8

BRACKLEY

Top Station
Road Ind
Est

Burwell
Farm

The Sidings
Ind Est

ST DAVID'S
CT

VALLEY
CRES

VALLEY
RISE

YEOMANS
CL

ST PETER'S

EGERTON
RD

CHURCH

PEBBLE
LA

Old
Town

7

37

WESTMINSTER
RD

WILLOW RD

BUCKINGHAM RD

WESTMINSTER
CL

Buckingham
Road
Ind Est

BOULTON RD

BOROUGH
RD

NIGEL CT

BOROUGH RD

SHIRES RD

COUNTY RD

The Shires
Bsns Pk

A422

6

A43 M40 Junc. 10

A43

5

36

PH

Turweston
Manor

Turweston Fields

Oatleys
Hall

Turweston

PO

CHAPEL LA

SOUTH
BANK

MAIN RD

1 CAESARS GATE
2 HADRIAN'S GATE
3 FLAVIUS GATE
4 ROMULUS WAY
5 REMUS GATE
6 BUCKINGHAM CT

Glebe
Farm

Ash Furlong La

Oatleys Farm

Grove Farm

A422

Hopcrafts
Farm

Turweston Hill
Farm

1 LINCOLN PK
2 BARRINGTON CT
3 AYOSBURY CT

Grovehill Farm

NN13

A422   BRACKLEY RD

River Great Ouse

4

Works

MILL LA

WESTBURY
MILL

Ash Beds

3

Hill Ground
Spinney

South Ground
Covert

Evenley Hill
Farm

35

2

Hollow Barn

1

Mixbury Hall
Farm

Mixbury
Hall

Mossycorner La

Mossycorner
Spinney

Mixbury

Beaumont Castle
(remains of)

SLADE
HILL

EVENLEY RD

CHURCH LA

Glebe Farm

34

59   A   60   B   C   60   C   61   D   E   61   E   F   F

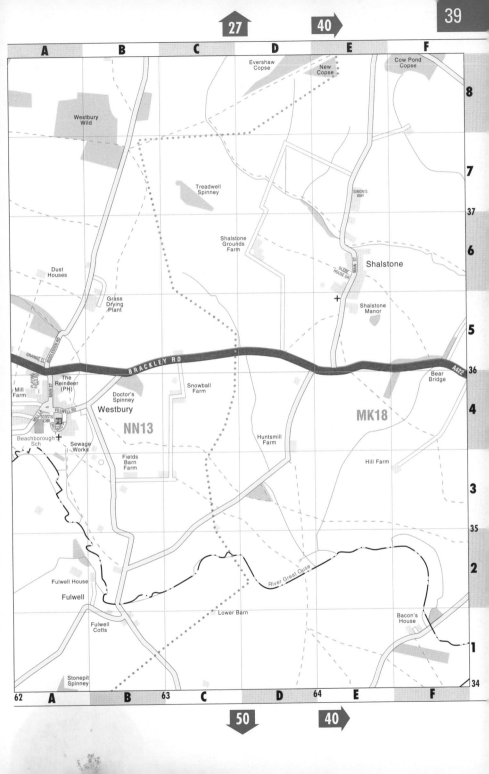

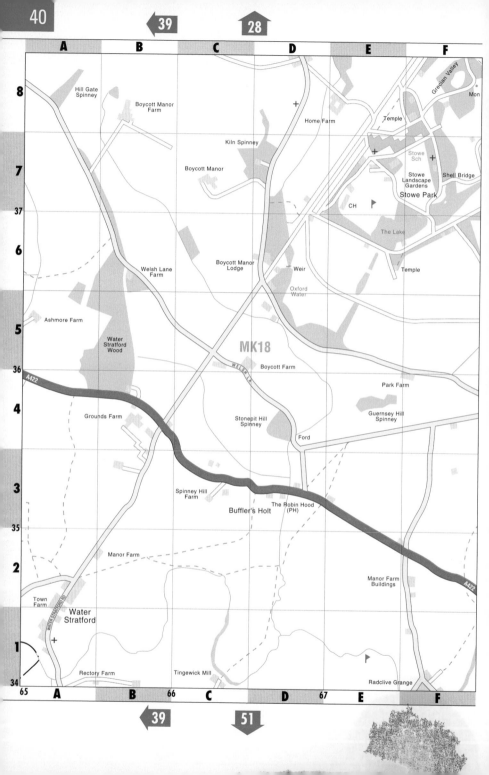

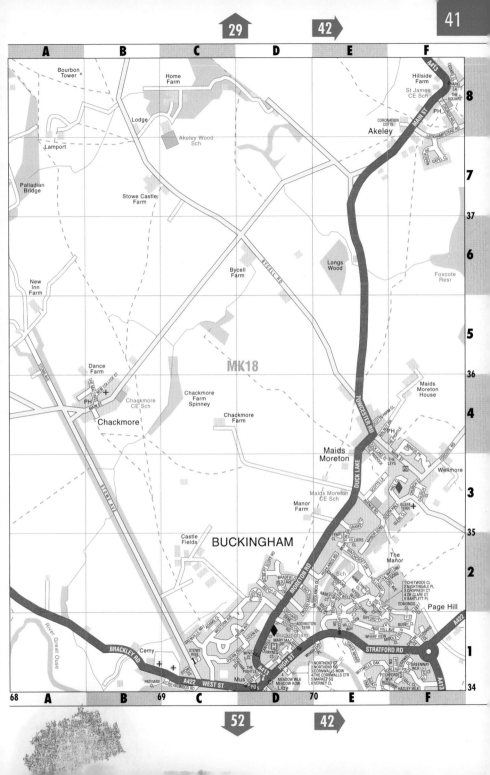

A B C D E F

8

Chapel La
Duck End
Akeley
Willow Farm
The Close
Leckhampstead Rd
Oak Tree Farm
Manor Farm
Church End
Manor House
Middle End
Valley Farm
Limes End Bridge
The Limes
Wicken Rd

P Leckhampstead
Weatherhead Farm
Barretts End
Limes End Farm

7

37

Foxcote Wood
Home Farm
South End
Lower Farm

6

Foxcote Resr

Grove Spinney

Foxcott Wood Farm

MK18

A422

5

Ash Close Spinney

36

Foscote Manor
Foscote
FOSCOTE COTTS

4

Leckhampstead Wharf House

Hydelane Farm

Thornborough Mill

3

Home Farm

STRATFORD RD

Buckingham Canal Nature Reserve

Reservoir

River Great Ouse

35

College Farm

2

A422

Old Mill House

1

34

Sewage Works

Thornborough Grounds

71 A B 72 C D 73 E F

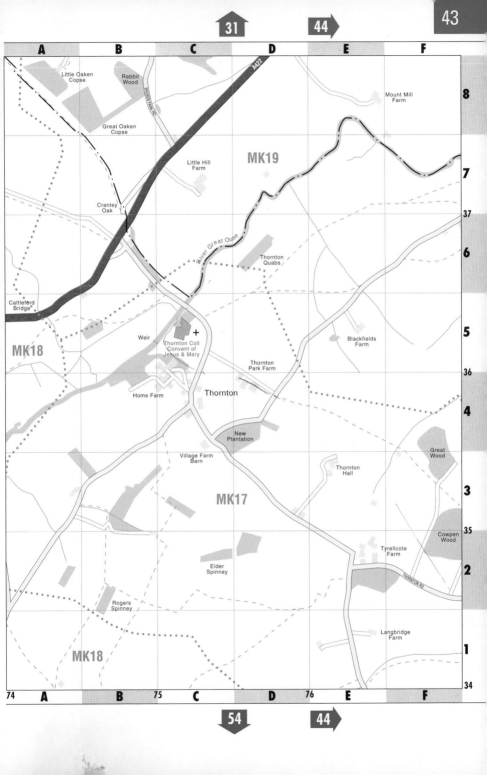

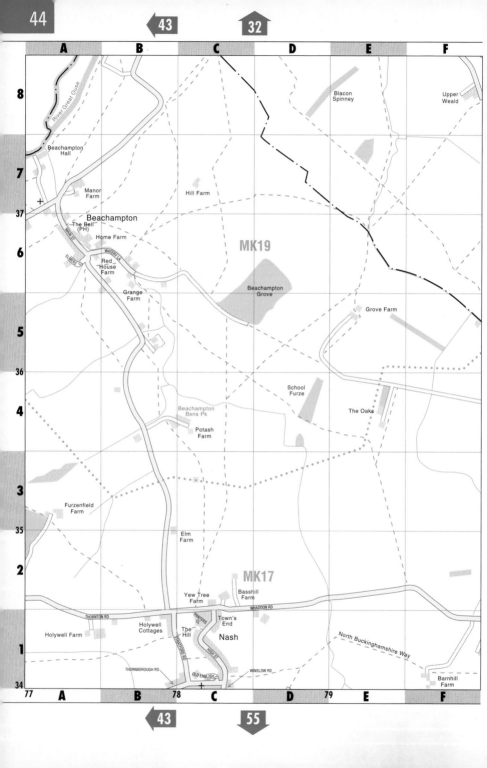

A   B   C   D   E   F

8

River Great Ouse

Blacon
Spinney

Upper
Weald

Beachampton
Hall

7

Manor
Farm

Hill Farm

37

Beachampton

The Bell
(PH)

Home Farm

MK19

6

WATERY LA

ELMERS CT

MAIN ST

Red
House
Farm

Grange
Farm

Beachampton
Grove

Grove Farm

5

36

School
Furze

The Oaks

4

Beachampton
Bsns Pk

Potash
Farm

3

Furzenfield
Farm

35

Elm
Farm

2

MK17

Yew Tree
Farm

Basshill
Farm

WHADDON RD

THORNTON RD

Holywell
Cottages

PAYNES CL

Town's
End

North Buckinghamshire Way

1

Holywell Farm

The
Hill

Nash

STRATFORD RD

HIGH ST

34

THORNBOROUGH RD

OLD ENGLISH

WINSLOW RD

Barnhill
Farm

77   A   B   78   C   D   79   E   F

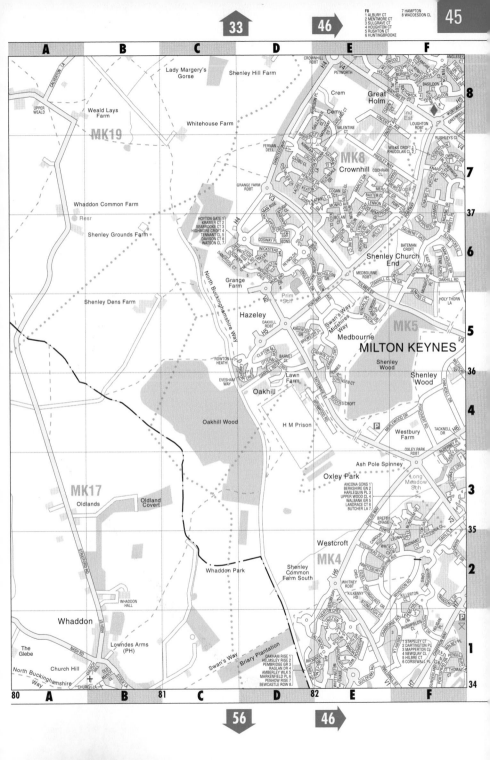

A   B   C   D   E   F

8
7
37
6
5
36
4
35
3
2
1
34

MK9
Leisure Plaza
Elder Gate
Oldbrook
Winterhill
Little Loughton Manor
Loughton
Loughton Manor
Loughton Middle Sch
The Grove Ind Sch
South Loughton Valley Park
Knowlhill
Milton Keynes Coll
MK6
Coffee Hall
St Pauls RC Sch
Peartree La
Hamlins
Denbigh Sch
Glastonbury Thorn Fst Sch
Knowlhill Rdbt
Shenley Lodge
Ind Est
The National Bowl
Bleak Hall
Ind Est
The Bowl Rdbt
Hotel
Elfield Park
MK5
Shenley Rdbt
L Ctr
Trad Est

MILTON KEYNES

Furzton Lake
Furzton
Furzton Rdbt
Caroline Haslett Comb Sch
Coldharbour Spinney
Denbigh Hall Ind Est
Cold Harbour CE Comb Sch
Denbigh Hall Ind Est
The Valley Farm
Emerson Farm House
Shenley Brook End Sch
Shenley Brook End
MK4
Emerson Valley Sch
Emerson Valley
Wellsmead Mid Sch
MK3
Wellsmead Fst Sch
Howe Park Wood
Tattenhoe
Romans Field Sch
Field Sch
STANDING WAY
Westcroft Rdbt
Hornby Chase

B2
1 GROSMONT CL
2 GOATHLAND CROFT
3 LITTLE HABTON
4 LOWICK PL
5 STAGSHAW GR
6 TARNBROOK CL
7 HAZELHURST

1 DUNGENESS CT
2 LANGNEY GR
3 OLDCASTLE CROFT
4 BLYTH CT

1 BLANSBY CHASE
2 EVERLEY CL
3 EDSTONE PL
4 HAWKSHEAD GR
BURHOLME

83   A   B   84   C   D   85   E   F

45   57

A3
1 UPPER WOOD CL

B3
1 ALSTONEFIELD
2 GILLAMOOR CL
3 FADMOOR PL
4 APPLETON MEWS

C2
1 GREYSTONLEY
2 DENCHWORTH CT
3 HOLLINWELL CL
4 FERNBOROUGH HAVEN
5 SPARSHOLT CL

D1
1 HUNGERFORD HO
2 ASHBURNHAM CL
3 HOLLINWELL CL
4 DUNBAR CL
5 RIBBLE CRES

F1
1 DURHAM HO
2 PEMBROKE HO
3 RUTLAND HO
4 WALTHAM HO
5 SAWLEY HO
6 NORFOLK HO
7 FLINT HO

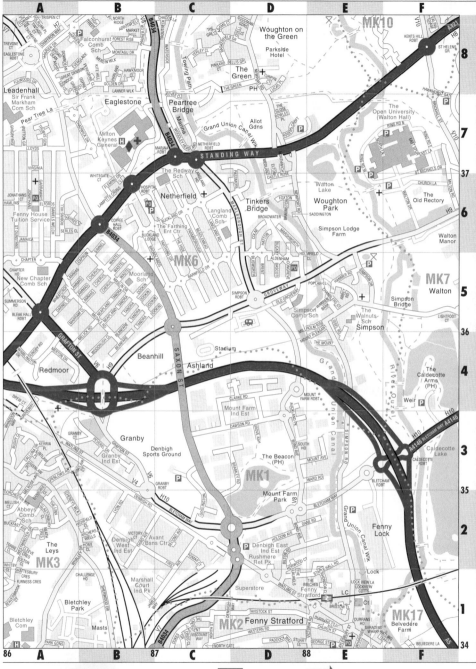

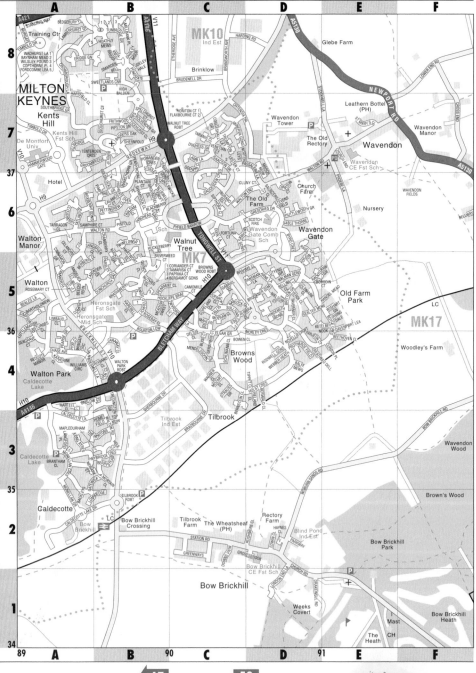

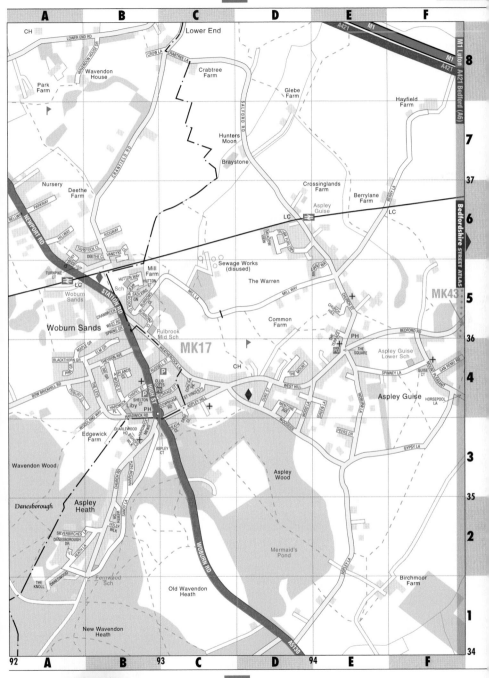

Lower End

CH

Park
Farm

Wavendon
House

Crabtree
Farm

Glebe
Farm

Hayfield
Farm

LOWER END RD

WAVENDON HOUSE DR

CROW LA

CRABTREE LA

SALFORD RD

Hunters
Moon

Braystone

Nursery

Deethe
Farm

CRANFIELD RD

Crosslands
Farm

Berrylane
Farm

Aspley
Guise

LC

BIRCH LA

LC

BELLVUE

NEWPORT RD

PARKWAY

HILLWAY

RIDGWAY

TAVISTOCK CL

DEETHE CL

VANDYKE

Mill
Farm

Sewage Works
(disused)

The Warren

MEADOW
VIEW

TRUNK FURLONG

BRICKHILL WAY

GURNEY CT

TURNPIKE
CT

LC

Woburn
Sands

HUTTON WAY

HUTTON
CT

SADLEIG
GN

MILL LA

MILL WAY

Common
Farm

CHURCH
HILL

PH

BEDFORD RD

MK43

STATION RD

Woburn Sands

CRANBROOK CT

SPRING GR

Fulbrook
Mid Sch

MK17

THE
TERRACE

PD

THE
SQUARE

Aspley Guise
Lower Sch

SPINNEY LA

SAN REMO RD

MAPLE GR

ELM GR

THEYDON AVE

TREE GR

ASPLANDS

RUSSELL ST

CHAPEL
RD

HEATHERBROOK

CH

THE MOUNT

WOBURN LA

GUISE
CT

Aspley Guise

HORSEPOOL
LA

BLACKTHORN GR

THE LEYS

WOODLAND WAY

CLUB
COTTS

COWMAN
RD

ST VINCENTS

Aspley Hill

WEST HILL

DUKE ST

GREEN LA

PEERS DR

BOW BRICKHILL RD

ZOBURY CL

HARDWICK
PL

SHELTON
CT

Liby

PH

HARDWICK RD

MENTONE
AVE

WOODSIDE

GYPSY LA

Edgewick
Farm

CHARLWOOD
HO

WALK

HIGH ST

ASPLEY
CT

HEATH
DENE

Wavendon Wood

CHURCH RD

MARSTON PATH

SANDY LA

Aspley
Wood

Danesborough

Aspley
Heath

SILVERBIRCHES

DANESBOROUGH
DR

KEITH WK

HOLLY
WLK

WOBURN RD

THE
KNOLL

DANESWOOD

Fernwood
Sch

Mermaid's
Pond

Birchmoor
Farm

TAVEY LA

New Wavendon
Heath

Old Wavendon
Heath

A5130

A421

M1

A421

M1

Bedfordshire STREET ATLAS

M1 Luton A421 Bedford (A6)

8

7

37

6

5

36

4

3

35

2

1

34

92   93   93   94

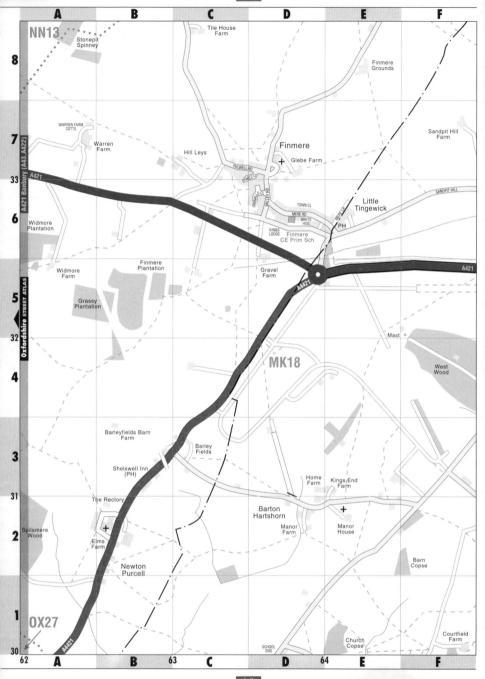

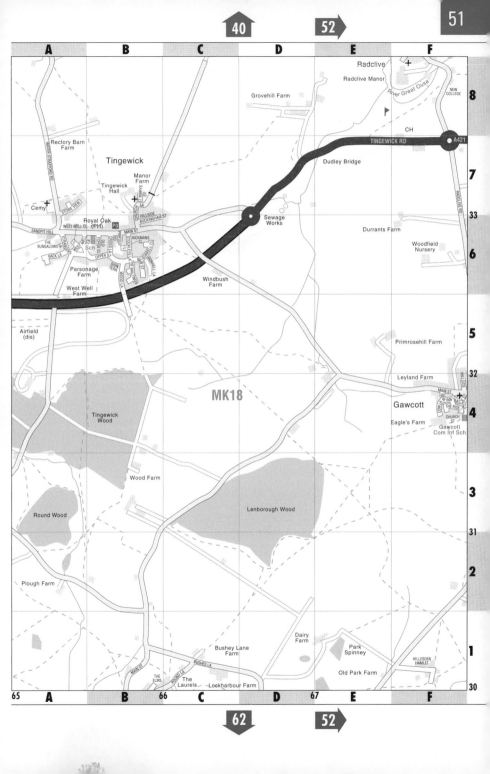

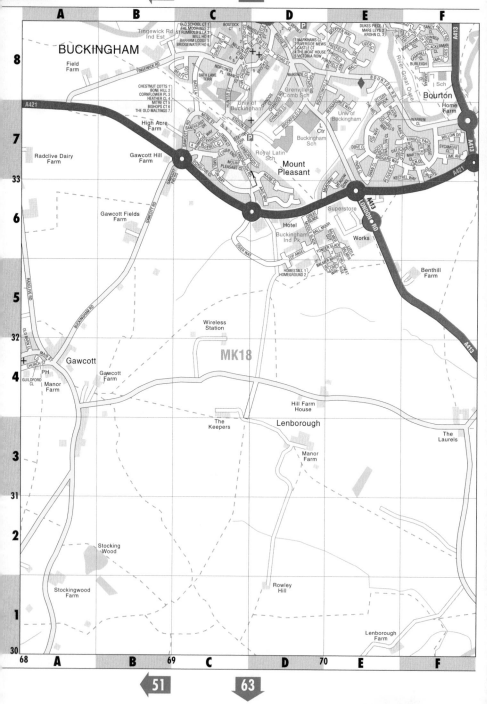

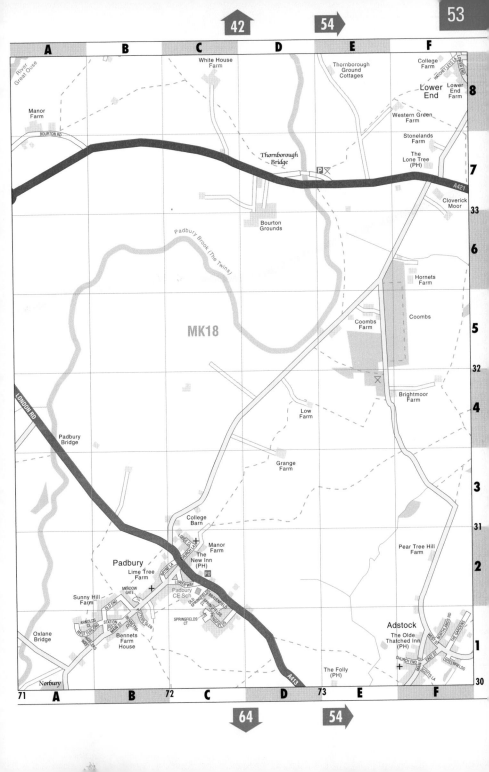

53
43

A **B** **C** **D** **E** **F**

BACK ST
Ford
Home Farm
PETERS MOOR

8
LOWER ST
HIGH ST
CHAPEL LA
Thornborough
Inf Sch
THE GREEN
THORNHILL
Coates Farm
Brakes Farm

NASH RD
THORNBOROUGH RD
Thornborough
The Two
Brewers
(PH)
Willow Farm
Dancer's
Grave
Nansley's
Brake
Bungalow Farm

Nash End Farm
Middle Shelspit
Farm

7
MK18
Lower Shelspit
Upper Shelspit
Farm

33
A421
The Folly
Priory Farm

6
Maywynn Farm
A421

Mangland Farm

5
Poultry Farm
Singleborough

32
Dean Farm
Laurel
Farm

4
Pilch Farm
MK17
PACH LA

Great Furze House

3
Sch
SCHOOL END 1
SINGLEBOROUGH LA 2

31
Home Farm
B4033

2
Adstockfields House
Adstockfields Farm
Wigwell Farm

Midshires Way
WINSLOW RD
North Buckinghamshire Way

1
B4033

30
74 **A** **B** 75 **C** **D** 76 **E** **F**

53
65

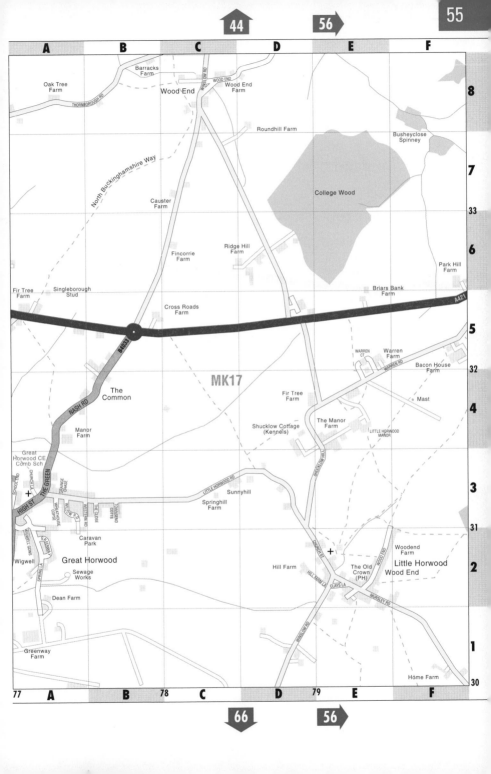

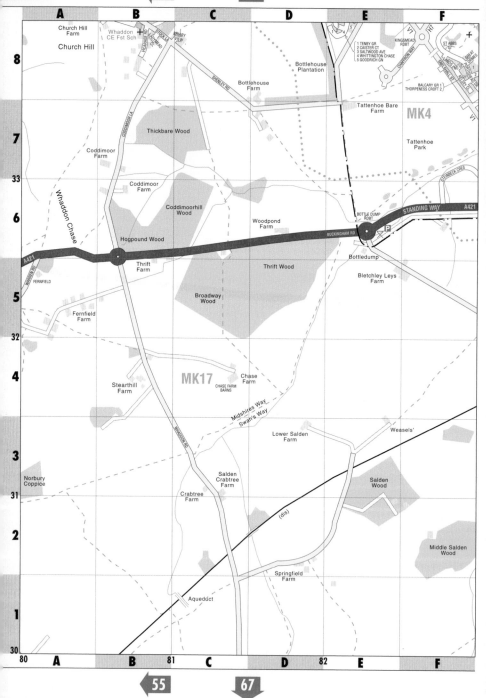

Church Hill Farm

Church Hill

Whaddon CE Fst Sch

BRIARY VIEW

Bottlehouse Plantation

Bottlehouse Farm

Thickbare Wood

SHENLEY RD

1 TENBY GR
2 CAISTER CT
3 SALTWOOD AVE
4 WHITTINGTON CHASE
5 GOODRICH GN

KINGSMEAD RDBT

ST ABBS CT

GREAT DUNES

BALCARY GR 1
THORPENESS CROFT 2

MK4

Tattenhoe Bare Farm

Tattenhoe Park

Coddimoor Farm

Coddimoor Farm

Coddimoorhill Wood

STEINBECK CRES

Whaddon Chase

Hogpound Wood

Woodpond Farm

STANDING WAY   A421

BOTTLE DUMP RDBT

BUCKINGHAM RD

Bottledump

Bletchley Leys Farm

Thrift Farm

Thrift Wood

A421

WHADDON RD

FERNFIELD

Fernfield Farm

Broadway Wood

MK17

Stearthill Farm

Chase Farm

CHASE FARM BARNS

Midshires Way

Swan's Way

Lower Salden Farm

Weasels'

Salden Wood

Norbury Coppice

WHADDON RD

Salden Crabtree Farm

Crabtree Farm

(dis)

Middle Salden Wood

Springfield Farm

Aqueduct

80   81   82

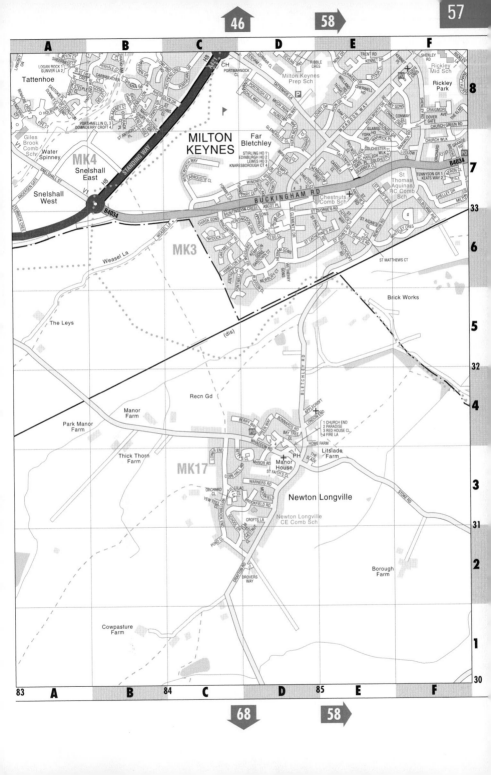

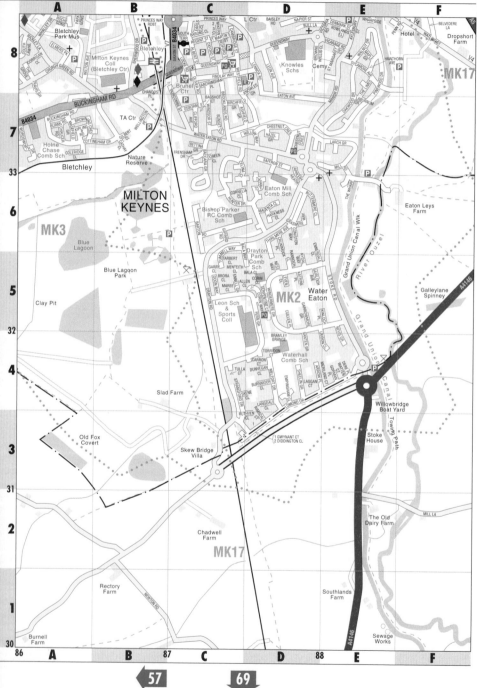

C8
1 ALEXANDER HO   7 Agora Ctr
2 LEE HO
3 CHRISTINE HO
4 WOODWARD HO
5 STANIER SQ
6 THE CONCOURSE

57   47

MILTON KEYNES

MK3

MK2

MK17

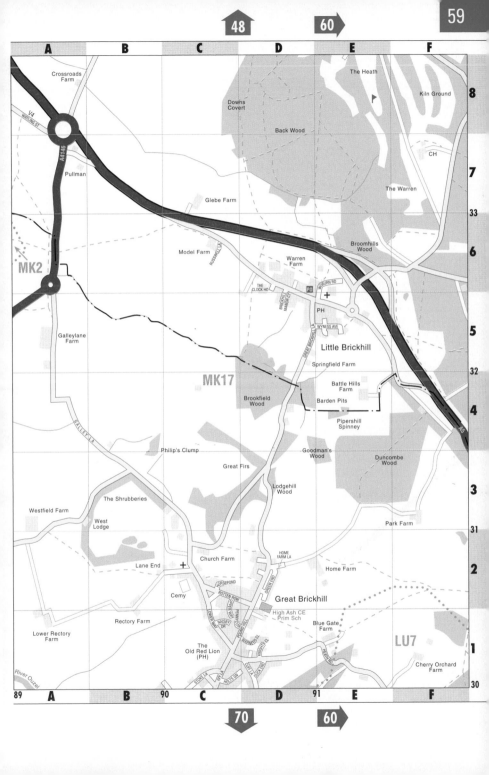

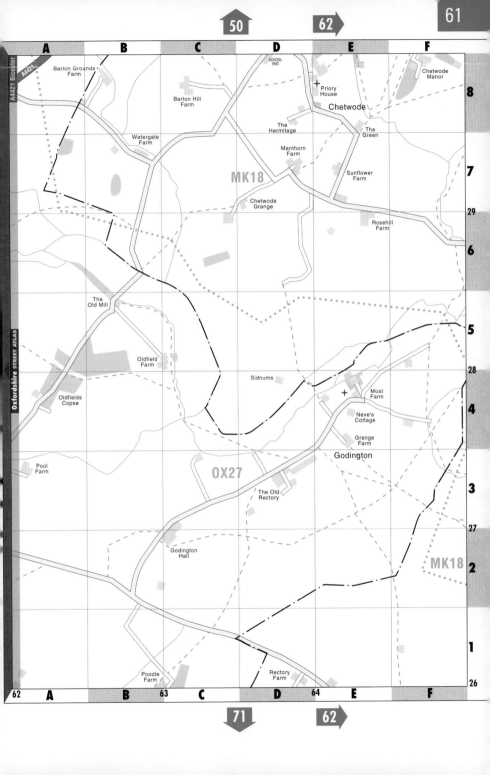

62

61

51

A B C D E F

8 Preston Bissett
Church Farm
Old Hat (PH)
SCHOOL LA
The Laurels
The Common
POUND YD
THE SQUARE
Thorpes Farm
Poplars Farm
MAIN ST

College Farm
Copperhouse Farm
Buryfield Spinney
Fir Tree Cottage
Jubilee Farm House
Jubilee Farm

7

29

6
Casemore Farm

Westfield Farm
Manor Farm

5 MK18

28

OX27

4
Cowley Farm
Cowley Old House
Cowley Lodge

3
Twyford Mill

27
Three Bridge Mill

2
Church View Farm
Twyford CE Sch
MILL LA
CHURCH ST
GRANGE
SCHOOL
Seven Stars (PH)

1 OX27
Twyford
Home Farm Hall
BICESTER RD
Crown (PH)
MANOR CT
PO
PORTWAY RD
ROSEHILL CRES
Portway Cottages

26
65 A B 66 C D 67 E F

61 72

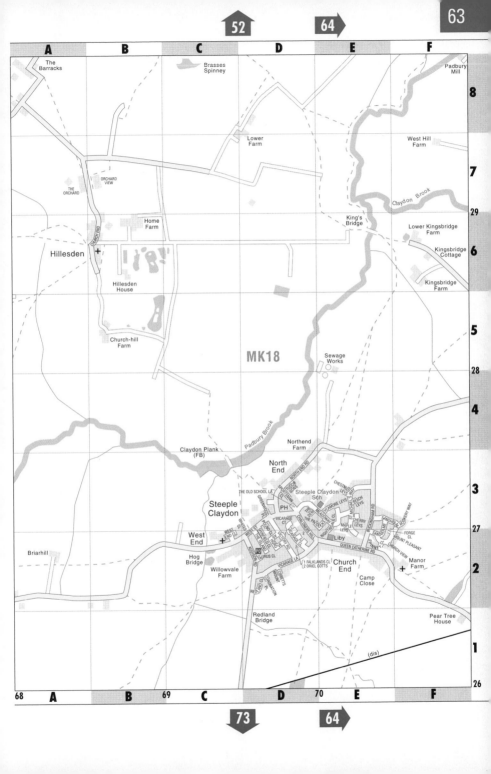

63
53

Folly Farm

A413

WR ST

Adstock Manor

A413

8

Wardens Farm

7

Padburyhill Farm

White Bridge

29

Hill Farm
Cottages

6

Hill Farm

Claydon Brook

5

MK18

Herd's Hill
Cottage

28

Claydon Hill Farm
No 6

Claydon Hill Farm

Claydon Hill Farm
No 5

Swan's Way

Jubilee Bridge

4

Windmillhill Farm

Verney
Junction

3

Littleworth Farm

The Verney Arms
(Hotel)

JUBILEE
COTTS

Littleworth

(dis)

Ashmore Farm House

27

2

Mount Pleasant
Farm

Greenacres

Sandhill

Sandhill

Sandhill Farm

RAILWAY
COTTS

North Buckinghamshire Way

LC

1

Rectory Farm

26

71   **A**   **B**   72   **C**   **D**   73   **E**   **F**

63
74

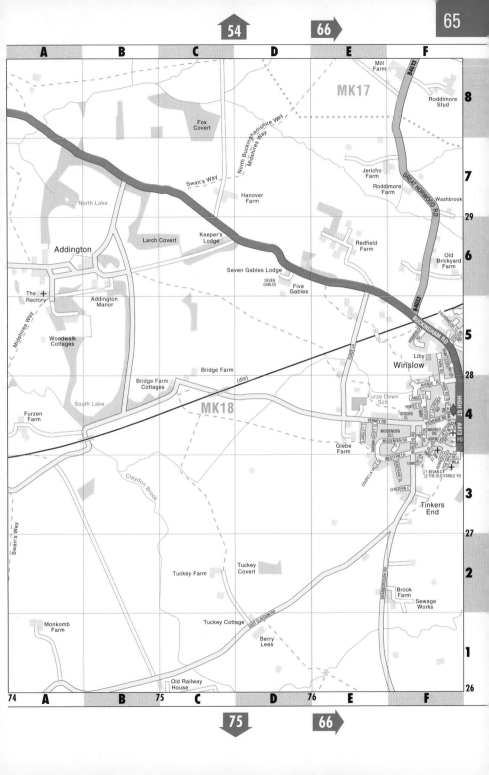

A B C D E F

8 Greenway Farm

Mount Pleasant

The Hollows

Horwood House

7 Osierbed Spinney

Fishpond Spinney

29 The White House

(dis)

Roddimore Covert

6 Moco Farm

Clare Farm Canada

1 STATION COTTS
2 OLD STATION CL

TANK HOUSE MAGPIE WAY

Foxhole Farm

COMBERFORD WAY
MCLERNON WAY THE SPINNEY
FLEDGELINGS
WLK RUDDS CL
G'WELL LA

Station Rd Ind Est

Spring Corner

MK17 Dodley Hill Farm

Midshires Way

5 Old Mill Furlong
SCOTT EVANS

LONGLANDS RD
KEACH CL
ELM LA JONES WAY
METERIN RD

Winslow CE Comb Sch

Redhall Farm

Abovemead Farm

28 +
P
CRICKETERS ROW

MK18

4 +
P
GREYHOUND CT
GREYHOUND CT

Winslow

Ivy Farm

OLD END
CHARLTON CL

Duck End

Shipton Mead Farm

B4032 WINSLOW RD

A413 SHEEP ST
Hotel
CLAYCUTTERS

B4032
SHIPTON

Rands Farm

3 Jubilee Cottages

Shipton Farm

27

Swanbourne House Sch

2 Shipton Bridge ✕

Claydon Brook

1 Haybush Farm

Midshires Way
Swan's Way

Bennett's Hill

26 North Hill Farm A413

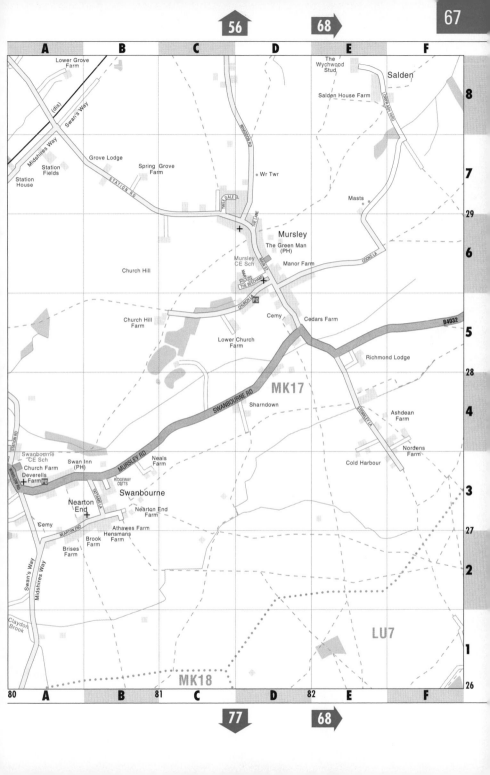

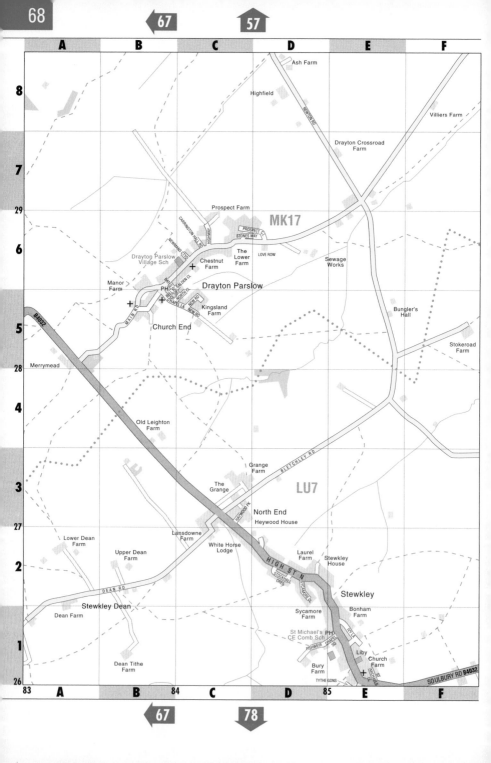

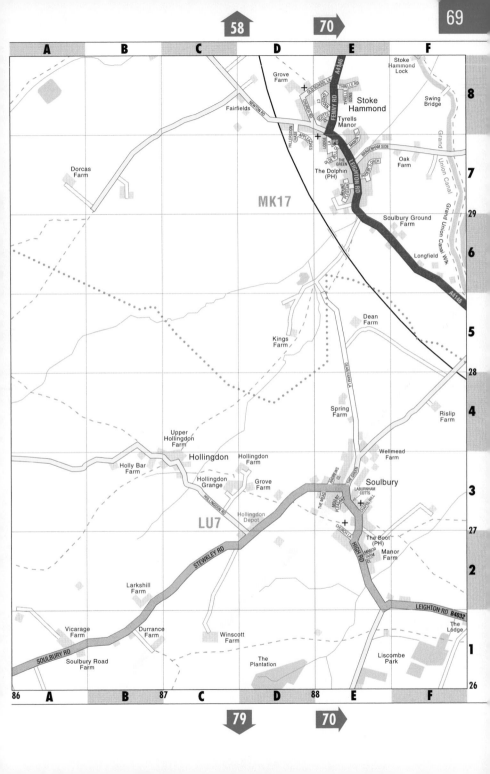

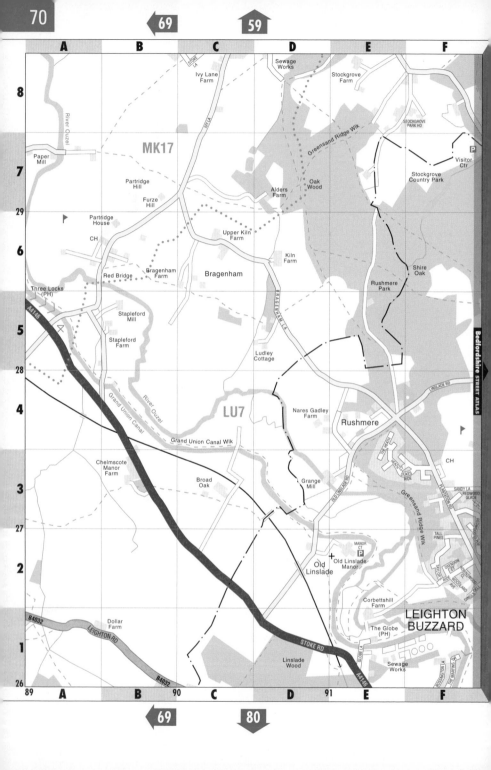

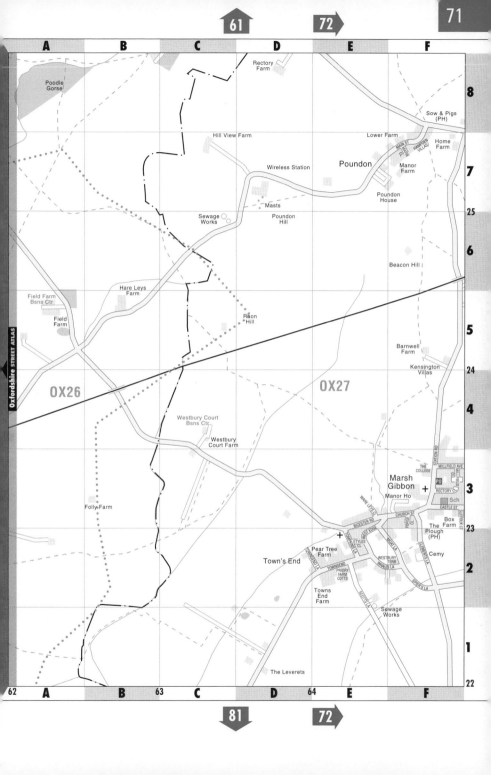

71
62

| A | B | C | D | E | F |

Red Furlong Farm

Twyford Lodge

MK18

Rosehill Farm

PORTWAY RD

Portway Farm

8

7

25

Grebe Lake

6

Windmill Hill

Lawn Farm

BARCLAY CL
HAMPDEN HILL
WOOTTON GN
BEATRICE

Charndon

CHESHIRE COTTS

SCHOOL HILL

MAIN ST

Station House

Charndon Grounds

5

Middle Farm

Valley Farm

Hill Farm

24

OX27

4

LITTLE MARSH RD

Swan Farm

SCOTTS CL

SWAN LA

Little Marsh

Gubbinshole Ditch

HP18

Rectory Farm

ST MICHAELS...

3

CASTLE ST

CASTLE CL

Leopold Farm

23

Summerstown

Edgcott

LEONARDS CL

BLENDONHAM RD

2

New Swan Farm

Gubbin's Hole

P

BRESTON RD

LAWN HOUSE LA

Gubbins Hole Farm

Lower Farm

1

22

| 65 | A | B | 66 | C | D | 67 | E | F |

71
82

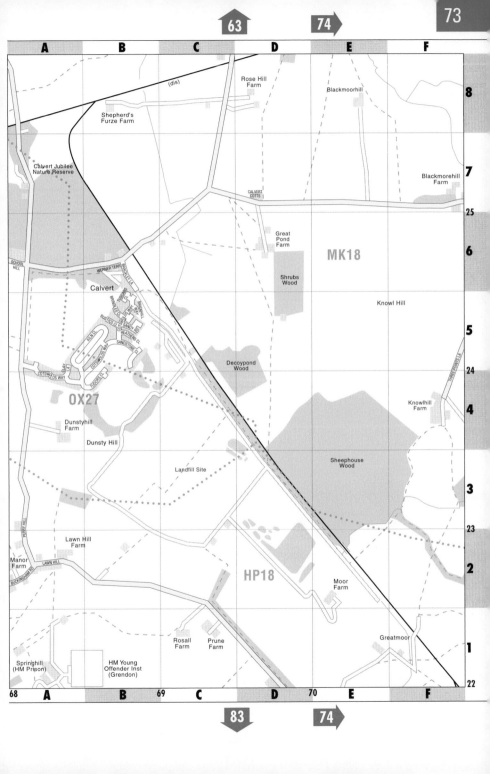

73
64

A   **B**   **C**   **D**   **E**   **F**

8

Home Farm
TOWNSEND COTTS
Cemy
Middle Claydon

Weir
The Old Brick Yard (disused)
Claydon Park

Verney Farm
New Farm
CHURCH
Swan's Way
East Claydon
EMERALD CL
CHESTNUT CL
ST MARYS CL

7

Catherine Farm

Claydon House

East Claydon Sch
Ivy Nook

25

South Lodge

Phoenix Fruit Farm

Botolph Farm

6

Botolph Farm
ORCHARD WAY
Botolph Claydon

MK18

Bernwood Farm

5

Home Wood

Muxwell Farm

24

4

Claydon Lawn

Romer Wood

Hogshaw Farm

3

Balmore Wood

Runt's Wood

Coppice Lowhill Farm

23

Three Points La

Hogshaw Farm

2

Greatsea Wood

HP22

HP18

Finemerehill House

1

Kitehill Farm

22

71 **A**   **B** 72 **C**   **D** 73 **E**   **F**

73
84

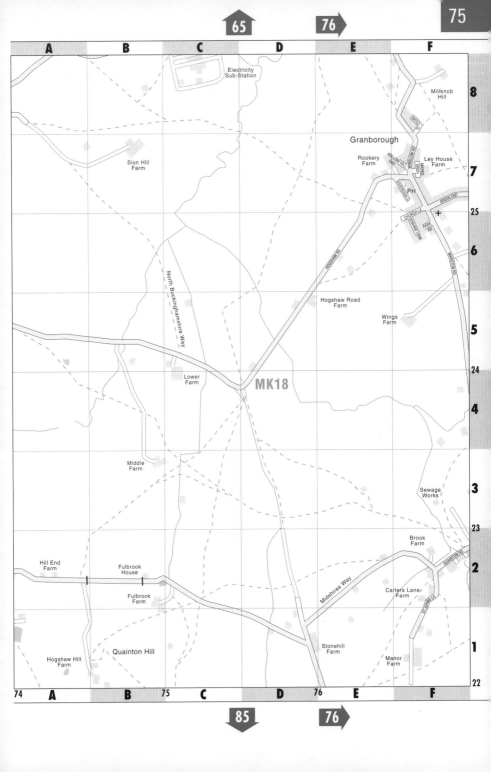

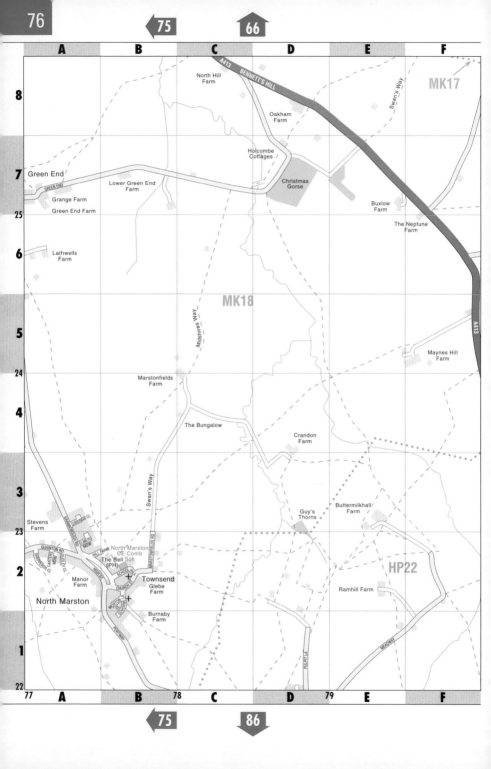

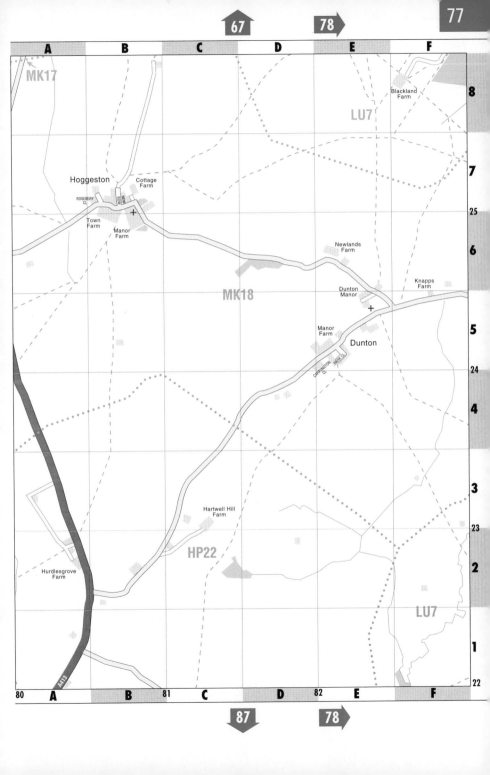

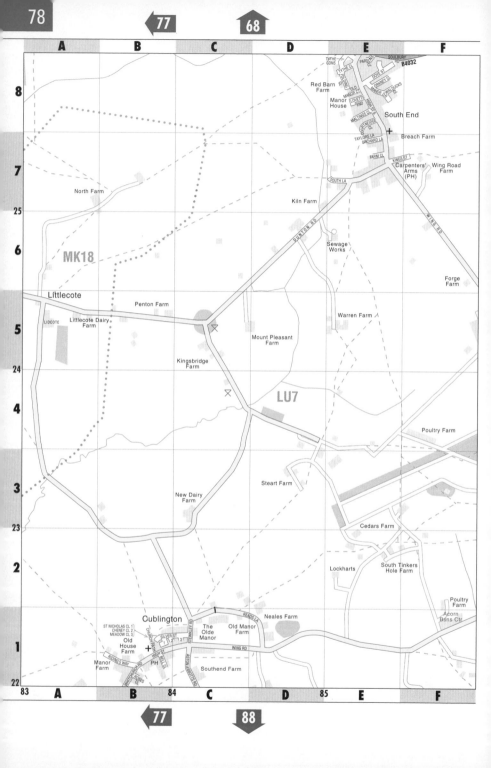

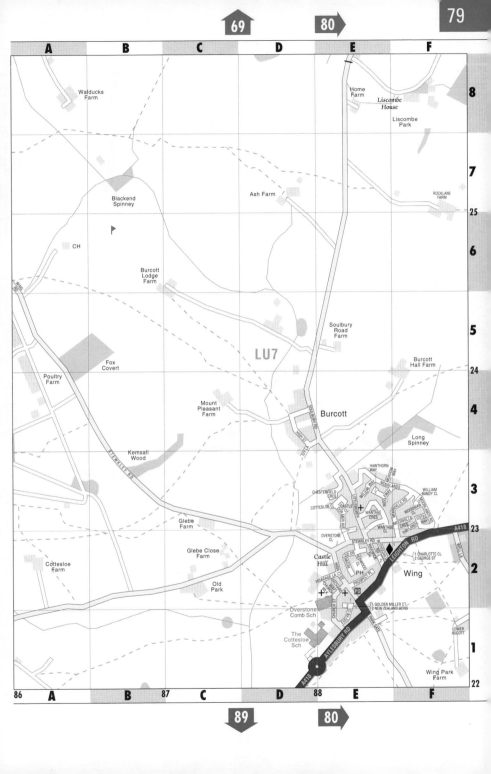

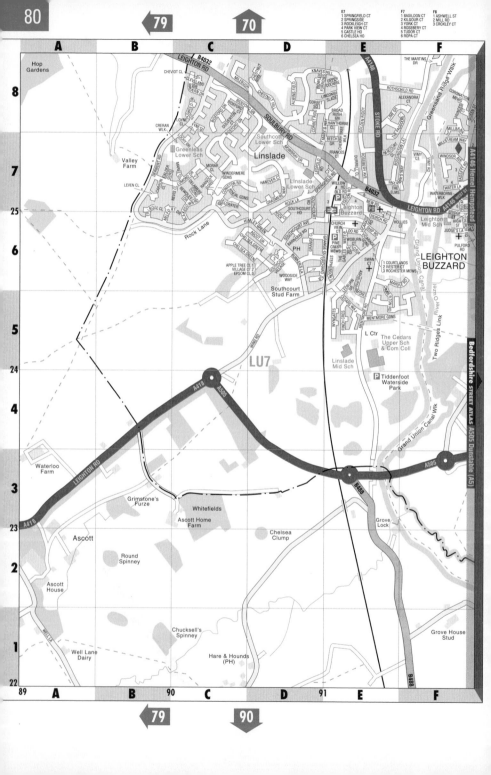

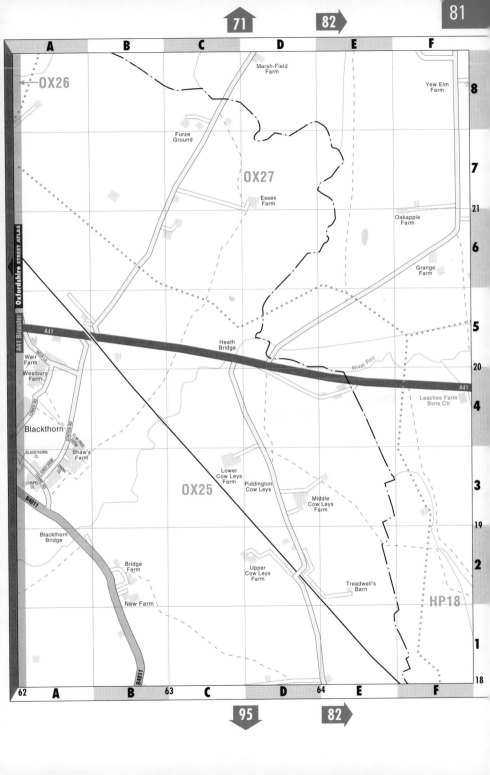

71 82 95 82

OX26

Marsh-Field Farm

Yew Elm Farm

Furze Ground

OX27

Essex Farm

Oakapple Farm

Grange Farm

A41

Weir Farm

Heath Bridge

River Ray

Westbury Farm

Leaches Farm Bsns Ctr

Blackthorn

Shaw's Farm

BLACKTHORN CL

CHAPEL CL

Lower Cow Leys Farm

Piddington Cow Leys

OX25

Middle Cow Leys Farm

B4011

Blackthorn Bridge

Bridge Farm

Upper Cow Leys Farm

Treadwell's Barn

HP18

New Farm

Oxfordshire STREET ATLAS

A41 Bicester

B4011

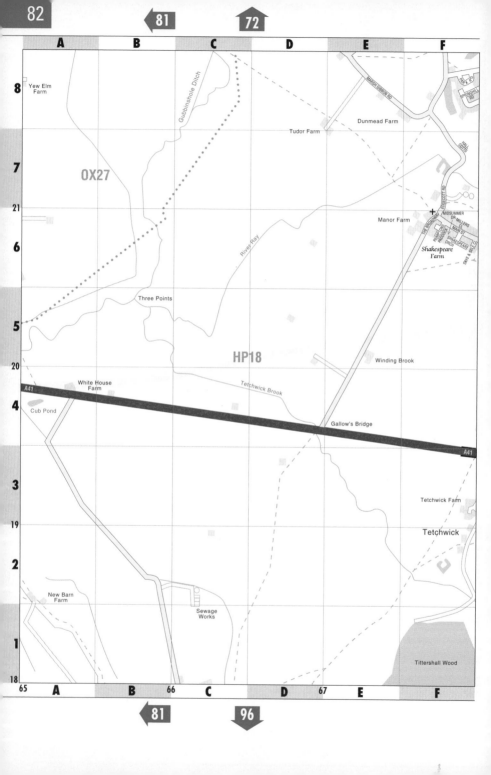

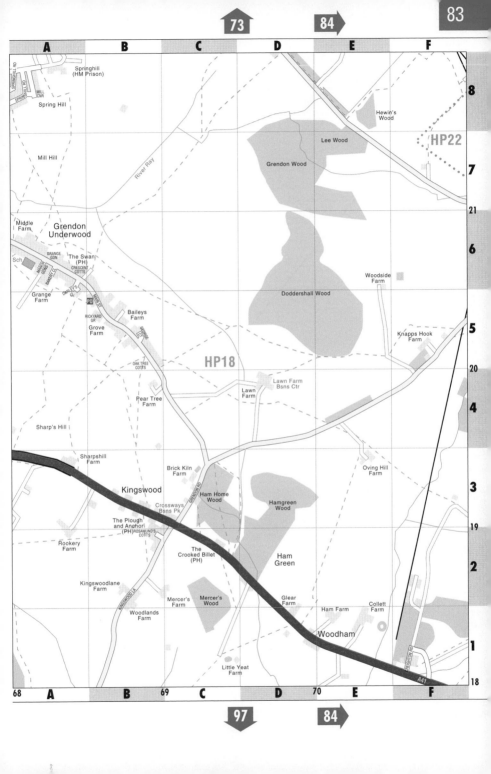

73
84

A B C D E F

8

7

21

6

5

20

4

3

19

2

1

18

Springhill (HM Prison)

SPRINGHILL RD
MILL CNR
SPRING HILL RD

Spring Hill

Mill Hill

Hewin's Wood

HP22

Lee Wood

Grendon Wood

River Ray

Middle Farm

Grendon Underwood

Sch

GRANGE GDN
MARSH GDNS
BAKER'S CL
OAKLEY'S CL

The Swan (PH)
CRESCENT COTTS

Grange Farm

RICKYARD GR

Baileys Farm

VAULT ST

GEORGE ST

Grove Farm

OAK TREE COTTS

Doddershall Wood

Woodside Farm

Knapps Hook Farm

HP18

Pear Tree Farm

Lawn Farm Bsns Ctr

Lawn Farm

Sharp's Hill

Sharpshill Farm

Brick Kiln Farm

GRENDON RD

Kingswood

Ham Home Wood

Hamgreen Wood

Oving Hill Farm

Crossways Bsns Pk

The Plough and Anchor (PH)
ROSAMUND'S COTTS

Rookery Farm

The Crooked Billet (PH)

Ham Green

KINGSWOODLA

Kingswoodlane Farm

Mercer's Farm

Mercer's Wood

Glear Farm

Ham Farm

Collett Farm

Woodlands Farm

Woodham

BRIGHTON RD

Little Yeat Farm

A41

68 A B 69 C D 70 E F 18

97
84

83
74

A B C D E F

HP18

Finemere Wood

River Ray

Dry Leys Farm

MK18

8

Shipton Lee

Woodlands Farm

7

Middle Farm

Lee House

Hill Farm

21

Woodlands Cottages

Lee Bridge Cottage

Grange Hill

6

North Farm

Grange Farm

LEE RD

5

Railway Cottage

HP22

Doddershall House

20

Fieldside Farm

4

Knapps Hook Wood

Lower South Farm

3

Upper South Farm

Factory

STATION RD

Binwell Farm

19

HP18

Quainton Road

P

Buckinghamshire Railway Centre

2

Mast

1

Lower Farm

18

UPPER BARN FARM

71 A B 72 C D 73 E F

83
98

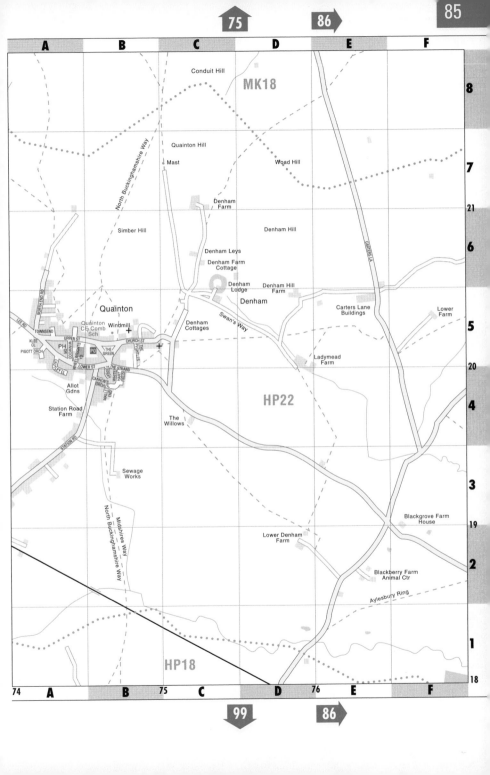

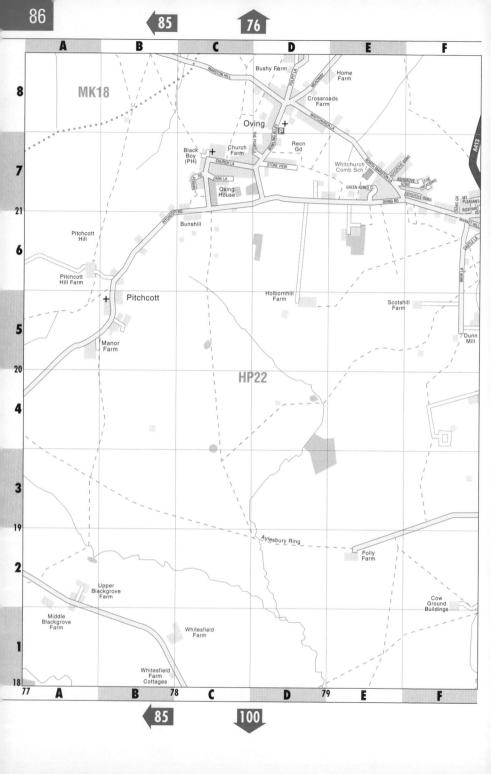

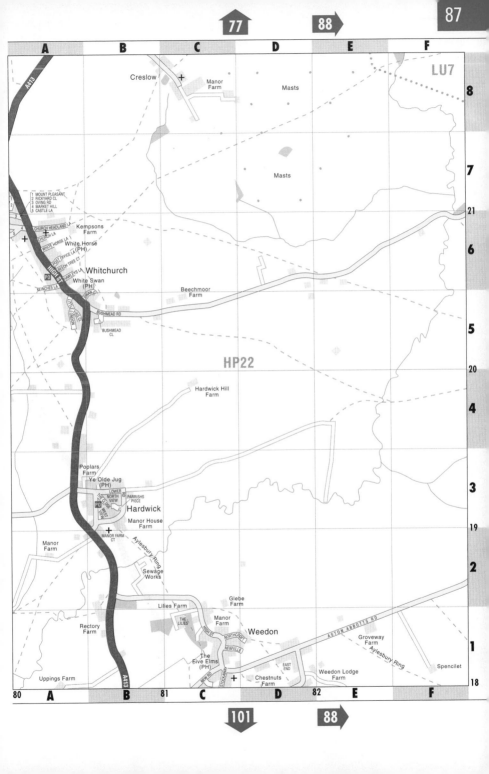

LU7

Creslow

Manor Farm

Masts

Masts

8

7

21

1 MOUNT PLEASANT
2 RICKYARD CL
3 OVING RD
4 MARKET HILL
5 CASTLE LA

CHURCH HEADLAND LA
CHURCH LA
WHITE HORSE LA
Kempsons Farm
White Horse (PH)
POST OFFICE LA
BEECH TREE CT
BEECH TREE LA
HIGH ST
HAWLEYS LA
Whitchurch
PO
White Swan (PH)
REINCHES LA
SWAN CL
Beechmoor Farm

6

BUSHMEAD RD
LITTLE LONDON
BUSHMEAD CL

5

HP22

20

Hardwick Hill Farm

4

Poplars Farm
Ye Olde Jug (PH)
LOWER RD
NORTH VIEW
WEST END
PARRISHS PIECE
PO
Hardwick
Manor House Farm

3

19

Manor Farm
MANOR FARM CT
Aylesbury Ring

Sewage Works

2

A413

Lilies Farm
THE LILIES
Glebe Farm
HIGH ST
Manor Farm
NORTHCROFT
NEWVILLE
Weedon
ASTON ABBOTS RD
Groveway Farm
Aylesbury Ring

1

Rectory Farm
The Five Elms (PH)
NEW RD
STOCKWELL FURLONG
EAST END
Chestnuts Farm
Weedon Lodge Farm
Spencilet

Uppings Farm
A413

18

A   B   C   D   E   F

8

7

21

6

5

20

4

3

19

2

1

18

Sewage
Works

LU7

Red Barn

Willow Brook
Farm

Red Barn
Farm

The Hay Barn
Bsns Pk

Vicarage
Farm

Longmoor
Farm

Works

Freemasons
Wood

Church
Farm

Aston
Abbotts

THE
OLD BAKERY

Norduck
Farm

The
Abbey

NASHS
FARM

PH

Windmill Hill
Farm

NEW
ZEALAND
COTTS

WINGRAVE RD

WINGRAVE
CROSS RDS

HP22

WINSLOW RD

THE LINES

Windmill
Hill

LINES HILL

Fox
Covert

Barns
Farm

A418

Lower Burston
Farm

Burston Hill
Farm

Manor
Farm

Burston Hill

BREWHOUSE LK

Aylesbury Ring

A418

Hale Farm

83   A   B   84   C   D   85   E   F

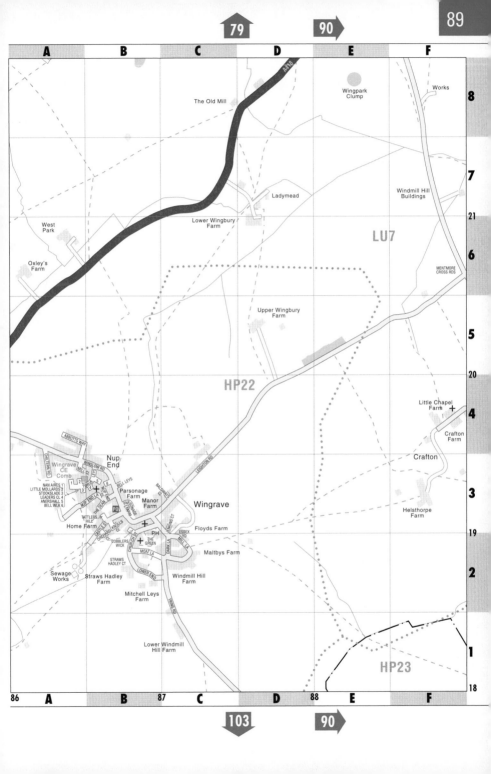

A   B   C   D   E   F

8

7

21

6

20

5

4

3

19

2

1

18

The Old Mill

Wingpark
Clump

Works

Windmill Hill
Buildings

Ladymead

Lower Wingbury
Farm

West
Park

LU7

MENTMORE
CROSS RDS

Oxley's
Farm

Upper Wingbury
Farm

HP22

Little Chapel
Farm

Crafton
Farm

Crafton

ABBOTTS WAY

Nup
End

Wingrave
CE
Comb

NAN AIRES 1
LITTLE MOLLARDS 2
STOOKSLADE 3
LEADERS CL 4
ANERSHALL 5
BELL WLK 6

WINSLOW RD

CHILTERN RD

MILL CL

BELL END LA

BELL LEYS

LEIGHTON RD

BALDWAY CL

Parsonage
Farm

Manor
Farm

Wingrave

PO

Helsthorpe
Farm

TATTLERS
HILL

Home Farm

DOBBLERS
WICK

CHURCH ST

CHURCH LA

ORCHARD CL

SELLS CL

PH
THE
GREEN

DARK LA

LOWING CT

ESSEX
YD

Floyds Farm

MOAT LA

Maltbys Farm

STRAWS
HADLEY CT

Sewage
Works

Straws Hadley
Farm

LOWER END

TRING RD

Windmill Hill
Farm

Mitchell Leys
Farm

Lower Windmill
Hill Farm

HP23

86   A   B   87   C   D   88   E   F

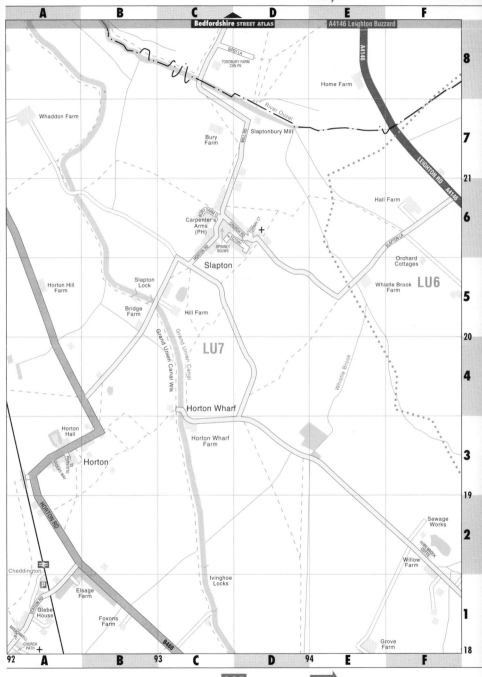

Bedfordshire STREET ATLAS

A4146 Leighton Buzzard

A4146

LEIGHTON RD

A4146

8

Home Farm

Whaddon Farm

River Ouzel

7

GIPSY LA
TODDBURY FARM
CVN PK

Bury
Farm

MILL RD

Slaptonbury Mill

21

Hall Farm

6

BURY FARM CL

Carpenter's
Arms
(PH)

HORTON RD

CHURCH RD

LA

ELM CT

+

SLAPTON LA

Orchard
Cottages

SPINNEY
BGLWS

Slapton

Whistle Brook
Farm

LU6

Horton Hill
Farm

Slapton
Lock

Hill Farm

Whistle Brook

5

Bridge
Farm

LU7

20

Grand Union Canal Wlk

Grand Union Canal

4

Horton Wharf

3

Horton
Hall

Horton Wharf
Farm

TO TODDURY WAY

Horton

HORTON RD

19

Sewage
Works

2

HOPE BROOK COTTS

Willow
Farm

Cheddington

P

Ivinghoe
Locks

STATION RD

Elsage
Farm

1

Glebe
House

Foxons
Farm

B488

BRIDEWELL

CHURCH
PATH

+

Grove
Farm

18

91

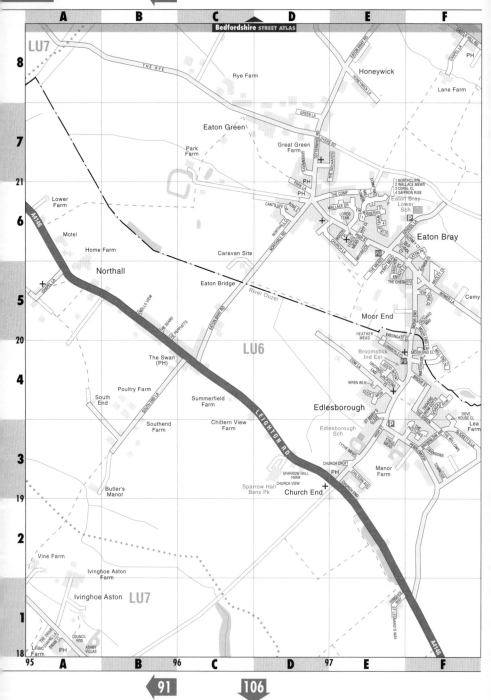

Bedfordshire STREET ATLAS

LU7

8

THE RYE

Rye Farm

Honeywick

Lane Farm

PH

CASTLE HILL RD

CHAPEL LA

HONEYWICK LA

GREEN LA

EATON BRAY RD

DYKES RD

Eaton Green

7

Park
Farm

Great Green
Farm

SUMMERLEYS

THE ORCHARDS

OTTERHILL RD

GREEN LA

COMP SIDE

21

PARK LA

PH

PH

THE COMP

WALLACE DR

1 NORTHCLIFFE
2 WALLACE MEWS
3 CORAL CL
4 SAFFRON RISE

Eaton Bray
Lower
Sch

P

Lower
Farm

A4146

CANTILUPE CL

RYE CL

NORTHALL RD

LORDS
TERR

NURSERY CL

THE

TOTTERNHOE RD

6

Motel

Home Farm

CHURCH LA

HIGH ST

THE KNOLLS

WOODSIDE

SEABROOK

Eaton Bray

PO

EATON PK

Northall

Caravan Site

THE MOSS

PEDDY'S WLK

KNIGHTSFIELD

KIMPT

THE CHEQUERS

YEW

BOWER LA

Cemy

CHAPEL LA

Eaton Bridge

Eaton Bridge

River Ouzel

MOOR END

DALE
TREE RD

5

CINKLE'S VIEW

THE SEARS

Moor End

HEATHER
MEAD

EATONGATE CL

MOOR END RD

20

THE PEPPATTS

EATON BRAY RD

LU6

Broomstick
Ind Est

SUMMERLEYS

MOOR END CL

PO

WHITEHALL

BROOK LA

ORCHARD
END

LOW LA

LAKESIDE

THE GREEN

4

Poultry Farm

SOUTH END LA

Summerfield
Farm

WREN WLK

COOK'S MDW

Edlesborough

DOVE
HOUSE CL

Lea
Farm

SLICKETTS LA

South
End

Southend
Farm

Chiltern View
Farm

LEIGHTON RD

Edlesborough
Sch

P

LINDEN
MEAD

THE
PASTURES

PEBBLEMOOR

BROWNLOW RD

THE WILLOWS

TOWN MEAD

BASONS
LA

EDENS CT

TEBWORTH

3

Church Croft

PH

TYTHE MEWS

Manor
Farm

CHILTERN AVE

19

Butler's
Manor

SPARROW HALL
FARM

CHURCH VIEW

Sparrow Hall
Bsns Pk

Church End

CHURCH END

ST MARY'S
GLEBE

2

Vine Farm

Ivinghoe Aston
Farm

Ivinghoe Aston

LU7

IVINGHOE
WAY

ST LEONARD'S WAY

A4146

1

THE DRIVE

CHAPEL CL

SWAN CL

PH

COUNCIL
HOS

ASHBY
VILLAS

18

Lilac
Farm

The Swan
(PH)

95

A

B

96

C

D

97

E

F

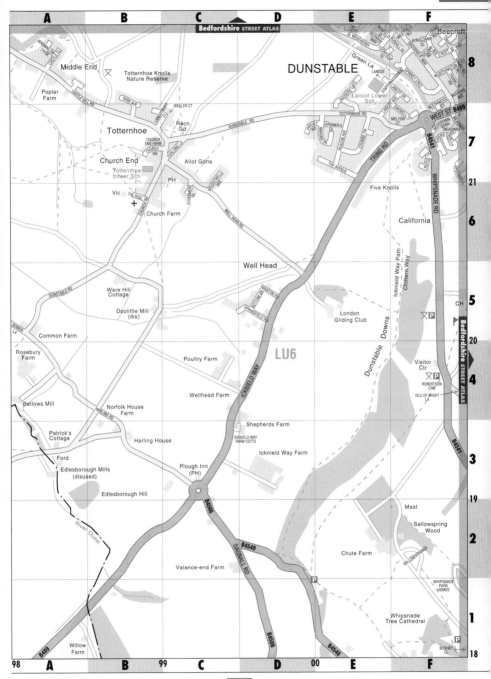

Bedfordshire STREET ATLAS

DUNSTABLE

Beecroft

Middle End

Totternhoe Knolls
Nature Reserve

Green La

Poplar
Farm

Lancot Lower
Sch

Weller Ct

Recn
Gd

Totternhoe

Dunstable Rd

Totternhoe Rd

Five Knolls

Church End

Allot Gdns

California

Totternhoe
Lower Sch

PH

Vic

Well Head Rd

Well Head

Icknield Way Path

Ware Hill
Cottage

Chiltern Way

CH

Doolittle Mill
(dis)

London
Gliding Club

P

Common Farm

LU6

Rosebury
Farm

Poultry Farm

Visitor
Ctr

Dunstable Downs

P

Bellows Mill

Wellhead Farm

Norfolk House
Farm

ROBERTSON
CRF

ISLE OF WIGHT
LA

Patrick's
Cottage

Shepherds Farm

Harling House

ICKNIELD WAY
FARM COTTS

Icknield Way Farm

Ford

Plough Inn
(PH)

Mast

Edlesborough Mills
(disused)

B4506

Sallowspring
Wood

Edlesborough Hill

B4540

Chute Farm

River Ouzel

DAGNALL RD

GALLOWSPRINGS

WHIPSNADE
PARK
HOMES

Valance-end Farm

Whipsnade
Tree Cathedral

P

B4506

B4540

BUSHEY
CL

Willow
Farm

B489

Bedfordshire STREET ATLAS

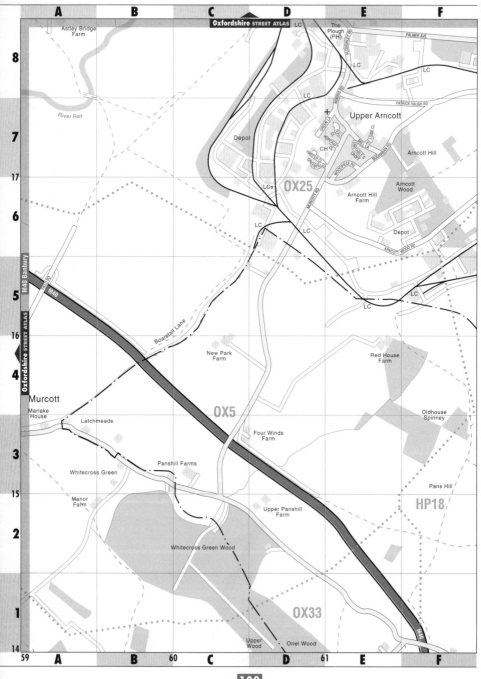

Astley Bridge Farm

River Ray

The Plough (PH)

PALMER AVE

LC

LC

PATRICK HAUGH RD

Upper Arncott

Depot

CH

Arncott Hill

Arncott Wood

OX25

LCs

Arncott Hill Farm

LC

LC

Depot

ARNCOTT WOOD RD

M40 Banbury

M40

Oxfordshire STREET ATLAS

LC

LC

LC

Boarstall Lane

New Park Farm

Red House Farm

Murcott

Marlake House

Latchmeads

OX5

Oldhouse Spinney

Four Winds Farm

Whitecross Green

Panshill Farms

Pans Hill

Manor Farm

HP18

Upper Panshill Farm

Whitecross Green Wood

OX33

M40

Upper Wood

Oriel Wood

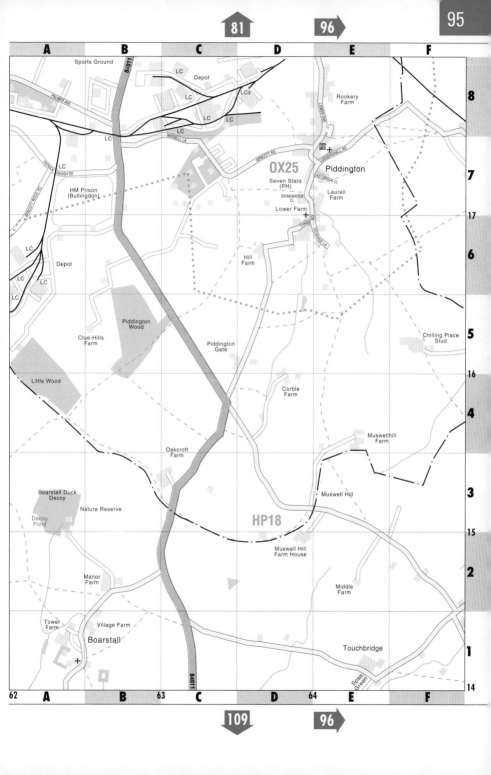

81 96

A B C D E F

8
7
17
6
5
16
4
3
15
2
1
14

Sports Ground

PALMER AVE

LC
Depot
LCs
LC
LC
LC
LC
WIDNELL LA

Rookery Farm

ARNCOTT RD

LOWER END

LC

OX25

Seven Stars (PH)

DRINKWATER CL

Piddington

EASTBROOK CL

LUGGERSHALL RD

PO

PATRICK HAUGH RD

LC
HM Prison (Bullingdon)

Laurell Farm

Lower Farm

THAME

ARNCOTT WOOD RD

LC
Depot
LC
LC
LC

Hill Farm

ROAD

TORBRIDGE LA

Clue-Hills Farm

Piddington Wood

Piddington Gate

Chilling Place Stud

Little Wood

Corble Farm

Muswellhill Farm

Oakcroft Farm

Boarstall Duck Decoy

Nature Reserve

Muswell Hill

HP18

Decoy Pond

Muswell Hill Farm House

Manor Farm

Middle Farm

Tower Farm

Village Farm

Boarstall

Touchbridge

B4011

Span Green

62 A B 63 C D 64 E F

109 96

A **B** **C** **D** **E** **F**

8

Nursery

Kings Farm

D'Oyley's Farm

Rookery Farm

The Green

Bridge Farm

Ludgershall

Tittershall Wood

PODINGTON RD

BICESTER RD

DUCK LA

SALTERS CL

Bull & Butcher (PH)

WHITE HART

HIGH ST

SALTERS LA

BROOK CL

Manor Farm

Glebe Farm

7

Eastfield Farm

BRILL RD

CHURCH LA

Ludgershall Farm

WOTTON END

17

6

Clearfields Farm

KINGSWOOD LA

The Lake

5

HP18

Poletrees Farm

Lapland Farm

Long Wood

The Warrells

16

Fivearch Wood

Fivearch Bridge

4

Rushbeds Wood Nature Reserve

Grenville's Wood

3

Tramway Farm

Rid's Hill

Lawn Farm

15

Brillbury Hall Farm

TRAM HILL

Coldharbour Farm

2

Dorton Park Farm

Brill Common

NORCOTTS KILN COTTS

THE AVENUE

GODFREYS CL

1

Windmill

NORTH HILLS

WINDMILL ST

HIGH ST

LA

CL

Brill

Chinkwell Wood

Dorton

Brook Farm

SOUTH HILLS

PH

Brill CE Comb Sch

14

65

A **B** 66 **C** **D** 67 **E** **F**

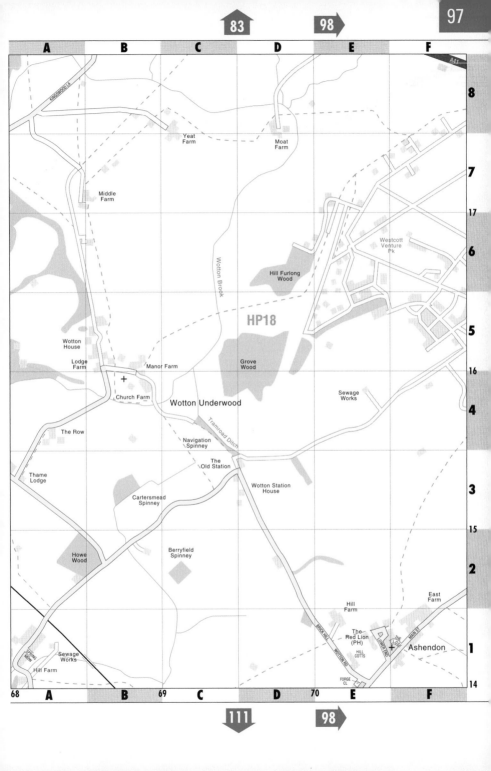

A B C D E F

8

7

17

6

5

16

4

3

15

2

1

14

KINGSWOOD LA

Yeat Farm

Moat Farm

Middle Farm

Wotton Brook

Hill Furlong Wood

Westcott Venture Pk

HP18

Wotton House

Lodge Farm

Manor Farm

Grove Wood

Sewage Works

Church Farm

Wotton Underwood

The Row

Tramroad Ditch

Navigation Spinney

Thame Lodge

The Old Station

Wotton Station House

Cartersmead Spinney

Berryfield Spinney

Howe Wood

East Farm

Hill Farm

The Red Lion (PH)

Ashendon

BRICK HILL

NETLOW RD

MAIN ST

HILL COTTS

THE CLOSE

LOWER END

FORGE CL

Sewage Works

Hill Farm

SPRING MDW

A41

97
84

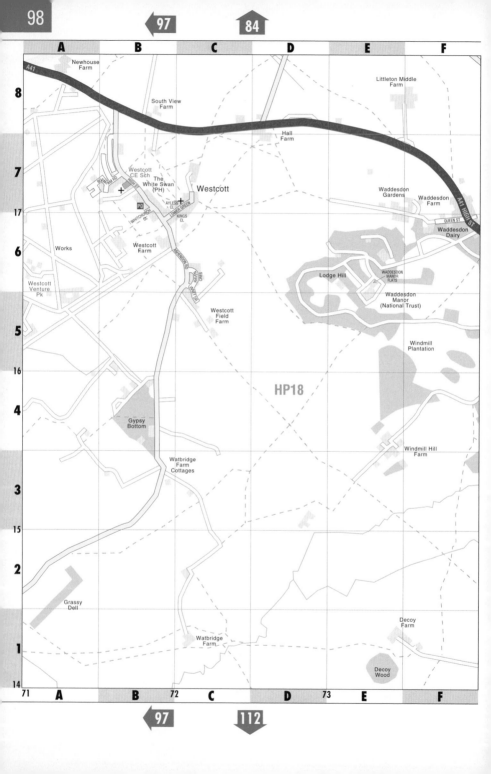

A B C D E F

8

7

17

6

5

16

4

15

3

2

14

1

A41
Newhouse Farm
South View Farm
Littleton Middle Farm
Hall Farm
Westcott CE Sch
The White Swan (PH)
Westcott
Waddesdon Gardens
Waddesdon Farm
AYLES CL
KINGS CL
LOWER GREEN
WHITCHURCH CE
PO
QUEEN ST
Waddesdon Dairy
A41 HIGH ST
Works
Westcott Farm
ASCENDEN RD
APPLE CRES
MIST CRES
Westcott Field Farm
Lodge Hill
WADDESDON MANOR FLATS
Waddesdon Manor (National Trust)
Westcott Venture Pk
Windmill Plantation
HP18
Gypsy Bottom
Windmill Hill Farm
Watbridge Farm Cottages
Grassy Dell
Decoy Farm
Watbridge Farm
Decoy Wood

71 A B 72 C D 73 E F

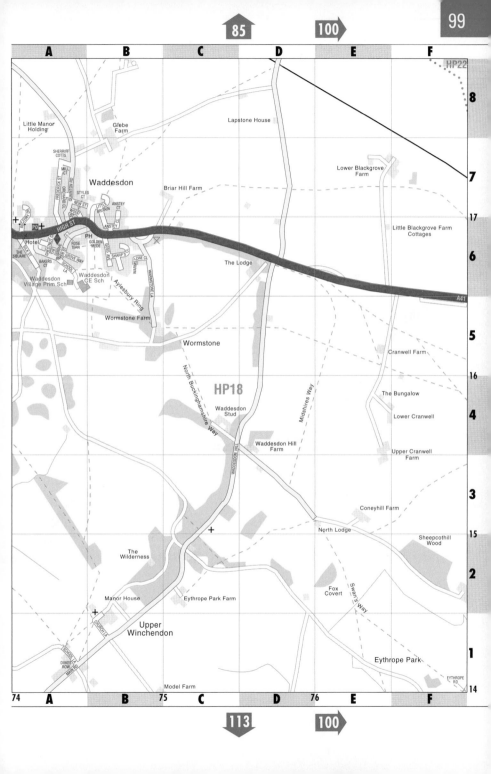

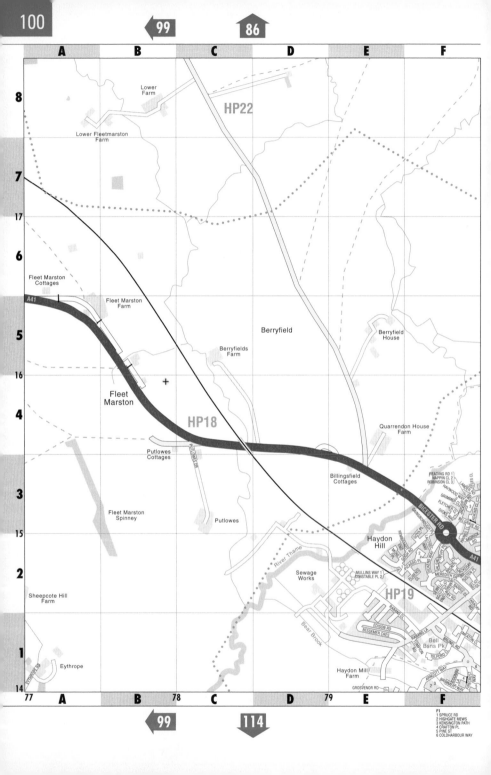

	A	B	C	D	E	F

8

Lower Farm

HP22

Lower Fleetmarston Farm

7

17

6

Fleet Marston Cottages

Fleet Marston Farm

A41

5

Berryfields Farm

Berryfield

Berryfield House

16

Fleet Marston

+

4

HP18

Quarrendon House Farm

Putlowes Cottages

3

Fleet Marston Spinney

Putlowes

Billingsfield Cottages

READING RD 1
NAPPIN CL 2
ROBINSON CL 3
HAYWOOD WAY
GRIMMER CL
FLETCHER
DICKENS
BICESTER RD

15

Haydon Hill

A41

2

Sheepcote Hill Farm

Sewage Works

River Thame

MULLINS WAY 1
CONSTABLE PL 2

HP19

MEREDITH GDNS

1

EDISON RD
BESSEMER CRES

Bell Bsns Pk

TELFORD

14

EYTHROPE RD

Eythrope

Bear Brook

Haydon Mill Farm

GROSVENOR RD

ARNCOTT WAY
BRIMMERS WAY

77	A	B	78	C	D	79	E	F

F1
1 SPRUCE RD
2 HIGHGATE MEWS
3 KENSINGTON PATH
4 CRAFTON PL
5 PINE ST
6 COLDHARBOUR WAY

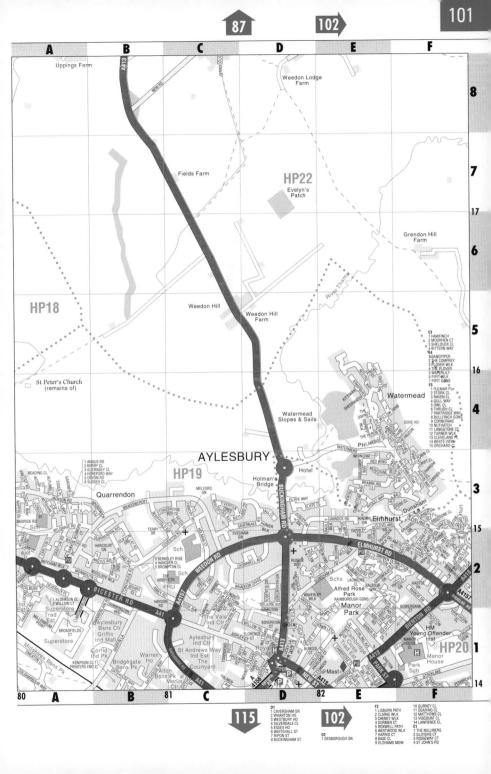

A   B   C   D   E   F

8

7

17

6

Uppings Farm

Weedon Lodge
Farm

HP22

Fields Farm

Evelyn's
Patch

Grendon Hill
Farm

HP18

Weedon Hill

Weedon Hill
Farm

River Thame

St Peter's Church
(remains of)

5

E3
1 HAWFINCH
2 MOORHEN CT
3 SHELDUCK CL
4 BITTERN WAY
E4
1 SANDPIPER
2 THE COMFREY
3 PLOVER WLK
4 THE PLOVER
5 WAVERILLY
6 PIPIT WLK
7 PIPIT GDNS
F3
1 FULMAR PL
2 STORK CL
3 RAVEN CL
4 GULL WAY
5 OWL CL
6 THRUSH CL
7 PARTRIDGE WAY
8 BULLFINCH GDNS
9 CORNCRAKE
10 NUTHATCH
11 LANGSTONE CL
12 TURNER WLK
13 CLEVELAND PL
14 WHITE VIEW
15 ORCHARD CL

16

Watermead

Watermead
Slopes & Sails

AYLESBURY

Hotel

Dunsham

HP19

1 ANGUS RD
2 KERRY CL
3 GUERNSEY CL
4 HEREFORD WAY
5 DEVON RD
6 SUSSEX CL

Quarrendon

Holman's
Bridge

MELFORD
GN

Elmhurst

ELMHURST RD

4

3

15

Manor
Park

Alfred Rose
Park

2

14

1 CAVERSHAM GN
2 WHARTON HO
3 WESTBURY HO
4 SILVERDALE CL
5 ESSEX HO
6 WHITEHALL ST
7 RIPON ST
8 BUCKINGHAM ST

HM
Young Offender
Inst

HP20

Manor
House

Park
Sch

READING CL

BADRICK RD
Sch

ELIOT

BICESTER RD

Superstore
Trad Est

1 ALDERSON CL
2 WILLOW CT

BROADFIELDOS
CT

Superstore

Midshires Bsns Pk

Aylesbury
Bsns Ctr

Griffin
Ind Mall

Corrid
Ind Pk

Bridgegate
Bsns Pk

Warren
Ho

Alton
Bsns Ctr

Merlin
Ctr

The
Courtyard

Aylesbury
Ind Ctr

St Andrews Way
Ind Est

PRU

Sch

1 BERKELEY RISE
4 HANOVER CL
5 BROMPTON CL

The Vale
Ind Ctr

WEEDON RD

A4157

A41

RAINBOROUGH GDNS

A413

A4157

BIERTON RD

A4157

A418

PARK ST

A41

A41

KEMPSON CL 1
PRINTERS END 2

80   A   81   B   C   82   D   E   F

D1
1 CAVERSHAM GN
2 WHARTON HO
3 WESTBURY HO
4 SILVERDALE CL
5 ESSEX HO
6 WHITEHALL ST
7 RIPON ST
8 BUCKINGHAM ST

D2
1 DESBOROUGH GN

F2
1 LISBURN PATH
2 CLARKE WLK
3 CHENEY WLK
4 DORNER CT
5 ROXWELL PATH
6 WESTWOOD WLK
7 HARRIS CT
8 BASE CL
9 OLDHAMS MDW

10 GURNEY CL
11 DEARING CL
12 MATTHEWS CL
13 VISCOUNT CL
14 LAWRENCE CL
E1
1 THE MILLINERS
2 GLOVERS CT
3 RIDGEWAY CT
4 ST JOHN'S RD

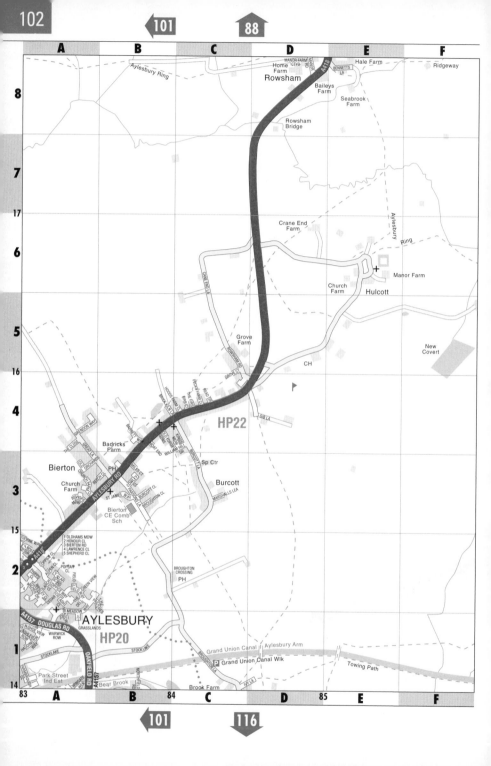

101
88

A B C D E F

8

7

17

6

5

16

4

HP22

3

15

2

1 OLDHAMS MDW
2 HONOUR CL
3 BIERTON RD
4 LAWRENCE CL
5 SHEPHERD CL

1

14

83 A B 84 C D 85 E F

101
116

Aylesbury Ring

Home
Farm
Rowsham

Hale Farm

Ridgeway

Baileys
Farm

Seabrook
Farm

Bennetts
LA

MANOR FARM

Rowsham
Bridge

Crane End
Farm

Aylesbury

Ring

Manor Farm

Church
Farm

Hulcott

CRANE END LA

Grove
Farm

New
Covert

GROVE
RD

CH

PECKS HANDS LA
RED CL
The FIRS
FIRS CL

CUB LA

HOODS MINI CL
BROOK CL

BADGER WALK
BOAT END

Badricks
Farm

WILLOWS END
WILLIAM HILL
BRISCOTT LA

Sp Ctr

Bierton

PH

THE CLOSE
BRENT LA
DEAN CL
ORCHARDS

Burcott

Church
Farm

AYLESBURY RD

COWLEY CL

MARSHALLS LEA

BISHOPS
MDW
BRISCOTT LA
ST JAMES
BURCOTT CL
BROUGHTON CL

Bierton
CE Comb
Sch

THORNE WAY
A418
VICARAGE CL
COPPER LA
POPLAR
CL

FIELD
GREEN VIEW

BROUGHTON
CROSSING
PH

W MEADOW
GRASSLANDS

AYLESBURY

DOUGLAS RD
A4157

HP20

WARWICK
ROW

STOCKLAKE

OAKFIELD RD
A4157

STOCKLAKE

NORTH FIELD
CL

BRIDGE CL
BRIDGE CL
CUB LA

Grand Union Canal Aylesbury Arm

P Grand Union Canal Wlk

Towing Path

Park Street
Ind Est

Bear Brook

Brook Farm

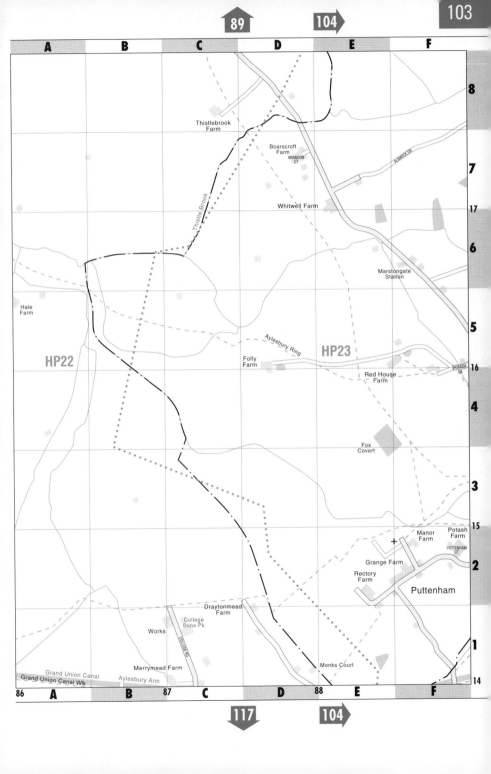

89
104
117
104

A B C D E F

8
7
17
6
5
16
4
3
15
2
1
14

Thistlebrook Farm

Boarscroft Farm
BRANDON CT

ALNWICK DR

Whitwell Farm

Thistle Brook

Marstongate Station

Hale Farm

HP22

Aylesbury Ring

HP23

Folly Farm

Red House Farm

POTASH LA

Fox Covert

Manor Farm

Potash Farm

PUTTENHAM CT

Grange Farm

Rectory Farm

Puttenham

Draytonmead Farm

College Bsns Pk

Works

COLLEGE RD

Monks Court

Merrymead Farm

Grand Union Canal
Grand Union Canal Wlk
Aylesbury Arm

86 A B 87 C D 88 E F

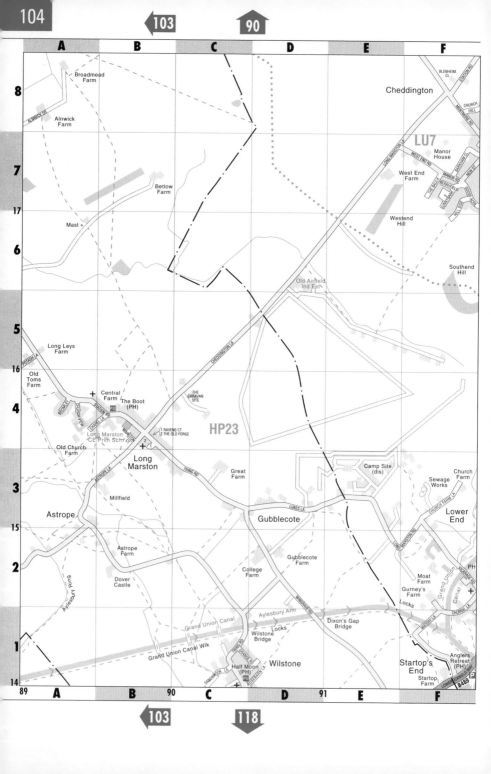

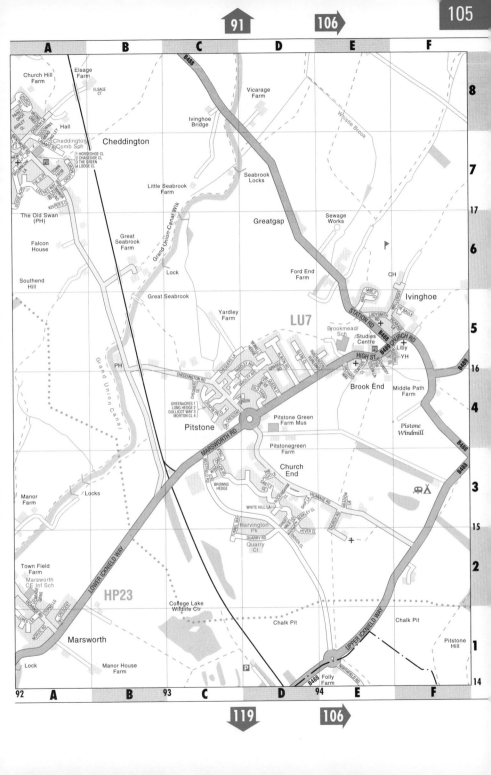

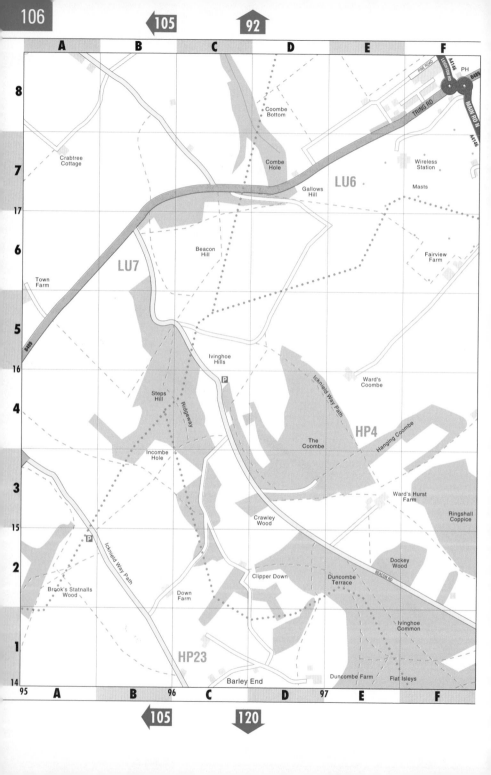

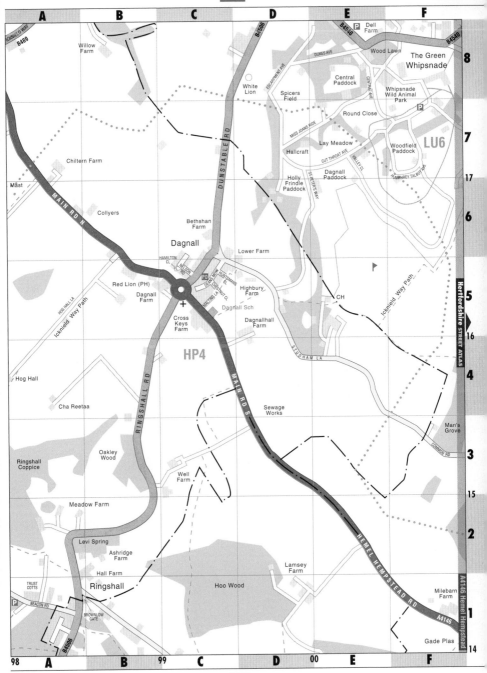

A B C D E F

ICKNIELD WAY
B489

Willow
Farm

8

White
Lion

Dell
Farm

Wood Lawn

The Green
Whipsnade

Spicers
Field

DUKES AVE

Central
Paddock

Whipsnade
Wild Animal
Park

Chiltern Farm

Round Close

LU6

7

MISS JOAN'S RIDE

Lay Meadow

Woodfield
Paddock

Mast

Hallcraft

CUT THROAT AVE

Dagnall
Paddock

HUMPHREY TALBOT AVE

17

Collyers

Holly
Frindle
Paddock

ST PETER'S WAY

VALLEY CL

CH

6

Bethshan
Farm

Icknield Way Path

MAIN RD N

Dagnall

Lower Farm

DUNSTABLE RD

B506

Red Lion (PH)

HAMILTON
CL

NELSON RD

PO

Highbury
Farm

5

HOG HALL LA

Icknield Way Path

Dagnall
Farm

GLEBE CRES

NEW
RD

HUNTSMANS
PL

MARTINS LA

NUT CL

Dagnall Sch

Hertfordshire STREET ATLAS

Cross
Keys
Farm

Dagnallhall
Farm

16

HP4

Hog Hall

STUDHAM LA

4

Cha Reetaa

MAIN RD S

Sewage
Works

RINGSHALL RD

Man's
Grove

Ringshall
Coppice

Oakley
Wood

Well
Farm

COMMON RD

3

Meadow Farm

15

Levi Spring

2

Ashridge
Farm

Lamsey
Farm

HEMEL HEMPSTEAD RD

Hall Farm

Hoo Wood

TRUST
COTTS

Ringshall

Milebarn
Farm

A4146 Hemel Hempstead

P

BEACON RD

BROWNLOW
GATE

A4146

1

B506

Gade Plas

14

A B C D E F

98 99 00

94

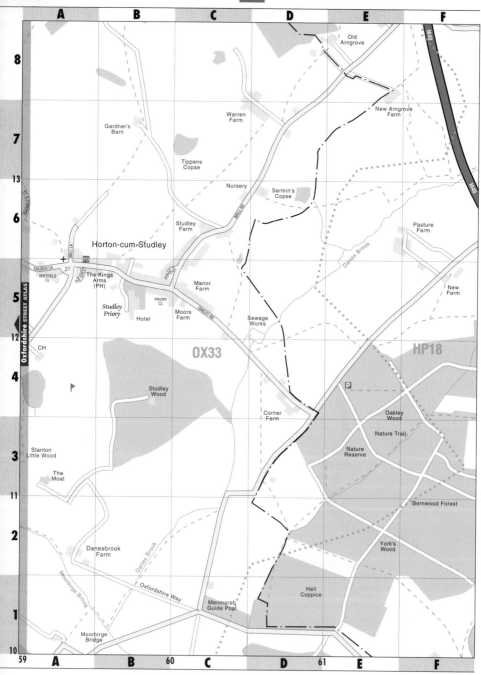

122

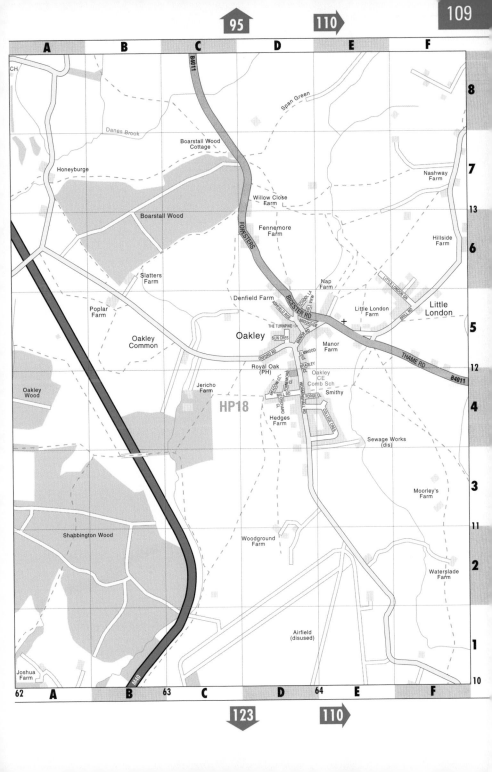

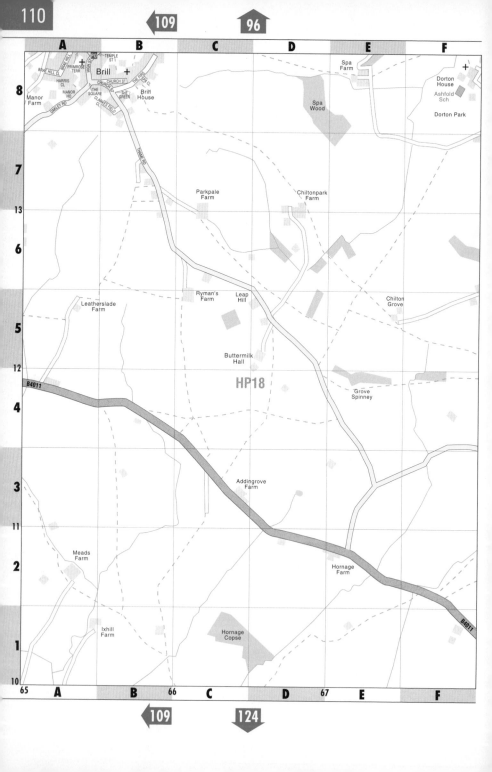

109

96

A **B** **C** **D** **E** **F**

8

Manor
Farm

Spa
Farm

Dorton
House

Ashfold
Sch

Dorton Park

OAKLEY RD

BRAE HILL CL

PRIMROSE
TERR

HARRIS
CL

MANOR
HO

THE SQUARE

THE GREEN

CLAYRES FIELD
CL

BRILL HILL

HIGH ST

CHURCH ST

TEMPLE
ST

THE END

SPA CL

PO

Brill

Brill
House

Spa
Wood

7

THAME RD

13

Parkpale
Farm

Chiltonpark
Farm

6

Leatherslade
Farm

Ryman's
Farm

Leap
Hill

Chilton
Grove

5

12

Buttermilk
Hall

HP18

Grove
Spinney

B4011

4

Addingrove
Farm

3

11

Meads
Farm

Hornage
Farm

B4011

2

Ixhill
Farm

Hornage
Copse

1

10

65 **A** **B** 66 **C** **D** 67 **E** **F**

109

124

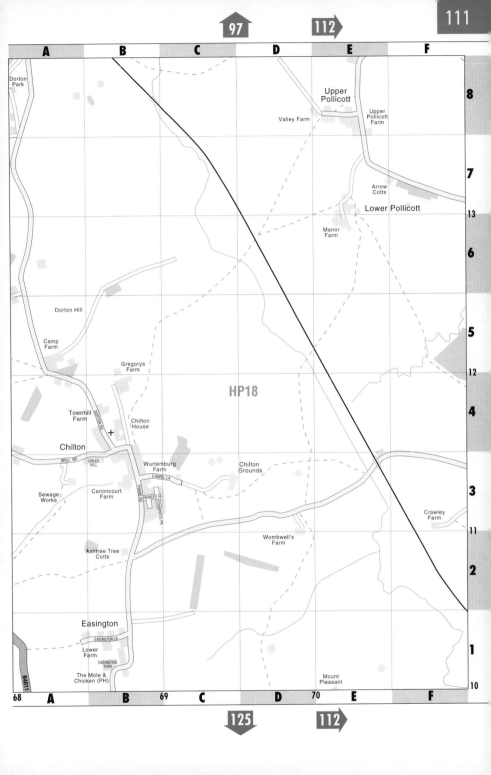

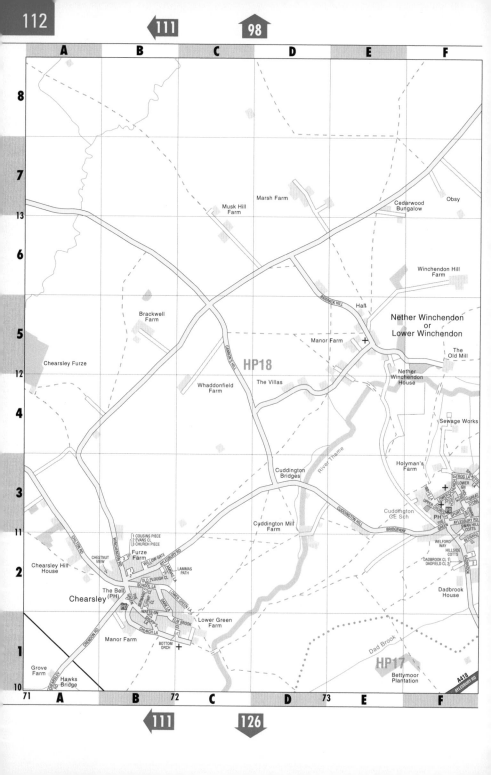

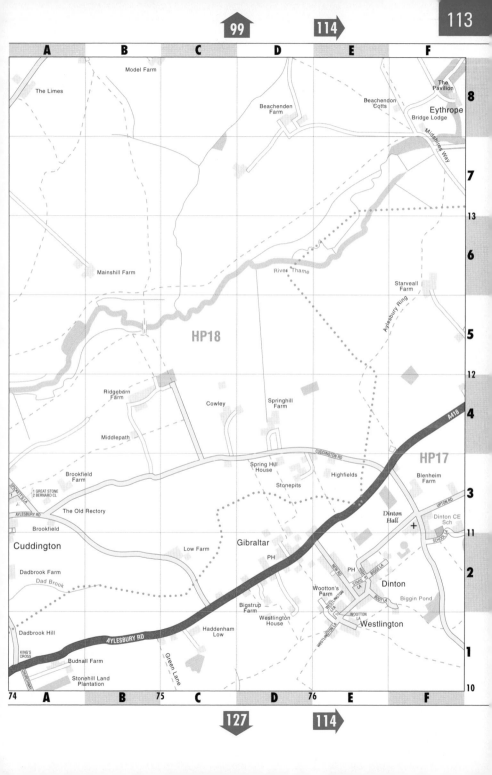

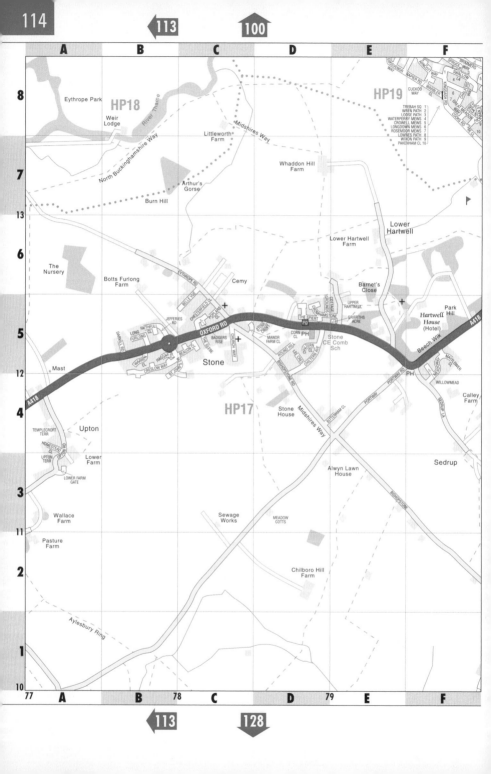

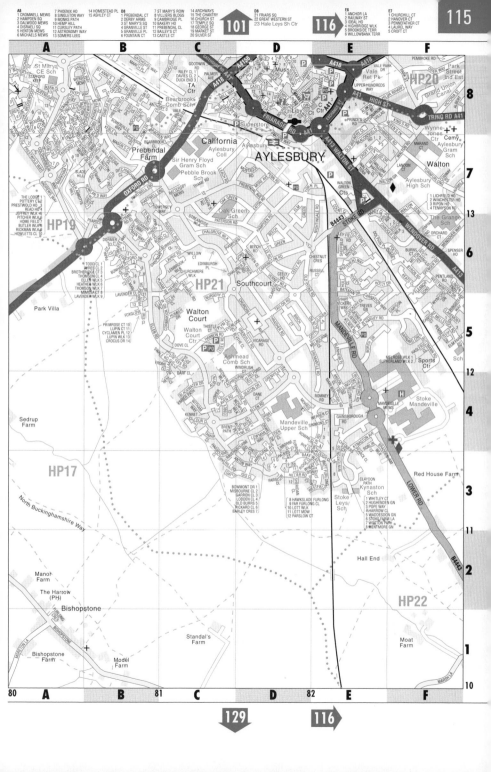

115
102

A B C D E F

8

Park Street
Ind Est

HP20

Oak Farm

Oak Farm
Rare Breeds Park

Broughton
Inf Sch

Broughton

Manor Farm

Victoria
Park

Broughton
Jun Sch

AYLESBURY

A41

TRING RD

Cemy

St Joseph's
RC Inf
Sch

Weston Mead
Farm

7

13

St Edward's
RC Jun Sch

Turnfurlong
Inf & Jun
Schs

TURNFURLONG
ROW

CHADWELL
PATH

ASTON CLINTON RD

Hotel

Liby

A41

6

Bedgrove
Jun Sch

Bedgrove
Inf Sch

WESTEND DITCH

1 RINGSTEAD WAY
2 LYNWOOD RD

A413

5

12

Bedgrove

HP21

Bedgrove Park

NEW RD

Rectory Farm

HP22

4

MARSHAM CL 1
THORPE CL 2
LOWBROOK CL 3

EDWARD
WLK

DIANE WLK

Hampden Hall
Coll

CH

3

11

WENDOVER RD

WALNUT TREE
CT

Weston
Turville

Weston Turville
CE Sch

PH

2

Stoke
Mandeville

Malthouse
Farm

STATION RD

A4010

Manor
Farm

PH

LOWER RD

Stoke
Mandeville

Manor
Farm

LODGE
FARM
CL

West End
Farm

WILLOW
END

1

Stoke
Mandeville
Comb Sch

B4443

RISBOROUGH RD

Wool Pack
(PH)

A4010

A413

Alberta
Farm

CHAPEL LA

10

83 A B 84 C D 85 E F

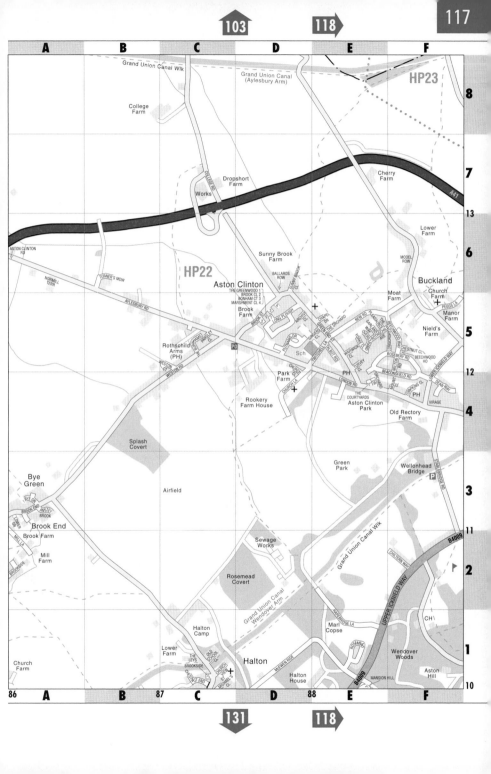

A **B** **C** **D** **E** **F**

Grand Union Canal Wlk

Grand Union Canal
(Aylesbury Arm)

HP23

8

College
Farm

7

Cherry
Farm

A41

13

Dropshort
Farm

Works

Lower
Farm

6

ASTON CLINTON
RD

Sunny Brook
Farm

MODEL
ROW

NORMILL
TERR

TURNER'S MDW

HP22

BALLARDS
ROW

Buckland

Aston Clinton

Moat
Farm

Church
Farm

5

AYLESBURY RD

THE GREENWOOD 1
BROOK CL 2
BONHAM CT 3
MARSHMENT CL 4

Manor
Farm

Brook
Farm

LONG PLOUGH

NEW RD

Nield's
Farm

WESTON CL

Rothschild
Arms
(PH)

PO

PULLMANS DR

BEECHWOOD
HO

CHESTNUT CL

ROSEBERY RD

WESTON RD

Sch

Park
Farm

PH

BEACONSFIELD RD

12

CHURCH

LONDON RD

PH

DEAN WAY

Rookery
Farm House

CHURCH LA

THE
COURTYARDS
Aston Clinton
Park

PH

VIRAGE

4

Old Rectory
Farm

Splash
Covert

Green
Park

Wellonhead
Bridge

3

Bye
Green

BYE GN

Airfield

P

STABLEBRIDGE RD

BROOK END

BROOK

B4009

11

Brook End

Brook
Farm

Sewage
Works

Grand Union Canal Wlk

2

Mill
Farm

Rosemead
Covert

CHELTERN WAY

UPPER ICKNIELD WAY

Church
Farm

Grand Union Canal
Wendover Arm

Marl
Copse

Halton
Camp

MARSHBRIDGE LA

CH

1

Lower
Farm

THE
LEYS

OLD
SCHOOL
LA

Halton

Wendover
Woods

Aston
Hill

BROOKSIDE

Halton
House

B4009

MANSION HILL

10

A 86 **B** 87 **C** **D** 88 **E** **F**

117 104

	A	B	C	D	E	F

8

B488

Chapel End
CHAPEL FIELDS
CHAPEL WELL RD
NEW RD
THE SCHOOL
Wilstone Great Farm
James Farm
Startop's End Resr

Chapelend Farm
Manor Farm
Wilstone Green

BUCKLANDS CROFT

Cemy
Tringford

WINDMILL RD
TRING FORD RD
WHARFE LA

7

LOWER ICKNIELD WAY
P
Wilstone Little Farm
Tringford Resr

Tringford Farm

13
A41

Wilstone Resr
(Nature Reserve)

Landing Stage
Little Tring Farm
Little Tring

B489

LITTLE TRING RD

6

Lower Farm

Drayton Beauchamp

Upper Farm

Grand Union Canal Wlk

HP23

5

B488

Miswell Farm
Miswell House

12

BISHOP RD
CHESHIRE GATE
THORNE WAY
LONDON RD
WENWELL CL

HP22

Bridge Farm
GREEN PATH

Drayton Bridge
Church Hill Farm

Broadview Farm

Icknield Farm

ICKNIELD WAY
Mast
Tring Bsns Ctr
Windmill

BUNSTRUX
OSMINGTON CL
WINDMILL PL

4

Bucklandwharf
WHARF ROW

THORNCLOSES

Rye Hill Farm

Beeches Farm

Factories

Goldfield fhf Sch
ELLISON CT 1
POPE CT 2

ACACIA WLK

BEECHWOOD CT
GRAVEL DR

Hotel
TRING HILL
B4009

B488

B4635

AYLESBURY RD
Sch

STANLEY GDNS
CONVENT CT

B4635
WESTERN RD
PARK RD

3

UPPER ICKNIELD WAY

Lodge Farm

Icknield House

Cemy

CHILTERN VILLAS
HOME FARM

11

B4009

DRAYTON BEAUCHAMP RD

Drayton Manor

WhiteCloud House

A41

2

Daniel's Hole

Astonhill Coppice

Fox Lane

MUCKHATCH LA
West Leith
West Leith Farm

Stud Farm
THE BARNS

West Leith
Stubbing's Wood

1

P
Forest Wlk

Buckland Hoo

Deacon's Hill Wood

Hastoe Hill
HASTOE HILL

10
Aston Hill Farm

89	A	B	90	C	D	91	E	F

117 132

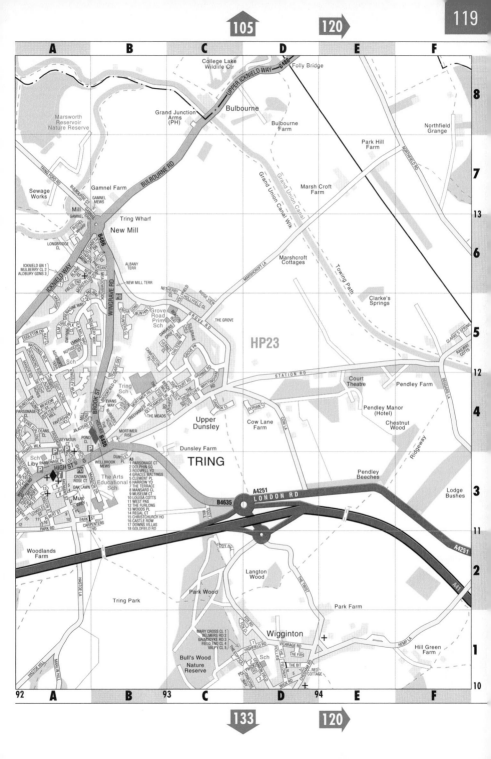

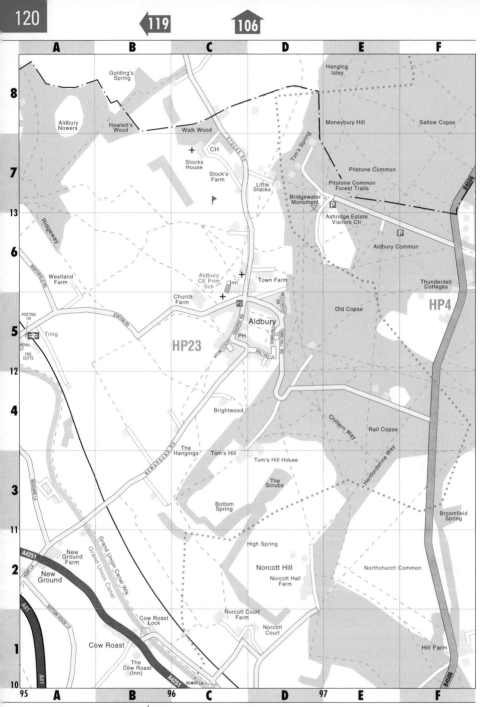

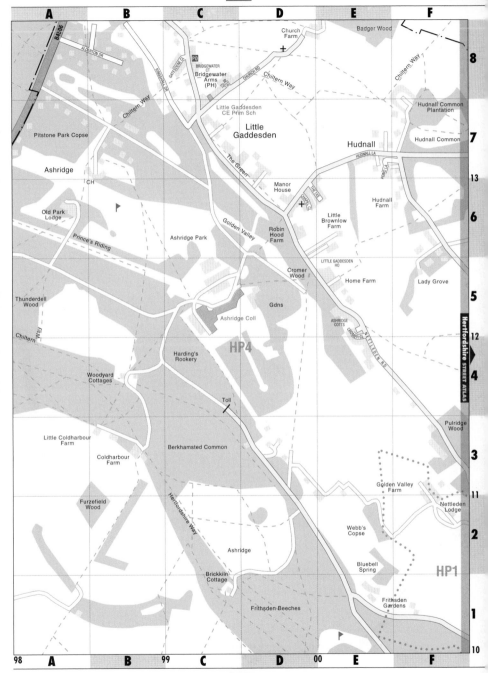

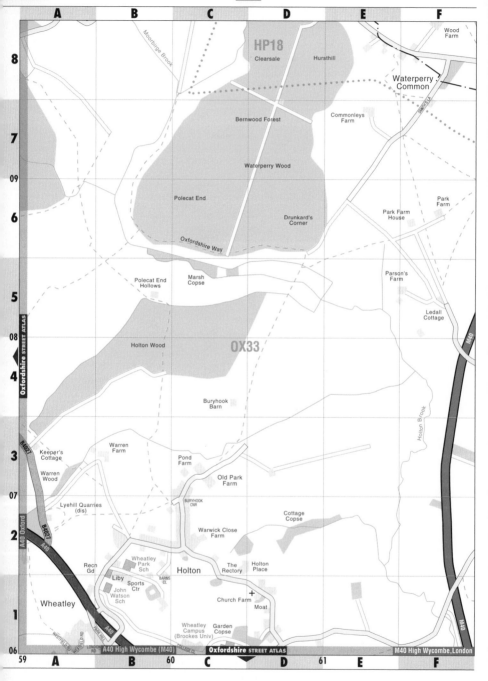

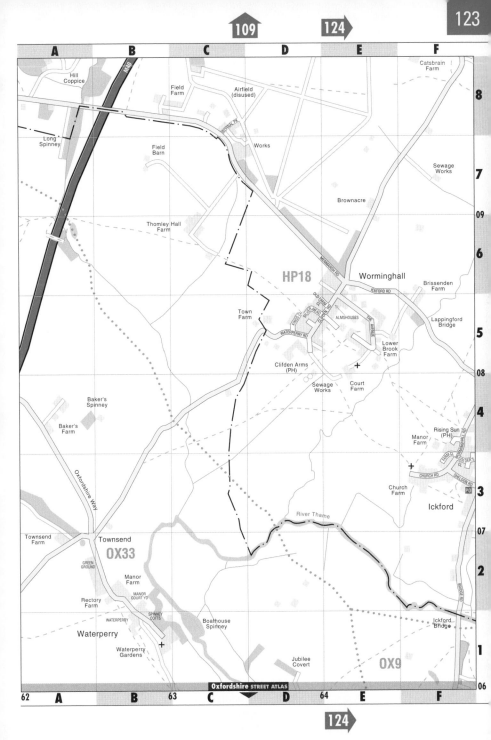

Hill
Coppice

Long
Spinney

Field
Farm

Airfield
(disused)

Catsbrain
Farm

WORNAL PK

Works

8

Field
Barn

Sewage
Works

7

Brownacre

Thomley Hall
Farm

09

6

HP18

Worminghall

Brissenden
Farm

MERMAISH RD

ICKFORD RD

Lappingford
Bridge

Town
Farm

OLD CLARK CL

KING'S CL

SILL MEAD

ALMSHOUSES

THE AVENUE

5

WATERPERRY RD

Lower
Brook
Farm

Clifden Arms
(PH)

Sewage
Works

Court
Farm

08

Baker's
Spinney

Baker's
Farm

Manor
Farm

Rising Sun
(PH)

4

Oxfordshire Way

TRESM CL

GOYDER'S

PLOWRIGHT RD

CHURCH RD

SHELSON RD

Church
Farm

PO

Ickford

3

River Thame

Townsend
Farm

Townsend

07

OX33

GREEN
GROUND

Manor
Farm

MANOR
COURT YD

Rectory
Farm

WATERPERRY

SPINNEY
COTTS

Boathouse
Spinney

Ickford
Bridge

BRIDGE RD

2

Waterperry

Waterperry
Gardens

Jubilee
Covert

OX9

1

06

62   A   B   63   C   D   64   E   F

	A	B	C	D	E	F

8

Woodway Farm

7

Westfield Farm

Lower
Peppershill Farm

09

Peppershill

Crendon
House

Hill
Farm

6

Peppershill Farm

5

HP18

08

Peacehaven
Farm

Lower
Farm

4

Ickford

Upper
Farm

GOLDER'S CL

SCHOOL CL

SHELDON RD

TURNFURLERS

THE BIRDHAMS

LOWER
FARM
CL

LONG CRENDON RD

MARSH RD

HOME CL

MORTON KING
CL

3

Ickford
Comb Sch

BULLS LA

Marsh
Farm

Sewage
Works

Shabbington

Little
Ickford

Rookery
Farm

Village
Farm

THE RYE

07

LIMES WAY

SCHOOL LA

ICKFORD RD

DUKES CL

KING WELLS CL

PO

2

Franklins
Farm

+

River Thame

Old
Fisherman
(PH)

OX9

1

OX9

River Thame

Manor Farm

North
Weston

06

65	A		B	66	C		D	67	E		F

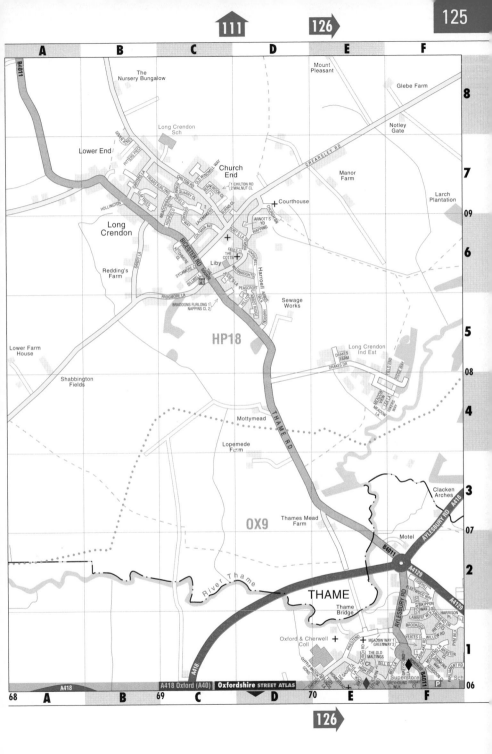

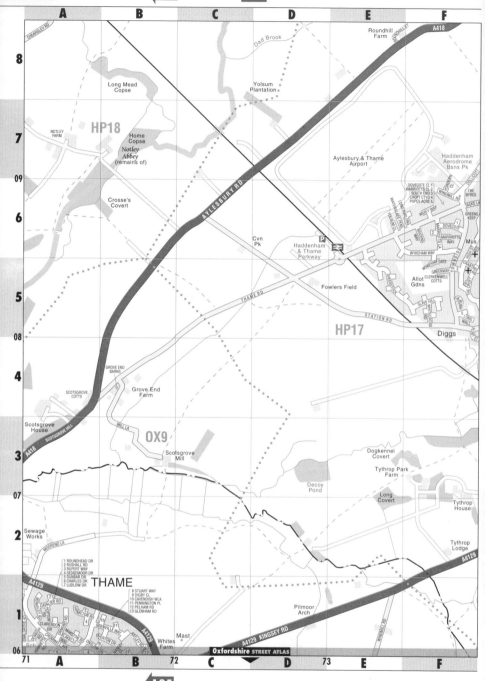

125

112

A B C D E F

8

7

HP18

09

6

5

08

HP17

4

3

07

OX9

2

1

06

71 A B 72 C D 73 E F

125

Dad Brook

Roundhill Farm

A418

Long Mead Copse

Yolsum Plantation

NOTLEY FARM

Home Copse

Notley Abbey (remains of)

Aylesbury & Thame Airport

Haddenham Aerodrome Bsns Pk

Crosse's Covert

AYLESBURY RD

DOVECOTE CL
MARRIOTTS CL
SOUTH END
CROFT CTYD
POPES ACRE

WINDMILL RD

THE BYRES

TACKS LA

GREENS KEEP

Cvn Pk

Haddenham & Thame Parkway

DOVECOTE

Mus

Fowlers Field

THAME RD

MARRIOTTS WAY

WYKEHAM WAY

WYNDHAM GATE

GREENWAY

Allot Gdns

CLERKENWELL COTTS

STATION RD

SLADE HILL

THE SCRUB

LONG WALL

Diggs

GROVE END BARNS

SCOTSGROVE COTTS

Grove End Farm

Scotsgrove House

SCOTSGROVE MILL

A418

MILL LA

Scotsgrove Mill

Dogkennel Covert

Tythrop Park Farm

Long Covert

Tythrop House

Decoy Pond

Tythrop Lodge

A4129

Sewage Works

MOOREND LA

THAME

1 ROUNDHEAD DR
2 RUSHALL RD
3 RUPERT WAY
4 SEDGEMOOR DR
5 DUNBAR DR
6 CHARLES DR
7 LUDLOW DR

8 STUART WAY
9 DIGBY CL
10 CAVENDISH WLK
11 PENNINGTON PL
12 PELHAM RD
13 GLENHAM RD

A4129

GRENVILLE WAY

OVERTON DR

ANSTEY RD

Mast

Whites Farm

A4129 KINGSEY RD

Pilmoor Arch

WINDMILL RD

A4129

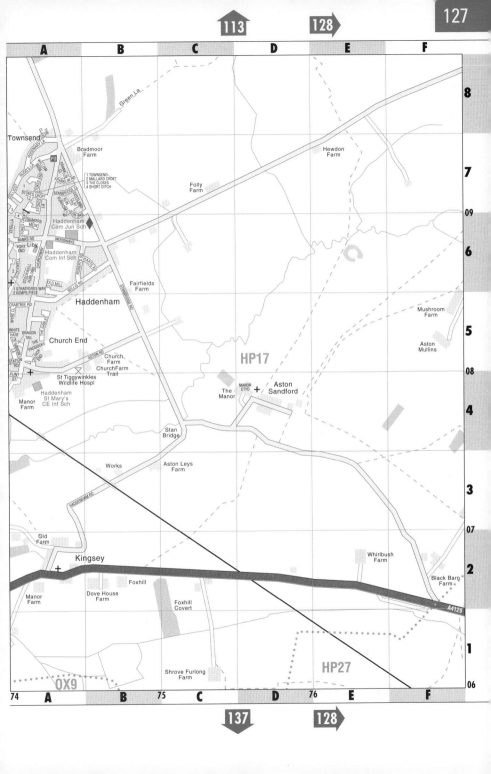

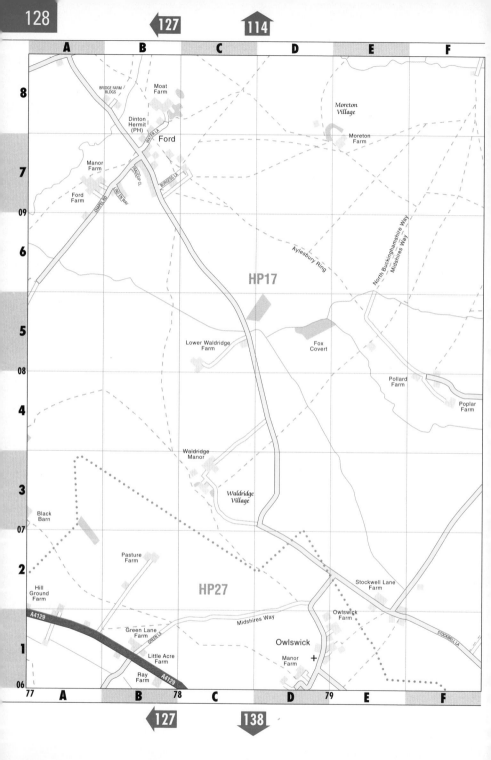

127
114

A   B   C   D   E   F

8

7

09

6

HP17

5

08

4

3

07

2

HP27

A4129

1

06

77   A   B   78   C   D   79   E   F

Moat
Farm

BRIDGE FARM
BLDGS

Dinton
Hermit
(PH)

WATER LA

Ford

Manor
Farm

BRADLEY CL

BURGESS LA

Ford
Farm

CHAPEL RD

LINCOLN WAY

Moreton
Village

Moreton
Farm

Aylesbury Ring

North Buckinghamshire Way

Midshires Way

Lower Waldridge
Farm

Fox
Covert

Pollard
Farm

Poplar
Farm

Waldridge
Manor

Waldridge
Village

Black
Barn

Pasture
Farm

Hill
Ground
Farm

A4129

Green Lane
Farm

GREEN LA

Little Acre
Farm

Ray
Farm

Stockwell Lane
Farm

Midshires Way

Owlswick
Farm

Owlswick

Manor
Farm

STOCKWELL LA

127
138

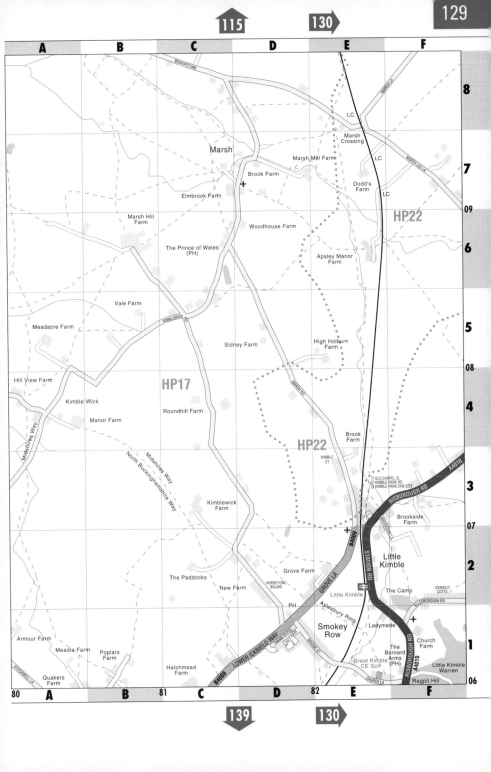

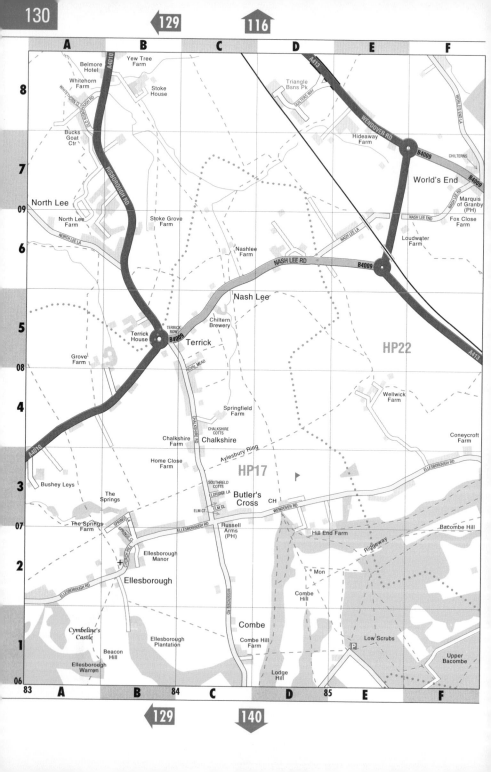

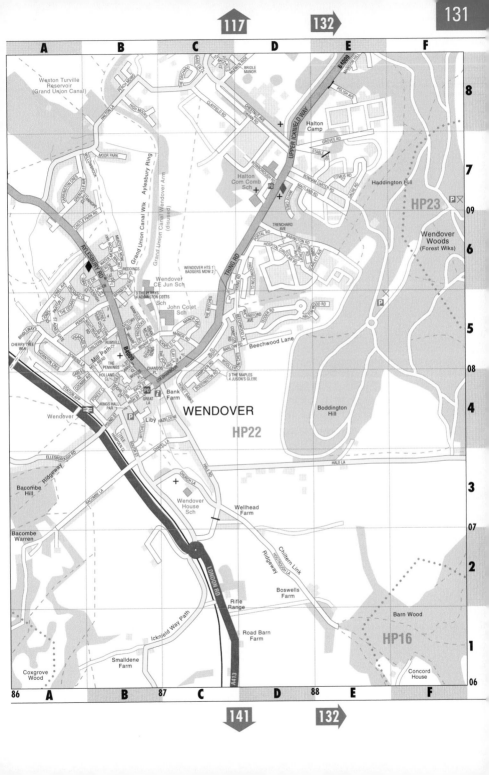

117
132

A B C D E F

8

7

HP23 09

6

5

08

4

3

07

2

1

06

WENDOVER

HP22

HP16

Weston Turville
Reservoir
(Grand Union Canal)

Halton
Camp

Haddington Hill

Wendover
Woods
(Forest Wlks)

Boddington
Hill

Wendover

Bacombe
Hill

Bacombe
Warren

Coxgrove
Wood

Smalldene
Farm

Road Barn
Farm

Rifle
Range

Boswells
Farm

Barn Wood

Concord
House

Wellhead
Farm

Wendover
House
Sch

Bank
Farm

Liby

Halton
Com Comb
Sch

Wendover
CE Jun Sch

John Colet
Sch

Ridgeway

Chiltern Link
Ridgeway

Icknield Way Path

Mill Path

Aylesbury Ring

Grand Union Canal Wlk

Grand Union Canal Wendover Arm
(disused)

UPPER ICKNIELD WAY

TRING RD

LONDON RD

A413

B4009

Beechwood Lane

HALE LA

ELLESBOROUGH RD

Ridgeway

WENDOVER HTS 1
BADGERS MDW 2

3 THE PERRYS
4 ADDINGTON COTTS

3 THE MAPLES
4 JUSON'S GLEBE

141
132

131
118

	A	B	C	D	E	F

8

Ashton Hill

HP22

Coombe Hill

Dancersend

Terrier's End

Leafy Lane

Grove Wood

Riding Stables

7

Bradnidge Wood

Spencersgreen

Nature Reserve

Bittam's Wood

Painsend Farm

Hanghill

Pavis Wood

Drayton Hollow

Hastoe House

Hastoe

GADMORE LA

HASTOE FARM BARNS

HASTOE HILL

BROWN'S LA

Tatnall's Wood

09

Works

6

The Crong

Water Works

Northhill Wood

Oakengrove

Longcroft

SHIRE LA

Mast

5

Halton Wood Forest Wlks

Chivery Hall Farm

Ridgeway

BRIDGEWAY

Hengrove Wood

08

Chivery

HP23

Leylands Farm

4

Chivery Farm

Milesfield

Lanes End

Buckland Wood

Beechwood Farm

3

HALE LA

The Hale

St Leonard's Common

COPPICE FARM PK CVN SITE

The Plantation

GILBERT'S HILL

St Leonards

Bucklandwood Farm

BOTTOM RD

LITTLE TRING RD

TAYLOR'S LA

07

Hale Wood

HP22

Chambers Green Farm

Buckland Grange

CHAPEL LA

White Lion (PH)

BROWN'S RISE

JENKINS LA

OAK LA

Cock's Hill

Franklands

2

Baldwin's Wood

Ashen Grove

Dundridge Manor

Stonehill Wood

1

HP16

Old Brun's Farm

ARREWIG LA

Great Widmoor Wood

Brun Grange

Lady Grove

HP5

06

	A	B	C	D	E	F
	89		90		91	

131
142

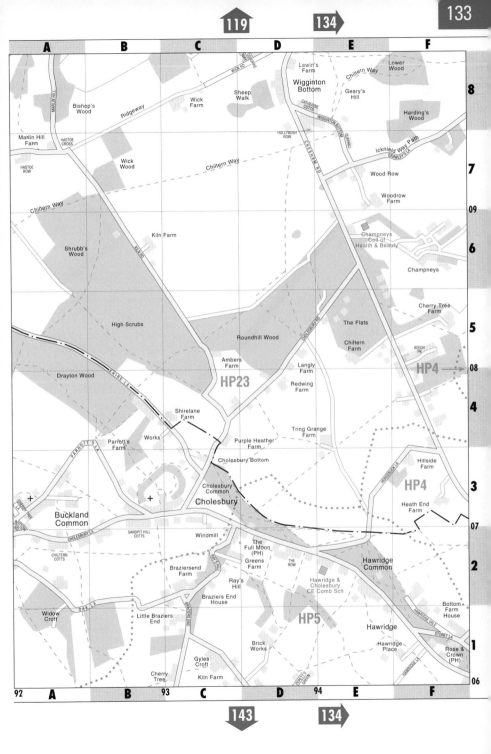

119
134

A **B** **C** **D** **E** **F**

8

Lewin's Farm

Wigginton Bottom

Chiltern Way

Lower Wood

Geary's Hill

Harding's Wood

Bishop's Wood

Wick Farm

Sheep Walk

WICK RD

CATHERINE COTTS

WHITE HILL

MARLIN HILL

Ridgeway

CATHERINE COTTS

WIGGINTON BOTTOM

CLAYHILL

Icknield Way Path

DARMLEY LA

7

Marlin Hill Farm

HASTOE CROSS

HASTOE ROW

Wick Wood

Chiltern Way

Wood Row

Woodrow Farm

09

Chiltern Way

Kiln Farm

KILN RD

Champneys Coll of Health & Beauty

6

Shrubb's Wood

Champneys

High Scrubs

CHOLESBURY RD

Roundhill Wood

The Flats

Cherry Tree Farm

5

Ambers Farm

Chiltern Farm

BEECH PK

HP4

Drayton Wood

SHIRE LA

HP23

Langly Farm

Redwing Farm

HP4

08

4

Shirelane Farm

Works

Purple Heather Farm

Tring Grange Farm

HORSELOCK LA

Hillside Farm

HP4

3

PARROTT'S LA

Parrott's Farm

Cholesbury Bottom

Heath End Farm

07

Cholesbury Common

Cholesbury

BOTTOM LA

CHOLESBURY TREE LA

Buckland Common

CHOLESBURY LA

SANDPIT HILL COTTS

Windmill

The Full Moon (PH)

THE ROW

2

CHILTERN COTTS

Braziersend Farm

RAY'S HILL

Greens Farm

Hawridge & Cholesbury CE Comb Sch

Hawridge Common

HAWRIDGE VALE

Bottom Farm House

STONEY LA

OAK LA

Ray's Hill

Braziers End House

Hawridge

Rose & Crown (PH)

1

Widow Croft

Little Braziers End

WIGGINS END

Brick Works

HP5

Hawridge Place

HAWRIDGE LA

Cherry Tree

Gyles Croft

Kiln Farm

PEPETT'S GREEN

06

92 **A** **B** 93 **C** **D** 94 **E** **F**

143
134

133
120

A B C D E F

8

Iknield Way
Park
CRAWLEYS LA
A41
Tinker's Lodge

Crawley's Lane Farm

White Farm

TINKERS LA

HP23

Newsetts Wood

A4251
WOSE LA

Hamberlins Farm

Rothschild Ct

Hamberlins House

Hamberlins Wood

HAMBERLINS LA

DARR LA
SHOOTERSWAY

Shootersway Farm

The Shrubbery

Lodge Farm

Windbush

HP23

Tring Lodge

Oak Corner

COCK GR

HP4

Cock Grove

Rossway Home Farm

Rossway

Heath End

Glebe Farm

Hill Farm

HP5

Woodfield Spring Farm

Hadden's Plantation

Marlin Chapel Farm

The Old Farm

Hog Lane Farm

Johns Lane Farm

HOG LA

NORTHCHURCH LA

HP5

Pancake Wood

Hockeridge Wood

Hockeridge Bottom

A416
CHESHAM RD

LINKS LA

CROSS OAK RD

A41

Dudswell

TRING RD

Grand Union Canal
Grand Union Canal Wlk
River Bulbourne

HOME FARM RD

HIGH ST

Gorseside

Northchurch Common
Ashridge

B4506

Northchurch House

NEW RD

CHILTERN VIEW 1
CONNAUGHT GDNS 2

St Mary's CE Fst Sch
Northchurch

B4506

Works
CANALSIDE

COMPASS POINT 1
EXHIMS MEWS 2
TUDOR ORCH 3
APPLECROFT 4
SEYMOUR CT 5
EGGLESFIELD CL 6

THE BENTONS 7
STONEY CL 8
CHILTERNS 9
THOMAS CT 10

GRANVILLE RD

BELL LA

DURRANTS LA

The Rookery

Woodcock Hill

The Lodge

Egerton-Rothesay Sch

Shootersway

Westfield Fst Sch

A4251

Greenway Fst Sch

OAKWOOD

SHOOTERSWAY

BLEGBERRY GDNS
BALCARY GDNS

95 96 97

07

06

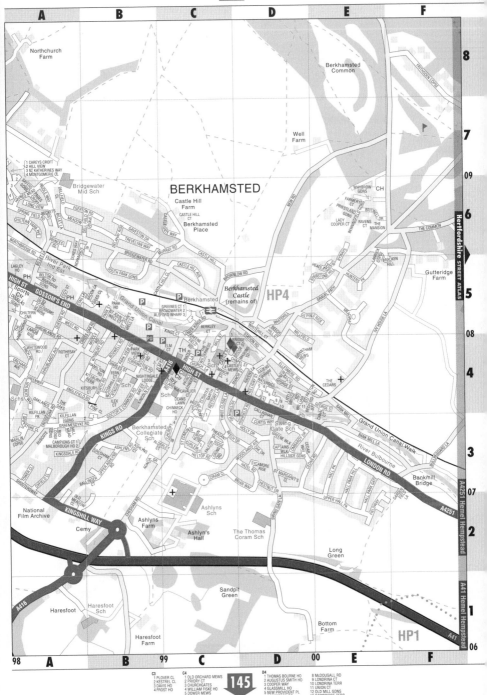

BERKHAMSTED

C3
1 PLOVER CL
2 KESTREL CL
3 DAVIS HO
4 FROST HO

C4
1 OLD ORCHARD MEWS
2 PRIORY CT
3 CHURCHGATES
4 WILLIAM FISKE HO
5 DOWER MEWS

D4
1 THOMAS BOURNE HO
2 AUGUSTUS SMITH HO
3 COOPER WAY
4 GLASSMILL HO
5 NEW PROVIDENT PL
6 ROBERTSON RD
7 COSTINS WLK
8 McDOUGALL RD
9 LONDRINA CT
10 LONDRINA TERR
11 UNION CT
12 OLD MILL GDNS
13 CAMBRIDGE TERR

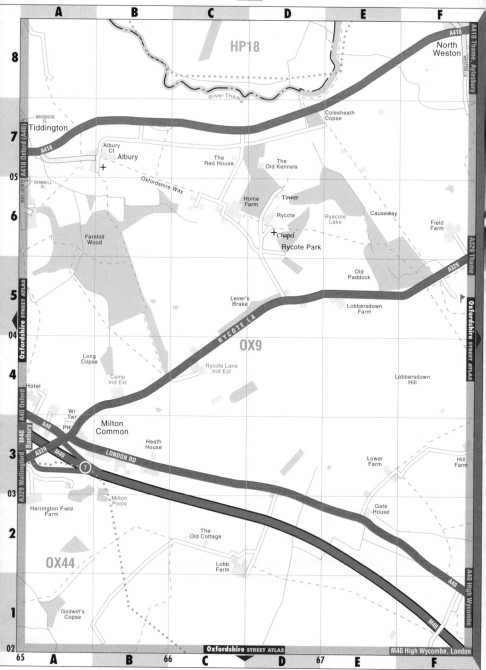

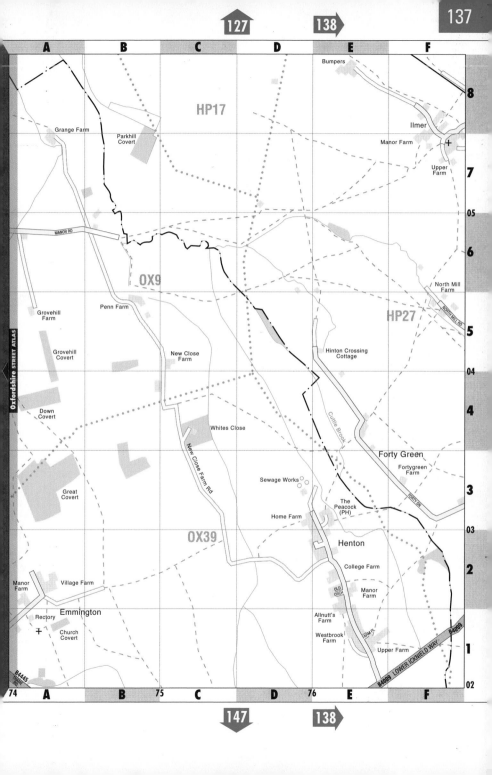

A B C D E F

8

Bumpers

Ilmer

HP17

Grange Farm

Parkhill
Covert

Manor Farm

Upper
Farm

7

05

MANOR RD

6

OX9

North Mill
Farm

Penn Farm

Grovehill
Farm

NORTH MILL RD

HP27

5

Grovehill
Covert

New Close
Farm

Hinton Crossing
Cottage

04

Down
Covert

Cuttle Brook

4

New Close Farm Rd

Whites Close

Forty Green

Fortygreen
Farm

FORTY GN

Great
Covert

Sewage Works

The
Peacock
(PH)

3

03

Home Farm

OX39

Henton

College Farm

2

Manor
Farm

Village Farm

Manor
Farm

OLD
ORCH

Allnutt's
Farm

Rectory

Emmington

Westbrook
Farm

Church
Covert

FARM PL

Upper Farm

B4009

LOWER (ICKNELD WAY)

1

B4009

02

B4445

74 A B 75 C D 76 E F

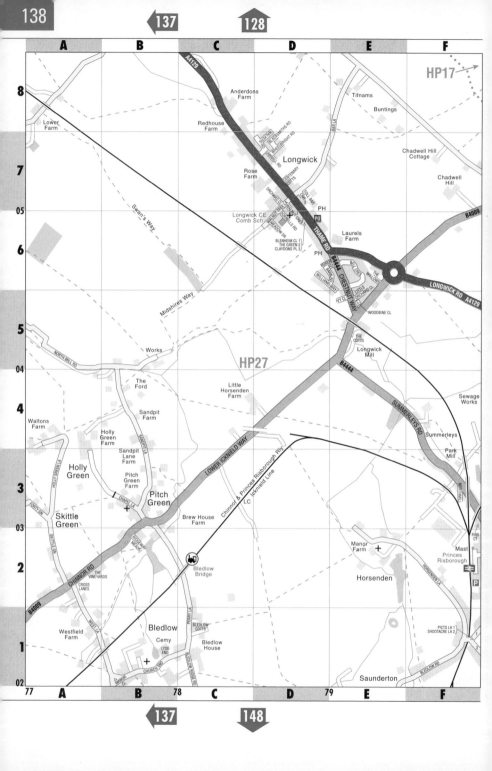

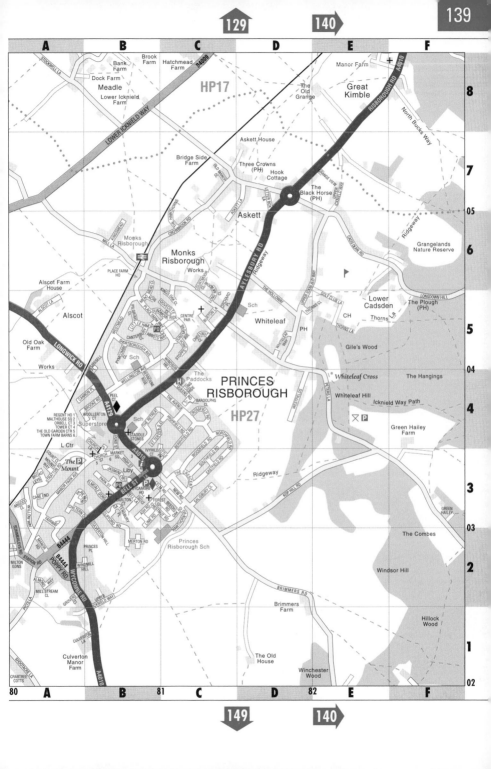

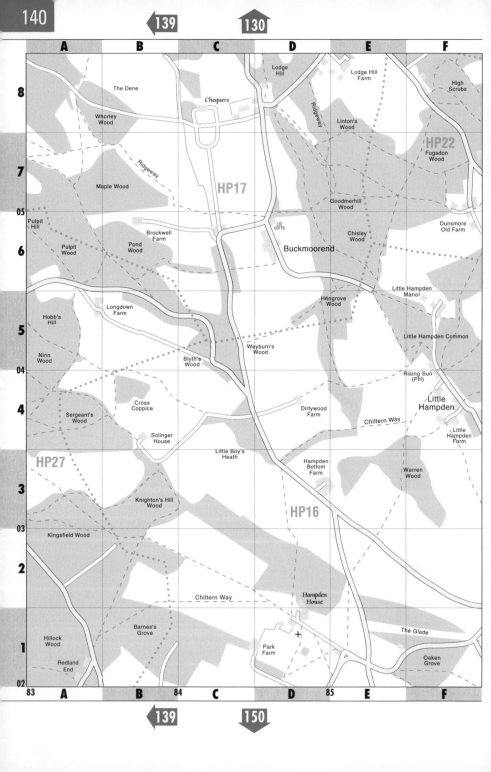

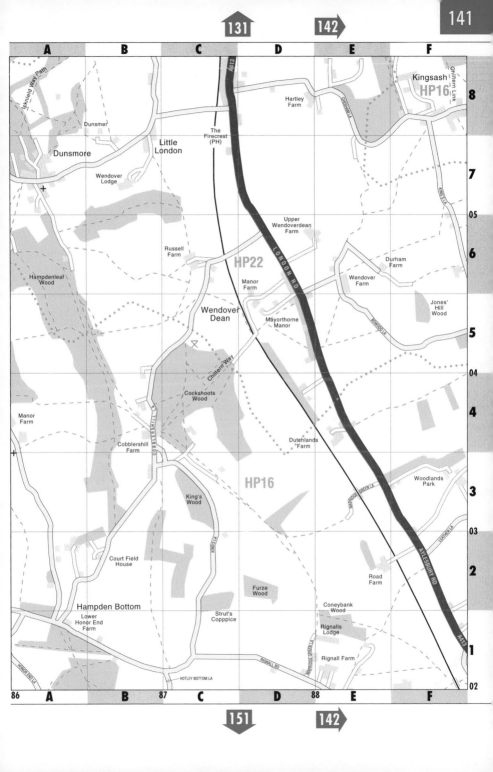

141 132

A B C D E F

8

HP23

Lordling Wood

Chiltern Way

PH

Kingswood

ARRIWIG LA

Erriwig Farm

HP23

HP5

7

The Gate (PH)

Lee Gate

Kingsgate Farm

Swan Bottom

Three Gates Farm

05

Gwenfa Farm

Bray's Wood

6

HP22

Chiltern Link

Lownde's Wood

Lee Clump

The Lee

Home Farm

Lee Clump House

The Bugle (PH)

5

Church Farm

Church (restored)

Hawthorn Farm

Cock and Rabbit (PH)

Lee Common CE Sch

OXFORD ST

ST MARYS

CRICKETS LA

KING'S LA

Bassibones Farm

Lower Bassibones Farm

Rushmoor Wood

HP16

Lee Common

MARTIN DELL COTTS

CHERRY TREE LA

04

KING'S LA

Hunt's Green

Pipers

SLY CNR

4

Hunt's Green Farm

Field End Grange

Ballinger Bottom

Chiltern Link

3

LEATHER LA

Hammonds Hall Farm

BALLINGER ROW

SOMME LA

BLACK LA

CHILTERN RD

BLACKFIELD

Ballinger Common

03

Springfield Farm

Ballinger Farm

BALLINGER GRANGE

2

Wr Twr

Ballinger Grove

HERBERTS HOLE

Havenfields

POTTER ROW

Park Farm

Ballinger Bottom (South)

1

A413

MEADOW LA

BALLINGER RD

MARRIOTTS AVE

02

89 A B 90 C D 91 E F

Bury Farm

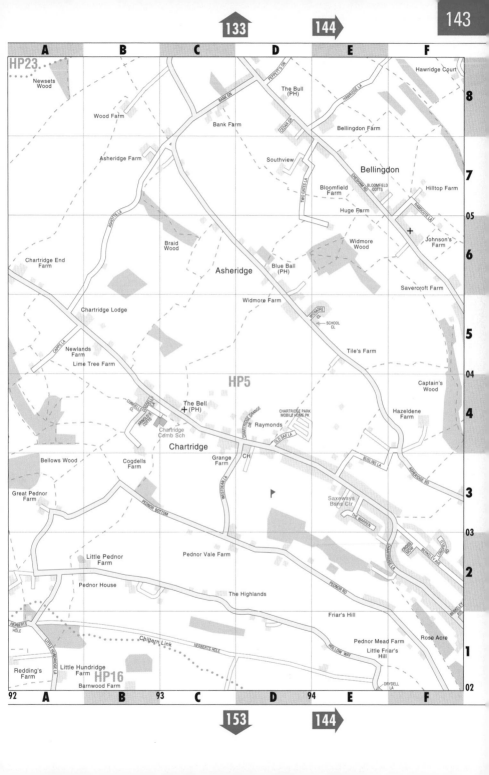

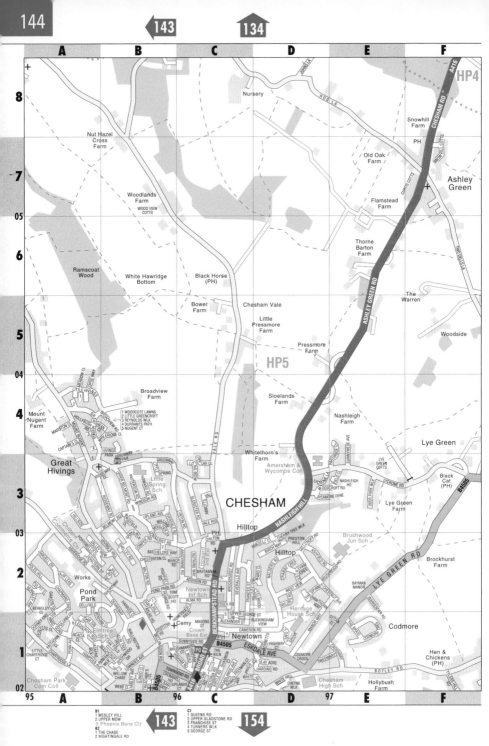

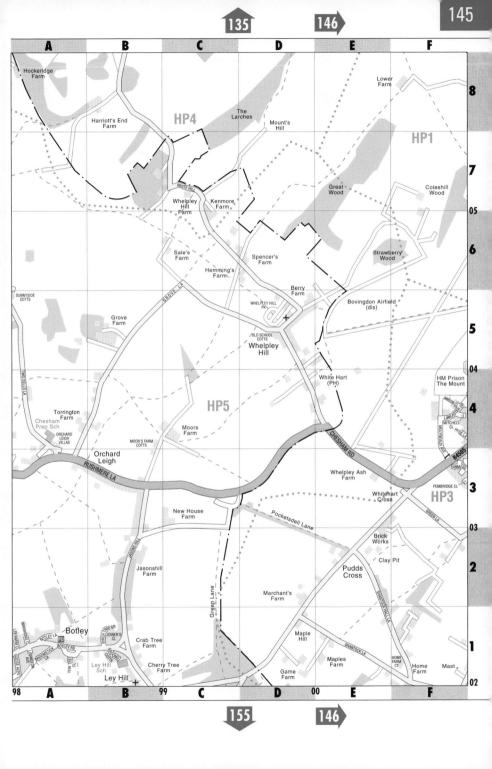

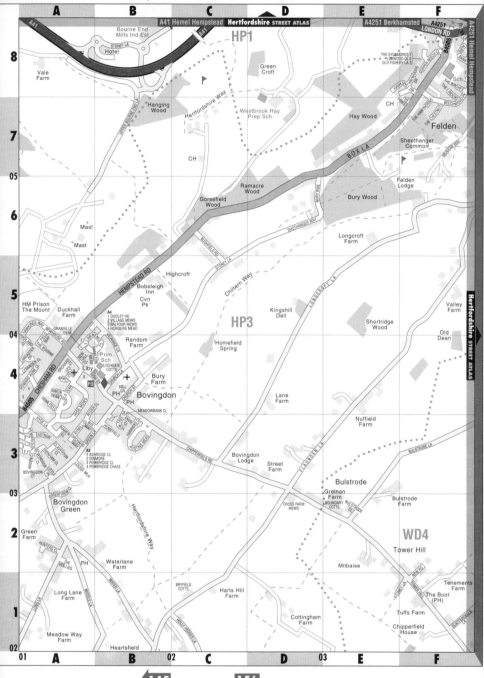

145

A41 Hemel Hempstead **Hertfordshire** STREET ATLAS A4251 Berkhamsted

HP1

Bourne End
Mills Ind Est

Vale
Farm

Hotel

STONEY LA

Green
Croft

Hanging
Wood

Hertfordshire Way

Westbrook Hay
Prep Sch

THE SYCAMORES 1
FOXWOOD CL 2
OLD FISHERY LA 3

QUEENS BEECH

THE BIRCHES

Sch J

THE BEECHWOOD

CH

Hay Wood

Felden

CH

Sheethanger
Common

BOX LA

Ramacre
Wood

Gorsefield
Wood

Felden
Lodge

Bury Wood

Mast

Mast

Longcroft
Farm

BURY RISE

SMITHANGER WAY

BUSFIELD RD

STONEY LA

Highcroft

Chiltern Way

HEMPSTEAD RD

Bobsleigh
Inn
Cvn
Pk

HP3

Kingshill
Dell

Shortridge
Wood

Valley
Farm

LONGCROFT LA

Old
Dean

HM Prison
The Mount

Duckhall
Farm

A4
1 DUDLEY HO
2 VILLAGE MEWS
3 BALFOUR MEWS
4 HONOURS MEAD

GRANVILLE
DENE

Random
Farm

Homefield
Spring

LANGCROFT

NEWCROFT RD

THE BOURNE

Prim
Sch

Liby

LYCHGATE
COTTS

Bury
Farm

CHURCH ST

Bovingdon

Lane
Farm

B456

CHESHAM RD

PO

PH

PH

BELL

MEADOWBANK CL

Nuffield
Farm

BULSTRODE LA

A3
1 ASHRIDGE CL
2 DINMORE
3 PEMBRIDGE CL
4 PEMBRIDGE CHASE

HYDE MEADS

AUSTINS MEAD

CHIPPERFIELD RD

Bovingdon
Lodge

Street
Farm

FLAUNDEN LA

Bulstrode

Greinan
Farm

Bulstrode
Farm

BOVINGDON
CT

GREEN VIEW CT

CROSS FARM
MEWS

BOUNDARY
COTTS

BULSTRODE LA

Bovingdon
Green

Hertfordshire Way

WD4

Green
Farm

Tower Hill

HUNTERS CL

THE
HOLLIES

PH

Waterlane
Farm

WATER LA

Milbaise

HOW RD

Tenements
Farm

LONGA LA

Long Lane
Farm

BRIDLE LA

BRYFIELD
COTTS

HOLLY HEDGES LA

Harts Hill
Farm

Cottingham
Farm

FLAUNDEN LA

TOWER HILL

Tuffs Farm

Chipperfield
House

The Boot
(PH)

SCATTERELLS

Meadow Way
Farm

Heartsfield

145   156

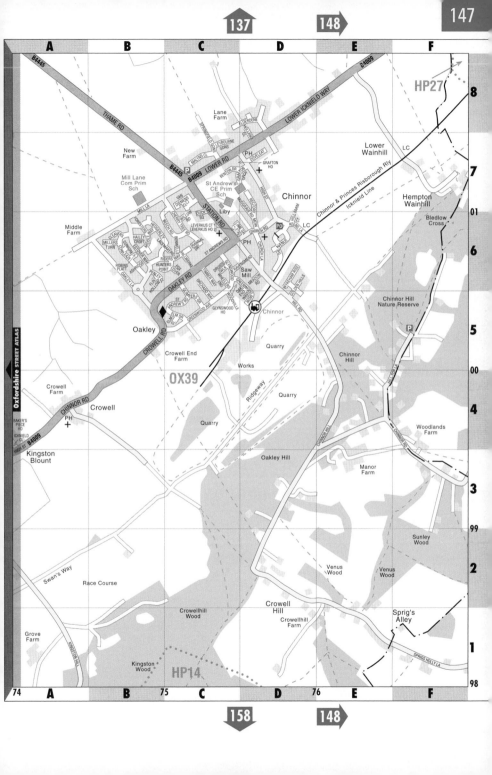

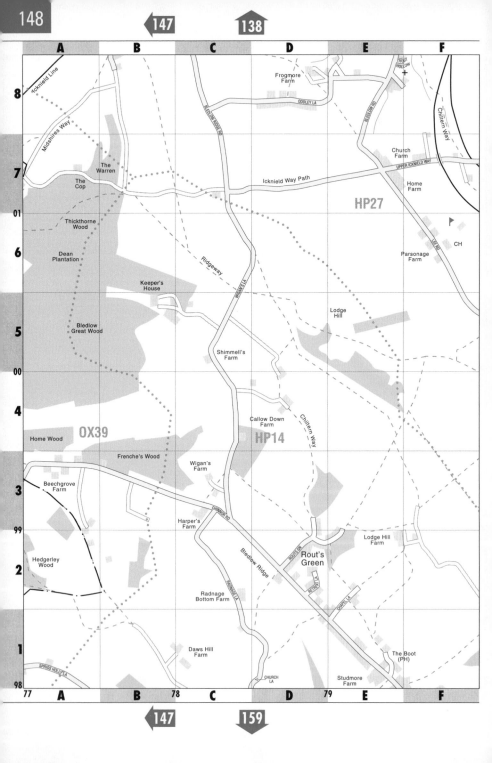

4cknield Line

Midshires Way

8

The Warren

The Cop

7

01

Thickthorne Wood

Dean Plantation

6

Keeper's House

Bledlow Great Wood

5

Ridgeway

Shimmell's Farm

WIGANS LA

00

4

Home Wood

OX39

Frenche's Wood

Callow Down Farm

HP14

Chiltern Way

3

Beechgrove Farm

Wigan's Farm

99

Harper's Farm

CHINNOR RD

Hedgerley Wood

2

Bledlow Ridge

RADNAGE LA

Radnage Bottom Farm

BOTTOM LA

Rout's Green

BETHEL Y

CHAPEL LA

Lodge Hill Farm

1

Daws Hill Farm

The Boot (PH)

98

SPRIGS HOLLY LA

CHURCH LA

Studmore Farm

Frogmore Farm

ODDLEY LA

BLEDLOW RIDGE RD

BLEDLOW RD

FRONT HOLLOW

Chiltern Way

Church Farm

UPPER ICKNIELD WAY

Icknield Way Path

Home Farm

HP27

CH

LEE RD

Parsonage Farm

Lodge Hill

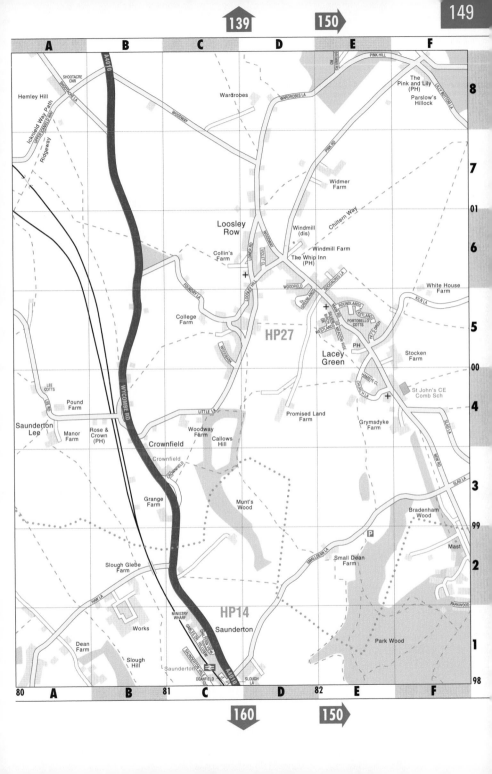

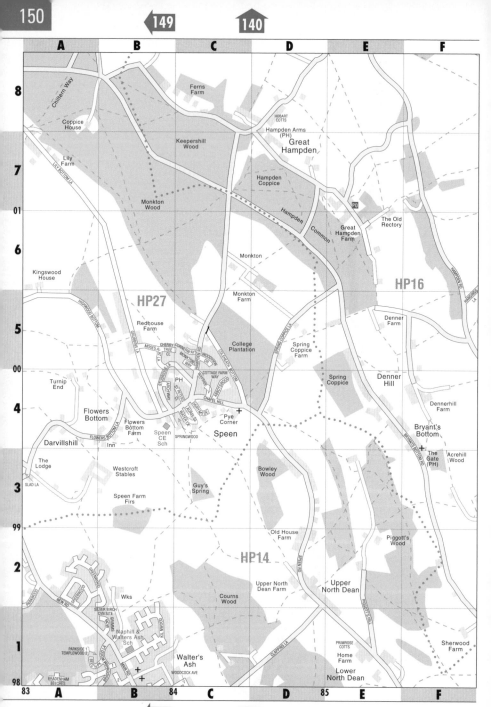

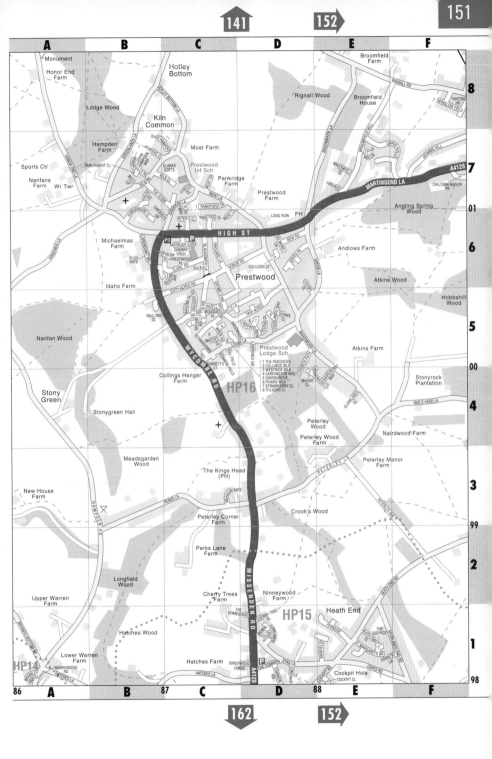

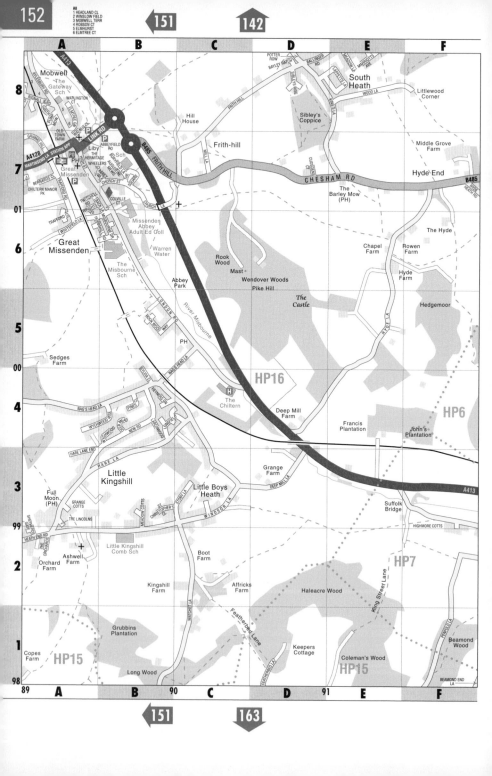

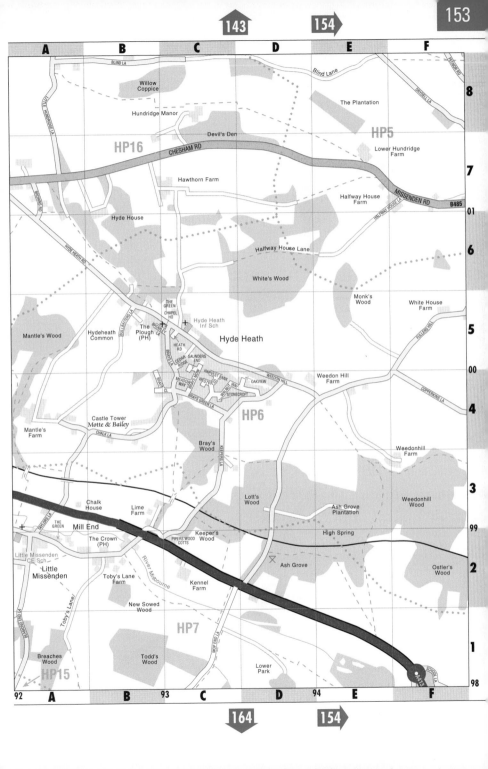

153
144

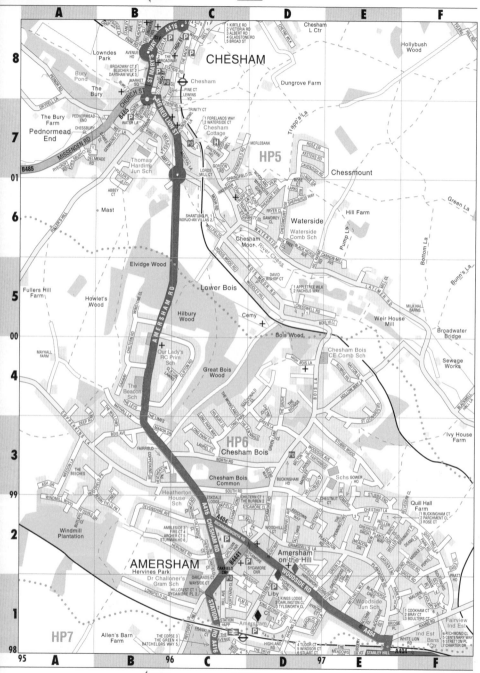

CHESHAM

1 KIRTLE RD
2 VICTORIA RD
3 ALBERT RD
4 GLADSTONE ST
5 BROAD ST

Chesham
L Ctr

Hollybush
Wood

Lowndes
Park

Bury
Pond

The
Bury

BROADWAY CT 1
BLUCHER ST 3
DARSHAM WLK 3

MARKET
SQ

Dungrove Farm

The Bury
Farm

Pednormead
End

PEDNORMEAD
END

CHESSBURY
RD

WATER LA

Chesham

PINE CT
LEWINS
YD

TRINITY CT

1 FORELANDS WAY
2 WATERSIDE CT
Chesham
Cottage

HP5

MERLEBANK

Trapp's La

ROSE DR
KESTERS RD

CAVENDISH RD

Chessmount

MISSENDEN RD

B485

ABBEY
CT

CHILTERN
CL

GORDON
RD

INKERMAN
ROW

SPRINGFIELD CL

WORDLING
RD

ROSE
CT

RICE GR
LARKS
LA

SHEPHERDS WAY

Mast

SHANTUNG PL 1
NORJO-AN VILLAS 2

FRYER CL
GAWDREY
CL

Waterside

Hill Farm

WATERSIDE

Chesham
Moor

River Chess

Waterside
Comb Sch

Pump La

Elvidge Wood

David
Bishop CT

BLACK HORSE
AVE

CANNON MILL
AVE

LATIMER RD

Bottom La

Bunn's La

Fullers Hill
Farm

Howlet's
Wood

Hilbury
Wood

Lower Bois

MOOLEY HILL

1 APPLETREE WLK
2 RACHELS WAY

CRESSWELL RD

Cemy

Bois Wood

BOIS HILL

Weir House
Mill

MILK HALL
BARNS

Broadwater
Bridge

MAYHALL
FARM

Our Lady's
RC Prim
Sch

CLAYTON
GROVE

The
Beacon
Sch

Great Bois
Wood

BOIS LA

HIGH
BOIS LA

Chesham Bois
CE Comb Sch

Sewage
Works

COPPERKINS LA

THE LEYS

Amersham RD

AMERSHAM RD

The
Limes

MANOR DR

LONG PARK CL

LAUREL CT

THE RISE

GREEN
LA

ST JOHNS RD

The
Beeches

BOIS AVE

FAIRFIELD

HP6

Chesham Bois

NORTH RD

THE
GROVE

THE
RIDINGS

STUBBS WOOD

Ivy House
Farm

WINDMILL WOOD

Heatherton
House
Sch

Chesham Bois
Common

SOUTH RD

Buckingham
HO

WOODSIDE AVE

Schs GOWER
RD

STUBBS END

Quill Hall
Farm

Windmill
Plantation

DEVONSHIRE AVE

AMBLESIDE 3
FIRS CT 4
ARCHER CT 5
STURMAN HO 6

A416 CHESHAM RD

RICKMANSWORTH RD

CHILTERN CT 1
THE BURREN 2

SYCAMORE CL

ASHDOWN
RD

WOODHILL
CT

CHESTNUT LA

WELLER RD

CHESTNUT CT

AMERSHAM

Hervines Park

Dr Challoner's
Gram Sch

OAKLANDS CT

OAKFIELD
CNR

BA431

SYCAMORE
CNR

WOODSIDE RD

B4441

Liby

Amersham
on the Hill

Woodside
Jun Sch

1 COOKHAM CT
2 BRAY CT
3 BOULTERS CT

HP7

Allen's Barn
Farm

STATION RD

LONGFIELD CL

SYCAMORE PL

HILLCREST CT 1
WAYSIDE CT

HILL AVE

ELM RD

STATION RD A416

FRANKLIN RD

THE CORSE 3
THE GREEN 4
BATCHELORS WAY 5

Amersham

THE
AVENUE

KINGS LODGE
DARLINGTON CL
TYLSWORTH CL

CT

HIGHLAND
RD

THE DRIVE

4 TUDOR CT
5 WINDSOR CT
6 STUART CT

THE
MEADOWS

A404

WHITE LION
RD

STANLEY HILL

1 RICHMOND CL
2 CENTENARY WAY
3 STRETTON PL
4 CHARTER DC

Ind Est
Bsns
Ctr

Fairview
Ind Est

153
165

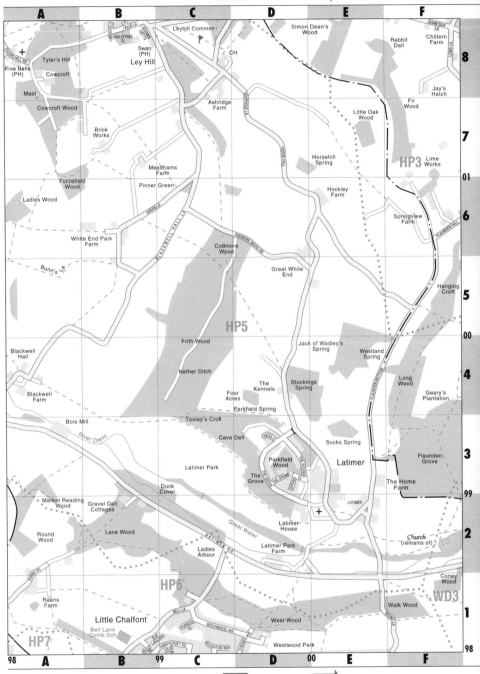

8

Leybill Common
CH
Simon Dean's Wood
Rabbit Dell
Chiltern Farm
SHANTOCK LA
LONG LA

Five Bells (PH)
Tyler's Hill
Cowcroft
Swan (PH)
Ley Hill
KILN LA
COLONIAL COTTS
HOLLYTREE CL
LETCHFIELD

Jay's Hatch

Mast
Cowcroft Wood
Ashridge Farm
Little Oak Wood
Fir Wood

7

Brick Works
Horsehill Spring
HP3
Lime Works

Meadhams Farm
Pinner Green
Furzefield Wood
Hockley Farm
01

Ladies Wood
White End Park Farm
GREEN LA
BLACKWELL HALL LA
HORSE HILL
ASHRIDGE LA

6

Codmore Wood
COODMORE WOOD RD
Springview Farm
FLAUNDEN HILL

Bunn's
Great White End

5

Hanging Croft

HP5
Jack of Wadley's Spring
Westland Spring
00

Blackwell Hall
Frith Wood
Long Wood
Geary's Plantation

4

Blackwell Farm
Nether Ditch
The Kennels
Stockings Spring
FLAUNDEN BOTTOM

Bois Mill
Four Acres
Parkfield Spring

River Chess
Tooley's Croft
Socks Spring
Flaunden Grove

3

Cave Dell
CHESS CL
Parkfield Wood
Latimer

Latimer Park
Duck Cover
The Grove
THE RIDINGS
THE DELL
THE GROVE
ORCHARD
LATIMER
The Home Farm
99

Market Reading Wood
Gravel Dell Cottages
Latimer House
Church (remains of)

2

Round Wood
Lane Wood
Great Water
Latimer Park Farm
RAANS RD
LATIMER RD

Ladies Arbour
Coney Wood
WD3

1

Raans Farm
HP6
Bell Lane Comb Sch
BELL LA
CHANDOS CL
THE LADIES
SANDYCROFT RD
BEECH LA
CHENIES AVE
BEECHWOOD AVE
BOUGHTON WAY
West Wood
Westwood Park
Walk Wood
STONY LA

HP7
Little Chalfont

98

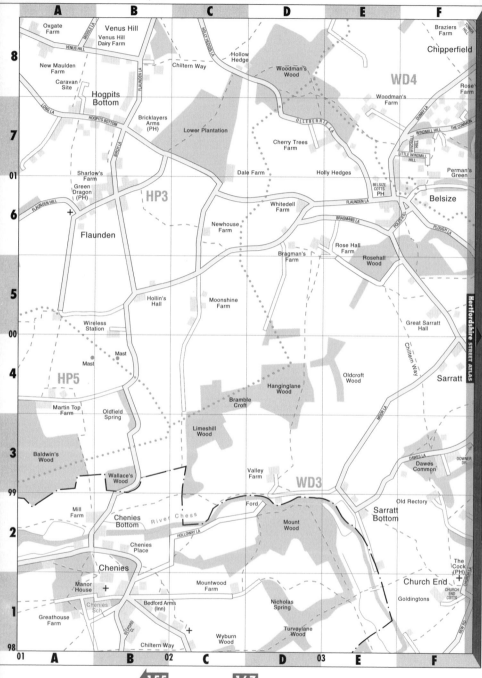

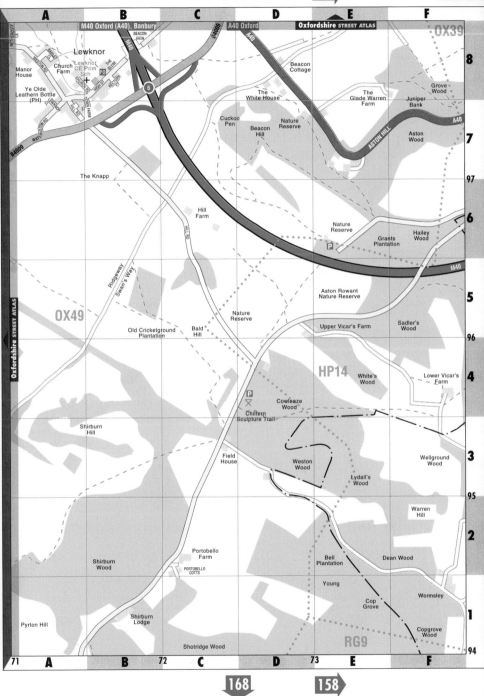

Oxfordshire STREET ATLAS

OX39

M40 Oxford (A40), Banbury

A40 Oxford

Lewknor

Manor House

Ye Olde Leathern Bottle (PH)

Church Farm

Lewknor CE Prim Sch

BEACON VIEW

Beacon Cottage

The White House

The Glade Warren Farm

Grove Wood

Juniper Bank

Cuckoo Pen

Beacon Hill

Nature Reserve

ASTON HILL

Aston Wood

A40

The Knapp

Hill Farm

Nature Reserve

Grants Plantation

Hailey Wood

M40

Ridgeway

Swan's Way

OX49

Aston Rowant Nature Reserve

Old Cricketground Plantation

Bald Hill

Nature Reserve

Upper Vicar's Farm

Sadler's Wood

HP14

White's Wood

Lower Vicar's Farm

Shirburn Hill

Cowleaze Wood

Chiltern Sculpture Trail

Field House

Weston Wood

Lydall's Wood

Wellground Wood

Warren Hill

Shirburn Wood

Portobello Farm

PORTOBELLO COTTS

Bell Plantation

Dean Wood

Young

Wormsley

Pyrton Hill

Shirburn Lodge

Cop Grove

Copgrove Wood

Shotridge Wood

RG9

Oxfordshire STREET ATLAS

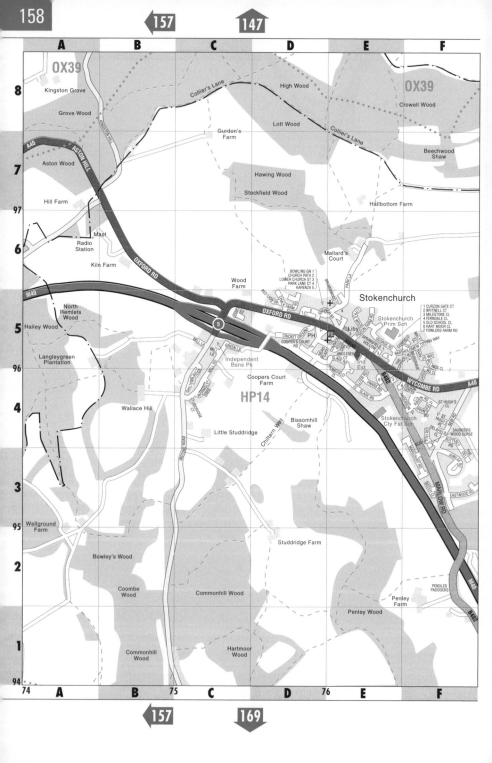

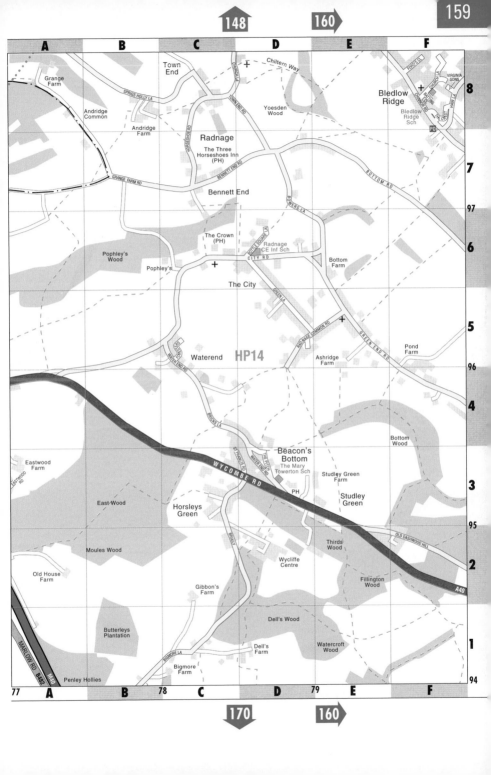

159
149

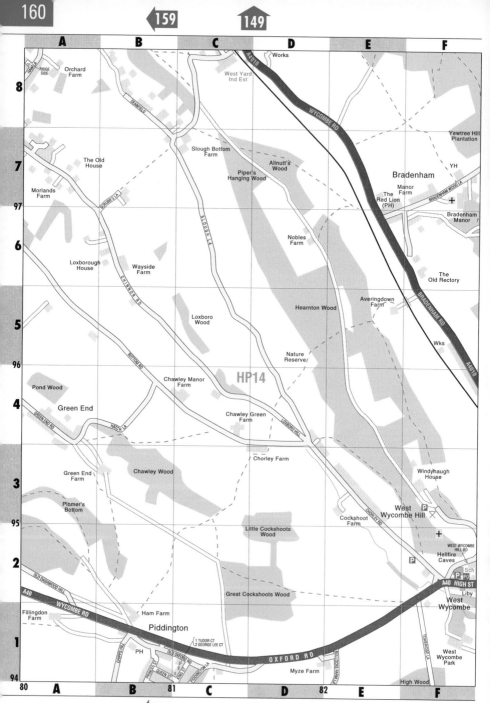

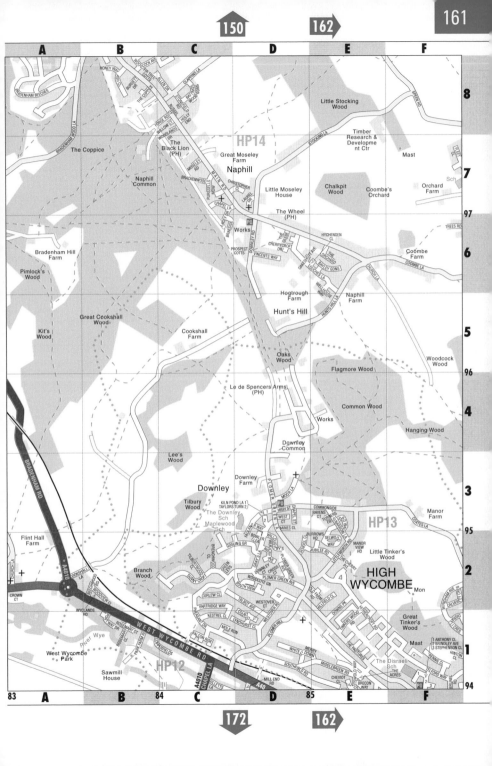

150
162

A   B   C   D   E   F

8

Little Stocking
Wood

Timber
Research &
Developme
nt Ctr

Mast

7

HP14

The Coppice

HONEY WAY

The Black Lion
(PH)

Great Moseley
Farm

Naphill

Chalkpit
Wood

Coombe's
Orchard

Orchard
Farm

Sch

Bradenham Beeches

Naphill
Common

Little Moseley
House

97

Bradenham Hill
Farm

Pimlock's
Wood

Works

The Wheel
(PH)

Cherrycroft
Dr

Vincents Way

Coombe
Wood

Coombe La

TREES RD

6

Kit's
Wood

Great Cookshall
Wood

Cookshall
Farm

Hogtrough
Farm

Hunt's Hill

Naphill
Farm

5

Oaks
Wood

Flagmore Wood

Woodcock
Wood

96

Le de Spencers Arms
(PH)

Common Wood

4

Lee's
Wood

Works

Hanging Wood

Downley
Common

Downley

Downley
Farm

3

Tilbury
Wood

The Downley
Sch
Maplewood
Sch

KILN POND LA 1
TAYLORS TURN 2

Commonside
Ravens
Ct

HP13

Manor
Farm

95

Flint Hall
Farm

CHURCH LA

CROWN
CT

A4010

COOKSHALL LA

Branch
Wood

MANOR
VIEW
HO

Little Tinker's
Wood

HIGH
WYCOMBE

Mon

2

WYCLANDS
HO

Bradenham Rd

River Wye

West Wycombe
Park

Sawmill
House

HP12

CHAPEL LA
A4010

WEST WYCOMBE RD

CURLEW CL

PARTRIDGE WAY

KESTREL CL

MOLE RUN

SOUTH VIEW

WESTOVER
CT

A40

MILL END
RD

SOUTH RD

CHEVIOT
WAY

BRECON
WAY

Great
Tinker's
Wood

Mast

1 ANTHONY CL
2 BRINDLEY AVE
3 STEPHENSON CL

The Disraeli
Sch
THE
ACRES

1

94

172
162

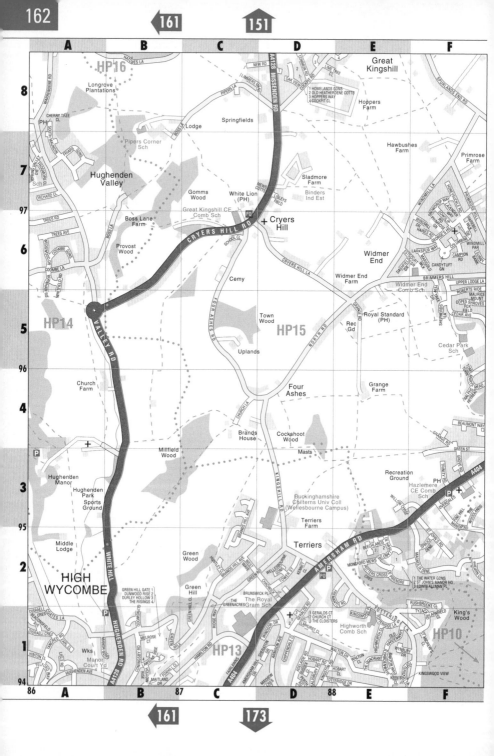

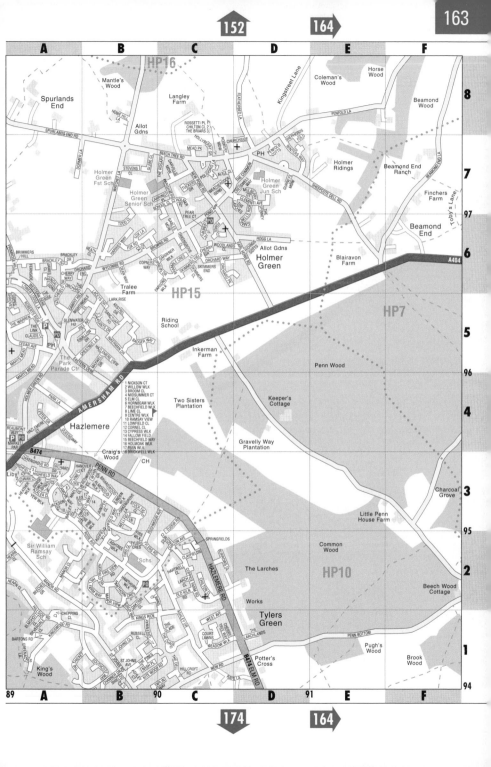

152
164
174
164

HP16

Spurlands
End

Mantle's
Wood

Langley
Farm

Allot
Gdns

Coleman's
Wood

Horse
Wood

Beamond
Wood

Rossetti PL 1
CHILTON CL 2
THE BRIARS 3.

Holmer Green
Fst Sch

Stevens
Cl

Holmer
Green
Senior Sch

Holmer
Green Jun Sch

Holmer
Ridings

Beamond End
Ranch

Fincher's
Farm

Pear
Tree Ct

Beamond
End

Brimmers
Hill

Brackley

Tralee
Farm

Holmer
Green

Allot Gdns

Blairavon
Farm

A404

HP15

The Park
Parade Ctr

Riding
School

Inkerman
Farm

Penn Wood

HP7

1 NICKSON CT
2 WILLOW WLK
3 BROOM CL
4 MIDSUMMER CT
5 ELM CL
6 HORNBEAM WLK
7 BEECHFIELD WLK
8 LIME CL
9 CENTRE WLK
10 RAMSAY VIEW
11 LOWFIELD CL
12 CORNEL CL
13 CYPRESS WLK
14 FALLOW FIELD
15 BEECHFIELD WAY
16 HOLMOAK WLK
17 FERN WLK
18 BRICKWELL WLK

Two Sisters
Plantation

Keeper's
Cottage

Gravelly Way
Plantation

Hazlemere

Craig's
Wood

CH

AMERSHAM RD

PENN RD

Charcoal
Grove

Little Penn
House Farm

B474

Sir William
Ramsay
Sch

Schs

Springfields

Common
Wood

HP10

The Larches

HAZLEMERE RD

Beech Wood
Cottage

Works

Tylers
Green

Penn Bottom

Pugh's
Wood

Brook
Wood

Chepping
Cl

Bartons Rd

King's
Wood

St Johns
Ave

Court
Lawns

Potter's
Cross

Hillcroft

B474 ELM RD

89   90   91

94   95   96   97

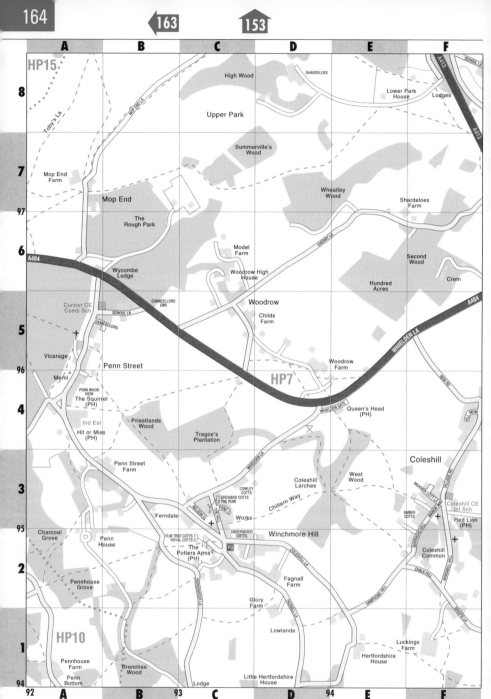

163
153

HP15

8

High Wood

SHARDELOES

Lower Park House

Lodges

Upper Park

SCHOOL LA

A413

Toby's La

7

Summerville's Wood

Mop End Farm

Wheatley Wood

Shardeloes Farm

97

Mop End

The Rough Park

6

A404

Model Farm

CHERRY LA

Second Wood

Wycombe Lodge

Woodrow High House

Crem

Hundred Acres

A404

WHIELDEN LA

Curzon CE Comb Sch

CHANCELLORS CNR

Woodrow

SCHOOL LA

Childs Farm

5

CHANCELLORS

Woodrow Farm

NEW RD

Vicarage

96

Meml

Penn Street

HP7

Woodrow Farm

MOW

HILL RD

PENN WOOD VIEW
The Squirrel (PH)

WHIELDEN GATE

Queen's Head (PH)

4

Ind Est
Hit or Miss (PH)

Priestlands Wood

Tragoe's Plantation

WHIELDEN LA

Coleshill

Penn Street Farm

Coleshill Larches

West Wood

MEADOW COTTS

Coleshill CE Inf Sch

VILLAGE RD

3

COWLEY COTTS
1 ORCHARD COTTS
2 THE ROW

Chiltern Way

AMBER COTTS

Red Lion (PH)

Ferndale

PONDL CL

NELSON CL

THE HILL

Works

UNDERWOOD COTTS

MAGPIE LA

MAIN RD

Charcoal Grove

95

Penn House

ELM TREE COTTS 1
ROYAL COTTS 2

Winchmore Hill

Coleshill Common

BARRACKS HILL

The Potters Arms (PH)

PO

HORSEMOOR LA

COLESHILL LA

CHALK HILL

2

Pennhouse Grove

Fagnall Farm

PUGHS LA

SAMPAGES BET

1

HP10

Glory Farm

Lowlands

Luckings Farm

MAGPIE LA

Pennhouse Farm

Branches Wood

Hertfordshire House

Penn Bottom

Lodge

Little Hertfordshire House

94

92 A

B 93

C

D 94

E

F

163
175

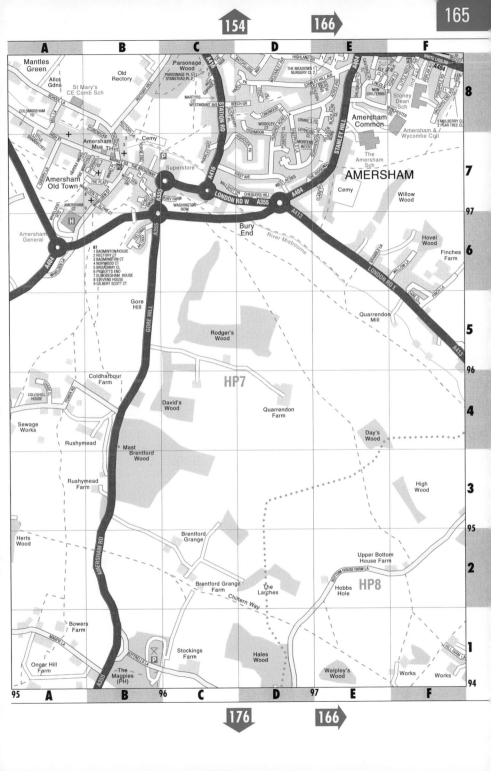

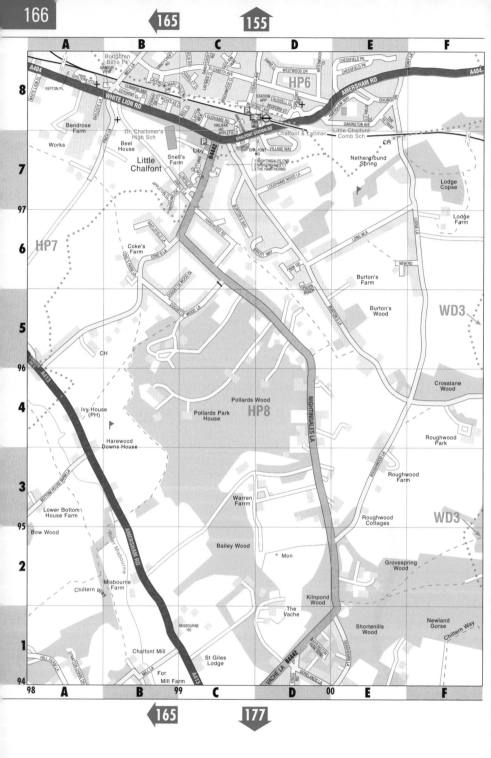

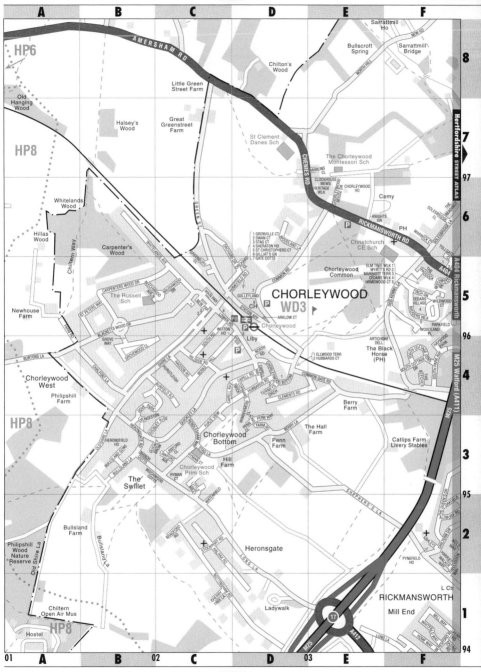

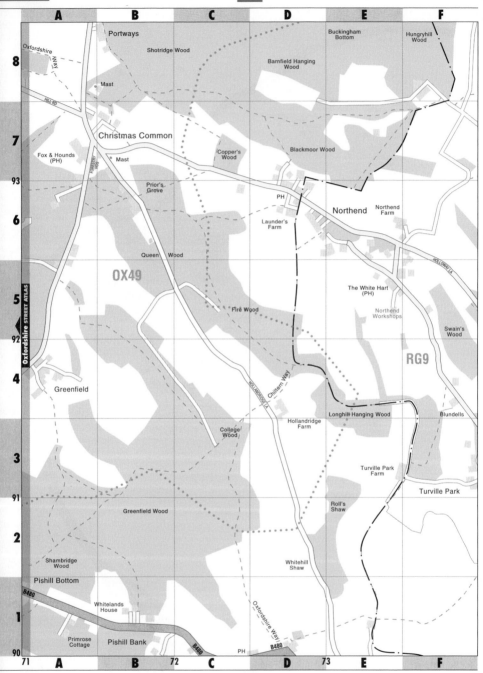

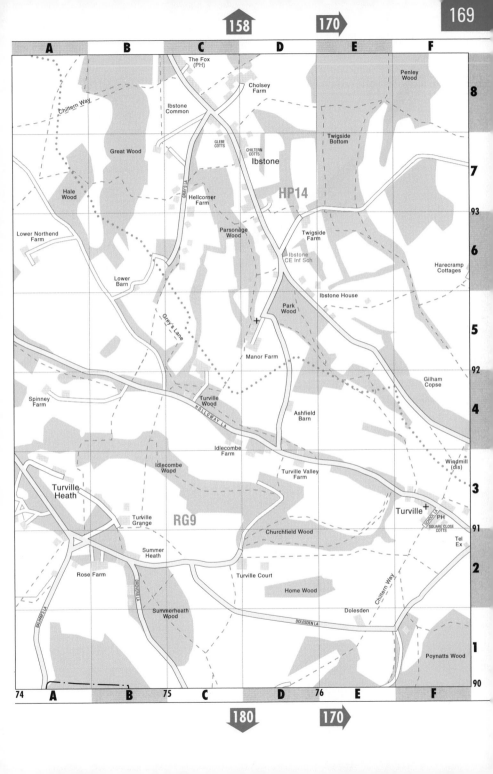

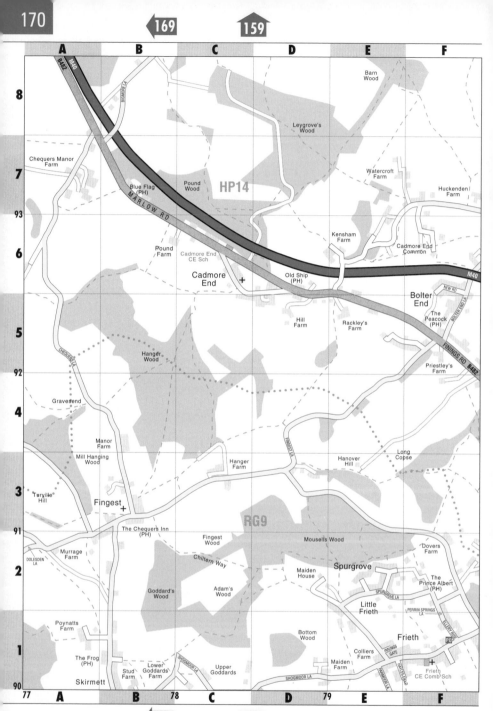

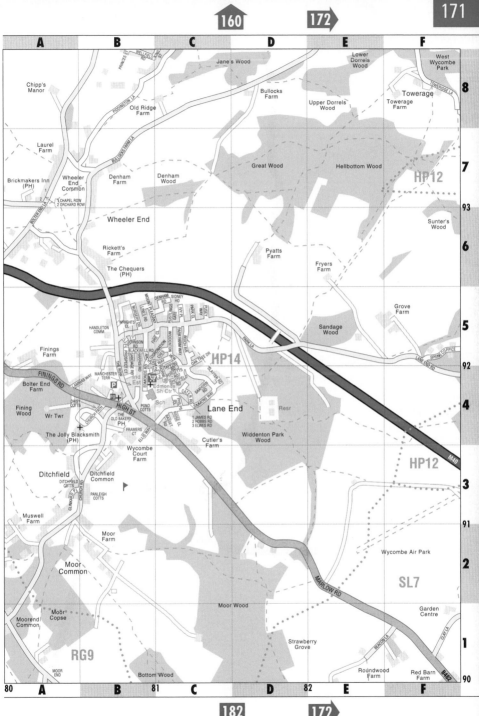

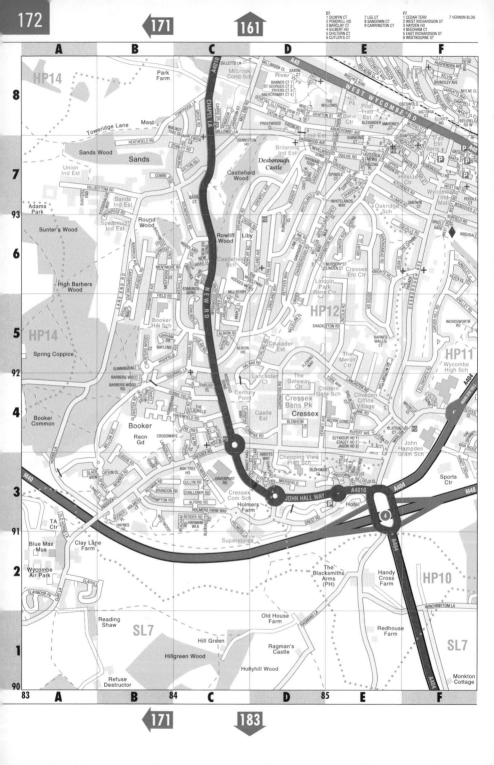

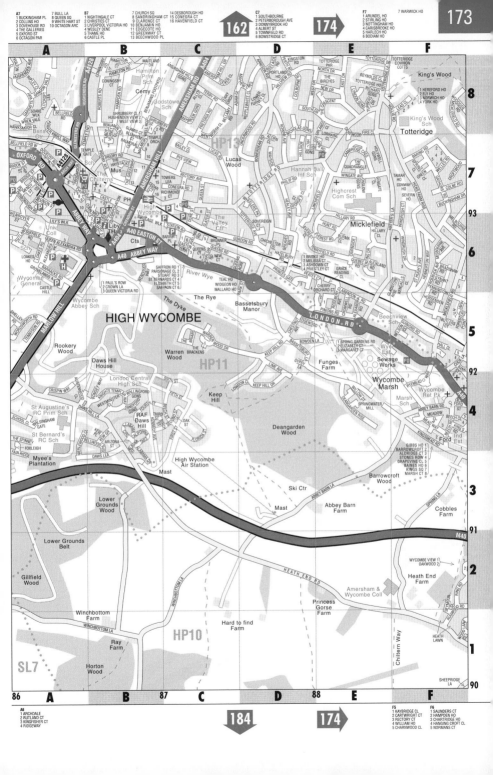

162
174

173

184
174

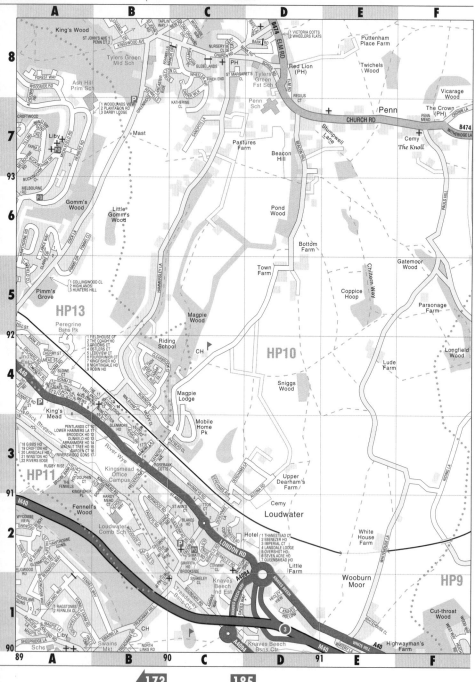

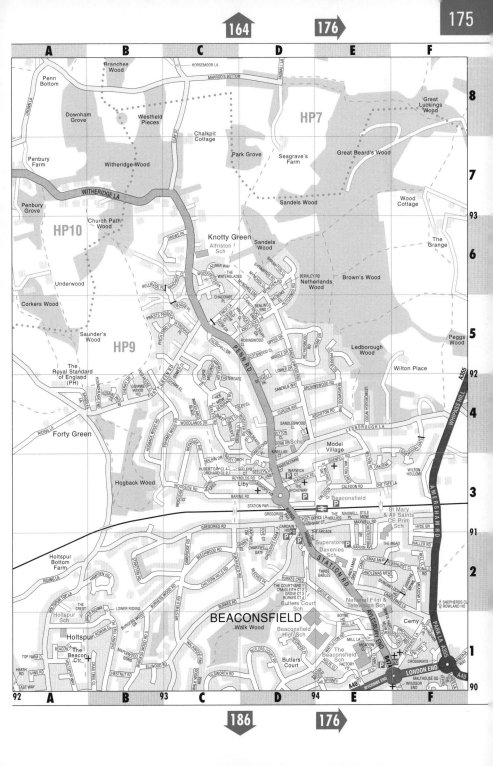

164
176

| A | B | C | D | E | F |

8

HP7

Penn Bottom

Branches Wood

HORSEMOOR LA

MARROD'S BOTTOM

Downham Grove

Westfield Pieces

Chalkpit Cottage

Great Luckings Wood

Penbury Farm

Witheridge Wood

Park Grove

Seagrave's Farm

Great Beard's Wood

7

WITHERIDGE LA

Penbury Grove

93

Sandels Wood

Wood Cottage

HP10

Church Path Wood

Knotty Green

Alfriston Sch

Sandels Wood

The Grange

6

Underwood

THE WATERGLADES

Berkley Rd

Netherlands Wood

Brown's Wood

Corkers Wood

Saunder's Wood

HP9

Robinswood Cl

Upper Rd

Peggs Wood

5

The Royal Standard of England (PH)

PENN RD

Ledborough Wood

Wilton Place

92

A355

Forty Green

SANDELS WAY

BROWNSWOOD RD

WHITEPASS HILL

4

Hogback Wood

Model Village

LEDBOROUGH LA

Wilton Hollow

AMERSHAM RD

Liby

The Broadway

Beaconsfield

One Tree La

3

WOODSIDE RD

BARING RD

Station Par

GREGORIES RD

POST OFFICE LA

St Mary & All Saints CE Prim Sch

91

Holtspur Bottom Farm

RIDING LA

Superstore

Davenies Sch

THE MEAD

WALLER RD

HYDE GN

2

CAMBRIDGE RD

BEECHWOOD RD

CHARTWELL GATE

BURKES CRES

THE COURTYARD

National Film & Television Sch

Holtspur Sch

The Crest

Lower Riding

BURKES RD

BEACONSFIELD

Walk Wood

Butlers Court Sch

Beaconsfield High Sch

Cemy

PARK LA

A355

1

Holtspur

The Beacon Ctr

CHESTNUT RD

Butlers Court

The Beaconsfield Sch

STATION RD

AYLESBURY END

B474

LONDON END

WYCOMBE END

WINDSOR END

A40

90

| A | 93 | B | C | 94 | D | E | F |

92

175
165

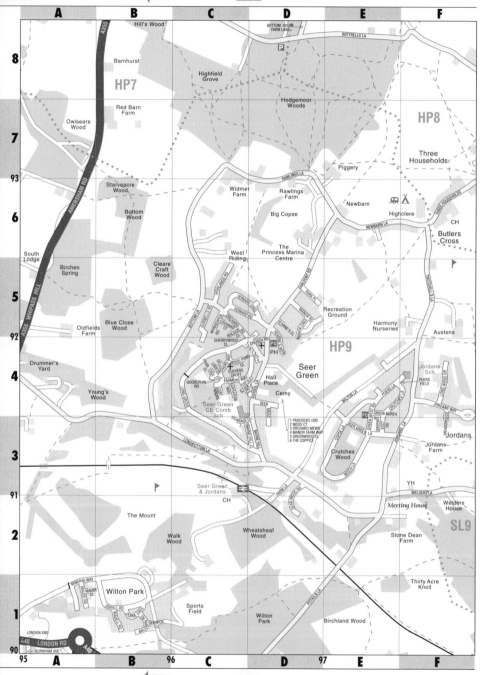

175
187

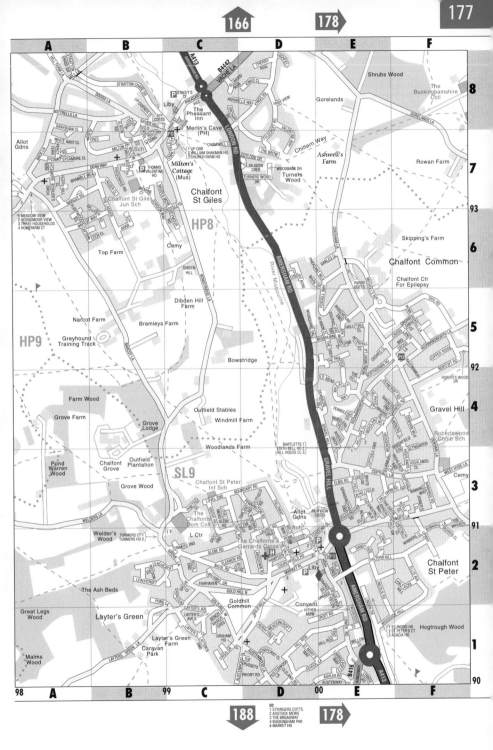

166
178
188
178

A B C D E F

8

HP8

Bottom
Wood

Ladywalk
Wood

Buckinghamshire Chilterns
Univ Coll

Newland
Park

Five
Plantations

7

GORELANDS LA

Model
Farm

Pollardshill
Wood

Woodoaks
Farm

Froghall
Farm

Chalfont
Shire Horse Ctr

93

Brawlings
Farm

6

Hillview

Horn Hill

Maple
Cross

PH

Maplelodge
Farm

Springwell
Lake

The
Dumb Bell
(PH)

Beechen
Wood

DUMBLETONS

River Colne

Longlees

Recn
Gd

Sewage
Works

5

Springview
Farm

Mast

BUTTLEHIDE

ASH VALE

Franklin's
Spring

WOODLAND RD

Lynsters

BY-WOOD END

THE
HAWTHORNS

BIRCH DR

Sch

ROBERT'S
WOOD DR

92

SL9

WD3

4

Round Rocket
Plantation

DENHAM WAY

Lynsters
Lake

CHALFONT LA

SUNNYHILL
RD

Royal Oak
(PH)

COPPERMILL LA

Cemy

Bloom
Wood

91

BUTTERFIELD
COTTS

PLEASANT
PL

Pynesfield Lake

West Hyde

Warren
Farm

UB9

2

Chalfont Heights
Scout Camp

UB9

TILEHOUSE LA

1

Mopes
Farm

West Hyde
House

90

01 A B 02 C D 03 E F

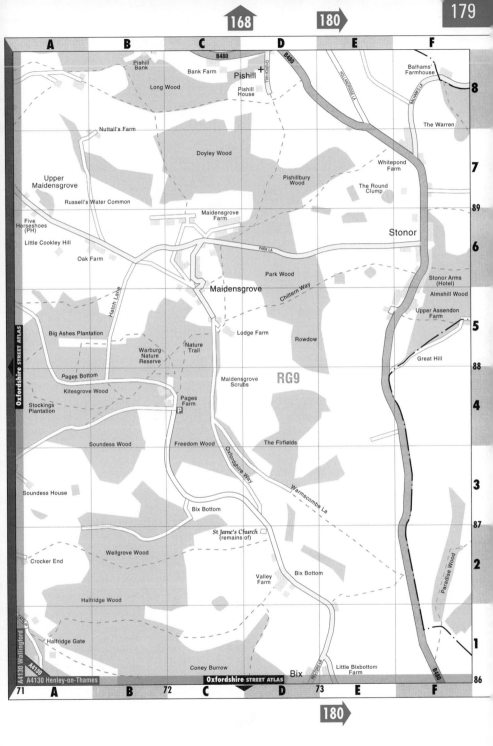

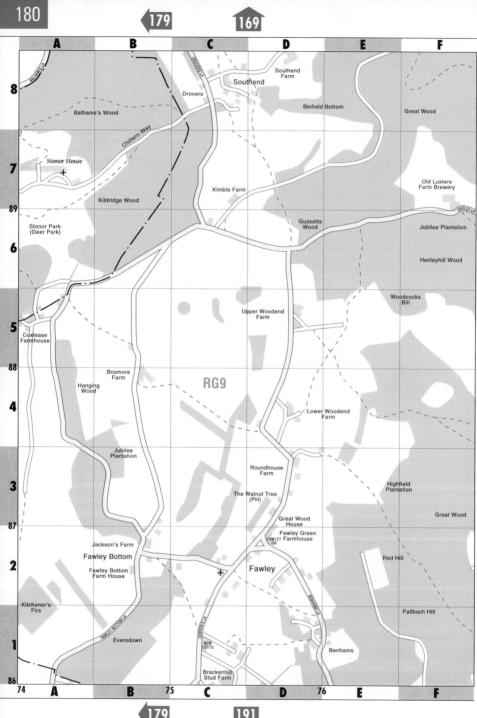

A B C D E F

8

Southend

Drovers   Southend Farm

Balhams's Wood   Binfield Bottom   Great Wood

Chiltern Way

7

Stonor House

Old Luxters Farm Brewery

Kildridge Wood   Kimble Farm

89   HENLEY LA

Stonor Park (Deer Park)   Gussetts Wood   Jubilee Plantation

6

Henleyhill Wood

Woodcocks Bill

5

Coxlease Farmhouse   Upper Woodend Farm

88

Bosmore Farm   RG9

Hanging Wood

4   Lower Woodend Farm

Jubilee Plantation

Highfield Plantation

3   Roundhouse Farm

The Walnut Tree (PH)   Great Wood

87   Great Wood House

Fawley Green Farmhouse

Jackson's Farm   FAWLEY GN

Fawley Bottom   Fawley   Red Hill

2   Fawley Bottom Farm House

Kitchener's Firs   Pallbach Hill

1   Eversdown

NEW COTTS

Benhams

86   Brackenhill Stud Farm

74   A   B   75   C   D   76   E   F

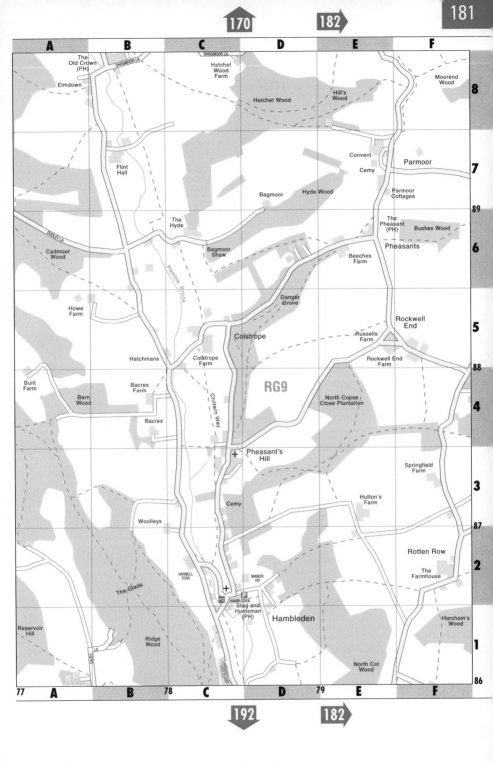

170
182

A   B   C   D   E   F

8
7
89
6
5
88
4
3
87
2
1
86

SHOGMOOR LA

The
Old Crown
(PH)

Elmdown

SHOGMOOR LA

Hatchet
Wood
Farm

Hatchet Wood

Hill's
Wood

Moorend
Wood

Flint
Hall

Convent

Cemy

Parmoor

Parmoor
Cottages

Bagmoor

Hyde Wood

DUDLEY LA

The Hyde

Cadmoor
Wood

Bagmoor
Shaw

The
Pheasant
(PH)

Bushes Wood

Pheasants

Beeches
Farm

Hamble Brook

Howe
Farm

Danger
Grove

Colstrope

Russells
Farm

Rockwell
End

Hatchmans

Colstrope
Farm

Rockwell End
Farm

RG9

Built
Farm

Barn
Wood

Bacres
Farm

Chiltern Way

North Copse /
Close Plantation

Bacres

Pheasant's
Hill

Springfield
Farm

Cemy

Hutton's
Farm

Woolleys

Rotten Row

The
Farmhouse

The Glade

VARNELL
TERR

MANOR
RD

PO
HAMBLEDEN

Stag and
Huntsman
(PH)

Hambleden

Harcham's
Wood

Reservoir
Hill

Ridge
Wood

DAIRY LA

North Cot
Wood

77   A   B   78   C   D   79   E   F   86

192
182

181
171

	A	B	C	D	E	F

8

Moorend Wood

HP14

Bottom Wood

Beacon Farm

B482

Finnamore La

Beacon La

7

HM Young Offender Inst (Finnamore Wood Camp)

Finnamore Wood

Bluey's Farm

The Roost

89

Chisbridge

Chisbridge Cross

Copy Green

6

Shillingridge Wood

Woodlands

Holme Wood Cottage

Holme Wood

Denelands Farm

SHILLINGRIDGE PK

5

Kent's Wood

Holme Wood

Oaklands Farm

Mundaydean Bottom

FRIETH RD

MUNDAYDEAN LA

Bottom House

Woodend House

Hawkins Farm

88

RG9

SL7

4

Fountain's

Woodend Farm

Holywick

Arbon

Lower Woodend

3

Heath Wood

Walnut Tree Farm

Lord's Wood

Marlow Common

MARLOW COMM

87

Homefield Wood

2

Rogues Plantation

Chiltern Way

Davenport Wood

Bockmer End Farm

Pullingshill Wood

1

Woodland Plain

Bockmer House

Bockmer End

BOCKMER LA

Hook's Farm

86

Widefield

80	A		B	81	C		D	82	E		F

181
193

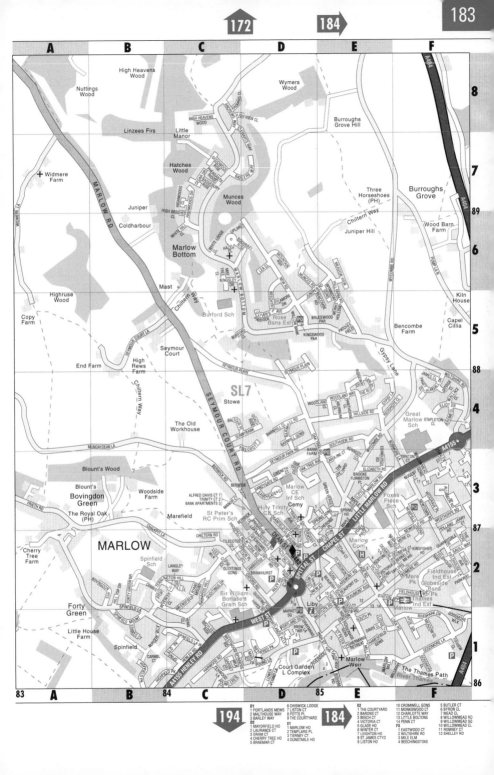

183

173

HP10

8

Horton Wood

Bloom Wood

New
Farm

Chiltern Way

PH

Sheepridge

7

Chiltern Way

Bloom
Farm

Pigeon House
Farm

89

Merton's Hole
Cottage

6

SL7

Fern
House

Cemy

FERN
COTTS

Fern

Well End

ABBEY
MEAD

5

Wilton
Farm

Little Marlow
CE Sch

Coronach

MARLOW RD

Little
Marlow

WELL END
COTTS

88

Pump
Farm

The
Kings Head
(PH)

Thame Valley
Falconry &
Conservation
Ctr

SL8

The
Abbey

4

A4155

Manor
House

The Spade Oak
(PH)

Abbotsbrook

LC

LC

1 BUTLER CT
2 BRISTOW CT
3 GRATTON CT
4 DOUGLAS CT
5 RAVENSCOURT

SPADE OAK
FARM

MILL
ELM

3

WESTHORPE PARK
CVN SITE

Westhorpe
House

Sewage
Works

The Moor

River Thames

87

6 HOBART CT
7 MARCHANT CT
8 WASHINGTON CT
9 SWALLOW RD
10 SWIFT HO

Westhorpe
Farm

The Thames Path

Noah's
House

Cock Marsh

2

Patches

SL6

Coney
Copse

Stone
House

1

Winter
Hill

Harvest
Moon

Greythatch

86

183

195

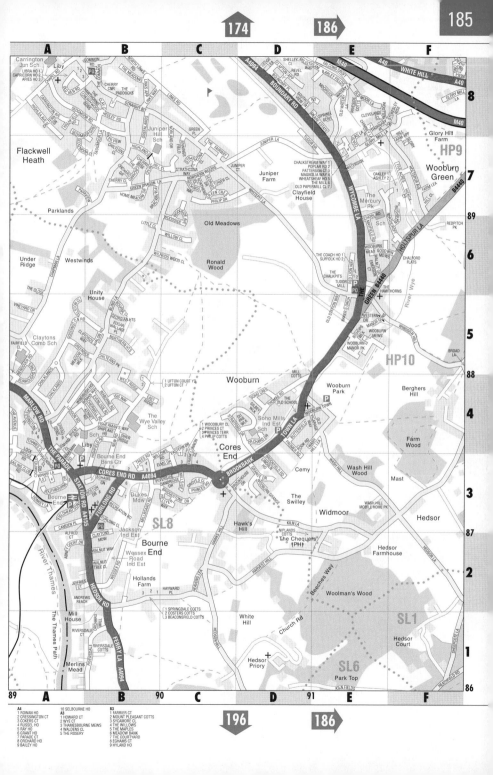

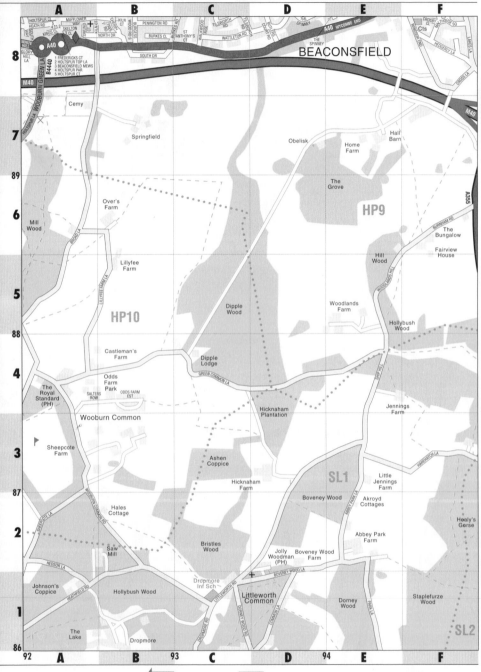

1 FREDERICKS CT
2 HOLTSPUR TOP LA
3 BEACONSFIELD MEWS
4 HOLTSPUR PAR
5 HOLTSPUR CT

BEACONSFIELD

Cemy

Springfield

Obelisk

Home
Farm

Hall
Barn

The
Grove

HP9

Over's
Farm

Mill
Wood

The
Bungalow

Fairview
House

Lillyfee
Farm

Hill
Wood

HP10

Dipple
Wood

Woodlands
Farm

Hollybush
Wood

Castleman's
Farm

Dipple
Lodge

Odds
Farm
Park

ODDS FARM
EST

GREEN COMMON LA

Hicknham
Plantation

Jennings
Farm

The
Royal
Standard
(PH)

SALTERS
ROW

Wooburn Common

Sheepcote
Farm

Ashen
Coppice

Hicknham
Farm

SL1

Little
Jennings
Farm

Boveney Wood

Akroyd
Cottages

Hales
Cottage

Healy's
Gerse

Saw
Mill

Bristles
Wood

Jolly
Woodman
(PH)

Boveney Wood
Farm

Abbey Park
Farm

Johnson's
Coppice

Hollybush Wood

Dropmore
Inf Sch

Littleworth
Common

Dorney
Wood

Staplefurze
Wood

The
Lake

Dropmore

SL2

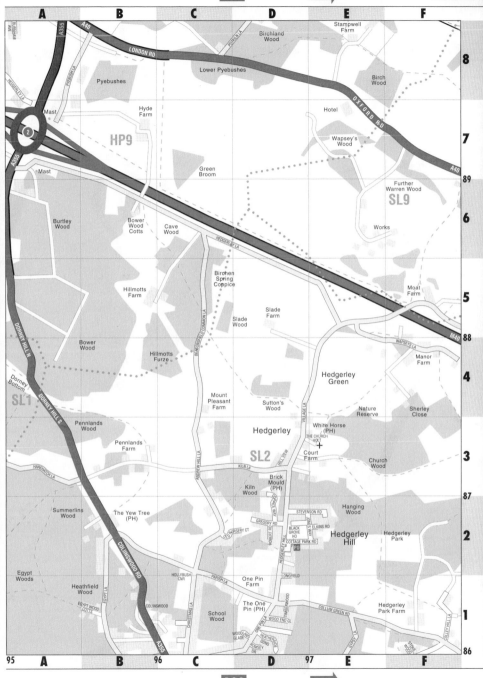

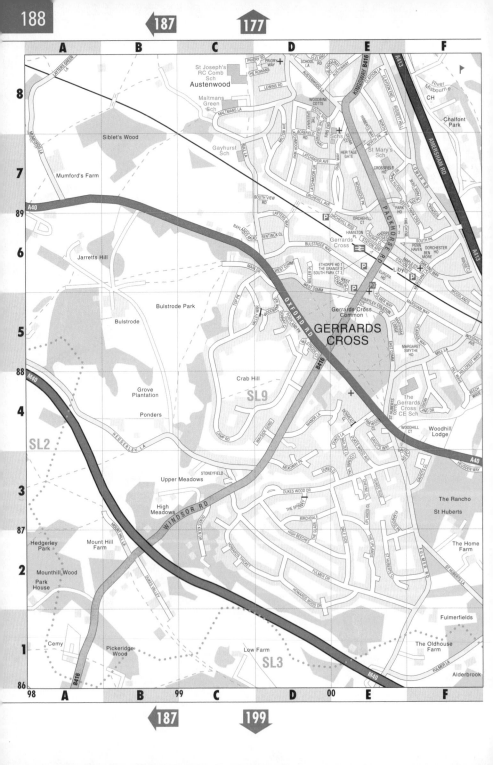

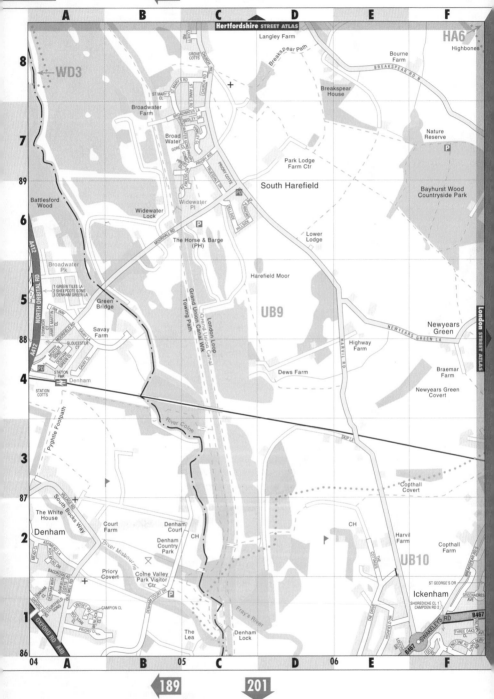

Hertfordshire STREET ATLAS

HA6

WD3

Langley Farm

Breakspear Path

Highbones

BREAKSPEAR RD N

Bourne
Farm

Breakspear
House

St Mary's Rd
St Mary's CL
St Anne's Rd

Broadwater
Farm

BROADWATER LA

BIRDLEY GDN

Broad
Water

GORSE CL

PRIORY CL

PRIORY DR

PRIORY AVE

PRIORY COTTS

THE CEDARS

Park Lodge
Farm Ctr

Nature
Reserve

P

89

South Harefield

Bayhurst Wood
Countryside Park

Widewater
Pl

Battlesford
Wood

Widewater
Lock

P

FELLSIDE

HILLSIDE

MOORHALL RD

P

The Horse & Barge
(PH)

Lower
Lodge

6

Broadwater
Pk

NORTH ORBITAL RD

A412

1 GREEN TILES LA
2 SHEEPCOTE GDNS
3 DENHAM GREEN LA

Green
Bridge

Grand Union Canal

London Loop

Towing Path

Harefield Moor

UB9

Newyears
Green

NEWYEARS GREEN LA

Highway
Farm

HARVIL RD

London STREET ATLAS

5

FOXMOOR
LIME WAY
JAMES MARTIN CL
SASSE CL
MOORFIELD RD

Savay
Farm

GLOUCESTER
CT

SAXON CL

Dews Farm

Braemar
Farm

88

STATION
FARM

Denham

Newyears Green
Covert

4

A412

P

STATION
COTTS

Pyghtle Footpath

River Colne

SKIP LA

3

Copthall
Covert

87

BUCKS WAY

South Bucks Way

The White
House

Court
Farm

Denham
Court

CH

CH

Harvil
Farm

Copthall
Farm

2

Denham

ASHMEAD LA

WEST CL

River Misbourne

Denham
Country
Park

Colne Valley
Park Visitor
Ctr

CH

UB10

THE COTTAGES

THE DRIVE

Ickenham

ST GEORGE'S DR

GREENACRES
AVE

BACONSMEAD LA

Priory
Covert

P

BREAKSPEAR COURT DR

HIGHFIELD DR

SHOREDICHE CL 1
CAMPDEN RD 2

THREE OAKS
AVE

B467

1

OXFORD RD A40

CAMPION CL

LINDSEY RD

PRIORY CL

The Lea

Denham
Lock

Fray's River

SWAKELEYS

B467

B467

SWAKELEYS RD

MILESTONE RD

86

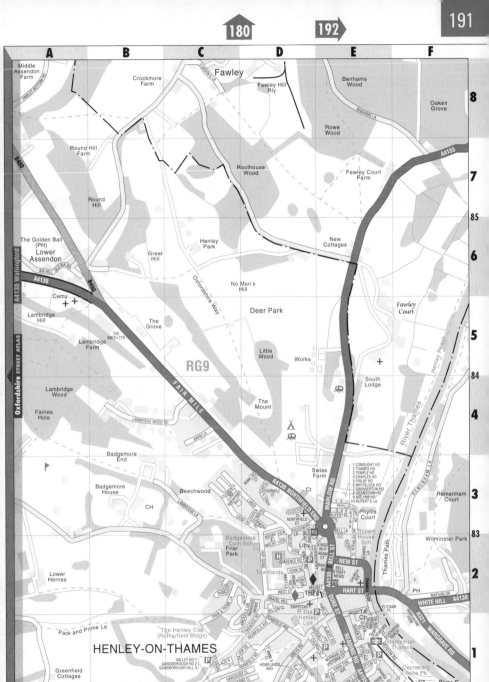

D2
1 CEDAR
2 BEECH
3 ACACIA
4 MOUNT VIEW CT
5 MARKET PLACE MEWS

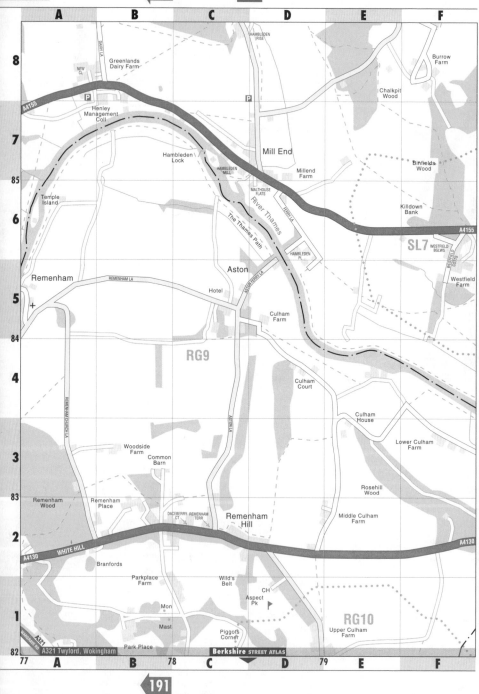

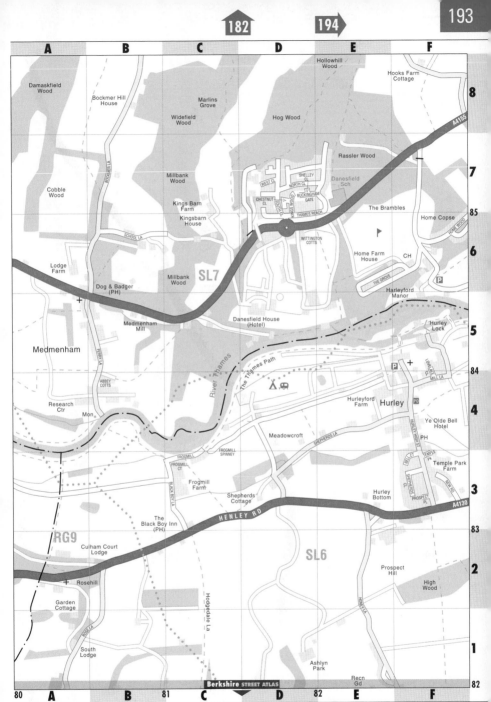

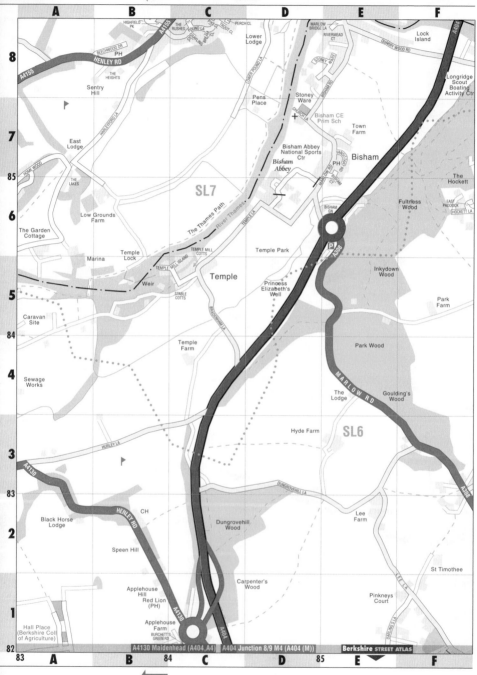

A **B** **C** **D** **E** **F**

HIGHFIELD PK
THE RUSHES
ROUND LA
PERCH CL
TOTT CT TROUT CL
MARLOW BRIDGE LA
RIVERMEAD CT
Lock Island
QUARRY WOOD RD
Longridge Scout Boating Activity Ctr

BEECHWOOD DR
8 PH
HENLEY RD
A4155
THE HEIGHTS
Lower Lodge

Sentry Hill
QUIET WATERS LA
Pens Place
Stoney Ware
ST STONEY WARE
BISHAM WOOD RD
Bisham CE Prim Sch
Town Farm
The Hockett

7
East Lodge
HARLEYFORD LA
Bisham Abbey National Sports Ctr
VANSITTART RD
MARLOW RD
Bisham
EAST PADDOCK
HOCKETT LA

85
HOME WOOD
THE LAKES
SL7
Bisham Abbey
PH
CHURCH LA
OLD MARSH
LA
Fultress Wood

6
Low Grounds Farm
The Thames Path
River Thames
TEMPLE LA
BISHAM GN
P
A308
Inkydown Wood

The Garden Cottage
Temple Lock
Marina
TEMPLE MILL ISLAND
TEMPLE MILL COTTS
Temple Park
Park Farm

5
Weir
STABLE COTTS
Temple
Princess Elizabeth's Well

Caravan Site
RACTON MALL LA

84
Temple Farm
Park Wood

4
Sewage Works

MARLOW RD
The Lodge
Goulding's Wood

3
HURLEY LA
Hyde Farm
SL6
A308

83
A4130
HENLEY RD
CH
DUNGROVEHILL LA
Lee Farm
St Timothee

2
Black Horse Lodge
Speen Hill
Dungrovehill Wood
LEE LA

Applehouse Hill
Red Lion (PH)
Carpenter's Wood
Pinkneys Court
GOULDING LA

1
Hall Place (Berkshire Coll of Agriculture)
A4130
Applehouse Farm
BURCHETT'S GREEN RD
A404

82
A4130 Maidenhead (A404,A4)
A404 Junction 8/9 M4 (A404 (M))
Berkshire STREET ATLAS

83 **A** **B** **84** **C** **D** **85** **E** **F**

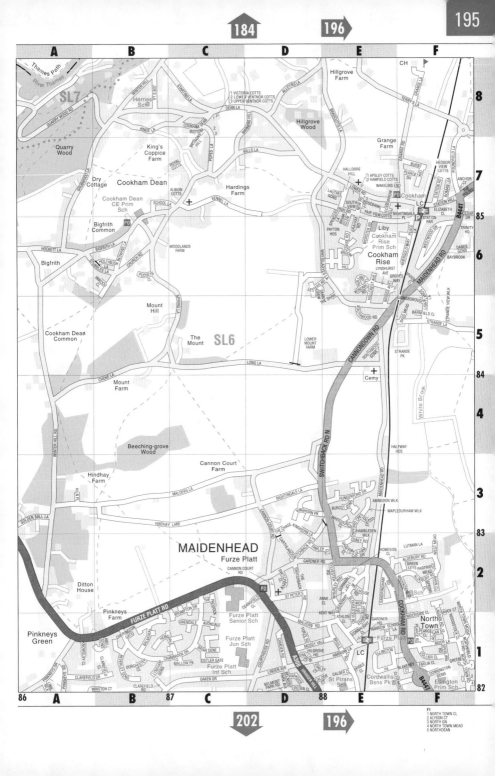

195
185

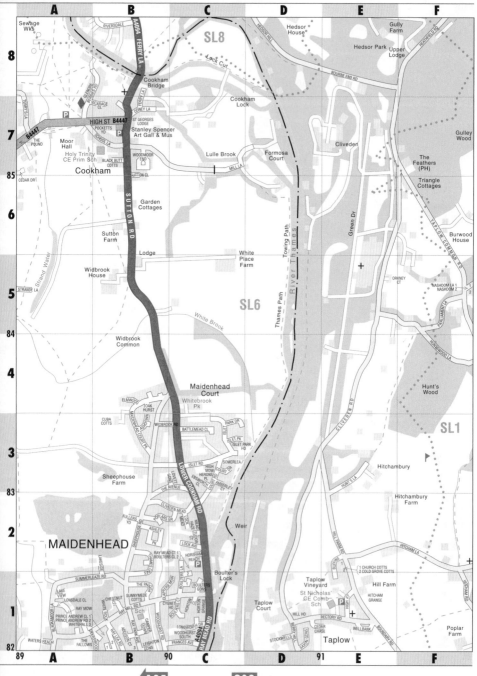

195
203

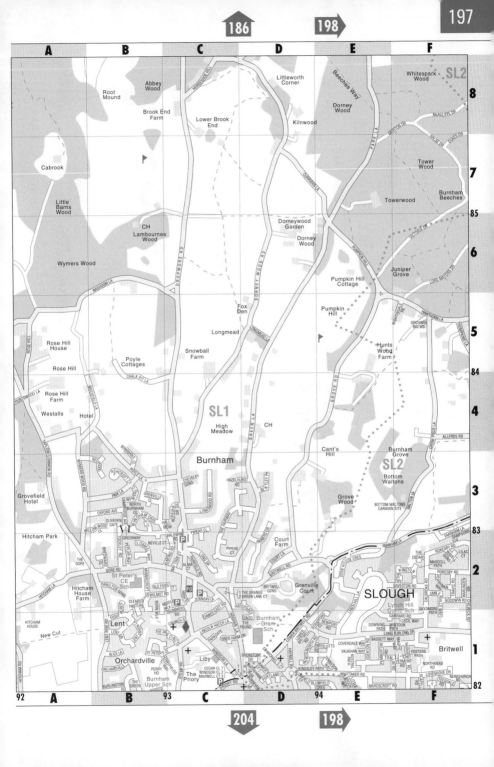

197
187

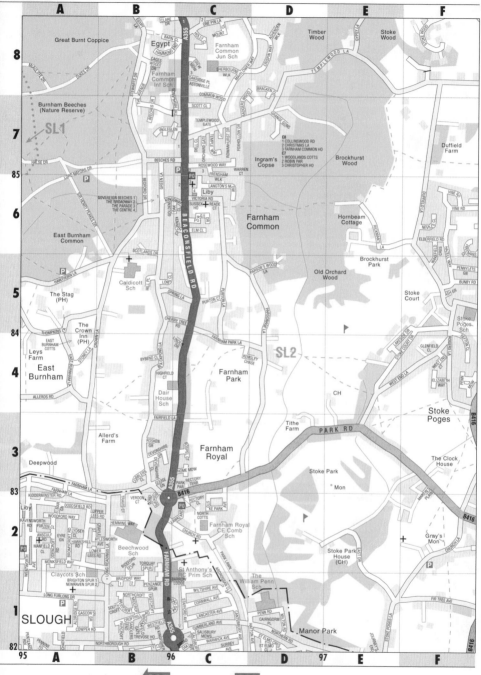

197
205

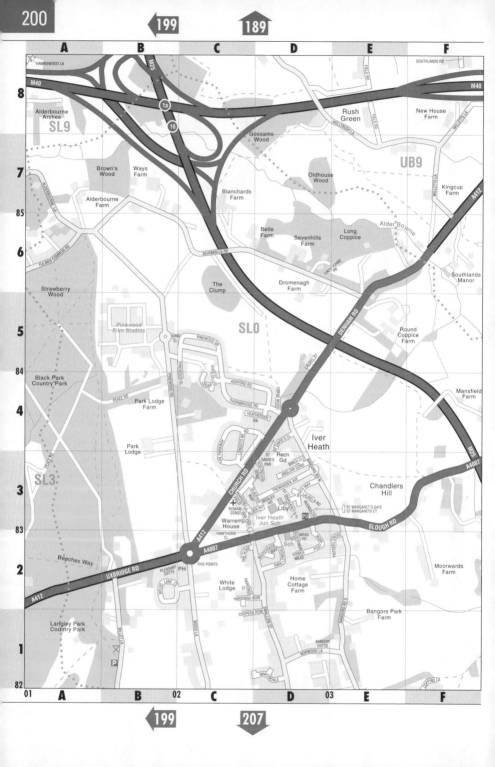

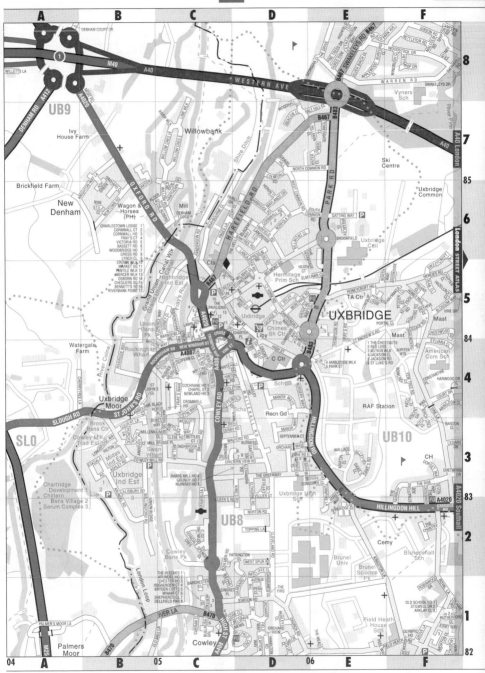

F7
1 WHITE HART RD
2 Nicholsons Sh Ctr
3 REGENT CT
4 FROGMORE CT
5 WHITCHURCH HO
6 KINGSWAY HO

7 WILBERFORCE MEWS
8 SYGNUS CT
9 PROVIDENCE PL
10 ST MARY'S WLK
11 OLD POST OFFICE LA
12 QUEEN'S LA

F6
1 BERKSHIRE LODGE
2 WILTSHIRE LODGE
3 SOMERSET LODGE
4 BUCKINGHAM HO
5 MARLBOROUGH HO
6 KENT LODGE
7 SUSSEX LODGE
8 HAMPSHIRE LODGE
9 DORSET LODGE
10 DEVONSHIRE LODGE
11 CORNWALL LODGE
12 HENLEY LODGE
13 MARLOW LODGE
14 COURTLANDS
15 COOKHAM LODGE

MAIDENHEAD

SL6

Cox Green

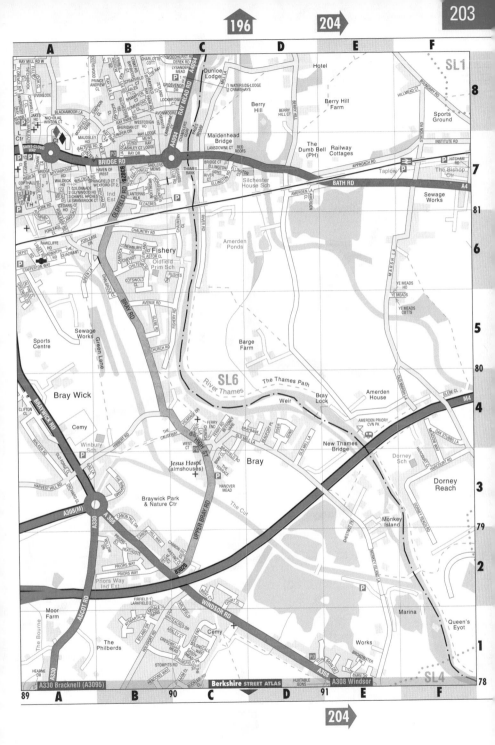

Berkshire STREET ATLAS

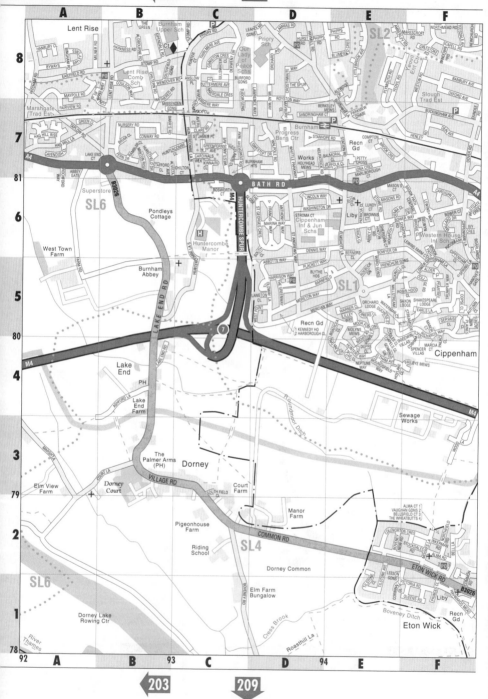

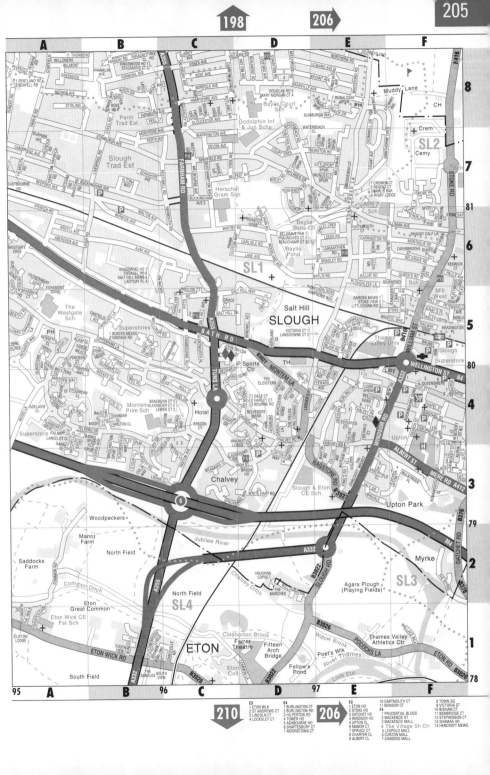

A B C D E F

8

7

81

6

5

80

4

3

79

2

1

78

98 A 99 B C 99 D 00 E F

Place labels

THE LODGE
Wexham Sch
WEXHAM WOODS
GRANGEWOOD
CHURCH GR
NORWAY DR
FARM
HILLERSDON
ALMONDS
MANOR
Wexham Court Prim Sch
OLD HOUSE CT
Stone's Wood
ALL SOULS COTTS
George Green
George Green Dr
Avenue Dr
A412
Upton Lea
Arbour Vale Sch
RC Prim Sch
CHURCHFIELD
Five Rivers (PH)
BEAUMONT CT
The George (PH)
Westfield Lane
AUGUST END
CORONATION
HARVEY HO
RC High Sch
CHARLES
DUNBAR CT
KOLA HO
THE FRITHE
CLARENDON CT 1
GRASMERE PAR 2
COPPERFIELD TERR 3
PICKWICK TERR 4
SHAGGY CALF LA
KENDAL DR
SL2
MIRADOR CRES
CANNON GATE
HOLMEDALE
Home Farm
MIDDLE GR
Convent
Nursery
TROUTBECK CL
Lea Inf & Jun Schs
GRASMERE AVE
GLANMOR RD
ELMWOOD RD
BROADMARK RD
Middle Green
Trenches Farm
THE PIPPINS
PICKFORD DR
PICKFORD CL
BLENHEIM CL
MORELLO CL
ST JOHNS RD
GALLOWAY CHASE
ST PAULS AVE
The Bsns Village
Works
HAZELMERE RD
SERMED
WARREN PAR
Lavender Farm
SL3
The Orchards
Grand Union Canal
Slough Arm
Grand Union Canal Wlk
NURSERY LA
The Langley Manor Sch
Slough Interchange Ind Est
LEITH CL
RICHMOND CRES
WELLESLEY RD
DIAMOND RD
VICTORIA RD
EASTRIDGE
GOODMAN PK
Middlegreen Trad Est
Marish Wharf Ind Est
Deserento
Langley Bsns Pk
WATERS
A4
WELLINGTON ST
A412
St Bernard's Prep Sch
HALKINGCROFT
RICKENFORDS
CHERRY AVE
LAUREL AVE
SEYMOUR HO
ALDERBURY RD
Slough Mus
Superstore
SL1
St Bernard's Convent Sch
FOXHERNE
SUTTON AVE
DOWNS RD
BANNISTER
Mobile Home Site
MERTON RD
MERTON
Upton
SUSSEX PL
CHICHESTER
JUNIPER
DOLPHIN CT
BEVERLEY CT
CAMBRIA
FIELDING GDNS
Ryvers Prim Sch
LAMBERT
PADSTOW
TORSYTHIA GDNS
Langleywood Sch
Coll
SPRINGFIELD
Sch
HARDWICKE
PURLEY LN
LARCHWOOD
PALMERSTON AVE
WARREN CL
RYVERS RD
Long Close Prep Sch
WHEATSTONE
PARKSTONE LODGE
PARK LA
GLENVILLE
Liby
PARRY GREEN
SLOUGH
Upton Court Rd
UPTON COURT RD
LONDON RD
Kedermister Park
Langley Gram Sch
BROOM HO
DENNY RD
Upton Court Park
Castleview Prim Sch
Green Dr
NASH
Cricket Gd
Ditton Park
MILBERRY DR
POPLAR
RANDALL
B376 DATCHET RD
SLOUGH RD A376
M4
B3026
Longmead Bridge
DITTON PARK CVN SITE
CONDUIT LA
A4
DITTON RD
B376

A3	A4	10 ELIZABETH CT	C3	F1	9 GIBSON CL
1 GROVE CL	1 COLONIAL RD	B4	1 STARWOOD CT	1 CALDER CL	10 SHERWOOD CT
2 CHATHAM CT	2 QUEENSMERE RD	1 AUSTRALIA RD	2 BLACKTHORN DELL	2 BESSEMER CL	
3 EASTFIELD CL	3 ALPHA ST N	2 PRINCES ST	3 APPLETREE LA	3 TYLER WLK	
4 ALBERT ST	4 MILFORD CT	3 CONNAUGHT RD	4 LA ROCHE CL	4 OWEN CL	
5 PRIORS CL	5 CLIFTON RD	4 SELIM CT	5 KINGSWAY	5 BECKET CHASE	
6 NIGHTINGALE CT	6 BELGRAVE PL	5 CLEMENTS CL	6 RED COTTAGE MEWS	6 DAVIDSON RD	
7 MOUNTBATTEN CL	7 CLIFTON LODGE	6 CHESHIRE CT	7 FLEMING CT	7 CHAPLIN MEWS	
8 HORNBEAM GDNS	8 LASCELLES HO	7 SUSSEX KEEP		8 SHARMAN ROW	
9 CHURCH VIEW	9 RYE CT				

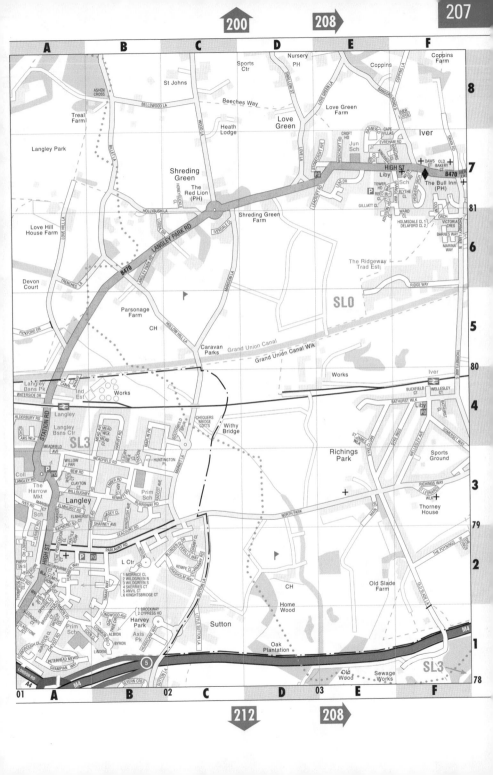

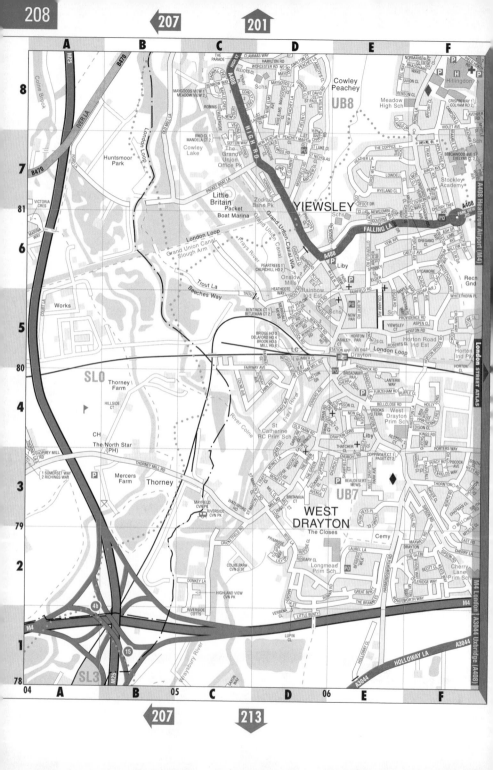

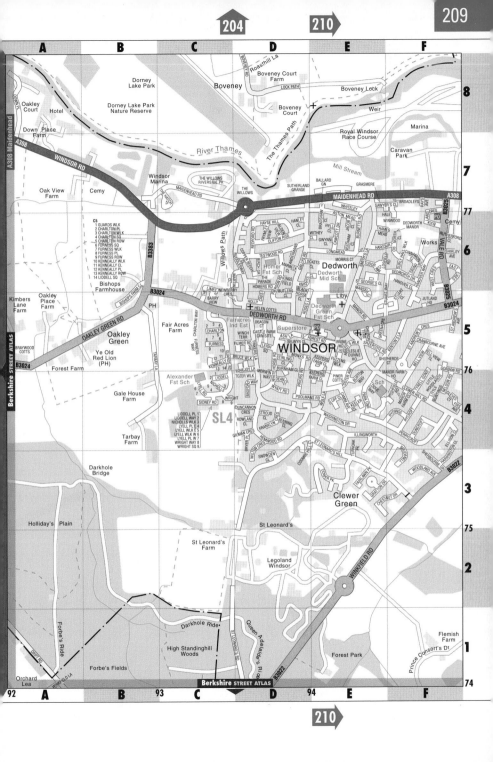

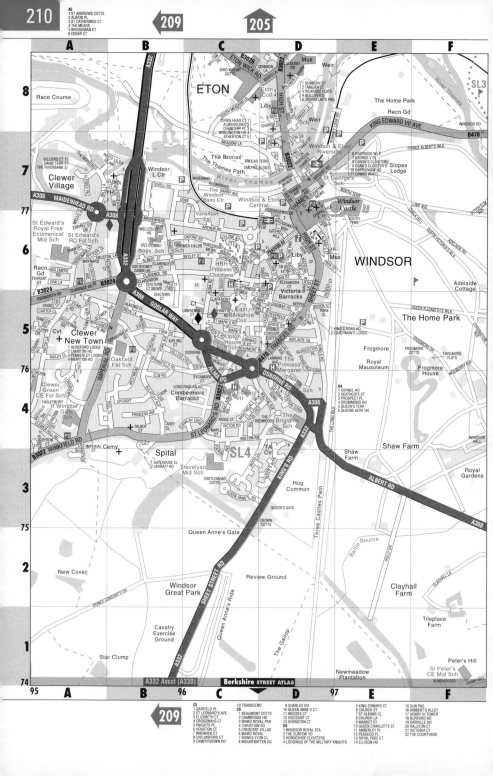

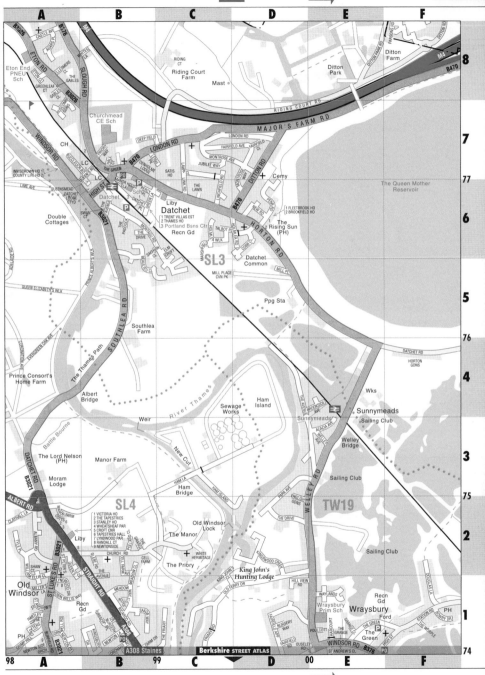

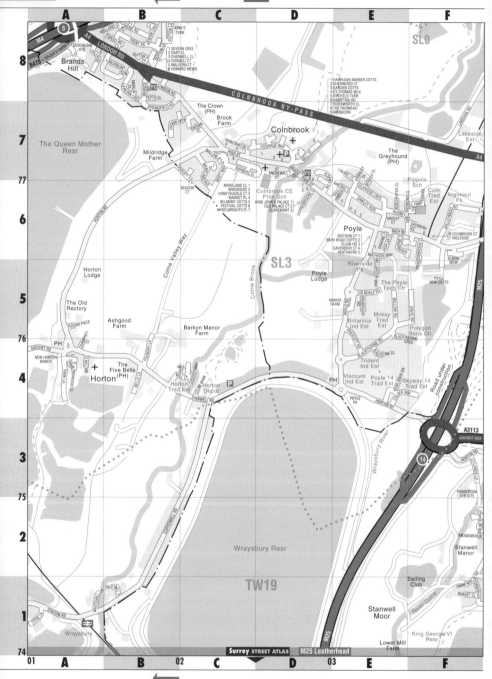

SL0

8

7

77

6

5

76

4

3

75

2

1

74

A   B   C   D   E   F

01   02   03

M4

Brands Hill

B470 MAJOR'S FARM

SOVEREIGN HTS

LONDON RD

LABURNUM

KING'S TERR

1 SEVERN CRES
2 DART CL
3 CHERWELL CL
4 DISRAELI CT
5 MALVERN CT
6 HOWARD MEWS

WELLAND CL
MORE RD
SUTTON LA
TRENT HO
TWEED LA
SUTTON LA

COLNBROOK BY-PASS

1 HARRISON BARBER COTTS
2 SHERWOOD CT
3 GARDEN COTTS
4 ST.THOMAS WLK
5 RYEFIELD TERR
6 HAMPTON HO
7 RUDSWORTH CL
8 THE FAIRMEAD
9 ABINGDON

Lakeside Est

A4

The Queen Mother Resr

Mildridge Farm

The Crown (PH)

Brook Farm

Colnbrook

The Greyhound (PH)

Pippins Sch

Coln Trad Est

Argonaut Pk

HUNSTANTON CL

HIGH ST

VICARAGE WAY

ST ANDREWS CT

RAYNERS CL

PO

MORELAND CL 1
BROOKSIDE 2
HONEYSUCKLE CT 3
MARKET PL 4
BELMONT COTTS 5
FESTIVAL COTTS 6
WHEELWRIGHTS PL 7

Colnbrook CE Prim Sch

KING JOHN'S PALACE 1
OLD PALACE CT 2
CLAREMONT 3

COLNBROOKE CRES

LAUREL CT

AINTREE CT

DAWLEY RIDE

HADLEY

BATH RD

DAVENTRY

MATHISEN WAY

Poyle

IBOTSON CT 1
BATH ROAD COTTS 2
ELGIN HO 3
CAVENDISH CT 4
HEATHACRE 5

6 COLNBROOK CT
7 INGLESIDE

ELBOW MDW

Colne Valley Way

BEACON CT

Horton Lodge

The Old Rectory

Ashgood Farm

Berkyn Manor Farm

Colne Brook

SL3

Riverside Pk

Poyle Lodge

The Poyle Tech Ctr

POYLE NEW COTTS

M25

MANOR FARM

COLNDALE RD

Britannia Ind Est

Mckay Trad Est

Polygon Bsns Ctr

BLACKTHORNE

PICKINS PIECE

DATCHET RD

CHIMNEY L

NEW HORTON MANOR

PARK LA

DARK LA

BIRCHWOOD CL

MILTON R

FOUNDRY LA

BELLS LA

MILL ST

STANWELL RD

COLNE BANK

Horton Trad Est

Horton Depot

PH

Trident Ind Est

Viscount Ind Est

Poyle 14 Trad Est

Skyway 14 Trad Est

OLD WAY

HORTON RD

POYLE PK

The Five Bells (PH)

Horton

PH

Road under construction

A3113

AIRPORT WAY

14

PONDEROSA CVN SITE

MEADOWVIEW

Stanwell Manor

Wraysbury River

PEPPERMILL RD

Wraysbury Resr

TW19

Sailing Club

River Colne

FARM WAY

RUSSET CL

OLD M

WHITEHALL LA

TITHE LA

STATION RD

Wraysbury

M25

Stanwell Moor

Lower Mill Farm

King George VI Resr

Surrey STREET ATLAS   M25 Leatherhead

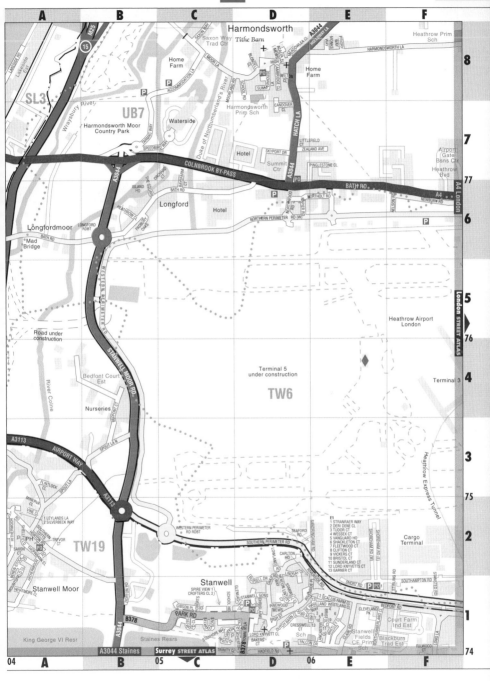

Heathrow Prim Sch

Harmondsworth

Tithe Barn

Home Farm

Saxon Way Trad Ctr

SL3

Wraysbury River

UB7

Harmondsworth Moor Country Park

Waterside

Duke of Northumberland's River

Harmondsworth Prim Sch

Home Farm

HATCH LA

LITTLEFIELD

SKYPORT DR

ZEALAND AVE

Hotel

Summit Ctr

Airport Gate Bsns Ctr

Heathrow Blvd

COLNBROOK BY-PASS

Longford Rdbt

Longfordmoor

BATH RD

Mad Bridge

Longford

Hotel

BATH RD.

NEWBURN RD

A4

A4 London

Pinglestone Cl

NORTHERN PERIMETER RD (W)

Road under construction

WESTERN PERIMETER RD

STANWELL MOOR RD.

Heathrow Airport London

London STREET ATLAS

River Colne

Bedfont Court Est

Nurseries

Terminal 5 under construction

TW6

Terminal 3

A3113

AIRPORT WAY

A3113

Western Perimeter Rd Rdbt

Heathrow Express Tunnel

FLEETLOCK

MINERVA CL

1 LEYLANDS LA
2 SILVERBECK WAY

TW19

Southern Perimeter Rd

SEAFORD

SANDRINGHAM RD

Cargo Terminal

E1
1 STRANRAER WAY
2 DERI DENE CL
3 TUDOR CT
4 WESSEX CT
5 VANGUARD HO
6 SHACKLETON CT
7 FLEETWOOD CT
8 CLIFTON CT
9 VICKERS CT
10 BRISTOL CT
11 SUNDERLAND CT
12 LORD KNYVETTS CT
13 GARNER CT

Stanwell Moor

Stanwell

PARK RD

B378

Staines Resrs

King George VI Resr

SOUTHAMPTON RD

Court Farm Ind Est

Stanwell Fields CE Prim Sch

Blackburn Trad Est

A3044 Staines

Surrey STREET ATLAS

Index

Church Rd **6** Beckenham BR2.......... **53** C6

Place name	**Location number**	**Locality, town or village**	**Postcode**	**Page and**
May be abbreviated	Present when a number	Shown when more than one	**district**	**grid square**
on the map	indicates the place's	place has the same name	District for the indexed place	Page number and grid
	position in a crowded area			reference for the standard
	of mapping			mapping

Public and commercial buildings are highlighted in magenta   **Places of interest** are highlighted in blue with a star★

Abbreviations used in the index

Acad	**Academy**	Comm	**Common**	Gd	**Ground**	L	**Leisure**	Prom	**Promenade**
App	**Approach**	Cott	**Cottage**	Gdn	**Garden**	La	**Lane**	Rd	**Road**
Arc	**Arcade**	Cres	**Crescent**	Gn	**Green**	Liby	**Library**	Recn	**Recreation**
Ave	**Avenue**	Cswy	**Causeway**	Gr	**Grove**	Mdw	**Meadow**	Ret	**Retail**
Bglw	**Bungalow**	Ct	**Court**	H	**Hall**	Meml	**Memorial**	Sh	**Shopping**
Bldg	**Building**	Ctr	**Centre**	Ho	**House**	Mkt	**Market**	Sq	**Square**
Bsns, Bus	**Business**	Ctry	**Country**	Hospl	**Hospital**	Mus	**Museum**	St	**Street**
Bvd	**Boulevard**	Cty	**County**	HQ	**Headquarters**	Orch	**Orchard**	Sta	**Station**
Cath	**Cathedral**	Dr	**Drive**	Hts	**Heights**	Pal	**Palace**	Terr	**Terrace**
Cir	**Circus**	Dro	**Drove**	Ind	**Industrial**	Par	**Parade**	TH	**Town Hall**
Cl	**Close**	Ed	**Education**	Inst	**Institute**	Pas	**Passage**	Univ	**University**
Cnr	**Corner**	Emb	**Embankment**	Int	**International**	Pk	**Park**	Wk, Wlk	**Walk**
Coll	**College**	Est	**Estate**	Intc	**Interchange**	Pl	**Place**	Wr	**Water**
Com	**Community**	Ex	**Exhibition**	Junc	**Junction**	Prec	**Precinct**	Yd	**Yard**

Index of localities, towns and villages

A

Addington 65 A6
Adstock 53 F1
Akeley 41 E8
Albury 136 B7
Aldbury 120 D5
Alderton 9 A2
Alscot 139 A5
Amersham 154 B2
Amersham Common ..165 E8
Amersham Old Town ..165 A7
Amersham on the Hill .154 D2
Ascott 80 A2
Ashendon 97 F1
Asheridge 143 C6
Ashley Green 144 F7
Ashton 9 E8
Askett 139 D6
Aspley Guise 49 F4
Aspley Heath 49 A2
Aston 192 C5
Aston Abbotts 88 D5
Aston Clinton 117 D6
Aston Sandford 127 D4
Astrope 104 A3
Astwood 16 A3
Atterbury 36 A4
Austenwood 188 C8
Aylesbury 115 D7

B

Baker's Wood 189 D3
Ballinger Common 142 E3
Bancroft 33 F5
Barretts End 42 F7
Barton Hartshorn 50 D2
Beachampton 44 B6

Beacon's Bottom 159 D3
Beaconsfield 175 D1
Beamond End 163 F6
Beanhill 47 B4
Bedgrove 116 C5
Bedlam 14 C1
Beecroft 93 F8
Bellingdon 143 E7
Belsize 156 F6
Bennett End 159 C7
Berkhamsted 135 C6
Berryfield 100 D5
Biddlesden 27 D5
Bierton 102 A3
Birchmoor Green 60 E8
Bisham 194 E7
Bishopstone 115 A1
Bix 179 D1
Blackthorn 81 A4
Blakelands 22 B1
Bleak Hall 46 F5
Bledlow 138 B1
Bledlow Ridge 159 F8
Bletchley 58 A7
Boarstall 95 B1
Bockmer End 182 C1
Bolbeck Pk 35 A7
Bolter End 170 F5
Booker 172 B4
Botley 145 A1
Botolph Claydon 74 F6
Bourne End 185 B2
Bourton 52 F8
Boveney 209 D8
Bovingdon 146 B4
Bovingdon Green 146 A2
Bow Brickhill 48 C1
Boyne Hill 202 D6
Brackley 38 A8
Bradenham 160 F7

Bradville 34 B7
Bradwell 34 A4
Bradwell Abbey 33 F3
Bradwell Common 34 B3
Bragenham 70 C6
Brands Hill 212 A8
Bray 203 D3
Bray Wick 203 A4
Brill 96 B1
Britwell 197 F1
Broad Green 25 B3
Brook End
  Ivinghoe 105 E4
  North Crawley 23 F5
  Weston Turville ...117 A3
Broughton
  Aylesbury 116 D8
  Milton Keynes 36 A3
Browns Wood 48 C4
Bryant's Bottom 150 F4
Buckingham 41 D2
Buckland 117 F6
Buckland Common 133 A3
Bucklandwharf 118 B4
Buckmoorend 140 D6
Buffler's Halt 40 C3
Bulbourne 119 C8
Bullingdon End 20 C7
Bulstrode 146 E3
Burcott 79 E4
Burnham 197 C3
Bury End 165 D6
Butlers Cross 176 F6
Butler's Cross 130 C3
Bye Green 117 A3

C

Cadmore End 170 C6

Caldecote 22 E1
Caldecotte 48 A2
California
  Aylesbury 115 C7
  Dunstable 93 F6
Calvert 73 B6
Calverton 32 E3
Campbell Park 35 A3
Castlethorpe 19 E5
Central Milton Keynes .34 D1
Chackmore 41 B4
Chalfont Common 177 F6
Chalfont St Giles ...177 C7
Chalfont St Peter ...177 F2
Chalkshire 130 C4
Chalvey 205 C3
Chandlers Hill 200 E3
Chapel End 118 C8
Charndon 72 E6
Chartridge 143 C4
Chearsley 112 A2
Cheddington 105 B7
Chenies 156 B2
Chenies Bottom 156 B2
Chesham 154 C8
Chesham Bois 154 C3
Chessmount 154 E7
Chetwode 61 E8
Chicheley 23 C8
Chilton 111 A4
Chinnor 147 D7
Chipperfield 156 F8
Chisbridge Cross 182 D6
Chivery 132 C4
Cholesbury 133 C3
Chorleywood 167 D5
Chorleywood Bottom ..167 C3
Chorleywood West ...167 A4
Christmas Common ...168 B7

Church End
  Chorley Wood 156 F1
  Drayton Parslow 68 B5
  Haddenham 127 A5
  Hanslope 11 A2
  Long Crendon 125 C7
  Pitstone 105 D3
  Steeple Claydon 63 E2
  Totternhoe 93 B7
Church Hill 56 A8
Cippenham 204 F4
Clewer Green 209 E3
Clewer New Town 210 A5
Clewer Village 210 A7
Clifton Reynes 7 C3
Codmore 144 E1
Coffee Hall 46 F7
Cold Brayfield 8 A5
Coleshill 164 F3
Colnbrook 212 D1
Colstrope 181 D5
Combe 130 C1
Common The 55 B4
Conniburrow 34 E4
Cookham 196 A7
Cookham Dean 195 B7
Cookham Rise 195 E6
Cores End 185 C4
Cosgrove 19 D2
Cowley 202 C3
Cowley Peachey 208 E8
Cow Roast 120 E1
Cox Green 202 C3
Crafton 89 F3
Cranfield 25 B1
Creslow 87 B8
Cressex 172 D4
Crofts End 14 A1
Crowell 147 B4
Crowell Hill 147 D2

Crowfield 26 F8
Crowfield 149 B4
Crownhill 45 E7
Cryers Hill 162 D6
Cublington 78 B1
Cuddington 113 A2

D

Dadford 28 D1
Dagnall 107 C6
Darvillshill 150 A4
Datchet 211 C6
Deanshanger 31 D4
Dedworth 209 E6
Denham
  Denham Green 190 A2
  Quainton 85 D5
Denham Green 189 E5
Denner Hill 150 E4
Diggs 126 F5
Dinton 113 F2
Ditchfield 171 A3
Dorney 204 C3
Dorney Reach 203 F3
Dorton 96 F1
Downend Park 35 B5
Downley 161 C3
Downs Barn 35 A5
Drayton Beauchamp 118 B5
Drayton Parslow 68 C6
Duck End
  Akeley 42 A8
  Swanbourne 66 F4
Dudswell 134 D8
Dunsmore 141 A7
Dunstable 93 E8
Dunton 77 E5

E

Eaglestone 47 B7
Eakley Lanes 4 D2
Easington 111 B1
East Burnham 198 A4
East Claydon 74 E8
East End
  Cranfield 25 C1
  North Crawley 24 F6
Eaton Bray 92 E6
Eaton Green 92 C7
Edgcott 72 F2
Edlesborough 92 E4
Egypt 198 B8
Ellesborough 130 B2
Elmhurst 101 E3
Emberton 13 E8
Emerson Valley 46 B2
Emmington 137 A1
Eton 210 C8
Eton Wick 204 F1
Eythrope 113 F8

F

Far Bletchley 57 D7
Farnham Common 198 D6
Farnham Park 198 C4
Farnham Royal 198 C3
Fawley 191 C4
Fawley Bottom 180 B2
Felden 146 F7
Fenny Lock 47 E2
Fern 184 E5
Filgrave 13 C5
Finmere 50 D7
Fishermead 35 A1
Flackwell Heath 185 A7
Flaunden 156 A6
Fleet Marston 100 B4
Flowers Bottom 150 A4
Ford 128 B7
Forty Green
  Beaconsfield 175 A4
  Princes Risborough 137 F3
Foscote 42 B4
Four Ashes 162 D4
Fox Milne 35 F4
Franklin's Spring 178 D5
Frieth 170 F1
Frith-hill 152 C7
Fullers Slade 33 A4
Fulmer 199 C8
Fulwell 39 A2
Furtho 19 A3
Furze Platt 195 C2
Furzton 46 D4

G

Gawcott 51 F4
Gayhurst 12 D2
George Green 206 E8
Gerrards Cross 188 E5
Gibraltar 113 D2
Giffard Park 22 A2
Godlington 61 E3
Gossard's Green 25 C4
Grafton Regis 9 D2
Granborough 75 E7
Granby 47 B3
Gravel Hill 177 F4
Great Brickhill 59 D2
Greatgap 105 D6
Great Hampden 150 D7
Great Hivings 144 A3
Great Holm 45 E8
Great Horwood 55 A1
Great Kimble 139 E8
Great Kingshill 162 E8
Great Linford 34 E8
Great Missenden 152 A6
Green End
  Granborough 76 A7
  High Wycombe 160 A4
Greenfield 168 A4
Greenleys 33 B5
Grendon Underwood 83 A6
Gubblecote 104 D3

H

Haddenham 127 B5
Halton 117 D1
Hambleden 181 D1
Ham Green 83 D2
Hampden Bottom 141 B2
Hanslope 11 B3
Hardmead 15 D3
Hardwick 87 B3
Harmondsworth 213 D8
Harrold 3 F6
Hartwell 10 D8
Hastoe 132 F7
Haversham 20 E2
Hawridge 133 E1
Hawridge Common 133 E2
Haydon Hill 100 E2
Hazeley 45 D5
Hazelmere 163 B4
Heath End
  Cholesbury 134 A2
  Prestwood 151 E1
Hedgerley 187 D3
Hedgerley Green 187 E4
Hedgerley Hill 187 D2
Hedsor 185 F3
Heelands 34 C4
Hempton Wainhill 147 F7
Henley-on-Thames 191 B1
Henton 137 E2
Heronsgate 167 D2
Higham Cross 10 D3
Higher Denham 189 C4
Highway 202 B7
High Wycombe 173 B5
Hillesden 63 A6
Hillesden Hamlet 51 F1
Hilltop 144 D2
Hoggeston 77 B7
Hogpits Bottom 156 B7
Hollingdon 69 C3
Holly Green 138 A3
Holmer Green 163 D6
Holton 122 C2
Holtspur 175 A1
Honeywick 92 E8
Horn Hill 178 B6
Horsenden 138 E2
Horsleys Green 159 C3
Horton
  Cheddington 91 B3
  Wraysbury 212 A4
Horton-cum-Studley 108 B6
Horton Wharf 91 C4
Hotley Bottom 151 C8
Hughenden Valley 162 B7
Hulcote 37 E2
Hulcott 102 E6
Huntgate End 10 C1
Hunt's Hill 161 D5
Hurley 193 E4
Hurst End 24 A3
Hyde End 152 F7
Hyde Heath 153 C5

I

Ibstone 169 D7
Ickenham 190 F1
Ickford 124 A3
Ilmer 137 F8
Iver 207 F7
Iver Heath 200 D4
Ivinghoe 105 F5
Ivinghoe Aston 92 A1

J

Jordans 176 F3

K

Kents Hill 48 A7
Kiln Common 151 B8
Kiln Farm 33 B3
Kingsey 127 B2
Kingston 36 C2
Kingston Blount 147 A3
Kingswood 83 B3
Knotty Green 175 C6
Knowlhill 46 D6

L

Lacey Green 149 E5
Lake End 204 B4
Lane End 171 C4
Lanes End 132 C4
Langley 207 A3
Lathbury 22 C7
Latimer 155 E3
Lavendon 7 F7
Layter's Green 177 B1
Leadenhall 47 A8
Leckhampstead 42 E7
Ledburn 90 D8
Lee Common 142 D5
Lee Gate 142 A7
Leighton Buzzard 80 F6
Lenborough 52 D3
Lent 197 B1
Lent Rise 204 A8
Lewknor 157 B8
Ley Hill 145 B1
Lillingstone Dayrell 29 F4
Lillingstone Lovell 30 B5
Linslade 80 D7
Little Boys Heath 152 C3
Little Brickhill 59 E5
Little Britain 208 C7
Little Chalfont 155 B1
Littlecote 78 A5
Little End 23 B8
Little Frieth 170 E2
Little Gaddesden 121 D7
Little Hampden 140 F4
Little Horwood 55 F2
Little Kimble 129 E2
Little Kingshill 152 B3
Little Linford 21 C5
Little London
  Oakley 109 F5
  Wendover 141 C7
Little Marlow 184 D5
Little Marsh 72 A3
Little Missenden 153 A2
Little Row 202 A5
Little Tingewick 50 E6
Little Tring 118 F6
Littleworth Common 186 D1
Long Crendon 125 B6
Longford 213 C6
Longfordmoor 213 A6
Long Marston 104 B3
Long Street 10 F4
Longwick 138 D7
Loosley Row 149 C6
Loudwater 174 D2
Loughton 46 A8
Love Green 207 D8
Lower Assendon 191 A6
Lower Bois 154 C5
Lower Cadsden 139 E5
Lower End
  Long Crendon 125 B7
  Marsworth 104 F3
  Thornborough 53 F8
  Woburn Sands 49 C8
Lower Hartwell 114 E6
Lower North Dean 150 E1
Lower Pollicott 111 F7
Lower Wainhill 147 E7
Lower Weald 32 E2
Lower Woodend 182 D4
Ludgershall 96 D8
Lye Green 144 F4

M

Maidenhead 202 F4
Maidenhead Court 196 C4
Maidensgrove 179 C5
Maids Moreton 41 E4
Manor Park
  Aylesbury 101 E2
  Slough 198 D1
Mantles Gn 165 A8
Maple Cross 178 D6
Marlow 183 B2
Marlow Bottom 183 C6
Marlow Common 182 F3
Marsh 129 C7
Marsh Gibbon 71 F3
Marsworth 105 A1
Meadle 139 B8
Medbourne 45 E5
Medmenham 193 A5
Mentmore 90 D4
Micklefield 173 E6
Middle Claydon 74 C8
Middle End
  Leckhampstead 42 D8
  Totternhoe 93 A8
Middle Green 206 E5
Middleton 35 E3
Middle Weald 32 E1
Mill End
  Henley-on-Thames 192 D7
  Little Missenden 153 A3
  Rickmansworth 167 F1
Milton Common 136 B3
Milton Keynes 34 D5
Milton Keynes Village 35 E2
Mixbury 38 D1
Mobwell 152 A8
Monks Risborough 139 C6
Monkston 36 A1
Monkston Park 35 E1
Moor Common 171 A2
Moor End
  Eaton Bray 92 E5
  Yardley Gobion 18 D6
Mop End 164 B7
Moulsoe 36 D8
Mount Pleasant
  Buckingham 52 D7
  Stoke Goldington 12 B7
Mundaydean Bottom 182 E5
Murcott 94 A4
Mursley 67 D6
Myrke 205 F2

N

Naphill 161 D7
Nash 44 C1
Nash Lee 130 C5
Nearton End 67 A3
Neath Hill 34 F6
Netherfield 47 C6
New Bradwell 33 F8
New Denham 201 A6
New Ground 120 A2
Newland Park 178 A7
New Mill 119 B6
Newport Pagnell 22 B5
Newton 144 C1
Newton Blossomville 8 A4
Newton Longville 57 D3
Newton Purcell 50 B2
Newyears Green 190 F5
Norcott Hill 120 D2
Northall 92 B5
Northchurch 134 C5
North Crawley 24 A6
Northend 168 E6
North End
  Stagsden 16 E8
  Steeple Claydon 63 D3
  Stewkley 68 D3
Northfield 35 D3
North Lee 130 A7
North Marston 76 A2
North Town 195 F1
North Weston 136 F8
Nup End 89 B3

O

Oakgrove 35 D2

Oakhill 45 D4
Oakley
  Brill 109 D5
  Chinnor 147 B5
Oakley Green 209 B5
Oldbrook 46 E8
Old Farm Park 48 E5
Old Linslade 70 D2
Old Stratford 32 B7
Old Town 38 A7
Old Windsor 211 A1
Old Wolverton 33 D8
Olney 6 E4
Orchard Leigh 145 B3
Orchardville 197 B1
Oving 86 D8
Owlswick 128 D1
Oxley Park 45 E3

P

Padbury 53 B2
Page Hill 41 F2
Palmers Moor 201 A1
Parmoor 181 F7
Passenham 32 C4
Paulerspury 17 B7
Pednormead End 154 A7
Penn 174 E7
Penn Street 164 B5
Pennyland 35 A6
Peppershill 124 D6
Petsoe End 14 A7
Pheasants 181 E6
Pheasant's Hill 181 D3
Piddington
  Blackthorn 95 E7
  High Wycombe 160 B1
  Northamptonshire 4 B8
Pimlico 26 F6
Pindon End 10 C4
Pineham 35 E7
Pinfoldpond 60 E6
Pinkneys Green 195 A1
Pishill 179 D8
Pishill Bank 168 B1
Pishill Bottom 168 A1
Pitchcott 86 B5
Pitch Green 138 B3
Pitstone 105 C4
Plumpton End 17 C7
Pond Park 144 A2
Portways 168 B8
Potterspury 18 D2
Poundon 71 E7
Poyle 212 E6
Prebendal Farm 115 B7
Preston Bissett 62 B8
Prestwood 151 D6
Princes Risborough 139 D4
Pudds Cross 145 E2
Pury End 17 A7
Puttenham 103 F2
Puxley 31 D7

Q

Quainton 85 B5
Quainton Hill 75 B1
Quarrendon 101 B3

R

Radclive 51 E8
Radnage 159 C7
Radstone 26 A6
Ram Alley 12 B5
Ravenstone 5 D2
Redmoor 47 A4
Remenham 192 A5
Remenham Hill 192 C2
Richings Park 207 B3
Rickmansworth 167 F1
Ringshall 107 B1
Rockwell End 181 F5
Rooksley 34 B2
Rotten Row 181 F2
Rout's Green 148 D2
Rowsham 102 D8
Rush Green 200 E8
Rushmere 70 E4

S

St Leonards 132 E3
Salcey Green 11 B7
Salden 67 F8

Salford 37 C3
Salt Hill 205 D5
Sandhill 64 E2
Sands 172 B7
Sarratt 156 F4
Saunderton
  Bledlow Ridge 149 C1
  Princes Risborough 138 E1
Saunderton Lee 149 A4
Sedrup 114 F3
Seer Green 176 D4
Shabbington 124 D3
Shalstone 39 E6
Sheeplane 60 C2
Sheepridge 184 E7
Shenley Brook End 46 A2
Shenley Church End 45 E6
Shenley Lodge 46 C5
Shenley Wood 45 F4
Sherington 14 A2
Shipton 66 B3
Shipton Lee 84 D7
Shootersway 134 E4
Shreding Green 207 C7
Singleborough 54 F5
Skirmett 170 A1
Skittle Green 138 A3
Slapton 91 C5
Slough 205 D5
Snelshall East 57 B7
Snelshall West 57 A7
Soulbury 69 E3
Southcourt 115 D6
Southend 180 C8
South End
  Leckhampstead 42 E7
  Stewkley 78 E8
South Harefield 190 D6
South Heath 152 E8
Speen 150 C4
Spencersgreen 132 C7
Spital 210 B3
Sprig's Alley 147 F1
Springfield 35 B2
Spurgrove 170 E2
Spurlands End 163 A8
Stacey Bushes 33 E4
Stagsden 16 F6
Stagsden West End 16 F4
Stantonbury 34 D7
Stanwell 213 C1

Stanwell Moor 212 E1
Startop's End 104 F1
Steeple Claydon 63 C3
Stewkley 68 E2
Stewkley Dean 68 B1
Stoke Bruerne 9 B8
Stoke Goldington 12 A6
Stoke Green 199 B1
Stoke Hammond 69 E8
Stoke Mandeville 116 A2
Stokenchurch 158 E5
Stoke Poges 198 F4
Stone 114 C5
Stonebridge 33 F7
Stonor 179 F6
Stony Green 151 A4
Stowe Park 40 F7
Studley Green 159 E3
Summerstown 72 B2
Sunnymeads 211 E4
Sutton 207 C1
Swanbourne 67 B3
Syresham 27 B8

Tinkers Bridge 47 D6
Tinkers End 65 F3
Tongwell 35 C8
Totteridge 173 F8
Totternhoe 93 B7
Touchbridge 95 E1
Towerage 171 F8
Tower Hill 146 F2
Town End 159 C8
Townsend
  Haddenham 127 A7
  North Marston 76 B2
Town's End 71 D2
Tring 119 C3
Tringford 118 F8
Turvey 8 F6
Turville 169 F3
Turville Heath 169 A3
Turweston 38 C8
Two Mile Ash 33 D2
Twyford 62 C1
Tylers Green 163 D1
Tyringham 12 F2

Taplow 196 E1
Tathall End 11 E2
Tatling End 189 B3
Tattenhoe 57 A8
Temple 194 C5
Terrick 130 C5
Terriers 162 D2
Tetchwick 82 F2
Tew's End 17 C8
Thame 125 E2
The City 159 D6
The Green
  Milton Keynes 47 D8
  Newport Pagnell 22 C3
  Whipsnade 107 F8
The Swillet 167 B3
Thornborough 54 A8
Thorney 208 B3
Thornton 43 C4
Three Households 176 F7
Tickford End 22 F4
Tiddington 136 A7
Tilbrook 48 C3
Tingewick 51 B7

Up End 24 A8
Upper Arncott 94 E7
Upper Dunsley 119 C4
Upper Maidensgrove . . .179 A7
Upper North Dean 150 E2
Upper Pollicott 111 E8
Upper Winchendon 99 B1
Upton
  Slough 206 B3
  Stone 114 A4
Upton Lea 206 A7
Upton Park 205 F3
Uxbridge 201 E5
Uxbridge Moor 201 B4

Venus Hill 156 B8
Verney Junction 64 F4
Victoria Park 116 B8

Waddesdon 99 B7
Walnut Tree 48 C6
Walter's Ash 150 C1
Walton
  Aylesbury 115 F7
  Milton Keynes 47 F5
Walton Court 115 C5
Walton Manor 48 A6
Walton Park 48 A4
Warrington 2 B1
Water Eaton 58 D5
Waterend 159 C5
Watermead 101 F4
Waterperry 123 B1
Waterperry Common . . .122 F8
Waterside 154 D6
Water Stratford 40 A1
Wavendon 48 E7
Wavendon Gate 48 D6
Weedon 87 D1
Well End 184 F5
Well Head 93 D5
Wendover 131 C4
Wendover Dean 141 C5
Westbury 39 B4
Westcott 98 C7
Westcroft 45 E2
West Drayton 208 D3
West End 63 C2
West Hyde 178 E3
West Leith 118 F2
Westlington 113 E1
Weston Turville 116 E3
Weston Underwood 6 B1
West Wycombe 160 F2
Wexham Street 199 C4
Whaddon 45 A1
Wharley End 24 D1
Wheatley 122 A1
Wheeler End 171 B6
Whelpley Hill 145 D5
Whipsnade 107 F8
Whitchurch 87 B6
Whiteleaf 139 D5
Whitfield 26 D3
Wicken 31 B3
Widmer End 162 E6
Widmoor 185 E3

Wigginton 119 D1
Wigginton Bottom 133 D8
Willen 35 D7
Willen Park 35 C6
Willowbank 201 C7
Wilstone 104 D1
Wilstone Green 118 D8
Wilton Park 176 B1
Winchmore Hill 164 D2
Windsor 210 E6
Wing 79 F2
Wingrave 89 C3
Winslow 66 B4
Winterhill 46 D8
Woburn 60 F7
Woburn Sands 49 A5
Wolverton 33 C5
Wolverton Mill 33 A6
Wooburn 185 D4
Wooburn Green 185 F7
Wooburn Moor 174 E1
Woodburn Common 186 B3
Wood End
  Little Horwood 55 E2
  Nash 55 C8
Wood Green 27 F2
Woodham 83 E1
Woodrow 164 D5
Woolstone 35 D3
Wootton Bourne End 25 F8
World's End 130 F7
Worminghall 123 E6
Wormstone 99 C5
Wotton Underwood 97 C4
Woughton On The Green .47 D8
Woughton Park 47 E6
Wraysbury 211 E1
Wycombe Marsh 173 F4
Wymbush 33 F2

Yardley Gobion 18 E5
Yardley Hastings 1 B6

Abbey Barn La HP10 .....173 E3
Abbey Barn Rd HP11 ....173 F4
Abbey Cl SL1 ....204 E6
Abbey Cotts SL7 ....193 B4
Abbey Ct HP5 ....154 B6
Abbey Ctr The HP19 .....101 B2
Abbey Gate SL6 ....204 A7
Abbey Park La SL1 ....186 E2
Abbey Rd Aylesbury HP19 .101 B2
  Bourne End SL8 ....184 F5
  Marlow Bottom SL7 ....
  Milton Keynes,Bradwell
  MK13 ....34 A4
  Milton Keynes,Simpson MK6 .47 E5
  Syresham NN13 ....27 C7
Abbey Sq MK43 ....8 E5
Abbey Terr MK16 ....22 D4
Abbey Way
  High Wycombe HP11 .....173 A6
  Milton Keynes MK13 ....34 B6
  Ravenstone MK46 ....5 E2
Abbey Wlk HP16 ....152 B7
Abbey's Comb Sch MK43 .47 A2
Abbeydore Gr MK10 ......35 F1
Abbeyfield Ho HP16 .....152 A7
Abbeyhill Rdbt MK12 ....33 E4
Abbot Ridge HP18 ....125 D5
Abbot Wlk HP18 ....125 D5
Abbot's Wlk SL4 ....209 E5
Abbots Cl MK13 ....34 B6
Abbots Way
  High Wycombe HP10 .....172 D3
  Monks Risborough HP27 .139 C5
Abbotsbury MK4 ....45 E2
Abbotsfield MK6 ....47 B8
Abbotswood HP27 ....150 C4
Abbott's Cl UB8 ....208 D8
Abbotts Cl HP20 ....101 E1
Abbotts Rd HP20 ....101 E1
Abbotts Vale HP5 ....144 C3
Abbotts Way Slough SL1 .204 D5
  Wingrave HP22 ....89 A4
Abell Gdns SL6 ....195 B1
Abercromby Ave HP12 ...172 E8
Abercromby Ct HP12 .....172 D8
Aberdeen Ave SL1 ....205 A6
Aberdeen Cl MK3 ....46 F2
Abingdon Cl Thame OX9 .125 F1
  Uxbridge UB10 ....201 F4
Abingdon Wlk SL6 ....195 E3
Abington Cl SL2 ....204 C6
Abney Court Dr SL8 .....185 A2
Abraham Cl MK15 ....35 C6
Abrahams Rd RG9 ....191 C3
Abstacle Hill HP23 ......118 F3
Acacia 3 RG9 ....191 D2
Acacia Ave
  West Drayton UB7 ......208 F6
  Wraysbury TW19 ....211 F3
Acacia Cl HP5 ....144 A1
Acacia Gr HP4 ....135 B3
Acacia Ho SL9 ....177 E2
Acacia Mews UB7 ....213 D8
Acacia Wlk HP23 ....118 E3
Accommodation La
  UB7 ....213 C8
Ackerman Cl MK18 ....52 F8
Ackroyd Pl MK5 ....46 B5
Acorn Bsns Ctr LU7 ......78 F1
Acorn Cl HP13 ....173 D7
Acorn Gdns HP12 ....172 E4
Acorn Ho MK9 ....34 D2
Acorn Wlk MK9 ....34 E2
Acre Pas SL4 ....210 D6
Acre The SL7 ....193 B4
Acres End SL9 ....188 D8
Acres End HP7 ....165 E8
Acres The HP13 ....161 E1
Adam Cl
  High Wycombe HP13 ....173 D8
  Slough SL5 ....205 A5
Adam Ct RG9 ....191 E2
Adams Cl MK18 ....44 C1
Adams Ct MK6 ....47 C8
Adams Way HP27 ....119 B6
Addington Cl SL4 ....210 A4
Addington Cotts HP22 ...131 B5
Addington Rd MK18 ......41 D1
Addington Terr MK18 ....41 D1
Addison Cl SL0 ....207 E6
Addison Ct SL6 ....196 B1
Addison Rd
  Chesham HP5 ....144 C2
  Steeple Claydon MK18 ..63 D2
Adelaide Cl SL1 ....205 A4
Adelaide Rd
  High Wycombe HP13 ....162 D1
  Windsor SL4 ....210 F6
Adelaide Sq SL4 ....210 D5
Adelphi Gdns SL1 ....205 E4
Adelphi St MK9 ....34 F4
Adkins Cl HP19 ....100 F3
Adkins Ct HP14 ....158 E5
Admiral Way HP4 ....134 F6
Adrians Wlk SL2 ....205 F5
Adstock Mews 2 SL2 ...177 D2
Agars Pl SL3 ....211 A8
Agora Ctr
  7 Milton Keynes MK2 ..58 C8
  Milton Keynes,Wolverton
  MK12 ....33 D7
Aidan Cl HP21 ....116 A4
Ailward Rd HP19 ....101 A2
Ainsdale Cl MK3 ....46 D1

Aintree Cl
  Milton Keynes MK3 .....57 C6
  Poyle SL3 ....212 E6
Airport Gate Bsns Ctr
  UB7 ....
Airport Way TW19 ....213 A3
Aiston Pl HP20 ....101 F2
Ajax Ave SL1 ....205 B6
Akeley Wood Jun Sch
  MK19 ....31 A1
Akeley Wood Lower Sch
  MK18 ....29 B4
Akeley Wood Sch MK18 .41 C7
Akeman St MK23 ....119 A3
Akerman Cl MK12 ....33 B5
Akister Cl MK18 ....52 E8
Alabama Circ HP11 ......173 B4
Alabama Dr HP11 ....173 B3
Alan Way SL3 ....206 E7
Alaska St HP11 ....173 B4
Albany Cl MK14 ....34 D7
Albany Gate HP5 ....144 B1
Albany Pk SL3 ....212 D7
Albany Pl HP19 ....101 A2
Albany Rd
  Old Windsor SL4 ....211 A2
  Windsor SL4 ....210 D5
Albany Terr HP23 ....119 B6
Albert Cl 9 SL1 ....205 F3
Albert Pl SL4 ....205 A1
Albert Rd Chesham HP5 .154 C8
  Henley-on-T RG9 ....191 E1
  West Drayton UB7 .....208 E5
  Windsor SL4 ....210 E3
Albert St Aylesbury HP20 .116 A8
  4 High Wycombe HP13 .173 C7
  Maidenhead SL6 ....202 F7
  Milton Keynes MK2 .....58 C8
  Slough SL1 ....205 F3
  Tring HP23 ....119 A3
  Windsor SL4 ....210 B6
Albion Cl SL2 ....206 A5
Albion Cotts SL6 ....195 C7
Albion Cres HP8 ....177 B7
Albion Ho MK10 ....43 A4
Albion Pl
  Milton Keynes MK9 ....35 A3
  2 Windsor SL4 ....210 A5
Albion Rd
  Chalfont St Giles HP8 ..177 B8
  High Wycombe HP13 ....172 C5
  Pitstone LU7 ....105 D5
Albright Cl SL2 ....204 A5
Albury Ct 3 MK8 ....33 F1
Albury View OX9 ....136 A6
Aldborough Spur SL1 ...205 E7
Aldbourne Rd SL1 ....204 B8
Aldbury CE Prim Sch
  HP23 ....120 C6
Aldbury Gdns HP23 ......119 B6
Aldbury Rd WD3 ....167 F2
Aldebury Rd SL6 ....195 F2
Alden View SL4 ....209 D6
Aldene Rd MK11 ....11 B3
Aldenham MK6 ....47 D5
Alder Cl SL1 ....204 F3
Alder Rd Iver Heath SL0 .200 D3
  New Denham UB9 ....204 A5
Alderbourne La SL3 .....199 E8
Alderbourne Manor
  SL9 ....189 A1
Alderbury Rd SL3 ....207 A4
Alderbury Rd W SL3 .....206 F4
Aldergill MK13 ....34 C5
Alderley Ct MK4 ....135 C3
Aldermead MK12 ....33 E5
Alderney Pl MK5 ....45 F4
Alders The UB9 ....201 C6
Alderson Cl HP19 ....101 A2
Alderton Dr HP4 ....121 B8
Aldin Ave N SL1 ....206 A4
Aldin Ave S SL1 ....206 A4
Aldrich Dr MK15 ....35 E7
Aldridge Ct HP11 ....173 F4
Aldridge Rd SL2 ....198 A1
Aldwick Dr SL4 ....209 C5
Aldwycks Cl MK5 ....45 F6
Alexander Ct
  High Wycombe HP12 ....172 E8
  Slough SL5 ....205 C4
Alexander Fst Sch SL4 ..209 C4
Alexander Ho 1 MK2 ....58 C8
Alexander Rd HP20 .....101 E1
Alexander St HP5 ....144 C1
Alexandra Ct
  Leighton Buzzard LU7 ...80 F8
  Milton Keynes MK14 ....34 A4
  Windsor SL4 ....210 D5
Alexandra Dr MK16 ......22 C2
Alexandra Pk HP11 ......173 A6
Alexandra Rd
  High Wycombe HP13 ....173 E5
  Maidenhead SL6 ....202 D8
  Slough SL1 ....205 D3
  Uxbridge UB8 ....201 D3
  Windsor SL4 ....210 D5
Alford Rd HP12 ....172 C3
Alfred Cl SL3 ....185 B3
Alfred Davis Ct SL7 .....183 D3
Alfriston Sch HP9 ....175 C6
Alham Rd HP21 ....115 C6
Alice Cl HP15 ....162 E1
Alice La 1 SL1 ....197 B1
All Saints CE Jun Sch
  SL6 ....202 C6
All Saints View MK5 ....46 B8
All Saints' Ave SL6 .....202 D7

All Souls Cotts SL3 .....206 E8
Alladale Pl MK12 ....33 D4
Allanson Rd SL7 ....183 F3
Allen Cl MK2 ....58 C5
Allen Dr HP14 ....161 C8
Allerds Rd SL2 ....198 A4
Allerford Cl MK4 ....46 C4
Alleyns La SL6 ....195 D8
Allhusen Gdns SL3 ......199 E8
Allington Circ MK4 ......45 E1
Allington Ct SL2 ....205 F6
Allison Ct MK15 ....35 C1
Alkins Ct SL4 ....210 D5
Allonby Way HP21 ....116 B7
Allyn Cl HP13 ....173 C8
Alma Ct Burnham SL1 ...197 C2
  Eton Wick SL4 ....204 F2
Alma Rd
  Berkhamsted HP4 ......134 E6
  Chesham HP5 ....144 C2
  Eton Wick SL4 ....204 F2
  Windsor SL4 ....210 C6
Almshouses MK14 ....21 E1
Almond Cl
  Newport Pagnell MK16 ..22 B3
  Windsor SL4 ....210 B5
Almond Rd SL1 ....197 C2
Almond Way MK27 ......139 A2
Almond Wlk HP15 ....163 B3
Almons Way SL2 ....206 B8
Almshouses Eton SL4 ...210 D7
  Old Windsor SL4 ....210 F1
  Worminghall HP18 .....123 E5
Alnwick Dr HP23 ....103 F7
Alpha Ct HP7 ....165 B7
Alpha St N 8 SL1 ......206 A4
Alpha St S SL1 ....206 A3
Alpine Cl SL6 ....203 A6
Alpine Croft MK5 ....46 A3
Alscot La SL7 ....139 A5
Alsford Wharf HP4 .....135 C5
Alston Dr MK13 ....33 F3
Alston Gdns SL6 ....202 E7
Alstonefield 1 MK4 .....46 B3
Althorpe Cres MK3 .....34 B6
Alton Bsns Pk HP19 .....101 B1
Alton Gate MK41 ....
Altona Way SL1 ....205 B7
Altwood Bailey SL6 .....202 B5
Altwood CE Sec Sch
  SL6 ....202 B5
Altwood Cl
  Maidenhead SL6 ....202 B5
  Slough SL1 ....204 E8
Altwood Dr SL1 ....204 E8
Altwood Rd
  Maidenhead SL6 ....202 B5
  Maidenhead SL6 ....202 C5
Alverton MK14 ....34 F8
Alvescot Rd SL4 ....209 D7
Alvista Ave SL6 ....204 B7
Alwin Cl HP21 ....115 C4
Alwins Field LU7 ....80 D8
Alwyn Inf Sch SL6 ......202 C8
Alwyn Rd SL6 ....202 B8
Alyngton HP4 ....134 E7
Alyson Ct 2 SL6 ....195 F1
Amanda Ct SL3 ....206 D3
Amber Cotts HP7 ....164 F3
Ambergate MK16 ....36 B4
Amberley Cl SL6 ....196 C3
Amberley Pl 11 SL4 .....210 D6
Amberley Way UB10 ....201 E3
Amberley Wlk MK4 ......45 E1
Ambers Way MK18 ......53 A1
Ambleside
  Amersham HP6 ....154 C2
  Aylesbury HP21 ....115 B6
Ambleside Wlk UB8 .....201 D4
Ambridge Gr MK6 ....35 C1
Ambrose Ct SL6 ....35 C2
Amelias La MK9 ....35 A3
Amerden Cl SL6 ....203 D7
Amerden La SL6 ....203 D7
Amerden Priory Cvn Pk
  SL6 ....203 E4
Amerden Way SL1 ....205 A4
American Com Sch
  UB10 ....201 F4
Amersham & Wycombe Coll
  Amersham HP7 ....165 F8
  Chesham HP5 ....144 D3
  Flackwell Heath HP10 ..173 E2
Amersham Ct SL7 ....165 A7
Amersham Hill HP13 ....173 B7
Amersham Hill Dr HP13 .173 B7
Amersham Hill Gdns
  HP13 ....173 C8
Amersham Mus* HP7 ....165 B7
Amersham Rd
  Beaconsfield HP7 ......176 A6
  Chalfont Common HP8,SL9 .177 D6
  Chalfont St Giles HP8 ..166 A8
  Chalfont St Peter SL9 ..177 E2
  Chesham HP5 ....154 E5
  Chorleywood WD3 ......167 C8
  Denham Green SL9 .....189 A4
  Gerrards Cross SL9 ....188 F7
  Hazlemere HP15 ....162 E2
  High Wycombe HP13 ....173 C8
  Little Chalfont HP6 .....166 E8

Amersham Sch The
  HP7 ....165 F7
Amersham Way HP6 .....166 E8
Ames Cl MK6 ....46 F8
Amherst Ct MK15 ....35 C7
Amos Ct MK13 ....34 A6
Ampleforth MK10 ....36 F1
Amy La HP5 ....154 B7
Ancastle Gn RG9 ....191 D1
Ancell Rd MK11 ....32 E5
Anchor Ct SL6 ....195 F7
Anchor La 1 HP20 ......115 E8
Ancona Gdns MK5 ......45 F3
Andermans SL4 ....209 D6
Anderson Gate MK4 .....47 C2
Anderson Rd HP14 ......158 F4
Anding Cl MK6 ....6 E4
Andover Cl UB8 ....201 B3
Andrew Hill La SL2 .....187 C3
Andrews Croft MK14 ....34 F8
Andrews Cl LU7 ....69 E3
Andrews Reach SL8 ....185 A2
Andrews Way
  Aylesbury HP19 ....115 A7
  Marlow Bottom SL7 ....183 C8
Anershall HP22 ....89 B3
Angel Cl MK2 ....35 A4
Angelica Cl UB7 ....208 F7
Angelica Ct MK7 ....48 A5
Angels Cl MK18 ....65 F4
Anglefield Rd HP4 ......135 B4
Anglesey Ct
  Milton Keynes MK8 .....46 A8
  Stokenchurch HP14 ....158 C5
Angood Cl HP27 ....139 A3
Angora Cl MK5 ....46 A3
Angstrom Cl MK5 ....46 B5
Angus Dr MK3 ....46 F2
Angus Rd HP19 ....101 A3
Anne Cl SL6 ....195 E2
Annes Gr MK14 ....21 D1
Annesley Rd MK16 ......22 B3
Anns Cl Aylesbury HP21 .116 A4
  Tring HP23 ....118 E3
Anscull Rd SL2 ....198 A2
Ansell Cl HP18 ....99 B6
Anslow Pl SL1 ....204 C8
Anson Cl Aylesbury HP21 .115 E4
  Bovingdon HP3 ....145 F4
Anson Rd MK13 ....33 C6
Anstey Brook HP22 .....117 A3
Anstey Cl HP18 ....99 B6
Anstey Ct HP18 ....99 B7
Anthony Cl HP13 ....161 F1
Anthony Cl MK11 ....32 D5
Anthony Way SL1 ....204 D6
Anton Way HP21 ....115 D3
Anvil Cl HP3 ....146 B3
Anvil Ct SL3 ....207 A2
Anxey Way HP17 ....126 F6
Aplin Rd HP21 ....116 C6
Apple Cotts HP3 ....146 A4
Apple Tree Cl LU7 ......80 D6
Appleacres MK17 ....69 D8
Appleby Heath MK2 .....58 C6
Applecroft
  Berkhamsted HP4 ......134 E6
  Maidenhead SL6 ....202 C3
  Newton Longville MK17 .57 D4
Appledore HP21 ....115 B6
Appleton Cl HP27 ......166 B7
Appleton Mews 4 MK4 ..46 B3
Appletree Ave SL6 ......208 F7
Appletree La 3 SL3 ....206 C3
Applewick La HP12 .....172 C8
Applewood Cl UB10 ....201 E6
Approach Rd SL6 ....203 E7
Approach The MK8 ......33 E2
Apsley Cotts SL6 ....195 E7
Apsley Ho MK9 ....35 A4
Aran Hts HP8 ....177 B6
Arborfield Cl SL1 ......205 F4
Arbour Vale Sch SL2 ...205 F7
Arbour View HP7 ....166 B8
Arbroath Cl MK3 ....34 D3
Arbrook Ave MK13 .....34 D3
Arcade The HP9 ....175 D3
Arch Way
  High Wycombe HP13 ....173 A7
  Speen HP27 ....150 B4
Archdale 1 MK13 ....173 A6
Archer Cl HP13 ....173 D7
Archer Ct HP6 ....154 C2
Archer Dr HP20 ....102 A2
Archer Terr UB7 ....208 E6
Archers Way HP14 .....171 B5
Archers Wells MK5 .....47 B2
Archive Cl HP22 ....117 D5
Archways 14 HP20 .....115 F8
Arden Cl HP3 ....146 A3
Arden Gr 7 MK4 ....33 B7
Ardenham La HP19 .....101 C1
Ardenham St HP19 .....101 C1
Ardleigh 2 SL2 ....198 C1
Ardley Mews MK10 .....36 B3
Ardrossan Cl SL2 ......198 C1
Ardwell La MK42 ....6 A8
Argyle Ct MK5 ....46 B8
Argonaut Pk SL3 ....212 F6
Argyle Ave HP19 ....101 B2
Argyll Ave SL1 ....205 A6
Argyll Ho MK3 ....46 F1
Aries Ho HP20 ....115 F8
Aris Way MK18 ....52 D6
Arizona St HP11 ....173 B4
Arklay Cl UB8 ....201 F1

Arkley Ct SL6 ....203 C1
Arklow Ct WD3 ....167 D5
Arkwright Rd SL3 ......212 E5
Arlington Cl SL6 ......202 A8
Arlington Ct MK4 ......46 E3
Ariott Cres MK6 ....46 F8
Armourer Dr MK14 .....34 F6
Armstrong Cl MK8 .....45 E7
Armstrong Ho SL2 .....206 C7
Arncliffe Dr MK13 .....34 B5
Arncott Rd OX25 ......95 D7
Arncott Way HP10 .....100 F1
Arncott Wood Rd OX25 .94 E6
Arne La MK7 ....48 D5
Arnison Ave HP13 .....162 D1
Arnold Cl HP22 ....116 C2
Arnold Cott MK19 .....32 C7
Arnold Ct HP21 ....115 F6
Arnold's Cotts HP5 ....143 B4
Arnolds Cl MK18 ......53 A1
Arnott's Yd HP18 .....125 D6
Arranmore Ho HP11 ...174 B4
Arrewig La HP5 ....142 E8
Arrow Pl MK2 ....58 D4
Arthur Rd Slough SL1 ..205 D4
  Windsor SL4 ....210 C6
Artichoke Dell WD3 ...167 E4
Arts Educational Sch
  HP23 ....119 B3
Arundel Cl SL3 ....202 A8
Arundel Ct SL3 ....206 D2
Arundel Gn HP20 ......101 F2
Arundel Gr MK3 ....57 E7
Arundel Ho
  High Wycombe HP13 ....173 F7
  Uxbridge UB8 ....201 C1
Arundel Rd
  High Wycombe HP12 ...172 B6
  Uxbridge UB8 ....201 B2
Ascot Dr LU7 ....80 D6
Ascot Ho MK9 ....34 C2
Ascot Pl MK3 ....57 D7
Ascot Rd Aylesbury HP20 .101 E1
Ascott Cl HP20 ....101 E1
Ascott Ho* LU7 ....80 A2
Ascott Rd HP20 ....101 E1
Ash Cl Aylesbury HP20 ..102 A2
  Slough SL3 ....207 B3
  Walter's Ash HP14 ....161 B8
Ash Gn UB9 ....201 B6
Ash Gr Amersham HP6 ..154 A2
  Aylesbury HP21 ....116 A7
  Stoke Poges SL2 ......198 F5
  West Drayton UB7 .....208 F6
Ash Hill Prim Sch HP14 .174 A7
Ash Hill Rd HP14 ......22 B4
Ash La SL4 ....209 D5
Ash Mead Dr UB9 ......190 A2
Ash Rd
  High Wycombe HP12 ...172 C4
  Princes Risborough HP27 .139 B3
  Tring HP23 ....118 F4
Ash Tree Ho HP21 .....172 C4
Ash Vale WD3 ....178 D5
Ashbourne End HP21 ..115 C4
Ashbourne Gr SL6 .....
Ashbourne Ho MK8 ....205 E4
Ashbrook Fst Sch MK8 .33 E1
Ashburnham Cres LU7 ..80 E6
Ashby MK6 ....47 A8
Ashby Rd HP4 ....134 D7
Ashby Villas LU7 ......92 A1
Ashcroft Cl SL1 ....197 B3
Ashcroft Dr UB9 ......189 F4
Ashcroft Rd SL6 ......202 C8
Ashcroft Terr HP23 ...119 A5
Ashdown SL6 ....196 B3
Ashdown Cl MK14 .....35 A8
Ashdown Ct HP13 .....173 D6
Ashdown Rd HP13 .....174 A8
Ashdown Way HP6 .....154 C2
Ashen Cross SL3 ......207 B8
Ashenden Wlk SL2 ....198 D8
Ashendon Rd HP18 ....98 C6
Asheridge Rd HP5 .....144 A2
Ashfield MK14 ....34 D8
Ashfield Cl HP15 .....163 B2
Ashfield Cotts HP13 ...190 A1
Ashfield Gr MK2 ......58 C7
Ashfield Rd HP5 ......144 B2
Ashfield Rise HP18 ...109 D5
Ashfield Way HP13 ...163 B3
Ashfold Sch HP18 ....110 F8
Ashford Cl HP21 ......116 A5
Ashford Cres MK8 ....45 D6
Ashford La SL4 ......204 B4
Ashford Rd MK8 ......45 D6
Ashgrove SL18 ....63 D2
Ashgrove Gdns HP22 ..86 E7
Ashlea MK46 ....6 E3
Ashlea Rd SL9 ....177 E1
Ashleigh Ct HP17 ....165 E8
Ashley Cl
  High Wycombe HP19 ...115 A8
  Maidenhead SL6 ....203 B7
  Tylers Green HP15 ....163 B1
  West Drayton UB7 .....208 E5
Ashley Dr HP10 ....163 C1
Ashley Green Rd HP5 ..144 E5
Ashley Pk SL6 ....196 B2
Ashley Rd UB8 ....201 B3
Ashley Row HP20 .....102 A1

Ashleys WD3 ....167 F2
Ashlyns Ct HP4 ....135 B3
Ashlyns Rd HP4 ....135 B3
Ashlyns Sch HP4 ......135 C2
Ashmead Comb Sch
  HP21 ....115 C5
Ashmead La UB9 ....190 A2
Ashotts La HP5 ....143 B6
Ashpole Furlong MK5 ...46 B7
Ashridge OX39 ....147 B6
Ashridge Cl
  1 Bovingdon HP3 ..146 A3
  Milton Keynes MK2 ....57 D7
Ashridge Coll Gdns*
  HP4 ....121 D5
Ashridge Cotts HP4 ..121 E5
Ashridge Coll Visitor Ctr*
  HP4 ....120 E6
Ashridge Man Coll HP4 121 C5
Ashridge Rise HP4 ...134 F5
Ashton Pl SL6 ....202 A6
Ashton Rd NN13 ....9 D8
Ashtree Wlk HP15 .....163 B2
Ashwell St **1** LU7 ....80 F8
Ashwells HP10 ....174 B8
Ashwells Manor Dr
  HP10 ....174 C8
Ashwells Way HP6 .....177 D8
Ashwood MK13 ....34 A7
Ashwood Dr HP5 ....144 B1
Askett La HP27 ....139 D7
Aspen Cl Aylesbury HP20 102 A2
  Slough SL2 ....205 B8
  West Drayton UB7 ....208 F5
Asplands Cl MK17 .....49 B4
Aspley Ct Aylesbury HP21 101 C1
  Woburn Sands MK17 ...49 E7
Aspley Guise Lower Sch
  MK17 ....49 E4
Aspley Guise Sta MK17 ..49 D6
Aspley Hill MK17 .....49 C4
Aspley La MK17 ....49 E2
Aspreys MK46 ....6 E4
Assheton Rd HP9 .....175 E4
Asthenhope MK8 ....33 F2
Astley Rd OX9 ....126 B1
Aston Abbotts Rd
  Cublington LU7 ....78 C1
  Weedon HP22 ....87 E1
Aston Cl Aylesbury HP19 101 A3
  Milton Keynes MK5 ...46 B5
Aston Clinton Rd HP22 116 C6
Aston Clinton Sch HP22 117 D5
Aston Ferry La RG9 ..192 D5
Aston Hill OX49 .....157 E7
Aston La RG9 ....192 C3
Aston Rd HP17 ....127 B5
Aston Rowant Nature
  Reserve* HP14 ....157 E5
Astonville SL2 ....198 C8
Astor Cl SL4 ....203 B6
Astronomy Way **12**
  HP19 ....115 A8
Astrope La HP23 .....104 B3
Astwood Rd MK43 ......25 C7
Atherstone Ct MK8 ....33 C2
Atherton Cl TW19 ....213 D1
Atherton Ct SL4 .....210 D7
Athlone Cl SL6 ......195 E1
Athlone Sq SL4 ......210 C5
Atkins Cl MK13 ....34 B3
Atlas Ho HP5 ....144 B1
Atterbrook MK13 ......34 A4
Attingham Hill MK8 ...34 A1
Atwell Cl MK4 ....45 E7
Auckland Cl SL6 .....203 B8
Auckland Pk MK1 ......47 D4
Auckland Rd HP13 ....173 E6
Auden Cl MK16 ....22 A5
Audley Dr SL6 ....202 B6
Audley Mead MK13 .....34 B3
August End SL3 ......206 E7
Augustine Cl SL3 ....212 E4
Augustine Mews HP16 .152 C5
Augustus Rd MK11 .....32 E4
Augustus Smith Ho **2**
  HP4 ....135 D4
Austen Ave MK46 ....7 A4
Austen Pl HP19 ......100 F2
Austenway SL9 ....188 E8
Austenwood Cl
  Chalfont St Peter SL9 177 C1
  High Wycombe HP11 ..173 A4
Austenwood La
  Chalfont St Peter SL9 177 D1
  Gerrards Cross SL9 ..188 D8
Austin Waye UB8 .....201 C4
Austins Mead HP3 ....146 B3
Australia Ave SL6 ...202 F8
Australia Rd SL1 ....206 B4
Austwick La MK4 ......46 B2
Autumn Cl
  Aylesbury HP19 ......101 A3
  Slough SL1 ....204 F5
Autumn Wlk SL6 ......202 A5
Auxiliaries Way UB9 .189 F6
Avalon Rd SL8 ....185 B5
Avant Bsns Ctr MK1 ...47 C2
Avebury Cl SL1 ......205 A6
Avebury Mrd MK9 ......34 E2
Avebury Rdbt MK9 .....34 D1
Aveling Rd HP13 .....173 C6
Avenue Cl UB7 ....208 D3

Avenue Dr
  Iver Heath SL3 ......199 F1
  Slough SL3 ....206 F8
Avenue Ho HP5 ....154 B8
Avenue Rd
  Buckingham MK18 .....41 E3
  Maidenhead SL6 .....203 B5
  Winslow MK18 ....65 F4
Avenue The
  Amersham HP7 ....154 C1
  Bourne End SL8 .....184 F4
  Chinnor OX39 ....147 D6
  Datchet SL3 ....211 B6
  Dunstable LU6 ....93 E7
  Farnham Common SL2 .198 B8
  Windsor SL4 ....210 A5
Avery Cl
  High Wycombe HP13 ..173 C7
  Maidenhead SL6 .....202 F7
  Windsor SL4 ....210 A5
Bailey Ho **8** SL4 .185 A4
Bailey's Ct HP27 ....115 D8
Baily Ct MK5 ....46 A5
Baines Ho HP11 ......173 F4
Baird Cl SL1 ....205 B4
Baisley Ho MK2 ....58 D8
Baker St
  High Wycombe HP11 ..172 F7
  Waddesdon HP18 ....99 A6
Baker's Orch HP10 ...185 E5
Baker's Piece Ho OX39 147 A4
Baker's Rd UB8 ......201 D5
Bakers Cl
  Stoke Goldington MK16 ..12 B5
  Turvey MK43 ....8 E5
Bakers Ct Stanwell TW19 213 D1
  Waddesdon HP18 ....99 A6
Bakers La NN12 ....9 A8
Bakers Wlk HP22 .....116 F2
Bakers Wood UB9 .....189 D3
Bakery Cl Cranfield MK43 .25 B1
  Grendon Underwood HP18 .83 A6
Bakery Ho **10** HP20 .115 D8
Bala Cl MK2 ....58 C5
Bala Way MK2 ....58 C5
Balcary Gdns HP4 ....134 F3
Balcary Gr MK4 ....56 F8
Baldways Cl HP22 .....89 C3
Baldwin Cres MK16 ....22 C3
Baldwin Pl SL6 ......202 C7
Baldwin Rd
  Beaconsfield HP9 ...176 B1
  Burnham SL1 ....197 C2
Baldwin's Shore SL4 .210 D8
Balfe Mews MK7 ....48 D4
Balfour Mews HP3 ....146 A4
Balfour Pl SL7 ......183 D4
Balfour Way HP20 ....101 E2
Balham's La RG9 .....179 F8
Ball Moor MK18 ....52 D6
Ballantine Ho **2** HP11 .116 B5
Ballard Gn SL4 ......209 E7
Ballards Row HP27 ...117 D6
Ballinger Ct HP4 ....135 B3
Ballinger Grange HP16 142 E2
Ballinger Rd HP16 ...142 C2
Ballinger Row HP16 ..142 D3
Balmer Bridge MK18 ...52 E5
Balmer Cut MK18 ......52 E5
Balmerino Cl MK10 ....36 B2
Balmoral SL6 ....195 B1
Balmoral Cl SL1 .....204 E7
Balmoral Ct
  High Wycombe HP11 ..173 B7
  Newport Pagnell MK16 ..22 B3

Badgers Way
  Buckingham MK18 .....52 E7
  Marlow Bottom SL7 ..183 D7
Badgers Wlk WD3 .....167 F5
Badgers Wood SL2 ....198 C7
Badmington Ct **8** HP7 .165 B7
Badminton Ho **1** HP7 .165 B7
Badminton Rd SL6 ....202 B6
Badminton View MK8 ...34 A1
Badrick Rd HP19 .....100 F2
Bagley Cl UB7 ....208 E4
Bagshot Ct MK2 ....58 C7
Bailey Cl
  High Wycombe HP13 ..173 C7
  Maidenhead SL6 .....202 F7
  Windsor SL4 ....210 A5
Baric Cl HP21 ....114 A6
Barlee Cres UB8 .....208 C8
Barley Cl
  Hazelmere HP15 .....163 A3
  Lewknor OX49 ....157 A8
Weston Turville HP22 .116 F2
Barley Cres HP21 ....115 D3
Barley Fields HP10 ..185 E8
Barley Hill Prim Sch
  OX9 ....126 A1
Barley Mead SL6 .....202 A5
Barley Way **3** SL2 ..183 D1
Barleycroft MK4 ......46 E4
Barlow Rd HP22 ......131 C5
Barn Cl
  Farnham Common SL2 .198 B8
  Maidenhead SL6 .....195 F2
Barn Ct HP12 ....172 C7
Barn Dr SL6 ....202 A4
Barn Farm SL7 ....183 D3
Barn La RG9 ....191 C4
Barn Rd HP27 ....138 E6
Barnabas Rd LU7 ......80 D6
Barnard Cres HP21 ...115 F5
Barnards Hill SL7 ..183 C2
Barncroft MK43 ......8 E6
Barncroft Rd HP4 ...134 F3
Barnes Ave HP15 .....144 C1
Barnes Pl MK6 ....46 E8
Barnes Wallis Ct HP12 172 E5
Barnes Way SL0 .....207 F6
Barnet Cl MK5 ....45 D5
Barnett Way HP22 ...102 B4
Barnfield Iver SL0 ..207 E7
  Slough SL1 ....204 D5
Barnfield Cl SL6 ....195 F5
Barnfield Dr MK6 .....47 C5
Barnhill Cl SL7 .....183 D4
Barnhill Gdns SL7 ..183 D4
Barnhill Rd SL7 ....183 D4
Barns Cl OX33 ....122 B1
Barns The HP23 .....118 F1
Barnsbury Ave HP20 ..116 B8
Barnsbury Gdns MK16 ..22 C2
Barnsdale Dr MK4 .....45 F2
Barnsfield Pl UB8 ..201 C5
Barnstable Ct MK4 ....46 D3
Baroma Way RG9 .....191 E2
Barons Cl MK2 ....58 C8
Barons Ct SL2 ......183 E2
Barons Mead RG9 ....191 D2
Baronsmead RG9 .....191 D2
Baronsmead Rd HP12 .172 E6
Barr's Rd SL6 ....204 B7
Barrack Hill HP18 ...112 E5
Barrack La SL4 .....210 D6
Barracks Hill HP7 ..164 F2
Barracks Rd HP11 ...173 A6
Barrards Way HP9 ...176 C4
Barrett Pl
  High Wycombe HP11 ..173 C6
  Milton Keynes MK5 ...45 F6
Barrie Ct HP19 ......100 F2
Barrington Dr NN13 ...38 A5
Barrington Mews **4** MK8 .34 C1
Barrington Park Gdns
  HP8 ....166 D1
Barrow Lodge SL2 ...198 C1
Barrowcroft HP11 ...173 F4
Barry Ave Eton SL4 .210 C7
  Milton Keynes MK4 ...34 C7
Barry Cl HP12 ....172 C4
Barry View SL4 ......203 B7
Bartelotts Rd SL2 ..183 D1
Bartholomew Cl MK7 ..48 A5
Bartholomew Tipping Way
  HP14 ....158 F5
Bartlett Pl MK18 .....41 E1
Bartletts Cl SL3 ....177 E3
Barton Rd
  Milton Keynes MK2 ...58 C6
  Slough SL3 ....206 F4
Barton Way HP13 .....162 E1
Bartons Rd HP10 ....163 A1
Bascote MK6 ....47 D5
Base Cl **8** HP20 ...101 F2
Basil Ave MK6 ....47 D5
Basildon Ho **2** HP13 ..209 D4
Basildon Ct
  1 Leighton Buzzard LU7 ..80 F7
  Milton Keynes MK8 ...45 F8
Basing Rd WD3 ......167 F1
Baskerfield Gr MK6 ..47 C8
Bass Mead SL6 ......195 F5
Basset Rd HP14 .....171 C4
Bassetsbury La HP11 173 D5
Bassett Ct
  Leighton Buzzard LU7 ..80 F7
  Uxbridge UB8 ....201 C5
Bassett Sq SL2 .....197 E1
Batchelor Cl HP20 ..101 F2
Batchelors Way
  Amersham HP7 ......165 D8
  Chesham HP5 ....144 A2
Bateman Croft MK5 ...45 F6
Bateman Rd HP21 ....115 E5
Bates Cl
  Granborough MK18 ....75 D3
  Milton Keynes MK15 ..35 D7

Barham Lodge MK18 ...52 C8
Baring Cres HP9 ....175 C3
Baring Rd
  Beaconsfield HP9 ...175 D3
  High Wycombe HP13 ..173 F7
Barkers Croft MK12 ...33 C4
Barkestone Cl MK4 ...46 C1
Barkham Cl LU7 .....104 F7
Barkus Way HP14 ....158 F5
Barlee Cres UB8 ....208 C8

(continued)

Bates Cl continued
  Slough SL3 ....206 E7
Bates Ct HP20 ....101 F2
Bates Gdns MK17 ......68 B6
Bates La HP22 ....116 F2
Bath Ct SL6 ....202 C6
Bath La MK18 ....52 C8
Bath Lane Terr MK18 ..52 C8
Bath Rd
  Harmondsworth UB7 ..213 C6
  Harmondsworth UB7 ..213 E6
  Maidenhead SL6 .....202 C6
  Poyle SL3 ....212 E6
  Slough SL1,SL6 .....204 D6
  Taplow SL6 ....203 F7
Bath Road Cotts SL3 212 E6
Bathurst Cl SL0 ....207 F4
Bathurst Wlk SL0 ...207 F4
Batt Furlong HP21 ...115 E3
Battersby Mews HP21 .115 C7
Batting Cl HP14 .....159 F8
Battings Wood Gdns
  HP14 ....161 C8
Battle Cl MK46 ....13 F8
Battlemead Cl SL6 ..196 C3
Battoney Vare SL6 ..203 C4
Baulk The
  Cheddington LU7 ....104 F7
  Ivinghoe LU7 ....105 F5
Bawtree Rd UB8 .....201 D6
Baxter Cl
  Loudwater HP11 .....174 B2
  Newton Longville MK17 .57 D4
Bay Cl HP4 ....5 D2
Bay La MK46 ....5 D2
Bay Tree Cl
  Loudwater HP11 .....174 B2
  Milton Keynes MK8 ...45 E7
Baybrook SL6 ....195 F6
Bayburst Wood Countryside
  Pk* UB9 ....190 F6
Bayley Cres SL1 ....204 A8
Bayley Gdns HP14 ...161 E6
Bayley Hatch HP14 ..152 D8
Baylis Bsns Ctr SL1 205 D6
Baylis Court Sch SL1 205 D8
Baylis Par SL1 .....205 E7
Baylis Rd SL1 ......205 E7
Bayman Manor HP5 ...144 E2
Bayne Hill HP9 .....176 D3
Bayne Hill Cl HP9 ..176 D3
Baynham Mead MK7 ...48 B8
Baysfarm Ct UB7 ....213 C6
Beacham Rd HP4 ....135 C5
Beachampton Bsns Pk
  MK19 ....44 C4
Beachborough Sch NN13 .39 A4
Beacon Ave LU6 ......93 E7
Beacon Cl
  Beaconsfield HP9 ...175 A1
  Chalfont St Peter SL9 .177 E3
  Stone HP17 ....114 C5
  Uxbridge UB8 ....201 D7
Beacon Ct Colnbrook SL3 212 C7
  Milton Keynes MK6 ...46 D2
Beacon Hill HP10 ...174 D7
Beacon La SL7 ......171 E1
Beacon Rd HP4 .....106 E2
Beacon Sch The HP6 .154 B4
Beacon View OX49 ...157 B8
Beacon Way HP23 ...119 C5
Beaconsfield Ave HP13 162 A1
Beaconsfield Common La
  SL7 ....187 D5
Beaconsfield Cotts SL8 .185 B2
Beaconsfield High Sch
  HP9 ....175 D1
Beaconsfield Mews
  HP9 ....186 A8
Beaconsfield Pl MK16 .22 C4
Beaconsfield Rd
  Aston Clinton HP22 .117 F4
  Aylesbury HP21 .....115 C8
  Farnham Common SL2 .198 C5
  Tring HP23 ....118 F3
Beaconsfield Sch The
  HP9 ....175 E1
Beaconsfield Sta HP9 175 E3
Beadlemead MK6 ......47 C6
Beales La MK7 ....48 A5
Bealings End HP9 ...175 D5
Beamish Way MK18 ....66 B5
Beamond End La HP7,
  HP15 ....163 F7
Beanfare MK6 ....47 B4
Bearbrook Cl HP21 ..115 C7
Bearbrook Comb Sch
  HP19 ....115 C8
Bearswood End HP9 .175 E4
Beatrice Ct OX27 ....72 E6
Beauchamp Cl MK14 ..34 E6
Beauchamp Ct SL1 ..205 D6
Beaudesert Mews UB7 208 E4
Beaufort Cl
  Aylesbury HP21 .....116 D7
  Marlow SL7 ....183 E2
Beaufort Dr MK15 ....35 C7
Beaufort Gdns SL3 ..183 E2
Beaufort Pl SL6 ....203 D4
Beaulieu Cl SL3 ....211 B5
Beaumaris Ct SL1 ..205 C8
Beaumaris Gr MK5 ...46 A6
Beaumont Cl SL6 ...202 A3
Beaumont Cotts **1** SL1 .210 C6
Beaumont Ct HP7 ...165 A7
Beaumont Rd
  Slough SL2 ....205 D8

B

Babington Cl MK10 ....36 A3
Babington Rd HP22 ..131 D6
Baccara Gr MK2 ......58 C7
Bachelors Acre SL4 .210 D6
Back Dr MK16 ....12 F3
Back La
  Chalfont St Giles HP8 177 A7
  Great Missenden HP16 152 B7
  Tingewick MK18 ......51 A5
Back St Gawcott MK18 .51 F4
  Thornborough MK18 ...54 A8
  Wendover HP22 ......131 B4
Backleys MK7 ....48 A2
Backs The HP5 ......154 C8
Bacombe La HP22 ....131 B3
Bacon Hill MK46 ......6 E3
Baconsmead UB9 ....190 A2
Bad Godesberg Way
  SL6 ....202 F7
Badgebury Rise SL7 .183 C7
Badgemore Com Sch
  RG9 ....191 D2
Badgemore Ct MK8 ...33 C2
Badger La RG9 ......191 E4
Badger Way HP15 ....163 B5
Badgers Gate LU6 ....93 E8
Badgers Mdw HP22 ..131 C5
Badgers Oak MK7 .....48 B7
Badgers Rise HP17 ..114 C5

Beaumont Rd *continued*
Windsor SL4 210 C5
Beaumont Rise SL7 183 E2
Beaumont Way HP15 162 F4
Beaver Cl MK18 52 E7
Beaverbrook Ct MK3 47 A1
Bec La MK15 35 B7
Beckets Sq HP4 135 A6
Beckett Chase 5 SL3 206 F1
Beckings Way HP10 185 C7
Beckinsale Gr MK8 45 E7
Beckwell Rd SL1 205 C4
Bedder Rd HP12 172 C3
Beddoes Croft MK5 45 E4
Bede Ct HP4 121 C8
Bedfont Court Est TW19 213 B4
Bedfont Rd TW19 213 F1
Bedford Ave
Little Chalfont HP6 166 D8
Slough SL1 205 A7
Bedford Cl Chenies WD3 156 B1
Maidenhead SL6 202 A3
Bedford Ct HP6 166 D8
Bedford Dr SL2 198 B6
Bedford Rd
Aspley Guise MK17 49 F5
Cold Brayfield MK46 8 B5
Cranfield MK43 25 C2
Sherington MK16 14 A1
Bedford Rd E NN7 1 D5
Bedford Rd W NN7 1 A6
Bedford St
Berkhamsted HP4 135 D4
Milton Keynes,Bletchley MK2 58 C8
Milton Keynes,Wolverton MK12 33 D6
Woburn MK17 60 F7
Bedgebury Pl MK7 48 A8
Bedgrove HP21 116 C6
Bedgrove Inf Sch HP21 116 C5
Bedgrove Jun Sch HP21 116 C6
Bedlam La MK16 14 C1
Bedlam Wlk MK16 14 C1
Bedwins La SL6 195 B6
Bedwyn Wlk HP21 115 D4
Beech 2 RG9 191 D2
Beech Ave
Lane End HP14 171 C5
Olney MK46 6 E3
Beech Cl Bierton HP22 102 B3
Buckingham MK18 41 D2
Flackwell Heath HP10 174 A2
High Wycombe HP11 173 F4
Maidenhead SL6 202 B8
Stokenchurch HP14 158 F3
Beech Ct
Berkhamsted HP4 135 D4
3 Marlow SL7 183 E2
Beech Dr HP4 135 C3
Beech Fern MK7 48 A5
Beech Gn HP21 115 D6
Beech Gr Amersham HP7 165 D8
Leighton Buzzard LU7 80 E7
Tring HP23 119 C4
Beech Hill Ct HP4 135 D5
Beech House Dr NN12 18 F4
Beech La
Prestwood HP16 151 B7
Seer Green HP9 176 E3
Beech Leys MK18 63 E3
Beech Pk
Little Chalfont HP6 155 B1
Naphill HP14 150 A1
Wigginton HP23 133 F5
Beech Rd
Aylesbury HP21 115 D6
Chinnor OX39 147 C6
High Wycombe HP11 173 F4
Newport Pagnell MK16 22 B3
Princes Risborough HP27 139 C3
Slough SL3 206 E4
Beech St HP11 173 C4
Beech Tree Cl MK19 20 D2
Beech Tree Ct HP22 87 A6
Beech Tree Rd HP15 163 C7
Beech Waye SL9 189 A4
Beech Wlk HP23 119 B4
Beechams The MK17 67 D6
Beechcroft HP4 135 C3
Beechcroft Rd
Chesham HP5 144 B1
Milton Keynes MK3 57 E6
Beeches Dr SL2 198 B7
Beeches Gr HP10 163 A2
Beeches Pk HP9 175 D2
Beeches Rd SL2 198 B7
Beeches The
Amersham HP6 154 A3
Chorleywood WD3 167 F4
Deanshanger MK19 31 E3
Milton Keynes MK1 47 E1
Tring HP23 119 C4
Uxbridge UB8 201 C1
Wendover HP22 131 C5
Beeches Way SL1 197 C2
Beechfield Pl SL6 202 C4
Beechfield Way HP15 163 B3
Beechfield Wlk HP15 163 A3
Beechingstoke 4 SL7 183 F3
Beechlands HP15 162 E2
Beechtree Ave SL7 183 D5
Beechview Sch HP13 173 E5
Beechwood Ave
Chorleywood WD3 167 B5
Little Chalfont HP6 155 C1
Beechwood Ave *continued*
Uxbridge UB8 208 F7
Beechwood Cl HP6 166 C8
Beechwood Cotts WD3 167 B3
Beechwood Ct
Aston Clinton HP22 118 A3
Dunstable LU6 93 F7
Beechwood Dr
Aldbury HP23 120 D5
Maidenhead SL6 202 A6
Marlow SL7 194 B8
Beechwood Gdns SL1 205 E4
Beechwood Ho HP22 117 F5
Beechwood La HP22 131 D5
Beechwood Pk
Chorleywood WD3 167 F5
Felden HP3 146 F7
Beechwood Pl 13 HP13 173 B7
Beechwood Rd
Beaconsfield HP9 175 C2
High Wycombe HP12 161 B2
Slough SL2 205 D8
Beechwood Sch SL2 198 B2
Beechwood Way HP22 117 F5
Beecroft Lower Sch LU6 93 F8
Beecroft Way LU6 93 F8
Beehive Cl UB10 201 F5
Beel Cl HP7 166 C8
Beethoven Cl MK7 48 E4
Beeward Cl MK12 33 A5
Beggars La HP23 119 F4
Bekonscot Ct MK14 21 F1
Bekonscot Model Village* HP9 175 E4
Belfast Ave SL1 205 D7
Belgrave Mews UB8 201 D1
Belgrave Par SL1 205 E6
Belgrave Pl 6 SL1 206 A4
Belgrave Rd
Aylesbury HP19 101 A3
Slough SL1 205 F6
Bell Ave UB7 208 F3
Bell Bsns Ctr SL6 202 F6
Bell Bsns Pk HP19 100 F1
Bell Cl Beaconsfield HP9 175 F2
Cublington LU7 78 B1
Drayton Parslow MK17 68 B6
Princes Risborough HP27 139 B3
Slough SL2 206 B8
Thame OX9 125 E1
Bell Cres HP27 138 E6
Bell Ct SL6 193 F3
Bell Gn HP3 146 B4
Bell La Berkhamsted HP4 134 E5
Eton Wick SL4 204 F2
Henley-on-T RG9 191 E3
Little Chalfont HP6 155 C1
Princes Risborough HP27 139 B3
Syresham NN13 27 B8
Thame OX9 125 F1
Bell Lane Comb Sch HP6 155 B1
Bell Leys HP22 89 B3
Bell St Henley-on-T RG9 191 E2
Maidenhead SL6 202 F6
Princes Risborough HP27 139 B3
Bell Street Mews RG9 191 E2
Bell View SL4 209 F5
Bell View Cl SL4 209 F5
Bell Wlk Wingrave HP22 89 B3
Winslow MK18 65 F3
Bellamy Rd HP13 173 C8
Bellclose Rd UB7 208 E4
Belle Vue HP17 114 C5
Bellfield Rd HP13 173 A8
Bellfield Rd W HP11 172 F7
Bellfounder Ho MK13 34 B4
Bellingdon Rd HP5 144 B1
Bellini Cl MK7 48 D5
Bellis Gr MK6 47 C8
Bellridge Pl HP9 175 B6
Bells Hill SL2 199 A4
Bells Hill Gn SL2 199 A5
Bells La SL3 212 B4
Bells Mdw MK15 35 B7
Bellsfield Ct SL4 204 F2
Bellswood La SL0 207 B8
Bellway MK17 49 A6
Bellwether MK11 33 A4
Bellwood Rise HP11 173 B4
Belmers Rd HP23 119 D1
Belmont SL2 205 A8
Belmont Cl UB8 201 D6
Belmont Cotts SL3 212 C7
Belmont Cres SL6 202 D8
Belmont Ct MK8 33 C2
Belmont Dr SL6 202 D8
Belmont Park Ave SL6 202 D8
Belmont Park Rd SL6 202 D8
Belmont Rd
Chesham HP5 144 B3
Maidenhead SL6 202 D8
Uxbridge UB8 201 D5
Belmont Vale SL6 202 D8
Belsize Ave MK6 35 B1
Belsize Cotts WD3 156 E6
Belton Rd HP4 135 A5
Belvedere Cl HP6 154 F2
Belvedere La MK17 58 F8
Belvedere Mans SL1 205 D4
Belvedere Rdbt MK9 34 F4
Belvoir Ave MK4 46 C1
Bembridge Ct 11 SL1 205 F4
Ben More SL9 188 F6
Benacre Croft MK4 57 A8
Benbow Ct MK5 46 A7
Benbow Way UB8 208 C8
Bench Manor Cres SL9 177 C1
Bencombe Rd SL7 183 E5
Benen-Stock Rd TW19 213 A2
Benham Cl HP5 144 B1
Benhams La RG9 180 D2
Benison Ct 11 SL1 205 F3
Benjamin Ho 10 HP13 173 B7
Benjamin Rd HP13 173 B8
Benjamins Footpath HP13 173 B8
Bennet Cl MK11 32 D4
Bennet's Yd UB8 201 D5
Bennett End Rd HP14 159 C7
Bennett's Hill MK18 76 C8
Bennetts HP5 144 D1
Bennetts Cl Padbury MK18 53 B1
Slough SL1 205 A5
Bennetts La HP22 102 E8
Benning Ave LU6 93 F8
Benning Cl SL4 209 D4
Benningfield Gdns HP4 135 E6
Bens Cl MK19 19 F5
Benson Cl Slough SL2 206 A5
Uxbridge UB8 208 E8
Bentall Cl MK15 35 C7
Bentinck Cl SL9 188 D6
Bentinck Ct UB7 208 D5
Bentinck Rd UB7 208 D5
Bentley Ct SL6 202 D5
Bentley Pk SL1 197 D3
Bentley Rd SL1 205 A5
Benton Dr OX39 147 C7
Bentons The HP4 134 F6
Benwell Cl MK13 33 F5
Benwells OX39 147 C6
Berberis Cl MK7 48 A5
Berberis Wlk UB7 208 E2
Bercham MK8 33 E2
Beresford Ave
Aylesbury HP19 101 C3
Slough SL2 206 C6
Beresford Cl MK4 46 B3
Beresford Rd WD3 167 F1
Beretun MK8 33 E1
Bereville Ct MK10 35 E3
Berevilles La MK10 35 E3
Bergamot Gdns MK7 48 B5
Berkeley Ave HP5 143 F1
Berkeley Cl
Chesham HP5 144 A1
Stoke Goldington MK16 12 B6
Berkeley Mews
Marlow SL7 183 F2
Slough SL1 204 E7
Berkeley Rd
Loudwater HP10 174 C2
Thame OX9 126 A1
Berkeley Rise HP19 101 B2
Berkhampstead Rd HP5 144 C2
Berkhamsted Castle* HP4 135 D5
Berkhamsted Collegiate Sch
Berkhamsted HP4 135 B4
Berkhamsted HP4 135 C4
Berkhamsted Sta HP4 135 C5
Berkley Cl
Maidenhead SL6 202 A8
Pitstone LU7 105 D3
Berkley Ct HP4 135 C4
Berkley Rd HP9 175 D6
Berks Hill WD3 167 C4
Berkshire Ave SL1 205 B7
Berkshire Gn MK5 45 F3
Berkshire Lodge 1 SL6 202 F6
Berling Rd MK8 33 F2
Bernard Cl HP18 112 F2
Bernard's Cl HP18 112 B2
Bernardines Way MK18 52 E7
Bernards Cl HP16 152 A7
Bernards Way HP10 174 A2
Bernay Gdns MK15 35 B7
Berndene Rise HP27 139 B4
Berners Cl SL1 204 E6
Bernewode Cl HP18 125 C7
Bernstein Cl MK7 48 C4
Bernwood Forest Nature Reserve HP18 108 E3
Berrell's Ct MK46 6 F3
Berries Rd SL6 196 A8
Berry Field SL2 206 C7
Berry Field Pk HP6 154 B2
Berry Hill SL6 203 D8
Berry Hill Ct SL6 203 D8
Berry La
Aspley Guise MK17 49 F6
Chorleywood WD3 167 D3
Berry Way MK17 57 D4
Berryfield LU7 104 F7
Berryfield Rd
Aylesbury HP19 101 B3
Princes Risborough HP27 139 C4
Berrystead MK7 48 B3
Bertram Cl MK13 34 B8
Berwald Cl MK7 48 D4
Berwick Ave SL1 205 B6
Berwick Cl
Beaconsfield HP9 176 B1
Marlow SL7 183 D3
Berwick Dr MK3 46 F2
Berwick La SL7 183 D3
Berwick Rd SL7 183 C3
Bessemer Cl 2 SL3 206 E1
Bessemer Cres HP19 100 E1
Bessemer Ct MK14 22 A1
Bestobell Rd SL1 205 C7
Betjeman Ct UB7 208 D5
Bettina Gr MK2 58 C7
Bettles Cl UB8 201 C3
Bettles Ct UB8 201 C3
Betty's Cl MK17 57 D3
Betty's La HP23 119 A4
Bevan Ct MK18 65 F4
Bevan Hill HP5 144 B2
Bevelwood Gdns HP12 172 D7
Beverley Cl SL7 183 B2
Beverley Ct SL1 206 B4
Beverley Gdns SL6 195 B1
Beverley Pl MK6 35 B2
Bewcastle Row MK4 45 E1
Bewdley Dr LU7 80 C7
Bexley St SL4 210 C6
Bicester Rd
Aylesbury HP19 101 B2
Long Crendon HP18 125 C6
Ludgershall HP18 96 C8
Marsh Gibbon OX27 71 E3
Oakley HP18 109 D5
Twyford MK18 62 C1
Bickleigh Cres MK4 46 D3
Biddles Cl SL1 204 E5
Biddlesden Rd NN13 39 A5
Bideford Ct LU7 80 C8
Bideford Gn LU7 80 C8
Bideford Spur SL2 198 B2
Bierton CE Comb Sch HP22 102 B3
Bierton Rd HP20 101 F1
Bigfrith La SL6 195 B6
Biggs La HP17 113 E2
Bigmore La
Beacon's Bottom HP14 170 B8
Stokenchurch HP14 159 C1
Bignell Croft MK5 34 B1
Biko Cl UB8 208 C7
Bilbrook La MK4 46 C4
Billet La
Berkhamsted HP4 135 A6
Iver SL0,SL3 207 B7
Billings Cl HP14 158 F5
Billingwell Pl MK6 35 B2
Billwell HP18 125 C6
Bilton Rd MK1 47 D2
Binders Ind Est HP15 162 D7
Bingham Cl MK4 46 C1
Bingham Rd SL1 204 A8
Binghams The SL6 203 B3
Birch Ave UB7 208 F7
Birch Cl Amersham HP6 154 E2
Iver Heath SL0 200 D3
Birch Cres UB10 201 F4
Birch Ct HP21 115 D5
Birch Dr WD3 178 D5
Birch Gdns HP7 165 E8
Birch Gr Slough SL2 205 B8
Windsor SL4 209 D6
Birch La HP3 156 B7
Birch Rd HP4 134 D7
Birch St HP11 173 B3
Birch Tree Gr HP5 145 B1
Birch Way Chesham HP5 144 D2
Tylers Green HP10 163 B1
Birchdale SL9 188 D3
Birchen Lee MK4 46 C2
Birches Rise HP12 172 E8
Birches The Felden HP3 146 F8
High Wycombe HP13 173 E8
Birchfield Gr MK2 58 C7
Birchington Rd SL4 210 A5
Birchmoor Gn MK17 60 F8
Birchwood Chase HP15 151 D1
Birchwood Cl HP12 172 B6
Bird Mount Cotts SL4 210 C8
Birdcage Wlk HP13 173 B6
Birdlip La MK7 48 B7
Birds La MK16 12 B6
Birdwood Rd SL6 202 B7
Birfield Rd HP10 174 C2
Birinus Ct HP12 172 C5
Birkdale Cl MK3 57 D7
Birkett Way HP8 166 D6
Birley Rd SL1 205 D7
Bisham Abbey National Sports Ctr SL7 194 D7
Bisham CE Prim Sch SL7 194 D7
Bisham Ct Bisham SL7 194 E6
10 Slough SL1 205 F4
Bisham Gn SL7 194 E6
Bisham Rd Bisham SL7 194 E8
Marlow SL7 183 E1
Bishop Ct SL6 202 D6
Bishop Ctr The SL6 203 F7
Bishop Parker RC Comb Sch MK2 58 C6
Bishop Wood CE Jun Sch HP23 119 A3
Bishops Ct MK18 52 C7
Bishops Farm Cl SL4 209 B6
Bishops Field HP22 118 A4
Bishops Ho HP9 175 D3
Bishops Mdw HP22 102 A3
Bishops Orch SL2 198 B2
Bishops Rd SL1 206 A4
Bishops Wlk
Aylesbury HP21 115 F6
Woburn Sands MK17 49 B3
Wooburn Green HP10 185 E5
Bishopshalt Sch UB8 201 F2
Bishopstone
Milton Keynes MK13 34 B5
Stone HP17 115 A1
Bishopstone Rd HP17 114 D5
Bissley Dr SL6 202 A3
Bit The HP23 119 D1
Bittenham Cl HP17 114 D4
Bittern Way 4 HP20 101 E3
Bix Hill RG9 191 A6
Bix La SL6 194 F1
Black Acre Cl HP7 165 E8
Black Boy La SL6 193 C3
Black Butt Cotts SL6 196 B7
Black Horse Ave HP5 154 D6
Black Horse Cl SL4 209 D5
Black Horse Pl UB8 201 C4
Black Park Ctry Pk* SL0,SL3 200 A4
Black Park Ctry Pk Visitor Ctr* SL3 199 F2
Black Park Rd SL3 199 E4
Blackamoor La SL6 203 A8
Blackberry Ct MK7 48 B6
Blackburn Trad Est TW19 213 F1
Blackdown MK11 32 F4
Blacketts Wood Dr WD3 167 B5
Blackfield La HP16 142 E3
Blackham Ct MK6 46 E7
Blackheath Cres MK13 34 D3
Blackhill Dr MK12 33 A6
Blackhorse Cl HP6 154 E1
Blackhorse Cres HP6 154 E1
Blackmoor Gate MK4 46 E2
Blackmore Gate HP22 118 A4
Blackmore Way UB8 201 D6
Blackpond La SL2 198 B4
Blacksmith La HP16 151 C6
Blacksmith Row SL3 207 A2
Blacksmith's La UB9 189 D2
Blacksmiths Rd HP27 138 D7
Blackthorn Cl OX25 81 A3
Blackthorn Dell 2 SL3 206 C3
Blackthorn Gr MK17 49 A4
Blackthorne Cres SL3 212 E5
Blackthorne Ind Pk SL3 212 E5
Blackthorne La HP16 142 E3
Blackthorne Rd SL3 212 E4
Blackwater Dr HP21 115 C4
Blackwell End NN12 18 C3
Blackwell Hall La HP5 155 C6
Blackwell Pl MK5 46 A4
Blackwell Rd HP14 171 B5
Blackwells Yd NN7 1 B6
Blackwood Cres MK13 33 E6
Blaine Cl HP23 119 A6
Blair Rd SL1 205 E5
Blairmont St MK9 34 F4
Blake Way OX9 126 A1
Blakedown Rd LU7 80 C6
Blakeney Ct
Maidenhead SL6 195 F1
Milton Keynes MK4 57 B8
Blakes Ho HP10 174 C2
Blanchland Circ MK10 36 A1
Blandford Cl SL3 206 D3
Blandford Ho SL6 202 C8
Blandford Rd N SL3 206 D3
Blandford Rd S SL3 206 D3
Blansby Chase MK4 46 C3
Blatherwick Ct MK5 45 F7
Blaydon Cl MK3 57 D6
Bleak Hall Rdbt MK6 47 A5
Bleasdale MK13 34 C5
Bledlow Bridge Halt* HP27 138 C2
Bledlow Cotts HP27 138 C1
Bledlow Rd HP27 148 E8
Bledlow Ridge Rd HP14 148 C8
Bledlow Ridge Sch HP14 159 F8
Blegberry Gdns HP4 134 E4
Blenheim Ave MK11 32 E4
Blenheim Cl
Cheddington LU7 104 F8
Longwick HP27 138 D6
Slough SL3 206 F5
Blenheim Ct HP13 173 B7
Blenheim Pl
Aylesbury HP21 115 E5
Syresham NN13 27 C7
Blenheim Rd
High Wycombe HP12 172 D4
Maidenhead SL6 202 B8
Slough SL3 206 D2
Bletcham Rdbt MK1 47 E3
Bletcham Way
Milton Keynes MK1 47 C2
Milton Keynes MK1 47 E2
Walton Park MK7 48 B4
Bletchley Com Hospl MK3 47 A1
Bletchley Park Mus* MK3 58 A8
Bletchley Rd
Milton Keynes MK5 46 B4
Newton Longville MK17 57 D4
Stewkley LU7 68 D3
Bletchley Sta MK3 58 B8
Blinco La SL3 206 E7
Blind La
Bourne End HP10,SL8 185 B5
South Heath HP16 153 B8
Blind Pond Ind Est MK17 48 D2
Bliss Ave MK43 25 C2
Bliss Ct MK7 48 C4
Blisworth MK6 47 D5
Blondell Cl UB7 213 D8
Bloomfield Cotts HP5 143 E7
Bloomfield Rd SL6 202 A5
Bloomsbury Cl MK17 60 F6
Blossom Way UB10 201 F5
Blucher St HP5 154 B8

Blue Max Mus* SL7 ....172 A2
Bluebell Cl MK18 ....52 C7
Bluebell Croft MK7 ....48 B6
Blumfield Cres SL4 ....204 E8
Blumfield Ct SL1 ....197 D1
Blundells Rd MK13 ....34 C6
Blunden Dr SL3 ....207 C2
Blyth Ct MK4 ....57 A8
Blythe Cl Aylesbury HP21 ....115 C5
  Iver SL0 ....207 F7
  Newport Pagnell MK16 ....22 D3
Blythe Hos SL1 ....204 D5
Blyton Cl HP9 ....175 D4
Boadicea Cl SL1 ....204 E5
Boarlands Cl SL1 ....204 F6
Boarstall Duck Decoy*
  HP18 ....95 A3
Boathouse Reach RG9 ....191 E1
Bobmore La SL7 ....183 F3
Bockmer La SL7 ....193 B7
Boddington Rd HP22 ....131 C4
Bodenham Ct MK18 ....52 F8
Bodiam Cl
  Aylesbury HP21 ....116 B5
  Milton Keynes MK5 ....46 A5
Bodiam Ho 6 HP13 ....173 F7
Bodle Cl MK15 ....35 A7
Bodley Ho SL0 ....200 D3
Bodmin Ave SL2 ....205 A8
Bodnant Ct MK4 ....45 F2
Bois Ave HP6 ....154 B3
Bois Hill HP5 ....154 E5
Bois La HP6 ....154 D4
Bois Moor Rd HP5 ....154 D5
Bolan Ct MK8 ....45 E6
Bold's Ct SL2 ....199 A5
Bolter End La HP14 ....171 A6
Bolton Ave SL4 ....210 D4
Bolton Cl MK3 ....47 A2
Bolton Cres SL4 ....210 C4
Bolton Rd SL4 ....210 C4
Boltwood Gr MK5 ....45 E5
Bond Ave MK1 ....47 D3
Bond Cl Aylesbury HP21 ....115 B6
  Iver Heath SL0 ....200 B5
  West Drayton UB7 ....208 F7
Bone Hill MK18 ....52 C7
Bonham Carter Rd
  HP22 ....131 E7
Bonham Cl HP21 ....115 B6
Bonham Ct HP22 ....117 D5
Bonnards Rd MK17 ....57 D4
Bonnersfield HP18 ....125 C7
Booker Ave MK13 ....34 D4
Booker Hill Sch HP12 ....172 B5
Booker La HP12 ....172 D7
Booker Pl HP12 ....172 B3
Bookerhill Rd HP12 ....172 C6
Boot La HP17 ....113 C2
Booth Pl LU6 ....92 E6
Borderside SL2 ....206 A7
Borodin Ct MK7 ....48 D5
Boroma Way RG9 ....191 E2
Borough Cl MK16 ....22 B3
Borough Rd NN13 ....38 A5
Borough Wlk MK9 ....34 E3
Bosanquet Cl UB8 ....201 D1
Boss La
  Great Kingshill HP15 ....162 B8
  Hughenden Valley HP14 ....162 B6
Bossiney Pl MK6 ....34 F1
Bossington La LU7 ....80 E7
Bostock Ct MK18 ....52 C8
Boston Dr SL8 ....185 B3
Boswell Cl MK14 ....46 C8
Boswell Ct MK18 ....31 E4
Boswick La HP4 ....134 D8
Bosworth Cl MK3 ....46 E2
Bosworth Ct SL1 ....204 C6
Botham Dr SL1 ....205 E3
Botley La HP5 ....145 A1
Botley Rd HP5 ....144 E1
Bottlefield Ct MK3 ....56 E6
Bottle Dump Rdbt MK12 ....56 E6
Bottle Square La MK14 ....159 D6
Bottom Dr LU6 ....93 D5
Bottom House Farm La
  HP8 ....165 E2
Bottom House La HP23 ....120 A1
Bottom La HP9 ....176 C5
Bottom Orch HP18 ....112 C1
Bottom Rd
  Bledlow Ridge HP14 ....160 B5
  Buckland Common HP23 ....132 C1
Bottom Waltons Caravan Site
  SL2 ....197 F3
Bottrells La HP8 ....176 E8
Botyl Rd MK18 ....52 E6
Boughton Bsns Pk HP6 ....166 B8
Boughton Way HP5 ....155 C1
Boulevard The MK9 ....34 E2
Boulmer Rd UB8 ....201 C2
Boulters Cl
  Maidenhead SL6 ....196 C1
  Slough SL1 ....205 A4
Boulters Ct
  Amersham HP6 ....154 E1
  Maidenhead SL6 ....196 C1
Boulters Gdns SL6 ....196 C1
Boulters La SL6 ....196 C1
Boulters Lock MK14 ....21 F2
Boundary Cres MK11 ....32 E6
Boundary Pl HP10 ....185 D8

Boundary Rd
  Brackley NN13 ....38 A6
  Chalfont St Peter SL9 ....177 D3
  Loudwater HP10 ....174 C1
  Taplow SL6 ....203 F8
  Wooburn Green HP10 ....185 D8
Boundary The MK6 ....46 F8
Bounds Croft MK12 ....33 C4
Bounty St MK13 ....33 F7
Bouquet Cl HP16 ....151 C5
Bourbon St HP20 ....115 D8
Bourne Ave SL4 ....210 C3
Bourne Cl SL8 ....185 B5
Bourne End MK43 ....25 C6
Bourne End Bsns Ctr
  SL8 ....185 B3
Bourne End Mills Ind Est
  HP1 ....146 B8
Bourne End Rd
  Cranfield MK43 ....25 C4
Bourne End Sta SL8 ....185 A3
Bourne Rd
  Berkhamsted HP4 ....134 F5
  Slough SL1 ....205 D4
Bourne The HP3 ....146 A4
Bourton Low MK7 ....48 B5
Bourton Meadow Sch
  MK18 ....52 F8
Bourton Rd MK18 ....52 E8
Bourtonville MK18 ....52 D8
Bouverie Way SL3 ....206 E2
Boveney Cl SL1 ....205 A4
Boveney New Rd SL4 ....204 E2
Boveney Rd SL4 ....204 C1
Boveney Wood La SL1 ....186 D1
Bovingdon Ct HP3 ....146 A3
Bovingdon Hts SL7 ....183 B2
Bovingdon Prim Sch
  HP3 ....146 B4
Bow Brickhill CE Fst Sch
  MK17 ....48 D2
Bow Brickhill Rd MK17 ....48 F3
Bow Brickhill Sta MK7 ....48 B2
Bowden La HP11 ....173 D5
Bowen Cl MK7 ....48 C5
Bower Cl LU6 ....92 F5
Bower Ct SL1 ....204 F6
Bower La LU6 ....92 F5
Bower Way SL1 ....204 E6
Bowerbank Ct HP20 ....101 F1
Bowerdean Rd HP13 ....173 D7
Bowers La HP14 ....159 D7
Bowers Rd MK16 ....22 C3
Bowes-Lyon Cl 7 SL4 ....210 C6
Bowl Rdbt The MK4 ....46 D5
Bowland Dr MK4 ....46 B1
Bowler Lea HP13 ....161 D2
Bowler Rd HP21 ....115 E4
Bowler's Orch HP8 ....177 A7
Bowles Pl MK6 ....47 D7
Bowling Alley HP22 ....86 D7
Bowling Cl UB10 ....201 F4
Bowling Ct RG9 ....191 D3
Bowling Gn HP14 ....158 D5
Bowling Leys MK10 ....35 C1
Bowmans Cl SL1 ....197 B3
Bowmont Dr HP21 ....115 D4
Bowood Ct 5 MK8 ....33 F1
Bowood La HP27 ....139 C6
Bowry Dr TW19 ....211 F1
Bowstridge Ct 8 HP13 ....173 C7
Bowstridge La HP8 ....177 C5
Bowyer Cres UB9 ....189 F5
Bowyer Dr SL1 ....204 E6
Bowyers Mews MK14 ....34 F6
Box La HP3 ....146 F7
Box Tree Cl HP5 ....154 E7
Boxberry Gdns MK7 ....48 A6
Boxer Rd HP27 ....138 E6
Boxgrove Ct MK10 ....36 A1
Boxmoor House Com Specl
  Sch HP3 ....146 F8
Boxwell Rd HP4 ....135 B4
Boxwood Cl UB7 ....208 F4
Boyce Cres MK7 ....48 B5
Boycott Ave MK6 ....34 E1
Boyle Cl UB10 ....201 F3
Boyn Hill Ave SL6 ....202 D6
Boyn Hill Cl SL6 ....202 D6
Boyn Hill Rd SL6 ....202 D6
Boyn Valley Rd SL6 ....202 D7
Boyndon Rd SL6 ....202 D7
Boyne Hill CE Inf Sch
  SL6 ....202 D6
Boyne Ho HP9 ....175 E1
Bozenham Mill La NN7 ....9 F5
Bracken Cl SL2 ....198 D8
Bracken Hill HP4 ....135 C5
Bracken Rd SL6 ....202 C4
Bracken Way
  Aylesbury HP21 ....115 B8
  Flackwell Heath HP10 ....185 B7
Brackenforde SL3 ....206 C4
Brackens The HP11 ....173 C5
Brackenwood HP14 ....161 C7
Brackley Dr HP15 ....163 A6
Brackley La MK18 ....73 B6
Brackley Rd
  Chackmore MK18 ....41 B1
  Hazelmere HP15 ....163 A6
  Westbury NN13 ....39 B5
Bradbery SL0 ....200 D5
Bradbury Cl MK13 ....34 A3
Bradbury Gdns SL3 ....199 D8
Bradcutts La SL6 ....195 E8

Braddenham Wlk HP21 ....115 E4
Braddons Furlong HP18 ....125 C6
Braden Cl HP21 ....116 A6
Bradenham Beeches
  HP14 ....161 A8
Bradenham La SL7 ....194 C5
Bradenham Rd HP14 ....161 A3
Bradenham Wood La
  Naphill HP14 ....150 B1
  Walter's Ash HP14 ....161 A7
Bradfield Ave MK18 ....41 D2
Bradford Gdns MK5 ....46 B4
Bradford Rd
  Heronsgate WD3 ....167 C2
  Slough SL2 ....205 B8
Bradley Cl HP18 ....109 D5
Bradley Gn MK4 ....46 B2
Bradley Rd SL1 ....205 A6
Bradshaw Cl SL4 ....209 E6
Bradshaw Rd HP18 ....173 F6
Bradshawe Waye U88 ....208 F8
Bradvue Cres MK13 ....34 B6
Bradwell Common Bvd
  MK13 ....34 C3
Bradwell Rd
  Milton Keynes MK5,MK8 ....34 A1
  Milton Keynes,Bradville
  MK13 ....34 A6
  Milton Keynes,Loughton
  MK5 ....46 B8
Bradwell Village Mid Sch
  MK13 ....34 B4
Bradwell Village YH*
  MK13 ....34 A3
Brae Hill HP18 ....110 A8
Brae Hill Rd HP18 ....110 A8
Braeburn Ct SL1 ....205 C4
Braemar Ct 5 SL1 ....183 D2
Braemar Gdns SL1 ....205 A4
Braeside HP14 ....161 C6
Braford Gdns MK5 ....46 B4
Bragenham La LU7,MK17 ....70 D5
Bragenham Side MK17 ....69 F7
Bragmans La WD4 ....156 E6
Brahms Cl MK7 ....48 C5
Braid The HP5 ....144 E1
Brakynbery HP4 ....134 F5
Bramber Cl MK3 ....57 E7
Bramber Ct SL1 ....205 A5
Bramble Ave MK4 ....34 E4
Bramble Cl
  Chalfont St Peter SL9 ....177 E4
  Uxbridge UB8 ....208 F7
Bramble Cres HP15 ....163 C6
Bramble Dr SL6 ....202 A4
Bramble La HP7 ....165 E6
Bramble Mead HP8 ....177 B7
Brambles The UB7 ....208 E2
Brambleside HP11 ....174 A4
Brambling HP19 ....101 E3
Bramcote Cl HP20 ....116 C8
Bramley Chase SL6 ....202 C4
Bramley Ct SL6 ....202 C3
Bramley Ct MK43 ....3 F6
Bramley End HP14 ....151 A1
Bramley Grange MK2 ....58 D4
Bramley Mdws MK16 ....22 B3
Bramley Rd MK1 ....47 D3
Brammas Cl SL1 ....205 C3
Brampton Ct
  Maidenhead SL6 ....203 B8
  Milton Keynes MK13 ....34 A6
Branch Rd HP10 ....174 B2
Brandon Ct HP23 ....103 D7
Brandon Rd HP22 ....116 C2
Brands Hill Ave HP13 ....162 C2
Brands Rd SL3 ....212 B8
Brandville Rd UB7 ....208 E4
Branssill Ct MK13 ....34 A3
Bransworth Ave MK10 ....48 C8
Brantham Ct MK7 ....48 A3
Braunston MK6 ....47 D6
Bravenfield MK18 ....53 C2
Brawlings La SL9 ....178 A6
Bray Cl SL6 ....203 C3
Bray Ct Amersham HP6 ....154 F2
Bray Rd SL6 ....203 B5
Braybank SL6 ....203 B5
Braybourne Cl UB8 ....201 C6
Braybrooke Dr MK4 ....46 E4
Brayfield Ho MK46 ....8 B5
Brayfield Rd SL6 ....202 C4
Brays Cl HP6 ....153 C4
Brays Green La HP6 ....153 C4
Brays La HP6 ....153 C4
Brays Mdw HP6 ....153 C4
Brayton Ct MK5 ....46 A4
Braywick Park & Nature Ctr*
  SL6 ....203 B3
Braywick Rd SL6 ....203 A4
Braywood Cotts SL4 ....209 B5
Braziers End HP5 ....133 C1
Breachwell Pl LU7 ....91 A1
Breakspear Rd N UB9 ....190 E8
Breakspear Rd S UB10 ....190 F2
Bream Cl SL7 ....194 C8
Breamore Ct MK8 ....45 F8
Brearley Ave MK6 ....46 E7
Brearley Cl UB8 ....201 E6
Breckland MK14 ....34 C8
Brecon Ct
  Milton Keynes MK10 ....35 F1
  Slough SL1 ....205 C4
Brecon Way HP13 ....172 C8
Bredward Cl SL1 ....197 B2
Bremen Gr MK5 ....46 A4
Brenchwood Cl HP13 ....161 C2

Brendon Ct MK4 ....46 D2
Brent Ho MK46 ....47 D5
Brent Path HP21 ....115 D4
Brent Rd SL8 ....185 A4
Brentwood Way HP21 ....116 B6
Bretby Chase MK4 ....45 F3
Breton MK11 ....32 E6
Brew Twr SL7 ....183 D1
Brewhouse La HP22 ....88 E1
Brewster Cl MK5 ....45 D5
Briaily HP14 ....159 C2
Briar Cl SL6 ....204 B7
Briar Dene SL6 ....195 C1
Briar Glen SL6 ....195 E6
Briar Hill MK12 ....33 E4
Briar Lodge MK12 ....33 D5
Briar Way
  Berkhamsted HP4 ....135 D3
  Slough SL2 ....205 B8
Briars Cl HP19 ....101 E2
Briars The
  High Wycombe HP11 ....173 C5
  Holmer Green HP15 ....163 C7
  Slough SL3 ....206 F1
Briarswood HP15 ....163 B3
Briarswood Cl HP14 ....158 E5
Briary View MK17 ....56 C8
Brices Mdw MK5 ....46 A3
Brick Cl MK11 ....33 C2
Brick Hill HP18 ....97 E1
Brick Kiln La HP22 ....102 B4
Brickfield La SL1 ....197 B4
Brickfields Way UB7 ....208 F3
Brickhill Manor Ct MK17 ....59 D5
Brickhill St
  Giffard Park MK14 ....22 A1
  Milton Keynes,Monkston Park
  MK10 ....35 E2
  Milton Keynes,Willen Park
  MK15 ....35 C6
  Walton Park MK7 ....48 A4
Brickhill Way MK18 ....73 B5
Bricks La HP14 ....159 C4
Brickwell Wlk HP15 ....163 B3
Bricstock HP22 ....88 D4
Bridens Way HP17 ....126 F6
Bridge Ave
  Cookham Rise SL6 ....195 E6
  Maidenhead SL6 ....203 A7
Bridge Bank Cl HP11 ....174 A3
Bridge Cl SL1 ....204 F6
Bridge Ct
  Berkhamsted HP4 ....135 D4
  Maidenhead SL6 ....203 C7
Bridge Farm Bldgs
  HP17 ....128 B8
Bridge Ho
  High Wycombe HP13 ....173 D6
  West Drayton UB7 ....208 D5
Bridge Pl HP6 ....154 F1
Bridge Rd Cosgrove MK19 ....19 E2
  Ickford HP18 ....123 F2
  Maidenhead SL6 ....203 B7
  Stoke Bruerne NN12 ....9 A8
  Uxbridge UB8 ....201 C3
Bridge St
  Berkhamsted HP4 ....135 D4
  Buckingham MK18 ....52 D8
  Colnbrook SL3 ....212 D7
  Great Kimble HP17 ....129 D1
  High Wycombe HP11 ....173 A7
  Leighton Buzzard LU7 ....80 F7
  Maidenhead SL6 ....203 A7
  Milton Keynes MK13 ....33 F7
  Olney MK46 ....6 F2
  Thornborough MK18 ....54 B8
  Turvey MK43 ....8 E4
Bridge Wlk MK19 ....31 E4
Bridgeford Ct MK6 ....46 E8
Bridgegate Bsns Pk
  HP19 ....101 B1
Bridgeman Ct 5 SL4 ....210 A5
Bridgeman Dr SL4 ....210 A5
Bridgestone Dr SL8 ....185 C3
Bridgeturn Ave MK12 ....33 D8
Bridgewater Ct
  Little Gaddesden HP4 ....121 C8
  Slough SL3 ....207 A2
Bridgewater Hill HP4 ....121 C8
Bridgewater Ho MK18 ....52 C8
Bridgewater Mid Sch
  HP4 ....135 A6
Bridgewater Monument*
  HP4 ....135 B6
Bridgewater Rd HP4 ....135 B5
Bridgewater Terr SL4 ....210 D6
Bridgewater Way SL4 ....210 D6
Bridgeway
  Cuddington HP18 ....112 C3
  Milton Keynes MK13 ....34 A7
Bridgnorth Dr MK4 ....45 E1
Bridle Cl Maidenhead SL6 ....195 C1
  Slough SL1 ....205 A6
Bridle Gate HP11 ....172 F6
Bridle Manor HP12 ....131 C8
Bridle Rd SL6 ....195 E1
Bridle Way HP4 ....134 A6
Bridleway
  Buckland Common HP22 ....132 C5
  Weston Turville HP22 ....116 F2
  West Drayton UB7 ....208 D5
Bridlington Cres MK10 ....36 A1
Bridlington Spur SL1 ....205 B4
Bridport Way SL2 ....198 B1
Briery Way HP6 ....154 E1
Brighton Spur SL2 ....198 B1
Brightwell Ave LU6 ....93 C7

Brill CE Comb Sch HP18 ....96 B1
Brill Cl Maidenhead SL6 ....202 D3
  Marlow SL7 ....183 C2
Brill Ho SL6 ....202 C3
Brill Pl MK13 ....34 C3
Brill Rd Chilton HP18 ....111 A3
  Horton-cum-S OX33 ....108 B6
  Ludgershall HP18 ....96 B7
  Oakley HP18 ....109 F5
Brimmers Hill HP15 ....162 F6
Brimmers Rd HP27 ....139 D2
Brimmers Way HP19 ....114 F8
Brimstone Way HP4 ....134 F6
Brindlebrook MK8 ....33 E1
Brindles Cl MK18 ....73 B5
Brindles La HP9 ....175 A4
Brindley Ave HP13 ....161 F1
Brinkburn Chase MK10 ....36 A1
Brinkhurst SL7 ....183 D2
Brinklow Rdbt MK10 ....36 C1
Briskman Way HP21 ....115 B6
Bristle Hill MK18 ....52 C8
Bristol Cl TW19 ....213 E1
Bristol Ct 10 TW19 ....213 E1
Bristol Way SL1 ....205 F5
Bristow Cl MK2 ....47 E1
Britannia Ct UB7 ....208 D3
Britannia Ind Est
  High Wycombe HP12 ....172 D7
  Poyle SL3 ....212 E5
Britannia Rd 6 HP5 ....154 B7
Britannia St HP20 ....115 E8
Britnell Ct HP14 ....158 E5
Britten Gr MK7 ....48 D5
Brittens The MK46 ....7 C3
Brittons La MK17 ....37 C3
Britwell Dr HP4 ....135 E6
Britwell Gdns SL1 ....197 D2
Britwell Rd SL1 ....197 D2
Broad Arrow Cl MK14 ....34 E7
Broad Dean MK6 ....47 A8
Broad Gn MK43 ....25 C3
Broad La HP9,HP10 ....186 A6
Broad Leys HP27 ....139 A3
Broad Oak SL2 ....198 C1
Broad Oak Ct SL2 ....198 C1
Broad Platts SL3 ....206 D8
Broad Rush Gn LU7 ....80 E8
Broad St Chesham HP5 ....144 C1
  Newport Pagnell MK16 ....22 C4
  Syresham NN13 ....27 B8
Broadfields Ct HP19 ....101 A1
Broadlands MK6 ....47 C5
Broadlands Ave HP5 ....144 C1
Broadleys SL4 ....209 F7
Broadmark Rd SL2 ....206 B6
Broadpiece MK15 ....35 A7
Broadview Rd HP5 ....144 B4
Broadwater
  Berkhamsted HP4 ....135 C5
  Milton Keynes MK6 ....47 D6
Broadwater Gdns UB9 ....190 C7
Broadwater La UB9 ....190 C7
Broadwater Pk
  Denham Green UB9 ....190 A5
  Maidenhead SL6 ....203 E1
Broadway SL6 ....202 F7
Broadway Ave SL4 ....21 F2
Broadway Ct 5 HP7 ....165 B7
Broadway Par
  Amersham HP7 ....165 B7
  Beaconsfield HP9 ....175 D3
  3 Chalfont St Peter SL9 ....177 D2
  Chesham HP5 ....154 B8
Broadway The
  Farnham Common SL2 ....198 C6
  Grendon Underwood HP18 ....82 F6
Brocas St SL4 ....210 D7
Brocas Terr SL4 ....210 D7
Brocas Way SL1 ....91 A3
Brock La SL6 ....202 F7
Brockhampton MK15 ....35 B6
Brockhurst Rd HP5 ....144 C2
Brockton Ct SL6 ....202 F6
Brockwell MK16 ....22 C4
Broddick Ho HP11 ....174 B4
Broken Furlong SL4 ....205 B1
Broken Gate La UB9 ....189 C3
Bromham Mill* MK14 ....21 F2
Bromley HP23 ....104 A4
Bromley La HP5 ....153 C5
Brompton Cl MK10 ....36 A1
Brompton Cres HP19 ....101 B2
Brompton Dr SL6 ....195 C2
Bromycroft Rd SL2 ....198 A2
Bronsdon Way UB9 ....189 F2
Bronte Cl HP19 ....100 F2
Brook Bsns Ctr UB8 ....201 B3
Brook Cl
  Aston Clinton HP22 ....117 D5
  Ludgershall HP18 ....96 C8
Brook Cres SL1 ....204 E7
Brook End
  North Crawley MK16 ....24 A6
  Weston Turville HP22 ....117 A3
Brook Ho Slough SL1 ....205 D3
  West Drayton UB7 ....208 D5
Brook St
  Aston Clinton HP22 ....117 D5

Brook St *continued*
Edlesborough LU6 92 F4
High Wycombe HP11 173 A7
Tring HP23 119 B4
Windsor SL4 210 D5
Brookbank HP10 185 D3
Brookdene Cl SL6 195 F2
Brooke Cl MK3 57 F7
Brooke Furmston Pl SL7 183 E3
Brooke Rd HP27 139 B4
Brookfield UB8 201 E6
Brookfield Cl HP23 119 B4
Brookfield Ho SL3 211 D6
Brookfield La MK18 52 D7
Brookfield Rd
Haversham MK19 20 D2
Newton Longville MK17 57 D3
Wooburn HP10 185 D3
Brookhouse Dr HP10 185 C3
Brooklands Rd MK2 58 C7
Brooklyn Way UB7 208 D3
Brookmead Sch LU7 105 E5
Brooks Ct MK18 52 D8
Brookside Colnbrook SL3 212 C7
Halton HP22 117 C1
Lillingstone Lovell MK18 30 A6
Loudwater HP10 174 C2
Milton Keynes MK12 33 D4
Oakley HP18 109 D5
Slough SL3 206 E7
Thame OX9 125 F1
Uxbridge UB10 201 F5
Weston Turville HP22 117 A2
Brookside Ave TW19 211 E4
Brookside Cl
Old Stratford MK19 32 B6
Tiddington OX9 136 A7
Brookside La HP17 129 E3
Brookside Terr 5 HP21 115 E8
Brooksward Comb Sch MK14 34 F7
Brookway MK19 31 E4
Broom Cl HP15 163 A3
Broom Hill
Cookham Rise SL6 195 E6
Stoke Poges SL2 199 A5
Broom Ho SL3 206 F2
Broombarn La HP16 151 E7
Broomfield MK12 33 D4
Broomfield Cl HP16 151 E7
Broomfield Gate SL2 198 B1
Broomfield Hill HP16 151 E7
Broomlee MK13 34 A5
Broomstick Ind Est LU6 92 E4
Broomstick La HP5 145 A1
Brora Cl MK2 58 C5
Brotheridge Ct HP21 115 B6
Brough Cl MK5 46 A5
Broughton Ave HP20 116 B8
Broughton Cl HP22 102 B3
Broughton Crossing HP22 102 C2
Broughton Fields Comb Sch MK10,MK16 36 B4
Broughton Grounds Com Woodlands* MK16 36 E6
Broughton Inf Sch HP20 116 B8
Broughton Jun Sch HP20 116 B8
Broughton La HP20, HP22 116 C8
Broughton Manor Bsns Pk MK16 36 B4
Broughton Rd MK17 37 C3
Brow The HP8 177 D7
Brown's La HP23 132 F7
Brown's Rise HP23 132 F3
Brownbaker Ct MK14 34 F6
Browne Willis Cl MK2 58 D8
Brownfield Gdns SL6 202 E5
Browning Cl MK16 22 A4
Browning Cres MK3 58 A7
Brownlow Ave LU6 92 F3
Brownlow Gate HP4 107 A1
Brownlow La LU7 105 A7
Brownlow Rd HP4 135 C5
Brownlow Ride LU6 93 A8
Browns Ct SL1 204 E6
Browns Hedge LU7 105 C3
Browns Rd
Holmer Green HP15 163 C6
South Heath HP16 153 A7
Browns Way MK17 49 E5
Browns Wood Rdbt MK7 48 C5
Brownset Dr MK4 45 E1
Brownsfield Rd NN12 18 E6
Brownswood Dr NN12 18 D3
Brownswood Rd HP9 175 E4
Broxbourne Cl MK14 21 F2
Bruce Cl SL1 205 A5
Bruce Wlk SL4 209 D5
Brucewood Par SL7 183 E5
Bruckner Gdns MK7 48 D5
Brudenell SL4 209 F3
Brudenell Dr
Milton Keynes MK10 48 C8
Stoke Mandeville HP22 116 B1
Brunel Cl SL6 202 E5
Brunel Ctr
Maidenhead SL6 202 D5
Milton Keynes MK2 58 C8
Brunel Rd
Aylesbury HP19 100 F1
High Wycombe HP13 161 F1
Maidenhead SL6 202 D5
Brunel Science Pk UB8 201 E2
Brunel Univ UB8 201 E2
Brunel Way SL1 205 F5
Brunleys MK11 33 B3
Brunner Pl HP13 173 C6
Brunswick Cl HP19 101 B3
Brunswick Pl HP13 162 D2
Brushford Cl MK4 46 D3
Brushmakers Ct HP5 144 B1
Brushwood Dr WD3 167 C5
Brushwood Jun Sch HP5 144 E2
Brushwood Rd HP5 144 E2
Bryans Cres MK16 24 A6
Bryanston Ave HP20 101 F2
Bryant Ave SL2 205 E8
Bryants Acre HP22 131 B6
Bryants Bottom Rd HP16 150 F4
Bryden Cotts UB8 201 C1
Bryer Pl SL4 209 D4
Bryfield Cotts HP3 146 C1
Bryne La MK18 53 B2
Bryony Cl UB8 208 F8
Bryony Pl MK14 34 E5
Bsns Ctr The HP6 154 F1
Bsns Village The SL2 206 B5
Buccleuch Rd SL3 211 B7
Buchan Cl UB8 201 C2
Buchanan Rd OX25 94 E7
Buckby MK6 47 D6
Buckfast Ave MK3 47 A2
Buckfield Ct SL0 207 F4
Buckingham Ave SL1 205 B7
Buckingham Ave E SL1 205 C7
Buckingham Canal Nature Reserve* MK18 42 D3
Buckingham Cl HP13 174 A7
Buckingham Ct
Amersham HP6 154 E2
Brackley NN13 38 A6
Newport Pagnell MK16 22 B3
Buckingham Dr HP13 174 A7
Buckingham Gate
Medmenham SL7 193 D7
Milton Keynes MK6 35 B1
Buckingham Gdns SL1 205 F4
Buckingham Ho
Amersham HP6 154 D3
4 Maidenhead SL6 202 F6
Buckingham Hospl MK18 41 D1
Buckingham Ind Pk MK18 52 D6
Buckingham Par 4 SL9 177 D2
Buckingham Pl 1 HP13 173 A7
Buckingham Prim Sch MK18 41 E2
Buckingham Rd
Aylesbury HP19,HP20 101 D3
Brackley NN13 38 A6
Deanshanger MK19 31 E2
Edgcott HP18 72 F2
Gawcott MK18 52 A5
Milton Keynes MK3 57 D7
Milton Keynes,Church Hill MK17 56 E6
Steeple Claydon MK18 63 E3
Tring HP23 118 E3
Winslow MK18 65 F5
Buckingham Road Ind Est NN13 38 A6
Buckingham Sch MK18 52 D7
Buckingham Sq MK9 34 C2
Buckingham St
8 Aylesbury HP20 101 D1
Milton Keynes MK12 33 D7
Tingewick MK18 51 B6
Buckingham View HP5 144 C1
Buckingham Way HP10 174 A1
Buckinghamshire Chilterns Univ Coll
Chalfont St Peter HP8 178 A7
High Wycombe HP11 173 A6
Buckinghamshire Chilterns Univ Coll (Wellesbourne Campus) HP13 162 D3
Buckinghamshire County Mus* HP20 115 D8
Buckinghamshire Railway Ctr* HP22 84 F2
Buckland Ave SL3 206 B3
Buckland Cres SL4 209 F6
Buckland Dr MK6 47 C6
Buckland Gate SL3 199 B2
Buckland Lodge MK6 47 B6
Buckland Rd HP22 118 A4
Bucklands Croft HP23 118 C8
Bucklebury Cl SL6 203 C1
Buckley Ct MK11 32 F4
Buckman Cl MK12 33 B5
Buckmaster Rd HP12 172 C3
Bucks Goat Ctr* HP22 130 A7
Buckthorn MK12 33 E5
Budge Rd NN12 18 F5
Buffins SL6 196 E2
Bulbourne Cl HP4 134 F6
Bulbourne Ct HP23 119 A7
Bulbourne Rd HP23 119 B7
Bulkeley Ave SL4 210 B4
Bull La
Gerrards Cross SL9 188 C7
7 High Wycombe HP11 173 A7
Milton Keynes MK2 58 D8
Bullbaiters La HP6 153 B5
Bullbeggars La HP4 135 F3
Bullfinch Gdns 8 HP19 101 F3
Bullington End Rd MK19 20 A6
Bullocks Farm La HP14 171 B7
Bullrush Gr UB8 201 C1
Bulls La HP18 124 A3
Bullsland Gdns WD3 167 B3
Bullsland La WD3 167 B3
Bulmer Cl MK10 36 B3
Bulstrode Cl WD4 146 E2
Bulstrode Ct SL9 188 D5
Bulstrode La WD4 146 F3
Bulstrode Pl SL1 205 F3
Bulstrode Way SL9 188 D6
Bunby Rd SL2 198 F5
Bunces Cl SL4 205 B1
Bunces Ct HP20 101 D1
Bungalows The MK18 51 A6
Bunhill Cl LU6 93 F8
Bunkers La LU7 80 D6
Bunsen Pl MK5 46 C4
Bunstrux HP23 119 A4
Bunsty Ct MK11 32 F5
Bunten Meade SL1 205 B5
Bunyan Cl HP23 119 B5
Burano Cl MK7 48 C6
Burchard Cres MK5 46 A6
Burchett's Green Rd SL6 194 C1
Burcot Gdns SL6 195 E3
Burcott Cl HP22 102 B3
Burcott La HP22 102 C3
Burdeleys La MK5 46 A4
Burdett Dr HP14 161 B8
Burdock Ct MK16 21 F4
Burewelle MK8 33 D1
Burfield Rd
Chorleywood WD3 167 C4
Old Windsor SL4 211 A1
Burford Cl
Ickenham UB10 201 E8
Marlow Bottom SL7 183 C5
Burford Gdns SL1 204 C8
Burford Ho 18 SL4 210 D6
Burford Sch SL7 183 C5
Burgess Gdns MK16 22 B2
Burgess La HP17 128 B7
Burgess Wood Gr HP9 175 B1
Burgess Wood Rd HP9 175 B2
Burgess Wood Rd S HP9 175 B1
Burgett Rd SL1 205 B3
Burghley Ct MK8 45 F8
Burholme MK4 46 C3
Burke Rd HP22 131 C5
Burkes Cl HP9 186 B8
Burkes Cres HP9 175 D2
Burkes Ct HP9 175 D2
Burkes Par HP9 175 D3
Burkes Rd HP9 175 C2
Burleigh Ct MK18 52 F8
Burleigh Piece MK18 41 F1
Burleys Rd MK18 65 F4
Burlington Ave SL1 205 E4
Burlington Ct 1 SL1 205 E4
Burlington Rd
Burnham SL1 197 B1
2 Slough SL1 205 E4
Burma Cl HP13 173 E6
Burn Wlk SL1 197 B1
Burners La MK11 33 B4
Burners Lane S MK11 33 B3
Burness Cl UB8 201 D3
Burnet MK14 34 C7
Burnetts Ct HP16 151 C5
Burnetts Rd SL4 209 E6
Burnham Ave HP9 176 A1
Burnham Beeches (Nature Reserve)* SL2 198 A7
Burnham Cl
Bourne End SL8 185 A4
High Wycombe HP12 172 D6
Windsor SL4 209 D5
Burnham Ct SL6 202 F8
Burnham Dr MK13 34 C3
Burnham Gram Sch SL1 197 D1
Burnham Hts SL1 204 C7
Burnham La SL1 204 E7
Burnham Pl NN13 27 B8
Burnham Rd
Beaconsfield HP9 186 F6
Hughenden Valley HP14 162 A6
Westcott HP18 98 B7
Burnham Sta SL1 204 D7
Burnham Upper Sch SL1 204 B8
Burnhams Field HP22 116 E7
Burnhams The
Aston Clinton HP22 117 C5
Shabbington HP18 124 D3
Burnmoor Cl MK2 58 D4
Burns Cl
Long Crendon HP18 125 D7
Newport Pagnell MK16 22 A4
Burns Ct HP21 115 F6
Burns Rd MK3 58 A7
Burnt Oak SL6 195 F7
Burrell Cl HP21 115 C6
Burren The HP6 154 D2
Burroughs Cres SL8 185 A4
Burroway Rd SL3 207 B3
Burrows Cl
Tylers Green HP10 163 C2
Woburn Sands MK17 49 B5
Burrows Ho HP13 161 E2
Burt's La HP18 125 D6
Burton La HP27 139 C5
Burton Way SL4 209 E4
Burton's La HP8 166 E5
Burton's Way HP8 166 C7
Burtons La WD3 167 A4
Burtree Cl MK12 33 D5
Bury Ave MK16 22 C4
Bury Cl MK16 22 C4
Bury Farm HP7 165 C7
Bury Farm Cl LU7 91 C6
Bury La HP5 154 B8
Bury Lawn Sch MK14 34 D7
Bury Rise HP3 146 D6
Bury St MK16 22 C4
Buryfield La HP16 152 B7
Buryhook Cnr OX33 122 C2
Busby Cl MK18 41 F1
Buscot Pl MK8 45 F8
Bush The HP17 126 F5
Bushel Wharf HP23 119 A6
Bushes La MK18 51 C1
Bushey Bartrams MK5 46 A3
Bushey Cl
Buckingham MK18 41 F1
High Wycombe HP12 172 E7
Whipsnade LU6 93 F1
Bushfield Mid Sch MK12 33 D6
Bushfield Rd HP3 146 C6
Bushfields MK12 33 D6
Bushmead Cl HP22 87 B5
Bushmead Rd HP22 87 B5
Bushy Cl MK3 47 A3
Buslins La HP5 143 E3
Butcher La MK5 45 F3
Bute Brae MK3 46 E2
Butler Ct 5 SL7 183 F3
Butler Wlk HP19 115 A7
Butlers Cl
Amersham HP6 154 A2
Windsor SL4 209 D6
Butlers Court Rd HP9 175 D1
Butlers Court Sch HP9 175 D1
Butlers Ct HP13 173 F5
Butlers Gr MK14 34 D8
Butterfield HP10 185 D4
Butterfield Cl MK15 35 C2
Butterfield Cotts WD3 178 E3
Butterly Rd HP14 158 F4
Buttermere HP21 116 B7
Buttermere Ave SL1 204 C8
Buttermere Cl MK2 58 D6
Buttfurlong HP17 127 A7
Buttlehide WD3 178 D5
Button Gr MK6 47 A7
Buzzacott La MK4 46 C3
By-Wood End SL9 178 A5
Bybend Cl SL2 198 B4
Bycell Rd MK18 41 C6
Bye Gn HP22 117 A3
Byerly Ho MK14 34 F5
Byerly Pl MK14 34 F5
Byford Way MK18 65 F4
Byland Dr SL6 203 B1
Byrd Cres MK7 48 D6
Byres The HP17 126 F6
Byron SL3 207 B1
Byron Cl 6 Marlow SL7 183 F3
Milton Keynes MK3 57 F7
Byron Ct SL4 210 A4
Byron Dr MK16 22 A4
Byron Rd HP21 115 F6
Byron Way UB7 208 F2
Byward Cl MK14 34 E7
Byways Berkhamsted HP4 135 E5
Burnham SL1 204 A8

C

Cadeby Ct MK10 36 B3
Cadman Sq MK5 46 C5
Cadmore End CE Sch HP14 170 C6
Cadsdean Rd HP27 139 E6
Cadwell Dr SL6 202 D3
Caernarvon Cres MK3 57 E7
Caesars Cl MK13 34 A5
Caesars Gate NN13 38 A6
Cages Wood Dr SL2 198 B8
Cairngorm Gate MK6 46 D8
Cairngorm Pl SL2 198 D1
Cairnside HP13 173 E6
Caister Ct MK4 56 E8
Caithness Ct MK3 46 E2
Calamus Ct MK7 48 B6
Calbroke Rd SL2 197 F2
Caldecote La MK16 22 F2
Caldecote St MK16 22 C4
Caldecotte La MK7 48 A3
Caldecotte Lake Dr MK7 48 A2
Caldecotte Rdbt MK7 47 F3
Calder Cl SL6 195 E1
Calder Ct
Maidenhead SL6 195 D1
1 Slough SL3 206 F1
Calder Gdns LU7 80 B7
Calder Vale MK3 46 E1
Calder Way SL3 212 E4
Caldewell MK8 33 D1
Caldicot Cl HP21 116 B6
Caldicott Sch SL2 198 B5
Caledon Cl HP9 175 E3
Caledon Rd HP9 175 E3
Caledonian Rd MK13 33 E7
Calewen MK8 33 E1
California Circ HP11 173 B4
Callaghan Ct HP4 135 D4
Callis Farm Cl TW19 213 E1
Calluna Dr MK3 47 A3
Calumet HP9 175 D3
Calvards Croft MK12 33 C4
Calverleigh Cres MK4 46 D3
Calverley Cres HP13 161 F2
Calvert Cotts MK18 73 D7
Calvert Jubilee Nature Reserve* MK18,OX27 73 A7
Calverton La MK19 33 B1
Calverton La Rdbt MK11 33 B2
Calverton Rd MK11 32 D4
Calves Cl MK5 46 A3
Cam Ct MK3 57 E8
Cam Mead HP21 116 B6
Camber Cl MK3 57 E7
Camberton Rd LU7 80 E6
Camborne Ave HP21 116 B5
Cambria Ct SL3 206 C4
Cambridge Ave
Burnham SL1 197 B3
Slough SL1 205 A7
Cambridge Cl
Aylesbury HP20 101 E1
Harmondsworth UB7 213 D8
Cambridge Close Trad Est HP20 101 E1
Cambridge Cres HP13 173 E7
Cambridge Ho 2 SL4 210 C6
Cambridge Pl 9 HP20 115 D8
Cambridge Rd
Beaconsfield HP9 175 C2
Marlow SL7 183 D2
Uxbridge UB8 201 D6
Cambridge St
Aylesbury HP20 101 E1
Milton Keynes,Bletchley MK2 58 C8
Milton Keynes,Wolverton MK12 33 C6
Cambridge Terr 13 HP4 135 D4
Cambron MK8 33 D2
Camden Ct HP19 101 C1
Camden Pl SL8 185 A3
Camden Rd SL6 195 D1
Cameron Rd HP5 144 C1
Camfield Ct SL6 202 A8
Camlet Gr MK14 34 D7
Camley Gdns SL6 202 A8
Camm Ave SL4 209 E4
Camomile Ct MK7 48 C5
Camomile Way UB7 208 E6
Camp Ind Est OX9 136 B4
Camp Rd SL9 188 C4
Campania Cl MK10 36 A2
Campbell Cl
Buckingham MK18 52 F8
High Wycombe HP13 172 F8
Campbell Dr HP9 175 C5
Campbell Park Rdbt MK9 34 F3
Campbells Ride HP15 163 D7
Campden Rd UB10 190 F1
Camperdown SL6 196 B1
Camperdown Ho 9 SL4 210 C5
Campion MK14 21 E2
Campion Cl
Aylesbury HP20 116 C8
Denham UB9 190 A1
Uxbridge UB8 208 F8
Campion Rd HP15 162 F6
Campions Ct HP4 135 B3
Canada Rd SL1 206 B4
Canal Ct HP4 135 E4
Canal Mus The* NN12 9 A8
Canal Wharf SL3 207 A4
Canalside
Berkhamsted HP4 134 F6
Old Stratford MK19 32 C7
Stoke Bruerne NN12 9 A8
Canalside Rdbt MK9 35 B4
Candlemas La HP9 175 E2
Candlemas Mead HP9 175 E2
Candlemas Oaks HP9 175 E2
Candlewicks MK7 48 B6
Candover Cl UB7 213 D7
Candy La MK5 46 B4
Candytuft Gn HP15 162 F6
Cane End HP27 139 A3
Cane End La HP22 102 C6
Canford Ct HP21 115 F5
Cannock Cl SL6 203 B6
Cannock Rd HP20 101 E3
Cannon Court Rd SL6 195 D3
Cannon Gate SL2 206 C6
Cannon Hill Cl SL6 203 C2
Cannon La SL6 202 A6
Cannon Mill Ave HP5 154 E5
Cannon Pl HP27 139 B4
Cannon's Hill HP18 112 C5
Cannon's Orch HP22 85 B4
Cannondown Rd SL6 195 E5
Canon Harnett Ct MK12 32 F6
Canon Hill Dr SL6 203 B3
Canon Hill Way SL6 203 B2
Canon's Cloisters SL4 210 D7
Canons Rd MK12 33 C7
Canons The MK16 22 E3
Cantell Cl MK18 41 D1
Canterbury Ave SL2 198 C1
Canterbury Cl
Amersham HP7 165 E8
Monks Risborough HP27 139 B5
Cantilupe Cl LU6 92 D6
Cantle Ave MK14 35 A5
Cantley Cl HP20 101 E2
Cape Villas SL0 207 E7
Capel Cl MK18 41 F7
Capel Dr MK14 34 F5
Capell Ave WD3 167 C4
Capell Rd WD3 167 D4
Capell Way WD3 167 D4
Capian Wlk MK8 33 E1

Capital Dr MK14 ....34 E6
Capps La HP5 ....143 A5
Capricorn Ho HP10 .....185 A8
Capron MK6 ....47 B5
Capswood Bsns Ctr
UB9 ....189 C3
Captain Cook Cl HP8 ...177 B6
Captain's Cl HP5 ....144 A4
Captains Wlk HP4 .....135 D3
Caravan Site The HP23 ..104 C4
Caraway Cl MK7 ....48 B4
Cardain Ho HP9 ....175 D3
Cardigan Cl
Milton Keynes MK3 .....46 F1
Slough SL1 ....205 D6
Cardinals Wlk SL6 .....204 C7
Cardwell Cl MK4 ....46 C2
Carey Cl Aylesbury HP21 .115 D4
Windsor SL4 ....210 B4
Carey Way MK46 ....7 A4
Careys Croft HP4 ....135 A7
Careys Rd NN12 ....17 A8
Carhampton Ct MK4 .....46 D3
Carisbrooke Ave HP12 ..172 B6
Carisbrooke Cl SL6 .....202 C6
Carisbrooke Ct
Buckingham MK18 ....41 E2
Slough SL1 ....205 F6
Carisbrooke Ho **4**
HP13 ....173 F7
Carisbrooke Way MK46 ..45 E1
Carleton Gate MK15 ....35 E7
Carlina Pl MK14 ....34 D3
Carlisle Rd SL1 ....205 D6
Carlton Cl
Aylesbury HP19 ....101 A2
Newport Pagnell MK16 ..22 E4
Carlton Ct HP27 ....139 B3
Carlton Ho TW19 ....213 D2
Carlton Rd Slough SL2 ..206 B6
Turvey MK43 ....8 E7
Carlyle Ave HP21 ....115 F7
Carlyle Cl MK16 ....22 A4
Carman Ct HP23 ....118 F3
Carmarthen Rd SL1 .....205 E6
Carmel Ct SL7 ....183 B1
Carnation Way HP21 ....115 E5
Carne The MK1 ....32 E5
Carnot Cl MK5 ....46 C4
Carnoustie Cl MK3 .....57 C7
Carnweather Ct MK4 ....57 B8
Caroline Cl SL8 ....208 D4
Caroline Ct SL7 ....183 E3
Caroline Haslett Comb Sch
MK5 ....46 B4
Carolus Creek MK15 ....35 A7
Carpenter Ct MK14 .....34 F6
Carpenters Wood Dr
WD3 ....167 B5
Carpenters Yd HP23 ....119 B3
Carr Cl HP19 ....101 A2
Carrick Rd MK6 ....34 F1
Carriers Cl MK19 ....11 A2
Carrington Ave HP10 ...185 A8
Carrington Cl MK18 ....77 E5
Carrington Cres HP22 ..131 A7
Carrington Ct **9** HP12 .172 E7
Carrington Hall Rd MK17 .68 C6
Carrington Inf Sch The
HP10 ....174 A1
Carrington Jun Sch
HP10 ....185 A8
Carrington Pl
Holmer Green HP15 .....163 C7
Tring HP23 ....119 B5
Carrington Rd
Aylesbury HP21 ....115 D6
High Wycombe HP12 ....172 D6
Newport Pagnell MK16 ..22 B3
Slough SL1 ....205 E6
Carrington Way HP16 ...151 C5
Carroll Cl MK16 ....22 A5
Carron Cl LU7 ....80 B7
Carron Ct MK12 ....58 C4
Carrs Dr HP12 ....172 C8
Carter Cl SL4 ....210 A5
Carter Wlk HP10 ....174 C8
Carteret Cl MK15 ......35 E7
Carters Cl MK16 ....13 F1
Carters La
Long Crendon HP18 .....125 B7
Milton Keynes MK11 ....33 A3
Quainton HP22,MK18 ....85 E6
Carters Mdw MK16 .....76 A2
Carters Ride HP22 .....116 B2
Cartmel Cl MK3 ....57 C6
Cartwright Ct **2** HP13 .173 F5
Cartwright Pl MK6 .....46 E8
Carver Hill Rd HP11 ...172 F5
Carvers Mews MK14 ....34 F6
Cascadia Cl HP11 ....174 B2
Cashmere Cl MK5 ....46 A4
Casterton Cl MK13 ....34 C4
Castle Acre MK10 ......35 F1
Castle Ashby Rd NN7 ....1 B7
Castle Ave Datchet SL3 .211 A8
West Drayton UB7 .....208 F6
Castle Cl
Marsh Gibbon OX6 .....72 A3
Pitstone LU7 ....105 D3
Totternhoe LU6 ....93 A8
Wing LU7 ....79 E3
Castle Ct
13 Aylesbury HP20 ....115 D8
Buckingham MK18 ......52 D8

Castle Ct continued
Maidenhead SL6 ....202 D7
Castle Dr SL6 ....202 D7
Castle Est HP12 ....172 D4
Castle Farm Cvn Site
SL4 ....209 D5
Castle Gate Way HP4 ..135 C6
Castle Hill
Berkhamsted HP4 ....135 C4
High Wycombe HP11 ....173 A6
Maidenhead SL6 ....202 E7
Windsor SL4 ....210 D6
Castle Hill Ave HP4 ...135 C5
Castle Hill Cl HP4 ....135 C5
Castle Hill Ct HP4 ....135 C5
Castle Hill Rd LU6 ....93 A8
Castle Hill Terr SL6 ..202 E7
Castle Ho **6** LU7 .....80 E7
Castle La HP27 ....86 F6
Castle Lodge SL6 ......202 F7
Castle Mdw SL4 ....211 B2
Castle Meadow Cl MK16 .22 E4
Castle Mews
Berkhamsted HP4 ....135 C4
Maidenhead SL6 ....202 E7
Castle Park Rd HP22 ...131 B6
Castle Pl **6** HP13 ...173 B7
Castle Rd HP27 ....86 F6
Castle Rose MK6 ....47 D6
Castle Row **11** HP23 ..119 A3
Castle St Aylesbury HP20 .115 D8
Berkhamsted HP4 ....135 C4
Buckingham MK18 ......52 D8
High Wycombe HP13 ....173 B7
Marsh Gibbon OX27 ....72 A3
Slough SL1 ....205 F3
Wingrave HP22 ....89 B3
Castle View MK18 .....172 D7
Castlefield Sch HP12 ..172 C6
Castlefields HP22 .....116 C3
Castlemead Cotts SL4 ..210 C3
Castlesteads MK13 .....34 B4
Castlethorpe Fst Sch
MK19 ....19 F5
Castlethorpe Rd MK19 ..11 A2
Castleton Ct SL7 .....183 E2
Castleview Ho SL4 .....210 D7
Castleview Prim Sch
SL3 ....206 D2
Castleview Rd SL3 .....206 D2
Caswell La MK17 ......60 F7
Catchpole Cl MK12 ....33 B5
Cater Rd HP14 ....171 C4
Catesby Croft MK5 ....46 C8
Cathay Cl MK3 ....58 B7
Catherine Cotts HP23 ..133 E8
Catherine Ct MK18 ....41 E2
Catherines Cl UB7 ....208 D4
Catkin Cl HP12 ....172 B3
Catslip RG9 ....179 A1
Causeway The Bray SL6 .203 C4
Marlow SL7 ....183 E1
Cautley Cl HP22 ....85 A5
Cavalier Ct HP4 ....135 C4
Cavalier Rd OX9 ....126 A1
Cavalry Cres SL4 .....210 C4
Cavendish Cl
Burnham SL6 ....204 A7
Little Chalfont HP6 ...166 B8
Wendover HP22 ....131 B6
Cavendish Ct
Milton Keynes MK5 ....46 A7
Poyle SL3 ....212 E6
Cavendish Rd HP5 .....154 D7
Cavendish Wlk HP6 ....126 B1
Cavenham MK8 ....33 F2
Cawardon MK14 ....34 C7
Cawcott Dr SL4 ....209 E6
Cawdor Rise MK4 ......45 E2
Cawkwell Way MK2 ....58 C8
Caxton Ct RG9 ....191 E1
Caxton Dr UB8 ....201 D3
Caxton Rd MK12 ....33 B7
Cecil Rd SL0 ....207 E7
Cecil Way SL2 ....197 F1
Cecily Ct MK5 ....46 A5
Cedar **1** RG9 ....191 D2
Cedar Ave
Hazelmere HP15 ....163 A5
West Drayton UB7 .....208 F6
Cedar Chase SL6 ......196 D1
Cedar Cl Aylesbury HP20 .102 A2
Burnham SL1 ....197 C1
Chesham HP5 ....144 E1
Iver Heath SL0 ....200 C4
Cedar Ct
Gerrards Cross SL9 ...188 E7
High Wycombe HP13 ...173 B7
Maidenhead SL6 ....202 D7
Marlow SL7 ....183 E2
6 Windsor SL4 ....210 A5
Cedar Dr Chesham HP5 ..144 A1
Cookham SL6 ....196 A7
Cookham Rise SL6 ....195 F7
Marlow Bottom SL7 ...183 C7
Cedar Gr Amersham HP7 .165 D8
Cedar Lodge Dr MK12 ..33 D7
Cedar Park Sch HP15 ..162 F5
Cedar Rd HP4 ....135 D3
Cedar Ridge HP6 ....153 C5
Cedar Terr **1** HP11 ..172 F7
Cedar Way
Berkhamsted HP4 ....135 D3
Slough SL3 ....206 B8
Cedars Cl Akeley MK18 ..41 F8
Chalfont St Peter SL9 ..177 E5

Cedars Dr UB10 ....201 F3
Cedars Ho SL6 ....203 A7
Cedars Rd SL6 ....203 A7
Cedars The
Berkhamsted HP4 ....135 E4
Slough SL2 ....197 F2
Wendover HP22 ....131 A5
Cedars Upper Sch & Com
Coll The LU7 ....80 E5
Cedars Village WD3 ...167 F5
Cedars Way
Leighton Buzzard LU7 ..80 E5
Newport Pagnell MK16 ..22 C4
Cedars Wlk WD3 ....167 F5
Ceely Ho HP21 ....115 D6
Ceely Rd HP21 ....115 D6
Celandine Ct MK7 ......48 A5
Celina Cl MK2 ....58 C7
Cell Farm Ave SL4 .....211 B2
Cell Farm Ave SL4 .....211 B2
Centenary Bsns Pk RG9 .191 F1
Centenary Cotts HP27 ..138 D7
Centenary Way HP6 ...154 F1
Central Ave
Cranfield MK43 ....24 E2
Whipsnade LU6 ....107 E8
Wooburn SL8 ....208 A7
Central Ct SL4 ....202 E7
Central Park Bsns Ctr
HP13 ....173 A8
Centre Par HP27 ....139 C5
Centre The SL2 ....198 C6
Centre Wlk HP15 ....163 A3
Centurion Ct MK11 ....33 C2
Century Ave MK6 ......46 E8
Century Point HP12 ...172 C4
Cestreham Cres HP5 ...144 D2
Chackmore CE Sch MK18 .41 B4
Chacombe Pl HP19 .....175 D5
Chadbone Cl HP20 .....115 D8
Chadds La MK6 ....47 C8
Chadwell Path HP21 ...116 C6
Chadwick Dr MK6 ......47 B7
Chadwick St HP13 .....162 D2
Chaffinch HP19 ....101 F4
Chaffron Way
Leadenhall MK6 ....46 F7
Milton Keynes,Oakgrove
MK6,MK10,MK15 ....35 D1
Milton Keynes,Shenley Lodge
MK4,MK5,MK6 ....46 C5
Chairborough Rd HP12 ..172 C4
Chalcot Pl MK8 ....45 F8
Chalcott SL1 ....205 E3
Chalet Cl HP4 ....134 F4
Chalfont & Latimer Sta
HP7 ....166 C8
Chalfont Ave HP6 .....166 D8
Chalfont Cl MK13 .....34 A6
Chalfont Ho HP7 ......166 D7
Chalfont La
Chorleywood WD3 .....167 B4
Maple Cross WD3 .....178 D3
Chalfont Rd
Flackwell Heath HP10 ..185 A8
Ford HP17 ....128 A7
Chalfont Row HP14 ...171 A7
Chalfont Shire Horse Ctr*
HP8 ....178 A7
Chalfont St Giles Inf Sch
HP8 ....177 B7
Chalfont St Giles Jun Sch
HP8 ....177 B7
Chalfont St Peter CE Sch
SL9 ....177 D2
Chalfont St Peter Inf Sch
SL9 ....177 C3
Chalfont Station Rd
HP7 ....166 C7
Chalfont Way HP12 ...172 D3
Chalfonts & Gerrards Cross
Hospl The SL9 ....177 D2
Chalfonts Com Coll The
SL9 ....177 C3
Chalford Flats HP10 ..185 F6
Chalford Way HP19 ...114 F8
Chalgrove Cl SL6 .....203 B6
Chalgrove End HP22 ...116 B1
Chalgrove Rd OX9 ....126 A1
Chalgrove Wlk HP21 ...115 C6
Chalk Farm Rd HP14 ..158 D5
Chalk Hill Chesham HP5 .144 B2
Coleshill HP7 ....164 C3
Windsor SL4 ....210 F6
Chalk Pit La SL1 .....197 B4
Chalkdell Dr MK5 .....45 F4
Chalklands SL8 ....185 A4
Chalkpit La SL7 ....183 B3
Chalkpits The HP10 ...185 E6
Chalkshire Cotts HP17 .130 C4
Chalkshire Rd HP17 ...130 C4
Chalkstream Way HP10 .185 E7
Challacombe MK4 .....46 D2
Challener Rd HP12 ....172 C3
Challenge Ho MK3 .....47 B1
Challow Ct SL6 ....195 D1
Chalmers Ave MK19 ...20 D2
Chaloner Pl HP21 .....115 D6
Chaloner Rd HP21 ....115 D6
Chaloners Hill MK18 ..63 D3
Chalvey Gdns SL1 ....205 E4
Chalvey Gr SL1 ....205 B4
Chalvey Pk SL1 ....205 E4
Chalvey Rd E SL1 ....205 E4
Chalvey Rd W SL1 ....205 D4
Chalwell Ride HP22 ...46 B4
Chamberlain Rd HP19 ..101 B1
Champflower MK4 .....46 D3

Champney Cl SL3 .....212 A4
Champneys Coll of Health &
Beauty HP23 ....133 E6
Chancellors HP7 ....164 E6
Chancellors Cnr HP7 ..164 B5
Chancery Cl MK13 .....34 A6
Chancery Pl SL4 ......210 D7
Chandlers Ct MK6 .....47 C5
Chandlers Quay SL6 ...203 C8
Chandos Cl
Buckingham MK18 .....52 D7
Little Chalfont HP6 ...155 C1
Chandos Ct MK16 ......52 D7
Chandos Mall **7** SL1 .205 F4
Chandos Pl
Milton Keynes MK2 ....58 B8
Wendover HP22 ....131 B4
Chandos Rd MK18 .....52 D8
Channer Dr HP10 ......163 B1
Channory Cl MK4 .....46 A1
Chantry Cl
West Drayton UB7 ....208 D6
Windsor SL4 ....210 A6
Woburn Sands MK17 ...49 A6
Chantry Rd HP19 .....101 C3
Chantry Sch UB7 .....208 E6
Chantry The
1 Aylesbury HP20 ..115 D8
Uxbridge UB8 ....201 F2
Chapel Arches SL6 ....202 F6
Chapel Cl Blackthorn OX25 .81 A3
Little Gaddesden HP4 ..121 D6
Chapel Cotts SL2 ....199 B5
Chapel Crofts HP4 ...134 E6
Chapel Ct SL6 ....202 D4
Chapel Dr HP22 ....117 E5
Chapel End La HP23 ..118 C8
Chapel Farm NN7 .....10 C6
Chapel Fields HP23 ..118 C8
Chapel Hill Soulbury LU7 .69 E3
Speen HP27 ....150 C4
Windsor SL4 ....210 D6
Chapel Ho HP6 ....153 C5
Chapel La Akeley MK18 ..41 F8
Chilton HP18 ....111 B3
Drayton Parslow MK17 ..68 B5
High Wycombe HP12 ...172 C8
Ivinghoe Aston LU7 ...92 A1
Long Marston HP23 ...104 B4
Northall LU6 ....92 A5
Pitch Green HP27 .....138 B3
Rout's Green HP14 ...148 E2
St Leonards HP23 ....132 D3
Stoke Bruerne NN12 ...9 A8
Stoke Mandeville HP22 .116 A1
Stoke Poges SL2 .....199 B5
Thornborough MK18 ...54 B8
Totternhoe LU6 ....92 F8
Turweston NN13 ....38 B7
Walter's Ash HP14 ...161 C7
Wendover HP22 ....131 B4
Whitfield NN13 ....26 D3
Chapel Rd
Flackwell Heath HP10 ..185 A8
Ford HP17 ....128 A7
Chapel Row HP14 ....171 A7
Chapel Sq LU7 ....68 E1
Chapel St
Berkhamsted HP4 .....135 D4
High Wycombe HP13 ...161 D3
Marlow SL7 ....183 E2
Slough SL1 ....205 F4
Tring HP23 ....118 F3
Uxbridge UB8 ....201 C4
Woburn Sands MK17 ...49 B4
Chapels Cl SL1 ....204 A5
Chaplin Gr MK8 ......45 D7
Chaplin Mews **2** SL3 .206 F1
Chapman Ave MK14 ...35 A6
Chapman Cl
Aylesbury HP21 ....115 B6
West Drayton UB7 ....208 F3
Chapman La HP8,HP10 .185 A6
Chapmans Cres HP5 ..144 A2
Chapmans Dr MK19 ....32 B7
Chapmans Lea HP22 ...88 D5
Chappel Mdw HP23 ...119 B6
Chapter MK6 ....47 A5
Chapter Cl UB10 .....201 F5
Chapter Ho MK6 ......47 A5
Chapter Mews SL4 ...210 D7
Charbray Cres MK5 ...46 A4
Chardacre MK8 ....33 E1
Charlbury Rd UB10 ...190 F1
Charles Cl HP21 .....116 B4
Charles Ct SL4 ....210 D7
Charles Dr OX9 ......126 A1
Charles Gdns SL2 ....206 A7
Charles Ho
Henley-on-T RG9 .....191 E3
Windsor SL4 ....210 C6
Charles St
Berkhamsted HP4 .....135 B4
Tring HP23 ....119 A3
Windsor SL4 ....210 D6
Charles Way MK16 ...22 C4
Charlestown Lodge
UB8 ....201 D6
Charlewood Ho MK17 ..49 B3
Charlock Ct MK16 ...21 F4
Charlotte Ave SL2 ...205 F6
Charlotte Cl LU7 ....79 F2
Charlotte Cott SL6 ..203 B8
Charlotte Way **12** SL7 .183 E2
Charlton SL4 ....209 C5
Charlton Cl Slough SL4 .205 B4
Swanbourne MK17 ....66 F3
Charlton Pl **2** SL4 .209 C5
Charlton Row **3** SL4 .209 C5

Charlton Sq **4** SL4 ...209 C5
Charlton Way SL4 ....209 C5
Charlton Wlk **8** SL4 .209 C5
Charmfield Rd HP21 ...116 A5
Charnwood Cl **8** HP13 .173 F5
Charsley Cl HP6 ......166 E8
Charter Dr HP6 ....154 F1
Charter Pl UB8 ....201 D5
Charter Rd SL1 ....204 E6
Chartley Ct MK5 ....46 B4
Chartridge Comb Sch
HP5 ....143 C4
Chartridge Development
UB8 ....201 B3
Chartridge Grange Dr
HP5 ....143 D4
Chartridge Ho **3** HP13 .173 F6
Chartridge La HP5 ....143 F2
Chartridge Park Mobile
Home Pk HP5 ....143 D4
Chartwell Gate HP9 ...175 D2
Chartwell Rd MK16 ...22 E4
Chase Ave MK7 ....48 A4
Chase Cl HP7 ....165 A4
Chase Farm Barns MK17 .56 C4
Chase Park Rd NN7 ....1 A5
Chase The
1 Chesham HP5 ....144 B2
Maidenhead SL6 ....195 D3
Marlow SL7 ....184 A3
Tylers Green HP10 ....163 C1
Chaseport Cl MK46 ....5 D2
Chaseside Cl LU7 ....105 A7
Chatfield SL2 ....205 A8
Chatham Ct **2** SL1 ..206 A3
Chatsworth MK8 ......33 F1
Chatsworth Cl SL6 ...202 C6
Chaucer Cl
Berkhamsted HP4 .....134 F5
Newport Pagnell MK16 ..22 A4
Windsor SL4 ....210 D4
Chaucer Dr HP21 .....115 F6
Chaucer Rd MK3 ......58 A7
Chaucer Way SL1 ....205 F5
Chauntry Cl SL6 .....203 C6
Chauntry Rd SL6 ....203 B6
Chawton Cres MK8 ...33 F1
Cheapside La UB9 ...189 F2
Chearsley Rd HP18 ...125 E7
Cheddington Comb Sch
LU7 ....105 A7
Cheddington La HP23 ..104 C5
Cheddington Rd LU7 .105 C4
Cheddington Sta LU7 ..91 A2
Chelmsford Ct **8** SL4 .210 C5
Chelsea Gn LU7 ......80 D6
Chelsea Ho **6** LU7 ..80 E7
Cheltenham Gdns MK3 .57 D6
Cheney Cl LU7 ....78 B1
Cheney Rd SL4 ....205 B4
Cheney Wlk **8** HP20 .101 F2
Cheneys Wlk MK3 .....47 A2
Chenies Ave HP6 .....166 D8
Chenies Manor Ho*
WD3 ....156 A1
Chenies Par HP7 .....166 C7
Chenies Rd WD3 .....167 D7
Chenies Sch WD3 ....156 B1
Chepping Cl HP10 ....163 A3
Chepping View Prim Sch
HP12 ....172 D3
Chepstow Dr MK3 .....57 D6
Chequers Bridge Cotts
SL0 ....207 C4
Chequers Cl LU7 ....105 C4
Chequers Ct SL6 ....203 D3
Chequers Dr HP16 ...151 C6
Chequers End MK18 ..66 A4
Chequers Hill HP27 ..165 D2
Chequers La
Ibstone HP14,RG9 ....170 A5
North Crawley MK16 ..24 B6
Pitstone LU7 ....105 C5
Prestwood HP16 ......151 C7
Chequers Orch SL0 ..207 F7
Chequers Sq UB8 ....201 C5
Chequers The
Castlethorpe MK19 ....19 F5
Eaton Bray LU6 ....92 F5
Cherington Gate SL6 ..195 B1
Cheriton MK4 ....46 E3
Cheriton Cl SL6 ......203 A7
Cherries The SL2 ....206 A7
Cherry Acre SL9 .....177 D6
Cherry Ave SL3 ....206 D4
Cherry Cl
Flackwell Heath HP10 ..185 B7
Prestwood HP16 ......151 D6
Cherry Cnr HP10 .....185 B8
Cherry Dr HP9 ....175 B4
Cherry Gdns HP23 ...118 F3
Cherry Gr HP15 .....163 C6
Cherry La Amersham HP7 .165 A7
West Drayton UB7 ....208 F2
Woodrow HP7 ....164 D6
Cherry Lane Prim Sch
UB7 ....208 F2
Cherry Leys HP18 ....63 E3
Cherry Orch
Amersham HP6 ....154 E2
Olney MK46 ....6 E4
Prestwood HP16 .....151 C6
Stoke Poges SL2 ....199 A5
West Drayton UB7 ...208 E4
Cherry Orchard Ct
HP13 ....173 E6
Cherry Pit The HP13 ..161 E2

Cherry Rd MK16 ....22 B3
Cherry Rise
Chalfont St Giles HP8 ....177 D8
Flackwell Heath HP10 ....185 B7
Cherry St HP13 ....174 A4
Cherry Tree Ave UB7 ....208 F7
Cherry Tree Cl
Great Kingshill HP15 ....151 D1
Hughenden Valley HP14 ....162 A7
Speen HP27 ....150 B5
Cherry Tree Ho 4 SL7 ....183 D2
Cherry Tree La
Buckland Common HP23 ....133 A3
Fulmer SL3 ....199 F6
Heronsgate WD3 ....167 C1
Lee Common HP16 ....142 E4
Cherry Tree Rd
Beaconsfield HP9 ....175 B1
Chinnor OX39 ....147 C6
Farnham Common SL2 ....198 C5
Cherry Tree Way HP10 ....163 C1
Cherry Tree Wlk
Chesham HP5 ....144 D2
Leighton Buzzard LU7 ....80 E7
Wendover HP22 ....131 A5
Cherry Way
Hazelmere HP15 ....163 A6
Horton SL3 ....212 C4
Cherrycroft Dr HP14 ....161 D6
Cherrytree La
Chalfont St Peter SL9 ....177 D1
Iver Heath SL0 ....201 A4
Cherrywood Cl HP9 ....176 D5
Cherrywood Gdns HP10 ....185 B8
Chervil MK6 ....47 B5
Cherwell Cl
Maidenhead SL6 ....203 A8
Slough SL3 ....212 B8
Cherwell Ho MK3 ....57 E8
Cherwell Rd
Aylesbury HP21 ....115 C6
Bourne End SL8 ....185 B4
Chesham Ave MK13 ....34 C3
Chesham Bois CE Comb Sch HP6 ....154 D4
Chesham Cottage Hospl HP5 ....154 C7
Chesham High Sch HP5 ....144 D1
Chesham La
Chalfont St Peter SL9 ....177 E6
Wendover HP22,HP16 ....141 E8
Chesham Park Com Coll HP5 ....144 A1
Chesham Prep Sch HP5 ....145 A4
Chesham Rd
Amersham HP6 ....154 C2
Ashley Green HP4,HP5 ....144 F8
Bellingdon HP5 ....143 E7
Berkhamsted HP4 ....135 B2
Bovingdon HP3,HP5 ....145 E4
Hyde Heath HP16 ....153 C7
Wigginton HP23 ....133 D7
Chesham Sta HP5 ....154 C8
Cheshire Cotts OX27 ....72 F6
Cheshire Ct 6 SL1 ....206 B4
Cheshire Rise MK3 ....46 E1
Cheslyn Gdns MK14 ....35 A8
Chesney Wold MK6 ....46 F5
Chess Cl Aylesbury HP21 ....115 D3
Latimer HP5 ....155 D3
Chessbury Cl HP5 ....154 A7
Chessbury Rd HP5 ....154 A7
Chessfield Pk HP6 ....166 E8
Chessmount Rise HP5 ....154 D6
Chester Cl MK3 ....57 D7
Chester Ho UB8 ....201 C1
Chester Rd SL1 ....205 D7
Chesterfield Cl HP17 ....114 C5
Chesterfield Cres LU7 ....79 E3
Chesterfield Pl HP19 ....115 B8
Chesterholm MK13 ....33 F5
Chesterton Cl HP5 ....144 B2
Chesterton Gn HP9 ....175 E2
Chestnut Ave
Chesham HP5 ....144 E2
Halton HP22 ....131 D8
High Wycombe HP11 ....173 D5
Slough SL3 ....206 E4
West Drayton UB7 ....208 F6
Chestnut Cl
Amersham HP6 ....154 D2
Aston Clinton HP22 ....117 F5
Chalfont St Peter SL9 ....177 F2
Dagnall HP4 ....107 C5
Maidenhead SL6 ....196 B1
Medmenham SL7 ....193 D7
Milton Keynes MK11 ....32 D5
Monks Risborough HP27 ....139 C5
Newton Longville MK17 ....57 D2
Waddesdon HP18 ....99 A6
Chestnut Cotts MK18 ....52 C7
Chestnut Cres
Aylesbury HP21 ....115 D6
Milton Keynes MK2 ....58 D7
Chestnut Ct HP6 ....154 D2
Chestnut Dr
Berkhamsted HP4 ....135 D3
Windsor SL4 ....209 F3
Chestnut End HP22 ....117 C1
Chestnut Gn NN13 ....26 E4
Chestnut Hill LU7 ....80 D8
Chestnut La
Amersham HP6 ....154 E2
Hazelmere HP15 ....163 B5
Chestnut Lane Sch HP6 ....154 E3
Chestnut Leys MK18 ....63 E3
Chestnut Pk SL6 ....203 E3
Chestnut Rd
Beaconsfield HP9 ....175 B1
Princes Risborough HP27 ....139 C3
Yardley Gobion NN12 ....18 F6
Chestnut Rise LU7 ....80 D8
Chestnut View
Chearsley HP18 ....112 B2
East Claydon MK18 ....74 F7
Chestnut Way
Longwick HP27 ....138 E6
Stoke Mandeville HP22 ....116 A1
Chestnut Wlk SL9 ....177 E3
Chestnuts Comb Sch MK3 ....57 E7
Chestnuts The
Castlethorpe MK19 ....19 F5
Felden HP3 ....146 F7
Uxbridge UB10 ....201 E5
Chestwood Gr UB10 ....201 F5
Chettle Pl NN12 ....18 E2
Chetwode Ave MK10 ....36 B1
Chetwode Cl MK18 ....41 E2
Chetwynd Dr UB10 ....201 F3
Chevalier Gr MK8 ....45 D7
Cheveley Gdns SL1 ....197 C3
Cheviot Cl
High Wycombe HP13 ....161 E1
Leighton Buzzard LU7 ....80 C8
Maidenhead SL6 ....203 B6
Cheviot Rd SL3 ....207 A1
Cheyne Cl
Amersham HP6 ....154 D3
Buckingham MK18 ....41 F1
Gerrards Cross SL9 ....188 E3
Pitstone LU7 ....105 D4
Cheyne Wlk HP5 ....154 D8
Chicheley Hall MK16 ....23 D8
Chicheley Hill MK16 ....23 A8
Chicheley Rd MK16 ....23 E7
Chicheley St MK16 ....22 E4
Chichester Cl HP13 ....173 D6
Chichester Ct SL1 ....206 A4
Chichester Row HP6 ....154 D2
Chicksands Ave MK10 ....36 A2
Chievely Ct MK4 ....46 C1
Chilcote La HP7 ....166 A8
Childs Way MK4,MK5,MK6, MK10 ....46 C7
Chillery Leys MK15 ....35 E7
Chillingham Ct MK5 ....46 A4
Chiltern Ave
Amersham HP6 ....154 D1
Edlesborough LU6 ....92 E3
High Wycombe HP12 ....172 D6
Stone HP17 ....114 D5
Chiltern Brewery* HP17 ....130 C5
Chiltern Bsns Village UB8 ....201 B3
Chiltern Cl
Berkhamsted HP4 ....134 F5
Princes Risborough HP27 ....139 A3
Stone HP17 ....114 D5
Wendover HP22 ....131 B5
Chiltern Cnr HP4 ....135 A5
Chiltern Commerce Ctr HP5 ....144 A2
Chiltern Cotts
Buckland Common HP23 ....133 A2
Ibstone HP14 ....169 D7
Chiltern Court Mews SL4 ....210 B6
Chiltern Ct
Amersham HP6 ....154 C2
Chesham HP5 ....144 A2
5 High Wycombe HP12 ....172 E7
Wendover HP22 ....131 B4
Windsor SL4 ....210 B6
Winslow MK18 ....65 F3
Chiltern Dr WD3 ....167 F2
Chiltern Gate Sch HP12 ....172 E4
Chiltern Gn HP10 ....185 A8
Chiltern Hill SL9 ....177 E2
Chiltern Hills Rd HP9 ....175 C2
Chiltern Ho HP5 ....154 C7
Chiltern Hospl The HP16 ....152 C4
Chiltern Hts HP7 ....166 A8
Chiltern Manor Pk HP16 ....152 A7
Chiltern Open Air Mus* HP8 ....167 A1
Chiltern Par HP6 ....154 C2
Chiltern Park Ave HP4 ....135 A6
Chiltern Rd
Amersham HP6 ....154 B4
Ballinger Common HP16 ....142 E3
Burnham SL1 ....204 B8
Maidenhead SL6 ....203 B6
Marlow SL7 ....183 C2
Wendover HP22 ....131 B5
Wingrave HP22 ....89 A3
Chiltern Ridge HP14 ....158 C4
Chiltern Sculpture Trail* OX49 ....157 D4
Chiltern St HP21 ....115 E6
Chiltern View
Berkhamsted HP4 ....134 F7
Saunderton HP14 ....149 C1
Chiltern View Rd UB8 ....201 D3
Chiltern Villas HP23 ....118 E2
Chiltern Way
Aston Clinton HP22 ....117 F2
Tring HP23 ....119 C5
Chilterns
Berkhamsted HP4 ....134 F6
World's End HP22 ....130 F7
Chilterns Cl HP10 ....185 B7
Chilterns Pk SL8 ....185 B5
Chilterns The HP13 ....173 A7
Chilton Cl
Holmer Green HP15 ....163 C7
Tylers Green HP10 ....163 C2
Chilton Ct SL6 ....204 C7
Chilton Pl HP20 ....101 E1
Chilton Rd
Chearsley HP18 ....112 A2
Chesham HP5 ....144 C2
Long Crendon HP18 ....125 C7
Chilwick Rd SL2 ....197 F1
Chimes Sh Ctr The UB8 ....201 D5
Chimes The HP12 ....172 E6
Chimney La HP10 ....185 E8
Chinalls Cl MK18 ....50 D6
Chingle Croft MK4 ....46 C2
Chinneck Ho HP4 ....135 C4
Chinnor & Princes Risborough Rly Icknield Line* OX39 ....147 E7
Chinnor Hill OX39 ....147 E4
Chinnor Hill Nature Reserve* OX39 ....147 F5
Chinnor Rd
Bledlow HP27 ....138 A2
Bledlow Ridge HP14 ....148 C3
Chinnor OX39 ....147 A4
Chinnor Sta* OX39 ....147 D5
Chippendale Cl HP13 ....162 D1
Chippendale Waye UB8 ....201 D5
Chippenham Dr MK10 ....36 C1
Chipperfield Cl MK13 ....34 A7
Chipperfield Rd HP3 ....146 C3
Chipping Vale MK4 ....46 C2
Chipstead SL9 ....177 C2
Chirbury Cl MK10 ....35 F1
Chislehampton MK15 ....35 C3
Chiswick Cl MK4 ....45 F2
Chiswick Lodge 6 SL7 ....183 D2
Choke La SL6 ....195 B4
Cholesbury La HP23 ....133 A2
Cholesbury Rd HP23 ....133 D5
Chorley Rd HP14 ....160 E3
Chorleywood Bottom WD3 ....167 D4
Chorleywood Ho WD3 ....167 E6
Chorleywood House Dr WD3 ....167 E6
Chorleywood Montessori Sch The WD3 ....167 E7
Chorleywood Prim Sch WD3 ....167 C3
Chorleywood Sta WD3 ....167 D5
Chrislaine Cl TW19 ....213 D1
Christ the King RC Fst Sch TW19 ....213 D1
Christchurch CE Sch WD3 ....167 F6
Christchurch Gr MK12 ....33 B6
Christchurch Ho 15 HP23 ....119 A3
Christchurch Rd HP23 ....118 F4
Christian Ct MK15 ....35 D7
Christian Smith Ho SL6 ....202 A1
Christian Sq 4 SL4 ....210 C6
Christie Cl MK16 ....22 A5
Christies Ct 2 HP13 ....173 B7
Christine Ho 6 MK2 ....58 C8
Christmas La SL2 ....187 C1
Christopher Cl HP14 ....161 D7
Christopher Ho 3 SL2 ....198 C7
Church Ave RG9 ....191 E2
Church Cl
Aston Clinton HP22 ....117 D5
Cuddington HP18 ....112 F3
Eton SL4 ....210 D8
Maidenhead SL6 ....202 D6
Maids Moreton MK18 ....41 F3
Uxbridge UB8 ....201 B3
West Drayton UB7 ....208 E3
Wicken MK19 ....31 B3
Church Cotts SL6 ....196 E2
Church Croft LU6 ....92 E3
Church Ct HP13 ....162 D1
Church Dr SL6 ....203 C4
Church End Adstock MK18 ....53 F1
Bledlow HP27 ....138 B1
Drayton Parslow MK17 ....68 B5
Edlesborough LU6 ....92 E3
Haddenham HP17 ....127 A5
Hillesden MK18 ....63 B6
Leckhampstead MK18 ....42 D8
Newton Longville MK17 ....57 D3
Potterspury NN12 ....18 E3
Sherington MK16 ....14 A2
Syresham NN13 ....27 C8
Wavendon MK17 ....48 E7
Church End Cotts WD3 ....156 F1
Church End Farm LU6 ....93 B7
Church End Rd MK5 ....46 A4
Church Farm Cl HP22 ....102 B3
Church Farm Cres MK14 ....34 E8
Church Farm Ho HP8 ....177 C7
Church Farm La HP23 ....104 F3
Church Farm Trail* HP17 ....127 B5
Church Gn
Long Crendon HP18 ....125 D7
Totternhoe LU6 ....93 B7
Church Gr
Little Chalfont HP6 ....166 E8
Slough SL3 ....206 C8
Church Green Rd MK3 ....58 A8
Church Headland La HP22 ....87 A6
Church Hill Akeley MK18 ....41 F8
Aspley Guise MK17 ....49 E5
Church Hill *continued*
Cheddington LU7 ....105 A8
Ellesborough HP17 ....130 B2
Milton Keynes MK8 ....33 F2
Pishill RG9 ....179 D8
South Harefield UB9 ....190 C8
Whaddon MK17 ....45 B1
Church Holt The SL2 ....187 E3
Church La Alderton NN12 ....9 A2
Aston Clinton HP22 ....117 D4
Berkhamsted HP4 ....135 C4
Bisham SL7 ....194 D7
Bledlow Ridge HP14 ....159 F8
Bovingdon HP3 ....146 B4
Bray SL6 ....203 C4
Chalfont St Peter SL9 ....177 D2
Chearsley HP18 ....112 B1
Cheddington LU7 ....105 A8
Chinnor OX39 ....147 D6
Clifton Reynes MK46 ....7 C3
Cryers Hill HP15 ....162 C4
Deanshanger MK19 ....31 E4
Eaton Bray LU6 ....92 E6
Edgcott HP18 ....72 F2
Emberton MK46 ....13 F7
Grafton Regis NN12 ....9 D2
Granborough MK18 ....75 F6
Great Horwood MK17 ....55 A3
Great Kimble HP17 ....129 E1
Great Missenden HP16 ....152 B7
Hastoe HP23 ....133 A7
Horton-cum-S OX33 ....108 A5
Lacey Green HP27 ....149 E4
Lillingstone Lovell MK18 ....30 A6
Ludgershall HP18 ....96 C7
Marsworth HP23 ....104 F1
Milton Keynes MK5 ....46 B8
Mixbury NN13 ....38 D1
Mursley MK17 ....67 D5
Newport Pagnell MK16 ....22 D7
Oving HP22 ....86 C7
Padbury MK18 ....53 C2
Potterspury NN12 ....18 E3
Princes Risborough HP27 ....139 B4
Radnage HP14 ....159 D8
Sarratt WD3 ....156 F1
Slough SL2,SL3 ....206 C8
Soulbury LU7 ....69 E2
Stoke Bruerne NN12 ....9 A8
Stoke Goldington MK16 ....12 A7
Stoke Poges SL2 ....198 F2
Thornborough MK18 ....54 A8
Tingewick MK18 ....51 B7
Upper Winchendon HP18 ....99 B1
Uxbridge UB8 ....201 B3
Walter's Ash HP14 ....161 E6
Walton MK7 ....47 F6
Wendover HP22 ....131 C3
West Wycombe HP14 ....161 A2
Weston Turville HP22 ....116 F1
Whaddon MK17 ....45 B1
Whitchurch HP22 ....87 A6
Wicken MK19 ....31 B3
8 Windsor SL4 ....210 D6
Yardley Hastings NN7 ....1 B7
Church Lees MK14 ....21 D1
Church Pas MK16 ....22 D4
Church Path
Cheddington LU7 ....91 A1
Cublington LU7 ....78 B1
Lane End HP14 ....171 B4
Prestwood HP16 ....151 D5
Stokenchurch HP14 ....158 D5
Church Piece HP18 ....112 B2
Church Rd
Aspley Heath MK17 ....49 B3
Bow Brickhill MK17 ....48 D1
Brackley NN13 ....38 A7
Chinnor OX39 ....147 D6
Cookham Dean SL6 ....195 B6
Farnham Royal SL2 ....198 C2
Ickford HP18 ....123 F3
Iver Heath SL0 ....200 C3
Ivinghoe LU7 ....105 F5
Lane End HP14 ....171 B3
Leighton Buzzard LU7 ....80 E6
Lewknor OX49 ....157 B8
Little Gaddesden HP4 ....121 D8
Little Marlow SL7 ....184 C5
Maidenhead SL6 ....203 B5
Old Windsor SL4 ....211 B2
Penn HP10 ....174 E7
Pitstone LU7 ....105 E3
Seer Green HP9 ....176 D4
Sherington MK16 ....13 F2
Slapton LU7 ....91 D6
South Harefield UB9 ....190 C8
Stoke Hammond MK17 ....69 D8
Stokenchurch HP14 ....158 D5
Thame OX9 ....125 E1
Totternhoe LU6 ....93 B6
Tylers Green HP10 ....174 C8
Uxbridge UB8 ....201 D1
West Drayton UB7 ....208 E3
Church Row SL3 ....199 D8
Church Sq
7 High Wycombe HP11 ....173 B7
Leighton Buzzard LU7 ....80 F6
Church St
Amersham HP7 ....165 B7
Aspley Guise MK17 ....49 E5
16 Aylesbury HP20 ....115 D8
Bovingdon HP3 ....146 B4
Brill HP18 ....110 B8
Buckingham MK18 ....52 C8
Burnham SL1 ....197 C1
Chesham HP5 ....154 B7
Gawcott MK18 ....52 A4
Church St *continued*
Great Missenden HP16 ....152 B7
Henley-on-T RG9 ....191 D1
High Wycombe HP11 ....173 B7
Little Horwood MK17 ....55 E2
Maids Moreton MK18 ....41 F3
Marsh Gibbon OX27 ....71 F3
Milton Keynes,Fenny Stratford MK2 ....47 E1
Milton Keynes,New Bradwell MK13 ....33 F7
Milton Keynes,Stony Stratford MK11 ....32 D5
Milton Keynes,Wolverton MK12 ....33 D7
North Marston MK18 ....76 B2
Olney MK46 ....7 A3
Princes Risborough HP27 ....139 B3
Quainton HP22 ....85 B5
Slough,Chalvey SL1 ....205 D4
Slough,Upton Park SL1 ....205 F4
Stokenchurch HP14 ....158 D5
Twyford MK18 ....62 C2
6 Windsor SL4 ....210 D6
Wing LU7 ....79 E2
Wingrave HP22 ....89 B2
Winslow MK18 ....65 F4
Church Terr Turvey MK43 ....8 E5
Windsor SL4 ....209 E5
Church View
Brackley NN13 ....38 A7
Edlesborough LU6 ....92 D3
Halton HP22 ....117 C1
Long Marston HP23 ....104 A4
Newport Pagnell MK16 ....22 D4
9 Slough SL1 ....206 A3
Steeple Claydon MK18 ....63 E2
Church View Ct LU7 ....80 E6
Church Views SL6 ....202 F8
Church Way
East Claydon MK18 ....74 F8
Stone HP17 ....114 C5
Church Wlk
Milton Keynes MK3 ....57 F7
North Crawley MK16 ....24 B6
Weston Turville HP22 ....116 F1
Wing LU7 ....79 E2
Winslow MK18 ....65 F4
Church Yd HP23 ....119 A3
Churchfield Mews SL2 ....206 A7
Churchfield Rd SL9 ....177 D2
Churchgates 3 HP4 ....135 C4
Churchill Ave HP21 ....115 D5
Churchill Cl HP10 ....185 B7
Churchill Ct 1 HP21 ....115 E7
Churchill Dr
Beaconsfield HP9 ....175 C5
Marlow SL7 ....183 F4
Churchill Ho UB7 ....208 D6
Churchill Rd SL3 ....206 F2
Churchmead CE Sch SL3 ....211 B7
Churchmere Wlk HP21 ....115 C6
Churchside HP15 ....163 D7
Churchway HP17 ....127 A6
Chyne The SL9 ....188 F6
Cinnamon Cl SL4 ....209 F6
Cinnamon Gr MK7 ....48 A5
Cippenham Cl SL1 ....204 F6
Cippenham Inf Sch SL1 ....204 D6
Cippenham Jun Sch SL1 ....204 D6
Cippenham La SL1 ....205 B5
City Rd HP14 ....159 D6
Clailey Ct MK11 ....32 F5
Claires Court Sch SL6 ....196 B1
Clammas Way UB8 ....208 D8
Clapham Pl MK13 ....34 C2
Clappers Mdw SL6 ....196 B1
Clappins La Naphill HP14 ....150 D1
Walter's Ash HP14 ....161 C8
Clapton App HP10 ....185 D8
Clare Croft MK10 ....36 A3
Clare Dr SL2 ....198 B8
Clare Pk HP7 ....165 E7
Clare Rd Maidenhead SL6 ....202 D6
Prestwood HP16 ....151 C6
Slough SL6 ....204 C7
Stanwell TW19 ....213 E1
Clarefield Cl SL6 ....195 B1
Clarefield Dr SL6 ....195 A1
Clarefield Rd SL6 ....195 A1
Claremont SL3 ....212 D6
Claremont Ave MK11 ....32 E4
Claremont Cl HP21 ....115 F5
Claremont Gdns SL7 ....183 E2
Claremont Rd
Marlow SL7 ....183 E2
Windsor SL4 ....210 C5
Clarence Cres SL4 ....210 C6
Clarence Ct
9 High Wycombe HP13 ....173 B7
Maidenhead SL6 ....202 E8
Windsor SL4 ....210 B6
Clarence Ho MK9 ....34 C2
Clarence Rd
Berkhamsted HP4 ....135 C4
Henley-on-T RG9 ....191 D2
Milton Keynes MK11 ....32 E5
Windsor SL4 ....210 B6
Clarendon Copse SL6 ....202 D6
Clarendon Ct Slough SL2 ....206 B6
Windsor SL4 ....210 B6
Clarendon Dr
Milton Keynes MK8 ....33 F2

Clarendon Dr continued
Thame OX9 ....126 A1
Clarendon Rd
High Wycombe HP13 ...173 E5
Prestwood HP16 ....151 B6
Claridge Dr MK10 ....36 A2
Clarke Ct HP20 ....101 F2
Clarke Dr HP13 ....174 A6
Clarke Rd MK1 ....47 D4
Clarke Wlk [2] HP20 ....101 F2
Clarke's Spring HP23 ...119 F5
Clarkes Dr UB8 ....208 E8
Clarkes Field HP18 ....110 B8
Clarks Cotts HP16 .....151 C7
Classon Cl UB7 ....208 E4
Clauds Cl HP15 ....163 A5
Claverton Cl HP21 ....146 A3
Clay Acre HP5 ....144 D1
Clay Cl HP10 ....185 B8
Clay Hill MK8 ....33 E2
Clay La Calvert OX27 ....73 A5
Marlow Bottom SL7 ....172 A2
Wendover HP22 ....131 C5
Clay St HP7,HP9 ....175 C7
Claycots Sch SL2 ....198 A1
Claycutters MK18 ....66 A4
Claydon Cl HP21 ....115 D6
Claydon Ct HP12 ....172 E4
Claydon End SL9 ....188 E8
Claydon Ho* MK18 ....74 C7
Claydon La SL9 ....188 E8
Claydon Path HP21 ....115 E3
Claydon Rd HP27 ......138 D7
Clayfield Rd HP22 .....131 C8
Clayfields HP10 ....163 C2
Clayhall La SL4 ....210 F2
Clayhill
Marlow Bottom SL7 .....172 A2
Wigginton HP23 ....133 E7
Claymoor Pk SL7 ......172 A2
Clays La MK17 ....55 E2
Clays The HP17 ....127 A7
Clayton Ct SL3 ....207 A3
Clayton Gate MK14 ......35 A8
Clayton Way UB8 ......201 D1
Clayton Wlk HP7 ......166 C8
Claytons Comb Sch SL8 185 A5
Claytons Mdw SL8 .....185 B8
Clearbrook Cl HP13 ....174 B4
Cleares Pasture SL1 ...197 B2
Cleavers OX39 ....147 B6
Cleavers Ave MK14 ......34 E3
Cleeve Cres MK3 ....47 A2
Clegg Sq MK5 ....46 B5
Cleland Rd SL4 ....177 D1
Clement Pl [5] HP23 ...119 A3
Clementi Ave HP15 ....163 D7
Clementi Cl [3] SL1 ...206 B4
Clements La OX27 ....71 F2
Clements Rd
Chorleywood WD3 ......167 D4
Henley-on-T RG9 ......191 C3
Clerkenwell Cotts HP17 .126 F5
Clerkenwell Pl MK6 .....35 B2
Clevehurst Cl SL2 .....199 A6
Cleveland MK13 ....34 B6
Cleveland Cl
Maidenhead SL6 ....203 B6
Wooburn Green HP10 ...185 E8
Cleveland Dr LU7 ....80 C8
Cleveland Pk
Aylesbury HP20 ....101 F3
Stanwell TW19 ....213 E1
Cleveland Pl [3] HP20 .101 F3
Cleveland Rd
Aylesbury HP20 ....101 E3
Uxbridge UB8 ....201 D2
Cleves Ct SL4 ....209 F4
Clewer Ave SL4 ....210 A5
Clewer Court Rd SL4 ..210 B7
Clewer Fields SL4 ....210 C6
Clewer Green CE Fst Sch
SL4 ....210 A4
Clewer Hill Rd SL4 ...209 F4
Clewer New Town SL4 .210 A5
Clewer Pk SL4 ....210 A7
Clickers Yd MK46 ....6 F4
Clifden Rd HP18 ......123 E5
Clifford Ave MK2 ....55 D7
Clifford Rd HP27 .....139 B3
Cliffords Way SL18 ...185 B5
Clifton Cl SL6 ....203 A4
Clifton Ct
High Wycombe HP11 ....172 E4
Olney MK46 ....7 A3
[1] Stanwell TW19 ....213 E1
Clifton Gn HP19 ......101 B2
Clifton Lawns HP6 ....154 C4
Clifton Lodge
Eton Wick SL4 ....205 A1
[1] Slough SL1 ....205 D4
Clifton Moor MK5 ....45 D5
Clifton Rd
Amersham HP6 ....154 C4
Newton Blossomville MK43 ..8 A4
[3] Slough SL1 ....205 F4
Clifton Rise SL4 .....209 D6
Cline Ct MK8 ....45 E6
Clinkard Pl HP14 .....171 A4
Clinton Cres HP21 ....116 A4
Clive Ct SL1 ....205 D4
Cliveden* SL6 ....196 E7
Cliveden Gate SL1 ....197 B3
Cliveden Mead SL6 ....196 C2

Cliveden Office Village
HP12 ....172 E4
Cliveden Rd SL6 ......196 E4
Clivemont Rd SL6 .....202 F8
Clock Ho The MK17 .....59 D6
Clockhouse Mews WD3 .167 E6
Cloebury Paddock MK15 .35 C3
Cloister Garth HP4 ...135 C4
Cloisters The
High Wycombe HP13 ...162 D2
Slough SL1 ....205 D4
Clonmel Way SL1 ......197 A8
Close The Akeley MK18 ..92 A8
Ashendon HP18 ....97 F1
Bierton HP22 ....102 A4
Bourne End SL8 ......185 A6
Great Horwood MK17 ...55 B3
Hardmead MK16 ....15 D4
Hardwick HP22 ....87 B3
Iver Heath SL0 ....200 C2
Lathbury MK16 ....22 D7
Milton Keynes,Bradwell
MK13 ....34 A4
Milton Keynes,The Green
MK6 ....47 D7
Newton Blossomville MK43 ..7 F3
Ravenstone MK46 ......5 F2
Slough SL1 ....205 D4
Weston Underwood MK46 ..6 A1
Closes The HP17 ....127 A7
Cloudberry MK7 ....48 A6
Cloutsham Cl MK4 ......46 D3
Clover Cl MK5 ....46 B8
Clover End MK18 ....52 C7
Clover La HP21 ....115 E5
Club Cotts MK17 ....49 B4
Cluny Ct MK7 ....48 D6
Clyde Pl MK3 ....46 E1
Clydesdale Pl MK14 ...34 F4
Coach Ho The
Loudwater HP11 ....174 A4
Wooburn Green HP10 ..185 E6
Coach Ride SL7 ....183 D4
Coach Yd MK17 ....18 E3
Coachmaker Ct MK14 ...34 F6
Coachman's Lodge SL4 210 D5
Coalmans Way SL1 ....204 A8
Coat Wicks HP9 ......176 C4
Coaters La HP10 .....185 E7
Coates La HP13 ......162 A1
Cobb Cl SL3 ....211 D6
Cobb Hall Rd MK17 ....57 C3
Cobb Rd HP4 ....134 F4
Cobbetts Mount MK18 ..63 D2
Cobbetts Ride HP23 ..118 F3
Cobblers Cl SL2 .....198 B3
Cobblers Wick HP27 ...89 B3
Cobblershill La HP16 .141 B4
Cobbs Gdn MK46 ....6 F4
Cobden Cl UB8 ....201 C4
Coberley La MK15 .....35 B6
Cobham Cl
Buckingham MK18 ....41 C1
Slough SL1 ....204 F5
Cochran Cl MK8 ....45 E7
Cochrane Ho UB8 .....201 C4
Cock Gr HP4 ....134 D4
Cock La HP10 ....174 A6
Cockerell Gr MK5 ......46 C5
Cockett Rd SL3 ......206 E3
Cockpit Cl HP15 .....151 E1
Cockpit Rd HP15 ....162 D8
Coddimoor La MK17 ....56 B7
Codmore Cres HP5 ....144 E1
Codmore Cross HP5 ..144 D1
Codmore Wood Rd HP5 .155 D6
Coe Spur SL1 ....205 B3
Coffee Hall Rdbt MK6 ..47 B6
Cofferidge Cl MK11 ....32 D5
Coftards SL2 ....206 C7
Cogan Cl MK46 ....45 E7
Cogdells Cl HP5 .....143 B4
Cogdells La HP5 .....143 B4
Coggeshall Gr MK7 ....48 C7
Coin Cl MK10 ....35 F3
Coke's Farm La HP8 ..166 B6
Coke's La HP8 ......166 B6
Cokers Ct [3] SL6 ...185 A4
Colborne Rd HP13 ....173 D8
Colchester Ct MK3 ....57 E7
Colchester Wlk MK3 ...57 E7
Cold Grove Cotts SL6 ..196 E2
Cold Harbour CE Comb Sch
MK3 ....46 F3
Coldeaton La MK4 .....46 B3
Coldharbour HP22 ....131 C4
Coldharbour Way HP19 .115 A7
Coldmoorholme La SL8 .184 E4
Coldmoreham Yd 165 A8
Cole Rd HP21 ....115 C5
Coleheath Bottom
HP27 ....150 C5
Colenorton Cres SL4 .204 E2
Coleridge Cl
Milton Keynes MK3 ....58 A7
Newport Pagnell MK16 .21 F4
Coleridge Cres SL3 ..212 E6
Coleridge Dr SL7 ....208 F2
Coles Hill HP18 ......111 B3
Colesbourne Dr MK15 ..35 B6
Coleshill CE Inf Sch
HP7 ....164 F3
Coleshill Ho HP7 ....165 A4
Coleshill La HP7 .....164 D2
Coleshill Pl MK13 .....34 C3
Colet Rd HP22 ....131 C5
Colgrain St MK9 ....35 A4
Colham Ave UB7 .....208 E5

Colham Mill Rd UB7 ...208 D5
Colham Rd UB8 ......201 F1
Colin Way SL1 ....205 B3
Colindale St MK9 ......35 E1
Colinswood SL2 ......187 B1
College Ave
Maidenhead SL6 .....202 E7
Slough SL1 ....205 E8
College Bsns Pk HP22 .103 C1
College Cl OX33 .....122 C1
College Cres
Oakley HP18 ....109 E4
Windsor SL4 ....210 B5
College Glen SL6 ....202 D7
College Lake Wildlife Ctr*
HP23 ....105 C1
College Rd
Aston Clinton HP22 ...117 C7
Cranfield MK43 ....24 E2
Maidenhead SL6 .....202 E7
Slough SL1 ....204 F5
College Rise SL6 ....202 D7
College The OX27 .....71 F3
Colley Hill MK13 ......34 A4
Colley Hill La SL2 ....187 F1
Colley Ho UB8 ....201 D4
Colleyland WD3 ......167 D5
Collier Cl SL6 ....195 F1
Collings Wlk HP16 ...151 C5
Collingwood Cl HP13 .174 A6
Collins Ho [2] HP11 ...173 A7
Collins Wlk MK16 ......22 A4
Collinswood Rd SL2 ..187 B2
Collum Green Rd SL2 .187 E1
Collyer Rd HP14 .....158 E4
Coln Cl SL6 ....202 F8
Coln Trad Est SL3 ....212 F6
Colnbrook By-Pass
Colnbrook SL3 ....212 D7
Harmondsworth UB7 ..213 C7
Colnbrook CE Prim Sch
SL3 ....212 D6
Colnbrook Ct SL3 ....212 F6
Colndale Rd SL3 .....212 E5
Colne MK6 ....47 D6
Colne Ave SL4 ......208 C4
Colne Bank SL3 ......212 C4
Colne Orch SL0 .....207 F6
Colne Park Cvn Site
UB7 ....208 C2
Colne Rd HP18 ......173 F7
Colne Reach TW19 ...212 F2
Colne Valley Park Visitor
Ctr* UB9 ....190 B1
Colnedale Rd UB8 ...200 E1
Colonial Rd [1] SL1 ..206 A4
Colonnade SL6 ......203 A7
Colsons Way MK46 .....6 F5
Colston Bassett MK4 ..46 C1
Colston Ct SL9 ......188 E5
Coltman Ave HP18 ...125 C6
Colts Holm Rd MK12 ...33 C8
Coltsfoot Dr UB7 ....208 E7
Coltsfoot Pl MK14 .....34 D3
Columbia Pl MK9 ......35 A3
Columbine Rd HP15 ..162 F6
Colville Ct HP13 .....152 B7
Colville Rd HP11 ....172 F6
Combe Martin MK4 .....46 D3
Combe Rise HP22 ....172 B7
Combermere Cl SL4 ..210 B5
Comerford Way MK18 ..66 A5
Comfrey Cl MK7 ....48 A5
Comfrey The [2] HP19 .101 E4
Common Field HP21 ..119 D1
Common Gate Rd WD3 .167 E4
Common La Eton SL4 ..205 D1
Hedgerley SL1 ....186 D1
Milton Keynes MK5 ....46 C8
Common Rd
Chorleywood WD3 ....167 D5
Dagnall LU6 ....107 F3
Dorney SL4 ....204 E4
Eton Wick SL4 ....205 A2
Flackwell Heath HP10 .185 B8
Great Kingshill HP15 ..151 D1
Slough SL3 ....207 A1
Common The 5 D1
Common The
Berkhamsted HP4 ....135 F6
Chipperfield WD4 ....156 F7
Flackwell Heath HP10 ..185 B8
Great Kingshill HP15 ..151 D1
Holmer Green HP15 ...163 D7
Stokenchurch HP14 ..158 E5
Common Wood SL2 ...198 C8
Commonside HP15 ....161 E3
Como Rd HP20 ......116 B8
Compass Point MK4 ..134 E6
Compton Ct
Moulsoe MK16 ....36 D8
Slough SL1 ....204 E7
Compton Dr SL6 ....202 A8
Concorde Cl UB10 ...201 E3
Concorde Rd SL6 ....202 D4
Concorde Way SL1 ...205 D4
Concourse The [6] MK2 .58 C8
Concrete Cows* SL4 ...33 F4
Condor Cl MK6 ....47 A8
Conduit La SL3 ......206 E1
Conegar Ct SL1 .....205 E5
Conegra Ct [5] HP13 .173 B7

Conegra Rd HP13 .....173 C7
Coneygere MK46 ....7 A3
Congreve MK6 ....47 D5
Conifer Rise HP12 ...172 E6
Conifers The SL6 ....202 A8
Conigre OX39 ....147 B6
Coningsby Cl SL6 ....202 D3
Coningsby Ct HP13 ..173 B8
Coningsby Rd HP13 ..162 B1
Coniston Cres SL1 ...204 C8
Coniston Gn HP20 ...101 D3
Coniston Rd LU7 ......80 C7
Coniston Way MK2 ....58 D6
Conkers SL6 ....203 B8
Connaught Cl SL6 ...195 E1
Connaught Gdns HP4 .134 F7
Connaught Rd
Aylesbury HP21 ......116 C8
[3] Slough SL1 ......204 F5
Conniburrow Bvd MK14 ..34 E4
Conniston Cl SL7 ....183 B2
Conought Ho RG9 ...191 E3
Consort Way UB9 ...189 F6
Constable Cl MK14 ....34 F7
Constable Pl HP19 ...100 F2
Constable's Croft OX25 ..94 A7
Constantine Pl UB10 .201 F4
Constantine Way HP13 ..33 F5
Convent Ct HP23 ....118 F3
Convent Rd SL4 ......210 A5
Conway Cl
Aylesbury HP21 ......115 F7
Loudwater HP10 .....174 C2
Milton Keynes MK3 ....57 F8
Conway Cres MK3 .....57 E8
Conway Ct SL9 ......189 B3
Conway Ho HP13 ....173 F7
Conway Rd SL6 ......204 B7
Cook Cl MK7 ....48 A8
Cook's Mdw LU6 ......92 E4
Cookfield Cl LU6 .....93 E8
Cookham Ct HP6 ....154 E1
Cookham Dean Bottom
SL6 ....195 C8
Cookham Dean CE Prim Sch
SL6 ....195 B7
Cookham Lodge [1] SL6 ..202 F6
Cookham Rd SL6 ....195 F1
Cookham Rise Prim Sch
SL6 ....195 E6
Cookham Sta SL6 ....195 F7
Cooks Cl NN7 ....9 F8
Cooks Cl MK19 ....67 E6
Cooks Rd HP19 .....114 F8
Cookshall La HP12 ...161 A2
Coombe Ave HP22 ...131 B4
Coombe Cl HP22 ....116 C2
Coombe Dr LU6 ....93 E7
Coombe Gdns
Berkhamsted HP4 ....134 F5
Hughenden Valley HP14 .162 A6
Coombe Hill Ct SL4 ..209 D4
Coombe Rd
Aylesbury HP19 .....100 F1
Walter's Ash HP14 ...161 F6
Coombe Vale SL9 ...188 E3
Cooper Rd RG9 .....191 D3
Cooper Way
Berkhamsted HP4 ....135 D4
Slough SL1 ....205 B3
Cooper's Court Rd
HP14 ....158 D5
Cooper's Yd HP20 ...101 D1
Coopers Ct MK16 ......22 C4
Coopers Mews MK14 ..34 F6
Coopers Row SL0 ...200 D1
Coote La MK18 ....52 E7
Cope Ct SL6 ....202 D7
Copeland Cl MK7 .....48 C5
Copes Haven MK5 ....46 B3
Copes Rd HP15 .....151 E1
Copes Shroves HP15 .162 F5
Copmans Wick WD3 ..167 D4
Copners Dr HP15 ....163 C6
Copners Way HP15 ..163 B6
Copper Beech Cl
Felden HP3 ....146 F8
Windsor SL4 ....209 D6
Copper Ridge SL9 ...177 F5
Copperfield Terr SL2 .206 B6
Copperfields
Beaconsfield HP9 ....175 E5
High Wycombe HP12 ..161 B1
Copperkins Gr HP6 ..154 B3
Copperkins La HP6 ..154 A3
Coppermill La WD3 ..178 F3
Coppermill Rd TW19 .212 B2
Coppice Cl HP20 ....102 A2
Coppice Farm Pk Cvn Site
HP23 ....132 D3
Coppice Farm Rd HP10 .163 C2
Coppice The
Great Kingshill HP15 ..151 E1
High Wycombe HP12 ..172 B4
Seer Green HP9 .....176 D4
Stokenchurch HP14 ..158 E5
Walter's Ash HP14 ...161 B8
West Drayton UB7 ...208 E7
Wigginton HP23 .....119 C1

Copse Cl continued
Slough SL1 ....204 F5
West Drayton UB7 ...208 D3
Copse Gate MK18 ......66 A4
Copse La HP9 ....176 E3
Copse The
Amersham HP7 ......154 C1
Beaconsfield HP9 ...175 C4
Copse Way HP5 .....144 A4
Copse Wood SL0 ....200 D4
Copthall Cl SL9 .....177 F3
Copthall Cnr SL9 ...177 E3
Copthall Ho SL6 ....203 A7
Copthall La SL9 .....177 E3
Copthorn Cl SL6 ....202 A4
Copthorne Pl MK7 ....48 B8
Copyground Ct HP12 .172 E7
Copyground La HP12 .172 E7
Coral Cl LU6 ....92 E6
Coram Cl HP4 ....135 C3
Corbet Rdbt LU7 ......80 D8
Corbet Sq LU7 ....80 D8
Corbett Cl MK15 ......35 D7
Cordons Cl SL9 .....177 D2
Cordwainer Ct MK14 ...34 F6
Cordwallis Bsns Pk SL6 .195 E1
Cordwallis Est SL6 ..202 F8
Cordwallis Rd SL6 ..202 E8
Cordwallis St SL6 ...202 E8
Cores End Rd SL8 ...185 B3
Corfe Cl HP21 ....115 E4
Corfe Cres MK3 ....57 F8
Corfe Gdns SL1 .....205 A6
Corfe Pl SL6 ....202 C7
Coriander Ct MK7 .....48 B5
Corin Cl MK2 ....58 D5
Corin Way MK2 ....58 D5
Corinium Ind Est HP6 .154 F1
Cork Pl MK3 ....46 E2
Corn Cl HP17 ....114 D5
Corn Hill MK8 ....33 E1
Corn Mkt HP11 ......173 B7
Cornbrook Rd HP21 ..115 C5
Cornbury Cres MK15 ..35 A6
Corncrake [9] HP19 .101 F3
Cornel Cl HP15 .....163 B3
Cornel Ho [8] SL4 ..210 D4
Cornel Cl MK2 ....58 C6
Cornerways HP27 ...150 C5
Cornfield Cl UB8 ....201 D3
Cornfield Cres HP4 .134 D7
Cornflower Pl MK18 ...52 C7
Cornhill Cty Fst Sch MK6 .47 A6
Cornish Ct SL2 ......198 C1
Cornwall Cl
Eton Wick SL4 ......204 E1
Maidenhead SL6 ....195 E2
Cornwall Ct UB8 ....201 D6
Cornwall Gr MK3 .....46 F1
Cornwall Ho UB8 ...201 D6
Cornwall Lodge [1] SL6 .202 F6
Cornwall Rd UB8 ...201 D6
Cornwalls Ctr The MK18 ..41 D1
Cornwalls Mdw MK18 ..41 D1
Cornwell Rd SL4 ....211 A1
Coronation Ave
Slough SL3 ....206 C7
Windsor SL4 ....211 A4
Coronation Cotts MK18 ..41 F8
Coronation Cres HP14 .171 C5
Coronation Mews LU7 ..80 F8
Coronation Pl MK18 ...63 D2
Coronation Rd
Cranfield MK43 ....25 B1
High Wycombe HP12 ..172 D4
Milton Keynes MK11 ...32 E5
Coronation Villas SL1 .115 E8
Corporation St HP13 .173 B7
Corrid Ind Pk HP19 ..101 B1
Corrigan Cl MK3 ......58 A8
Corsewall Pl MK4 .....45 F1
Corsham Ct [4] MK8 ...33 F1
Cosgrove Leisure Pk*
MK19 ....19 F1
Cosgrove Rd MK19 ...32 C7
Cosgrove Village Prim Sch
MK19 ....19 E2
Costers Cotts SL8 ...185 B2
Costins Wlk [7] HP4 .135 D4
Cosway Pl MK8 ....45 D6
Cotes Way LU7 ....79 F3
Cotman Cl MK12 ......33 B5
Cotswold Cl
Maidenhead SL6 ....203 B6
Slough SL1 ....205 B3
Uxbridge UB8 ....201 C4
Cotswold Ct HP12 ...172 F8
Cotswold Dr LU7 .....80 C8
Cotswold Gn HP20 ..101 E2
Cotswold Way HP13 .172 E8
Cotswolds Way MK18,
MK17 ....73 B5
Cottage Comm MK5 ...46 B8
Cottage Farm Way
HP27 ....150 C4
Cottage Grounds HP17 .114 D5
Cottage Park Rd SL2 .187 D2
Cottages The
Ickenham UB10 ......190 E2
Syresham MK17 ......27 C5
Cottesbrooke Cl SL3 .212 D6
Cottesloe Cl LU7 .....79 E3
Cottesloe Ct MK11 ...32 F5
Cottesloe Rd HP21 ..115 C5
Cottesloe Sch The LU7 .79 D1
Cottingham Gr MK3 ...58 A2
Cottisford Cres MK14 ..21 F1
Cottland Clay HP17 ..127 A4

Cotts The
Long Crendon HP18 . . . . .125 C6
Longwick HP27 . . . . .138 E5
Coulson Ave MK8,MK5 . . . .45 E4
Coulson Ct HP16 . . . . .151 D6
Coulson Way SL1 . . . . . . .204 B8
Council Hos LU7 . . . . .92 A1
Countisbury MK4 . . . . .46 D2
Country La HP15 . . . . .151 F1
Country Life Ho SL3 . . . . .211 B7
County Rd NN13 . . . . .38 A6
Cours La Ville Cl MK18 . . .65 E3
Court Cl Aylesbury HP21 . .115 E7
High Wycombe HP13 . . . . .161 D1
Maidenhead SL6 . . . . .113 C2
Princes Risborough HP27 .139 A3
Court Cnr MK46 . . . . .6 E3
Court Cres SL1 . . . . .205 D7
Court Dr Maidenhead SL6 .196 C3
Uxbridge UB10 . . . . .201 F4
Court Farm Ind Est
TW19 . . . . .213 F1
Court La Burnham SL1 . . . .197 D2
Dorney SL4 . . . . .204 B3
Iver SL0 . . . . .208 A5
Court Lawns HP10 . . . . . .163 C1
Court Rd Cranfield MK43 . .25 B1
Maidenhead SL6 . . . . .196 C3
Court The MK17 . . . . .37 C3
Courteneys Lodge MK4 . .46 E3
Courtfield Dr SL6 . . . . . . .202 C6
Courtfield Gdns UB9 . . . .190 A1
Courthouse* HP18 . . . . . .125 D7
Courthouse Cl MK16 . . . . .65 E5
Courthouse Jun Sch
SL6 . . . . .202 B8
Courthouse Mews MK16 . .22 C4
Courthouse Rd SL6 . . . . . .202 E7
Courtlands
Leighton Buzzard LU7 . . . .80 E6
14 Maidenhead SL6 . . . . .202 F6
Courtlands Ave SL3 . . . . .206 D2
Courtmoor Cl HP27 . . . . . .139 C6
Courtneidge Cl LU7 . . . . .78 E8
Courtney Ho UB9 . . . . . . .189 F5
Courtyard Arts Ctr*
MK14 . . . . .21 E1
Courtyard Cl HP6 . . . . . . .154 C1
Courtyard The
Aylesbury HP19 . . . . .101 C1
Beaconsfield HP9 . . . . . . .175 D2
7 Bourne End SL8 . . . . . .185 B3
8 Marlow SL7 . . . . .183 D2
1 Marlow SL7 . . . . .183 E2
22 Windsor SL4 . . . . .210 D6
Courtyards The HP22 . . . .117 E4
Cousins Cl UB7 . . . . .208 E6
Cousins Dr HP20 . . . . . . .101 F2
Cousins Piece HP18 . . . . .112 B2
Coventon Rd HP19 . . . . . .101 C2
Coverack Pl MK4 . . . . .57 B8
Coverdale MK11 . . . . .34 C5
Coverdale Way SL2 . . . . .197 E1
Covert Cl HP4 . . . . .134 D6
Covert Rd HP4 . . . . .134 D6
Cow La Edlesborough LU6 .92 E4
Gawcott MK18 . . . . .51 F4
Tring HP23 . . . . .119 D4
Cowdray Cl MK15 . . . . . . .35 C3
Cowleaze OX39 . . . . .147 B6
Cowley Bsns Pk UB8 . . . . .201 C2
Cowley Cl HP22 . . . . .102 B3
Cowley Cotts HP7 . . . . . . .164 C3
Cowley Cres UB8 . . . . . . .208 C8
Cowley Inf Sch UB8 . . . . . .208 D8
Cowley Mill Rd UB8 . . . . . .201 B3
Cowley Mill Trad Est
UB8 . . . . .201 B3
Cowley Rd UB8 . . . . .201 C4
Cowper & Newton Mus The*
MK46 . . . . .6 F3
Cowper Cl MK16 . . . . .22 A4
Cowper Rd
Berkhamsted HP4 . . . . . . .135 B4
Chesham HP5 . . . . .144 B2
Slough SL2 . . . . .198 A1
Cowper St MK16 . . . . .7 A5
Cowpers Orch MK46 . . . . . .6 A1
Cowslip Cl UB10 . . . . .201 E5
Cowslip Rd HP15 . . . . .162 F6
Cox Green La SL6 . . . . . . .202 C3
Cox Green Rd SL6 . . . . . . .202 D3
Cox Green Sch SL6 . . . . . .202 E4
Coxborrow Cl SL6 . . . . . . .195 E7
Coxfield Cl HP14 . . . . .158 F5
Coxwell Cl MK18 . . . . .41 F1
Coy Ct HP20 . . . . .116 A8
CR Bates Ind Est HP14 . .158 E5
Crab Tree Cl
Beaconsfield HP9 . . . . . . .175 B1
Olney MK46 . . . . .6 E5
Crabbe Cres HP5 . . . . . . .144 D2
Crabs Gr HP22 . . . . .86 F7
Crabtree Cotts HP27 . . . . .139 A1
Crabtree La MK17 . . . . . . .49 C8
Crabtree Rd MK17 . . . . . . .127 A5
Craddocks Cl MK13 . . . . . .34 B3
Cradley Wlk HP20 . . . . . . .101 E3
Crafton Pl 4 HP20 . . . . . .101 F3
Craigleith Ct HP9 . . . . . . .175 D2
Craigmore Ave MK3 . . . . . .57 F8
Craigwell Ave HP21 . . . . .116 C7
Cranberry Cl MK7 . . . . . . .48 B6
Cranborne Ave
Milton Keynes MK4 . . . . . . .45 E2
Milton Keynes MK4 . . . . . . .45 F1
Cranbourne Ave SL4 . . . .209 F5
Cranbourne Cl SL1 . . . . . .205 C5

Cranbourne Rd SL1 . . . . .205 C5
Cranbrook MK17 . . . . .49 B5
Cranbrook Dr SL6 . . . . . . .195 C1
Crane Ct MK5 . . . . .34 B1
Crane Way MK43 . . . . .25 C2
Cranes Cl MK43 . . . . .8 E5
Cransbill Pl MK14 . . . . . . .34 E4
Cranfield Innovation Ctr
MK43 . . . . .37 D8
Cranfield Lower Sch
MK43 . . . . .37 D8
Cranfield Rd
Astwood MK16,MK43 . . . . .16 B2
Cranfield MK43 . . . . .25 F3
Moulsoe MK16 . . . . .36 E8
Salford MK17 . . . . .37 D5
Wavendon MK17 . . . . .49 B7
Cranfield Tech Pk MK43 . .37 D8
Cranfield Univ MK43 . . . . . .24 E2
Cranwell Cl MK5 . . . . .45 F6
Craufurd Ct SL6 . . . . .202 E8
Craufurd Rise SL6 . . . . . . .202 E8
Craven The MK13 . . . . .34 C4
Crawley Rd
Cranfield MK43 . . . . .25 B3
Woburn MK17 . . . . .60 F8
Crawley's Cl HP23 . . . . . . .133 F7
Crawshays Cl MK4 . . . . . . .46 B3
Crayle St SL2 . . . . .198 B2
Creden Cl SL6 . . . . .195 D1
Creed St MK12 . . . . .33 D7
Creighton Rd HP18 . . . . . .83 F1
Crendon Rd HP18 . . . . . . .112 A1
Crendon St HP13 . . . . . . .173 B7
Creran Wlk LU7 . . . . .80 C7
Crescent Cl HP18 . . . . .83 A6
Crescent Dale SL6 . . . . . .202 F6
Crescent Dr SL6 . . . . .202 E7
Crescent The
Cranfield MK43 . . . . .24 E2
Haversham MK19 . . . . .20 C2
High Wycombe HP13 . . . . .173 E8
Maidenhead SL6 . . . . .202 F7
Marsworth MK23 . . . . .105 A1
Milton Keynes,Fenny Stratford
MK2 . . . . .47 C1
Milton Keynes,Giffard Park
MK14 . . . . .21 E2
Pitstone LU7 . . . . .105 C4
Princes Risborough HP27 .139 B3
Slough SL1 . . . . .205 E4
Crescent Villas **5** SL4 . . .210 C6
Creslow Cl MK11 . . . . .32 F5
Creslow Way HP17 . . . . . .114 B5
Cress Rd SL1 . . . . .204 E5
Cressex Bsns Pk HP12 . . .172 D4
Cressex Com Sch HP12 . . .172 E4
Cressex Ent Ctr HP12 . . . .172 E6
Cressex Rd HP12 . . . . .172 C3
Cressey Ave MK5 . . . . .46 B4
Cressington Ct 8 SL8 . . .185 A4
Cressington Pl SL8 . . . . . .185 A4
Cresswell Ct TW19 . . . . . .213 D1
Cresswell Rd HP5 . . . . . . .154 D5
Cresswell Way HP5 . . . . . .163 D7
Cresswells Mead SL6 . . . .203 C1
Crest Rd HP11 . . . . .172 D3
Crest The
Beaconsfield HP9 . . . . . . .175 A1
Bledlow Ridge HP14 . . . . .159 F8
Creswell Row SL7 . . . . . . .183 D2
Creswick Mdw HP11 . . . . .116 A5
Crew Curve HP4 . . . . .134 F7
Cricket Field Rd UB8 . . . .201 D4
Cricket Green Rdbt MK9 .35 B4
Cricket Ground HP21 . . . .158 D5
Cricketers Row MK18 . . . .66 A4
Cricketfield Rd UB7 . . . . . .208 C2
Cricklebeck MK13 . . . . . . .34 B5
Crimp Hill SL4 . . . . .211 A1
Crisp Rd RG9 . . . . .191 C3
Crispin Cl HP9 . . . . .175 C4
Crispin Field LU7 . . . . . . .105 C4
Crispin Way SL8 . . . . .34 B7
Crispin Way
Farnham Common SL2 . . . .198 D3
High Wycombe HP11 . . . . .173 A4
Uxbridge UB8 . . . . .208 F8
Criss Gr SL9 . . . . .177 C1
Crocketts La HP16 . . . . . . .142 D5
Crocus Dr HP21 . . . . .115 B5
Croft Cnr SL4 . . . . .211 A2
Croft Cl **5** HP21 . . . . .115 E7
Croft Ctyd HP17 . . . . .114 E6
Croft Gn LU6 . . . . .93 F8
Croft Ho SL0 . . . . .207 E7
Croft Mdws LU7 . . . . .105 A7
Croft Rd Aylesbury HP21 . .115 E7
Chalfont St Peter SL9 . . . .177 E1
Croft The
Haddenham HP17 . . . . . . .126 F5
Maidenhead SL6 . . . . .202 C5
Marlow SL7 . . . . .184 A3
Crofters SL4 . . . . .211 A1
Crofters Cl TW19 . . . . .213 D1
Crofthill Rd SL2 . . . . .198 B1
Crofton Ho HP11 . . . . .174 A4
Crofts End MK16 . . . . .14 A1
Crofts La MK17 . . . . .57 D3
Croftwood HP13 . . . . .162 E1
Cromarty Ct MK3 . . . . .46 E3
Cromer Cl HP4 . . . . .121 C5
Cromer St SL1 . . . . .205 E7
Cromhamstone HP17 . . . .114 D5
Cromwell Ave
Aylesbury HP21 . . . . .101 D4
Newport Pagnell MK16 . . . .22 A3
Thame OX9 . . . . .126 A1

Cromwell Cl HP8 . . . . .177 C7
Cromwell Cl MK18 . . . . . . .41 E2
Cromwell Dr SL1 . . . . .205 E7
Cromwell Gdns **10** SL7 . .183 E2
Cromwell Ho
Chesham HP5 . . . . .144 B1
Uxbridge UB8 . . . . .201 C4
Cromwell Mews 1
HP19 . . . . .115 A8
Cromwell Rd
High Wycombe HP13 . . . . .173 E5
Maidenhead SL6 . . . . .202 D7
Marlow SL7 . . . . .183 E2
Cropredy Crt MK18 . . . . . .41 E2
Cropton Rise MK4 . . . . . . .46 A2
Cropwell Bishop MK4 . . . .46 C1
Crosby Cl HP9 . . . . .186 F8
Crosby Ct MK8 . . . . .45 E6
Crosland Rd HP21 . . . . . . .116 A3
Cross Cl HP13 . . . . .161 D2
Cross End MK17 . . . . .48 F7
Cross Farm Mews HP3 . . .146 D2
Cross La
Beaconsfield HP9 . . . . . . .186 F8
Tingewick MK18 . . . . .51 F4
Weston Underwood MK46 . .6 B2
Cross Lanes
Bledlow HP27 . . . . .138 A2
Chalfont St Peter SL9 . . . .177 F5
Cross Lanes Cl SL9 . . . . . .177 F5
Cross Mdw HP5 . . . . .143 F2
Cross Oak SL4 . . . . .210 A5
Cross Oak Rd HP4 . . . . . . .135 A4
Cross Rd
High Wycombe HP12 . . . . .172 C6
Uxbridge UB8 . . . . .201 C5
Cross St
Newport Pagnell MK16 . . . .22 C4
Uxbridge UB8 . . . . .201 C5
Cross Tree Rd MK19 . . . . .31 B3
Crossfield Cl HP4 . . . . . . .134 F4
Crossfield Ho SL9 . . . . . . .188 E7
Crossfield Rd HP27 . . . . . .139 C4
Crosshills MK11 . . . . .32 D4
Crosslands MK14 . . . . .34 E8
Crossleys HP8 . . . . .177 C7
Crosslow Bank MK4 . . . . . .46 C3
Crossway HP21 . . . . .144 E1
Crossway The UB10 . . . . .201 F3
Crossways
Beaconsfield HP9 . . . . . . .175 F1
Berkhamsted HP4 . . . . . . .134 F3
High Wycombe HP12 . . . . .172 B4
Crossways Bsns Pk HP18 .83 C3
Crossways Cl SL4 . . . . . . .210 C5
Crosthwaite Way SL1 . . . .204 D8
Crow La MK17 . . . . .49 B8
Crow Piece La SL2 . . . . . .197 F4
Crowborough La MK7 . . . . .48 A8
Crowell Mews HP14 . . . . .114 F8
Crowell Rd OX39 . . . . .147 B5
Crown Bsns Est HP5 . . . . .144 C1
Crown Cl SL3 . . . . .212 C7
Crown Cotts Botley HP5 . .155 B8
Windsor SL4 . . . . .210 D3
Crown Ct HP14 . . . . .161 A2
Crown La
East Burnham SL2 . . . . . . .198 A4
High Wycombe HP11 . . . . .173 B6
Maidenhead SL6 . . . . .203 A7
Marlow SL7 . . . . .183 D2
Penn HP10 . . . . .174 F7
Crown Leys HP20 . . . . . . .101 E1
Crown Mdw SL3 . . . . .212 B7
Crown Rd SL3 . . . . .183 D2
Crown Rose Ct HP23 . . . . .119 A3
Crown Way UB7 . . . . .208 F5
Crown Wlk
Milton Keynes MK9 . . . . . . .34 E3
Uxbridge UB8 . . . . .201 C5
Crownfield HP27 . . . . .149 C3
Crownhill Rdbt MK4 . . . . . .45 E8
Crowther Ct MK5 . . . . .46 C5
Croxley Cl 3 LU7 . . . . .80 F8
Croxley Rise SL6 . . . . .202 D6
Croydon Cl MK4 . . . . .46 C3
Cruickshank Gr MK8 . . . . .45 E7
Crummock Cl SL1 . . . . . . .204 C7
Crummock Pl MK2 . . . . . . .58 D5
Crusader Est HP12 . . . . . .172 D5
Crutches La HP9 . . . . .176 E4
Cryers Hill La HP15 . . . . . .162 D6
Cryers Hill Rd HP15 . . . . .162 C4
Cuba Cotts SL6 . . . . .196 B3
Cubb Field HP19 . . . . .115 B7
Cublington Rd HP22 . . . . . .88 D6
Cuckoo Way HP19 . . . . . . .114 F8
Cuddington CE Sch
HP18 . . . . .112 F3
Cuddington Hill HP18 . . . .112 E3
Cuddington Rd HP17,
HP18 . . . . .113 E3
Cudsdens Ct HP16 . . . . . .152 D7
Cuff La MK17 . . . . .59 D1
Culbertson La MK13 . . . . . .33 E6
Culham Dr SL6 . . . . .195 E2
Cullen Pl MK2 . . . . .58 D5
Cullern's Pass HP16 . . . . .202 F6
Culley Way SL6 . . . . .202 A4
Cullyn Rd HP12 . . . . .172 C3
Culmstock Cl MK4 . . . . . . .46 D2
Culrain Pl MK12 . . . . .33 D4
Culross Gr MK10 . . . . .36 A2
Culvers Croft HP9 . . . . . . .176 C4
Culvert La UB8 . . . . .201 B3
Culverton Hill HP27 . . . . . .139 C3
Culverton La HP27 . . . . . .139 B1

Cumberland Ave SL2 . . . .198 C1
Cumberland Cl
Aylesbury HP21 . . . . .116 B7
Little Chalfont HP7 . . . . . . .166 B8
Cumbrae Cl SL2 . . . . .206 A5
Cumbria Cl
Maidenhead SL6 . . . . .202 A4
Milton Keynes MK3 . . . . . . .46 F1
Cumbrian Way
High Wycombe HP13 . . . . .172 F8
Milton Keynes MK8 . . . . . .201 D5
Curfew Yd The 2 SL4 . . .210 D6
Curlew HP19 . . . . .101 F3
Curlew Cl
Berkhamsted HP4 . . . . . . .135 C3
High Wycombe HP15 . . . . .161 C2
Curls La SL6 . . . . .202 E4
Curls Rd SL6 . . . . .202 E4
Curran Cl UB8 . . . . .201 C1
Currier Dr MK14 . . . . .34 F6
Curriers La SL1 . . . . .197 D7
Cursley Path 11 HP19 . . .115 A8
Curtis Cotts HP5 . . . . .144 F7
Curtis Croft MK5 . . . . .46 B3
Curtis Way HP4 . . . . .135 D3
Curzon Ave
Beaconsfield HP9 . . . . . . .175 D4
Tylers Green HP15 . . . . . .163 C2
Curzon CE Comb Sch
HP7 . . . . .164 A5
Curzon Cl HP15 . . . . .163 C2
Curzon Gate Ct HP14 . . . .158 E5
Curzon Mall 6 SL1 . . . . . .205 F4
Curzon Pl MK7 . . . . .48 D6
Cut Throat Ave HP6 . . . . .107 E7
Cutler's Ct 8 HP12 . . . . . .172 E7
Cutlers Mews MK14 . . . . . .34 F6
Cuttle Brook Gdns OX9 . .125 E1
Cyclamen Pl HP21 . . . . . .115 B5
Cygnet Ho SL6 . . . . .196 C1
Cypress Cl MK6 . . . . .22 A3
Cypress Ho SL3 . . . . .207 B1
Cypress Wlk HP15 . . . . . .163 B3

D

Daceberry Ct RG9 . . . . . . .192 C2
Dacre Rd HP22 . . . . .131 E7
Dadbrook HP18 . . . . .112 F2
Dadbrook Cl HP18 . . . . . . .112 F2
Dadfield Cl HP18 . . . . .112 F2
Dag La
Stoke Goldington MK16 . . .12 A7
Stoke Goldington MK16 . . .12 B6
Dagmar Rd SL4 . . . . .210 D5
Dagnall Cres UB8 . . . . . . .208 C8
Dagnall Rd Olney MK46 . . .6 E3
Dagnall Sch HP4 . . . . .107 C5
Dair House Sch SL2 . . . . .198 B4
Dairy La SL4 . . . . .192 B8
Dairymede HP22 . . . . .150 C4
Daisy Cotts HP14 . . . . . . .171 B4
Dale Cl SL6 . . . . .202 D7
Dalesford Rd HP21 . . . . . .116 A4
Dalgin Pl MK9 . . . . .35 A3
Dalston Cl HP20 . . . . .101 F2
Dalton Gate MK10 . . . . . . .35 F4
Dalvina Pl MK12 . . . . .33 D4
Dalwood Mews 9 HP19 . .115 A8
Daly Way HP20 . . . . .101 E3
Damask Cl HP22 . . . . .119 C4
Damson Gr SL1 . . . . .205 C4
Danbury Ct MK14 . . . . .34 E5
Dancers End La HP22,
HP23 . . . . .118 C2
Dandridge Cl SL3 . . . . . . .206 D2
Dandridge Ct MK8 . . . . . . .45 C6
Dandridge Dr SL8 . . . . . . .185 C3
Dane Cl HP7 . . . . .165 F6
Dane Ct HP21 . . . . .115 D4
Dane Rd MK1 . . . . .47 E2
Danes Cl SL6 . . . . .202 D7
Danes Gdns SL6 . . . . .195 F6
Danesborough Dr MK17 . .99 E6
Danesbrook Cl MK4 . . . . . .46 D4
Danesfield Sch MK17 . . . .193 E7
Danesfield Sch SL7 . . . . . .183 E3
Daneswood MK17 . . . . .49 A1
Daniels Welch MK6 . . . . . .47 A6
Dansteed Way
Milton Keynes,Bradwell Common
MK8,MK13,MK14,MK15 . . .34 C4
Milton Keynes,Crownhill
MK8 . . . . .45 D7
Danvers Croft HP23 . . . . . .119 C5
Darby Cl MK5 . . . . .46 B5
Darby Lodge HP13 . . . . . .174 A7
Darin Ct MK8 . . . . .45 E6
Dark La Chearsley HP18 . . .112 B2
Oving HP22 . . . . .86 C7
Wingrave HP22 . . . . .89 C2
Darley Cl HP21 . . . . .116 B6
Darley Gate MK14 . . . . . . .35 B1
Darling's La SL6 . . . . .194 E1
Darlington Cl HP6 . . . . . . .154 D1
Darnel Cl MK1 . . . . .47 A5
Darr's La HP4 . . . . .134 D6
Darrell Cl SL3 . . . . .206 F2
Darsham Wlk MK8 . . . . . . .154 B8
Dart Cl Aylesbury HP21 . . .116 B4
Newport Pagnell MK16 . . . .22 D4
Dartington Pl MK14 . . . . . .45 F1
Dartmouth Ct **10** SL1 . . . .205 F3

Dartmouth Rd MK46 . . . . . .6 F4
Darvell Dr HP5 . . . . .144 A2
Darvill Rd HP17 . . . . .114 B5
Darvill's La SL1 . . . . .205 D4
Darville Ho 10 SL4 . . . . . .210 D6
Darvills Mdw HP15 . . . . . .163 C7
Darwin Cl MK15 . . . . .45 E5
Darwin Rd SL3 . . . . .206 F4
Dashfield Gr HP15 . . . . . . .162 F6
Dashwood Ave HP12 . . . . .172 D2
Dashwood Cl SL3 . . . . . . .206 C2
Dashwood Ind Est HP12 .172 D7
Datchet Ho 3 SL1 . . . . . . .205 F3
Datchet Lodge Ctyd
SL3 . . . . .211 B6
Datchet Pl SL3 . . . . .211 B6
Datchet Rd Eton SL4 . . . . .205 F2
Horton SL3 . . . . .211 A3
Old Windsor SL4 . . . . .211 A3
Windsor SL4 . . . . .211 A3
Datchet St Mary's CE Prim
Sch SL3 . . . . .211 B6
Datchet Sta SL3 . . . . .211 B6
Daubeney Gate MK5 . . . . .45 F6
Davenies Sch HP9 . . . . . .175 E2
Davenport Lea MK7 . . . . . .48 E5
Davenport Rd HP22 . . . . . .172 C3
Daventry Cl SL3 . . . . .212 F6
David Bishop Ct HP5 . . . .154 D5
David Cl HP21 . . . . .116 A4
David St SL3 . . . . .212 F5
Davidge Pl HP9 . . . . .175 C5
Davidson Rd 6 SL3 . . . . . .206 F1
Davies Cl HP20 . . . . .115 D8
Davies Ct SL6 . . . . .172 D5
Davies Way HP10 . . . . . . .174 C1
Davis Cl SL7 . . . . .183 E1
Davis Ho 3 HP4 . . . . .135 C3
Daws Cl MK18 . . . . .45 D6
Davy Ave MK5 . . . . .46 D6
Dawe's Cl UB10 . . . . .201 E3
Dawe's Rd UB10 . . . . .201 E3
Dawes Cl HP5 . . . . .154 B7
Dawes East Rd SL1 . . . . . .197 C2
Dawes La WD3 . . . . .156 F3
Dawes Moor Cl SL2 . . . . . .206 C7
Dawley Ride SL3 . . . . .212 E6
Dawn Redwood Cl SL3 . . .212 A4
Dawney Cl HP21 . . . . .101 C2
Daws Ct SL0 . . . . .207 F7
Daws Hill La HP11 . . . . . . .173 A4
Daws Lea HP11 . . . . .173 B3
Dawson Ct SL4 . . . . .210 A5
Dawson Rd MK1 . . . . .47 D3
Daylesford Ct MK15 . . . . . .35 B5
De Clare Ct MK18 . . . . .41 E1
De Havilland Dr HP15 . . . .162 E2
De Havilland Way TW19 . .213 E1
De Montfort Univ MK7 . . . .48 A7
De Pirenore HP15 . . . . . . .162 E2
Deacon Cl HP22 . . . . .118 E5
Deacon Ct SL4 . . . . .209 D5
Deacon Pl MK10 . . . . .35 F3
Deadmarsh La HP8 . . . . . .166 E1
Deal Ave SL1 . . . . .204 F7
Dean Cl Aylesbury HP21 . .116 A5
High Wycombe HP11 . . . . .172 E6
Uxbridge UB10 . . . . .201 D4
Windsor SL4 . . . . .209 D4
Dean Farm La LU7 . . . . . . .91 B1
Dean Field HP3 . . . . .146 A4
Dean La SL6 . . . . .195 C8
Dean Rd LU7 . . . . .68 B2
Dean St SL7 . . . . .183 D2
Dean The HP22 . . . . .89 B3
Dean View HP15 . . . . .195 D6
Dean Way
Aston Clinton HP22 . . . . . .117 F4
Chalfont St Giles HP8 . . . .177 B7
Holmer Green HP15 . . . . . .163 B6
Dean Wood Rd HP9 . . . . . .176 D2
Dean's Cloisters SL4 . . . .210 D7
Dean's Rd MK12 . . . . .33 C7
Deanacre Cl SL9 . . . . .177 E4
Deancroft Rd SL9 . . . . . . .177 E4
Deanfield HP14 . . . . .161 C6
Deanfield Ave HP10 . . . . .191 D1
Deanfield Cl Marlow SL7 . .183 D2
Saunderton HP14 . . . . . . .149 C1
Deanfield Rd HP14 . . . . . .191 D1
Deangarden Rise HP11 . . .173 E4
Deans Cl Amersham HP6 . .154 F2
Tring HP23 . . . . .119 A4
Wexham Street SL2 . . . . . .199 B4
Deans Furlong HP23 . . . . .119 A4
Deans Lawn HP4 . . . . .135 C4
Deans Mdw HP4 . . . . .107 C5
Deansfield Cl SL6 . . . . . . .195 D2
Deanshanger Dr NN12 . . .17 F1
Deanshanger Prim Sch
MK19 . . . . .31 E3
Deanshanger Rd
Old Stratford MK19 . . . . . . .32 B6
Wicken MK19 . . . . .31 B3
Deansway HP5 . . . . .144 B2
Dearing Cl 11 HP20 . . . . .101 F2
Debbs Cl MK11 . . . . .32 E5
Deben Cl MK16 . . . . .22 E3
Decies Way SL2 . . . . .183 F2
Dedmere Ct SL7 . . . . .183 E2
Dedmere Rd SL7 . . . . .183 F2
Dedmere Rise SL7 . . . . . .183 E2
Dedworth Dr SL4 . . . . .209 F6
Dedworth Green Fst Sch
SL4 . . . . .209 E5

Dedworth Manor SL4 .....**209** F6
Dedworth Mid Sch SL4 ...**209** E6
Dedworth Rd SL4 ....**209** D5
Deeds Gr HP12 ....**172** E5
Deena CI SL1 ....**204** E6
Deep Acres HP6 ....**154** A3
Deep Field SL2 ....**211** B7
Deep Mill La HP16 ......**152** D3
Deepdale MK13 ....**34** C5
Deer Park Wlk HP5 ....**144** E3
Deer Wlk MK9 ....**34** F3
Deerfern CI MK14 ....**21** E1
Deerfield CI MK18 ....**52** E7
Deermead SL6 ....**152** B4
Deerswood SL6 ....**196** A1
Deethe CI MK17 ....**49** B6
Delafield CI HP14 ....**158** F4
Delaford CI SL0 ....**207** F7
Delaford Ho UB7 ....**208** D5
Delahay Rise HP4 ......**135** B6
Delamere CI HP20 .....**101** F2
Delamere Gdns LU7 .....**80** C7
Delaware Dr
  Milton Keynes MK15 .....**35** B8
  Tongwell MK15,MK16 .....**22** B1
Delius CI MK7 ....**48** C4
Dell CI SL2 ....**198** C7
Dell Field HP16 ....**151** C5
Dell Field Ave HP4 ....**135** B6
Dell Lees HP9 ....**176** C4
Dell Rd Berkhamsted HP4 **134** D7
  West Drayton UB7 ....**208** F3
Dell The Aylesbury HP20 **102** A2
  Chalfont St Peter SL9 ....**177** E4
  Maidenhead SL6 ....**202** A2
  Stokenchurch HP14 ......**158** F3
  Tylers Green HP10 ....**163** C1
  Uxbridge UB8 ....**201** C1
Dellfield HP5 ....**144** A2
Dellfield CI HP4 ....**135** A6
Dellfield Cres UB8 .....**201** C1
Dellfield Par UB8 ....**201** C1
Dells MK46 ....**6** F4
Dellside UB9 ....**190** C6
Delmeade Rd HP5 .....**154** A7
Deltic Ave MK13 ....**34** B2
Democran CI MK18 ....**65** F3

Denbigh East Ind Est
  MK1 ....**47** D2
Denbigh Hall MK3 ....**46** F3
Denbigh Hall Dr MK3 ...**46** F3
Denbigh Hall Ind Est
  MK3 ....**46** F3
Denbigh Rd
  Milton Keynes MK1 ....**47** B2
  Thame OX9 ....**126** A1
Denbigh Sch MK5 ....**46** A6
Denbigh Way MK2 ....**47** C1
Denbigh West Ind Est
  MK1 ....**47** B2
Denby Wlk HP20 ....**116** A8
Denchworth Ct 2 MK4 ...**46** C2
Dene CI Winslow MK18 ....**66** A3
  Woburn Sands MK17 ......**49** C4
Dene The MK18 ....**63** D3
Denewood HP13 ....**173** E8
Denham Ave UB9 ....**189** F3
Denham CI Denham UB9 **190** A1
  Maidenhead SL6 ....**202** C6
  Milton Keynes MK3 ....**57** D8
Denham Court Dr UB9 .**190** B1
Denham Ctry Pk* UB9 .**190** E6
Denham Garden Village
  UB9 ....**189** F5
Denham Golf Club Sta
  UB9 ....**189** D4
Denham Green CI UB9 .**190** A4
Denham Green La UB9 .**189** F5
Denham La SL9 ....**178** A2
Denham Lodge UB9 ....**201** C6
Denham Rd
  Iver Heath SL0 ....**200** E5
  Lane End HP14 ....**171** C5
Denham Sta UB9 ....**190** A4
Denham View MK18 ....**75** F6
Denham Village Inf Sch
  UB9 ....**189** F2
Denham Way (North Orbital
  Rd) WD3 ....**178** E4
Denham Way North Orbital
  Rd UB9 ....**189** F7
Denham Wlk SL9 ....**177** F4
Denholme Lodge SL3 ..**211** B7
Denison Ct MK7 ....**48** D6
Denmark St
  High Wycombe HP11 .....**173** A4
  Maidenhead SL6 ....**202** E8
  Milton Keynes MK2 ....**58** D8
Denmead MK8 ....**33** E2
Denmead Ct SL9 ....**188** E4
Dennis CI HP22 ....**118** A4
Dennis Way SL1 ....**204** D6
Denniston Ho HP12 .....**172** C8
Denny Rd SL3 ....**206** F2
Denny's La HP4 ....**134** F2
Denton Ct SL7 ....**183** F3
Depot Rd SL6 ....**203** A6
Derby Arms HP20 ....**115** D8
Derby Rd UB8 ....**201** D3
Dere PI MK2 ....**58** E4
Derehams Ave HP10 ...**174** C3
Derehams La HP10 ......**174** C2
Derek Rd SL6 ....**203** C8
Deri Dene CI 2 TW19 .**213** E1

Derwent CI
  Little Chalfont HP7 ....**166** B8
  Newport Pagnell MK16 ....**22** D4
Derwent Dr
  Maidenhead SL6 ....**202** D8
  Milton Keynes MK3 ....**57** E8
  Slough SL1 ....**204** C8
Derwent Rd
  Aylesbury HP21 ....**116** B6
  Leighton Buzzard LU7 ......**80** B7
Desborough Ave HP11 .**172** F6
Desborough Cres SL6 .**202** D5
Desborough Gn 3
  HP20 ....**101** D2
Desborough Ho 14
  HP13 ....**173** B7
Desborough Ind Pk
  HP12 ....**172** E8
Desborough Park Rd
  HP12 ....**172** E8
Desborough Rd HP11 ..**172** F7
Desborough Sch SL6 ..**202** E5
Desborough St HP11 ...**172** F7
Deseronto Wharf Ind Est
  SL3 ....**206** E4
Develin CI MK14 ....**34** F7
Devereux PI HP19 ....**101** A2
Devereux Rd SL4 ....**210** D5
Deverill Rd HP21 ....**115** C3
Deverills Way SL3 ....**207** C2
Devon Ave SL1 ....**205** C7
Devon CI MK3 ....**46** F1
Devon Rd HP19 ....**101** A3
Devon Way UB10 ....**201** E3
Devonshire Ave HP6 ..**154** B2
Devonshire CI
  Amersham HP6 ....**154** C2
  Farnham Royal SL2 ....**198** B3
Devonshire Gn SL2 ....**198** B3
Devonshire Lodge 10
  SL6 ....**202** F6
Dexter Ave MK6 ....**46** F8
Dexter Ho MK6 ....**46** F8
Dhoon Rise SL6 ....**202** F6
Diamond Rd SL1 ....**206** A4
Diana CI SL3 ....**206** E7
Diane CI HP21 ....**116** A4
Diane Wlk HP21 ....**116** A4
Dibden Hill HP8 ....**177** C6
Dickens CI MK43 ....**3** F6
Dickens Dr MK19 ....**32** B6
Dickens PI SL3 ....**212** E6
Dickens Rd MK12 ....**33** C8
Dickens Spinney MK46 ...**6** E4
Dickens Way HP19 .....**100** F2
Dickins PI SL3 ....**212** E6
Dickins Way HP19 ......**100** F3
Diddington CI MK2 ....**58** C3
Digby CI OX9 ....**126** B1
Digby Croft MK10 ....**35** E3
Dilwyn Ct 1 HP12 ....**172** E7
Dingle Dell LU7 ....**70** F2
Dinglederry MK46 ....**6** F4
Dinmore HP3 ....**145** F3
Dinton C E Sch HP17 ..**113** F3
Disraeli Cres HP13 .....**161** F1
Disraeli Ct SL3 ....**212** B8
Disraeli Pk HP9 ....**175** D4
Disraeli Sch The HP13 **161** F1
Disraeli Sq 4 HP19 ....**115** A8
Diswell Brook Way MK19 **31** E5
Ditchfield Cotts HP14 ..**171** A3
Ditton Pk SL3 ....**211** A6
Ditton Park Cvn Site
  SL3 ....**206** F1
Ditton Park Rd SL3 .....**211** E8
Ditton Rd Datchet SL3 .**211** D7
  Slough SL3 ....**211** F8
Dixie Ct HP20 ....**116** A8
Dixie La MK7 ....**48** C6
Dobbin PI HP21 ....**115** B6
Dobbins La HP22 ....**131** B5
Dobson's La UB9 ....**191** C8
Doctor's Commons Rd
  HP4 ....**135** A4
Dodds La HP8 ....**177** B8
Doddsfield Rd SL2 ......**198** A2
Dodkin MK6 ....**47** B5
Dodman Gn MK4 ....**57** B8
Dog Kennel La WD3 ....**167** F5
Doggetts Farm Rd UB9 **189** C4
Doggetts Wood CI HP8 **166** B6
Doggetts Wood La HP8 **166** B5
Dolben CI MK15 ....**35** D8
Dolesden La RG9 ....**169** D1
Dollicot HP17 ....**126** F6
Dolphin CI
  Loudwater HP11 ....**174** A3
  Slough SL1 ....**206** B4
Dolphin PI HP21 ....**115** E6
Dolphin Rd SL1 ....**206** B4
Dolphin Sq 2 HP23 ....**119** A3
Don The MK3 ....**46** D1
Donkey Dr SL8 ....**185** A3
Donkey La
  Bourne End SL8 ....**185** A3
  Tring HP23 ....**118** E2
  West Drayton UB7 ....**208** C2
Donnay CI SL3 ....**188** D5
Donnington MK13 ....**34** B6
Donnington Gdns SL6 .**195** F1
Donnybrook Ho 3
  HP13 ....**173** C7
Doon Way MK2 ....**58** C5
Dorchester Ave MK3 .....**47** A2
Dorchester CI
  Maidenhead SL6 ....**195** B1
  Stoke Mandeville HP22 ..**116** B2

Dorchester Ho SL9 ......**188** F6
Doreen CI MK2 ....**58** C7
Dorian CI HP21 ....**119** D4
Dorking PI MK5 ....**46** B4
Dormans CI MK10 ....**36** A2
Dormer Ave LU7 ....**79** E3
Dormer CI HP21 ....**115** B6
Dormer Ct HP20 ....**101** F2
Dormer La HP15 ....**163** B7
Dornels SL2 ....**206** C7
Dorney Ct SL4 ....**204** B3
Dorney End HP5 ....**144** B1
Dorney Hill N SL1,HP9 .**187** A4
Dorney Hill S SL2 ....**187** A4
Dorney Lake Park Nature
  Reserve* SL4 ....**197** D6
Dorney Lake Pk* SL4 .**209** B8
Dorney Lake Rowing Ctr*
  SL4 ....**204** A1
Dorney PI MK13 ....**34** C3
Dorney Reach Rd SL6 .**203** F3
Dorney Sch SL6 ....**203** F3
Dorney Wood Rd
  Burnham SL1 ....**197** D6
  Littleworth Common SL1 .**186** C1
Dorneywood Gdn* SL1 **197** D6
Dorrells Rd HP27 ....**138** D6
Dorrien's Croft HP4 .....**134** F7
Dorset CI
  Berkhamsted HP4 ....**134** F5
  Milton Keynes MK3 ....**46** F1
Dorset Lodge 9 SL6 ...**202** F6
Dorset PI HP21 ....**116** C6
Dorset Rd SL4 ....**210** C6
Dorset Way UB10 ....**201** F3
Dorton CI MK8 ....**33** F1
Dorton Rd HP18 ....**111** B4
Douglas Ave SL4 ....**184** A3
Douglas Gdns HP4 .....**135** A5
Douglas La TW19 ....**211** F1
Douglas PI MK6 ....**46** E8
Dove CI
  Aylesbury HP20 ....**102** A1
  Slough SL3 ....**205** D8
  Stanwell TW19 ....**213** D1
Doune Ho MK3 ....**46** F2
Dove CI Aylesbury HP21 **115** C5
  Buckingham MK18 ....**52** E7
  Newport Pagnell MK16 ....**22** D4
Dove Ct HP9 ....**175** D3
Dove Ho HP9 ....**101** F4
Dove House CI
  Edlesborough LU6 ....**92** F4
  Winslow MK18 ....**66** A4
Dove House Cres SL2 .**197** E2
Dove PI WD3 ....**167** B4
Dove St LU7 ....**78** E8
Dovecot Rd HP13 ....**173** A7
Dovecote
  Haddenham HP17 ....**126** F6
  Newport Pagnell MK16 ...**22** C4
Dovecote CI MK14 ....**21** E1
Dovecote Cotts MK5 ....**46** A4
Dovehouse Mews MK16 **12** B6
Dovehouse Rd 8 HP21 **173** A7
Doveleat OX39 ....**147** D7
Dover CI LU7 ....**105** D2
Dover Gate MK3 ....**57** E8
Dover Hedge HP21 ......**116** C7
Dover Rd SL1 ....**204** F7
Dovetail CI HP17 ....**172** D8
Dowding Rd UB10 ......**201** D6
Dower Ho HP15 ....**175** C5
Dower Mews 5 HP4 ....**135** C4
Down PI SL4 ....**209** E3
Down Rd SL4 ....**209** A8
Downdean MK6 ....**47** A8
Downderry Croft MK4 ...**57** B8
Downer CI MK18 ....**52** F8
Downer Dr WD3 ....**156** F3
Downham Rd MK17 ......**49** C4
Downing Path SL2 ....**197** E1
Downings Wood WD3 ..**178** D5
Downland MK8 ....**33** E2
Downley Ave MK13 ....**34** C3
Downley Ct HP13 ....**161** D2
Downley Rd HP14 ....**161** D6
Downley Sch The HP13 **161** D3
Downs Barn Fst Sch
  MK14 ....**34** D5
Downs Barn Rdbt MK14 **34** E5
Downs Pk HP13 ....**161** E2
Downs Rd SL3 ....**206** D4
Downs View MK17 ....**48** C2
Downs Villas 7 HP21 ..**119** A3
Dr Challoner's Gram Sch
  HP6 ....**154** C1
Dr Challoner's High Sch
  HP7 ....**166** B7
Dragon Tail HP17 ....**127** A5
Drake Ave SL3 ....**206** D2
Drake CI HP21 ....**115** B6
Drake's Rd HP7 ....**165** B8
Drakeloe CI MK17 ....**60** F8
Drakes Dr HP18 ....**125** E5
Drakes Farm HP18 ......**125** E5
Drakes Mews MK8 ....**45** F7
Drakewell Rd MK17 ....**48** D1
Draymans La SL7 ....**183** D1
Drayton CI MK18 ....**52** D7
Drayton Gdns UB7 ......**208** E4
Drayton Park Comb Sch
  MK2 ....**58** D5

Drayton Parslow Village Sch
  MK17 ....**68** C6
Drayton Rd
  Aylesbury HP20 ....**101** D2
  Milton Keynes MK2 ....**58** C5
  Newton Longville MK17 ....**57** C2
Dresser Rd HP16 ....**151** C5
Drew CI MK3 ....**47** A4
Drew Mdw SL2 ....**198** C8
Drews Pk HP9 ....**175** C6
Drey The SL9 ....**177** E5
Drift Rd SL4 ....**209** A1
Drift Way SL3 ....**212** C7
Drinkwater CI OX25 ......**95** D7
Drive The
  Amersham HP7 ....**154** D1
  Bourne End SL8 ....**184** F4
  Chalfont St Peter SL9 ....**177** F3
  Cranfield MK43 ....**24** D2
  Datchet SL3 ....**211** B6
  Ickenham UB10 ....**190** E1
  Ivinghoe Aston LU7 ....**92** A1
  Slough SL3 ....**206** E4
  Wraysbury TW19 ....**211** D2
Dropmore Inf Sch SL1 .**186** C1
Dropmore Rd
  Burnham SL1 ....**197** C5
  Littleworth Common SL1 .**186** C1
Drovers Croft MK2 ....**33** B4
Drovers La RG9 ....**169** B2
Drovers Way
  Dunstable LU6 ....**93** F8
  Newton Longville MK17 ....**57** D2
  Seer Green HP9 ....**176** C4
Druce End NN12 ....**18** E6
Druids Wlk OX39 ....**147** D8
Drummond Ho 4 SL4 ..**210** D4
Drummond Ride HP23 ..**119** A5
Drummond Hay MK15 ...**35** C7
Drydell La HP5 ....**153** F8
Dryden CI
  Aylesbury HP20 ....**101** E2
  Newport Pagnell MK16 ....**22** A4
Du Pre Wlk HP10 ....**185** D4
Duchess Gdns NN12 ...**18** D3
Duchess Gr MK7 ....**48** C7
Duchess St SL4 ....**204** E5
Duck End
  High Wycombe HP20 .....**115** C8
  Great Brickhill MK17 ....**59** D1
Duck La Ludgershall HP18 **96** C8
  Woburn MK17 ....**60** F7
Duck Lake MK18 ....**41** E3
Duck Lake CI MK18 ......**41** E4
Duck Sq OX39 ....**147** C6
Duckmore La HP23 .....**118** E2
Duckworth Ct MK6 ....**46** E7
Dudley CI MK18 ....**76** A2
Dudley Hill MK5 ....**206** A3
Dudley Hill MK5 ....**46** A6
Dudley Ho HP3 ....**146** A4
Dudley La RG9 ....**181** A6
Dudswell La HP4 ....**134** D7
Duffield La SL2 ....**198** F6
Duffield Pk SL2 ....**199** A2
Duke St Aspley Guise MK17 **49** F8
  Eton SL4 ....**210** C7
  Henley-on-Thames RG9 .**191** E2
  High Wycombe HP13 .....**173** C6
  Princes Risborough HP27 **139** B4
Dukes Ave LU6 ....**107** E8
Dukes CI
  Gerrards Cross SL9 ....**188** E3
  Shabbington HP18 ....**124** C2
Dukes Dr
  Farnham Common SL2 ...**198** A8
  Milton Keynes MK2 ....**47** C1
Dukes Kiln Dr SL9 ....**188** C3
Dukes La SL9 ....**188** E4
  Dukes Mdw SL8 ....**185** B3
Dukes PI Marlow SL7 ...**183** D2
  Slough SL1 ....**205** F6
Dukes Ride
  Gerrards Cross SL9 ....**188** E3
  Ickenham UB10 ....**201** E8
  Leighton Buzzard LU7 ....**70** F3
Dukes Row HP11 ....**99** A1
Dukes Valley SL9 ....**188** B2
Dukes Way
  Berkhamsted HP4 ....**135** A6
  Uxbridge UB8 ....**201** C4
Dukes Wood Ave SL9 ..**188** E3
Dukeswood Dr SL9 ......**188** D3
Dulverton Ct LU7 ....**80** C8
Dulverton Dr MK4 ....**46** D3
Dulwich CI MK16 ....**22** C2
Dumbletons WD3 ....**178** E6
Dumfries CI MK3 ....**46** F3
Dunbar CI
  Milton Keynes MK3 ....**57** D8
  Slough SL2 ....**206** A6
Dunbar Dr OX9 ....**126** A1
Duncan Gr MK5 ....**45** F6
Duncan Lock Ho HP9 ..**175** F2
Duncan Rd MK43 ....**24** E2
Duncannon Cres SL4 ..**209** D4
Dunchurch Dale MK7 ...**48** B5
Duncombe CI HP6 ....**154** E1
Duncombe St MK2 ....**58** C7
Duncroft SL4 ....**209** F4
Dundale Prim Sch
  HP23 ....**119** A5
Dundale Rd HP23 ....**119** A4
Dundee Rd SL1 ....**205** A8
Dungeness Ct MK4 ....**46** A1
Dungrovehill La SL7 ....**194** D3

Dunholme End SL6 ......**202** D3
Dunkeld Ho HP11 ....**174** B4
Dunkery Beacon MK4 ....**46** D3
Dunnet CI MK4 ....**57** A8
Dunny La WD4 ....**156** F7
Dunsby Rd MK6 ....**47** A4
Dunsham La HP20 ....**101** E2
Dunsley PI HP23 ....**119** B3
Dunsmore Ave HP27 ...**139** C5
Dunsmore Ride HP27 ..**139** C5
Dunstable Downs* LU6 ..**93** E4
Dunstable Ho 4 SL7 ....**183** E1
Dunstable Rd
  Dagnall HP4 ....**107** C7
  Eaton Bray LU6 ....**93** A5
  Totternhoe LU6 ....**93** D7
Dunster CI MK4 ....**46** E3
Dunster Gdns SL1 ......**205** A6
Dunston Hill HP23 ....**119** A4
Dunthorne Way MK8 .....**45** D6
Dunton Rd LU7 ....**105** A8
Dunvedin PI MK12 ....**33** D4
Dunvegan CI MK2 ....**58** D4
Dunwood Ct SL6 ....**202** C5
Dunwood Rise HP13 ...**162** B1
Duparc CI MK7 ....**48** C5
Dupre CI SL1 ....**204** E4
Dupre Cres HP9 ....**176** B1
Durant La MK4 ....**57** B8
Durgate MK7 ....**48** A8
Durham Ave SL1 ....**205** A7
Durham Ho 1 MK3 ....**46** F1
Durley Hollow HP13 .....**162** B1
Durlston End MK4 ....**57** A8
Durrans Ct MK2 ....**47** E1
Durrans Ho MK2 ....**47** E1
Durrants Path HP5 ....**144** A4
Durrants Rd HP4 ....**134** F5
Durrell CI LU7 ....**80** E7
Dutch Barn CI TW19 ....**213** D1
Dutch Elm Ave SL4 ......**210** F7
Dutton Way SL0 ....**207** E7
Dyers Mews MK14 ....**34** F6
Dyers Rd LU6 ....**92** D7
Dyersdale MK13 ....**34** C1
Dyson CI SL4 ....**210** B4

Eagle CI HP6 ....**154** F2
Eagle Way MK43 ....**3** F6
Eagle Wlk MK4 ....**34** F3
Eagles Rd HP20 ....**116** A8
Eaglestone Rdbt MK6 ...**47** A8
Ealing Chase MK10 ......**47** F8
Eames CI HP20 ....**101** F3
Eardley PI MK8 ....**45** D6
Earl CI HP13 ....**162** A1
Earl Howe Rd HP13 .....**163** D6
Earls CI MK2 ....**58** C8
Earls La SL1 ....**204** F5
Earls Willow MK13 ....**34** A8
Earlsfield SL6 ....**203** C2
Earlswood Ct HP21 .....**116** A5
Easby Gr MK10 ....**36** A1
Eascote Rd HP21 ....**116** B4
Easington La HP18 ......**111** B1
Easington Terr HP18 ...**111** B1
East Berkshire Coll
  Maidenhead SL6 ....**202** D6
  Slough SL3 ....**207** A3
  Windsor SL4 ....**210** C5
East Burnham Cotts
  SL2 ....**198** A4
East Burnham La SL2 ..**198** A4
East Chapel MK4 ....**57** B8
East Claydon Rd MK18 ..**65** D2
East Claydon Sch MK18 **74** E7
East Comm SL3 ....**188** E5
East Cres SL4 ....**209** F6
East Dales MK13 ....**34** C5
East Dr
  High Wycombe HP13 .....**173** E8
  Stoke Poges SL2 ....**198** E2
East End HP22 ....**87** D1
East Green CI MK5 ....**45** F6
East Hills MK43 ....**25** B1
East La MK7 ....**47** F7
East Paddock SL6 ....**194** F6
East Rd Cranfield MK43 ...**24** E2
  Maidenhead SL6 ....**202** E7
  West Drayton UB7 ....**208** D3
East Richardson St 6
  HP11 ....**172** F7
East Ridge SL8 ....**185** B4
East Spur MK7 ....**47** F7
East St Adstock MK18 ...**53** F1
  Chesham HP5 ....**154** B8
East Terr SL4 ....**210** E7
East View OX25 ....**81** A3
East Way HP9 ....**175** A1
East Wlk N MK9 ....**34** E2
East Wlk S MK9 ....**34** E2
Eastbourne Rd SL1 .....**205** A7
Eastbridge SL2 ....**206** B5
Eastbrook CI OX25 ....**95** E7
Eastbury Ct MK4 ....**46** D1
Eastcott CI MK4 ....**46** D1
Eastcroft SL2 ....**198** B1
Eastcroft Ct MK4 ....**46** C1
Eastern Dene HP5 ....**163** B5
Eastern Dr SL8 ....**185** C4
Eastern St HP20 ....**101** E1
Eastfield CI 3 SL1 ......**206** A3
Eastfield Cres NN12 ....**18** E5
Eastfield Dr MK18 ....**11** A3

Eastfield Rd
Aylesbury HP20 ....116 B8
Burnham SL1 ....204 A8
Princes Risborough HP27 .139 C3
Eastlands HP27 ....149 E5
Eastleigh Rd SL3 ....146 A3
Eastoke Pl MK4 ....57 A8
Easton St HP11 ....173 B6
Easton Terr HP13 ......173 C6
Eastwick Cres WD3 ....178 F8
Eastwood Ct 1 SL7 ....183 F3
Eastwood Rd HP14 .....158 F3
Eaton Ave
High Wycombe HP12 .....172 D8
Milton Keynes MK2 ......58 D7
Eaton Bray Lower Sch
LU6 ....92 F6
Eaton Bray Rd
Edlesborough LU6 ....92 C5
Honeywick LU6 ....92 E8
Eaton Mill Comb Sch
MK2 ....58 D6
Eaton Pk LU6 ....92 F6
Eaton Pl HP12 ....172 D8
Eaton Rd HP21 ....115 D7
Eatongate Cl LU6 ......92 E5
Ebble Cl HP21 ....115 C4
Ebbsgrove MK5 ....34 B1
Ebenezer Ho HP10 .....174 C2
Ebsworth Cl SL6 ....196 C3
Eddington Ct MK4 ......46 D1
Eddy St HP4 ....135 A5
Eden Cl Aylesbury HP21 .115 D4
Slough SL3 ....207 A1
Edgar Rd UB7 ....208 E5
Edgar Wallace Pl SL8 ..185 B5
Edge Hill Ct MK18 ......41 E2
Edgecombe Rd HP21 ....116 B5
Edgecote MK8 ....46 A8
Edgecote Ho 11 HP23 ...173 B7
Edgecott Rd HP18 ......82 F7
Edgehill OX9 ....125 F2
Edgewood HP11 ....173 D5
Edinburgh Ave SL1 .....205 D7
Edinburgh Dr UB9 ......189 F5
Edinburgh Gdns SL6 ....210 D5
Edinburgh Ho MK3 ......57 D7
Edinburgh Pl HP21 .....115 C6
Edinburgh Rd
Maidenhead SL6 ....195 C1
Marlow SL7 ....183 E3
Edison Cl UB7 ....200 B2
Edison Rd HP19 ....100 E1
Edison Sq MK5 ....46 C5
Edith Bell Ho SL9 ......177 E4
Edith Rd SL1 ....42 A1
Edlesborough Sch LU6 ..92 C3
Edlyn Cl HP4 ....134 F5
Edmonds Cl MK18 ......41 F1
Edmonds Ho HP14 ......171 B4
Edmonds Sh Ctr HP14 ..171 B4
Edmund Ct
Beaconsfield HP9 ....186 A8
Milton Keynes MK5 ......45 F7
Edmunds Cl HP12 ......172 C5
Edmunds Gdns HP12 ....172 C5
Edmunds Way SL2 ......206 B7
Edrich Ave MK6 ....46 F8
Edstone Pl MK4 ....46 C3
Edward Cl HP21 ....116 A4
Edward Wlk HP21 ......116 A4
Edwards Ct SL1 ....205 E4
Edwin Allman Pl SL7 ...162 E2
Edwin Cl MK17 ....48 D2
Edy Ct MK5 ....34 A1
Ezell Cres MK4 ....45 F8
Eelbrook Ave MK13 .....34 C2
Eeles Cl HP19 ....100 F3
Egerton Cl MK13 ....38 A7
Egerton Gate MK5 ......46 B4
Egerton Rd
Berkhamsted HP4 ....135 B6
Slough SL2 ....197 E1
Egerton-Rothesay Lower Sch
HP4 ....135 B4
Egerton-Rothesay Sch
HP4 ....134 C4
Egglesfield Cl HP4 .....134 E6
Eggleton Dr HP23 ......119 A5
Eghams Ct HP9 ....175 C4
Eghams Ct 8 SL8 ......185 B3
Eghams Gn SL8 ....185 B3
Eghams Wood Rd HP9 ..175 C4
Egmont Ave MK11 ......32 C4
Egremont Gdns SL1 ....205 A5
Egypt La SL2 ....187 B1
Egypt Way HP11 ....173 C6
Egypt Wood Cotts SL2 ..187 B1
Eider Cl MK18 ....52 E8
Eight Acres Burnham SL1 .197 B7
Tring HP23 ....119 A4
Elangeni Sch HP6 ......154 E3
Elbow Mdw SL3 ....212 F6
Elder Cl Loudwater HP11 .174 B3
West Drayton UB7 ......208 C5
Elder Gate
Milton Keynes,Rooksley
MK9 ....34 C1
Milton Keynes,Winterhill
MK9 ....46 C8
Elder Way HP15 ....163 B3
Elderdene OX39 ....147 D8
Elderfield Rd SL2 ......198 F6
Eldridge La HP17 ......130 C3
Eleanor Cl MK47 ....60 F7
Eleanor Gdns HP21 .....115 F6
Eleanor Rd SL9 ....177 C2

Eleanor Wlk MK17 ......60 F7
Elfords MK6 ....47 A6
Elgar Gr MK7 ....48 C4
Elgin Ho SL3 ....212 E6
Elgiva La HP5 ....154 B8
Elham Way HP21 ....116 A4
Eliot Cl Aylesbury HP19 ..100 F2
Newport Pagnell MK16 ....21 F5
Eliot Dr SL7 ....183 F4
Elizabeth Ave HP6 .....166 C8
Elizabeth Cl
Aylesbury HP21 ....116 B4
Milton Keynes MK2 ......58 D7
Elizabeth Ct
High Wycombe HP13 .....173 C6
High Wycombe, Wycombe Marsh
HP13 ....173 E5
10 Slough SL1 ....206 A4
3 Windsor SL4 ....173 D5
Elizabeth Dr HP23 .....119 B6
Elizabeth Rd Marlow SL7 .183 E3
Stokenchurch HP14 .....158 F4
Elizabeth Way SL2 .....198 F4
Elkins Rd SL2 ....187 E2
Ellen Pl HP21 ....115 C5
Ellen Rd HP21 ....115 C5
Ellen Wlk HP21 ....115 B6
Ellenstow MK13 ....34 A4
Ellesborough Gr MK8 ...33 D3
Ellesborough Rd
Butler's Cross HP17 .....130 C2
Ellesborough HP17 ......130 A2
Wendover HP22 ....131 A3
Ellesmere Cl
Datchet SL3 ....211 A8
Totternhoe LU6 ....93 C6
Ellesmere Rd HP4 ......135 D4
Elliman Ave SL2 ....205 F6
Ellington Ct SL6 ....203 C7
Ellington Gdns SL6 .....203 C7
Ellington Pk SL6 ....195 F1
Ellington Prim Sch SL6 ..203 C7
Ellington Rd SL6 ....203 C7
Elliots Cl UB8 ....208 C8
Elliott Ho HP11 ....172 F8
Ellis Ave
Chalfont St Peter SL9 ....177 F2
Slough SL1 ....205 E4
Ellis Way HP14 ....171 B4
Ellisgill Cl MK13 ....34 A4
Ellison Cl SL4 ....209 F4
Ellison Ct HP23 ....118 F3
Ellison Ho 14 SL4 ......210 D6
Ellsworth Rd HP11 .....172 F4
Ellwood Ho SL9 ....177 E2
Ellwood Rd HP9 ....175 B1
Ellwood Rise HP9 ......177 C8
Ellwood Terr WD3 ......167 D4
Elm Brook Cl HP4 ......112 C1
Elm Cl Amersham HP6 ..154 C1
Butler's Cross HP17 .....130 C3
Chinnor OX39 ....147 C5
Farnham Common SL2 ..198 C6
Hazelmere HP15 ....163 A3
Newton Longville MK17 ..57 C2
Weston Turville HP22 ....116 F2
Elm Croft SL3 ....211 C6
Elm Ct Berkhamsted HP4 .135 B4
Butler's Cross HP17 .....130 C3
Elm Dr Chinnor OX39 ...147 C5
Deanshanger MK19 ......31 D5
Elm Farm Rd HP21 .....116 A5
Elm Gn HP21 ....115 C4
Elm Gr Berkhamsted HP4 .135 C4
Maidenhead SL6 ....202 E7
West Drayton UB7 ......208 F6
Woburn Sands MK17 ....49 B4
Elm La SL8 ....184 F5
Elm Lawn Cl UB8 ......201 E5
Elm Rd
High Wycombe HP12 .....172 C4
Princes Risborough HP27 .139 C3
Tylers Green HP10 ......174 D8
Windsor SL4 ....210 B4
Elm St MK18 ....52 D8
Elm Tree Cotts HP7 ....164 C2
Elm Tree Farm OX25 ....81 A4
Elm Tree Wlk
Chorleywood WD3 ......167 F5
Tring HP23 ....119 A5
Elm Trees HP18 ....125 B7
Elmar Gn SL2 ....198 A2
Elmdale Gdns HP27 .....139 B3
Elmers Cl MK19 ....44 A6
Elmers Mdw MK18 ......76 A2
Elmers Pk MK3 ....58 A8
Elmfield Cl NN12 ....18 D3
Elmfields Gate MK18 ....66 A4
Elmhurst 8 HP16 ....152 A8
Elmhurst Cl
High Wycombe HP13 .....162 D1
Milton Keynes MK4 ......46 F4
Elmhurst Ct SL3 ....207 A3
Elmhurst Inf Sch HP20 ..101 C2
Elmhurst Jun Sch HP20 .101 C2
Elmhurst Rd
Aylesbury HP20 ....101 C2
Slough SL3 ....207 A3
Elmlea Dr MK46 ....6 E3
Elmodesham Ho 7 HP7 ..165 B7
Elmridge Ct MK46 ......46 C2
Elms Dr SL8 ....185 C3
Elms Rd SL9 ....177 E3
Elms The
Leighton Buzzard LU7 ....80 E7
Milton Keynes MK3 ......57 F8

Elms The continued
Preston Bissett MK18 ....51 B1
Elmshott Cl HP10 ......163 A1
Elmsmead La SL1 ......205 D4
Elmside MK18 ....66 A4
Elmslie Cl SL6 ....202 E7
Elmtree Ct 6 HP20 .....152 A8
Elmtree Gn HP16 ....152 A8
Elmtree Hill HP5 ....144 B1
Elmtree Sch HP5 ....144 B1
Elmwood
Maidenhead SL6 ....196 B4
Turvey MK43 ....8 E6
Elmwood Cl HP18 ......109 D5
Elmwood Pk SL9 ....188 E3
Elmwood Rd SL2 ....206 B6
Elora Rd HP13 ....173 E7
Elruge Cl UB7 ....208 D3
Elsage Ct LU7 ....105 B8
Elsmore Cl HP21 ....116 A4
Eltham Ave SL1 ....204 E4
Elthorne Rd UB8 ....201 D3
Elthorne Way MK16 ....22 C2
Elton MK6 ....47 D7
Elton Dr SL6 ....202 D8
Elwes Rd HP14 ....171 C4
Ely Ave SL1 ....205 D7
Ely Cl HP7 ....165 E8
Ely Ho HP13 ....173 F8
Ember Path HP21 ......115 C4
Ember Rd SL3 ....207 B3
Emberton Ctry Pk MK46 ...6 E1
Emberton Ctry Pk Visitors Ctr* MK46 ....6 E1
Embleton Way MK18 ....52 C7
Emerald Cl MK18 ....74 F8
Emerald La SL3 ....205 E4
Emerald Gate MK15 ....35 E5
Emerson Ct HP10 ......185 E6
Emerson Valley Sch MK4 ...46 C2
Emerton Ct HP4 ....134 E7
Emerton Garth HP4 ....134 E7
Emerton Gdns MK11 ....32 E5
Emilia Ct SL1 ....195 F1
Emlyns Bldgs SL4 ......210 D7
Emma Rothschild Ct
HP23 ....119 A5
Emmett Cl MK4 ....46 C1
Emperor Cl HP14 ......134 F2
Empingham Cl MK2 .....58 D4
Empstead Ct RG9 ......191 D2
Enborne Cl HP21 ....115 D4
Enfield Chase MK14 ....34 D5
Enfield Cl UB8 ....201 D3
Engaine Dr MK5 ....45 F7
English Gdns TW19 ....211 D2
Enmore Gate MK9 ......35 A3
Enmore Rdbt MK9 ......35 A3
Ennell Gr MK2 ....58 C5
Ennerdale Cl MK2 ......58 D6
Ennerdale Cres SL1 ....204 C8
Ensbury Path HP21 ....101 E2
Enterprise La MK9 .....35 A3
Epsom Cl LU7 ....80 D6
Epsom Gr MK3 ....57 D7
Eriboll Cl LU7 ....80 B6
Erica Cl SL1 ....204 D8
Eridge Gn MK7 ....48 A8
Errington Dr SL4 ....210 A4
Escarpment Ave LU6 ...107 D8
Esk Way MK3 ....58 B4
Eskdale Ave HP5 ....144 D1
Eskdale Gdns SL6 ......203 B2
Eskdale Lodge HP6 .....154 C2
Eskdale Rd
Stoke Mandeville HP22 ..116 B2
Uxbridge UB8 ....201 B3
Eskdale Way MK10 .....36 B3
Essenden Cl MK11 ......32 F5
Essex Ave SL2 ....205 C8
Essex Cl MK1 ....59 A5
Essex Ho 5 HP20 ....101 D1
Essex Pl HP19 ....100 F2
Essex Rd HP5 ....144 C2
Essex Yd HP22 ....89 C2
Estcourt Dr HP15 ......162 F6
Esther Cl MK13 ....34 A6
Eston Ct MK13 ....34 A5
Estover Way OX39 .....147 B6
Etheridge Ave MK10 ...48 C8
Ethorpe MK8 ....33 E1
Ethorpe Cl SL9 ....188 E6
Ethorpe Cres SL9 ......188 E6
Ethorpe Ho SL9 ....188 E6
Eton Cl SL3 ....211 A8
Eton Coll SL4 ....210 D8
Eton Cres MK12 ....33 A6
Eton Ct SL4 ....210 D7
Eton End PNEU Sch
SL3 ....211 A8
Eton Pl 1 SL1 ....205 F3
Eton Pl SL7 ....183 D2
Eton Porny CE Fst Sch
SL4 ....210 D8
Eton Rd SL3 ....211 A8
Eton Riverside SL4 .....210 D7
Eton Sq SL4 ....210 D7
Eton Wick CE Fst Sch
SL4 ....205 A1
Eton Wick Rd SL4 ......205 A1
Eton Wlk SL1 ....205 E3
Eunice Gr HP5 ....154 D7
Europa Bsns Pk MK10 ..36 C2
Europa Ho SL9 ....188 E6

Evans Cl Aylesbury HP21 .116 A4
Chearsley HP18 ....112 B2
Evans Gate MK6 ....46 E8
Evans Way SL3 ....119 B4
Evelyn Cl LU7 ....79 E1
Evelyn Pl MK13 ....34 A7
Evelyns Cl UB8 ....208 F7
Evenley Rd NN13 ......38 D1
Evenlode SL6 ....202 F8
Evenlode Cl SL8 ....185 B4
Everard Ave SL1 ....205 E4
Everest Cl HP13 ....173 D6
Everest Rd HP13 ....173 E6
Everglade MK6 ....47 A8
Evergreen Oak Ave SL4 .211 A4
Everley Cl MK47 ....46 C3
Evesham Gn HP19 .....101 C3
Evesham Way MK5 .....45 D5
Ewart Cl HP20 ....101 F1
Ewreham Rd SL0 ......207 E7
Exbury La MK4 ....45 F1
Exchange Ho MK9 ......34 E2
Exchange St HP20 .....115 E8
Exbridge MK4 ....46 A1
Exhims Mews HP4 .....134 E6
Exmoor Gate MK4 .....46 E2
Eynsford Terr UB7 .....208 F7
Eynsham Ct MK15 ......35 C2
Eyre Cl HP19 ....114 F8
Eyre Gn SL2 ....198 A2
Eythrope Rd HP18 .....100 A1
Eythrope HP18 ....100 A1
Stone HP17 ....114 C6

F

Factory Yd HP9 ....175 E1
Fadmoor Pl 3 MK4 .....46 B3
Fagnall La HP7 ....164 D2
Fair Acres HP16 ....151 D5
Fair Leas HP5 ....144 A2
Fair Mdw MK18 ....66 A4
Fair Mile Aylesbury HP21 .116 A7
Henley-on-T RG9 ....191 C4
Fair Ridge HP11 ....172 F4
Fair View Cotts
Chalfont St Peter SL9 ....177 F2
Cookham Rise SL6 ....195 E7
Faircross SL2 ....198 B1
Fairacres Ind Est SL4 ..209 D5
Faircroft SL2 ....198 B1
Fairfax MK13 ....34 C6
Fairfax Cres HP20 .....101 E2
Fairfax Mews HP7 .....165 A7
Fairfield HP6 ....154 B3
Fairfield App TW19 ....211 D1
Fairfield Ave SL3 ......211 A7
Fairfield Cl
Bourne End SL8 ....185 A5
Datchet SL3 ....211 D7
Olney MK46 ....7 A3
Fairfield La SL2 ....198 B3
Fairfield Rd
Burnham SL1 ....197 C2
Paulersbury NN12 ......17 B7
Uxbridge UB8 ....201 D6
West Drayton UB7 ......208 E6
Wraysbury TW19 ....211 D1
Fairfields HP15 ....151 E1
Fairford Cres MK15 ....35 B6
Fairford Leys Way HP19 .115 A7
Fairford Rd SL6 ....202 F8
Fairhaven SL7 ....177 F8
Fairhawn Pk SL4 ....209 E3
Fairlawns HP13 ....162 C1
Fairlea SL6 ....202 B3
Fairlie Rd SL1 ....205 A8
Fairlight Ave SL4 ......210 D5
Fairlight Dr UB8 ....201 D6
Fairmead The SL3 ......212 D7
Fairmile Ct RG9 ....191 D3
Fairthorn Cl HP23 .....118 E3
Fairview Ind Est
Amersham HP6 ....154 F1
High Wycombe HP11 .....173 F4
Fairview La HP10 ......174 A1
Fairview Rd
Burnham SL6 ....204 A7
Slough SL2 ....197 F1
Fairway HP27 ....139 A3
Fairway Ave UB7 ......208 D5
Fairway Cl SL3 ....211 A8
Fairway The
Burnham SL1 ....197 C3
Flackwell Heath HP10 ...185 C7
Maidenhead SL6 ....202 B3
Uxbridge UB10 ....201 F3
Fairways MK8 ....33 C2
Fairways Rdbt MK8 .....33 C2
Faith Terr UB7 ....114 C4
Faithfull Cl HP17 ....114 B5
Faithorn Cl HP5 ....144 A1
Falaise MK5 ....35 B7
Falcon Ave MK6 ....46 F7
Falcon Cl TW19 ....213 E1
Falcon Ridge HP4 ......135 C3
Falcon Rise HP13 ......161 C1
Falcon Way HP15 ......163 B3
Falconhurst Comb Sch
MK6 ....47 B8
Falcons Croft HP10 ....185 E8
Falkland Rd SL6 ....202 F8
Falklands Cl MK18 .....63 D2
Fall Cl HP19 ....101 D3
Falling La UB7 ....208 E6
Fallow Field HP15 .....163 B3

Fallows The SL6 ....196 A1
Fallowfield MK6 ....34 F1
Falmouth Rd SL1 ....205 A7
Fane Way SL6 ....202 D5
Fantail La HP23 ....118 F4
Far Furlong Cl HP21 ...115 D3
Faraday Cl SL2 ....205 B8
Faraday Dr MK5 ....46 C5
Faraday Rd
Aylesbury HP19 ....101 A1
Slough SL2 ....205 B8
Farinton MK8 ....33 F2
Farjeon Ct MK7 ....48 D4
Farm Cl
High Wycombe HP13 .....174 A7
Ickford HP18 ....123 F3
Little Chalfont HP6 ......166 D8
Maidenhead SL6 ....203 C1
Maidenhead, Highway SL6 .202 A2
Stewkley LU7 ....78 E7
Farm Cres SL2 ....206 C8
Farm Dr SL4 ....211 B1
Farm Gr HP9 ....175 E5
Farm La HP9 ....176 D3
Farm Lea HP10 ....185 F7
Farm Pl Berkhamsted HP4 .134 F5
Henton OX39 ....137 C1
Farm Rd Bourne End SL8 .184 F4
Brackley NN13 ....38 A6
Burnham SL6 ....204 A5
Chorleywood WD3 ......167 A3
Maidenhead SL6 ....202 A7
Farm Way TW19 ....212 F1
Farm Yd SL4 ....210 D7
Farmborough MK6 .....47 C6
Farmbrough Cl HP20 ...102 A1
Farmers Cl SL6 ....202 A4
Farmers Way
Maidenhead SL6 ....202 A4
Seer Green HP9 ....176 C4
Farmery Ct HP4 ....135 E6
Farnburn Ave SL1 .....205 B8
Farndale Gdns HP15 ...163 A6
Farnell Ct MK5 ....46 C8
Farnham Cl HP3 ....146 A5
Farnham Common Ho 3
SL2 ....198 C8
Farnham Common Inf Sch
SL2 ....198 B8
Farnham Common Jun Sch
SL2 ....198 C8
Farnham Cl MK8 ....33 F1
Farnham La SL2 ....198 A2
Farnham Park La SL2 ..198 C4
Farnham Royal CE Comb Sch
SL2 ....198 C2
Farnley Rd HP20 ......101 E2
Farrer Cl NN13 ....26 D4
Farrier Ct 1 SL8 ....185 B3
Farrier Pl MK14 ....35 A5
Farriers Cl HP3 ....146 A3
Farthing Ent Ctr The
MK6 ....47 C6
Farthing Gr MK6 ....47 C6
Farthing Green La SL2 ..199 B4
Farthingales The SL6 ..203 B7
Farthings The HP6 .....154 A3
Fassets Rd HP10 ....174 B2
Faulkner Way HP13 ....161 D3
Faulkner's Way LU7 ...80 E7
Fawcett Dr MK4 ....46 F4
Faversham Cl HP23 ....119 A4
Fawcett Rd SL4 ....210 B6
Fawley Bottom La RG9 .180 A1
Fawley Cl SL6 ....195 D2
Fawley Ct* RG9 ....191 E5
Fawley Gn RG9 ....190 F2
Fawley Hill Rly* RG9 ..191 D8
Fawsley Cl SL3 ....212 E7
Featherbed La HP15 ...163 D8
Featherstone Rd MK12 .33 A3
Fedden Ho MK43 ....24 D5
Fegans Ct MK11 ....32 C6
Felbridge MK7 ....48 A7
Felden La HP3 ....146 D8
Felden Ct HP18 ....125 D6
Fellstead Ct SL6 ....202 C6
Fences La MK16 ....13 A2
Fennel Dr MK14 ....34 E4
Fennels Farm Rd HP10 .174 A1
Fennels Rd HP11 ....174 A4
Fennels The HP11 .....174 A3
Fennels Way HP10 .....174 A1
Fennemore Cl HP18 ....109 D4
Fennings The HP6 .....154 D3
Fenny House Tuition Service
MK6 ....47 A6
Fenny Rd MK17 ....69 E8
Fenny Stratford Sta MK1 .47 E1
Fennymere MK8 ....33 D1
Fenton Ct MK8 ....45 F8
Fern Cotts SL7 ....184 E5
Fern Gr MK16 ....135 B4
Fern Dr SL6 ....204 B7
Fern La Fern SL7 ....184 E5
Haddenham HP17 ....127 A4
Fern Wlk HP15 ....163 B3
Fernan Dell MK8 ....45 D7
Fernborough Haven 4
MK4 ....46 B1
Ferndale Ave SL6 ......35 B1
Ferndale Cl HP14 ......158 F4
Ferndale Cres UB8 .....201 C2

Ferne Furlong MK46 ......6 F5
Fernes CI UB8 ....208 C7
Fernfield MK17 ....56 A5
Fernhill CI OX9 ....136 A6
Fernhurst CI HP9 ......175 F2
Fernie Fields HP22 ....172 C4
Fernlea CI HP10 ....174 A1
Fernley Ct SL6 ....195 D1
Ferns The HP9 ....175 F1
Fernside
  Great Kingshill HP15 ....151 E1
  Hazelmere HP15 ......163 A6
Fernsleigh CI SL9 ......177 E4
Fernwood Sch MK17 ....49 B2
Ferrers Ave UB7 ....208 D4
Ferrers CI SL1 ....204 E5
Ferry End SL6 ....203 C4
Ferry La Bourne End SL8 ..196 B8
  Medmenham SL7 ......193 B5
  Mill End RG9 ....192 D6
Ferry Rd SL6 ....203 C4
Festival Cotts SL3 ....212 C7
Fetty PI SL2 ....202 D4
Field CI Aylesbury HP20 ..102 A2
  Chesham HP5 ....144 E3
  Ickford HP18 ....A3
  Sherington MK16 ......14 A2
Field Ct MK5 ....46 B8
Field End HP18 ....125 F5
Field End CI HP23 ......119 D1
Field Farm Bsns Ctr
  OX26 ....71 A5
Field Hurst SL3 ....206 F1
Field La MK12 ....33 B5
Field Rd Denham UB9 ..189 E1
  Denham,Rush Green UB9 ..200 E8
  High Wycombe HP12 ..172 B5
  Murcott OX5 ....94 A5
Field Way
  Aylesbury HP20 ......102 A2
  Bovingdon HP3 ......146 A4
  Chalfont St Peter SL9 ..177 D2
  Uxbridge UB8 ....201 D1
Field Wlk MK9 ....34 F3
Fieldfare HP19 ....101 E4
Fieldhead Gdns SL8 ....185 A3
Fieldhouse Ct HP13 ....174 A4
  Fieldhouse Ind Est SL7 ..183 F2
Fieldhouse La SL7 ......183 F2
Fieldhouse Way SL7 ....183 F2
Fielding Gdns SL3 ....206 C4
Fielding Rd SL6 ......202 B8
Fields End HP23 ......119 A6
Fields The SL1 ....205 D4
Fieldway Amersham HP7 ..165 B6
  Berkhamsted HP4 ....135 E2
  Chalfont St Peter SL9 ..177 D3
  Wigginton HP23 ......119 D1
Fife Ct MK4 ....57 A8
Fife Ho MK3 ....46 F1
Fifth St HP11 ....173 C4
Filey Spur SL1 ....205 B4
Filgrave Sch MK16 ....13 C5
Filmer Rd SL4 ....209 D5
Finch CI HP10 ....35 F3
Finch Cres LU7 ....80 E5
Finch Ct SL6 ....202 D5
Finch End HP10 ......174 C8
Finch Gn WD3 ....167 F5
Finch La Amersham HP7 ..165 F5
  Beaconsfield HP9 ....175 C5
  Little Chalfont HP7 ....166 B7
Finch Rd HP4 ....135 A4
Findlay Way MK2 ......58 C8
Fingest La RG9 ....170 D4
Fingle Dr MK13 ....33 E7
Finians CI UB10 ......201 F5
Finings Rd HP14 ......171 A4
Finlay Dr RG9 ....191 E2
Finlay Ho RG9 ....191 E3
Finmere CE Prim Sch
  MK18 ....50 D6
Finmere Rd HP18 ......116 C5
Fir Tree Ave SL2 ......198 F1
Fir Tree Cotts HP14 ..161 B8
Fircroft CI SL2 ....199 A6
Fircroft Ct SL2 ....199 A6
Fire La MK17 ....57 D4
Firecrest Way HP19 ..100 F1
Firfield SL6 ....203 B1
Firs Ave SL4 ....209 F4
Firs CI Hazlemere HP15 ..163 B2
  High Wycombe HP13 ..173 E8
  Iver Heath SL0 ......200 C4
  Lane End HP14 ......171 C5
  Whitchurch HP22 ......87 A5
Firs Ct Amersham HP6 ..154 A1
  Bierton HP22 ....102 C4
  Princes Risborough HP27 ..138 F3
Firs Dr SL3 ....206 F5
Firs End SL9 ....188 D8
Firs Rise HP16 ....151 E7
Firs The Bierton HP22 ..102 C4
  Brill HP18 ....110 B8
  Maidenhead SL6 ......195 C1
  Uxbridge UB8 ....201 D1
  Wigginton HP23 ......119 D1
Firs View Rd HP15 ....163 B2
Firs Wlk HP15 ....163 B2
First Ave Amersham HP7 ..165 D7
  Marlow SL7 ....184 A2
  Milton Keynes MK1 ....47 C1
First Cres SL1 ....205 C8
First St HP11 ....173 C3
Firview CI SL7 ....183 F1

Fish Ponds La OX9 ....125 E1
Fisherman's Way SL8 ..185 B4
Fishermans CI MK46 ....6 E4
Fishermans Retreat SL7 ..183 E1
Fishermead Bvd MK6 ..35 A1
Fishers Field MK18 ....52 C8
Fishery Rd SL6 ....203 C5
Fishguard Spur SL1 ..206 B4
Fishweir LU7 ....68 D1
Fitzgeralds Way HP12 ..172 B7
Fitzhamon Ct MK12 ....33 A5
Five Acre Wood HP12 ..172 C6
Five Acres Chesham HP5 ..154 D6
  Woburn Green HP10 ..185 F7
Five Points SL0 ....200 C2
Flaggs Mdw MK46 ......6 E4
Flambard CI MK15 ......35 A7
Flamborough Spur SL1 ..205 A4
Flamingo Zoo Gardens Pk*
  MK18 ....6 B3
Flaunden Bottom HP5 ..155 E4
Flaunden Hill HP3 ....156 A6
Flaunden La
  Bovingdon HP3 ......146 D3
  Chipperfield WD3 ....156 E6
Flavius Gate NN13 ....38 A7
Flaxbourne Ct MK7 ....48 C7
Flaxen Field HP22 ....116 F2
Flaxley Gate MK10 ....36 B5
Fledgelings Wlk MK18 ..66 A5
Fleet CI Buckingham MK18 ..41 F2
  Walter's Ash HP14 ....161 F7
Fleet St HP20 ....101 D1
Fleet The MK6 ....35 B2
Fleetbrook Ho SL3 ....211 D6
Fleetwood CI HP8 ....177 A6
Fleetwood Ct TW19 ..213 E1
Fleetwood Rd SL2 ....205 F6
Fleetwood Spur SL1 ..125 F2
Fleming CI SL3 ....206 C3
Fleming Dr MK6 ....47 B6
Fleming Way HP12 ....172 D5
Fletcher CI HP19 ......100 F3
Fletchers Mews MK14 ..34 F6
Flint Ho MK3 ....46 F1
Flint Hollow OX39 ....147 B6
Flint St HP17 ....127 A5
Flint Way HP16 ....151 C7
Flintergill Ct MK13 ....34 B4
Flintlock Ct TW19 ....213 A3
Flitcroft Lea HP13 ....173 A8
Flitton Ct MK11 ....32 F5
Flora Thompson Dr
  MK16 ....21 F6
Florence Ave SL6 ......203 A8
Florence Ct HP19 ....101 D1
Florence Way UB8 ....201 C5
Florida St HP11 ......173 C4
Florin CI MK15 ....35 A7
Flowers Bottom La
  HP27 ....150 B4
Fog Cotts HP23 ......120 A5
Folding CI LU7 ....78 E8
Foley CI HP9 ....175 C4
Foliejohn Way SL6 ....202 A1
Folkestone Ct SL3 ....207 A1
Follet CI SL4 ....211 B1
Folly La Hartwell NN7 ..10 C8
  North Crawley MK16 ..24 B5
Folly Rd MK19 ....31 D4
Fontwell CI SL6 ......202 A8
Fontwell Dr MK3 ......57 C6
Forbes PI MK5 ....45 E4
Forches CI MK4 ....46 D2
Ford End UB9 ....189 F2
Ford La SL0 ....208 A8
Ford St Buckingham MK18 ..52 D8
  High Wycombe HP13 ..173 F4
Ford Way HP13 ....161 E3
Ford's CI HP14 ....159 F8
Fordcombe Lea MK7 ....48 B8
Forelands Way HP5 ....154 C7
Forest CI
  Princes Risborough HP27 ..139 B3
  Wendover HP22 ......131 B4
Forest Point HP13 ....173 F5
Forest Rd Hanslope MK19 ..10 F5
  Piddington (Northants) NN7 ..4 A4
  Windsor SL4 ....209 E5
Forest Rise MK6 ......47 B8
Forest Way HP13 ......174 A8
Foresters
  Beacon's Bottom HP14 ..159 C5
  Chinnor OX39 ....147 B6
  Oakley HP18 ....109 D6
Forestry Hos OX49 ....168 A7
Forfar Dr MK3 ....46 F2
Forge CI Ashendon HP18 ..97 E1
  Holmer Green HP15 ..163 C6
  Horton-cum-S OX33 ..108 B5
  Marsh Gibbon OX27 ..71 F3
  Oakley HP18 ....109 D4
  Steeple Claydon MK18 ..63 E2
Forge Dr SL2 ....198 C6
Forge End HP7 ....165 B7
Forge Rd HP14 ....161 C8
Forge The MK46 ....6 E5
Forgetts Rd HP14 ....171 C4
Forlease CI SL6 ......203 A6
Forlease Dr SL6 ......203 A6
Forlease Rd SL6 ......203 A6
Formby CI
  Milton Keynes MK3 ....57 C7
  Slough SL3 ....207 C2
Forrabury Ave MK13 ..34 C3
Forsythia Gdns SL3 ..206 E4
Fort End HP17 ....127 A6
Fortescue Dr MK5 ......46 B6

Forthill PI MK5 ....45 F7
Fortuna Ct MK7 ....48 C6
Forty Gn HP27 ....137 F3
Forty Green Dr SL7 ..183 B2
Forty Green Rd HP9 ..175 C4
Forum The MK14 ....34 E5
Foscot Way MK18 ......41 E2
Foscote Cotts MK18 ..42 B4
Foscote Rd MK18 ......41 F3
Fossey CI MK5 ....45 F3
Foster Ave SL4 ......209 E4
Foster CI HP20 ....101 F3
Fosters La SL4 ....34 A3
Fosters Path SL2 ....197 F1
Fotherby Ct SL6 ......203 A6
Fotheringay Gdns SL1 ..205 A6
Fotherley Rd WD3 ....178 F8
Founders Dr UB9 ......189 F5
Founders Mews MK14 ..34 F6
Foundry La Horton SL3 ..212 B4
  Lacey Green HP27 ....149 C5
Fountain Ct
  G Aylesbury HP20 ....115 D8
  Olney MK46 ....6 F3
Fountain Gdns SL4 ....210 D4
Fountaine CI MK14 ....34 E7
Fourdrinier Ct HP11 ..174 A4
Fourth Ave SL7 ....184 A2
Fourth St HP11 ....173 B4
Fowler MK14 ....34 C7
Fowler Rd HP19 ......115 B8
Fowlers Farm Rd HP14 ..158 E4
Fox CI HP23 ....119 D1
Fox Cover OX39 ......147 C6
Fox Field HP15 ....162 F5
Fox La HP15 ....163 B6
Fox Milne Rdbt MK10 ..35 F4
Fox Rd
  Holmer Green HP15 ..163 B6
  Slough SL3 ....206 D2
  Wigginton HP23 ......119 C2
Fox Way MK18 ....52 E7
Foxborough CI SL3 ..207 A1
Foxborough Ct SL6 ..202 E4
Foxborough Prim Sch
  SL3 ....207 A1
Foxcovert Rd MK5 ....45 F4
Foxdell Way SL9 ......177 E5
Foxes Piece SL7 ......183 E2
Foxes Piece Sch SL7 ..183 E3
Foxgate MK16 ....22 B4
Foxglove HP27 ....115 B5
Foxglove CI MK18 ....52 C7
Foxglove CI MK16 ....21 F4
Foxgoles CI MK19 ....31 F5
Foxherne SL3 ....206 C4
Foxhill MK46 ....6 E5
Foxhill CI HP13 ......162 B1
Foxhollow Dr SL2 ....198 C7
Foxhunter Dr MK14 ..34 E6
Foxleigh HP17 ....173 A4
Foxley PI MK5 ....46 C8
Foxmoor Ct UB9 ......190 A5
Foxton MK6 ....47 D6
Fraderica Cotts MK16 ..22 C3
Framers Ct HP14 ......171 B4
Framewood Manor SL2 ..199 C6
Framewood Rd SL2,SL3 ..199 C6
Framlingham Ct MK5 ..46 A5
Frampton Ct UB9 ....189 F5
France Furlong MK14 ..34 F8
Frances Ave SL6 ......196 C1
Frances Ct LU7 ....80 E7
Frances St SL4 ......210 D5
Franchise St HP5 ....144 C1
Francis CI MK5 ....46 B6
Francis Edmonds Comb Sch
  HP14 ....171 B4
Francis Way SL1 ......204 D6
Frank Atter Croft MK12 ..33 C5
Frank Howe Ct MK46 ..35 A1
Frank Lunnon CI SL8 ..185 C3
Frank Sutton Way SL1 ..205 D6
Franklin Ave SL2 ....205 B8
Franklin CI HP17 ......127 A7
Franklin Ct HP7 ......154 C1
Franklin Rd Dunstable LU6 ..93 F8
  Haddenham HP17 ....127 A7
Franklins Croft MK12 ..33 C5
Franklyn Cres SL4 ..209 D4
Frankston Ave MK11 ..32 E5
Frankswood Ave UB7 ..208 F7
Frantons The SL6 ....202 F7
Frascati Way SL6 ....202 F7
Fraser Rd HP12 ......128 B7
Fraucup Ct HP17 ......128 B7
Fray's Ct UB8 ....201 D5
Fray's Waye UB8 ......201 C4
Frays Ave UB7 ....208 D4
Frays CI UB7 ....208 D3
Frayslea UB8 ....201 C4
Frederick PI HP13 ....174 B3
Frederick Smith Ct MK12 ..33 D4
Frederick St HP18 ....99 A7
Fredericks CI HP9 ..186 A8
Freeman CI MK12 ......33 B5
Freeman Ct HP5 ......144 C1
Freemans CI SL2 ......199 A6
Freemans Gdns MK46 ..7 A3
Fremantle Dr
  Aylesbury HP21 ......115 E5
  High Wycombe HP13 ..162 E5
Frenchum Gdns SL1 ..204 E5
Frensham Dr MK2 ......58 C7

Frensham Wlk SL2 ....198 C6
Friarage Rd HP20 ....115 D8
Friars Field HP4 ......134 E7
Friars Furlong HP18 ..125 B7
Friars Gdns HP14 ....162 A2
Friars Rd HP20 ....115 D8
Friars Wlk
  Prestwood HP16 ....151 D5
  Tring HP23 ....119 A4
Friarscroft Way HP20 ..115 C8
Friary Gdns MK16 ......22 C2
Friary Rd TW19 ....211 C1
Friary The CI OX9 ....211 C1
Friday St OX9 ....125 F1
Friday St
  Henley-on-T RG9 ....191 E2
  Leighton Buzzard LU7 ..80 F7
Frieth CE Comb Sch
  RG9 ....170 F1
Frieth Rd SL7 ....182 E5
Fripp Gdns MK8 ......45 D6
Frith Hill
  Great Missenden HP16 ..152 B7
  South Heath HP16 ....152 C8
Frithe The SL2 ....198 C3
Frithsden Copse HP4 ..135 F8
Frithwood Cres MK7 ..48 B7
Frog La HP18 ....112 F3
Froggy La UB9 ....189 D1
Frogmill SL6 ....193 C3
Frogmill Ct SL6 ......193 C3
Frogmill Spinney SL6 ..193 C4
Frogmoor HP13 ......173 A7
Frogmore CI
  Hughenden Valley HP14 ..162 A7
  Slough SL1 ....205 A4
Frogmore Cotts SL4 ..210 E5
Frogmore Ct SL6 ....202 F7
Frogmore Dr SL4 ....210 F5
Frogmore Flats SL4 ..210 F5
Frogmore La HP18 ..125 C5
Frogmore St HP23 ....119 A3
Frome CI HP21 ....115 C5
Fromer Rd HP10 ......185 D4
Frost Ho HP4 ....135 C3
Foxfield CI MK4 ......46 A5
Fryday St MK6 ....46 E7
Fryer CI HP5 ....154 D6
Fryers Ct HP12 ......172 D8
Fryers La HP12 ......172 D8
Frymley View SL4 ....209 D6
Fulbrook Mid Sch MK17 ..49 B5
Fulbrook St SL6 ......203 A8
Fuller's CI HP5 ......154 B6
Fuller's Hill HP5,HP6 ..154 A6
Fullers Yd SL6 ....196 B2
Fulmar PI HP19 ......101 F3
Fulmer Chase SL1 ..199 C8
Fulmer Common Rd
  SL3,SL0 ....199 C6
Fulmer CI SL6 ....202 D8
Fulmer Dr SL9 ....188 D2
Fulmer Inf Sch SL3 ..199 E8
Fulmer La SL0 ....199 F7
Fulmer Rd SL3 ......188 E2
Fulmer St
  Milton Keynes,Emerson Valley
  MK4 ....46 C3
  Milton Keynes,Medbourne
  MK8,MK5 ....45 C3
Fulton CI HP13 ......173 A8
Fulwell Ct MK14 ......34 E8
Fulwell Rd Finmere MK18 ..50 F2
  Westbury NN13 ......39 A4
Fulwood Ct TW19 ....213 F1
Fulwoods Dr MK6 ......47 A8
Furlong CI SL8 ......185 B3
Furlong Cres HP17 ..115 A1
Furlong La LU6 ....93 C7
Furlong Rd SL8 ......185 B3
Furlong The I2 HP23 ..119 A3
Furness CI SL4 ......209 C5
Furness Cres MK3 ....47 A1
Furness PI I3 SL4 ....209 C5
Furness Row I3 SL4 ..209 C5
Furness Sq I3 SL4 ....209 C5
Furness Way SL4 ....209 C5
Furness Wlk I7 SL4 ..209 C5
Furnival Ave SL2 ....205 B8
Furrow CI HP21 ......115 D4
Furrow Way SL6 ......202 A4
Furrows The UB9 ....190 C6
Furtho CI MK19 ....32 B7
Furtho La NN12 ......18 E3
Fury CI MK8 ....45 F7
Furze Down Sch MK18 ..65 F4
Furze Field HP16 ....142 B8
Furze La HP15 ....65 E5
Furze Platt Halt SL6 ..195 E1
Furze Platt Inf Sch SL6 ..195 C1
Furze Platt Jun Sch
  SL6 ....195 C1
Furze Platt Senior Sch
  SL6 ....195 C2
Furze Rd SL6 ....195 D1
Furze View WD3 ......167 C4
Furzefield Rd HP9 ..175 C2
Furzeham Rd UB7 ....208 E4
Furzton CI SL2 ....198 A2
Furzton Rdbt MK4 ....46 C4
Fuzzens Wlk SL4 ....209 E5
Fyfield Barrow MK7 ..48 C6
Fyne Dr LU7 ....80 C8

G

Gable Thorne MK7 ....48 D6
Gables CI
  Chalfont St Peter SL9 ..177 E5
  Datchet SL3 ....211 A8
  Maidenhead SL6 ....203 B8
  Wendover HP22 ......131 A4
Gables Dr HP14 ......149 C1
Gables Mdw HP15 ....163 C6
Gables The Datchet SL3 ..211 A8
  Haddenham HP17 ....127 A5
  Leighton Buzzard LU7 ..80 E6
Gabriel CI MK7 ....48 C5
Gaddesden Cres MK7 ..48 C5
Gadge CI OX9 ....125 E1
Gadmore La HP23 ....132 F7
Gadsden CI MK43 ....25 D3
Gadsden Ct MK17 ....69 E8
Gage CI SL6 ....202 E4
Gainsborough CI SL6 ..195 F5
Gainsborough Ct MK8 ..45 D6
Gainsborough Dr SL6 ..202 D8
Gainsborough Hill RG9 ..191 D1
Gainsborough PI HP19 ..100 F3
Gainsborough Rd
  Aylesbury HP21 ......115 E4
  Henley-on-T RG9 ....191 D1
Gairloch Ave MK2 ....58 D5
Galahad CI SL1 ......205 A4
Gallagher Ct MK8 ....45 E6
Galleries The I4 HP13 ..173 A7
Galley Hill MK11 ......32 F5
Galley La MK17 ....59 A4
Galleymead Rd SL3 ..212 F6
Galloway HP19 ......101 A3
Galloway Chase SL2 ..206 A6
Galloway CI MK3 ......46 E2
Gallows La HP12 ......172 C8
Gallys Rd SL4 ....209 D6
Galsworthy PI HP19 ..100 F4
Galvin Rd SL1 ......205 C6
Gamnel HP23 ....119 A6
Gamnel Mews HP23 ..119 B7
Gamnel Terr HP23 ..119 A6
Gandon Vale HP13 ..173 A8
Gandon CI MK43 ......3 A8
Ganton CI MK4 ....46 B1
Garamonde Dr MK8 ..33 F2
Garbo CI MK8 ....45 D7
Garden CI Halton HP22 ..131 C8
  Maidenhead SL6 ....202 A5
Garden Cotts SL3 ....212 D7
Garden Ct HP11 ......174 B3
Garden End HP6 ......154 E2
Garden Field La HP4 ..135 E7
Garden Mews SL1 ..205 F5
Garden Reach HP8 ..166 D6
Gardener Wlk HP15 ..163 C6
Gardens CI HP14 ....158 F4
Gardens The MK18 ....53 F1
Gardiner Ct MK13 ....33 E6
Gardner CI
  Aylesbury HP19 ....101 A3
  Great Kingshill HP15 ..151 D1
Gardner Ho SL6 ......195 E1
Gardner's CI SL6 ....195 D2
Gardner's CI LU6 ......93 E7
Garfield PI I1 SL4 ....210 C5
Garland Ave MK18 ....45 E8
Garland Way HP22 ..117 E5
Garner Ct I8 TW19 ..213 E1
Garners CI SL9 ......177 F4
Garners End SL9 ....177 E4
Garners Rd SL9 ......177 E4
Garnet CI SL1 ....205 A4
Garnet Ct SL7 ....183 C1
Garrard Rd SL2 ......197 F1
Garraways MK6 ......47 A6
Garrett CI HP5 ......154 D6
Garrick Wlk MK9 ......34 F3
Garron CI HP21 ......115 D3
Garrowmore Gr MK2 ..58 D5
Garry CI MK2 ....58 C5
Garson Gr HP5 ......144 A2
Garston MK8 ....33 F1
Garth The HP10 ......174 B2
Garthlands SL6 ......195 D2
Garthwaite Cres MK5 ..46 A4
Garvin Ave HP9 ......175 E2
Garwood Cres
  Milton Keynes MK8 ....45 C8
  Milton Keynes MK8 ....45 D6
Gas La SL6 ....203 A3
Gascon's Gr SL2 ....198 A4
Gaskin Ct MK14 ......35 A5
Gatcombe MK8 ....33 F1
Gate Cotts WD3 ......167 D5
Gatehouse CI
  Aylesbury HP19 ....115 C2
  Windsor SL4 ....210 B4
Gatehouse Sch The
  MK14 ....34 D7
Gatehouse Way HP19 ..101 B1
Gatenbury PI HP27 ..139 B3
Gatesdene CI HP4 ..121 C8
Gateway Ctr The HP12 ..172 D4
Gateway Sch The HP16 ..152 A8
Gatewick CI SL1 ....205 E5
Gatewick La MK7 ......48 A3
Gatting Way UB8 ....201 F6
Gatward Ave SL6 ....202 A3
Gaveston Dr HP4 ....135 B6
Gaveston Rd SL2 ....197 F2
Gaviots CI SL9 ......188 F3
Gaviots Gn SL9 ......188 F3
Gaviots Way SL9 ....188 E4

Gawcott Com Inf Sch
MK18 .....51 F4
Gawcott Fields MK18 .....52 B7
Gawcott Rd MK18 .....52 B6
Gawdrey Cl HP5 .....154 D6
Gayal Croft MK5 .....46 B4
Gayhurst Ho MK16 .....12 D1
Gayhurst Rd HP13 .....173 F7
Gayhurst Sch SL9 .....188 C7
Gayton Cl HP6 .....154 E4
Gees Farm Cl NN7 .....1 A5
Gell Cl UB10 .....190 F1
George Cl SL7 .....183 F4
George Ct HP18 .....83 B5
George Green Dr SL3 .....206 F7
George Green Rd SL3 .....206 E7
George Inn Pl MK16 .....12 B6
George Lee Ct HP14 .....160 C1
George Rd HP14 .....158 E5
George St
18 Aylesbury HP20 .....115 D8
Berkhamsted HP4 .....135 D4
Berkhamsted HP4 .....135 E4
5 Chesham HP5 .....144 C1
High Wycombe HP11 .....172 F7
Milton Keynes MK2 .....47 E1
Uxbridge UB8 .....201 D5
Wing LU7 .....79 E2
Woburn MK17 .....60 F7
George V Pl SL4 .....210 D7
George Yd MK11 .....32 D5
George's Hill HP15 .....162 F6
Georges Dr HP10 .....185 C7
Georgian Cl UB10 .....201 E8
Georgian Hts SL8 .....185 B5
Geralds Ct HP13 .....162 D1
Geralds Rd HP13 .....162 D2
Gerard Cl MK13 .....34 A7
Germain St HP5 .....154 B7
Germains Cl HP5 .....154 B7
Germander Park Fst Sch
MK14 .....34 D4
Germander Pl MK14 .....34 D4
Gerrards Cross CE Sch The
SL9 .....188 F4
Gerrards Cross Rd SL2 .....199 A6
Gerrards Cross Sta SL9 .....188 E6
Gershwin Ct MK7 .....48 C4
Gervaise Cl SL1 .....204 F5
Ghlbert Way HP4 .....135 A4
Ghyll Gdns HP4 .....134 D7
Gib La HP22 .....102 D4
Gibbings Cl MK18 .....76 A3
Gibbs Cl HP13 .....172 F8
Gibbs Ho HP11 .....173 F4
Gibbwin MK14 .....34 E8
Gibraltar La SL6 .....184 C1
Gibson Ct 9 SL3 .....206 F1
Gibson La HP17 .....127 A5
Gibson Pl TW19 .....213 C1
Gibson Rd
High Wycombe HP12 .....172 B3
Ickenham UB10 .....201 F8
Gibsons Gn
Milton Keynes MK13 .....34 C4
Milton Keynes MK13 .....34 C4
Giffard Park Comb Sch
MK14 .....22 A2
Giffard Park Rdbt MK14 .....21 F3
Giffard Rd MK2 .....58 C6
Giffard Way HP18 .....125 C7
Gifford Gate MK14 .....34 E7
Gifford Pl MK18 .....41 E1
Gilbert Cl MK3 .....58 B7
Gilbert Ho 4 HP11 .....172 E7
Gilbert Scott Ct 9 HP7 .....165 B7
Gilbert Scott Rd MK18 .....41 D2
Gilbert's Hill HP23 .....132 E3
Gilbey Wlk HP10 .....185 D4
Gilders Mews MK14 .....34 F6
Giles Brook Comb Sch
MK4 .....57 A7
Giles Gate HP16 .....151 B6
Gillamoor Cl 2 MK4 .....46 B3
Gilletts La HP12 .....161 C1
Gillfield Cl HP11 .....172 E3
Gilliat Rd SL1 .....205 E6
Gilliat's Gn WD3 .....167 D5
Gilliatt Cl SL0 .....207 E7
Gillott Ct SL6 .....202 F8
Gilman Cres SL4 .....209 D4
Gilmore Cl SL3 .....206 C4
Gilmore Rd HP20 .....101 E3
Gilpin Way MK46 .....7 A4
Gilpin's Ride HP4 .....135 D5
Gingers Cl HP22 .....117 E5
Gipsy La LU7 .....91 D8
Gisburn Cl MK13 .....34 B5
Glade Ho 5 SL7 .....183 E2
Glade Rd SL7 .....183 E2
Glade The
Gerrards Cross SL9 .....188 D2
Tylers Green HP10 .....163 C1
Glade View HP12 .....172 A3
Gladstone Cl MK16 .....22 D3
Gladstone Ind Est SL6 .....202 E8
Gladstone Rd HP5 .....144 C1
Gladstone Rise HP13 .....173 F6
Gladstone Way SL1 .....205 A5
Glaisyer Way SL0 .....200 D3
Glamis Ct HP13 .....173 B8
Glamis Ho MK3 .....57 E7
Glamorgan Cl MK3 .....46 F1
Glanmor Rd SL2 .....206 B6
Glassmill Ho 4 HP4 .....135 D4
Glastonbury Cl MK3 .....47 A2
Glastonbury Thorn Fst Sch
MK5 .....46 B6
Glaven Rd HP21 .....115 C4
Glazier Dr MK14 .....34 F6
Glebe Cl
Chalfont St Peter SL9 .....177 D3
Dorney SL6 .....203 F4
Holmer Green HP15 .....163 B7
Maids Moreton MK18 .....41 F3
Milton Keynes MK5 .....46 A8
Pitstone LU7 .....105 D5
Glebe Cotts HP14 .....169 C7
Glebe Dr NN13 .....38 A7
Glebe Ho SL9 .....177 D3
Glebe House Dr MK18 .....39 E6
Glebe La MK19 .....10 E5
Glebe Rd
Chalfont St Peter SL9 .....177 C2
Deanshanger MK19 .....31 E5
Maidenhead SL6 .....203 B5
Old Windsor SL4 .....211 B2
Uxbridge UB8 .....201 C3
Glebe Rdbt MK9 .....35 B4
Glebe Terr MK18 .....41 F3
Glebe The Lavendon MK46 .....7 F8
Lewknor OX49 .....157 B8
Prestwood HP16 .....151 C7
Stone HP17 .....114 C5
Walter's Ash HP14 .....161 D6
West Drayton UB7 .....208 F2
Weston Turville HP22 .....116 F2
Glebe Way HP6 .....154 D3
Glebelands HP10 .....174 C8
Glebelands Cl HP16 .....151 E4
Gledfield Pl MK12 .....33 D4
Gleeman Cl MK12 .....33 A5
Glen The SL3 .....206 C2
Glenavon Gdns SL3 .....206 C3
Gleneagles Cl
Milton Keynes MK3 .....57 D7
Stanwell TW19 .....213 D1
Glenfield Cl
Aylesbury HP21 .....116 A5
Stoke Poges SL2 .....198 F4
Glenham Rd OX9 .....126 B1
Glenister Rd
Chesham HP5 .....144 C3
High Wycombe HP12 .....172 B4
Glenisters Rd HP13 .....173 A8
Glenmore Cl HP10 .....174 A2
Glenmore Ho HP11 .....174 B3
Glenore SL6 .....196 A8
Glenstal Pl MK9 .....35 A3
Glentworth Pl SL1 .....205 C5
Glenwater Ho HP15 .....163 A5
Glenwoods MK16 .....22 C3
Glimbers Gr OX39 .....147 C5
Globe Ho UB7 .....208 D5
Globe La LU7 .....70 E1
Globeside Bsns Pk SL7 .....183 F2
Glory Cl HP10 .....185 F7
Glory Mill La
Beaconsfield HP9 .....185 F8
Wooburn Green HP10 .....185 E7
Gloucester Ave SL1 .....205 C8
Gloucester Ct UB9 .....190 A4
Gloucester Pl SL4 .....210 D5
Gloucester Rd
Maidenhead SL6 .....195 E2
Milton Keynes MK12 .....33 D5
Glovers Ct 2 HP20 .....101 E1
Glovers La MK13 .....34 B4
Glyn Sq MK12 .....33 D7
Glyn St MK13 .....34 A7
Glynswood
Chalfont St Peter SL9 .....177 F3
Chinnor OX39 .....147 C6
High Wycombe HP13 .....162 B1
Glynswood Ho OX39 .....147 C6
Glynswood Rd MK18 .....41 C1
Glynwood Ho SL6 .....203 A7
Goathland Croft 2 MK4 .....46 B2
Goddards Croft MK12 .....33 C5
Goddington Rd SL8 .....185 A5
Godfreys Cl HP18 .....96 B1
Godolphin Inf Sch SL1 .....205 C7
Godolphin Jun Sch SL1 .....205 D7
Godolphin Rd
Seer Green HP9 .....176 C4
Slough SL1 .....205 D6
Godrevy Gr MK4 .....57 B8
Godstowe Sch HP13 .....173 B8
Godwin Cl MK7 .....48 C7
Gogh Rd HP19 .....100 F2
Gold Crest HP19 .....101 F4
Gold Hill E SL9 .....177 D1
Gold Hill N SL9 .....177 C2
Gold Hill W SL9 .....177 C1
Gold Oak Wlk MK9 .....34 F3
Gold St MK19 .....11 A2
Golden Ball La SL6 .....195 A3
Golden Dr MK6 .....47 B8
Golden Hills OX39 .....147 D6
Golden Mede HP18 .....99 B6
Golden Miller Ct LU7 .....79 E2
Golden Oak Cl SL2 .....198 C6
Golden Riddy LU7 .....80 E8
Golder's Cl HP18 .....123 F3
Goldfield Inf Sch HP23 .....118 F3
Goldfield Rd HP23 .....118 F3
Goldilocks MK7 .....48 B6
Goldmark Cl MK7 .....48 D5
Goldsmith Dr MK16 .....21 F4
Goldsworthy Way SL1 .....204 C7
Golf Club La HP27 .....139 E5
Golspie Croft MK12 .....33 C4
Gomm Pl HP13 .....174 A4
Gomm Rd HP13 .....174 A4
Gomms Wood Cl HP9 .....175 B4
Gomms Wood Ho HP9 .....175 B4
Good Intent LU6 .....92 E4
Goodacres La HP27 .....149 E6
Goodall Cl RG9 .....191 E1
Goodlake Ct UB9 .....189 F4
Goodman Gdns MK6 .....47 D8
Goodman Pk SL2 .....206 C5
Goodrich Gn MK4 .....56 E8
Goodwick Gr MK4 .....57 B8
Goodwin Mdws HP10 .....185 E6
Goodwin Rd
Aylesbury HP19 .....115 C8
Slough SL2 .....197 F2
Goodwin Villas SL1 .....204 F5
Goodwins Mead LU7 .....105 A7
Goodwood MK8 .....45 F8
Goodwood Rise SL7 .....183 C7
Goose Acre Botley HP5 .....145 A1
Cheddington LU7 .....105 A7
Goose Gn SL2 .....198 B3
Goosemere MK19 .....31 E4
Goosen Gn HP21 .....116 C6
Goran Ave MK11 .....32 E4
Gordale MK13 .....34 C5
Gordon Rd Chesham HP5 .....154 C7
High Wycombe HP13 .....173 D6
Maidenhead SL6 .....202 D7
West Drayton UB7 .....208 E6
Windsor SL4 .....209 F5
Gordon Way HP8 .....177 B7
Gore Cl UB9 .....190 C7
Gore Hill HP7 .....165 B5
Gore Rd SL1 .....197 B2
Gore The SL1 .....197 A2
Gorelands La HP8 .....177 F8
Gorell Rd HP9 .....176 B1
Goring MK14 .....34 C7
Gorman Pl MK2 .....58 E4
Gorrell Cl MK18 .....51 B6
Gorrell La MK18 .....51 B6
Gorricks MK11 .....32 D4
Gorse Meade SL1 .....205 B5
Gorse Rd SL6 .....195 E6
Gorse Wlk
Hazlemere HP15 .....163 A3
West Drayton UB7 .....208 E7
Goslar Way SL4 .....210 B5
Gosling Gn SL3 .....206 E3
Gosling Gr HP13 .....161 D2
Gosling Rd SL3 .....206 E3
Goslington MK1 .....47 C2
Goss Ave HP18 .....99 B6
Gossage Rd UB10 .....201 F5
Gossmore Cl SL7 .....183 F1
Gossmore La SL7 .....183 F1
Gossmore Wlk SL7 .....183 F1
Gossom's End HP4 .....135 A5
Gossoms Ryde HP4 .....135 A5
Goswell Hill SL4 .....210 D6
Goswell Rd SL4 .....210 D6
Goudhurst Ct MK7 .....48 B7
Governors Ave UB9 .....189 F6
Governors Cl HP6 .....154 F1
Gower Ho HP6 .....154 E3
Gowers Field HP19,
HP20 .....101 D1
Gowers The HP6 .....154 E2
Gowers Yd MK19 .....32 B7
Gowings Gn SL1 .....204 E4
Goya Pl HP19 .....100 F2
Grace Ave MK6 .....46 E8
Grace Ct SL1 .....205 C5
Grace Reading Cl HP13 .....173 E6
Graces Cl MK43 .....25 C3
Graces Maltings 4
HP23 .....119 A3
Graeme Ave HP16 .....151 C6
Grafham Cl MK14 .....35 A8
Grafton Cl
Maidenhead SL6 .....195 E2
Potterspury NN12 .....18 E3
Slough SL3 .....206 E7
Grafton Ct NN7 .....4 A8
Grafton Gate MK9 .....34 C1
Grafton Ho OX39 .....147 C7
Grafton Orch OX39 .....147 D7
Grafton Pk MK9 .....34 D1
Grafton Rd
Aylesbury HP19 .....101 A2
Yardley Gobion NN12 .....18 F6
Grafton St
High Wycombe HP12 .....172 D8
Milton Keynes,Bradwell
MK13 .....34 B4
Milton Keynes,Granby MK1 .....47 B3
Milton Keynes,New Bradwell
MK12,MK13,MK19 .....33 E8
Milton Keynes,Winterhill
MK6 .....46 E7
Graham Cl SL6 .....202 C5
Graham Dr HP12 .....172 B5
Graham Ho SL9 .....177 C1
Graham Rd SL6 .....195 E6
Grainge Chase MK17 .....55 A3
Grainge Cl NN13 .....39 A5
Grampian Gate MK6 .....46 E7
Grampian Way SL3 .....207 A1
Gramwell MK5 .....45 F7
Granary Cl MK19 .....21 A3
Granborough Rd
North Marston MK18 .....76 A2
Winslow MK18 .....65 E2
Granby Ct MK1 .....47 A3
Granby Ind Est MK1 .....47 B3
Granby Rdbt MK1 .....47 C3
Grand Union Office Pk The
UB8 .....208 C7
Grandison Ho RG9 .....191 E3
Granes End MK14 .....34 E8
Grange Cl
Chalfont St Peter SL9 .....177 E2
Leighton Buzzard LU7 .....80 D6
Maids Moreton MK18 .....41 E3
Twyford MK18 .....62 D2
Wraysbury TW19 .....211 E1
Grange Cotts HP16 .....152 A3
Grange Dr HP10 .....185 D3
Grange Farm Rd HP14 .....159 B7
Grange Farm Rdbt MK8 .....45 D7
Grange Fields SL9 .....177 E2
Grange Gdn HP18 .....83 A6
Grange Gdns
Farnham Common SL2 .....198 D7
Wendover HP22 .....131 B5
Grange La SL6 .....195 F8
Grange Rd
Chalfont St Peter SL9 .....177 E2
Cookham Rise SL6 .....195 F7
Hazlemere HP15 .....162 F4
Hazlemere, Widmer End
HP15 .....162 E5
Henley-on-T RG9 .....191 E1
Milton Keynes MK3 .....57 F7
Pitstone LU7 .....105 D5
Tring HP23 .....119 C4
Wilstone HP23 .....104 D1
Grange Sch The HP21 .....115 F6
Grange The
Burnham SL1 .....197 C2
Gerrards Cross SL9 .....188 E6
Old Windsor SL4 .....211 B2
Wraysbury TW19 .....211 E1
Grange View HP27 .....139 E7
Grange Way SL0 .....207 F7
Grangelands Nature
Reserve* HP27 .....139 F6
Grangers Croft MK12 .....33 C4
Grangewood SL3 .....206 C8
Grant Ave SL1 .....205 E7
Grant Ho 6 SL8 .....185 A4
Grantham Ct MK5 .....46 C5
Grantham Mews HP4 .....135 D4
Granville Ave SL2 .....205 D8
Granville Dene HP3 .....146 A4
Granville Pl 5 HP20 .....115 D8
Granville Rd HP4 .....134 E6
Granville Sq MK15 .....35 C7
Granville St 4 HP20 .....115 D8
Grapevine Cl HP11 .....173 F4
Grasholm Way SL3 .....207 C2
Grasmere
Aylesbury HP21 .....116 B5
Windsor SL4 .....209 E7
Grasmere Ave SL2 .....206 A6
Grasmere Par SL2 .....206 B6
Grasmere Way
Leighton Buzzard LU7 .....80 D7
Milton Keynes MK2 .....58 D6
Grass Hays HP21 .....116 C7
Grasscroft MK4 .....46 E4
Grassingham End SL9 .....177 E3
Grassingham Rd SL9 .....177 E3
Grassington MK13 .....34 A5
Grasslands HP20 .....102 A1
Grassy La SL6 .....202 E7
Grattan Ct SL7 .....184 A3
Gratton Ct MK4 .....46 C3
Gratton Dr SL4 .....209 E3
Gravel Dr HP23 .....118 B3
Gravel Hill
Chalfont St Peter SL9 .....177 E3
Henley-on-T RG9 .....191 D2
Uxbridge UB8 .....201 D7
Gravel Path HP4 .....135 E5
Gravel Wlk MK46 .....13 F7
Graveney Pl MK6 .....35 B2
Gray's La
High Wycombe HP13 .....161 D2
Ibstone HP14 .....169 C7
Gray's Mon* SL2 .....198 F2
Gray's Pl SL2 .....205 F5
Gray's Rd Slough SL1 .....205 F5
Uxbridge UB10 .....201 E5
Grayburn Cl HP8 .....177 A8
Grayling Cl SL7 .....194 C8
Grayling Ct HP4 .....134 F6
Grays Cl NN12 .....17 D8
Grays La Paulerspury NN12 .....17 D8
Yardley Gobion NN12 .....18 E6
Grays Park Rd SL2 .....199 A3
Grays Wlk HP5 .....144 B2
Greamesdyke Rd HP4 .....135 A3
Great Benty UB7 .....208 E2
Great Brickhill La MK17 .....59 D5
Great Denson MK6 .....47 A8
Great Ground MK14 .....34 E7
Great Hill Cres SL6 .....202 C6
Great Hivings HP5 .....144 A4
Great Horwood CE Comb Sch
MK17 .....55 A3
Great Horwood Rd MK18 .....65 F7
Great Kimble CE Sch
HP17 .....129 E1
Great Kingshill CE Comb Sch
HP15 .....162 C6
Great La Bierton HP22 .....102 A4
Wendover HP22 .....131 B4
Great Linch MK10 .....36 A2
Great Linford Comb Sch
MK14 .....34 E8
Great Linford Lakes Wildfowl
Ctr* MK14 .....21 C2
Great Marlow Sch SL7 .....183 F4
Great Meadow Way
Aylesbury HP19 .....114 F8
Aylesbury HP19 .....115 A8
Great Missenden CE Comb
Sch HP16 .....152 B7
Great Missenden Sta
HP16 .....152 A7
Great Monks St
Milton Keynes,Wolverton
MK12 .....33 C5
Milton Keynes,Wymbush
MK8 .....33 E2
Great Ormes MK4 .....56 F8
Great Pasture MK10 .....35 F3
Great Slade MK18 .....52 D6
Great Stone HP18 .....112 F3
Great Western St 22
HP20 .....115 D8
Greatchesters MK13 .....33 F5
Greatheed Dell MK7 .....48 D4
Greaves Rd HP13 .....173 D6
Grebe Cl HP19 .....101 F3
Grecian St HP20 .....116 A8
Green Acre HP21 .....116 A7
Green Acres Cl HP22 .....86 E7
Green Cl Burnham SL6 .....204 A7
High Wycombe HP13 .....173 F7
Maidenhead SL6 .....195 F1
Green Common La
HP10,HP9,SL1 .....186 C4
Green Cres HP10 .....185 C7
Green Dragon La HP10 .....185 B7
Green East Rd HP9 .....176 E3
Green End
Aylesbury HP20 .....115 D8
Granborough MK18 .....76 A7
Great Brickhill MK17 .....59 D2
Green End La MK19 .....11 A3
Green End Rd HP14 .....159 E5
Green End St HP22 .....117 E5
Green Farm Rd MK16 .....22 C4
Green Ground OX33 .....123 A2
Green Hailey HP27 .....139 F3
Green Hill HP13 .....162 B1
Green Hill Cl HP13 .....162 C1
Green Hill Gate HP13 .....162 B1
Green La Amersham HP6 .....154 E2
Aspley Guise MK17 .....49 E4
Botley HP5 .....155 B6
Bovingdon HP3 .....146 A3
Burnham SL1 .....197 D4
Chesham Bois HP6 .....154 D3
Datchet SL3 .....211 B6
Eaton Bray LU6 .....92 D7
Farnham Common SL2 .....198 B6
Ivinghoe LU7 .....105 E5
Maidenhead SL6 .....203 A6
Milton Keynes MK12 .....33 D6
Owlswick HP27 .....128 B1
Prestwood HP16 .....151 E6
Radnage HP14 .....159 D5
Stokenchurch HP14 .....158 C5
Upper Arncott OX6 .....94 E7
Windsor SL4 .....210 B5
Green Lane Cl HP6 .....154 D3
Green Lane Ct SL1 .....197 C2
Green Lane Rdbt MK9 .....35 B5
Green Leys
High Wycombe HP13 .....161 C2
Maidenhead SL6 .....195 F2
Green North Rd HP9 .....176 E4
Green Park Comb Sch
MK16 .....22 B3
Green Park Dr MK16 .....22 C3
Green Path HP22,HP23 .....118 D4
Green Pk HP16 .....151 D6
Green Pl HP10 .....185 C8
Green Rd HP13 .....162 C2
Green St
Chorleywood WD3 .....167 C6
Hazlemere HP15 .....162 F4
High Wycombe HP11 .....172 F7
Green The
Amersham HP7 .....154 C1
Aston Abbotts HP22 .....88 D4
Brill HP18 .....110 B8
Burnham SL1 .....197 B1
Chalfont St Giles HP8 .....177 C8
Chearsley HP18 .....112 B2
Cheddington LU7 .....105 A7
Cosgrove MK19 .....19 F2
Cranfield MK43 .....24 E2
Cuddington HP18 .....112 F3
Deanshanger MK19 .....31 E4
Edlesborough LU6 .....92 F4
Great Horwood MK17 .....55 A3
Hanslope MK19 .....11 A2
Horton-cum-S OX33 .....108 A5
Hyde Heath HP6 .....153 C5
Little Missenden HP7 .....153 A2
Longwick HP27 .....138 D6
Mentmore LU7 .....90 D4
Milton Keynes,Loughton
MK5 .....46 A8
Milton Keynes,The Green
MK6 .....47 C8
Newport Pagnell MK16 .....22 C4
Paulerspury NN12 .....17 B7
Pitstone LU7 .....105 D4
Quainton HP22 .....85 B5
Slough SL1 .....205 D4
Soulbury LU7 .....69 E3
Stoke Hammond MK17 .....69 E7
Thornborough MK18 .....54 A8
Turvey MK43 .....8 E5
West Drayton UB7 .....208 D3
Wingrave HP22 .....89 B2
Wooburn Green HP10 .....185 E5

Green The continued
Wraysbury TW19 ....211 E1
Green Tiles U89 ....189 F4
Green Tiles La U89 ....189 F5
Green Verges SL7 ....183 E3
Green View HP20 ....102 A2
Green View Cl HP3 ....146 A2
Green Way MK17 ....57 D4
Green West Rd HP9 ....176 E3
Greenacre SL4 ....209 E5
Greenacres LU7 ....105 C4
Greenacres Ave UB10 ....191 E1
Greenacres La HP10 ....163 A1
Greenacres The HP15 ....162 C1
Greenbury Cl WD3 ....167 C5
Greendale Mews SL2 ....206 A6
Greene Field Rd HP4 ....135 C4
Greene Wlk HP4 ....135 D3
Greenes Ct HP4 ....135 C5
Greenfern Ave SL1 ....204 C7
Greenfield End SL9 ....177 F3
Greenfield Rd MK16 ....22 A4
Greenfields Adstock MK18 ..53 F1
  Maidenhead SL6 ....203 A5
  Upper Arncott OX6 ....94 D7
Greenhill Cl MK5 ....46 A8
Greenlands
  Flackwell Heath HP10 ....185 B8
  Lacey Green HP27 ....149 D5
Greenlands Cl MK16 ....22 A3
Greenlands Ct SL6 ....202 B8
Greenlands La HP15 ....151 B7
Greenlaw Pl MK3 ....47 A3
Greenleaf Ct SL3 ....211 A8
Greenlees Lower Sch
  LU7 ....80 C7
Greenleys Fst Sch MK12 ..33 C5
Greenleys La MK12 ....33 C4
Greenleys Mid Sch MK12 ..33 C5
Greenleys Rdbt MK12 ....33 B6
Greenock Rd SL1 ....205 A7
Greenridge HP10 ....174 B8
Greenside Bourne End SL8 ..185 A5
  Prestwood HP16 ....151 C5
  Slough SL2 ....205 A8
Greenside Hill MK4 ....46 B1
Greenway
  Berkhamsted HP4 ....135 A4
  Burnham SL1 ....197 B3
  Chesham HP5 ....144 B3
  Great Horwood MK17 ....55 A2
  Haddenham HP17 ....126 F5
  Thame OX9 ....125 F1
Greenway Ct HP13 ....173 B7
Greenway Fst Sch HP4 ....134 F4
Greenway Par HP5 ....144 B3
Greenway The
  Gerrards Cross SL9 ....188 D8
  High Wycombe HP13 ....173 B7
  Slough SL1 ....204 D5
  Tring HP23 ....118 F5
  Tylers Green HP10 ....163 B1
  Uxbridge UB8 ....201 D3
Greenway Wlk MK18 ....41 F1
Greenways
  Bow Brickhill MK17 ....48 C2
  Eaton Bray LU6 ....92 D7
Greenways Dr SL6 ....202 A8
Greenwich Gdns MK16 .....22 C2
Greenwood HP14 ....150 A2
Greenwood Ave OX39 .....147 C5
Greenwood Cl
  Amersham HP6 ....154 E1
  Seer Green HP9 ....176 D4
Greenwood Mdw OX39 ...147 D6
Greenwood Pl MK18 ....63 D3
Greenwood The HP22 .....117 D5
Greenyard The MK7 ......1 B7
Greetham Rd HP21 ....116 C6
Gregories Ct HP5 ....144 C3
Gregories Dr MK7 ....48 D6
Gregories Farm La HP9 ..175 D2
Gregories Rd HP9 ....175 C3
Gregory Dr SL4 ....211 B1
Gregory Rd SL2 ....187 D2
Grenadine Way HP23 .....119 A5
Grendon Rd Edgcott HP18 .72 F1
  Kingswood HP18 ....83 C3
Grendon Underwood Comb Sch HP18 ....83 A6
Grendon Way HP22 ....102 A4
Grenfell Ave
  High Wycombe HP12 ....172 D7
  Maidenhead SL6 ....202 F6
Grenfell Pl SL6 ....202 F6
Grenfell Rd
  Beaconsfield HP9 ....175 E3
  Maidenhead SL6 ....202 E6
Grenville Ave HP22 ....131 A7
Grenville Cl SL1 ....197 B3
Grenville Comb Sch
  MK18 ....52 D7
Grenville Cl SL8 ....167 C5
Grenville Gn HP21 ....115 D4
Grenville Rd
  Aylesbury HP21 ....115 D5
  Buckingham MK18 ....41 C1
Grenville Way OX9 ....126 B1
Gresham Ct HP4 ....135 B3
Gresham Rd SL1 ....205 A7
Greyfriars Ct MK10 ....36 B2
Greyhound Ct MK18 ....66 A4
Greyhound La
  Thame OX9 ....125 F1
  Winslow MK18 ....66 A4
Greyhound Wlk OX9 .....125 F1
Greys Hill RG9 ....191 D1
Greys Rd RG9 ....191 D1
Greys The MK6 ....47 C8
Greystoke Cl HP4 ....135 A3
Greystoke Rd SL2 ....204 F8
Greystonley MK4 ....46 C2
Griffin Cl
  Maidenhead SL6 ....202 E5
  Slough SL1 ....205 C4
Griffin Ind Mall HP19 ...101 B1
Griffin La HP19 ....101 B1
Griffith Gate MK10 ....36 A3
Griffith Gate Rdbt MK10 ..36 A2
Griffith Ho HP10 ....174 C2
Griffiths Acre HP17 .....114 E5
Griffiths Yd HP5 ....144 B1
Griffon Cl MK4 ....47 A7
Grigby Rise MK6 ....47 A7
Griggs Orch MK14 ....34 C3
Grimbold Ct MK15 ....35 C7
Grimmer Cl HP19 ....100 F3
Grimms Hill HP16 ....151 F7
Grimms Mdw HP14 ....150 B1
Grimsdell's La HP6 ....154 D2
Grimsdyke Rd HP23 .....119 D1
Gringer Hill SL6 ....202 E8
Grizedale MK13 ....34 B5
Groom Rd HP16 ....151 C5
Groombridge MK7 ....48 A7
Grooms Cotts HP5 ....145 B1
Grooms Ct HP11 ....174 A4
Groomsby Dr LU7 ....105 E5
Grosmont Cl MK4 ....46 B2
Grosvenor Cl SL0 ....200 D2
Grosvenor Ct SL2 ....205 E7
Grosvenor Dr SL6 ....203 C8
Grosvenor Way HP19 ....114 E8
Groundsel Cl MK7 ....48 B6
Grove Ash MK1 ....47 D3
Grove Cl
  Chalfont St Peter SL9 .....177 C2
  Slough SL1 ....206 A3
Grove Cotts UB9 ....190 C8
Grove Ct
  Beaconsfield HP9 ....175 D2
  Bierton HP22 ....102 C5
  Maidenhead SL6 ....202 D7
  Turvey MK43 ....8 E6
Grove End SL9 ....177 C2
Grove End Barns OX9 ....126 B4
Grove Gdns HP23 ....119 B5
Grove Hill SL9 ....177 C3
Grove Ind Sch The MK5 ..46 C7
Grove La
  Ashley Green HP5 ....145 C5
  Chalfont St Peter SL9 .....177 C2
  Little Kimble HP17 ....129 E2
  Uxbridge UB8 ....201 D1
Grove Pk HP23 ....119 C5
Grove Rd Amersham HP6 ..154 F1
  Beaconsfield HP9 ....175 E2
  Burnham SL1,SL2 ....197 E4
  Hazlemere HP15 ....162 F3
  High Wycombe HP12 ....172 C8
  Maidenhead SL6 ....202 F7
  Tring HP23 ....119 C5
  Turvey MK43 ....8 E6
  Uxbridge UB8 ....201 D5
  Windsor SL4 ....210 D5
Grove Road Prim Sch
  HP23 ....119 C5
Grove The
  Amersham HP6 ....154 D4
  Hartwell MK1 ....155 D3
  Mednenham SL7 ....193 E6
  Milton Keynes,Bradwell
  MK13 ....34 A4
  Milton Keynes,Rickley Park
  MK3 ....58 A8
  Newport Pagnell MK16 ....22 B3
  Slough SL1 ....206 A4
  Tring HP23 ....119 C5
  Waddesdon HP18 ....99 A6
Grove Way
  Chorleywood WD3 ....167 B4
  Uxbridge UB8 ....201 D5
  Waddesdon HP18 ....99 A6
Grovelands HP11 ....173 A6
Grovers Ct HP27 ....139 A2
Groves Cl SL8 ....185 C3
Groves Rd HP22 ....131 E7
Groves Way SL6 ....195 E6
Grovesbrook MK17 ....48 D2
Groveway
  Bow Brickhill MK7 ....48 B7
  Milton Keynes,Redmoor
  MK3 ....47 A7
  Milton Keynes,Simpson
  MK6 ....47 D5
Grovewood Cl WD3 ....167 B4
Grubbins La HP27 ....150 B5
Grubwood La SL6 ....195 A7
Grundy Ho UB8 ....201 D3
Gryms Dyke HP16 ....151 D6
Guards Club Rd SL6 .....203 C7
Guards Rd SL4 ....209 C5
Guards View SL4 ....210 D6
Guards Wlk SL4 ....209 C5
Guernsey Cl HP19 ....101 A3
Guest Gdns MK13 ....34 B8
Guildford Ave MK4 ....45 E1
Guildford Cl MK18 ....52 A4
Guillemot Way HP19 ....101 E3
Guinea Orch MK46 ....6 E4
Guinions Rd HP13 ....173 F5
Guise Ct MK17 ....49 F4
Gull Way 4 HP19 ....101 F3
Gullicot Way LU7 ....105 C4
Gulliver's SL4 ....210 D8
Gulliver's Land* MK15 ..35 C4
Gun La MK16 ....14 A2
Gundale Ct MK4 ....46 B2
Gunmaker Ct MK14 ....34 F6
Gunthorpe Rd SL7 ....184 A3
Gunver La MK4 ....57 B8
Gurnard Cl UB7 ....208 D6
Gurnards Ave MK6 ....35 A2
Gurnells Rd HP9 ....176 C5
Gurney Cl
  Aylesbury HP20 ....101 F2
  Beaconsfield HP9 ....175 D2
  Milton Keynes MK5 ....46 A7
Gurney Ct LU6 ....92 F6
Gurneys Mdw HP15 ....163 D7
Guttmann Rd HP21 ....115 F5
Gwendale SL6 ....195 C1
Gweneth Ct SL7 ....183 D8
Gwent Cl SL6 ....202 B4
Gwynant Ct MK2 ....58 C3
Gwynne Cl Tring HP23 ...119 A5
  Windsor SL4 ....209 E6
Gynant Rd HP13 ....173 F6
Gyosei International Sch UK
  MK15 ....35 C5
Gypsy La
  Aspley Guise MK17 ....49 F3
  High Wycombe HP11 ....173 D5
  Marlow SL7 ....183 E4
  Stoke Poges SL2 ....187 E1

H

Haberley Mead MK13 .....34 B3
Hackett Pl MK16 ....24 A6
**Haddenham & Thame
  Parkway Sta** HP17 ......126 E6
**Haddenham Aerodrome Bsns
  Pk** HP17 ....126 F7
Haddenham Com Inf Sch
  HP17 ....127 A6
Haddenham Com Jun Sch
  HP17 ....127 A6
Haddenham Mus*
  HP17 ....126 F6
Haddenham Rd HP17 .....127 A3
**Haddenham St Mary's CE Inf
  Sch** HP17 ....127 A3
Haddington Cl
  Milton Keynes MK3 ....46 E2
  Wendover HP22 ....131 D6
Haddington Way HP20 ...102 A1
Haddon MK8 ....45 F8
Haddon Rd
  Chorleywood WD3 ....167 C4
  Maidenhead SL6 ....202 B8
Hadfield Rd TW19 ....213 D1
Hadland Cl HP3 ....146 A4
Hadley Cl SL3 ....212 E6
Hadley Pl MK13 ....34 C3
Hadlow Ct SL1 ....205 C5
Hadrian's Gate NN13 .....38 A7
Hadrians Dr MK13 ....34 A5
Hag Hill La SL6 ....204 A7
Hag Hill Rise SL6 ....204 A7
Haggar St HP17 ....114 B5
Haglis Dr HP22 ....131 B6
Haig Dr SL1 ....205 C4
Hailey Croft OX39 ....147 B6
Hailey Ct SL6 ....202 D7
Haileybury Ct SL4 ....210 A4
Haines Cl HP19 ....100 F2
Haines Rd HP15 ....162 F6
Haithwaite MK8 ....33 D1
Haldene MK8 ....33 E2
Hale Ave MK11 ....32 E5
Hale La HP22 ....131 E3
Hale Leys Ctr HP20 ......115 D8
Hale Leys Sh Ctr 28
  HP20 ....115 D8
Hale Rd HP22 ....131 C3
Hale St HP20 ....115 E8
Hales Croft HP21 ....116 B4
Halfacre Hill SL9 ....177 F1
Halfway Hos
  Hanslope MK19 ....10 F4
  Maidenhead SL6 ....195 E4
Halfway House La HP5 ...153 F7
Halifax Cl SL6 ....202 A8
Halifax Ho HP7 ....166 C8
Halifax Rd
  Heronsgate WD3 ....167 C2
  High Wycombe HP12 ....172 D5
  Maidenhead SL6 ....202 A8
Halifax Way SL6 ....202 A8
Halings La UB9 ....189 E7
Halkingcroft SL3 ....206 C4
Hall Cl
  High Wycombe HP13 ....173 F5
  Maids Moreton MK18 .....41 F3
  Old Stratford MK19 ....32 B6
Hall Cotts HP18 ....96 F7
Hall Cl SL3 ....211 B7
Hall La MK16 ....23 C8
Hall Mdw SL1 ....197 C3
Hall Park Gate HP4 ......135 C4
Hall Park Hill HP4 ....135 C3
Hall Pk HP4 ....135 E3
**Hall Place (Berkshire Coll of
  Agriculture)** SL6 ....194 A1
Halldore Hill SL6 ....195 E7
Halls Cnr HP10 ....174 A1
Halse Dr SL1 ....197 F7
Halswell Pl MK10 ....36 A3
Halton Com Comb Sch
  HP22 ....131 D7
Halton La HP22 ....131 B8
Halton Wood Forest Wlks*
  HP23 ....132 A5
Halton Wood Rd HP22 ...131 D5
Haltonchesters MK13 .....33 F6
Haly Cl MK13 ....34 B4
Ham Island SL4 ....211 C3
Ham La SL4 ....211 C3
Hamberlins La HP4,
  HP23 ....134 B7
Hamble Dr HP21 ....115 C6
Hambleden RG9 ....181 C2
Hambleden Mill RG9 .....192 C7
Hambleden Rise RG9 .....192 D6
Hambleden Rise RG9 .....192 D8
Hambleden Wlk SL6 ......195 E3
Hambleton Cl MK4 ....46 B2
Hambleton La MK4 ....46 B1
Hambling Pl LU6 ....93 F8
Hamburg Croft MK5 ....46 B3
Hambye Cl HP27 ....149 E4
Hamer Cl HP3 ....146 A3
Hamfield Cotts SL6 ......195 E7
Hamilton Ave RG9 ....191 E1
Hamilton Cl HP4 ....107 C5
Hamilton Ct
  Aylesbury HP19 ....101 D1
  High Wycombe HP13 ....173 B8
Hamilton Gdns SL1 ......197 B2
Hamilton La MK3 ....57 C6
Hamilton Mead HP3 .....146 A4
Hamilton Pk SL6 ....202 A6
Hamilton Pl SL9 ....188 E6
Hamilton Prim Sch
  HP13 ....173 B7
Hamilton Prim Sch (Annexe)
  HP13 ....173 B8
Hamilton Rd
  Berkhamsted HP4 ....135 B4
  High Wycombe HP13 ....162 C1
  Slough SL1 ....205 A7
  Thame OX9 ....126 A1
  Uxbridge UB8 ....201 D1
Hamlins MK6 ....47 C8
Hammersley La HP10,
  HP11 ....174 B5
Hammerwood Gate MK7 ..48 A7
Hammond Cres MK15 .....35 B6
Hammond La SL2 ....198 B8
Hampden Ave HP5 ....144 A1
Hampden Cl
  Aylesbury HP21 ....115 D6
  Stoke Poges SL2 ....199 A2
Hampden Gdns HP21 .....115 D6
Hampden Hall Coll
  HP22 ....116 C4
Hampden Hill
  Beaconsfield HP9 ....175 B2
  Charndon OX27 ....72 E6
Hampden Ho 2 HP13 ....173 B8
Hampden Rd
  Aylesbury HP21 ....115 D6
  Chalfont St Peter SL9 .....177 D2
  High Wycombe HP13 ....173 B8
  Hughenden Valley HP16 ..151 B3
  Maidenhead SL6 ....202 B8
  Slough SL3 ....206 C5
  Speen HP27 ....150 C5
  Stoke Mandeville HP22 ...116 B1
  Wendover HP22 ....131 C6
Hampden Sq 2 HP19 ....115 A8
Hampden Villas OX27 .....71 F7
Hampshire Ave SL1 ......205 C8
Hampshire Cl MK3 ....46 F2
Hampshire Lodge 8
  SL6 ....202 F6
Hampson Cl MK13 ....34 A5
Hampstead Gate MK13 ...34 C3
Hampton MK8 ....46 A8
Hampton Cl HP22 ....116 B1
Hampton Ho SL3 ....212 D7
Hanbury Cl SL1 ....204 A8
Handel Mead MK7 ....48 E5
Handleton Comm HP14 ..171 B5
Handley Page Cl MK43 ...24 E2
Handy Cross HP11 ....172 F3
Hangar Rd UB9 ....189 E7
Hanging Croft Cl 4
  HP13 ....173 D7
Hangings La HP16 ....151 A6
Hanley Cl SL4 ....209 D6
Hanmer Rd MK6 ....47 E5
Hannah Ball Inf Sch
  HP13 ....173 D7
Hannon Rd HP21 ....115 C5
Hanover Cl
  Aylesbury HP19 ....101 A2
  Slough SL1 ....206 A3
  Windsor SL4 ....209 F5
Hanover Ct
  2 Aylesbury HP21 ....115 E7
  Hazlemere HP15 ....163 B3
  Leighton Buzzard LU7 .....80 D7
  Milton Keynes MK14 ....34 D7
Hanover Gate SL1 ....204 F5
Hanover Mead SL6 ......203 C3
Hanover Way SL4 ....209 F6
Hanscomb Cl MK15 ....35 C2
Hansen Croft MK5 ....46 B5
Hanslope Comb Sch
  MK19 ....11 A3
Hanslope Rd MK19 ....19 F6
Hanson Cl UB7 ....208 F3
Hanson Way HP21 ....116 A4
Harborne Ct MK8 ....33 C2
Harborough Cl SL1 ......204 D5
Harbourne Ct HP21 .....115 C3
Harby Cl MK4 ....46 C1
Harcourt
  Milton Keynes MK15 ....34 A3
  Wraysbury TW19 ....211 E1
Harcourt Cl Dorney SL6 ..203 F3
  Henley-on-T RG9 ....191 C1
  Leighton Buzzard LU7 .....80 E7
Harcourt Gn HP19 ....101 B2
Harcourt Rd Dorney SL4 ..203 F3
  Tring HP23 ....119 C4
Harcourt Sq SL4 ....209 F6
Hardenwaye HP13 ....162 E1
Harding Rd
  Chesham HP5 ....144 D1
  Milton Keynes MK10 ....48 C8
Hardings Cl SL0 ....200 C2
Hardings Row SL0 ....200 D2
Hardmead Rd MK43 ....8 A3
Hardwick Cl SL6 ....202 A8
Hardwick Mews MK17 ...49 B3
Hardwick Pl MK17 ....49 B4
Hardwick Rd MK17 ....49 B4
Hardwicke Gdns HP6 ....154 E1
Hardy Cl Aylesbury HP21 ..115 E3
  Slough SL1 ....205 A5
Hardy Mead Ct HP11 ....174 B2
Hare Cl MK18 ....52 E7
Hare La HP16 ....152 B3
Hare Lane End HP16 .....152 A3
Hare Shoots SL6 ....202 E5
Harebell Cl MK7 ....48 B5
Harebell Wlk HP15 ......162 F6
Harebridge La HP22 .....117 C1
Hareden Croft MK4 ....46 B2
Harefield Rd
  Maidenhead SL6 ....202 A7
  Uxbridge UB8 ....201 D6
Harehatch La SL1 ....186 F3
Harescombe SL6 ....175 D3
Haresfoot Sch HP4 ....135 B1
Harewood Pl SL1 ....206 A3
Harewood Rd HP8 ....166 C6
Hargrave Rd SL6 ....202 B8
Hargreaves Nook MK14 ..22 B2
Harkness Cl MK2 ....58 D6
Harkness Rd SL1 ....204 B8
Harlans Cl MK6 ....47 B8
Harle Stone Ct MK14 .....22 A1
Harlech Ho 5 HP13 .....173 F7
Harlech Pl MK3 ....57 E7
Harlequin Pl MK5 ....45 F3
Harley Ct SL1 ....205 C4
Harleyford La SL7 ....194 B7
Harling Rd LU6 ....93 B4
Harlow Rd HP13 ....173 C6
Harman Terr HP12 ....172 D7
Harman Wlk HP12 ....172 D7
Harmondsworth La UB7 ..213 E8
Harmondsworth Prim Sch
  UB7 ....213 D8
Harmondsworth Rd
  UB7 ....208 E2
Harnett Dr MK12 ....32 F6
Harper Cl OX25 ....94 D7
Harpers La MK14 ....34 F8
Harrier Cl HP20 ....101 F3
Harrier Cl MK6 ....47 A8
Harrier Dr MK6 ....47 A8
Harries Cl HP5 ....144 B1
Harries Way HP15 ....163 B6
Harriet Walker Way
  WD3 ....167 F2
Harrington Cl SL4 ....209 F3
Harris Cl HP18 ....110 A8
Harris Ct HP20 ....101 F2
Harris Gdns SL1 ....205 C4
Harris Rd HP14 ....171 B5
Harrison Barber Cotts
  SL3 ....212 D1
Harrison Cl MK5 ....46 D6
Harrison Pl OX9 ....125 F1
Harrison Way SL1 ....204 D5
Harroell
  Long Crendon HP18 ....125 D5
  Long Crendon,Church End
  HP18 ....125 D6
Harrogate Ct SL3 ....207 A3
Harrold Lower Sch MK43 ..3 F6
Harrold Priory Mid Sch
  MK43 ....3 F6
Harrold Rd MK46 ....3 B1
Harrow Cl
  Aylesbury HP21 ....115 C4
  Maidenhead SL6 ....195 E1
Harrow La SL6 ....195 E1
Harrow Mkt The SL3 .....207 A3
Harrow Rd SL3 ....206 F3
Harrow Way 6 HP23 ....119 A3
Harrowden MK13 ....34 B7
Hart Moor Cl HP14 ......158 E4
Hart St RG9 ....191 E2
Hartdames MK5 ....46 A3
Hartfield Cl MK7 ....48 A7
Hartington Gr MK4 ....46 B3
Hartland Ave MK4 ....57 B8
Hartland Cl SL1 ....205 D5
Hartley Cl SL3 ....199 C4
Hartley Copse SL4 ......211 A1
Hartley Ct SL9 ....188 E5
Harts Rd HP17 ....127 B6
Hartwell Cl HP10 ....163 C2
Hartwell Dr HP9 ....175 D3

Hartwell End HP21 . . . . .115 B7
Hartwell Rd Ashton NN7 . . . .9 F8
Hanslope MK19 . . . . .10 E5
Hartwort Cl MK7 . . . . .48 B5
Harvard Cl MK14 . . . . .21 F2
Harvest Bank HP6 . . . . .153 C4
Harvest Hill HP10 . . . . .185 D2
Harvest Hill Rd SL6 . . . . . . .202 F3
Harvester Cl MK12 . . . . .33 B5
Harvey Dr MK46 . . . . .6 F1
Harvey Ho SL3 . . . . .206 E7
Harvey Orch HP9 . . . . .175 C3
Harvey Rd
  Aylesbury HP21 . . . . .115 E5
  Dunstable LU6 . . . . .93 D7
  Slough SL3 . . . . .207 B4
Harvil Rd U89,UB10 . . . . . . .190 E4
Harvington Pk LU7 . . . . .105 D3
Harwich Rd SL1 . . . . .205 A7
Harwood Dr UB10 . . . . .201 F4
Harwood Rd SL12 . . . . .183 C1
Harwood St MK13 . . . . .34 A7
Hasgill Cl MK13 . . . . .34 B4
Haslemere Rd SL4 . . . . .210 A6
Haslerig Cl HP21 . . . . .115 F5
Haslow Cl MK8 . . . . .33 E3
Hasting Cl SL6 . . . . .203 C2
Hastings MK11 . . . . .32 E5
Hastings Mdw SL2 . . . . . . .199 A4
Hastoe Cross HP23 . . . . . . .133 A7
Hastoe Farm Barns
  HP23 . . . . .132 F7
Hastoe Hill HP23 . . . . .132 F8
Hastoe La HP23 . . . . .119 A2
Hastoe Pk HP20 . . . . .101 F2
Hastoe Row HP23 . . . . .133 A7
Hatch La
  Harmondsworth UB7 . . . . . .213 D7
  Radnage HP14 . . . . .160 B4
  Windsor SL4 . . . . .210 A5
Hatch The SL4 . . . . .209 C7
Hatches La
  Great Kingshill HP15 . . . . . .151 C1
  Hughenden Valley HP15 . . . .162 B8
Hatchet Leys La MK18 . . . . .53 F8
Hatchgate Gdns SL1 . . . . . .197 D1
Hatchlands MK8 . . . . .33 F1
Hatfield Cl SL6 . . . . .202 C6
Hatfield Rd SL1 . . . . .206 A4
Hathaway Ct MK8 . . . . .45 E8
Hatter's La HP13 . . . . .173 F6
Hatton MK6 . . . . .47 D6
Hatton Ave SL2 . . . . .198 D1
Hatton Ct SL4 . . . . .210 C5
Hatton Gr UB7 . . . . .208 D4
Hauksbee Gdns MK5 . . . . . .46 D5
Havelock Boro Pk SL6 . . . . .202 C7
Havelock Cres SL6 . . . . . . .202 B7
Havelock Ct HP20 . . . . .101 D1
Havelock Rd SL6 . . . . .202 B7
Havelock St HP20 . . . . .101 D1
Haven Of Rest SL6 . . . . . . .203 B7
Haven Shaw Cl HP21 . . . . . .116 A5
Havenfield Ct 6 HP13 . . . . .173 B7
Havenfield Rd HP22 . . . . . . .172 C4
Haversham Fst Sch MK19 . .20 D1
Haversham Rd MK19 . . . . . .20 D1
Haw La HP14 . . . . .149 A2
Hawfinch 1 HP19 . . . . .101 E3
Hawker Ct SL3 . . . . .207 A3
Hawkhurst Gate MK7 . . . . . .47 F7
Hawkings Way HP3 . . . . . . .146 A5
Hawkins Cl MK11 . . . . .32 D5
Hawkmoor Cl MK6 . . . . .47 B8
Hawkridge MK4 . . . . .46 E3
Hawks Hill SL8 . . . . .185 C3
Hawkshead Dr MK4 . . . . . . .46 C3
Hawkshill Dr HP3 . . . . .146 F8
Hawkshill Rd SL2 . . . . .198 A2
Hawksdale Furlong
  HP21 . . . . .115 D3
Hawksmoor Cl MK11 . . . . . .173 A8
Hawkswood Cl SL3 . . . . .6 F5
Hawkswood Gr SL3 . . . . . . .199 F6
Hawkswood La SL3,SL9 . . . .199 F8
Hawkwell Dr HP23 . . . . .119 C4
Hawkwell Est MK19 . . . . . . .32 B7
Hawleys La HP22 . . . . .86 F5
Hawridge & Cholesbury CE
  Comb Sch HP5 . . . . .133 C2
Hawridge La HP5 . . . . .143 E8
Hawridge Vale HP5 . . . . . . .133 F1
Hawthorn Ave MK2 . . . . .58 E8
Hawthorn Cl
  Aylesbury HP20 . . . . .101 F2
  Iver Heath SL0 . . . . .200 C2
  Turvey MK43 . . . . .8 E6
Hawthorn Cres HP15 . . . . . .163 B2
Hawthorn Dr UB9 . . . . .201 C6
Hawthorn Gdns SL6 . . . . . .202 E5
Hawthorn La SL2 . . . . .198 A5
Hawthorn Pl HP10 . . . . .174 C8
Hawthorn Rd HP27 . . . . . . .139 C3
Hawthorn Way
  Chesham HP5 . . . . .144 D2
  Wing LU7 . . . . .79 E3
Hawthorne Cl
  Aylesbury HP21 . . . . .101 F2
  Marlow SL7 . . . . .183 E4
Hawthorne Cres
  Slough SL1 . . . . .205 F7
  West Drayton UB7 . . . . . . .208 F4
Hawthorne Gdns HP10 . . . .174 A2
Hawthorne Rd HP13 . . . . . .174 A6
Hawthorns The
  Berkhamsted HP4 . . . . .135 A5
  Cranfield MK43 . . . . .25 B1

Hawthorns The continued
Felden SL6 . . . . .146 F7
Little Chalfont HP8 . . . . .166 C7
Maple Cross WD3 . . . . .178 D5
Monks Risborough HP27 . . .139 C6
Poyle SL3 . . . . .212 F6
Wooburn Green HP10 . . . . .185 D2
Hawtrey Cl SL1 . . . . .206 B4
Hawtrey Rd SL4 . . . . .210 C5
Hay Barn Bsns Pk The
  HP22 . . . . .88 C6
Hay La SL3 . . . . .199 D8
Hayden Ho 3 HP11 . . . . . .172 F7
Haydock Cl MK3 . . . . .57 C6
Haydon Abbey Comb Sch
  HP19 . . . . .101 C2
Haydon Cl SL6 . . . . .202 E6
Haydon Rd HP19 . . . . .101 C2
Hayes Pl SL7 . . . . .183 D1
Hayes Rd MK19 . . . . .31 F5
Hayfield Dr HP15 . . . . .163 B2
Hayles Field RG9 . . . . .170 E1
Haymaker Cl UB10 . . . . . . .201 F5
Hayman Rise MK8 . . . . .45 D6
Haynes Cl
  Bow Brickhill MK17 . . . . . . .48 D2
  Slough SL3 . . . . .206 F1
Haynes Ho HP12 . . . . .172 B3
Haynes Mead HP4 . . . . .135 A6
Hayse Hill SL4 . . . . .209 D6
Haystacks The HP13 . . . . . .173 B7
Haythorp Cl MK15 . . . . .35 B6
Hayward Pl SL8 . . . . .185 C2
Haywards Cl RG9 . . . . .191 C1
Haywards Croft MK12 . . . . . .33 B5
Haywards Mead SL4 . . . . . .204 F1
Haywood Pk
  Chorleywood WD3 . . . . . . .167 F4
  Stewkley LU7 . . . . .68 C3
Haywood Way HP19 . . . . . .100 F3
Haywoods Dr HP3 . . . . .146 F8
Hazel Cl SL2 . . . . .183 C6
Hazel Ct WD3 . . . . .178 E5
Hazel Gr MK2 . . . . .58 D7
Hazel Rd HP4 . . . . .135 D3
Hazelbury Rd HP13 . . . . . . .173 D6
Hazelcroft Cl UB10 . . . . . . .201 F5
Hazeldene HP22 . . . . .131 C4
Hazeley Sch MK8 . . . . .45 D6
Hazelhurst 7 MK4 . . . . . . .46 B2
Hazelhurst Rd SL1 . . . . . . .197 D3
Hazell Ave HP21 . . . . .116 A7
Hazell Cl SL6 . . . . .202 F8
Hazell Pk HP7 . . . . .165 D8
Hazell Rd HP6 . . . . .151 C5
Hazell Way SL2 . . . . .198 F6
Hazelwood MK14 . . . . .34 F8
Hazelwood Cl HP5 . . . . . . .144 D2
Hazely HP23 . . . . .119 C4
Hazlehurst Dr HP21 . . . . . . .116 A6
Hazlemere CE Comb Sch
Hazlemere Rd
  Slough SL3 . . . . .206 B5
  Tylers Green HP10 . . . . . . .163 C3
Hazlemere View HP15 . . . . .163 B5
Hazley Wlk MK18 . . . . .41 F1
Headington Cl SL6 . . . . . . .202 A7
Headington Pl SL2 . . . . . . .198 E6
Headington Rd SL6 . . . . . . .202 A7
Headland Cl 1 HP16 . . . . . .152 A8
Headlands Dr HP4 . . . . .135 C5
Healey Ave HP13 . . . . .173 D7
Heaney Cl MK16 . . . . .22 A5
Hearn Cl HP10 . . . . .162 F2
Hearne Ct HP8 . . . . .177 B7
Hearne Dr SL6 . . . . .203 A1
Hearne Pk MK6 . . . . .46 F8
Hearne's Mdw HP9 . . . . . . .176 D5
Hearnes Cl HP9 . . . . .176 D5
Heath Cl Aylesbury HP21 . .116 B5
  Holmer Green HP15 . . . . . .163 B6
  Stanwell TW19 . . . . .213 C1
  Woburn Sands MK17 . . . . . .49 C3
Heath Ct
  Leighton Buzzard LU7 . . . . .70 E3
  Uxbridge UB8 . . . . .201 D5
Heath End Cl HP15 . . . . . . .151 E1
Heath End Rd
  Flackwell Heath HP10 . . . .174 A1
  Great Kingshill HP15,HP10 .151 E2
  Little Marlow HP10 . . . . . . .173 D2
Heath La MK17 . . . . .49 A2
Heath Lawn HP10 . . . . .173 F1
Heath Rd
  Beaconsfield HP9 . . . . .186 A8
  Great Brickhill MK17,LU7 . . .59 E1
  Hyde Heath HP6 . . . . .153 C5
Heath The LU7 . . . . .70 E4
Heath Way SL0 . . . . .200 C2
Heathacre SL3 . . . . .212 E6
Heathcote SL6 . . . . .203 B2
Heathcote Ct 2 SL4 . . . . . .210 D4
Heathcote Way UB7 . . . . . .208 D5
Heather Cl
  Buckingham MK18 . . . . .52 C7
  Uxbridge UB8 . . . . .208 F8
Heather La UB7 . . . . .208 E7
Heather Mead LU6 . . . . .92 E5
Heather Wlk
  Aylesbury HP21 . . . . .115 B6
  Hazelmere HP15 . . . . .163 A3
Heathercroft MK14 . . . . .34 E7
Heatherden Gn SL0 . . . . . .200 D4
Heathers Cl SL6 . . . . .73 B5
Heatherside Gdns SL2 . . . .187 D1

Heatherton House Sch
  HP6 . . . . .154 C3
Heatherton Pk HP6 . . . . . . .154 B3
Heathfield MK41 . . . . .33 E4
Heathfield Rd
  High Wycombe HP12 . . . . .172 B7
  Taplow SL1 . . . . .186 A1
Heathlands Dr SL6 . . . . . . .202 A6
Heathrow Bvd UB7 . . . . . . .213 F7
Heathrow Cl UB7 . . . . .213 B6
Heathrow Prim Sch
  UB7 . . . . .213 F8
Heavens Lea SL8 . . . . .185 C2
Hedge Lea HP10 . . . . .185 D8
Hedgerley SL6 . . . . .199 B6
Hedgerley Hill SL2 . . . . . . .187 D2
Hedgerley La
  Beaconsfield HP9 . . . . .186 F8
  Gerrards Cross SL9 . . . . . .188 B4
  Hedgerley SL2 . . . . .187 D6
Hedgerow Way MK4 . . . . . . .46 E4
Hedgerows The MK4 . . . . . . .46 E4
Hedges Ct MK5 . . . . .46 A8
Hedingham Ct MK5 . . . . . . .46 A5
Hedingham Mews SL6 . . . .202 D7
Hedley Cl HP22 . . . . .118 A4
Hedley Rd HP10 . . . . .185 B8
Hedley View HP10 . . . . .174 D1
Hedsor Hill SL8 . . . . .185 C3
Hedsor La Hedsor HP10 . . .185 A2
  Taplow SL1 . . . . .186 A2
Hedsor Rd SL8 . . . . .185 B2
Hedsor View Cotts SL6 . . . .195 F7
Heelands Fst Sch MK13 . . .34 B4
Heights The SL7 . . . . .194 B8
Hele Cl MK7 . . . . .48 B3
Helen Cotts SL4 . . . . .209 D5
Helen Rd SL4 . . . . .210 D5
Helena Cl HP21 . . . . .115 D4
Helford Pl MK6 . . . . .35 A1
Heligan Pl MK4 . . . . .45 F1
Hellfire Caves* HP14 . . . . .160 F2
Hellyer Way SL8 . . . . .185 C3
Helmsley Rise MK4 . . . . . . .45 E1
Helston La SL4 . . . . .210 B6
Helston Pl MK6 . . . . .34 F1
Hemel Hempstead Rd
  HP4 . . . . .107 F1
Hemingway Cl MK16 . . . . . .21 F5
Hemingway Rd HP10 . . . . . .100 F2
Hemming Way SL2 . . . . . . .198 B2
Hemmings The HP4 . . . . . . .134 F3
Hemp Hill 10 HP19 . . . . . . .115 A8
Hempson Ave SL3 . . . . .206 C3
Hempstead Rd HP3 . . . . . . .146 B5
Hemsdale SL6 . . . . .195 B1
Hemwood Rd SL4 . . . . .209 D4
Hencroft Mews 14 SL1 . . .205 F4
Hencroft St N SL1 . . . . .205 F4
Hencroft St S SL1 . . . . .205 F3
Henders MK11 . . . . .32 E5
Hendon Way TW19 . . . . . . .213 D1
Hendons Way SL6 . . . . .203 B1
Hendrix Dr MK8 . . . . .45 D7
Hengistbury La MK4 . . . . . . .46 A1
Henley Coll The RG9 . . . . . .191 D1
Henley Coll The (Rotherfield
  Bldgs) RG9 . . . . .191 C1
Henley Lodge 12 SL6 . . . . .202 F6
Henley Rd Hurley SL6 . . . . .193 D3
  Maidenhead SL6,SL7 . . . . .194 B2
  Marlow SL7 . . . . .194 B8
  Slough SL1 . . . . .204 F7
Henley-on-Thames Sta
  RG9 . . . . .191 E1
Hennerton Way HP13 . . . . . .173 F6
Henrietta Rd OX9 . . . . .126 A1
Henry III Twr 9 SL4 . . . . . .210 D6
Henry Rd Aylesbury HP20 . .116 B8
  Slough SL1 . . . . .205 D4
Henry St HP23 . . . . .119 B3
Hensman Gate MK10 . . . . . .35 F4
Henson Cl MK4 . . . . .24 E3
Henton Mews 5 HP19 . . . .115 A8
Hepleswell MK8 . . . . .33 E1
Hepplewhite Cl HP13 . . . . .173 D8
Herbert Rd HP13 . . . . .173 E7
Herberts Hole
  Chesham HP5 . . . . .143 C1
  South Heath HP5,HP16 . . .142 F1
Hercies Rd UB10 . . . . .201 F5
Herd's Hill MK8 . . . . .64 A4
Herdman Cl MK12 . . . . .33 B5
Hereford Ho HP13 . . . . .173 F8
Hereford Way HP19 . . . . . . .101 A3
Heritage Cl UB8 . . . . .201 C1
Heritage Gate SL8 . . . . . . .188 E7
Heritage House Sch
  HP5 . . . . .144 D1
Heritage Wlk WD3 . . . . .167 E6
Hermitage Cl SL3 . . . . .206 C3
Hermitage La SL4 . . . . .210 A4
Hermitage Prim Sch
  UB8 . . . . .201 D5
Hermitage The
  Great Missenden HP16 . . . .152 A7
  Uxbridge UB8 . . . . .201 D5
Heron Cl Aylesbury HP20 . .116 C8
  Uxbridge UB8 . . . . .201 D6
  Heron Dr SL3 . . . . .207 B2
Heron Lodge MK14 . . . . .34 C6
Heron The HP19 . . . . .101 E4
Herons Elm HP4 . . . . .134 F5
Herons Pl
  Maidenhead SL6 . . . . .196 C3
  Marlow SL7 . . . . .183 E3
Heronsford Ho WD3 . . . . . .167 B3

Heronsgate Fst Sch MK7 . .48 B5
Heronsgate Mid Sch
  MK7 . . . . .48 B5
Heronsgate Rd WD3 . . . . . .167 B3
Herries Sch SL6 . . . . .195 B8
Herriot Cl MK16 . . . . .22 A5
Herschel Gram Sch SL1 . . .205 C7
Herschel St SL1 . . . . .205 F4
Herston Cl HP21 . . . . .116 B5
Hertford Pl MK7 . . . . .46 F2
Hervines Ct HP6 . . . . .154 C2
Hervines Rd HP6 . . . . .154 C2
Hesketh Rd MK12 . . . . .18 E6
Het's Orch HP27 . . . . .139 A5
Hetherington Cl SL2 . . . . . .197 F2
Hetherington Way MK18 . .201 E8
Hetton Cl MK13 . . . . .34 C4
Heusden Way SL1 . . . . .205 E7
Hever Cl Maidenhead SL6 . .202 C6
  Pitstone LU7 . . . . .105 D2
Hewgate Ct RG9 . . . . .191 E1
Heybridge Cres MK7 . . . . . .48 B3
Heydon Ct MK13 . . . . .34 A7
Heynes Gn SL6 . . . . .202 B3
Heythrop Dr UB10 . . . . .201 F8
Heywood Ave SL6 . . . . .202 A2
Heywood Court Cl SL6 . . . .202 A2
Heywood Gdns SL6 . . . . . .202 A1
Hibbert Rd SL6 . . . . .203 B4
Hibbert's Alley 16 SL4 . . . .210 D6
Hibberts Way SL9 . . . . .188 E8
Hickman St HP19 . . . . .114 F8
Hickmans Cl MK18 . . . . .51 B6
Hickox Ct HP10 . . . . .185 F7
Hicks Farm Rise HP13 . . . .173 F7
Hidcote Dr MK4 . . . . .45 F1
Higgins Mdw The MK6 . . . . .47 C6
Higgs Ct MK4 . . . . .46 A8
High Ash CE Prim Sch
  MK17 . . . . .59 D2
High Beeches
  Gerrards Cross SL9 . . . . . .188 D2
  High Wycombe HP12 . . . . .172 C6
High Beeches Cl SL7 . . . . .183 C7
High Bois La HP6 . . . . .154 D4
High Coppice HP7 . . . . .165 C8
High Halden MK7 . . . . .48 B8
High Heavens Wood
  SL7 . . . . .183 C8
High Land Cl HP18 . . . . .96 A1
High March Sch HP9 . . . . . .175 D4
High Mdw SL6 . . . . .196 C3
High Moors HP22 . . . . .131 B8
High Park Dr MK12 . . . . .33 A6
High Rd
  Cookham Rise SL6 . . . . . . .195 E7
  Soulbury LU7 . . . . .69 C2
  Uxbridge UB8 . . . . .208 C7
High St Amersham HP7 . . .165 A7
  Aylesbury HP20 . . . . .115 E8
  Berkhamsted, HP4 . . . . . . .135 C4
  Berkhamsted,Northchurch
  HP4 . . . . .134 E6
  Bovingdon HP3 . . . . .146 A4
  Bray SL6 . . . . .203 C4
  Brill HP18 . . . . .110 A8
  Buckingham MK18 . . . . .41 D1
  Burcott LU7 . . . . .79 D4
  Chalfont St Giles HP8 . . . .177 D8
  Chalfont St Peter SL9 . . . .177 E2
  Chalvey SL1 . . . . .205 D3
  Cheddington SL7 . . . . .105 A7
  Chesham HP5 . . . . .154 B8
  Chinnor OX39 . . . . .147 D7
  Chinnor,Kingston Blount
  OX39 . . . . .147 A4
  Colnbrook SL3 . . . . .212 C7
  Cookham SL6 . . . . .196 B7
  Cranfield MK43 . . . . .25 B1
  Cranfield MK43 . . . . .37 F8
  Cublington LU7 . . . . .78 B1
  Datchet SL3 . . . . .211 B6
  Deanshanger MK19 . . . . . .31 F7
  Dinton HP17 . . . . .113 E2
  Eaton Bray LU6 . . . . .92 E6
  Edlesborough LU6 . . . . .92 E3
  Eton SL4 . . . . .210 D8
  Great Horwood MK17 . . . . .55 A3
  Great Missenden HP16 . . . .152 A7
  Haddenham HP17 . . . . . . .126 F6
  Hanslope MK19 . . . . .11 A2
  Harmondsworth UB7 . . . . .213 D8
  Harrold MK43 . . . . .3 E6
  Haversham MK19 . . . . .21 A3
  High Wycombe HP11 . . . . .173 B6
  High Wycombe, Downley

High St continued
Newport Pagnell MK16 . . . .22 D4
North Crawley MK16 . . . . . .24 B6
North Marston MK18 . . . . . .76 A2
Olney MK46 . . . . .6 F3
Paulerspury NN12 . . . . .17 C8
Pottersbury NN12 . . . . .18 D3
Prestwood HP16 . . . . .151 D6
Princes Risborough HP27 . .139 B3
Sherington MK16 . . . . .14 A2
Slough SL3 . . . . .207 A2
Slough,Upton SL1 . . . . . . .205 F4
Stanwell TW19 . . . . .213 D1
Stoke Goldington MK16 . . . .12 B6
Syresham NN13 . . . . .27 B7
Taplow SL6 . . . . .196 E1
Thame OX9 . . . . .125 E1
Thornborough MK18 . . . . . .54 A8
Tring HP23 . . . . .119 A3
Turvey MK43 . . . . .8 E5
Uxbridge UB8 . . . . .201 D5
Uxbridge,Cowley UB8 . . . .201 C1
Waddesdon HP18 . . . . .99 A6
Weedon HP22 . . . . .87 C1
Wendover HP22 . . . . .131 B4
West Drayton UB7 . . . . . . .208 E6
West Wycombe HP14 . . . . .160 F2
Westcott HP18 . . . . .98 B7
Weston Underwood MK46 . . .6 B2
Whaddon MK17 . . . . .45 B1
Whitchurch HP22 . . . . .87 A6
Windsor SL4 . . . . .210 D6
Wing LU7 . . . . .79 E2
Winslow MK18 . . . . .66 A5
Woburn Sands MK17 . . . . . .49 B4
Wraysbury TW19 . . . . .211 F1
Yardley Gobion NN12 . . . . .18 F6
Yardley Hastings NN7 . . . . . .1 B6
High St N LU7 . . . . .68 D2
High St S Olney MK46 . . . . . .6 F3
  Stewkley LU7 . . . . .78 E8
High St The MK8 . . . . .33 E1
High Town Rd SL6 . . . . .202 F7
High Trees MK46 . . . . .47 B8
High View
  Chalfont St Giles HP8 . . . .177 D8
  Deanshanger MK19 . . . . . .31 E5
High View Cl SL7 . . . . .183 C8
High Wycombe CE Comb Sch
  HP11 . . . . .173 A6
Higham Cross Rd MK19 . . . .10 E4
Higham Mead HP5 . . . . . . .144 C1
Higham Rd HP5 . . . . .144 C1
Highbridge Ind Est UB8 . . .201 C5
Highbridge Rd HP21 . . . . . .115 E8
Highbridge Wlk 4
  HP21 . . . . .115 E8
Highbury La MK9 . . . . .35 B3
Highcrest Com Sch
  HP13 . . . . .173 E7
Highcroft Cl MK12 . . . . .18 E6
Highfield
  Chalfont St Giles HP8 . . . .177 D8
  Long Crendon HP18 . . . . . .125 C7
Highfield Ave HP12 . . . . . . .172 B5
Highfield Cl
  Amersham HP6 . . . . .154 C2
  Milton Keynes MK3 . . . . . . .47 B2
  Newport Pagnell MK16 . . . .22 E4
Highfield Ct
  Farnham Royal SL2 . . . . . .198 B4
  Hazelmere HP15 . . . . .163 A3
Highfield Dr UB10 . . . . .190 E1
Highfield La SL6 . . . . .202 A4
Highfield Pk SL7 . . . . .183 B1
Highfield Rd
  Berkhamsted HP4 . . . . .135 D4
  Bourne End SL8 . . . . .185 B4
  Chesham HP5 . . . . .144 B2
  Flackwell Heath HP10 . . . .185 B8
  Princes Risborough HP27 . .139 C4
  Tring HP23 . . . . .118 E3
  Wigginton HP23 . . . . .119 D1
  Windsor SL4 . . . . .209 F4
  Winslow MK18 . . . . .65 F5
Highfield Sch SL6 . . . . .202 E7
Highfields
  Flackwell Heath HP10 . . . .185 B4
  High Wycombe HP19 . . . . .174 A5
Highlands Cl SL9 . . . . .177 F3
Highlands La SL9 . . . . .177 F3
Highlands Rd
  Buckingham MK18 . . . . .41 E2
  Seer Green HP9 . . . . .176 C5
Highlands The SL2 . . . . . . .198 C2
Highlea Ave HP10 . . . . .185 A8
Highley Gr MK10 . . . . .36 B3
Highmoor HP7 . . . . .165 D8
Highmore Cotts HP7 . . . . . .152 F3

Highmore Croft MK8 .....45 D6
Highover Pk HP7 .....165 D7
Highveer Ctr MK4 .....46 B1
Highway MK17 .....68 C6
Highway Ave SL6 .....202 A6
Highway Ct
  Beaconsfield HP9 .....175 D3
  Chesham HP5 .....144 D1
Highway Rd SL6 .....202 B6
Highway The HP9 .....175 D2
Highwood Ave HP12 .....172 B5
Highwood Bottom
  HP27 .....150 A5
Highwood Cres HP12 .....172 B6
Highwoods Cl SL7 .....183 C7
Highwoods Dr SL7 .....183 C7
Highworth Cl HP13 .....162 E1
Highworth Comb Sch
  HP13 .....162 E1
Hikers Way HP18 .....125 D4
Hilbre Ct MK4 .....45 F1
Hilbury Cl HP6 .....154 C3
Hilda Wharf HP20 .....115 F8
Hildreth Rd HP16 .....151 C5
Hilgrove Ho SL6 .....195 D1
Hiljon Cres SL9 .....177 E2
Hill Ave Amersham HP6 .....154 C1
  Hazelmere HP15 .....163 B5
Hill Cl HP10 .....185 F7
Hill Cotts HP18 .....97 E1
Hill Farm MK18 .....76 A2
Hill Farm App HP10 .....185 F7
Hill Farm Ct OX39 .....147 D6
Hill Farm La
  Chalfont St Giles HP8 .....166 A1
  Little Horwood MK17 .....55 E2
Hill Farm Rd
  Chalfont St Peter SL9 .....177 E3
  Chesham HP5 .....154 D5
  Marlow Bottom SL7 .....183 E5
  Taplow SL6 .....196 E2
Hill Farm Way HP15 .....163 B2
Hill Gr SL9 .....177 E3
Hill Ho SL6 .....196 D1
Hill House Cl SL9 .....177 E3
Hill Mdw HP7 .....164 F4
Hill Mead HP4 .....135 A3
Hill Pl SL2 .....198 B5
Hill Rd Chinnor OX39 .....147 D5
  Christmas Common OX49 .....168 A8
  Lewknor OX49 .....157 A7
  Lewknor OX49 .....157 C6
Hill Rise SL9 .....177 D1
Hill Rise Cres SL9 .....177 E1
Hill Side LU7 .....104 F7
Hill St HP13 .....174 A5
  Winchmore Hill HP7 .....164 C3
Hill Top Dr SL7 .....183 B2
Hill Top La OX39 .....147 F4
Hill View
  Berkhamsted HP4 .....135 A6
  Great Kimble HP17 .....129 D1
  Hedgerley SL2 .....187 D3
  Newport Pagnell MK16 .....22 A3
  Oakley HP18 .....109 D5
Hill View Rd TW19 .....211 D1
Hill Waye SL9 .....188 F4
Hillary Cl Aylesbury HP21 .....116 A5
  High Wycombe HP13 .....173 E6
Hillary Rd
  High Wycombe HP13 .....173 E6
  Slough SL3 .....206 E4
Hillbeck Gr MK10 .....35 E3
Hillbottom Rd HP12 .....172 B7
Hillcrest MK43 .....25 C2
Hillcrest Ave SL6 .....195 E6
Hillcrest Cl MK5 .....46 B6
Hillcrest Ct HP6 .....154 C1
Hillcrest Rise MK18 .....52 E6
Hillcrest Way MK18 .....52 E5
Hillcrest Waye SL9 .....188 F5
Hillcroft Rd
  Chesham HP5 .....144 D2
  Tylers Green HP10 .....163 C1
Hillersdon SL2 .....206 B8
Hillesden Hamlet MK17 .....69 D8
Hillesden Hamlet MK18 .....51 F1
Hillesden Way MK18 .....41 E1
Hillfield Cl HP13 .....161 E2
Hillfield Sq SL9 .....177 E3
Hillgate Dr SL7 .....183 D3
Hilliard Dr MK13 .....34 A3
Hilliards Rd UB8 .....208 D7
Hillier Rd HP21 .....115 D3
Hillingdon Hill UB10 .....201 E2
Hillingdon Hospl UB8 .....208 F8
Hillingdon Rd UB10 .....201 E3
Hillingdon Tuition Ctr
  UB7 .....208 E5
Hillington Cl HP19 .....115 B7
Hillman Cl UB8 .....201 E7
Hillmead Ct SL6 .....203 F8
Hillrise SL3 .....212 A8
Hills Cl MK14 .....34 E7
Hills La SL6 .....195 D7
Hillside Chesham HP5 .....144 A3
  Gawcott MK18 .....51 F2
  High Wycombe HP13 .....173 D7
  Maidenhead SL6 .....202 D5
  Slough SL1 .....205 E4
  South Harefield UB9 .....190 C6
  Tingewick MK18 .....51 B6
Hillside Cl
  Chalfont St Giles HP8 .....177 B7

Hillside Cl continued
  Chalfont St Peter SL9 .....177 E4
  Upper Arncott OX25 .....94 E7
Hillside Cotts HP18 .....112 F2
Hillside Ct SL0 .....208 B4
Hillside Ctr HP11 .....172 F7
Hillside Gdns
  Amersham HP7 .....165 E7
  Berkhamsted HP4 .....135 D3
  High Wycombe HP13 .....173 D7
Hillside Rd
  Chorleywood WD3 .....167 C4
  Marlow SL7 .....183 E4
  Tylers Green HP10 .....163 A2
Hilltop HP18 .....125 D5
Hilltop Ave MK18 .....41 E2
Hilltop Fst Sch SL4 .....209 E4
Hilltop Rd HP4 .....135 C3
Hillview Saunderton SL4 .....149 C1
  Sherington MK16 .....14 A1
Hillview Rd HP13 .....173 D8
Hillway Amersham HP7 .....165 B6
  Woburn Sands MK17 .....49 A6
Hillwerke SL9 .....147 C6
Hillyer Ct MK6 .....35 C1
Hilperton Rd SL1 .....205 E4
Hilton Ave HP20 .....101 E2
Hilton Cl UB8 .....201 B3
Himley Gn LU7 .....80 D6
Hindemith Gdns MK7 .....48 D5
Hindhay La SL6 .....195 B3
Hindhead Knoll MK7 .....48 B6
Hinds Way HP21 .....115 B6
Hinkley Cl UB9 .....190 C7
Hinksey Cl SL3 .....207 B3
Hinton Ct MK3 .....46 F1
Hinton Rd Slough SL1 .....204 E6
  Uxbridge UB8 .....201 C4
Hipwell Ct MK46 .....6 F3
Hitcham Grange SL6 .....196 E1
Hitcham Ho SL1 .....197 A1
Hitcham La SL6,SL1 .....196 F2
Hitcham Rd SL1,SL6 .....204 A8
Hither Mdw SL9 .....177 E1
Hithercroft Rd HP13 .....161 E1
Hithermoor Rd TW19 .....213 A2
Hiving's Hill HP5 .....144 A2
Hivings Pk HP5 .....144 A3
HM Prison (Bullingdon)
  OX25,HP18 .....95 A7
HM Prison (The Mount)
  HP3 .....145 F4
HM Young Offender Inst
  (Finnamore Wood Camp)
  SL7 .....182 D7
HM Young Offender Inst
  (Grendon) HP18 .....73 B1
Hoathly Mews MK7 .....48 B8
Hobart Cl HP13 .....162 E1
Hobart Cotts HP16 .....150 D8
Hobart Cres MK15 .....35 B7
Hobart Ct SL7 .....184 A3
Hobart Rd HP13 .....162 D1
Hobarts Dr UB9 .....189 F5
Hobbis Dr SL6 .....202 A6
Hobbs Rd HP14 .....171 C4
Hobbshill Rd HP16 .....152 B6
Hobsons Wlk HP23 .....118 F5
Hockett La SL6 .....195 A6
Hockley La SL2 .....199 B4
Hockliffe Brae MK7 .....48 C5
Hodder La MK4 .....46 C2
Hodds Wood Rd HP5 .....154 C6
Hodge Lea La MK12 .....33 D4
Hodgemoor View HP8 .....177 A7
Hodgemore Ct MK14 .....21 F2
Hodges Mews HP12 .....172 C6
Hoe Mdw HP9 .....175 C4
Hog Hall La HP4 .....107 A5
Hog La Ashley Green HP5 .....144 D8
  Berkhamsted HP5 .....134 C2
Hogarth Cl SL1 .....204 E6
Hogarths Ct 9 MK8 .....33 F1
Hogback Wood Rd HP9 .....175 B4
Hogfair La SL1 .....197 C1
Hogg La HP15 .....163 D6
Hoggets Bottom HP3 .....156 E7
Hogshaw Rd MK18 .....75 E6
Hogtrough La HP22 .....131 D2
Holborn Cres MK4 .....57 A8
Holdom Ave MK1 .....47 D2
Holes La MK46 .....6 F4
Holiday La MK19 .....10 F4
Holland Cl Chinnor OX39 .....147 D7
  Wendover HP22 .....131 B4
Holland Rd
  Aylesbury HP19 .....101 B2
  Marlow SL7 .....183 F3
Holland Way HP14 .....161 E7
Hollandridge La OX49,
  RG9 .....168 D4
Holliday Cl MK8 .....45 E7
Holliday St HP4 .....135 D4
Hollies Ct LU7 .....80 E7
Hollies The
  Beaconsfield HP9 .....175 E3
  Bovingdon HP3 .....146 A2
  Tring HP23 .....119 D1
Hollin La MK12 .....33 E4
Hollington Bspl Ct HP10 .....69 D2
Hollington Rd LU7 .....69 C3
Hollington HP18 .....125 D7
Hollinwell Cl 3 MK4 .....46 D1
Hollis Rd HP13 .....173 F8
Hollister Chase MK5 .....46 B4
Hollow Hill End MK18 .....75 F7
Hollow Hill La SL0 .....207 C5

Hollow Rise HP13 .....162 B1
Hollow Way HP5 .....143 E1
Hollow Way La HP5,HP6 .....154 E4
Hollow Wood MK46 .....6 E3
Holloway Cl UB7 .....208 E1
Holloway Dr MK18 .....41 E2
Holloway La
  Chenies WD3 .....156 C2
  Turville Heath RG9 .....169 C4
  West Drayton UB7 .....208 D1
Holloway The
  Monks Risborough HP27 .....139 D5
  Tring HP22,HP23 .....118 C4
Holly Cl
  Farnham Common SL2 .....198 C8
  Milton Keynes MK8 .....45 E6
Holly Cres SL4 .....209 D5
Holly Dr Aylesbury HP21 .....115 E6
  Berkhamsted HP4 .....135 D3
  Maidenhead SL6 .....202 F8
  Windsor SL4 .....210 E2
Holly End HP14 .....161 C8
Holly Gdns UB7 .....208 F4
Holly Green La HP27 .....138 A3
Holly Hedges La HP3 .....156 C8
Holly Pl HP11 .....174 A3
Holly Tree La HP18 .....112 F3
Holly Wlk MK17 .....49 B2
Hollyberry Gr HP15 .....163 C7
Hollybush Cnr SL2 .....187 C2
Hollybush Hill SL2 .....199 B6
Hollybush La
  Amersham HP6 .....154 D3
  Cookham Dean SL6 .....195 B6
  Denham UB9 .....200 E8
  Iver SL0,SL3 .....207 B7
Hollybush Rd HP5 .....144 A4
Hollybush Row HP23 .....133 D8
Hollyfield HP23 .....119 C5
Hollyfield Cl HP22 .....119 C5
Hollytree Cl Astrop HP5 .....155 B8
  Chalfont St Peter SL9 .....177 E5
Holm Gate MK5 .....46 A8
Holman St HP19 .....101 C2
Holmanleaze SL6 .....203 A8
Holmedale SL2 .....206 C6
Holmer Green Fst Sch
  HP15 .....163 B7
Holmer Green Jun Sch
  HP15 .....163 B7
Holmer Green Rd HP15 .....163 A4
Holmer Green Senior Sch
  HP15 .....163 B7
Holmer Pl HP15 .....163 C7
Holmers Ct HP12 .....172 B3
Holmers Farm Way
  HP12 .....172 C3
Holmers La HP12 .....172 C3
Holmewood MK4 .....46 E4
Holmfield Cl MK6 .....47 D5
Holmlea Rd SL3 .....211 D6
Holmlea Wlk SL3 .....211 C6
Holmoak Wlk HP15 .....163 B3
Holmsdale Cl SL0 .....207 F7
Holmwood Cl SL6 .....202 B5
Holmwood Fst Sch MK8 .....33 F1
Holne Chase Comb Sch
  MK3 .....58 A7
Holst Cres MK7 .....48 D4
Holt Gr MK5 .....46 A8
Holt The MK18 .....52 E7
Holton Hall MK4 .....46 C4
Holton Rd MK18 .....41 D2
Holts Gn MK17 .....59 C1
Holtspur Ave HP10 .....185 F7
Holtspur Cl HP9 .....186 A8
Holtspur La HP10 .....185 F6
Holtspur Par HP9 .....186 A8
Holtspur Top La HP9 .....175 A1
Holtspur Top La HP9 .....175 A2
Holtspur Way HP9 .....175 A1
Holy Family RC Prim Sch
  SL3 .....206 F1
Holy Thorn La MK5 .....46 A5
Holy Trinity CE Prim Sch
  SL6 .....196 B7
Holy Trinity CE Sch SL7 .....183 D3
Holyhead Cres MK3 .....57 C8
Holyhead Mews SL1 .....204 D7
Holyport Rd SL6 .....203 B1
Holyrood MK8 .....45 E8
Holywell CE Mid Sch
  MK43 .....25 B1
Holywell Gdns HP13 .....173 E7
Holywell Pl MK6 .....35 C2
Holywell Rd MK43 .....25 C1
Home Cl
  Milton Keynes MK3 .....47 B2
  Shabbington HP18 .....124 D3
  Weston Turville HP22 .....116 F2
Home Ct MK10 .....36 A3
Home Farm
  Newton Longville MK17 .....57 D4
  Tring HP23 .....118 F2
Home Farm Ct
  Bovingdon HP3 .....145 F1
  Emberton MK46 .....13 E8
Home Farm La HP17 .....59 D2
Home Farm Rd HP4 .....134 D7
Home Farm Way SL3 .....199 C4
Home Field
  Aylesbury HP19 .....115 A7
  Bow Brickhill MK7 .....48 B3
Home Mdw SL2 .....198 C3
Home Meadow Dr HP10 .....185 E7
Home Way WD3 .....167 F1
Home Wood SL7 .....193 F6

Homefarm Ct HP8 .....177 A7
Homefield HP3 .....146 B3
Homefield Cl HP14 .....158 E4
Homefield Rd WD3 .....167 D5
Homeground MK18 .....52 E6
Homelands Gdns HP15 .....162 D8
Homelands Way RG9 .....191 D1
Homer Fst Sch SL4 .....209 D6
Homeridings Ho MK13 .....34 B4
Homers Rd SL4 .....209 D6
Homeside Cl SL6 .....195 E2
Homestall MK18 .....52 D6
Homestall Cl MK18 .....52 D6
Homestead Cl HP17 .....114 A4
Homestead Pl 14 HP19 .....115 A8
Homestead Rd SL6 .....202 D4
Homestead Way
  Great Kingshill HP15 .....151 D1
  High Wycombe HP12 .....172 D3
  Milton Keynes MK5 .....46 A8
  Thame OX9 .....125 E1
Homestead Way NN12 .....18 E3
Homeward Ct MK5 .....46 B7
Homewood SL3 .....206 D7
Homewood Ct WD3 .....167 F5
Honey Banks HP22 .....131 C4
Honey Hill Emberton MK46 .....13 F7
  Uxbridge UB10 .....201 F5
Honey Hill Dr MK19 .....31 E1
Honey La SL6 .....193 E2
Honey Way HP14 .....161 B8
Honeycroft Hill UB10 .....201 E5
Honeypot Cl MK13 .....34 B4
Honeysuckle Cl SL0 .....207 F7
Honeysuckle Ct SL3 .....212 C7
Honeysuckle Field HP5 .....154 B6
Honeysuckle Rd HP15 .....162 F7
Honeywick La LU6 .....92 E8
Honiton Ct MK7 .....48 C7
Honor End La HP16 .....151 A7
Honor Rd HP16 .....151 D6
Honorwood Cl HP16 .....151 B6
Honour Cl HP20 .....102 A2
Honours Mead MK43 .....146 A4
Hoods Farm Cl HP22 .....102 C4
Hooke The MK15 .....35 D7
Hooper Gate MK15 .....35 C7
Hop Gdns RG9 .....191 D2
Hopcraft Cl OX25 .....94 E7
Hope Brook Cotts LU7 .....91 F2
Hopkins Cl MK10 .....36 A2
Hopkins Ct HP20 .....101 F2
Hoppers Mdw MK5 .....46 A8
Hoppers Way HP15 .....162 D8
Hopton Gr MK16 .....22 F3
Hopton Rd OX9 .....126 A1
Hordern Cl HP17 .....126 F6
Horn La MK11 .....32 D5
Horn St MK16 .....13 B8
Hornbeam MK16 .....22 A3
Hornbeam Cl HP12 .....172 B4
Hornbeam Gdns 8 SL1 .....206 A3
Hornbeam Wlk HP15 .....163 A3
Hornbill Cl UB8 .....208 D7
Hornby Chase MK4 .....46 B2
Horners Croft MK12 .....33 C5
Hornhill Rd WD3 .....178 D5
Horns La
  High Wycombe HP12 .....172 A3
  Princes Risborough HP27 .....139 B3
Horse Hill HP5 .....144 B2
Horsebuck La HP23 .....133 E3
Horsefair Gn MK11 .....32 D5
Horseguards Dr SL6 .....203 B7
Horsemoor Cl SL3 .....207 A2
Horsemoor La HP17 .....164 C2
Horsenden La HP27 .....138 F2
Horsenden Rd HP13 .....173 F5
Horsepond MK17 .....59 C2
Horsepool La MK17 .....49 F4
Horseshoe Cl MK17 .....105 A7
Horseshoe Cloisters 3
  SL4 .....210 D6
Horseshoe Cres HP9 .....175 F1
Horseshoe Hill SL1 .....197 C8
Horseshoe Rd HP14 .....159 C7
Horstone Bglws HP7 .....129 D2
Horsham Reach SL6 .....196 C2
Horsleys SL3 .....178 D5
Horton Bridge Rd UB7 .....208 F5
Horton Cl
  Aylesbury HP19 .....115 A7
  Maidenhead SL6 .....196 C1
  West Drayton UB7 .....208 F5
Horton Depot SL3 .....212 C4
Horton Gate MK14 .....21 F2
Horton Gdns SL3 .....211 F4
Horton Grange SL6 .....196 C1
Horton Ind Pk UB7 .....208 E5
Horton Par UB7 .....208 E5
Horton Rd Datchet SL3 .....211 D6
  Horton SL3 .....212 A6
  Ivinghoe LU7 .....91 A2
  Slapton LU7 .....91 C6
  Stanwell TW19 .....213 A2
  West Drayton UB7 .....208 E5
  Poyle SL3 .....212 E4
Horton Road Ind Est
  UB7 .....208 E5
Horton Trad Est SL3 .....212 B6
Hortonsfield Rd NN12 .....18 F5
Hospital Circular Rd
  HP22 .....131 D6
Hospital Hill HP5 .....154 C7
Hospital Rdbt MK6 .....47 B6
Hotch Croft MK43 .....25 C3

Hotley Bottom La HP16 .....151 C8
Houghton Ct 4 MK8 .....45 F8
Housman Cl MK16 .....22 A5
Houston Ct 6 SL4 .....210 C5
How's Cl UB8 .....201 C4
How's Rd UB8 .....201 C4
Howard Agne Cl HP3 .....146 A4
Howard Ave
  Aylesbury HP21 .....116 B6
  Slough SL2 .....205 E8
Howard Cres HP9 .....176 D5
Howard Cl 1 SL8 .....185 A3
Howard Ind Est HP5 .....144 C2
Howard Mews SL3 .....212 B8
Howard Rd Chesham HP5 .....144 B3
  Seer Green HP9 .....176 D5
Howards Thicket SL9 .....188 D2
Howards Wood Dr SL9 .....188 D2
Howarth Rd SL6 .....203 A6
Howe Cl MK10 .....36 A3
Howe Dr HP9 .....175 E5
Howe Hill La HP15 .....163 B8
Howe Park Fst Sch MK4 .....46 B1
Howe Rock PH MK4 .....46 B1
Howell Hill Cl LU7 .....90 D5
Howitt Dr MK13 .....34 B8
Howland Pl MK17 .....60 F7
Howletts Cl HP19 .....115 A7
Hoylake Cl
  Milton Keynes MK3 .....57 D7
  Slough SL1 .....204 E4
Hoyton Gate MK8 .....45 D6
HRH Princess Christians
  Hospl SL4 .....210 D5
Hubbard Cl MK18 .....41 F1
Hubbards Ct WD3 .....167 D4
Hubbards Rd WD3 .....167 D4
Hubert Day Cl HP9 .....175 D3
Hubert Rd SL3 .....206 D3
Huckleberry Cl MK7 .....48 B6
Hudnall La HP4 .....121 E7
Hudson La MK8 .....45 D7
Hudsons Ave UB9 .....189 F6
Hugh Park Cl MK5 .....46 C8
Hughenden Ave HP13 .....173 A8
Hughenden Cl SL6 .....202 C6
Hughenden La UB8 .....201 C1
Hughenden Gn HP21 .....115 E4
Hughenden Inf Sch
  HP14 .....162 A7
Hughenden Manor*
  HP14 .....162 A3
Hughenden Rd
  High Wycombe HP13 .....162 B1
  Slough SL1 .....205 D7
Hughenden View HP13 .....173 B8
Hulbert End HP21 .....116 D5
Hulcombe Wlk HP20 .....101 E2
Hull Cl Aylesbury HP21 .....115 E6
  Slough SL1 .....205 C4
Hulton Dr MK46 .....13 F8
Humber Cl UB7 .....208 D5
Humber Dr HP21 .....115 C5
Humber Way
  Milton Keynes MK3 .....46 E1
  Slough SL3 .....207 A2
Humphrey Talbot Ave
  LU6 .....107 F7
Humphries Cl HP22 .....88 D5
Hundred Acres La HP7 .....165 D8
Hungerford Ave SL2 .....205 E8
Hungerford Rd SL6 .....195 E3
Hungerford Ho 1 MK4 .....46 D1
Hunsdon Cl MK14 .....34 D6
Hunsford Lodge SL4 .....210 A4
Hunstanton Cl SL3 .....212 C7
Hunstanton Way MK3 .....57 D8
Hunt Rd HP13 .....173 E6
Hunt's La SL6 .....196 E3
Hunter Cl SL1 .....204 C8
Hunter Dr MK2 .....58 C8
Hunter St MK18 .....52 C8
Huntercombe Cl SL6 .....204 C7
Huntercombe La N SL6 .....204 C6
Huntercombe La S SL6 .....204 C6
Huntercombe Manor Hospl
  SL6 .....204 C5
Huntercombe Spur SL6 .....204 C6
Hunters Cl
  Bovingdon HP3 .....146 A2
  Chesham HP5 .....144 A1
  Tring HP23 .....119 B5
Hunters Hill HP13 .....173 F5
Hunters Mews SL4 .....210 C6
Hunters Pk HP4 .....135 E5
Hunters Point OX39 .....147 C6
Hunters Reach MK13 .....34 A3
Hunters Way SL1 .....204 E6
Huntingbrooke 6 MK8 .....45 F8
Huntingdon Cres MK3 .....57 D6
Huntington Pl SL3 .....207 B3
Huntley Cl HP13 .....162 C2
Huntley Cres MK9 .....35 A3
Hunts Hill La HP14 .....161 E5
Huntsman Gr MK14 .....22 A2
Huntsmans Ct MK4 .....107 C5
Huntswood La SL6,SL1 .....196 F4
Hurley Croft MK10 .....36 B1
Hurley High St SL6 .....193 F4
Hurley La SL7 .....194 B3
Hurlstone Gr MK4 .....46 D3
Hurricane Way SL3 .....207 B1
Hurst Rd SL1 .....204 D8
Hurstfield Dr SL6 .....203 B7
Hurstleigh WD3 .....167 C4
Hurworth Ave SL3 .....206 C3
Hutchings Cl MK15 .....46 A8

Hutchings Rd HP9 ....175 D5
Hutton Ave MK6 ....34 F1
Hutton Ct MK17 ....49 B5
Hutton Way MK17 ....49 B5
Huxley Cl
  Newport Pagnell MK16 ....21 F4
  Uxbridge UB8 ....201 D1
Huxtable Gdns SL6 ....203 E1
Hyacinth Dr UB10 ....201 E5
Hychenden Cl HP14 ....161 E6
Hyde Cl MK16 ....22 C2
Hyde Gn
  Beaconsfield HP9 ....175 D3
  Marlow SL7 ....183 F1
Hyde Heath Inf Sch
  HP6 ....153 C5
Hyde Heath Rd HP6,
  HP10 ....153 A6
Hyde La Bovingdon HP3 ...146 A3
  South Heath HP16 ....152 E5
Hyde Mdws HP3 ....146 A4
Hyde The HP22 ....116 F2
Hyland Ho 3 SL8 ....185 B3
Hylle Cl SL4 ....209 E6
Hylton Rd HP12 ....172 C2
Hyrons Cl HP6 ....154 E1
Hyrons La HP6 ....154 E1
Hyrons La HP6 ....154 D1
Hythe The MK8 ....33 E3

I

Ibotson Ct SL3 ....212 E6
Ibstone Ave MK13 ....34 C3
Ibstone Ct LU7 ....49 B5
Ibstone CE Inf Sch
  HP14 ....169 D6
Ibstone Rd HP14 ....158 C3
Ickford Comb Sch HP18 ..124 A3
Ickford Rd
  Shabbington HP18 ....124 C2
  Worminghall HP18 ....124 C2
Icknield Cl Chinnor OX39 ..147 A4
  Wendover HP22 ....131 C5
Icknield Cotts HP17 ....129 F2
Icknield Gn HP23 ....119 A6
Icknield Way
  Dunstable LU6 ....93 D4
  Tring HP23 ....118 E4
Icknield Way Farm Cotts
  LU6 ....93 C3
Ideal Ho 3 HP20 ....115 C3
Iffley Cl UB8 ....201 D5
Ilchester Ct SL6 ....202 C5
Ilex Cl HP15 ....163 B3
Ilex Ct HP4 ....135 B4
Illingworth SL4 ....209 E4
Illingworth Pl MK6 ....46 F8
Imperial Ct
  Henley-on-T RG9 ....191 E1
  Loudwater HP10 ....174 C2
  Windsor SL4 ....210 A4
Imperial Rd SL4 ....210 A5
In The Ray SL6 ....203 B8
Independent Bsns Pk
  HP14 ....158 C5
India Rd SL1 ....206 B4
Ingleglen SL2 ....198 B7
Ingleside SL3 ....212 F6
Ingleton Cl MK13 ....34 C4
Ingram Ave HP21 ....116 C5
Inkerman Dr HP15 ....163 B5
Inkerman Rd SL4 ....204 F2
Inkerman Terr HP5 ....154 C4
Inn Farm Ct MK16 ....22 D7
Innes Ct MK8 ....34 F6
Innholder Ct MK14 ....34 F6
Innings Gate RG9 ....170 E1
Inniscrown Ho SL3 ....211 B7
Institute Rd Marlow SL7 ...183 E1
  Taplow SL6 ....203 F7
Intalbury Ave HP19 ....101 A2
Inverness Cl MK3 ....46 F2
Inwood Cl SL6 ....195 B6
Iona Cres SL1 ....204 E7
Ipswich Rd SL1 ....205 A7
Ireland Cl MK7 ....48 C4
Ireton Ct OX9 ....125 F1
Iris Cl HP21 ....115 B5
Iris Ct HP20 ....116 B8
Ironmonger Ct MK14 ....34 F6
Irvine Dr HP22 ....116 A2
Irvine Ho SL4 ....209 E5
Irving Cres SL4 ....105 A8
Irving Dale MK7 ....48 E5
Isaacson Dr MK7 ....48 C7
Isambard Cl UB8 ....201 D1
Isis Cl HP21 ....115 D3
Isis Way SL8 ....185 B4
Isis Wlk MK3 ....46 E1
Island Ho MK7 ....213 B6
Island The MK18 ....63 D2
Isle Of Wight La SL6 ....93 F4
Islet Ct SL6 ....196 C3
Islet Park Ho SL6 ....196 C3
Islet Pk SL6 ....196 C3
Islet Rd SL6 ....196 C3
Isling Brook MK5 ....46 B3
Ivanhoe Cl UB8 ....200 D8
Iver Ct MK18 ....52 C7
Iver Heath Inf Sch SL0 ....200 D3
Iver Heath Jun Sch SL0 ...200 D2
Iver La SL0 ....208 A8
Iver Lodge SL0 ....207 F8
Iver Sta SL0 ....207 F4
Iver Village Inf Sch SL0 ...207 F7
Iver Village Jun Sch The
  SL0 ....207 E7

Iverdale Cl SL0 ....207 C6
Ives Rd SL3 ....207 A3
Ivester Ct LU7 ....80 E6
Ivinghoe View HP20 ....101 F1
Ivinghoe Way LU6 ....92 E1
Ivinghoe YH* LU7 ....105 E5
Ivins Rd HP9 ....175 A1
Ivy Cl Longwick HP27 ....138 E5
  Newport Pagnell MK16 ....22 E4
Ivy Cotts HP8 ....177 B8
Ivy Cres SL1 ....204 F6
Ivy House La HP4 ....135 C5
Ivy La Bierton HP22 ....102 D1
  Burcott LU7 ....79 D4
  Great Brickhill MK17 ....70 C8
  Newton Longville MK17 ....57 C3
  Stewkley LU7 ....68 E1
Ivy Pl HP14 ....171 C5
Ivybridge Cl UB8 ....201 E2
Ivyhill Cl HP27 ....139 B3

J

Jack's La MK43 ....8 E5
Jacks Cl MK46 ....7 E7
Jackson Cl UB10 ....201 E5
Jackson Ct SL1 ....163 A3
Jackson Ind Est SL8 ....185 B2
Jackson Rd
  Aylesbury HP19 ....101 A3
  Uxbridge UB10 ....201 E5
Jacksons Cl LU6 ....92 E4
Jacob Cl SL4 ....209 E6
Jacobs Cl MK14 ....34 D7
Jakeman Way HP21 ....115 B6
Jakes Ho SL6 ....203 A8
Jamaica MK6 ....47 A6
James Cl
  Hazelmere HP15 ....163 A6
  Marlow SL7 ....183 F4
James Elliman Sch SL2 ...205 E6
James Martin Ct UB9 ....190 A5
James Rd HP14 ....171 B4
James St SL4 ....210 D6
James Way MK1 ....47 B1
Jane Cl HP21 ....116 A6
Jansel Sq MK21 ....116 B6
Japonica La MK15 ....35 C6
Jardine Cotts SL2 ....199 A8
Jarman Ct MK18 ....52 F8
Jarratt Rd SL4 ....210 B4
Jarry Ct SL7 ....183 F3
Jarvis Cl HP21 ....116 A6
Jasmine Cl HP27 ....139 B3
Jasmine Cres HP27 ....139 B3
Jasmine Wlk HP5 ....144 A1
Jason Ho HP12 ....172 E4
Jasons Hill HP5 ....145 B2
Jeeves Ct MK6 ....47 C7
Jefferies Rd HP17 ....114 B5
Jeffrey Cl HP23 ....119 A3
Jeffrey Wlk HP19 ....115 A7
Jeffries Ct SL8 ....185 B2
Jellicoe Cl SL1 ....205 B4
Jenkins Cl MK5 ....45 F5
Jenkins Ct HP23 ....89 C3
Jenkins La HP23 ....132 E3
Jenna Way MK16 ....23 A3
Jenner Rd HP21 ....115 C6
Jennery La SL1 ....197 C2
Jennings MK14 ....34 C7
Jennings Field HP10 ....185 C7
Jennings Wharf SL4 ....210 D7
Jerome Ct SL7 ....183 F4
Jersey Rd MK12 ....33 C6
Jesse's La HP18 ....125 D6
Jesus Hospl (almshos)
  SL6 ....203 C3
Job's La SL6 ....195 B8
John Colet Sch HP21 ....131 C5
John Hall Way HP11 ....172 D3
John Hampden Gram Sch
  HP11 ....172 F4
John Hampden Sch The
  HP22 ....131 B5
John Hampden Way
  HP16 ....151 B7
John Hellins Prim Sch
  NN12 ....18 D3
John Taylor Ct SL1 ....205 C5
John Watson Sch OX33 ...122 B1
Johns La HP5 ....134 E1
Johnson Cl HP21 ....171 B5
Johnsons Field MK46 ....6 C4
Johnston Pl MK6 ....46 E8
Joiner's Cl Botley HP5 ...145 B1
  Chalfont St Peter SL9 .....177 F3
Joiner's La SL9 ....177 E3
Joiners La SL9 ....177 F3
Joiners Way
  Chalfont St Peter SL9 .....177 E3
  Lavendon MK46 ....7 B
Jonathan Ct SL6 ....202 E7
Jonathans MK6 ....47 A6
Jonathans Ct MK6 ....47 A6
Jones Way SL2 ....187 C2
Joplin Ct MK5 ....45 F7
Jordans La HP9 ....176 E3
Jordans Rd HP9 ....176 F4
Jordans Way HP9 ....176 F4
Joules Ct MK5 ....46 C5
Jourdelay's Pas SL4 ....210 D8
Journeys End SL2 ....205 E8
Jubilee Cotts MK18 ....64 C7
Jubilee Rd
  High Wycombe HP11 .....172 E7

Jubilee Rd continued
  High Wycombe, Downley
  HP13 ....161 E2
  Stokenchurch HP14 ....158 F3
Jubilee Terr MK11 ....32 E5
Jubilee Way SL3 ....211 C7
Judge's La LU7 ....80 F6
Juniper Cl HP15 ....163 B3
Juniper Ct
  Flackwell Heath HP10 .....185 C7
  Slough SL1 ....206 B4
Juniper Dr
  High Wycombe HP12 ....172 C5
  Maidenhead SL6 ....203 B8
Juniper Gdns MK7 ....48 E7
Juniper Hill Sch HP10 .....185 B7
Juniper La HP10 ....185 D7
Juniper Rd SL7 ....183 D5
Jupiter Hts UB10 ....201 F4
Juson's Glebe HP22 ....131 C5
Jutland Ho SL4 ....209 F5

K

Kalman Gdns MK7 ....48 E5
Kaplan Cl MK5 ....46 B5
Karenza HP14 ....158 E5
Katherine Cl
  Tylers Green HP10 ....174 C8
  Walton MK7 ....48 A4
Katrine Cl MK2 ....58 D5
Kay Cl HP23 ....119 A5
Kaybridge Cl 1 HP13 ....173 F5
Kaywood Cl SL3 ....206 C3
Keach Cl MK18 ....66 A5
Keasden Ct MK4 ....46 B2
Keaton Cl MK8 ....45 D7
Keats Cl Aylesbury HP21 ..115 F6
  High Wycombe HP13 ....172 F6
  Newport Pagnell MK16 ....22 A4
Keats La SL4 ....210 C8
Keats Way
  Milton Keynes MK3 ....57 F7
  West Drayton UB7 ....208 F2
Keble Cl HP19 ....115 B8
Keble Rd SL6 ....202 E8
Keel Dr SL1 ....205 C4
Keeler Cl SL4 ....209 E4
Keen Cl HP19 ....115 A8
Keen's Cl HP13 ....162 E1
Keens La OX39 ....147 D6
Keensacre SL0 ....200 D3
Keep Hill Dr HP11 ....173 D4
Keep Hill Rd HP11 ....173 D5
Keepers Cl LU7 ....105 A7
Keepers Farm Cl SL4 ....209 E5
Keepers La HP6,HP27 ....153 C3
Keinches La HP22 ....87 A6
Keith Park Rd UB10 ....201 F5
Kellan Dr MK6 ....35 A1
Kellet Cl MK11 ....33 B2
Kelpatrick Rd SL1 ....204 D7
Kelsey Cl
  Maidenhead SL6 ....202 D3
  Milton Keynes MK4 ....56 F8
Kelso Cl MK3 ....57 D6
Kelvin Cl HP13 ....172 F8
Kelvin Dr MK5 ....46 D6
Kemble Cl MK15 ....35 F6
Kempe Cl SL3 ....207 C2
Kemps Piece HP17 ....127 A6
Kempson Cl HP19 ....101 B1
Kempton Gdns MK3 ....57 D6
Kemsley Chase SL2 ....198 D4
Kenchester MK13 ....33 F5
Kendal Cl
  Aylesbury HP21 ....116 B6
  Slough SL2 ....206 A6
Kendal Dr SL2 ....206 A6
Kendal Gdns LU7 ....80 C7
Kendall Pl
  Maidenhead SL6 ....202 C4
  Milton Keynes MK5 ....45 E5
Kendalls Cl HP13 ....173 F6
Kendrick Rd SL3 ....206 B3
Kenilworth Cl SL1 ....205 F3
Kenilworth Dr
  Aylesbury HP21 ....101 D2
  Milton Keynes MK3 ....57 E8
Kenneally SL4 ....209 C5
Kenneally Cl 11 SL4 ....209 C5
Kenneally Pl 12 SL4 ....209 C5
Kenneally Row 10 SL4 .....209 C5
Kenneally Wlk 10 SL4 .....209 C5
Kennedy Ave HP11 ....173 B4
Kennedy Cl
  Farnham Common SL2 ....198 C6
  Maidenhead SL6 ....202 C4
  Marlow SL7 ....183 E3
Kennedy Ho SL1 ....204 D5
Kennedy La SL6 ....195 C7
Kennet Dr
  Paulerspury NN12 ....17 D3
  Pottersbury NN12 ....18 A3
Kennet Cl
  Aylesbury HP21 ....115 C4
  High Wycombe HP13 ....162 D2
Kennet Dr MK3 ....57 E8
Kennet Rd MK3 ....57 F8
Kennet Rd
  Bourne End SL8 ....185 B4
  Maidenhead SL6 ....202 F8
Kennett Rd SL3 ....207 B3
Kennington Cl MK16 ....22 C3
Kennish Cl MK18 ....65 F4
Kensington Dr
  Great Holm MK8 ....46 A8

Kensington Dr continued
  Milton Keynes MK8 ....33 F1
Kensington Path 3
  HP19 ....100 F1
Kensington Pl MK46 ....6 F5
Kent Ave SL1 ....205 C8
Kent Cl UB8 ....201 C6
Kent Ho MK3 ....46 F2
Kent Lodge 6 SL6 ....202 F6
Kent Way SL6 ....195 E1
Kentmere Rd HP21 ....116 B7
Kenton Cl SL7 ....183 E2
Kenton Ct HP19 ....101 C2
Kenton's La SL4 ....209 F5
Kents Hill Fst Sch MK7 ....48 A7
Kents Hill Rdbt MK10 ....47 F8
Kents Rd MK14 ....34 D8
Kenway Dr HP7 ....166 B8
Kenwell Ct MK15 ....35 C3
Kenwood Cl SL6 ....202 A7
Kenwood Dr WD3 ....178 F8
Kenwood Gate MK6 ....35 B2
Keppel Ave MK19 ....20 D2
Keppel St SL4 ....210 D5
Kepwick MK8 ....33 E1
Kercroft MK8 ....33 E2
Kernow Cres MK6 ....35 A1
Kerria Pl MK3 ....47 A3
Kerry Cl HP19 ....101 A3
Kersey MK4 ....34 C8
Kesters Rd HP5 ....154 D7
Kestrel Cl
  2 Berkhamsted HP4 ....135 C3
  High Wycombe HP13 ....161 C1
Kestrel Dr HP15 ....163 B5
Kestrel Path SL2 ....197 E1
Kestrel Way
  Aylesbury HP21 ....101 A4
  Buckingham MK18 ....52 F7
Keswick Ct SL2 ....205 F6
Keswick Rd MK19 ....11 B2
Ketchmere Cl HP18 ....125 C6
Ketelbey Nook MK7 ....48 E5
Ketton Cl MK15 ....35 D7
Kew Cl MK8 ....33 F1
Kew Gr HP11 ....173 B4
Kew Rd HP11 ....173 B4
Keyes Way MK18 ....41 E2
Keynes Cl MK14 ....22 E4
Keys Pl SL6 ....202 F6
Khasiaberry MK7 ....48 B5
Kidd Cl MK3 ....45 E6
Kidderminster Rd SL2 ....198 A2
Kidderminster Wlk MK10 ..36 B2
Kidwells Cl SL6 ....202 E8
Kidwells Park Dr SL6 .....202 F7
Kildonan Pl MK12 ....33 D4
Kilfillan Gdns HP4 ....135 A3
Kilfillan Pk HP4 ....135 A3
Kilgour Ct 2 LU7 ....80 F7
Kilkenny Ho MK4 ....45 E2
Killarney Dr SL6 ....202 E7
Killerton Cl MK4 ....45 F2
Kiln Ave HP6 ....155 C1
Kiln Cl Calvert MK18,OX27 ..73 B5
  Prestwood HP16 ....151 C2
Kiln Croft Cl SL7 ....184 A3
Kiln Ct HP9 ....186 B8
Kiln Farm Ind Est MK11 ...33 B3
Kiln Farm Rdbt MK11 ....33 B3
Kiln Fields SL6 ....185 E1
Kiln La Botley HP5 ....155 B8
  Cores End SL8,HP10 .....185 D3
  Hedgerley SL2 ....187 D3
  Lacey Green HP27 ....149 F5
Kiln Pl SL6 ....195 F1
Kiln Pond La HP13 ....161 D3
Kiln Rd Hastoe HP23 ....133 B6
  Prestwood HP16 ....151 B7
Kiln The HP5 ....144 C1
Kilner Rd HP21 ....115 E5
Kilnwood HP14 ....150 B1
Kilpin Gn MK16 ....24 B6
Kilwinning Dr MK10 ....35 F1
Kimbells Cl HP18 ....124 D2
Kimber Cl SL4 ....210 A4
Kimber La SL6 ....202 E3
Kimberley Cl SL3 ....206 F2
Kimbers Dr SL1 ....197 D2
Kimble Ct HP22 ....129 E3
Kimble Park Cvn Site
  HP17 ....129 E3
Kimble Park Rd HP17 .....129 E3
Kimblewick Rd HP17 ....129 C5
Kimbolton Ct MK14 ....35 A8
Kincardine Dr MK3 ....46 F3
Kindermann Ct MK5 ....46 B5
Kindleton MK14 ....34 F8
Kinellan Ct HP9 ....175 D3
King Charles Cl MK18 ....41 E2
King Edward Ave HP21 ...116 D6
King Edward Ct 4 SL4 ....210 D6
King Edward St
  Milton Keynes MK3 ....33 F7
  Slough SL1 ....205 D4
King Edward VII Ave
  SL4 ....210 D8
King Edward VII Hospl
  SL4 ....210 C4
King George Cres MK3 ....57 E8
King George V Rd HP6 ....154 D1
King John's Cl TW19 ....211 C2
King Johns Rd SL3 ....212 D6
King St Chesham HP5 ....154 B7
  Maidenhead SL6 ....202 F6
  Maidenhead SL6 ....202 F7
  Milton Keynes MK11 ....32 E6
  Piddington HP14 ....160 C1

King St continued
  Tring HP23 ....119 A3
King Stable St SL4 ....210 D7
King's Cross HP18 ....113 A1
King's Gr SL6 ....202 E6
King's La
  Great Missenden HP16 ....141 C2
  Lee Common HP16,HP22 ..141 F7
  South Heath HP16 ....152 E8
King's Rd Aylesbury HP21 ..115 F3
  Henley-on-T RG9 ....191 D2
King's Road HP11 ....173 F4
  Loudwater HP11 ....174 A4
  Slough SL1 ....205 E3
  Uxbridge UB8 ....201 D3
King's Terr SL3 ....212 B8
King's Wood Sch HP13 ...173 F8
Kingfisher HP19 ....101 E4
Kingfisher
  3 High Wycombe HP11 ...173 A4
  Slough SL2 ....198 B1
Kingfisher Ctr The MK16 ..22 C3
Kingfisher Ho
  Loudwater HP11 ....174 A4
  Marlow SL7 ....183 F2
Kingfisher Pl HP11 ....174 B3
Kingfisher Rd MK18 ....52 F7
Kinghorn La SL6 ....195 D3
Kinghorn Pk SL6 ....195 D3
Kings Chase SL6 ....202 F6
Kings Cl
  Beaconsfield HP9 ....186 A8
  Buckingham MK18 ....52 F7
  Henley-on-T RG9 ....191 D2
  Westcott HP18 ....98 C6
  Worminghall HP18 ....123 D5
Kings Ct HP4 ....135 C5
Kings Farm Rd WD3 ....167 D3
Kings Hall Par HP22 ....131 B4
Kings La SL6 ....195 B8
Kings Lodge
  Amersham HP6 ....154 L1
  Finmere MK18 ....50 D6
Kings Mdw HP22 ....102 C4
Kings Mead LU6 ....92 E3
Kings Oak Ct HP27 ....139 C5
Kings Rd
  Berkhamsted HP4 ....135 B3
  Chalfont St Giles HP8 .....177 B8
  Henley-on-T RG9 ....191 D2
  West Drayton UB7 ....208 F4
Kings Ride HP10 ....163 B1
Kings Sq HP11 ....173 F4
Kings St LU7 ....78 E7
Kings Wlk RG9 ....191 D2
Kings Wood SL7 ....193 D7
Kingsash Rd HP19 ....114 F8
Kingsbridge MK4 ....46 D2
Kingsbrook Sch MK19 ....31 F4
Kingsbury HP20 ....115 D8
Kingsbury Dr SL4 ....211 B1
Kingscote Sch SL9 ....188 E8
Kingsdale Rd HP4 ....135 A3
Kingsey Rd OX9 ....126 D1
Kingsfield SL4 ....209 D6
Kingsfold MK13 ....34 B7
Kingsgate HP19 ....115 B8
Kingshill Dr MK19 ....31 E5
Kingshill Rd HP13,HP15 ..162 D3
Kingshill Way HP4 ....135 B2
Kingsland Rd HP21 ....116 A4
Kingsley Cl MK16 ....21 F1
Kingsley Cres HP11 ....172 F6
Kingsley Dr SL7 ....183 C6
Kingsley Path SL2 ....197 D1
Kingsley Wlk HP23 ....119 A4
Kingsmead HP27 ....139 B6
Kingsmead SL1 ....205 C6
Kingsmead Office Campus
  MK ....
Kingsmead Rd HP11 ....174 B3
Kingsmead Rdbt MK4 ....56 F8
Kingsoe Leys MK10 ....36 A2
Kingston Ave
  Milton Keynes MK11 ....32 E5
  West Drayton UB7 ....208 F4
Kingston La
  Uxbridge UB8 ....201 E2
  West Drayton UB7 ....208 F4
Kingston Rd HP13 ....162 D1
Kingston Rdbt MK10 ....36 D1
Kingsway
  Farnham Common SL2 ....198 C6
  Gerrards Cross SL9 ....188 E8
  Iver SL0 ....207 D3
Kingsway Ho 3 SL6 ....206 C3
Kingswood Ave HP10 ....174 A8
Kingswood Creek TW19 ..211 D1
Kingswood Ct SL6 ....202 D5
Kingswood Ho SL2 ....205 C8
Kingswood La
  Kingswood HP18 ....83 B2
  Ludgershall HP18 ....96 F6
Kingswood Par SL7 ....183 D5
Kingswood Pl HP13 ....162 A1
Kingswood Rd HP10 ....163 A1
Kingswood View HP13 ....162 E1
Kinloch Pl MK2 ....58 E5
Kinnaird Cl SL1 ....204 C7
Kinnear Cl MK8 ....45 E7

Kinross Dr MK3 ....46 E2
Kinson Gn HP20 ....101 E3
Kipling Ct SL4 ....210 B5
Kipling Dr MK16 ....21 F4
Kipling Rd MK3 ....58 A7
Kippell Hill MK46 ....6 F5
Kirby Est LU7 ....208 D6
Kirby Way UB8 ....201 F1
Kirke Cl MK5 ....46 A5
Kirkeby Cl MK14 ......34 D6
Kirkham Ct MK5 ....46 C8
Kirkstall Pl MK6 ......46 D8
Kirkwall Spur SL1,SL2 .205 E8
Kirkwood Gr MK5 ....45 D5
Kirtle Rd HP5 ....144 C1
Kirtlington MK15 ......35 B5
Kitchener Cl MK46 .....7 A3
Kitchener Rd HP11 ...172 E7
Kite Field HP4 ....134 E7
Kite Hill MK6 ....47 B8
Kite Wood Rd HP10 ..163 B1
Kitelee Cl MK19 ....11 A3
Kitsbury Ct HP4 ......135 B4
Kitsbury Rd HP4 ......135 B4
Kitsbury Terr HP4 ....135 B4
Kittiwake HP19 ....101 E4
Klee Cl HP22 ....85 A5
Klondyke SL7 ....183 D2
Knapp Gate MK5 ......45 F7
Knaresborough Ct MK3 .57 D7
Knaves Beech HP10 ...174 D1
Knaves Beech Bsns Ctr
  HP10 ....174 D1
Knaves Beech Ind Est
  HP10 ....174 C1
Knaves Beech Way
  HP10 ....174 C1
Knaves Hill LU7 ....80 D8
Knaves Hollow HP10 ..174 D1
Knebworth Gate MK14 ..22 A1
Knighton-Way La UB9 ..201 B6
Knights Cl Eaton Bray LU6 .92 E5
  Great Brickhill MK17 ..59 D1
  Windsor SL4 ....209 D6
Knights Ct LU6 ....92 E5
Knights Gn WD3 ......167 E6
Knights Hill HP12 ....172 E6
Knights Pl **5** SL4 ...210 C5
Knights Templar Way
  HP11 ....173 B4
Knightsbridge Ct SL3 .207 B4
Knoll Cl MK16 ....13 F2
Knoll The
  Aspley Heath MK17 ....49 A1
  Sherington MK16 ......13 F2
Knolls Cl HP22 ....89 B3
Knolls View LU6 ....92 B5
Knolton Way SL2 .....206 C2
Knottocks Cl HP9 ....175 D5
Knottocks Dr HP9 ....175 D5
Knottocks End HP9 ...175 D5
Knowl Gate MK5 ....46 C7
Knowle Way UB9 .....189 F5
Knowles Cl LU7 ......208 E5
Knowles Fst Sch MK2 ..58 D8
Knowles Gn MK2 ......58 C8
Knowles Mid Sch MK2 .58 D8
Knowlhill Rdbt MK5 ...46 C6
Knowsley Cl SL6 ......195 A1
Knox Bridge MK7 ......48 B8
Kola Ho Sl2 ....206 B6
Kop Hill Rd HP27 ....139 D3
Kramer Ct MK8 ....45 D6
Krohn Cl MK18 ....52 F8
Krypton Cl MK5 ....46 B6
Kynaston Ave HP21 ...115 E4
Kynaston Sch HP21 ...115 E3

L

La Roche Cl **4** SL3 ..206 C3
Laburnham Cotts LU7 ..69 C3
Laburnham Rd SL6 ...202 E6
Laburnum Ave UB7 ...208 F6
Laburnum Cl SL7 .....183 E4
Laburnum Gr
  Milton Keynes MK2 ....58 E7
  Slough SL3 ....212 B8
Laburnum Rd HP12 ...172 C5
Lace Mews MK46 ....7 A4
Lacemakers
  Chinnor OX39 ......147 C6
  Long Crendon HP18 ..125 C7
Lacey Dr HP14 ....161 C7
Laceys Dr HP15 ......163 B5
Lacy Dr MK15 ....35 A8
Ladbroke Cl HP20 ....101 E2
Ladbrooke Rd SL1 ...205 D3
Lady Cooper Ct HP4 ..135 E6
Lady Verney Ct HP13 .173 B8
Lady Yorke Pk SL0 ...200 D6
Ladybridge Terr MK43 ..8 E5
Ladyday Pl SL1 ......205 E4
Ladymead Cl MK17 ....56 B8
Ladymeadow CE MK10 .35 E3
Ladysmith Rd LU7 ....105 E5
Ladywalk WD3 ....178 A6
Laggan Ct MK2 ....58 D4
Laggan Sq SL6 ....195 F1
Laggan Sq **1** SL6 ..195 F1
Lagger Cl HP8 ....177 B7
Lagger The HP8 ......177 B7
Lagley Ho HP4 ....135 A5
Lagonda Cl MK16 ......22 E4

Laidon Cl MK2 ....58 D4
Lake Ave SL1 ....205 D6
Lake Cl MK18 ....66 B6
Lake End Ct SL6 .....204 A7
Lake End Rd SL4,SL6 .204 B5
Lake View SL6 ....196 A1
Laker Ct MK6 ....46 E7
Lakes Cotts LU7 ....90 C8
Lakes La
  Beaconsfield HP9 ....186 F8
  Newport Pagnell MK16 .22 B5
Lakes The SL7 ....194 A6
Lakeside Aylesbury HP19 .101 E4
  Maidenhead SL6 .....196 B1
  Tring HP23 ....119 A5
Lakeside Dr SL2 .....198 F4
Lakeside Est SL3 ....212 F7
Lakeside Rd SL3 ....212 F7
Lamb Cl MK6 ....46 E8
Lamb La MK7 ....48 C7
Lambe Rd HP22 ......131 C5
Lamberhurst Gr MK7 ..48 A8
Lambert Ave SL3 ....206 E3
Lambert Wlk OX9 ....125 F1
Lamberts Croft MK12 ..33 C5
Lamborne Ave MK4 ...46 D2
Lambourne Ave HP21 .115 D3
Lambourne Ct
  Maidenhead SL6 .....203 C8
  Uxbridge UB8 ....201 B4
Lambourne Dr SL6 ...202 C3
Lambridge La RG9 ...191 C1
Lambridge Wood Rd
  RG9 ....191 B4
Lambscroft Way SL7 ..177 E1
Lambton Ho SL4 .....210 A4
Lambtons Way MK18 ..66 B5
Lamesley Ho SL6 ....202 E6
Lammas Ave SL4 ....210 C5
Lammas Ct SL4 ......210 C5
Lammas La HP18 .....112 B2
Lammas Path HP18 ..112 B2
Lammas Rd
  Cheddington LU7 ...105 A7
  Slough SL1 ....204 D8
Lammas Way
  Lane End HP14 .....171 A4
  Loudwater HP10 .....174 E2
Lampitts Cross MK6 ...47 B6
Lamport Ct MK8 ....46 A8
Lamva Ct MK11 ....32 F5
Lanark Ho MK3 ....46 F1
Lancaster Ave SL2 ..198 C1
Lancaster Cl TW19 ..213 E1
Lancaster Ct LU7 ....172 D4
Lancaster Dr HP3 ...145 F4
Lancaster Gdns MK3 ..57 E7
Lancaster Rd
  Aylesbury HP21 ....116 B6
  High Wycombe HP12 ..172 E4
  Maidenhead SL6 ....202 B8
  Uxbridge UB8 ....201 D5
Lancaster Ride HP10 ..174 B8
Lancastria Mews SL6 .202 D7
Lancewood Way MK18 .174 A6
Lancelot Cl SL1 ......205 A4
Lanchester Rd MK43 ..24 D2
Lancot Ave LU6 ....93 F8
Lancot Dr LU6 ....93 F8
Lancot Lower Sch LU6 .93 F8
Lancot Pl LU6 ....93 F8
Lancotbury Cl LU6 ....93 C7
Lancresse Cl UB8 ...201 D6
Lander Rd HP19 .....100 F3
Landon Ct HP21 .....115 F7
Landrace Ct MK5 .....45 F3
Lands End Gr MK4 ....56 F8
Lands The LU7 ....79 F3
Landsborough Gate
  MK15 ....35 C7
Lane End HP4 ....134 F4
Lane End Ind Est HP14 .171 A4
Lane End Rd HP12 ...172 B6
Lane The
  Grafton Regis NN12 ...9 D2
  Mursley MK17 ....67 D6
Lane Wood Cl HP7 ...165 F8
Lanercost Cres MK10 ..36 B1
Lanfranc Gdns MK15 ..35 B7
Langcliffe Dr MK13 ...34 C5
Langdale Cl
  Maidenhead SL6 ....203 A6
  Milton Keynes MK2 ...58 D4
Langdale Ho HP11 ...174 A4
Langdale Lodge HP11 .174 C2
Langdon Ave HP21 ...115 E3
Langdon St SP23 ....119 A3
Langerstone La MK4 ..46 B1
Langford Pl MK4 ......48 A3
Langland Comb Sch MK6 .47 C6
Langland Ho MK6 .....47 C6
Langland Rd MK6 .....47 C6
Langlands MK46 ....7 E7
Langley Broom SL3 ..206 F1
Langley Bsns Ctr SL3 .207 A4
Langley Bsns Pk SL3 .207 A4
Langley Cl MK18 ......65 E4
Langley Cnr SL2 .....199 F6
Langley Manor Sch The
  SL3 ....206 E5
Langley Park Ctry Pk*
  SL0,SL3 ....200 A1
Langley Park Rd SL3 .207 B6
Langley Rd SL3 ......206 E3
Langley Sta SL3 .....206 E3
Langley Way MK7 ....183 C2

Langleywood Sch SL3 .206 E3
Langmuir Ct MK5 ......46 C4
Langney Gn MK4 ......57 A8
Langport Cres MK5 ...45 D5
Langston Ct HP12 ...172 C8
Langstone Ct HP20 ..101 F3
Langstone Dr **11** HP20 .101 F3
Langton Cl
  Maidenhead SL6 ....202 D8
  Slough SL1 ....204 D5
Langton Dr MK8 ....33 E3
Langton's Mdw SL2 ..198 C6
Lanner Wlk MK6 ....47 B8
Lanrick Copse HP4 ..135 E5
Lansdell Ave HP12 ...172 B3
Lansdown Rd SL9 ...177 D2
Lansdowne Ave SL1 .205 E5
Lansdowne Ct
  Maidenhead SL6 ....203 C7
  Slough SL1 ....205 E5
Lansdowne Rd
  Aylesbury HP20 .....101 D2
  Chesham HP5 ....144 C2
Lansdowne Way HP11 .172 E3
Lantern Way UB7 ....208 E4
Lantern Wlk SL6 ....203 B7
Lanthorn Cl MK14 .....34 C6
Lappetts La HP16 ....152 E8
Larch Cl Aylesbury HP20 .102 A2
  Slough SL2 ....205 B8
  Tylers Green HP10 ..163 C2
Larch Dr MK2 ....58 E7
Larch Rise HP4 ......135 A5
Larches The
  Berkhamsted HP4 ...134 D5
  Holmer Green HP15 .163 D7
  Little Chalfont HP6 ..155 B1
Larchfield Prim Sch
  SL6 ....202 E4
Larchfield Rd SL6 ...202 E5
Larchmoor The HP10 .163 D1
Larchmoor Pk Sl2 ...199 A7
Larchwood HP16 ....152 B4
Lark Cl MK18 ....52 E7
Lark Rise HP15 ......163 B5
Lark Vale HP19 ......101 E3
Larkfield SL6 ....203 B1
Larkfield Cl HP13 ...162 F1
Larkin Cl MK16 ....22 A5
Larkings La Sl2 ......199 B4
Larks Rise HP5 ......154 D6
Larkspur Ave MK14 ...34 E5
Larkspur Way HP15 .162 F6
Larwood Pl MK4 ......34 F1
Lasborough Rd MK10 ..36 C1
Lascelles Cl MK15 ....35 B7
Lascelles Ho **8** SL1 .206 A4
Lascelles Rd SL3 ....206 B3
Laser Cl MK5 ....46 C6
Lashlake Rd OX9 ....125 F1
Lassell Gdns MK6 ...203 B7
Lastingham Gr MK4 ..46 B2
Latchmoor Ave SL9 ..188 D7
Latchmoor Gr SL9 ...188 D7
Latchmoor Way SL9 .188 D7
Latimer Latimer HP5 .155 E2
  Milton Keynes MK11 ..32 E4
Latimer Ct HP6 ......166 C8
Latimer Rd HP20 ....116 A8
Latimer Rd Chesham HP5 .154 E5
  Little Chalfont HP5 ..155 C2
Latimer Way HP9 ....175 C6
Laud's Cl RG9 ....191 C1
Launceston WD3 ....167 B3
Launceston Ct MK5 ..46 B6
Launde **11** MK7 ......36 B1
Laurance Ct **2** SL7 .183 D2
Laurel Ave SL3 ......206 E4
Laurel Bank HP3 ....146 F8
Laurel Cl
  Milton Keynes MK8 ...45 D7
  Poyle SL3 ....212 E7
  Prestwood HP16 ....151 B7
  Speen HP27 ....150 C4
Laurel Dr
  Loudwater HP11 ....174 B3
  Walter's Ash HP14 ..161 D7
Laurel La UB7 ....208 E2
Laurel Rd SL9 ....177 D2
Laurel Way **4** HP21 .115 E7
Laurels Cl SL0 ......200 D3
Laurels The
  High Wycombe HP12 .172 C4
  Milton Keynes MK1 ..47 D1
Lautrec Way HP19 ..100 D2
Lautree Gdns SL6 ...195 E7
Lavender Cl HP21 ...115 B5
Lavender Gr MK7 .....48 A5
Lavender Rd UB8 ....208 F8
Lavender Way HP15 .162 F7
Lavender Wlk HP21 ..115 B5
Lavendon Comb Sch MK46 .7 F8
Lavric Rd HP21 ......115 C6
Lawford Ave WD3 ...167 C3
Lawford Cl WD3 .....167 C3
Lawkland SL2 ....198 C2
Lawn Ave UB7 ......208 D4
Lawn Cl SL3 ....211 C7
Lawn Farm Bsns Ctr
  HP18 ....83 D4
Lawn Hill HP18 ....73 A2
Lawn House La HP19 ..72 F1
Lawn Rd UB8 ....201 C5
Lawn St SL3 ....211 C6
Lawns The Brill HP18 ..96 B1

Lawns The continued
  Tylers Green HP10 ..163 B2
Lawnsmead Gdns MK16 .22 D5
Lawrence Cl HP20 ...102 A2
Lawrence Ct SL4 ....210 C5
Lawrence Gr HP16 ..151 D5
Lawrence Way SL1 ..204 D8
Lawrence Wlk MK16 ..21 F5
Lawson Cl MK14 ....8 A5
Lawson Pl MK5 ....46 B5
Lawsone Rise HP13 ..162 B1
Laxton Gn SL6 ......202 C3
Lay Rd HP19 ....101 B2
Layburn Cres SL3 ...212 B8
Layer's Ave SL9 ....177 C1
Layter's Ave S SL9 .177 C1
Layter's Gn SL9 ....177 C1
Layter's End SL9 ...177 C1
Layters Green La SL9 .177 B1
Layters Way SL9 ....188 D6
Lea Cl SL7 ....183 D6
Lea HP7 ....165 F8
Lea Inf Sch SL2 .....206 B6
Lea Jun Sch SL2 ....206 B6
Lea La MK18 ....125 F4
Leaberry MK13 ....34 A8
Leach Rd HP21 ......115 C7
Leachcroft SL9 ......177 B2
Leaches Farm Bsns Ctr
  HP18 ....81 F4
Leacort Cl UB7 .....208 E6
Leacroft Rd SL0 .....207 E7
Leadenhall Rdbt MK6 .46 E7
Leaders Cl HP22 .....89 B3
Leafield Rise MK8 ....33 D2
Leafy La HP23 ......118 E1
Leaholme Gdns SL1 .204 D8
Leapingwell La MK18 ..66 B5
Leary Cres MK16 .....22 E4
Leas Cl HP13 ....173 F8
Leas Dr SL0 ....207 E7
Leaside MK5 ....12 B6
Leasowe Pl MK13 ....34 C3
Leather La HP16 ....142 A3
Leaver Rd RG9 .....191 C1
Leckhampstead Rd MK18 .42 A8
Leckhamstead Rd MK19 .31 A3
Ledborough Gate HP9 .175 F4
Ledborough La HP9 ..175 E4
Ledborough Wood HP9 .175 E4
Ledburn LU7 ....90 C8
Ledburn Gr LU7 ......80 E6
Ledbury MK14 ....21 E1
Ledeview Ct HP11 ...174 A4
Ledger's Rd SL1 ....205 D4
Lee Common CE Sch
  HP16 ....142 D5
Lee Cotts
  Buckmoorend HP17 ..140 D6
  Lacey Green HP27 ..149 A4
Lee Cres HP17 ......114 C5
Lee Ct **7** HP12 ....172 E7
Lee Farm Cl HP5 ....145 A1
Lee Ho **2** MK4 ......46 B2
Lee La **6** SL4 .....194 F1
Lee Rd Aylesbury HP21 .115 D6
  Quainton HP22 ......84 F5
  Saunderton HP27 ...148 F6
Leeches Way LU7 ...105 A7
Leeds Rd SL1 ....205 E6
Lees Cl SL6 ....202 B5
Lees Gdns SL6 .....202 B5
Lees Wlk SL7 ....183 C2
Leeson Gdns SL4 ...204 E2
Legoland Windsor*
  SL4 ....209 D2
Leicester Cl RG9 ...191 D3
Leigh Hill MK4 ....46 A2
Leigh Pk SL3 ....211 B7
Leigh Rd SL1 ....205 B6
Leigh Sq SL4 ....209 D5
Leigh St **1** HP11 .172 F7
Leighton Buzzard Sta
  LU7 ....80 E7
Leighton Gdns SL6 ..196 B1
Leighton Rd **7** SL7 .183 E2
Leighton Mid Sch LU7 ..80 F6
Leighton Rd
  Edlesborough LU6 ...92 D4
  Leighton Buzzard LU7 .80 F7
  Soulbury LU7 ....70 B1
  Stoke Hammond MK17 ..69 E7
  Wing LU7 ....80 A3
  Wingrave HP22 ......89 C3
Leighton St MK17 .....60 E6
Leiston Spur SL1 ...205 E7
Leisure Plaza* MK9 ..46 C8
Leith Cl SL1 ....206 A5
Leith Rd HP19 ......115 A8
Lembrook Wlk HP21 .115 C6
Lenborough Cl MK18 ..52 C7
Lenborough Ct MK15 ..35 C2
Lenborough Rd MK18 ..52 C7
Lennon Dr MK8 ....58 D7
Lent Gn SL1 ....197 B1
Lent Green La SL1 ..197 B1
Lent Rise Comb Sch
  SL1 ....204 B8
Lent Rise Rd SL1 ...204 B8
Lenthall Cl MK13 .....34 A5
Leominster Gate **4**
  MK13 ....36 A1
Leon Ave MK2 ....58 D8
Leon Sch & Sports Coll
  MK2 ....58 C5
Leonards Cl HP18 ....72 F2
Leonardslee MK4 .....45 F2

Leopard Dr MK15 .....35 A7
Leopold Mall **5** SL1 .205 F4
Leopold Rd LU7 ......80 D7
Lerwick Dr SL1 .....205 E8
Leslie Dunne Ho SL4 .209 E5
Lester Ct MK7 ....48 C7
Lester Gr HP15 ......163 A4
Lesters Rd SL6 .....195 D6
Letchfield HP5 ......155 B8
Letter Box La HP27 .139 D7
Leven Cl
  Leighton Buzzard LU7 .80 B7
  Milton Keynes MK2 ..58 D5
Levens Hall Dr MK4 ..45 F1
Leverkus Ct OX39 ..147 C6
Leverkus Ho OX39 ..147 C6
Levings Cl HP19 ....101 A3
Levens Croft MK16 ..16 A3
Lewes Cl SL1 ....54 B8
Lewes Ho MK3 ....57 D7
Lewins Farm Ct SL1 .204 F4
Lewins Rd SL9 ......188 D8
Lewins Way SL1 ....204 F6
Lewins Yd HP5 .....154 B8
Lewis Cl MK16 ....21 F5
Lewis La SL9 ....177 E2
Lewknor CE Prim Sch
  OX49 ....157 B8
Lewknor Cl OX49 ...157 A7
Lexham Gdns HP6 ..154 C2
Lexington Ave SL6 ..202 D5
Ley Field Rd HP21 ..115 E6
Ley Hill Sch HP5 ....145 B1
Leybourne Gdns MK19 .147 C7
Leyburne Cl LU7 .....90 C8
Leyland Pl **3** MK6 ..34 C1
Leylands La TW19 ..213 A2
Leys Ct MK5 ....46 B8
Leys La MK18 ....62 B8
Leys Rd MK5 ....46 B8
Leys The Amersham HP6 .154 B4
  Buckingham MK18 ...41 F3
  Halton HP22 ....117 C1
  Tring HP23 ....119 B4
  Woburn Sands MK17 ..49 B4
Leys View MK16 ......13 F1
Leywood Cl HP7 ....165 E7
Libra Ho HP10 ......185 A8
Lichfield Down MK7 ..48 B5
Lichfield Ho HP21 ..115 F6
Lidcote LU7 ....78 A5
Liddall Way UB7 ....208 F5
Liddell SL4 ....209 C4
Liddell Pl SL4 ......209 C4
Liddell Sq **14** SL4 .209 C4
Liddell Way SL4 ....209 C4
Liffre Dr HP22 ......131 B6
Lightfoot Ct MK7 ....47 F5
Lightlands La SL6 ..195 F5
Ligo Ave HP22 ......116 C2
Lilac Cl MK17 ....57 C3
Lilac Ct SL2 ....197 F2
Lilac Pl UB7 ....208 F6
Lilies The HP22 ......87 C1
Lilleshall Ave MK10 ..35 F1
Lilley Way SL1 .....204 E5
Lillibrooke Cres SL6 .202 A3
Lilly Hill MK46 ....6 F5
Lillyfee Farm La HP10 .186 B5
Lily Bottom La HP27 .150 A7
Lily Dr UB7 ....208 D2
Lily Hill Rd HP21 ...173 A6
Limbaud Cl MK7 ......48 A5
Lime Ave
  Buckingham MK18 ...52 F7
  High Wycombe HP11 .173 D5
  West Drayton UB7 ..208 F6
  Windsor SL4 ....210 F7
Lime Cl Hazelmere HP15 .163 A6
  Newport Pagnell MK16 .22 B3
Lime Gr Chinnor OX39 .147 D6
  Leighton Buzzard LU7 .80 E8
  Woburn Sands MK17 ..49 B4
Lime Rd
  Princes Risborough HP27 .139 B3
  Yardley Gobion NN12 .18 E6
Lime St MK46 ....6 F3
Lime Tree Cl HP15 ..162 D8
Lime Tree Wlk HP7 .165 F8
Lime Wlk
  Maidenhead SL6 ....202 A8
  New Denham UB9 ...201 C7
Limerick La MK9 ......35 B3
Limes Ave HP21 ....116 B3
Limes The
  Amersham HP6 .....154 B3
  Milton Keynes MK11 ..32 B5
  Milton Keynes,Fenny Stratford
    MK2 ....58 E8
  Stoke Mandeville HP22 .116 B2
  Windsor SL4 ....209 C6
Limes Way HP18 ....124 D2
Limit Home Pk HP4 .134 D7
Limmer La HP12 ....172 B3
Limmers Mead HP15 .162 D8
Linceslade Gr MK5 ...34 B1
Linchfield HP13 .....211 C6
Linchfield Rd SL3 ..211 C6
Lincoln MK14 ....34 D8
Lincoln Cl HP22 .....116 B2
Lincoln Ct
  Berkhamsted HP4 ...135 B4
  6 Slough SL1 ....205 E3
Lincoln Hatch La SL1 .197 C1
Lincoln Ho HP10 ...185 D3
Lincoln Park Bsns Ctr
  HP12 ....172 D6

Lincoln Pk
 Amersham HP7 ....165 E8
 Brackley NN13 ....38 A5
Lincoln Rd
 Chalfont St Peter SL9 ....177 E2
 High Wycombe HP12 ....172 E3
 Maidenhead SL6 ....202 B8
Lincoln Way SL1 ....204 D6
Lincolns The HP16 ....152 A3
Lincolnshire Cl MK3 .....46 E1
Lincombe Slade LU7 .....80 A8
Lincroft MK43 ....25 B1
Lincs SL3 ....207 B1
Linden Ave SL6 ....195 D1
Linden Ct HP12 ....172 D6
Linden Dr
 Chalfont St Peter SL9 ....177 E1
 Farnham Royal SL2 ....198 C4
Linden End HP21 ....115 F6
Linden Gr MK14 ....34 E8
Linden Lea MK12 ....131 B6
Linden Way HP17 ....128 B7
Linden Wlk HP15 ....163 B3
Lindens The HP7 ....153 B2
Lindisfarne Dr MK10 ....36 A1
Lindo Cl HP5 ....144 B1
Lindores Croft MK8 .....36 B1
Lindsay Ave HP22 ....172 E7
Lindsay Cl TW19 ....213 D2
Lindsey Rd UB9 ....190 A1
Lines Hill HP22 ....88 B3
Lines Rd HP14 ....171 B5
Lines The HP22 ....88 C4
Linfields HP17 ....166 C7
Linford Ave MK16 ....22 A4
Linford Day Hospl MK12 .33 C5
Linford La
 Milton Keynes,Willen MK15 .35 D7
 Milton Keynes,Woolstone
  MK15 ....23 C3
Linford Lakes (Nature
 Reserve)* MK14 ....21 D3
Lingfield MK12 ....33 E4
Lingfield Cl HP13 ....174 A5
Lingholm Cl SL6 ....202 C6
Linington Ave HP15 .....145 A1
Link Cl HP12 ....172 D6
Link Rd Datchet SL3 .....211 C6
 Great Missenden HP16 ...152 A7
 High Wycombe HP12 ....172 D6
Link The Hazelmere HP15 .163 A5
 Slough SL2 ....206 B7
Link Way UB9 ....190 A5
Links App HP10 ....185 B8
Links Rd HP10 ....185 C8
Links Way HP10 ....185 B8
Linkswood Rd SL1 ....197 C3
Linnet Cl HP12 ....172 B3
Linnet Dr HP18 ....98 C5
Linney Ct MK4 ....46 A1
Linslade Lower Sch LU7 ..80 D7
Linslade Mid Sch LU7 ...80 E5
Linslade Rd LU7 ....70 F4
Lintlaw Pl MK3 ....47 A3
Linton Cl MK13 ....34 C4
Lintott Ct TW19 ....213 D1
Linx The MK3 ....47 A2
Lionel Ave HP22 ....131 A6
Lionel Cl HP22 ....131 A5
Lipscomb La MK5 ....46 A7
Lipscombe Dr MK18 ....41 E1
Lisburn Path **1** HP20 ..101 F2
Lisle Rd HP13 ....162 A1
Lisleys Field HP15 ......162 D7
Lismore Pk SL2 ....205 F7
Lissel Rd MK4 ....47 E5
Lisset Rd SL6 ....203 A6
Lister Gn HP21 ....115 E5
Liston Ct **7** SL7 ....183 D2
Liston Ho **9** SL7 ....183 D2
Liston Rd SL7 ....183 D2
Litcham Spur SL1 ....205 D7
Little Balmer MK18 .....52 E6
Little Benty UB7 ....208 D1
Little Boltons **15** SL7 ...183 E2
Little Bridge Rd HP4 ...135 E4
Little Britain HP18 ......99 B7
Little Buntings MK4 ....209 F4

Little La
 Lacey Green HP27 ....149 C4
 Yardley Hastings NN7 ....1 A7
Little Linford La MK16,
 MK19 ....21 E4
Little London
 Deanshanger MK19 ......31 E4
 Whitchurch HP22 ....87 A5
Little Marlow CE Sch
 SL7 ....184 C5
Little Marlow Rd SL7 ...183 E3
Little Marsh Rd OX7 ....72 A3
Little Mdw MK5 ....46 C7
Little Missenden CE Sch
 HP7 ....153 A2
Little Mollards HP7 .....146 C4
Little Orchard Cl HP27 .138 E5
Little Orchs HP20 ....101 F3
Little Pk Bovingdon HP3 .146 A4
 Princes Risborough HP27 .139 C3
Little Reeves Ave HP7 ..150 A8
Little Shardeloes HP7 ...165 A8
Little Spinney MK43 ....25 C3
Little Spring HP5 ....144 B3
Little Spring Sch HP5 ...144 B3
Little St NN7 ....1 B6
Little Stanton MK14 ....34 D8
Little Stocking MK5 ....46 A3
Little Sutton La SL3 ....207 C1
Little Tring Rd HP23 ....118 F6
Little Twye HP23 ....132 F3
Little Twye Rd HP23 ....132 F3
Little Windmill Hill
 WD4 ....156 F7
Little Wood HP4 ....158 E5
Little Woodlands SL4 ..209 A4
Littlebrook Ave SL2 ....204 E8
Littlecote MK8 ....34 A1
Littledown Rd SL1 ......205 F5
Littledown Sch SL1 .....205 F6
Littlefield Ct UB7 ......213 D7
Littleport Spur SL1 ....205 E7
Littleworth LU7 ....79 E3
Littleworth Rd
 Hedgerley SL1 ....186 C1
 High Wycombe HP13 ....161 E2
Litton Cl HP10 ....174 C2
Liverpool Rd SL1 ....205 B7
Liverpool Victoria Ho **3**
 HP13 ....173 B7
Livesey Hill MK5 ....46 B5
Livingstone Dr MK15 ...35 C5
Llanbury Cl SL9 ....177 E3
Lloyds MK6 ....47 A7
Loakes Ho HP11 ....173 A6
Loakes Rd HP11 ....173 A6
Lochinvar Cl SL1 ....205 B4
Lochnell Rd HP4 ....134 C6
Lochy Dr LU7 ....80 C7
Lock Ave SL6 ....196 C2
Lock Bridge Rd SL6 ....195 F6
Lock La Cosgrove MK19 ..19 E2
 Maidenhead SL6 ....202 C4
Lock Mead SL6 ....196 C2
Lock Path SL4 ....209 D8
Lock Rd SL3 ....203 C8
Lock View La MK1 ......47 E1
Lockbridge Ct SL6 .....203 D8
Locke Cl HP19 ....101 A2
Locke Gdns SL3 ....206 C4
Locke Rd MK4 ....58 C8
Lockets Cl SL4 ....209 D6
Lockton Cl **4** SL1 ....46 B3
Lockton Ct MK4 ....46 B3
Lockview Cotts MK1 ....47 E1
Lodden Cl HP21 ....115 D3
Loddon Dr SL6 ....196 C1
Loddon Rd SL8 ....185 A4
Loddon Spur SL1 ....205 E7
Lodge Cl
 Cheddington LU7 ....105 A7
 Marlow SL7 ....183 E1
 Padbury MK18 ....53 C2
 Slough SL1 ....206 B8
 Uxbridge UB8 ....201 C1
Lodge Farm Bsns Ctr
 MK19 ....20 C3
Lodge Farm Cl HP22 ....116 E2
Lodge Farm Ct MK19 ...19 F6
Lodge Gate MK14 ......34 E7
Lodge La
 Little Chalfont HP8 .....166 F6
 Prestwood HP16 ....151 D5
 Stoke Hammond MK17 ..69 E7
Lodge Park The MK16 ..22 C4
Lodge Rd MK43 ....37 F8
Lodge The
 Aylesbury HP19 ....115 A7
 Slough SL3 ....206 B8
Lodge Way SL4 ....209 A4
Lodges of the Military
 Knights **4** SL4 ....210 D6
Lodore Gn UB10 ....190 E1
Logan Rock MK4 ....57 B8
Logans Cl HP6 ....154 C2
Lombardy Dr HP4 ......135 D3
Lomond Dr
 Leighton Buzzard LU7 ...80 C7
 Milton Keynes MK2 .....58 D4
London Central High Sch
 HP11 ....173 B4
London End
 Newton Longville MK17 .175 F1
 Woburn MK17 ....60 F6
London End La MK17 ...48 D1

London Ho MK11 ....32 D5
London Rd
 Aston Clinton HP22 ....117 E4
 Beaconsfield HP9 ......187 B8
 Buckingham MK18 .....52 E6
 Chalfont St Giles HP8 ..177 C7
 Datchet SL3 ....211 C7
 Felden HP3 ....146 F8
 High Wycombe HP11 ...173 E5
 Little Kingshill HP16 ...152 B5
 Loughton MK5 ....46 A7
 Milton Common OX9 ...136 B3
 Milton Keynes MK16 ...36 B5
 Milton Keynes,Stony Stratford
  MK11 ....32 C5
 Newport Pagnell MK16 .22 F3
 Old Stratford MK19 ....32 C7
 Slough,Brands Hill SL3 .212 B8
 Slough,Langley SL3 ....206 D2
 Tring HP23 ....119 C3
 Wendover HP22 ....141 D6
 Wheatley OX33 ....122 B1
 Slough SL3 ....212 B8
London Rd E HP7 ......165 E6
London Rd W HP7 .....165 C7
Londrina Ct **9** HP4 ....135 D4
Londrina Terr **10** HP4 ..135 D4
Long Ayres MK7 ....48 A3
Long Cl SL2 ....198 B5
Long Close Prep Sch
 SL3 ....206 A2
Long Crendon Ind Est
 HP18 ....125 E5
Long Crendon Rd HP18 .124 D3
Long Crendon Sch
 HP18 ....125 C7
Long Croft Rd WD3 ....178 D5
Long Dr SL1 ....197 C2
Long Furlong
 Haddenham HP17 ......126 F6
 Stone HP17 ....114 B5
Long Furlong Dr SL2 ...197 E1
Long Gr HP9 ....176 C4
Long Gr La HP7 ....105 C3
Long Hale LU7 ....105 A5
Long Hedge LU7 ....105 C4
Long Hide HP27 ....139 C4
Long La Bovingdon HP3 .155 F8
 Cookham Rise SL6 .....195 D5
 Heronsgate WD3 ....167 D2
 Olney MK46 ....6 F4
 Wooburn Moor WD3 ...167 F1
Long Leys HP19 ....115 A8
Long Ley LU7 ....105 A7
Long Leys HP19 ....115 A8
Long Lional HP20 ......115 D8
Long Marston CE Prim Sch
 HP23 ....104 B4
Long Marston La LU7 ..104 C4
Long Marston Rd LU7 ..104 F2
Long Massey MK46 .....6 E5
Long Mdw
 Aylesbury HP21 ....116 B6
 Chesham HP5 ....144 C3
Long Meadow Sch HP5 .45 F3
Long Orchard Dr HP10 .174 C8
Long Park Cl HP6 .....154 C3
Long Park Way HP6 ...154 C3
Long Pk HP6 ....154 C3
Long Plough HP22 .....117 D5
Long Readings La SL2 ..198 B2
Long Ride HP27 ....139 C3
Long Row
 Leckhampstead MK18 ..30 E1
 Prestwood HP16 ....151 D6
Long View HP4 ....135 A6
Long Walk The* SL4 ...210 D4
Long Wall HP17 ....126 F5
Long Wlk HP8 ....166 E6
Long Wood Dr HP9 ....176 F4
Longborns MK43 ....25 C2
Longbottom La HP9 ...176 C3
Longboat Quay SL4 ....209 D6
Longbridge Gr HP23 ...119 A6
Longbridge Way UB8 ..201 B3
Longcroft HP22 ....117 F5
Longcroft Ave HP22 ...131 D6
Longcroft La
 Bovingdon HP3 ....146 D5
 Paulerspury NN12 .....17 C8
Longcross MK15 ....35 A6
Longdown Hill HP17 ...139 F5
Longdown Mews HP19 .114 F8
Longfellow Dr MK16 ...22 A4
Longfield Hedgerley SL2 .187 D1
 Little Kingshill HP16 ...152 B4
Longfield Dr HP6 ......154 B1
Longfield Gdns HP23 ..118 E3
Longfield Rd
 Chesham HP5 ....143 F2
 Tring HP23 ....118 F3
Longford Rdbt UB7 ....213 B6
Longhedge MK7 ....48 A2
Longland Way HP21 ...172 D5
Longlands Ct MK16 ....66 A5
Longlands Wlk MK16 ..60 A5
Longlat Cl MK7 ....33 F1
Longleat Gdns SL6 ....202 D6
Longlees WD3 ....178 D5
Longmead La SL1 ......197 D5
Longmead Prim Sch
 UB7 ....208 E2
Longmire MK46 ....7 F7
Longmore Cl WD3 .....178 F6
Longpeak Cl MK4 ......46 B1

Longridge Scout Boating
 Activity Ctr SL7 ....194 F8
Longstone Rd SL0 .....200 C4
Longview HP9 ....185 F8
Longville MK12 ....33 B7
Longwick CE Comb Sch
 HP27 ....138 D6
Longwick Rd
 Longwick HP27 ....138 F6
 Monks Risborough HP27 .139 A5
Longwood Ave SL3 ....207 B1
Longwood La HP7 .....165 A8
Longworth Dr SL6 .....196 C1
Lonsdale Cl SL6 ....196 A1
Lonsdale Way SL6 .....203 C1
Look Ahead SL1 ....205 E4
Loose Path HP19 ......114 F8
Loosen Dr SL6 ....202 A3
Loosley Hill HP27 .....149 D6
Lord Grey Sch MK3 ....46 F1
Lord Knyvett Cl TW19 .213 D1
Lord Knyvetts Ct **12**
 TW19 ....213 E1
Lord Mayors Dr SL2 ...198 A7
Lord Raglan Ho SL4 ...210 C4
Lords Cl MK2 ....47 C1
Lords Mead LU6 ....92 E6
Lords Mill Ct HP5 .....154 F2
Lords Terr LU6 ....92 E6
Lordsmead MK43 ......25 C2
Loriner Pl MK14 ....35 A6
Loring Rd
 Berkhamsted HP4 .....135 C3
 Dunstable LU6 ....93 F8
 Windsor SL4 ....209 F6
Lorne Cl SL1 ....205 C3
Lorraine Cl HP13 ......173 E8
Loseley Cl MK8 ....33 F1
Losfield Rd SL4 ....209 E6
Lossie Dr SL3 ....207 B6
Lothersdale MK13 .....34 B5
Lothian Cl MK4 ....46 E2
Lott Mdw HP21 ....115 D3
Loudhams Rd HP7 ....166 C8
Loudhams Wood La
 HP8 ....166 D7
Loudwater Comb Sch
 HP11 ....174 B2
Loughton Manor First Sch
 MK5 ....46 A8
Loughton Middle Sch
 MK5 ....46 A7
Loughton Rd MK13 ....34 A3
Loughton Rdbt MK8 ...45 F8
Louisa Cotts **10** HP23 ..119 A3
Louise Wlk HP3 ....146 A3
Lovat Mid Sch MK16 ..22 D3
Lovat St MK16 ....22 D4
Lovatt Dr MK3 ....57 E8
Love Green La SL0 ....207 B8
Love Hill La SL3 ....207 A6
Love La SL0 ....207 D7
Love Row MK17 ....68 D6
Lovegrove Dr SL2 .....197 F1
Lovejoy La SL4 ....209 B5
Lovel End SL9 ....177 C3
Lovel Mead SL9 ....177 C3
Lovel Rd SL9 ....177 C2
Lovelace Cl SL4 ....193 F4
Lovett Gdns SL6 ......196 C3
Lovett End LU7 ....78 E8
Lovibonds Ave UB7 ...208 F7
Lowbrook Cl HP21 ....116 A4
Lowbrook Dr SL6 .....202 A3
Lowbrook Prim Sch
 SL6 ....202 A3
Lowdell Cl UB7 ....208 E7
Lowdon Cl HP11 ......173 D4
Lower Ascott LU7 .....79 F1
Lower Ash Yd MK17 ...67 F8
Lower Boyndon Rd SL6 .202 E6
Lower End Ashendon HP18 .97 C1
 Lower End MK18 ....53 F8
 Newton Longville MK17 .57 C3
 Piddington OX25 ......95 E8
 Wingrave HP22 ....89 D3
Lower End Rd MK17 ...49 A8
Lower Farm Cl HP18 ..124 D3
Lower Farm Gate HP17 .114 A3
Lower Fourth St MK9 ..34 D1
Lower Furney Cl HP13 .173 D8
Lower Gn
 Cuddington HP18 ......112 F3
 Westcott HP18 ....98 C7
 Weston Turville HP22 ..117 A3
Lower Green La HP18 ..112 C2
Lower Hammersley La
 HP13 ....174 B4
Lower Icknield Way
 Chinnor OX39 ....147 D8
 Great Kimble HP17 ....129 D1
 Monks Risborough HP27 .139 B8
 Pitch Green HP27 .....138 C3
 Wilstone HP22,HP23 ..118 C7

Lower Kings Rd HP4 ...135 C5
Lower Lees Rd SL2 ....198 B2
Lower Lodge La HP15 .163 A5
Lower Mead SL0 ......200 D2
Lower Mount Farm SL6 .195 D5
Lower Ninth St MK9 ...34 E2
Lower Pound La SL7 ..194 D8
Lower Rd
 Aylesbury HP21,HP22 ..115 F3
 Blackthorn OX25 ......81 A4
 Chinnor OX39 ....147 C7
 Chorleywood WD3 ....167 D5
 Cookham Rise SL6 ....195 E7
 Denham UB9 ....189 D4
 Gerrards Cross SL9 ...188 F7
 Hardwick HP22 ....87 B3
 Lacey Green HP27 ....149 D6
 Little Kingshill HP16 ..152 B2
Lower Ridge SL8 ......185 B4
Lower Riding HP9 .....175 B2
Lower Second St MK9 .34 C1
Lower St Pury End NN12 .17 A7
 Quainton HP22 ....85 A5
Lower Stonehayes MK14 .34 F7
Lower Tenth St MK9 ..34 E1
Lower Third St MK9 ...34 D1
Lower Ventnor Cotts
 SL6 ....195 C8
Lower Ward SL4 ......210 D7
Lower Way
 Great Brickhill MK17 ..59 C1
 Padbury MK18 ....53 C2
Lower Weald MK19 ...32 E2
Lower Wharf MK18 ...41 E1
Lowes Cl HP14 ....158 C5
Lowestoft Dr SL1 .....204 D7
Lowfield Cl HP15 .....163 B3
Lowfield Way HP15 ...163 B3
Lowick Pl **4** MK4 ......46 A2
Lowland Rd MK3 ......57 C8
Lowlands Cres HP15 ..151 D3
Lowlands Rd TW19 ...213 D2
Lowman Way HP21 ...115 D4
Lowndes Ave MK5 ....144 B1
Lowndes Gr MK5 ......45 F7
Lowndes Way MK18 ..66 A5
Lownes Path HP19 ....114 F8
Loxbeare Dr MK4 .....46 C4
Loxboro Hill HP14 ....160 D4
Loxley Rd HP4 ....134 F6
Loxwood Cl HP3 ......146 F6
Loyne Cl LU7 ....80 C8
Lucas Pl MK6 ....47 D8
Lucas Rd HP13 ....173 C7
Luccombe MK4 ....46 C3
Lucky La or Cock La
 HP20 ....101 D1
Lucy La MK5 ....46 B8
Ludgate Milton Keynes MK6 .46 E7
 Tring HP23 ....118 F4
Ludgershall Rd OX25 ..95 E7
Ludlow Cl MK3 ....57 F7
Ludlow Ho SL6 ....202 A6
Ludlow Mews HP11 ...172 A4
Ludlow Rd SL6 ....202 A6
Ludlow Way HP10 ....116 B8
Ludlow Rd SL6 ....202 A6
Luff Cl SL4 ....209 E4
Lufford Pk MK14 ......35 F3
Luke Pk MK10 ....35 F3
Luker Ave RG9 ....191 D3
Lukes La HP23 ....104 D3
Lukes La HP21 ....105 A1
Lullingstone Dr MK13 .33 F5
Lumber La NN12 ......17 B7
Lundholme MK13 .....34 B5
Lundy Ct SL1 ....204 E6
Lupin Cl HP21 ....115 B5
Lupin Wlk HP21 ......115 B5
Lutman La SL6 ....195 F2
Luttlemarsh MK7 .....48 A5
Lutyens Gr MK7 ......48 D5
Luxborough Gr MK4 ..46 C4
Lychgate Cotts HP3 ..146 B4
Lycrome La HP5 ......144 D3
Lycrome Rd HP5 .....144 E3
Lyde End HP27 ....138 B1
Lydford Ave SL2 .....205 D8
Lydiard MK8 ....33 E1
Lydiard Cl HP21 ......116 A4
Lydsey Cl SL2 ....198 A8
Lye Green Cotts HP5 .144 E3
Lye The HP4 ....121 D6
Lyell Pl E SL4 ....209 C4
Lyell Pl W SL4 ....209 C4
Lyell Rd SL4 ....209 C4
Lyell Wlk E SL4 ......209 C4
Lyell Wlk W SL4 .....209 C4
Lyme Ave HP4 ....134 D7
Lynch Cl UB8 ....201 C5
Lynch Hill Comb Sch
 SL2 ....197 F2
Lynch Hill La SL2 ....197 E2
Lynch The MK8 ....45 B8
Lyndhurst Ave SL1 ...195 E6
Lyndhurst Ct HP13 ...173 A4
Lyndhurst Rd HP5 ....144 B2
Lyndon Cl HP15 ......163 B3
Lyndon Gdns HP13 ...173 E8
Lynfield HP4 ....135 B1
Lyndwood Dr SL4 ....211 A2
Lyndwood Par SL4 ...211 A2
Lyneham Gdns MK8 ..45 B8
Lynher Cl HP21 ....115 C4

Lynmouth Cres MK4 ....46 D4
Lynott Cl MK8 ....45 E6
Lynton Gn SL6 ....202 E7
Lynton Rd HP5 ....144 C3
Lynwood Ave SL3 .....206 D3
Lynwood Rd HP21 .....116 A5
Lyon Rd MK1 ....47 B2
Lysander Cl HP3 .....146 A4
Lysander Mead SL6 ...203 C8

M

Macdonald Cl HP6 ....154 D4
Mackenzie Mall 3 SL1 .205 F4
Mackenzie St 2 SL1 ..205 F4
Maconi Croft MK5 .....46 C5
Madeira Wlk SL4 .....210 D6
Madeley Cl HP6 ......154 D3
Madeley Rd HP21 .....115 E6
Magdalen Cl
  Milton Keynes MK11 ..32 D6
  Syresham NN13 ....27 C8
Magdalen Ho MK11 ....32 D6
Magenta Cl MK4 ......58 D6
Magnolia Dene HP15 .162 F2
Magnolia Gdns SL3 ...206 C3
Magnolia St SL7 .....208 D2
Magnolia Way HP16 ..185 E7
Magpie Cl
  Flackwell Heath HP10 .174 A1
  Milton Keynes MK5 ...46 B4
Magpie La Coleshill HP7 .165 A1
  Flackwell Heath HP10 .174 A1
  Loudwater HP13 ......174 B3
Magpie Way Slough SL2 .197 F1
  Winslow MK18 ....66 B6
Mahler Cl MK7 ....48 C5
Mahoney Cl HP11 ....172 F8
Maidenhead Ave MK13 .34 C3
Maidenhead Coll for Girls
  SL6 ....202 E7
Maidenhead Court Pk
  SL6 ....196 B3
Maidenhead Rd
  Cookham Rise SL6 ...195 F6
  Windsor SL4 ....209 E2
  Maidenhead Sta SL6 .202 F6
Maids Moreton CE Sch
  MK18 ....41 E3
Maidstone Rd MK10 ...36 C2
Main Dr
  Gerrards Cross SL9 ..188 C6
  Iver SL0 ....207 E3
  Potterspury NN12 ....18 B2
Main Par WD3 ....167 C5
Main Rd Astwood MK16 .16 B3
  Drayton Parslow MK17 .68 B5
  Lacey Green HP27 ...149 E5
  Syresham NN13 ......27 C7
  Upper Winchendon HP18 .99 A1
  Walter's Ash HP14 ..161 C7
Main Rd N HP4 ......107 A6
Main Rd S HP4 ......107 D4
Main St Adstock MK18 .53 F1
  Akeley MK18 ....41 F8
  Ashendon HP18 ......97 F1
  Beachampton MK19 ..44 A6
  Buckingham MK18 ....41 F3
  Chackmore MK18 ....41 B4
  Charndon OX27 .....19 E2
  Cosgrove MK19 ......19 E2
  Gawcott MK18 ....51 F4
  Grendon Underwood HP18 .83 B5
  Mursley MK17 ....67 D6
  Padbury MK18 ....53 B1
  Poundon OX27 ......71 F7
  Preston Bissett MK18 .62 B8
  Shalstone MK18 .....39 E6
  Tingewick MK18 ......38 C8
  Twyford MK18 ....62 C1
  Westbury NN13 ......39 A4
  Weston Turville HP22 .116 E2
Maitland Dr HP13 ...173 B8
Maitland Rd HP22 ...131 D7
Major's Farm Rd
  Datchet SL3 ....211 E8
  Slough SL3 ....212 A8
Malbons Ct MK6 ......46 E7
Malborough Ho HP4 ..135 A3
Malborough Way NN12 .18 F5
Malcolm Rd UB10 ....201 F8
Malden Cl HP6 ......154 F1
Malders La SL6 .....195 C3
Malet Cl HP14 ......158 F5
Malins Gate MK14 ...34 E8
Malkin Dr HP4 ......175 C3
Mallard Cl HP19 ....101 E4
Mallard Croft HP17 .127 A7
Mallard Dr
  Buckingham MK18 ....52 E8
  Slough SL1 ....204 F6
Mallard Ho HP11 ....173 C6
Mallets End HP22 ...85 B4
Malletts Cl MK11 ...32 E5
Mallow Gate MK14 ..34 E4
Mallow Pk SL6 .....195 C1
Malmers Well Rd HP13 .173 B7
Malpas Rd SL2 .....206 B6
Malt La NN13 ....27 C8
Malthouse Flats RG9 .192 D6
Malthouse Sq
  Beaconsfield HP9 ...186 F8
  Princes Risborough HP27 .139 B4

Malthouse Way 2 SL7 .183 D1
Malting Cl MK16 .....12 B6
Malting La Aldbury HP23 .120 D5
  Dagnall HP4 ....107 C5
Maltings Cl
  Cranfield MK43 ......25 A1
  Stewkley LU7 ....78 E8
Maltings Field MK19 .19 F5
Maltings The
  Chackmore MK18 ....41 B4
  Olney MK46 ....7 A3
  Tingewick MK18 ......41 B4
Maltmans Green Sch
  SL9 ....188 C8
Maltmans La SL9 ....188 C8
Malton Ave SL1 .....205 B6
Malton Cl MK10 .....35 F1
Malvern Cl HP13 ....172 E8
Malvern Ct SL3 .....212 A7
Malvern Dr
  Leighton Buzzard LU7 .80 C8
  Milton Keynes MK11 ..33 A4
Malvern Rd
  Aylesbury HP20 .....116 C8
  Maidenhead SL6 ....195 D1
Malyns Cl OX39 .....147 C7
Manchester Terr HP14 .171 B4
Mandela Ct UB8 .....208 C7
Mandelyns MK4 ......134 E7
Mandeville Dr MK16 .36 C2
Mandeville Mews HP21 .115 E4
Mandeville Rd
  Aylesbury HP21 .....115 E5
  Prestwood HP16 ....151 B7
Mandeville Upper Sch
  HP21 ....115 D4
Manfield Cl SL2 ....198 A2
Manifold La MK4,MK5 .46 B3
Manor Cl
  Berkhamsted HP4 ...135 C4
  Bledlow HP27 ....138 B1
  Cosgrove MK19 .....19 E2
  Hanslope MK19 ......11 A2
  Milton Keynes MK10 .35 F3
  Prestwood HP16 ....151 D4
  Salford MK17 ....34 A7
  Stoke Hammond MK17 .69 E7
  Tylers Green HP10 ..163 A2
Manor Cotts
  Chorleywood WD3 ...167 B3
  Milton Keynes MK12 .33 B7
Manor Court Yd
  High Wycombe HP13 .162 A1
  Waterperry OX33 ...123 B2
Manor Cres
  Seer Green HP9 ....176 D5
  Wendover HP22 .....131 C5
Manor Ct Emberton MK46 .13 F8
  Leighton Buzzard LU7 .70 E2
  Marlow SL7 ....183 C3
  Slough,Cippenham SL1 .204 F5
  6 Slough,Upton Park SL1 .205 F3
  Twyford MK18 ....62 C1
Manor Ctyd
  Haddenham HP17 ...127 D4
  Sherington MK16 ....13 F1
Manor Dr Amersham HP6 .154 B3
  Aylesbury HP20 .....101 F2
  Haversham MK19 ....20 E2
  Stewkley LU7 ....78 E8
Manor Farm Ct SL3 .212 E5
Manor Farm Cl
  Soulbury LU7 ....69 E2
  Stone HP17 ....114 C5
  Weston Turville HP22 .116 E2
  Windsor SL4 ....209 E2
Manor Farm Comm Inf Sch
  HP15 ....163 B2
Manor Farm Comm Jun Sch
  HP15 ....163 B2
Manor Farm Cotts SL4 .211 A2
Manor Farm Ct HP22 .87 B2
Manor Farm Ctyd HP22 .102 D8
Manor Farm Ho SL4 .209 F4
Manor Farm La LU7 ..90 C8
Manor Farm Way HP16 .176 D4
Manor Gdns
  Grendon Underwood HP18 .83 A6
  High Wycombe HP13 .162 A1
  Maids Moreton MK18 .41 E2
  Wooburn Green HP10 .185 E5
Manor Ho Brill HP18 .110 A8
  Hambleden RG9 ......181 D2
Manor House Cl HP20 .101 E2
Manor House Hospl
  HP20 ....101 F1
Manor House La SL3 .211 B6
Manor La
  Gerrards Cross SL9 .188 D4
  Maidenhead SL6 ....202 E4
Manor Park Ave HP27 .139 A3
Manor Pk MK18 ......41 E1
Manor Pound Rd LU7 .105 A7
Manor Rd Akeley MK18 .41 F7
  Aylesbury HP20 .....101 E1
  Cheddington LU7 ....104 F7
  Chesham HP5 ....144 C2
  Maidenhead SL6 ....202 E4
  Milton Keynes,Bletchley
  MK2 ....58 E8
  Milton Keynes,Wolverton
  MK12 ....33 B7
  Newport Pagnell MK16 .22 A4
  Newton Longville MK17 .57 D3
  Oakley HP18 ....109 D5
  Oving HP22 ....86 C7
  Princes Risborough HP27 .139 A2

Manor Rd continued
  Rowsham HP22 ....102 D8
  Seer Green HP9 ....176 D5
  Tring HP23 ....119 A5
  Tylers Green HP10 ..163 A2
  Wendover HP22 .....131 C5
  Windsor SL4 ....209 E5
Manor St
  Berkhamsted HP4 ...135 D4
  Buckingham MK18 ....52 C8
Manor View HP15 ....163 B2
Manor View Ho HP13 .161 E2
Manor Way
  Chesham HP5 ....144 D1
  Coleshill HP7 ....164 F3
  Yardley Gobion NN12 .18 E6
Manor Waye UB8 .....201 D4
Manorfields Rd MK19 .32 B6
Mansard Cl 8 HP23 .119 A3
Manse Cl MK11 ......32 D6
Mansel Cl Cosgrove MK19 .19 E2
  Slough SL2 ....206 B8
Mansell Ct
  Milton Keynes MK5 ...46 A6
  Windsor SL4 ....209 E6
Manshead Cl MK11 ..32 F5
Mansion Dr HP23 ...119 B3
Mansion Hill HP22 ..131 E8
Mansion La Harrold MK43 .3 F6
  Iver SL0 ....207 C6
Mansion The HP4 ...135 E6
Manton Rd LU6 .....93 D5
Maple Ave UB7 .....208 F5
Maple Cl
  Hazelmere HP15 ....163 A3
  High Wycombe HP12 .172 C5
  Maidenhead SL6 ....202 C5
Maple Cres SL2 ....206 B6
Maple Cross Jun, Mix & Inf
  Sch WD3 ....178 E5
Maple Ct
  Gerrards Cross SL9 .188 F6
  Marlow SL7 ....183 E3
  Windsor SL4 ....210 C4
Maple Gr
  Milton Keynes MK2 ...58 E8
  Woburn Sands MK17 .49 B4
Maple Leys MK18 ....63 E3
Maple Lodge Cl WD3 .178 E6
Maple Pl UB7 ......208 F5
Maple Rise SL7 ....183 E3
Maples The
  5 Bourne End SL8 ..185 B3
  Wendover HP22 .....131 C5
Maplewood Gdns HP9 .175 B1
Maplewood Sch HP13 .161 D3
Maplin Pk SL3 .....207 B4
Mapperton Cl MK4 ..45 F1
Mappridge Green La
  HP16 ....141 D1
Mara Pl MK9 ....35 A3
Marand Ct HP21 ....115 F8
Marbeck Cl SL4 ....209 D6
March Edge MK18 ...41 E1
March Mdw MK7 .....48 D7
March Pl HP19 .....115 B8
Marchant Ct SL7 ...184 A3
Marches The SL4 ...205 D2
Marcia Ct SL1 .....204 F5
Marcourt Rd HP14 ..158 F3
Mardle Rd LU7 .....80 E6
Mare Leys MK18 ....52 F8
Maree Cl
  Leighton Buzzard LU7 .80 C7
  Milton Keynes MK2 ...58 C5
Marefield Rd SL7 ..183 D2
Marescroft Rd SL2 .197 E1
Margam Cres MK10 ..36 A1
Margaret Ct HP13 ..173 A8
Margaret Powell Sq MK9 .34 F3
Margaret Smythe Ho
  HP13 ....173 A8
Marie Cl OX27 .....71 F7
Marigold Pl MK14 ..34 E4
Marigold Wlk HP15 .162 F6
Marina Dr Dunstable LU6 .93 E7
  Milton Keynes MK12 .33 D6
Marina Rdbt MK6 ...47 C7
Marina Way Iver SL0 .208 A6
  Slough SL1 ....205 C3
Marish Ct SL3 .....207 A3
Marish La UB9 .....189 D7
Marish Prim Sch SL3 .207 A3
Marish Wharf Ind Est
  SL3 ....206 E4
Marjoram Pl MK14 ..34 E4
Mark Dr SL9 ....177 E6
Markenfield Pl MK4 .45 E1
Market Hill
  Buckingham MK18 ....41 D1
  Milton Keynes MK6 ..47 B8
  Whitchurch HP22 ...86 F6
Market Ho 5 SL9 ..177 D2
Market La SL3 .....207 C3
Market Par HP15 ...163 A4
Market Pl
  Chalfont St Peter SL9 .177 D2
  Colnbrook SL3 .....212 C7
  Henley-on-T RG9 ...191 D2
  Olney MK46 ....6 F3
  Woburn MK17 ....60 F7
Market Place Mews 5
  RG9 ....191 D2

Market Sq
  Amersham HP7 ......165 B7
  Aylesbury HP20 .....115 D8
  Buckingham MK18 ....41 D1
  Chesham HP5 ....154 B8
  Hanslope MK19 ......11 A2
  Marlow SL7 ....183 D2
  Milton Keynes MK11 .32 D5
  Princes Risborough HP27 .139 B3
  Uxbridge UB8 ......201 C5
  Winslow MK18 ....65 F4
Market St
  Maidenhead SL6 ....202 F7
  9 Windsor SL4 .....210 D6
Markham Cl HP19 ...115 A7
Markhams Ct MK18 ..52 D8
Marks Orch MK18 ...75 F7
Marlborough Cl SL6 .202 A6
Marlborough Ct SL1 .204 E7
Marlborough Gate MK9 .34 F3
Marlborough Rd 5 SL6 .202 F6
Marlborough Rd
  Aylesbury HP21 .....115 E4
  Maidenhead SL6 ....202 A6
  Slough SL3 ....206 D2
Marlborough St
  Milton Keynes,Neath Hill
  MK14 ....34 E6
  Milton Keynes,Tinkers Bridge
  MK6 ....47 D6
Marlborough Trad Est
  HP11 ....172 F7
Marley Gr MK8 .....45 E7
Marlin Cl HP4 .....134 F5
Marlin Copse HP4 ..135 A3
Marlin Ct SL7 .....183 D1
Marlin Hill HP23 ..133 A8
Marlins Cl WD3 ....167 C3
Marlins End HP4 ...134 F3
Marlow Bottom SL7 .183 D6
Marlow Bridge La SL7 .194 E8
Marlow CE Inf Sch SL7 .183 D3
Marlow Com Hospl SL7 .183 E2
Marlow Comm SL7 ..182 F3
Marlow Dr Nr MK16 .22 A4
Marlow Hill HP11 ..173 A5
Marlow Ho 1 SL7 ..183 E1
Marlow Lodge 15 SL6 .202 F6
Marlow Mill SL7 ...183 E1
Marlow Rd Bisham SL7 .194 E7
  Henley-on-T RG9 ...191 E3
  High Wycombe HP11 .172 E4
  Lane End HP14,SL7 .171 E2
  Little Marlow SL7 ..184 C5
  Maidenhead SL6 ....202 F7
  Maidenhead,Furze Platt
  SL6 ....194 E4
  Stokenchurch HP14 .170 B6
  Marlow Sta SL7 ....183 F2
Marquis Ct MK17 ...60 F7
Marram Cl MK4 .....45 F7
Marriott Terr WD3 .167 F5
Marriott's Cl HP17 .126 F6
Marriott's La HP17 .126 F6
Marriotts Ave HP16 .142 E1
Marrod's Bottom HP7 .175 C8
Marron La MK12 ....33 C5
Marroway HP22 ....116 C2
Marsh Ct HP11 .....173 F4
Marsh Dr MK14 .....21 E1
Marsh End Rd MK16 .22 D3
Marsh Gibbon CE Inf Sch
  OX27 ....71 F3
Marsh Gibbon Rd HP18 .82 E8
Marsh La
  Stoke Mandeville HP22 .129 F8
  Taplow SL6 ....203 E6
Marsh Rd
  Great Kimble HP22 ..129 D4
  Shabbington HP18 ..124 D3
  Marsh Sch HP11 ....173 F4
Marshall Court Ind Pk
  MK1 ....47 B1
Marshalls La MK15 .35 C2
Marshalls Lea HP22 .102 C3
Marsham Cl HP21 ...116 A4
Marsham La SL9 ....188 F6
Marsham Lodge SL9 .188 E5
Marsham Way SL9 ..188 F5
Marshaw Pl MK4 ...46 C2
Marshaw Pl 3 MK4 .46 C2
Marshcroft La HP23 .119 D6
Marshfield SL3 ....211 C6
Marshgate Trad Est
  SL6 ....204 A7
Marshment Cl HP22 .117 D5
Marston Cl HP5 ....144 A4
Marston Ct HP23 ..104 B4
Marston Hill
  Cranfield MK43 .....25 F2
  Oving HP22 ....86 C8
Marston Rd
  Granborough MK18 ..75 F6
  Thame OX9 ....126 A1
Marstonfields Rd MK18 .76 B2
Marsworth CE Inf Sch
  HP23 ....105 A2
Marsworth Rd LU7 ..105 D4
Marsworth Reservoir (Nature
  Reserve)* HP23 ....119 A8
Martell Cl MK7 ....48 A3
Martin Cl
  Buckingham MK18 ....52 E7
  Milton Keynes MK14 .34 E6
  Uxbridge UB10 ......201 E3
  Windsor SL4 ....209 D6

Martin Dell Cotts HP16 .142 E4
Martin Rd
  Maidenhead SL6 ....202 F8
  Slough SL1 ....205 E3
Martin's Plain SL2 .198 F3
Martindale SL0 ....200 D1
Martingale Pl MK14 .34 F5
Martins Dr The LU7 .80 F8
Martinsend La HP16 .151 E7
Martyrs Ct HP7 ....165 C8
Marunden Gn SL2 ..197 F2
Marwood Cl MK4 ...46 D3
Mary Cross Cl HP23 .119 D1
Mary MacManus Dr
  MK18 ....41 D1
Mary Morgan Ct SL2 .205 D8
Mary Towerton Sch The
  HP14 ....159 D3
Marygold Wlk HP6 .166 C8
Maryland Coll MK17 .60 C6
Maryland Rd MK15 .35 B8
Maryport Ct MK16 ..13 F2
Marys Mead HP15 ..163 A5
Maryside SL3 ......206 E4
Mascoll Path SL2 ..197 F2
Masefield Cl
  Chesham HP5 ....144 B3
  Newport Pagnell MK16 .22 A7
Masefield Gr MK3 ..58 A7
Maslin Dr MK6 ....47 B5
Mason MK14 ....34 C8
Mason's Ct
  Aylesbury HP19 ....115 B7
  Slough SL4 ....204 E6
Masons Cl HP16 ...151 C5
Masons Ct HP5 ....144 C1
Masons Rd SL1 ....204 E6
Masons Yd MK14 ..135 D4
Massie Cl MK15 ...35 B6
Mathiesen Rd MK13 .134 A4
Mathisen Way SL3 .212 E6
Matilda Gdns MK5 .46 B5
Matlock Rd HP20 ..101 F2
Matson Dr RG9 ....191 F2
Matthew Ct MK5 ...46 B6
Matthews Cl 12 HP20 .101 F2
Maud Jane's Cl LU7 .105 C5
Maude Cl HP9 .....176 A1
Maude Rd HP9 ....176 A1
Maudsley Cl MK5 ..46 C6
Maudsley Ho SL6 .203 A7
Mauduit Cl MK19 ..11 A3
Maulden Gdns MK4 .45 E1
Maurice Mount HP15 .162 F5
Mavoncliff Dr MK4 .57 A8
Maxham MK5 ....46 A3
Maxwell Ct SL1 ...197 C1
Maxwell Dr HP15 ..163 B5
Maxwell Pl HP9 ...175 F3
Maxwell Rd
  Beaconsfield HP9 ..175 E3
  West Drayton UB7 .208 F2
May Cl LU6 ....92 E6
May Rd MK43 ....8 E6
May Tree Cl SL7 ..183 C6
Maybach Ct MK5 ..46 A6
Maybrook Gdns HP13 .173 C8
Maybury Ct SL1 ...204 D7
Maybush Gdns HP16 .151 C6
Maybush Wlk MK46 .6 A5
Mayditch Pl MK13 .34 C3
Mayer Gdns MK5 ..46 C5
Mayfield Cvn Pk UB7 .208 C3
Mayfield Dr SL4 ..210 A4
Mayfield Rd HP10 .185 E6
Mayflower Cl HP17 .114 F3
Mayflower Way
  Beaconsfield HP9 ..186 A8
  Farnham Common SL2 .198 D8
Maygoods Cl UB8 .208 D8
Maygoods Gn UB8 .208 D8
Maygoods La UB8 .208 D8
Maygoods View UB8 .208 D8
Mayhall Farm HP6 .154 A4
Mayhall La HP6 ...154 A4
Mayhew Cres HP13 .173 D8
Maylands Dr UB8 .201 D6
Maynard Cl MK13 .34 A3
Maynard Ct SL4 ..210 A6
Mayorfield Ho 1 SL7 .183 D2
Maypole Rd SL6 ..204 A8
Mays Way NN12 ....18 D3
McAuliffe Dr SL1,SL2 .197 F8
McConnell Dr MK12 .33 E6
McDougall Rd 1 HP4 .135 D4
McEwen Ride HP4 .117 D1
McKay Trad Est SL3 .212 D3
McKenzie Cl MK18 .52 D8
McLellan Pl HP12 .172 D5
McLernon Way MK18 .66 A5
Mead Acre HP27 ..139 B5
Mead Ave SL3 ....207 B4
Mead Cl Denham UB9 .190 A2
  7 Marlow SL7 ......183 F3
  Monks Risborough HP27 .139 B6
  Slough SL3 ....207 B4
Mead Haze SL6 ...196 C2
Mead Ho SL0 ......200 D2
Mead Pk HP15 ....163 C7
Mead Platt HP14 ..158 D5
Mead Rd UB8 .....201 D5
Mead St HP13 ....174 A4
Mead The
  Beaconsfield HP9 ..175 E2
  Soulbury LU7 ....69 E3
Mead Way
  High Wycombe HP11 .173 F4
  Slough SL1 ....204 D8

Mead Wlk SL3 ....207 B4
Meades La HP5 ....154 B7
Meadow Ave SL3 ......207 A3
Meadfield Rd SL3 .....207 B3
Meadfurlong Mid Sch
 MK6 ....34 F1
Meadow Bank [6] SL8 .185 B3
Meadow Cl
Aylesbury HP20 ....102 A1
Chesham HP5 ....144 A4
Cublington LU7 ....78 C1
High Wycombe HP11 ..173 F4
Marlow SL7 ....183 F1
Oakley HP18 ....109 D4
Old Windsor SL4 ......211 B2
Tring HP23 ....119 A4
Meadow Cotts
Beaconsfield HP9 .....175 E1
Little Kingshill HP16 ..152 B3
Stone HP17 ....114 D3
Meadow Ct MK46 ......5 D2
Meadow Dr
Amersham HP6 ....154 E2
Longwick HP27 ....138 D6
Meadow Gate
Padbury MK18 ....53 B2
Prestwood HP16 .....151 C3
Meadow Gdns MK18 ..52 E6
Meadow High Sch UB8 .208 E8
Meadow La
Beaconsfield HP9 .....175 F2
Eton SL4 ....210 C7
Long Crendon HP18 ..125 E4
Milton Keynes MK10 ..36 A3
Pitstone LU7 ....105 E3
South Heath HP16 ....152 E8
Meadow Pk HP22 .....116 C2
Meadow Rd
Berkhamsted HP4 .....135 B6
Chinnor OX39 ....147 D6
Henley-on-T RG9 .....191 E1
Slough SL3 ....206 E3
Meadow Rise HP27 ...149 E5
Meadow Row MK18 ..41 D1
Meadow View
Aspley Guise MK17 ...49 D6
Chalfont St Giles HP8 .177 A7
Long Crendon HP18 ..125 E4
Marlow Bottom SL7 ..183 E6
Pottersbury NN12 ....18 D3
Stanwell TW19 ....213 A2
Uxbridge UB8 ....208 C8
Meadow Way
Aylesbury HP20 ......102 A1
Dorney SL6 ....203 F4
Felden HP3 ....146 F7
Hyde Heath HP6 .....153 C4
Old Windsor SL4 .....211 B1
Thame OX9 ....125 F1
Wing LU7 ....79 E3
Meadow Wlk
Bourne End SL8 .....185 A5
Buckingham MK18 ...41 D1
Tylers Green HP10 ..163 C1
Meadoway
Steeple Claydon MK18 .63 E3
Stone HP17 ....114 F5
Meadowbank Cl
Bovingdon HP3 ....146 B3
Long Crendon HP18 ..125 C7
Meadowbrook HP23 ..119 B6
Meadowbrook Cl SL3 .212 F6
Meadowcott La HP7 .164 F3
Meadowcroft
Aylesbury HP19 ....101 B3
Berkhamsted HP4 ....134 D7
Chalfont St Peter SL9 .177 D1
Meadowlea Cl UB7 ...213 D8
Meadows Sch The HP10 .185 E7
Meadows The
Amersham HP7 ....154 E1
Flackwell Heath HP10 .185 B8
Old Stratford MK19 ..32 B6
Whitchurch HP22 .....86 F7
Meadowside HP9 ....176 F4
Meadowsweet MK7 ..48 B5
Meadowview TW19 ..212 F2
Meads Cl MK13 .....34 B8
Meads The
Berkhamsted HP4 ....134 F6
Eaton Bray LU6 ......92 E5
Stoke Poges SL2 .....199 A2
Tring HP23 ....119 B4
Uxbridge UB8 ....201 E1
[4] Windsor SL4 .....210 A5
Meadway
Berkhamsted HP4 ....135 E5
Buckingham MK18 ...52 D6
Dunstable LU6 ....93 F7
Oving HP22 ....76 E1
Meadway Ct LU6 ....93 F7
Meadway Pk SL3 ...188 D3
Meadway The MK5 ..46 A7
Meare Est HP10 ....185 E8
Meavy Cl HP13 ....174 B3
Medale Rd MK6 ...47 B5
Medallion Pl LU6 ..203 B7
Medbourne Rdbt MK8 .45 E6
Medeswell MK4 ...46 E3
Medhurst MK8 ....33 E2
Medland MK6 ......47 C6
Medley Cl LU6 ....92 F5
Medman Cl UB8 ..201 C3
Medway Cl MK16 ..22 E3
Meeting Oak La MK18 .66 B5
Megdale Pl HP20 ..101 D2
Melbourne Ave SL1 .205 C7
Melbourne Cl HP21 .115 E5

Melbourne Rd HP13 .173 F6
Melbourne Terr MK13 .34 A7
Melford Gn HP19 ...101 C3
Melfort Dr
Leighton Buzzard LU7 .80 B6
Milton Keynes MK2 ..58 D4
Melick Rd MK6 .....47 B4
Melissa Ct HP13 ...173 D6
Melksh Ct MK3 ....47 A2
Melstock Rd HP21 .115 E5
Melrose Ave MK3 ..47 A3
Melrose Ct HP13 ...162 B1
Melrose Wlk HP21 .115 F5
Melton MK14 ....34 C8
Melton Ct Dunstable LU6 .93 F7
Maidenhead SL6 ....202 F6
Mendelssohn Gr MK7 .48 C4
Mendip Cl SL3 .....207 A1
Mendip Way HP13 .172 F8
Mendy St HP11 ....173 A7
Menmarsh Rd HP18 .123 E6
Menteith Cl MK4 ..58 C5
Mentmore* LU7 ...90 C4
Mentmore Cl SL4 ..210 D5
Mentmore Cross Rds
LU7 ....89 F6
Mentmore Ct
Mentmore LU7 .....90 D5
[2] Milton Keynes MK8 .45 F8
Mentmore Gdns LU7 .80 F5
Mentmore Gn HP21 .115 E3
Mentmore Rd
Cheddington LU7 ...104 F8
High Wycombe HP12 .172 B6
Leighton Buzzard LU7 .80 E5
Mentmore View HP23 .118 F5
Mentone Ave MK17 .49 D4
Menzies Ct MK5 ...46 B4
Mercer Wlk UB8 ...201 C5
Mercers Dr SL3 ...34 B6
Mercers Mdw HP22 .131 B6
Merchant La
Cranfield MK43 .....25 A1
Cranfield, Wharley End
MK43 ....24 F2
Merchant Pl MK10 .35 E3
Mercia Rd SL6 .....202 C4
Mercian Way SL1 ..204 D5
Mercury Gr MK8 ...45 E7
Mercury Pk The HP10 .185 E7
Mere Cl SL7 ....183 F2
Mere La MK8 ......50 E6
Mere Pk SL7 ......183 F2
Mere Rd Finmere MK18 .50 D6
Slough SL1 ....205 F3
Merebrook Ct MK18 .43 E7
Mereck 46 C3
Meredith Dr HP19 .100 F2
Meriland Ct MK2 ..58 E4
Merlebank HP5 ....154 C7
Merlewood Cl HP11 .173 A4
Merlewood Dr MK5 .45 F4
Merlin Cl SL3 .....212 B8
Merlin Ct SL6 .....202 B8
Merlin Ctr HP19 ..101 C1
Merlin Ctr The HP12 .172 E5
Merlin Wlk MK6 ...47 B8
Merling Croft HP4 .134 E7
Merrivale Mews UB7 .208 D3
Merrydown HP13 ..161 D1
Merryfields UB8 ...201 D3
Mersey Cl MK3 ....46 E1
Mersey Way MK3 .46 E1
Merthen Gr MK4 ..57 B8
Merton Cl SL6 ....202 C3
Merton Ct SL1 ....206 A3
Merton Dr MK6 ...46 F5
Merton Rd
Princes Risborough HP27 .139 B2
Slough SL1 ....206 A3
Merwin Way SL4 ..209 D4
Meryton Ho SL4 ..210 A4
Messenger Cl HP21 .116 A6
Metcalfe Gr MK14 .22 B2
Mews Cotts HP15 ..162 D7
Mews Gamnel HP23 .118 E5
Mews The HP6 ....154 D3
Michael Cl SL6 ...202 C5
Michaels Mews [6]
HP19 ....115 A8
Michigan Dr
Milton Keynes MK15 .35 C8
Newport Pagnell MK15 .22 C1
Nicholls Ave SL9 ..177 E5
Micklefield Rd HP13 .174 A7
Mickleton MK15 ...35 A6
Mid Cross La SL9 .177 F5
Midas Ind Est UB8 .201 B3
Midcot Way HP4 ..134 F6
Midcroft SL2 ......198 B1
Middle Cl HP6 ....154 F2
Middle Cres UB9 ..189 D4
Middle Dr HP9 ....175 D5
Middle Field HP22 .116 F3
Middle Gn SL3 ...206 E6
Middle La HP3 ....146 A1
Middle Mdw HP8 .177 C7
Middle Rd
Aylesbury HP21 ...116 B7
Berkhamsted HP4 .135 B4
Denham UB9 ......189 D4
Middle Slade MK18 .52 D6
Middle Way OX39 .147 B6
Middle Weald MK19 .32 A3
Middle Wlk SL1 ..197 C2
Middlebrook Rd HP13 .161 E1
Middlefield Cl MK18 .41 F1
Middlegreen Rd SL3 .206 D5

Middlegreen Trad Est
SL3 ....206 D4
Middlesex Dr MK3 .46 F1
Middleton MK14 ..34 E7
Middleton Prim Sch
MK10 ....35 E3
Middleway The HP12 .172 C6
Midhurst Cl HP21 .116 B5
Midland Rd MK46 .7 A5
Midshires Bsns Pk
HP19 ....101 A1
Midsumer Ct HP15 .163 A3
Midsummer Arc MK9 .34 E2
Midsummer Bvd MK9 .34 E2
Midsummer Dr HP18 .82 F6
Midsummer Pl MK9 .34 E2
Midsummer Rdbt MK9 .34 C1
Miersfield HP11 ...172 D3
Mikern Cl MK2 ...58 C8
Milburn Ave MK6 .46 E8
Milburn Dr UB7 ..208 E6
Mildenhall Rd SL1 .205 E7
Mile Elm SL7 .....184 A3
Milebush LU7 ....80 C8
Milecastle MK13 .34 A5
Miles Cl Aylesbury HP21 .116 A7
Milton Keynes MK14 .22 A3
Miles Ct HP22 ....102 B3
Miles End HP21 ..115 B6
Milesmere MK8 ..33 D1
Milhayes MK14 ..34 F8
Millholm Rise MK6 .47 E5
Millington Gate MK15 .35 D7
Millshot Dr HP7 ..165 D7
Millside SL8 ......185 C3
Millstream Cl HP22 .116 F2
Millstream La SL1 .204 E5
Millstream Way
Leighton Buzzard LU7 .80 F7
Wooburn Green HP10 .185 E8
Milner Rd SL1 ....204 A8
Milton Ave SL9 ..188 D8
Milton Cl
Henley-on-T RG9 .191 D2
Horton SL3 ....212 A4
Milton Dr MK16 ..22 E4
Milton Fields HP8 .177 B7
Milton Gdns HP27 .139 A2
Milton Gr MK3 ...57 F7
Milton Hill HP8 ..177 B7
Milton Keynes Central Sta
MK9 ....34 C1
Milton Keynes Coll MK6 .46 F7
Milton Keynes Coll (Bletchley
Ctr) MK3 ....58 B8
Milton Keynes Coll
(Wolverton Ctr) MK12 .33 B6
Milton Keynes General Hospl
MK6 ....47 B7
Milton Keynes Materials
Recycling Factory*
MK12 ....33 C8
Milton Keynes Mus*
MK12 ....33 D5
Milton Keynes Prep Sch
MK3 ....57 D8
Milton Lawns HP6 .154 D3
Milton Rd
Aston Clinton HP22 .117 F5
Aylesbury HP21 ...115 F6
Chesham HP5 .....144 B2
Milton Keynes,Broughton
MK10 ....36 B3
Milton Keynes,Willen MK15 .35 D7
Slough SL2 ....198 D1
Walton MK7 ......47 F6
Milton Way UB7 .208 F2
Milton's Cottage (Mus)*
HP8 ....177 B7
Milverton Cl SL6 .202 B3
Mimosa Ct HP21 .115 B6
Mina Ave SL3 ....206 D4
Mineral La HP5 ..154 C7
Minerva Cl TW19 .213 A2
Minerva Gdns MK7 .48 C7
Minerva Way HP9 .176 A1
Minniecroft Rd SL1 .197 B2
Minorca Gr MK5 ..46 A4
Minshull Cl MK18 .41 D1
Minster Way SL3 .206 F4
Minstrel Ct MK13 .34 B7
Minton Cl MK14 ..22 A1
Minton Rise SL6 .204 B7
Mirador Cres SL2 .206 B6
Mirrie La UB9 ....189 C6
Misbourne Ave
Chalfont St Peter SL9 .177 E5
High Wycombe HP13 .173 F6
Misbourne Cl
Aylesbury HP21 ...115 D3
Chalfont St Peter SL9 .177 E5
Misbourne Ct SL3 .207 A2
Misbourne Dr HP16 .152 B6
Misbourne Ho HP16 .166 C1
Misbourne Mdws UB9 .189 D3
Misbourne Sch The
HP16 ....152 B6
Misbourne Vale SL9 .177 D5
Miss Joans Ride HP4 .107 D7
Missenden Abbey Adult Ed
Coll HP16 ....152 B6
Missenden Gdns SL1 .204 B7
Missenden Rd
Chesham HP5 .....154 A7

Missenden Rd continued
Ellesborough HP17 ...130 C2
Great Kingshill HP15 .151 D2
Winslow MK18 ......65 F4
Miswell La HP23 ...118 F3
Mitcham Pl MK13 ..34 D3
Mitcham Wlk HP19 .101 A2
Mitchell Cl
Bovingdon HP3 ....145 F4
Slough SL1 ....205 A4
Mitchell Rd MK43 .24 E2
Mitchell Wlk HP6 .154 E1
Mithras Gdns MK7 .48 C6
Mitre Cl MK18 ....52 C3
Mitre St MK18 ...52 C7
Moat Cl Prestwood HP16 .151 C6
Wendover HP22 ..131 B6
Moat Dr Prestwood HP16 .151 C7
Slough SL2 ....206 C8
Moat End HP22 ..102 B4
Moat House The HP18 .52 D8
Moat La
Aston Abbotts HP22 .88 D4
Marsh Gibbon OX27 .71 F2
Prestwood HP16 ..151 C7
Wingrave HP22 ..89 B2
Moat Pl UB9 ......201 B8
Mobwell Terr [3] HP16 .152 A8
Model Row HP22 .117 F6
Moeran Cl MK7 ...48 C4
Moffy Hill SL6 ...195 E2
Mole Run HP13 ..161 C1
Molyneaux Ave HP3 .145 F4
Molyns Ho RG9 ..191 E3
Molyns Mews SL1 .204 E5
Monellan Cres MK7 .48 A3
Monellan Gr MK7 .48 A3
Monet Pl HP19 ...100 E2
Money La UB7 ...208 D3
Monkey Island La SL6 .203 E2
Monks Hollow SL7 .183 E5
Monks Path [9] HP19 .115 A8
Monks Rd SL4 ...209 D5
Monks Risborough CE Prim
Sch HP27 ....139 C5
Monks Risborough Sta
HP27 ....139 B6
Monks Way
Harmondsworth UB7 .213 C8
Milton Keynes MK12, MK13,
MK14, MK15 ......34 C6
Monksfield Way SL2 .198 A2
Monkston Comb Sch
MK10 ....36 B1
Monkston Rdbt MK10 .36 B2
Monkswood Ct SL7 .183 E2
Monkton Way HP27 .150 C5
Monmouth Pl HP19 .101 A2
Monmouth Gr MK4 .45 E1
Monro Ave MK8 ..45 E7
Montabaur Rd NN13 .38 A7
Montagu Dr MK6 .47 B8
Montagu Rd SL4 .211 B6
Montague Rd
Aylesbury HP21 ..115 D7
Berkhamsted HP4 .135 B4
Slough SL1 ......205 F6
Uxbridge UB8 ...205 D5
Montem La SL1 .205 D4
Montem Prim Sch SL1 .205 B4
Montford Mews HP15 .162 E2
Montgomerie Cl HP4 .135 A6
Montgomery Cres .35 B7
Montgomery Pl SL2 .206 C7
Montpellier Cl SL4 .210 C5
Montrose Ave
Datchet SL3 .....211 C7
Slough SL1 ......205 B7
Montrose Dr SL6 .202 A6
Montrose Way SL3 .211 C7
Monument La SL9 .177 E5
Monycrower Dr SL6 .202 E7
Moon St MK12 ...33 D6
Moor End Eaton Bray LU6 .92 F5
Frieth RG9 ......171 A1
Moor End Cl LU6 .92 F4
Moor End La LU6 .92 F5
Moor Furlong SL1 .204 E5
Moor La
Harmondsworth UB7 .213 C8
High Wycombe HP13 .161 D3
Maidenhead SL6 .195 F1
Sarratt WD3 .....156 E3
Moor Pk
Milton Keynes MK3 .57 D8
Wendover HP22 .131 B7
Moor Rd HP5 ....154 C6
Moor The SL7 ...184 C4
Moor's Farm Cotts HP5 .145 B4
Moorbridge Rd SL6 .203 A7
Moorcroft Sch UB8 .208 F7
Moore Cl SL1 ....205 B4
Moore Rd HP4 ...134 F6
Moorend La Thame OX9 .125 F1
Thame OX9 .....126 A2
Moorend Rd NN12 .18 E6
Moores Hill MK46 .6 F5
Moores La SL4 ..204 F2
Moorfield MK17 .49 B4
Moorfield Rd
Denham Green UB9 .190 A5
Uxbridge UB8 ...208 D7
Moorfield Terr SL6 .203 A8
Moorfoot MK11 ..33 A4

Moorgate MK6 ....46 F7
Moorhall Rd UB9 ....190 B6
Moorhen Ct 2 HP20 ....101 E3
Moorhen Way MK18 ....52 E8
Moorhills Cres LU7 ....79 F3
Moorhills Rd LU7 ....79 F3
Moorings The
Buckingham MK18 ....52 C8
Windsor SL4 ....210 A7
Moorland Fst Sch MK6 ....47 B5
Moorland Rd UB7 ....213 C8
Moorlands LU7 ....79 E3
Moorlands Rd LU7 ....79 F3
Moors Cl MK19 ....31 E5
Moorside HP10 ....185 E8
Moorside Cl SL6 ....195 F1
Moorstown Ct 7 SL1 ....205 E4
Mop End La HP7 ....164 B7
Morar Cl LU7 ....80 C7
Moray Dr SL2 ....206 A7
Moray Pl MK3 ....46 F2
Mordaunt Cl MK43 ....8 E6
Mordaunts Ct MK15 ....35 C2
More Ave HP21 ....115 D7
Moreau Wlk SL3 ....206 E7
Morebath Gr MK4 ....46 C4
Morefields HP23 ....119 A6
Moreland Ave SL3 ....212 C7
Moreland Cl SL3 ....212 C7
Moreland Dr SL9 ....188 F4
Morello Dr SL3 ....206 F5
Moreton Dr MK18 ....41 E2
Moreton La HP17 ....115 A1
Moreton Rd MK18 ....41 D2
Moreton Way SL1 ....204 D5
Morland Dr MK8 ....45 D6
Morley Cl SL3 ....206 F4
Morley Cres MK7 ....48 D4
Morrell Cl MK5 ....46 B5
Morrice Cl SL3 ....207 A2
Morris Cl SL9 ....177 F2
Morris Ct
Aylesbury HP21 ....115 D4
Windsor SL4 ....209 E6
Morris Wlk MK16 ....22 A4
Morrison Ct MK8 ....45 E6
Mortain Cl MK7 ....48 B3
Mortain Dr HP4 ....134 F6
Morten Gdns UB9 ....190 A4
Mortens Wood HP7 ....165 E7
Mortimer Hill HP23 ....119 B4
Mortimer Rd SL3 ....206 D3
Mortimer Rise HP23 ....119 B4
Morton Cl
North Marston MK18 ....76 B2
Pitstone LU7 ....105 C4
Uxbridge UB8 ....201 F1
Morton Dr SL1 ....197 E8
Morton King Cl HP18 ....124 D3
Mortons Fork MK13 ....33 F6
Moseley Rd HP14 ....161 C7
Moses Plat La HP27 ....150 B5
Moss Ct HP9 ....176 D4
Mossdale MK13 ....34 B5
Mossway HP9 ....175 C5
Mossy Vale SL6 ....195 D1
Moundsfield Way SL1 ....204 E4
Mount Ave MK1 ....47 E3
Mount Cl
Aston Clinton HP22 ....117 F4
Farnham Common SL2 ....198 C8
High Wycombe HP12 ....172 E6
Mount Farm Ind Est MK1 ....47 D4
Mount Farm Rdbt MK1 ....47 D4
Mount Hill La SL9 ....188 B2
Mount La UB9 ....189 D2
Mount Nugent HP5 ....144 A4
Mount Pleasant
Aspley Guise MK17 ....49 F4
Aylesbury HP19 ....101 D1
Lane End HP14 ....171 B5
Milton Keynes MK6 ....47 E4
Soulbury LU7 ....69 E3
Steeple Claydon MK18 ....63 E2
Stoke Goldington MK16 ....12 B7
Stoke Hammond MK17 ....69 E7
Whitchurch HP22 ....86 F7
Yardley Gobion NN12 ....18 F6
Mount Pleasant Cl MK18 ....52 C7
Mount Pleasant Cotts 2
SL8 ....185 B3
Mount St HP20 ....115 D8
Mount The
Aspley Guise MK17 ....49 D4
Milton Keynes MK6 ....47 E4
Mount View RG9 ....191 D2
Mount View Ct 4 RG9 ....191 D2
Mount Way HP27 ....139 A3
Mountain Ash SL7 ....183 D6
Mountbatten Cl 7 SL1 ....206 A3
Mountbatten Sq 8 SL4 ....210 C6
Mounthill Ave MK19 ....32 B7
Mountsfield Cl
Newport Pagnell MK16 ....22 C3
Stanwell TW19 ....213 A2
Mow Mead MK46 ....6 F5
Mowbray Dr LU7 ....80 D7
Mowbray Rd HP20 ....101 D2
Mowhills MK43 ....3 F6
Moyleen Rise SL7 ....183 C1
Mozart Cl MK7 ....48 C4
Muddiford La MK4 ....46 D4
Muirfield Dr MK3 ....46 D1
Mulberry Ave SL4 ....210 F5
Mulberry Cl
Amersham HP7 ....165 F8
High Wycombe HP12 ....172 C5
Tring HP23 ....119 A5
Mulberry Ct HP15 ....163 D7
Mulberry Dr SL3 ....206 E1
Mulberry Wlk SL6 ....202 C8
Mullen Ave MK14 ....34 F4
Mullins Way HP19 ....100 E2
Mullion Pl MK6 ....35 A1
Mumfords La SL9 ....188 A7
Munces Rd SL7 ....183 D6
Munday's Farm HP21 ....116 B7
Mundaydean La SL7 ....183 B4
Mundesley Spur SL1 ....205 E7
Murcott Rd OX6 ....94 D6
Murray Rd HP4 ....135 C6
Murrey Cl MK5 ....46 C5
Murrin Rd SL6 ....202 C8
Mursley CE Sch MK17 ....67 D6
Mursley Ct MK11 ....32 F5
Mursley Rd
Little Horwood MK17 ....55 E2
Swanbourne MK17 ....67 B3
Mus of Eton Life The*
SL4 ....210 D8
Museum Ct 9 HP23 ....119 A3
Musgrave Rd OX39 ....147 D7
Musgrave Wlk HP14 ....158 F5
Musgrove Pl MK5 ....45 F6
Myddleton Rd UB8 ....201 C4
Mylne Cl HP13 ....172 F8
Mynchen Cl HP9 ....175 D6
Mynchen End HP9 ....175 D6
Mynchen Rd HP9 ....175 D6
Myrke The SL3 ....205 F2
Myrtle Bank MK12 ....33 E5
Myrtle Cl Poyle SL3 ....212 E6
Uxbridge UB8 ....208 F8
West Drayton UB7 ....208 F3
Myrtle Cres SL2 ....205 F6

N

Nag's Head La HP16 ....152 A4
Nailzee Cl SL9 ....188 E4
Nairdwood Cl HP16 ....151 E4
Nairdwood La HP16 ....151 D5
Nairdwood Way HP16 ....151 E4
Nairn Ct MK3 ....46 E2
Naisby Dr MK17 ....59 C1
Nalders Rd HP5 ....144 D2
Nan Aires HP22 ....89 A3
Nancy Hall Ct HP12 ....172 D3
Naphill & Walters Ash Sch
HP14 ....150 B1
Naphill Pl MK13 ....34 C3
Napier Cl UB7 ....208 F3
Napier Rd
Aylesbury HP19 ....114 F8
Harmondsworth TW6 ....213 D6
Maidenhead SL6 ....202 B6
Napier St MK2 ....58 D8
Nappin Cl HP19 ....101 A3
Nappins Cl HP18 ....125 D5
Narbeth Dr HP20 ....116 B8
Narcot La
Chalfont St Giles HP8 ....177 B5
Chalfont St Peter HP8 ....177 B5
Narcot Rd HP8 ....177 A7
Narcot Way HP8 ....177 B6
Narrow La HP13 ....161 E3
Narrow Path MK17 ....49 B3
Naseby Cl
Newport Pagnell MK16 ....22 A3
Thame OX9 ....126 B1
Naseby Ct
Buckingham MK18 ....41 E2
Milton Keynes MK13 ....34 B6
Nash Cl HP21 ....116 A4
Nash Croft MK4 ....57 B8
Nash Lee End HP22 ....130 F6
Nash Lee La HP22 ....130 E6
Nash Lee Rd
Nash Lee HP17 ....130 D6
World's End HP22 ....130 F7
Nash Pl HP10 ....163 B1
Nash Rd
Great Horwood MK17 ....55 A4
Slough SL3 ....207 A2
Thornborough MK18 ....54 B8
Whaddon MK17 ....45 A1
Nashdom SL1 ....196 F5
Nashdom La SL1 ....197 B6
Nashleigh Hill HP5 ....144 D3
Nashleigh Ho HP5 ....144 E3
Nashs Farm HP22 ....88 D4
Nathanial Cl MK5 ....46 B5
Nathaniel Wlk HP23 ....119 A5
National Badminton Ctr
MK8 ....34 A1
National Bowl The*
MK6 ....46 E5
National Film & Television
Sch HP9 ....175 E1
National Hockey Stad
MK9 ....34 C1
Natwoke Cl HP9 ....175 D5
Neal Cl SL9 ....189 B3
Neale Cl HP12 ....172 D3
Neapland MK6 ....47 B5
Near Town MK46 ....7 A3
Near Town Gdns MK46 ....7 A3
Nearton End MK17 ....67 A3
Neath Cres MK3 ....47 A2
Neath Hill Rdbt MK15 ....35 A6
Needham Cl SL4 ....209 E6
Needham Ct 4 HP11 ....172 F7
Neild Way WD3 ....167 F2
Neilson Ct MK7 ....48 C5
Nelson Cl
High Wycombe HP13 ....173 F5
Milton Keynes MK8 ....45 E6
Slough SL3 ....206 D2
Winchmore Hill HP7 ....164 C3
Nelson Ct MK18 ....52 C8
Nelson Rd Dagnall HP4 ....107 C5
Harmondsworth TW6 ....213 F6
Windsor SL4 ....209 F4
Nelson St MK18 ....52 C8
Nelson Terr HP20 ....115 D8
Nene Cl Aylesbury HP21 ....115 C4
Newport Pagnell MK16 ....22 D3
Nene Dr MK3 ....57 E8
Neptune Way SL1 ....204 E4
Ness Way MK2 ....58 D5
Nether Cl NN13 ....38 A7
Nether Gr MK5 ....46 B3
Nether Winchendon Ho*
HP18 ....112 E5
Netherby Cl HP23 ....119 C6
Nethercote La OX49 ....157 A8
Netherfield Rdbt MK6 ....47 C7
Netherwood Rd HP9 ....175 D5
Netley Ct MK10 ....36 A1
Nettlecombe MK4 ....46 C3
Nettleden Rd HP4 ....121 E4
Nettleton Rd UB10 ....201 F8
Neve Ho SL6 ....202 F8
Nevill Cl MK19 ....11 B2
Neville Cl SL2 ....198 F6
Neville Ct SL1 ....197 C2
Nevis Cl LU7 ....80 C7
Nevis Gr MK2 ....58 E4
New Bradwell Comb Sch
MK13 ....33 F7
New Chapter Comb sch
MK6 ....47 A5
New Chilterns HP7 ....165 E8
New Cl RG9 ....192 A8
New Coll MK18 ....51 F8
New College Ct MK18 ....41 B4
New Cotts RG9 ....180 C1
New Ct
High Wycombe HP13 ....173 C6
Marlow SL7 ....183 D2
New Dr HP13 ....173 E8
New Garden Dr UB7 ....208 E4
New Hall Cl HP3 ....146 A4
New Horton Manor SL3 ....212 A4
New Inn La MK18 ....51 F4
New Mdw HP21 ....116 C7
New Mill Terr HP23 ....119 B6
New Par
Chorleywood WD3 ....167 C5
West Drayton UB7 ....208 E5
New Peachey La UB8 ....208 D8
New Pond Rd HP15 ....163 C7
New Provident Pl 5
HP4 ....135 D4
New Rd Amersham HP6 ....154 E2
Aston Clinton HP22 ....117 E5
Berkhamsted HP4 ....135 D6
Berkhamsted,Northchurch
HP4 ....134 F7
Bolter End HP14 ....170 F6
Bourne End SL8 ....185 B4
Castlethorpe MK19 ....19 F5
Chipperfield WD4 ....146 F1
Coleshill HP7 ....164 F4
Cookham Rise SL6 ....195 E7
Datchet SL3 ....211 D6
Dinton HP17 ....113 E2
Drayton Parslow MK17 ....68 C5
Great Kingshill HP15 ....162 D8
Harrold MK43 ....3 E6
High Wycombe HP12 ....172 C5
Hurley SL6 ....193 F3
Leighton Buzzard LU7 ....80 E7
Little Chalfont HP8 ....166 F6
Little Kingshill HP16 ....152 B4
Marlow Bottom SL7 ....183 D6
Naphill HP14 ....150 A2
Prestwood HP16 ....151 D6
Princes Risborough HP27 ....139 C3
Sarratt HP8 ....156 F1
Slough SL3 ....207 A3
Stokenchurch HP14 ....158 F4
Tring HP23 ....119 B6
Tylers Green HP10 ....163 C1
Weedon HP22 ....101 B8
Weston Turville HP22 ....116 E5
Wilstone HP23 ....118 D8
New Road Cl HP12 ....172 C6
New Road Gdns HP12 ....172 C6
New Row Hoggeston MK18 ....77 B7
Lavendon MK46 ....7 E8
New Sq SL1 ....205 F4
New St Aylesbury HP20 ....101 D1
Berkhamsted HP4 ....135 D4
Cheddington LU7 ....104 F7
Henley-on-T RG9 ....191 E2
Milton Keynes MK11 ....32 D5
Tingewick MK18 ....51 B6
Waddesdon HP18 ....99 A7
New Windsor St UB8 ....201 C4
New Zealand Cotts HP22 ....88 E4
New Zealand Gdns LU7 ....79 E2
Newark Ct MK7 ....48 A3
Newbarn La HP9 ....176 E6
Newberry Cres SL4 ....209 D5
Newbery Way SL1 ....205 D4
Newbolt Cl
Newport Pagnell MK16 ....21 F5
Paulerspury NN12 ....17 B8
Newbridge Oval MK4 ....46 B3
Newbury Ct MK3 ....57 D6
Newbury Dr SL6 ....203 B6
Newbury Rd UB7 ....213 F6
Newby Pl MK4 ....46 B2
Newchurch Rd SL2 ....204 F8
Newcombe Rise UB7 ....208 E7
Newcourt UB8 ....208 C8
Newcroft Cl UB8 ....208 F8
Newell Cl HP21 ....116 A6
Newells Hedge LU7 ....105 D5
Newfield Gdns SL7 ....183 F3
Newfield Rd SL7 ....183 F3
Newfield Way SL7 ....183 F2
Newground Rd HP23 ....120 B3
Newhaven Spur SL2 ....198 B1
Newhouse Rd HP3 ....146 A4
Newland Ho UB8 ....201 C4
Newlands Dr
Maidenhead SL6 ....202 A7
Poyle SL3 ....212 E4
Newlands Girls Sch SL6 ....202 A7
Newlyn Pl MK6 ....35 A2
Newmans Cl MK14 ....21 E1
Newmans Ctyd MK17 ....68 C6
Newmarket Ct MK10 ....36 C2
Newmer Rd HP12 ....172 B3
Newport Pagnell Rd
MK43 ....16 C4
Newport Rd
Astwood MK16 ....15 C2
Emberton MK46 ....13 F6
Hanslope MK19 ....11 B2
Milton Keynes MK10 ....36 D1
Milton Keynes,New Bradwell
MK13 ....34 A8
Milton Keynes,Oakgrove
MK15 ....35 C2
Milton Keynes,Willen MK15 ....35 D7
Milton Keynes,Woughton on t G
MK6 ....35 D1
Moulsoe MK16 ....36 C7
Slough SL2 ....197 E1
Wavendon MK17 ....48 E7
Woburn MK17 ....60 F8
Woughton On T G MK6 ....47 D8
Woughton Park MK6 ....47 D6
Newquay Cl MK4 ....45 F1
Newton Blossomville CE Fst
Sch MK43 ....8 B4
Newton Cl SL3 ....206 F4
Newton Ct SL4 ....211 A1
Newton La SL4 ....211 B1
Newton Longville CE Comb
Sch MK17 ....57 D3
Newton Rd
Drayton Parslow MK17 ....68 D8
Milton Keynes MK3 ....57 E6
Stoke Hammond MK17 ....69 D8
Turvey MK43 ....8 E5
Newton Side Orch SL4 ....211 A1
Newton St MK46 ....7 A4
Newtonside SL4 ....211 A1
Newtown Inf Sch HP5 ....144 C2
Newtown Rd Marlow SL7 ....183 F3
New Denham UB9 ....201 B6
Newville HP22 ....87 C1
Newyears Green La
UB9 ....190 F5
Neyland Dr HP19 ....101 D3
Nicholas Gdns
High Wycombe HP13 ....173 D8
Slough SL1 ....204 E5
Nicholas Mead MK14 ....34 F8
Nicholas Winton Ct SL6 ....203 A8
Nicholls SL4 ....209 C4
Nicholls Wlk SL4 ....209 C4
Nicholson Gr MK8 ....45 E6
Nicholsons La SL6 ....202 F7
Nicholsons Shopping Ctr 2
SL6 ....202 F7
Nickson Ct HP15 ....163 A3
Nicol Cl SL9 ....177 C2
Nicol End SL9 ....177 C2
Nicol Rd SL9 ....177 C2
Nielson Ct MK7 ....48 D5
Nigel Ct NN13 ....38 A5
Nightingale Cl
Hazelmere HP15 ....163 B5
Steeple Claydon MK18 ....63 E3
Nightingale Cres MK13 ....34 A7
Nightingale Ct
1 High Wycombe HP13 ....173 B7
6 Slough SL1 ....206 A3
Nightingale Ho HP11 ....174 A4
Nightingale La SL6 ....195 D3
Nightingale Lodge HP4 ....135 B4
Nightingale Pk SL2 ....197 F5
Nightingale Pl
Buckingham MK18 ....41 E1
Cookham Rise SL6 ....195 F7
Nightingale Rd
Aylesbury HP21 ....115 E6
2 Chesham HP5 ....144 B2
Wendover HP22 ....131 B5
Nightingale Way UB9 ....189 F5
Nightingale Wlk SL4 ....210 C4
Nightingales Cnr HP7 ....166 C7
Nightingales Ct HP8 ....166 C7
Nightingales La HP8 ....166 D4
Nijinsky Ho UB8 ....201 D3
Nine Acres SL1 ....204 F5
Nine Elms Ave UB8 ....208 D8
Nine Elms Cl UB8 ....208 D8
Nine Stiles Cl UB9 ....201 B6
Ninnings Rd SL9 ....177 F3
Ninnings Way SL9 ....177 F3
Niplands Cotts HP10 ....185 D2
Nixey Cl SL1 ....206 A4
Nixons Cl MK6 ....46 E6
Noble Cl MK15 ....35 A7
Noble Ct SL2 ....205 F5
Noon Layer Dr MK10 ....35 E3
Norbrek MK8 ....33 E2
Norcotts Kiln Cotts HP18 ....96 A1
Norden Cl SL6 ....202 C4
Norden Mdws SL6 ....202 C5
Norden Rd SL6 ....202 C5
Norelands Dr SL1 ....197 C3
Norfolk Ave SL1 ....205 C8
Norfolk Ho 6 MK3 ....46 F1
Norfolk Park Cotts SL6 ....202 F8
Norfolk Rd
Maidenhead SL6 ....202 F8
Turvey MK43 ....8 E6
Uxbridge UB8 ....201 D6
Norfolk Terr HP20 ....101 E1
Norgrove Pk SL9 ....188 E7
Norjo-An Villas HP5 ....154 C6
Norland Dr HP10 ....185 C8
Norman Ave RG9 ....191 E1
Norman Cres MK10 ....35 E3
Norman Way LU6 ....93 E8
Normandy Dr HP4 ....135 B6
Normandy Way MK3 ....46 E2
Normans Cl UB8 ....208 F8
Normans Ct 5 HP13 ....173 F6
Normans The SL2 ....206 B7
Normanstead RG9 ....191 D1
Normill Terr HP22 ....117 A6
Norreys Dr SL6 ....202 D4
Norrington MK8 ....33 E2
Norris Ho SL6 ....202 E7
Norris Rd OX6 ....94 E8
North Burnham Cl SL1 ....197 B3
North Cl
Drayton Parslow MK17 ....68 C5
Medmenham SL7 ....193 D7
Windsor SL4 ....209 F6
North Common Rd UB8 ....201 D7
North Cotts SL2 ....198 C2
North Crawley CE Fst Sch
MK16 ....24 B6
North Crawley Rd MK16 ....23 C4
North Croft MK18 ....66 A4
North Ct MK10 ....36 B1
North Dr Aylesbury HP21 ....115 E5
Beaconsfield HP9 ....186 B8
High Wycombe HP13 ....173 E8
North Eastern Rd HP19 ....101 C2
North Eighth St MK9 ....34 E3
North Elder Rdbt MK9 ....34 C1
North Eleventh St MK9 ....34 E3
North End Rd
Quainton HP22 ....85 A5
Steeple Claydon MK18 ....63 D3
North Fifth St MK9 ....34 D2
North Fourteenth St MK9 ....34 F4
North Fourth St MK9 ....34 D2
North Gate MK2 ....47 C1
North Gn
3 Maidenhead SL6 ....195 F1
Slough SL1 ....205 E6
North Grafton Rdbt
MK13 ....34 C2
North Hill Dadford MK18 ....28 D2
Sarratt WD3 ....167 E8
North Hills HP18 ....96 A1
North La MK7 ....47 E7
North Lee La
North Lee HP22 ....130 A6
Stoke Mandeville HP22 ....129 F7
North Links Rd HP10 ....174 B1
North Marston CE Comb Sch
MK18 ....76 B2
North Marston La HP22 ....86 E7
North Mill Rd HP27 ....138 A5
North Ninth St MK9 ....34 E3
North Orbital Rd
Denham Green UB9 ....189 F4
Rickmansworth WD3 ....178 E7
North Overgate Rdbt
MK15 ....35 B5
North Pk
Gerrards Cross SL9 ....188 E8
Iver SL0 ....207 D3
North Rd Amersham HP6 ....154 C3
Berkhamsted HP4 ....135 B4
Chorleywood WD3 ....167 D4
Cryers Hill HP15 ....162 D5
Maidenhead SL6 ....202 E7
West Drayton UB7 ....208 F3
North Ridge MK6 ....35 B1
North Row Fulmer SL3 ....199 E8
Milton Keynes MK9 ....34 C2
Milton Keynes MK9 ....34 E3
North Saxon Rdbt MK14 ....34 D3
North Secklow Rdbt
MK14 ....34 E3
North Second St MK9 ....34 C2
North Seventh St MK9 ....34 D2
North Sixth St MK9 ....34 D2
North Skeldon Rdbt MK9 ....35 A4
North Sq MK16 ....22 D5
North St
Castlethorpe MK19 ....19 F5
Milton Keynes,Bradville
MK13 ....34 A7
Milton Keynes,Fenny Stratford
MK2 ....47 C1
Thame OX9 ....125 F1
North Star La SL6 ....202 C6
North Tenth St MK9 ....34 E3
North Terr SL4 ....210 E7
North Third St MK9 ....34 C2
North Thirteenth St MK9 ....34 F3

North Town Cl **1** SL6 ....195 F1
North Town Mead **4**
SL6 ....195 F1
North Town Moor SL6 ....195 F1
North Town Rd SL6 ....195 F1
North Twelfth St MK9 ....34 F3
North View HP22 ....87 B3
North Way
Deanshanger NN12 ....31 E5
Pottersbury NN12 ....18 E2
North Witan Rdbt MK13 ....34 D2
Northall Cl LU6 ....92 D6
Northall Rd LU6 ....92 D6
Northampton Ave SL1 ....205 C7
Northampton Rd
Brackley NN13 ....26 A1
Cosgrove MK19 ....19 C1
Cosgrove MK19 ....32 C8
Grafton Regis NN12 ....9 C3
Lathbury MK16 ....22 D6
Lavendon MK46 ....7 F8
Yardley Hastings NN7 ....1 A6
Northborough Rd SL2 ....198 B1
Northbridge Rd HP4 ....135 A6
Northchurch La HP5 ....134 D2
Northchurch St Mary's CE Fst
Sch HP4 ....134 B5
Northcliffe LU6 ....92 E6
Northcroft
Milton Keynes MK5 ....46 C6
Slough SL3 ....198 B1
Weedon HP22 ....87 C1
Wooburn Green HP10 ....185 F6
Northdean **5** SL6 ....195 F1
Northdown Rd SL9 ....177 E4
Northend MK46 ....5 E3
Northend Cl HP10 ....185 C7
Northend MK18 ....41 D1
Northend Sq MK18 ....41 D1
Northend Workshops
RG9 ....168 E5
Northern Hts SL8 ....185 B5
Northern Perimeter Rd (W)
TW6 ....213 D6
Northern Rd
Aylesbury HP19 ....101 C2
Slough SL1 ....198 D1
Northern Woods HP10 ....185 C7
Northfield Ct RG9 ....191 D3
Northfield Dr MK15 ....35 F5
Northfield Rd RG9 ....191 D3
Northfield Rd
Aylesbury HP20 ....116 B8
Eton Wick SL4 ....204 F2
Maidenhead SL6 ....195 F1
Princes Risborough HP27 ....139 C4
Tring HP23 ....119 F7
Northfield Rdbt MK10 ....36 A5
Northlands Rd MK18 ....53 F1
Northleigh MK4 ....46 D2
Northmead Rd SL2 ....204 F8
Northmill HP27 ....138 F3
Northolt Rd TW6 ....213 E6
Northumberland Ave
HP21 ....116 B6
Northumberland Ct
TW19 ....213 E1
Northumbria Rd SL6 ....202 B4
Northwich MK6 ....47 D7
Northwood Rd TW6 ....213 D6
Nortoft Rd SL9 ....177 F5
Norton Leys MK7 ....48 C7
Norton Rd UB8 ....201 D2
Norton's Pl MK18 ....52 C8
Nortons The MK7 ....48 B3
Norvic Rd HP23 ....105 A1
Norway Dr SL2 ....206 B8
Norwich Ho
High Wycombe HP13 ....173 F8
Maidenhead SL6 ....202 E8
Norwood Cl HP20 ....101 F2
Norwood Ct HP7 ....165 B7
Norwood La
Newport Pagnell MK16 ....22 C3
Uxbridge SL0 ....200 D1
Norwood Rd HP10 ....174 B2
Notley Farm HP18 ....126 A7
Nottingham Gr MK3 ....46 E2
Nottingham Ho **3** HP13 ....173 F7
Nottingham Rd WD3 ....167 C1
Nova Lodge MK4 ....46 B2
Novello Croft MK7 ....48 B4
Nugent Ct Chesham HP5 ....144 A3
Marlow SL7 ....183 F3
Nuneham Gr MK4 ....45 F3
Nup End Cl HP22 ....89 B3
Nup End La HP22 ....89 B3
Nurseries The LU6 ....92 E6
Nursery Cl
Amersham HP7 ....165 B8
Aylesbury HP21 ....115 C5
Tylers Green HP10 ....174 C8
Nursery Ct HP12 ....172 D6
Nursery Dr HP14 ....171 B5
Nursery Gdns
Milton Keynes MK13 ....34 A4
Tring HP23 ....119 B4
Nursery La Slough SL3 ....206 D5
Tylers Green HP10 ....174 C8
Nursery Pl SL4 ....211 B1
Nursery Rd SL6 ....204 B7
Nursery Way TW19 ....211 D1
Nursery Waye UB8 ....201 D4
Nursery Wlk SL7 ....183 B1
Nutfield La HP11 ....172 F8
Nuthatch **10** HP19 ....101 F3
Nutkin Wlk UB10 ....201 E5

Nutkins Way HP5 ....144 C2
Nutmeg Cl MK7 ....48 B5
Nye Way HP3 ....146 A3

O

O'Grady Way HP19 ....101 A3
O'Neill Rd MK8 ....45 D6
Oak Barn Cl MK43 ....25 A1
Oak Cres HP12 ....172 C4
Oak Ct MK9 ....34 E2
Oak Dr HP4 ....135 D3
Oak End Dr SL0 ....200 C3
Oak End Way
Chinnor OX39 ....147 D5
Gerrards Cross SL9 ....188 F6
Oak Farm Rare Breeds Pk*
HP22 ....116 D8
Oak Field HP5 ....144 B1
Oak Gn HP22 ....115 C7
Oak Green Sch HP21 ....115 C7
Oak La
Buckland Common HP3 ....133 A2
Windsor SL4 ....210 A6
Oak Lawn HP23 ....119 A3
Oak Rd HP27 ....139 C3
Oak St HP11 ....173 C4
Oak Stubbs La SL6 ....203 F4
Oak Tree Ave SL7 ....183 D3
Oak Tree Cl SL7 ....183 D3
Oak Tree Cotts HP18 ....83 B5
Oak Tree Dr
Lane End HP14 ....171 C5
Slough SL3 ....207 B1
Oak Tree Rd SL7 ....183 D4
Oak View HP15 ....162 D8
Oakdene HP9 ....175 E3
Oakdown Cres MK46 ....6 F3
Oaken Gr SL6 ....195 C1
Oaken Head MK4 ....46 C2
Oakengrove HP16 ....151 C5
Oakengrove Cl HP15 ....163 C6
Oakengrove La HP15 ....163 B3
Oakengrove Rd HP15 ....163 A3
Oakeshott Ave HP14 ....161 D6
Oakfield WD3 ....167 F2
Oakfield Ave SL1 ....205 B5
Oakfield Cl HP6 ....154 C2
Oakfield Cnr HP6 ....154 C2
Oakfield Fst Sch SL4 ....210 B5
Oakfield Rd
Aylesbury HP20 ....116 A8
Bourne End SL8 ....185 A3
Oakgrove Rdbt MK10 ....35 F2
Oakham Rise MK4 ....45 E1
Oakhill Cl
Maple Cross WD3 ....178 E6
Milton Keynes MK5 ....45 E6
Oakhill Rd
Maple Cross WD3 ....178 D6
Milton Keynes,Hazeley MK5 ....45 D5
Milton Keynes,Shenley Church End
MK5 ....45 F6
Oakhill Rdbt MK5 ....45 D5
Oakhurst SL6 ....196 B4
Oakington Ave HP6 ....166 E8
Oakland Way HP10 ....174 A1
Oaklands HP4 ....135 A4
Oaklands Cl HP6 ....154 C1
Oakley HP10 ....185 F7
Oakley CE Comb Sch
HP18 ....109 D4
Oakley Cres SL1 ....205 E6
Oakley Gdns MK15 ....35 B5
Oakley Green Rd SL4 ....209 B5
Oakley La OX39 ....147 B6
Oakley Rd Brill HP18 ....110 A3
Chinnor OX39 ....147 C6
Horton-cum-S OX33 ....108 C5
Oakridge MK4 ....46 E4
Oakridge Ct HP22 ....172 D6
Oakridge Pl SL2 ....198 C8
Oakridge Rd HP11 ....172 E7
Oakridge Sch HP11 ....172 E7
Oaks Rd TW19 ....213 D2
Oaks The HP4 ....135 A4
Oakside UB9 ....201 B6
Oaktree Cl HP10 ....163 B2
Oakview MK16 ....35 C7
Oakway Amersham HP6 ....154 B4
Winslow MK18 ....66 A4
Oakwell Cl LU6 ....93 F7
Oakwood
Berkhamsted HP4 ....134 F3
Flackwell Heath HP10 ....174 F4
Oatlands Dr SL1 ....205 D4
Oban Ct SL1 ....205 D4
Ockwells St SL6 ....202 C2
Octagon Arc **10** HP11 ....173 A7
Octagon Par **6** HP11 ....173 A7
Octavian Dr MK13 ....33 F5
Octavian Way NN13 ....38 A1
Oddley La HP27 ....148 D8
Odds Farm Est HP10 ....186 B4
Odds Farm Pk* HP10 ....186 B4
Oddy Hill Tring HP23 ....119 C3
Wigginton HP23 ....119 D4
Odell Cl MK6 ....47 C8
Odencroft Rd SL2 ....198 A2
Odney La SL6 ....196 B7
Offas La MK18 ....66 B5
Ogilvie Rd HP11 ....172 E7
Okeford Cl HP23 ....118 F4
Okeford Dr HP23 ....118 F4

Okeley La HP23 ....118 E3
Old Airfield Ind Est
HP23 ....104 D6
Old Amersham Rd SL9 ....189 B3
Old Bakery Ct SL0 ....207 F7
Old Bakery The
Aston Abbotts HP22 ....88 D5
Lane End HP14 ....171 B4
Old Barn Cl MK18 ....52 A4
Old Bix Rd RG9 ....191 A6
Old Brewery Cl HP21 ....115 E7
Old Burrs HP21 ....115 D3
Old Chapel Cl HP17 ....129 E3
Old Coach Dr HP11 ....174 A4
Old Court Cl SL6 ....202 B3
Old Dashwood Hill
HP14 ....159 F2
Old Dean HP3 ....146 A4
Old End MK18 ....53 B2
Old English Cl MK17 ....44 C1
Old Farm LU7 ....105 D4
Old Farm Cl
Beaconsfield HP9 ....175 C5
Slapton LU7 ....91 A3
Worminghall HP18 ....123 E5
Old Farm Rd
High Wycombe HP13 ....161 E2
West Drayton UB7 ....208 D4
Old Ferry Dr TW19 ....211 D1
Old Field Cl HP6 ....166 E8
Old Fishery La HP1 ....146 F8
Old Fives Ct SL1 ....197 C2
Old Forge Cl
Maidenhead SL6 ....203 A3
Tingewick MK18 ....51 B6
Old Forge Gdns HP22 ....102 B4
Old Forge Rd HP10 ....174 C2
Old Forge The HP23 ....104 A1
Old Gaol Mus* MK18 ....41 D1
Old Garden Ctr The
HP27 ....139 B3
Old Groveway MK6 ....47 D5
Old Hardenwaye HP13 ....162 E1
Old Heatherdene Cotts
HP15 ....162 D8
Old Horns La SL7 ....172 A3
Old House Ct SL3 ....206 D7
Old Kiln Rd
Flackwell Heath HP10 ....185 A8
Tylers Green HP10 ....163 C2
Old Linslade Rd LU7 ....70 E3
Old Lodge Dr HP9 ....175 E1
Old Maltings The
Buckingham MK18 ....52 C7
Thame OX9 ....125 E1
Old Manor Cl
Askett HP27 ....139 C7
Whaddon MK17 ....45 B1
Old Manor Ct LU7 ....78 E8
Old Marsh La SL6 ....203 F4
Old Mead SL9 ....177 F4
Old Meadow Cl HP4 ....135 A2
Old Mews The MK46 ....6 F4
Old Mill Cl HP17 ....127 A6
Old Mill Furlong MK18 ....66 A5
Old Mill Gdns **12** HP4 ....135 D4
Old Mill La
Maidenhead SL6 ....203 D4
Uxbridge UB8 ....208 B8
Old Mill Pl TW19 ....212 B1
Old Moor La HP13 ....162 A8
Old Nursery Ct SL2 ....187 C2
Old Oak Gdns HP4 ....134 E7
Old Orch OX39 ....137 E2
Old Orchard Mews **1**
HP4 ....135 C4
Old Orchards HP22 ....102 A3
Old Oxford Rd HP14 ....160 C1
Old Palace Cl SL3 ....212 D6
Old Papermill Cl HP18 ....185 E8
Old Plough Cl HP18 ....112 B2
Old Post Office La **11**
SL6 ....202 F7
Old Rd LU7 ....80 E7
Old Rectory La HP9 ....189 E4
Old Risborough Rd
HP22 ....130 A8
Old Sax La HP5 ....143 D4
Old School Cl
Halton HP22 ....117 C1
Stokenchurch HP14 ....158 E4
Old School Cotts HP5 ....145 C5
Old School La
Buckingham MK18 ....52 C8
Eaton Bray LU6 ....92 E7
Old School La MK17 ....69 E8
Old School Rd UB8 ....201 F1
Old School The HP10 ....185 D4
Old Shire La WD3 ....167 B3
Old Slade La SL0 ....207 F2
Old Springfields MK18 ....53 C2
Old Stable Yd MK19 ....32 C7
Old Stable Yd The MK18 ....65 F4
Old Station Cl MK18 ....66 A5
Old Station La TW19 ....212 A1
Old Station Way HP10 ....185 E5
Old Stoke Rd HP21 ....115 A4
Old Stratford Prim Sch
MK19 ....32 B6
Old Tan Yard Ct MK18 ....52 D7
Old Town NN13 ....38 A7
Old Town Cl HP9 ....175 E1
Old Town Farm HP16 ....152 A7
Old Uxbridge Rd WD3 ....178 E3

Old Vicarage Way HP10 ....185 D4
Old Watery La HP10 ....185 E8
Old Windmill Way HP18 ....125 C2
Old Wolverton Rd SL2 ....33 C8
Oldacres SL6 ....203 B7
Oldbrook Bvd MK6 ....46 E8
Oldbrook Fst Sch MK6 ....46 E8
Oldbury Gr HP9 ....175 D5
Oldicalle Croft MK4 ....46 A1
Olde Bell Cl MK17 ....69 C7
Olde Bell La MK5 ....46 A7
Oldershaw Mews SL6 ....202 B8
Oldfield Prim Sch SL6 ....203 B6
Oldfield Rd SL6 ....203 B7
Oldfield Road Ind Est
SL6 ....203 B7
Oldhams Mdw **8** HP20 ....117 D1
Oldhouse Cl HP11 ....172 E3
Oldway La SL1 ....204 D5
Oliffe Cl HP20 ....101 D3
Oliffe Way HP20 ....101 D3
Oliver Rd MK2 ....58 C8
Oliver's Paddock SL7 ....183 D5
Olivia Dr SL3 ....206 F1
Olivier Way HP20 ....116 A8
Olleberrie La WD4 ....156 D7
Olney Fst Sch MK46 ....6 E3
Olney Mid Sch MK46 ....6 F5
Olney Rd Emberton MK46 ....13 F8
Lavendon MK46 ....7 B8
Olson Cotts HP14 ....158 F4
Olympic Ho UB8 ....201 F1
One Pin La SL2 ....198 A6
One Tree La HP9 ....175 E3
Onslow Ct MK7 ....48 A4
Onslow Dr OX9 ....126 B1
Onslow Gdns HP13 ....173 E7
Onslow Mills UB7 ....208 D6
Opal Ct SL3 ....199 C1
Opal Dr MK15 ....35 C5
Open University (Walton
Hall) The MK7 ....47 F7
Opendale Rd SL1 ....204 B8
Oram Ct **3** SL7 ....183 D2
Orbell Ct HP27 ....139 B3
Orbison Ct MK8 ....45 D7
Orchard Ave
Berkhamsted HP4 ....135 A4
Slough SL1 ....204 D8
Windsor SL4 ....210 A6
Orchard Bglws SL2 ....197 F5
Orchard Cl
Aston Clinton HP22 ....117 C4
Chorleywood WD3 ....167 D5
Hazelmere HP15 ....163 A3
Leighton Buzzard LU7 ....80 D6
Uxbridge UB8 ....201 D1
Wooburn HP10 ....185 D4
Orchard End
Edlesborough LU6 ....92 E4
Hazelmere HP15 ....163 B6
Orchard End Ave HP7 ....165 F8
Orchard Gate SL2 ....198 C7
Orchard Gr
Chalfont St Peter SL9 ....177 C2
Flackwell Heath HP10 ....185 B7
HP22 ....130 A8
Orchard Ho
Bourne End SL8 ....185 A4
Milton Keynes MK12 ....33 D6
Orchard La
Amersham HP6 ....154 D1
Harrold MK43 ....3 D6
Prestwood HP16 ....151 C6
Stewkley LU7 ....78 E7
Orchard Leigh Villas
HP5 ....145 A4
Orchard Lodge SL1 ....204 E5
Orchard Mews HP9 ....176 D4
Orchard Mill SL8 ....185 B1
Orchard Pk HP15 ....163 C6
Orchard Pl
Monks Risborough HP27 ....139 C5
Uxbridge UB8 ....201 D5
Westbury NN13 ....39 A4
Orchard Rd
Beaconsfield HP9 ....175 C5
Chalfont St Giles HP8 ....177 C8
Loudwater HP14 ....174 A4
Orchard Rd SL4 ....211 B1
Seer Green HP9 ....176 D4
Orchard Rise MK46 ....6 F3
Orchard Row HP14 ....171 A4
Orchard The
Aston Clinton HP22 ....117 C5

Orchard The continued
Flackwell Heath HP10 ....185 B7
Halton HP22 ....131 C8
Hazelmere HP15 ....163 A6
Hillesden MK18 ....63 A7
Marlow SL7 ....183 C3
Pottersbury NN12 ....18 C3
Walter's Ash HP14 ....161 E6
Orchard View
Hillesden MK18 ....63 B7
Uxbridge UB8 ....201 D1
Orchard Way
Aylesbury HP20 ....101 F2
Bovingdon HP3 ....146 A3
Chinnor OX39 ....147 C5
Cranfield MK43 ....25 A1
East Claydon MK18 ....74 E6
Eaton Bray LU6 ....92 F5
Holmer Green HP15 ....163 C6
North Crawley MK16 ....24 A6
Pitstone LU7 ....105 E4
Slough SL3 ....206 D5
Stoke Goldington MK16 ....12 B7
Wing LU7 ....79 E2
Orchard Waye UB8 ....201 D3
Orchard Wlk MK46 ....7 F7
Orchards The
Eaton Bray LU6 ....92 E7
Little Kingshill HP16 ....152 A2
Slough SL3 ....206 B8
Tring HP23 ....118 F3
Orchardville SL1 ....197 B1
Orchehill Ave SL9 ....188 D7
Orchehill Ct SL9 ....188 E6
Orchehill Rise SL9 ....188 E6
Oregano Cl MK7 ....208 F6
Orford Ct MK5 ....46 B6
Oriel Cl MK12 ....33 B6
Oriel Cotts MK18 ....63 D2
Orkney Cl
Milton Keynes MK3 ....46 F2
Stewkley LU7 ....78 E8
Orkney Ct SL6 ....196 E5
Ormesby Cl MK4 ....116 A5
Ormond Rd OX9 ....126 A1
Ormonde Cl MK18 ....34 B5
Ormsgill Ct MK13 ....34 B5
Orne Gdns MK15 ....35 A7
Orpington Gr MK5 ....46 B4
Ortensia Dr MK7 ....48 C7
Orwell Cl Aylesbury HP21 ....115 D4
Newport Pagnell MK16 ....21 F5
Windsor SL4 ....210 D4
Orwell Dr HP21 ....115 D4
Osborn Rd UB8 ....201 C5
Osborn's Ct MK46 ....6 F3
Osborne Ct SL4 ....210 C5
Osborne Mews SL4 ....210 C5
Osborne Rd SL4 ....210 D4
Osborne St
Milton Keynes MK2 ....58 C7
Slough SL1 ....205 F4
Osborne Way HP23 ....119 D1
Osbourne St SL1 ....33 D6
Osier La MK5 ....46 B4
Osier Way
Aylesbury HP20 ....115 F8
Buckingham MK18 ....52 C6
Osmington Pl HP23 ....118 F4
Osney Rd SL6 ....195 E2
Osprey Cl
Milton Keynes MK6 ....47 B8
West Drayton UB7 ....208 E4
Osprey The HP21 ....101 E4
Osprey Wlk
Aylesbury HP19 ....101 E4
Buckingham MK18 ....52 F7
Ostler Cl SL9 ....195 C1
Ostler Gate SL6 ....195 C1
Ostlers Cl HP11 ....174 A4
Ostlers La MK11 ....32 D6
Otter Cl MK3 ....46 D1
Otterburn Cres MK5 ....45 D5
Otterfield Rd UB7 ....208 E6
Otters Brook MK18 ....52 E7
Otway Cl HP21 ....115 E3
Oulton Ct HP21 ....116 A5
Our Lady of Peace RC Inf Sch
SL1 ....204 C3
Our Lady of Peace RC Jun
Sch SL1 ....204 C3
Our Lady's RC Prim Sch
HP6 ....154 A4
Ousbank St MK16 ....22 D5
Ousebank Way MK11 ....32 D5
Ousedale Sch MK16 ....22 B3
Ouseley Rd TW19 ....211 D1
Outfield Rd SL9 ....177 D3
Outlook Dr HP8 ....177 D7
Ouzel Cl MK3 ....46 E1
Oval The MK6 ....46 E7
Oval Way SL9 ....188 E7
Over Hampden HP16 ....151 C7
Over The Misbourne
UB9 ....189 B5
Over The Misbourne Rd
UB9 ....189 C5
Overdale Rd HP5 ....144 B3
Overdales HP15 ....162 F3
Overend Cl MK13 ....34 A4
Overgate MK6,MK9,MK14 ....35 B4
Overhills MK46 ....6 E4
Overn Ave MK18 ....41 C1
Overn Cl MK18 ....41 D1
Overn Cres MK18 ....41 C1

Overshot Ho HP10 ....174 C2
Oversley Cl MK14 ....22 A1
Overstone Cl LU7 ....79 E2
Overstone Comb Sch
LU7 ....79 E2
Overstrand HP22 ....117 E5
Overstreet MK15 ....35 A6
Overton Dr OX9 ....126 B1
Oville Ct MK5 ....46 B5
Oving Rd HP22 ....86 E7
Ovitts Cl MK18 ....66 A5
Owen Cl [4] SL3 ....206 F1
Owl Cl [5] HP1 ....101 F3
Owlsears Cl HP9 ....175 D4
Oxendon Ct LU7 ....70 A2
Oxfield Cl HP4 ....135 A3
Oxfield Park Dr MK19 .....32 C7
Oxford & Cherwell Coll
OX9 ....125 C8
Oxford Ave Burnham SL1 ..197 B3
Slough SL1 ....204 F8
Oxford Gdns UB9 ....190 A1
Oxford Rd
Aylesbury HP17,HP21 .....115 B7
Denham UB9 ....189 D2
Gerrards Cross SL9 ....188 D5
High Wycombe HP11 ......173 A7
Marlow SL7 ....183 D2
Oakley HP18 ....109 D5
Piddington HP14 ....160 D1
Stokenchurch HP14 ......158 D5
Stone HP17 ....114 C5
Thame OX9 ....125 E1
Uxbridge UB8,UB9 ....201 B6
Windsor SL4 ....210 C6
Oxford Rd E SL4 ....210 C6
Oxford St
[8] High Wycombe HP11 ..173 A7
Lee Common HP16 ....142 D5
Milton Keynes,Fenny Stratford
MK2 ....58 C8
Milton Keynes,Stony Stratford
MK11 ....32 D5
Milton Keynes,Wolverton
MK12 ....33 D6
Oxhouse Ct MK5 ....46 A3
Oxley Park Rdbt MK5 .....45 F3
Oxleys 6 E4
Oxman La MK12 ....33 A5
Oxwich Gr MK4 ....57 B8

P

Pack & Prime La RG9 ....191 C2
Packet Boat La UB8 ......208 C7
Packhorse Rd SL9 ....188 E6
Padbury CE Sch MK18 ....53 C2
Padbury Oaks UB7 ....213 B6
Padcroft Rd UB7 ....208 D5
Paddock Cl
Maidenhead SL6 ....202 A2
Milton Keynes MK14 ......34 E8
Paddock Cotts SL6 ......202 A2
Paddock The
Aylesbury HP21 ....116 C7
Chalfont St Peter SL9 ....177 E5
Datchet SL3 ....211 B6
Emberton MK46 ....13 F8
Maidenhead SL6 ....195 C2
Maids Moreton MK18 ......41 E4
Paddock Way MK4 ....47 D1
Paddocks End HP9 ....176 C4
Paddocks Hospl The
HP27 ....139 C4
Paddocks The
Chorleywood WD3 ....167 F5
Flackwell Heath HP10 ....185 B8
Haddenham HP17 ....127 A5
High Wycombe HP12 .....172 B3
Leighton Buzzard LU7 .....80 F8
Prestwood HP16 ....151 C5
Steeple Claydon MK18 .....63 E3
Wendover HP22 ....131 B5
Padstow Ave MK6 ....34 F1
Padstow Cl
Aylesbury HP20 ....101 F1
Slough SL3 ....206 E3
Page Hill Ave MK18 ......41 E1
Pages Croft HP4 ....135 A6
Pages La UB8 ....201 C6
Pages Wharf SL6 ....203 C8
Paget Cl SL7 ....183 F4
Paget Ct UB7 ....208 E4
Paget Dr SL6 ....202 A4
Paget Rd SL3 ....206 F2
Pagg's Ct MK16 ....22 C6
Pagoda Rdbt MK15 ....35 C5
Pagoda The SL6 ....196 B1
Paines Orch LU7 ....105 A8
Pakenham Cl HP11 ....114 F8
Palace Cl SL1 ....204 F5
Palace Sq MK6 ....46 F7
Palliser Rd HP8 ....177 B6
Palmer Ave
Aylesbury HP19 ....115 C8
Upper Arncott OX25 ......94 F8
Palmer's Moor La SL0 ...201 A1
Palmers Cl SL6 ....202 D8
Palmers Moor MK18 ....54 A8
Palmers Rd MK46 ....7 A3
Palmerston Ave SL3 .....206 B3
Pankridge Dr HP16 ......151 C7
Panleigh Cotts HP14 .....171 B3
Pannier Pl MK14 ....35 A5

Panters Cl MK17 ....44 C1
Pantile Row SL3 ....207 A2
Pantile Wlk UB8 ....201 C5
Paprika Ct MK17 ....48 B5
Parade Ct [7] SL8 ....185 A4
Parade The
Bourne End SL8 ....185 A3
Farnham Common SL2 ....198 C6
High Wycombe HP11 .....172 F6
Uxbridge UB8 ....208 C8
Windsor SL4 ....209 D6
Paradise MK17 ....57 D4
Paradise Mews RG9 ......191 D2
Paradise Rd RG9 ....191 C1
Parchment Cl HP6 ....154 E2
Parish La SL2 ....187 C1
Parish Piece HP15 ....163 C7
Park Ave
Newport Pagnell MK16 .....22 B4
Totternhoe LU6 ....93 B8
Wraysbury TW19 ....211 D3
Park Cl Cosgrove MK19 ...19 F2
Dunton MK18 ....77 E5
Lane End HP14 ....171 C5
Windsor SL4 ....210 D5
Park Cnr SL4 ....209 E4
Park Ct UB8 ....201 D4
Park Farm Rd HP12 ......161 B1
Park Farm Way HP11 .....171 C5
Park Gate LU7 ....79 E1
Park Gdns MK3 ....47 A1
Park Gr HP8 ....166 D6
Park Hill OX33 ....122 B1
Park Ho
Berkhamsted HP4 ....135 B5
Gerrards Cross SL9 ......188 E7
Maidenhead SL6 ....202 E6
Park House Dr MK5 ....45 F6
Park La Beaconsfield HP9 .175 F1
Burnham SL1 ....197 E7
Eaton Bray LU6 ....92 D6
Hazlemere HP15 ....163 A4
Horton SL3 ....212 A4
Lane End HP14 ....171 D5
Maidensgrove RG9 ....179 D6
Paulersperry NN12 ....17 B7
Slough SL3 ....206 B3
Stokenchurch HP14 ......158 E6
Park Lane Ct MK14 ......158 E5
Park Lawn SL2 ....198 C2
Park Mdw HP27 ....139 A3
Park Par SL2 ....198 A5
Park Parade Ctr The
HP15 ....163 A5
Seer Green HP9 ....176 D5
Park Rd Amersham HP6 ...154 F1
Chesham HP5 ....154 B8
Farnham Royal SL2 ......198 E3
Granborough MK18 ....75 F6
Grendon Underwood HP18 .82 F8
Hanslope MK19 ....11 B1
Hartwell NN7 ....10 C8
Henley-on-T RG9 ....191 C1
Milton Keynes MK11 ......32 D5
Sherington MK16 ....14 A2
Stanwell TW19 ....213 C1
Tring HP23 ....118 F2
Uxbridge UB8 ....201 E6
Winslow MK18 ....65 F5
Park Rd E UB10 ....201 D3
Park Rd S MK18 ....65 F4
Park Rise HP4 ....134 E6
Park Sch HP20 ....101 F1
Park St Aylesbury HP20 ..115 F8
Berkhamsted HP4 ....135 B5
High Wycombe HP11 .....173 D6
Maidenhead SL6 ....202 F7
Poyle SL3 ....212 F6
Princes Risborough HP27 ..139 B3
Slough SL1 ....205 F4
Tring HP23 ....119 A3
Windsor SL4 ....210 D6
Woburn MK17 ....60 F7
Park Street Ind Est
HP20 ....115 F8
Park View
Newport Pagnell MK16 .....22 D4
West Drayton UB7 ....208 E6
Park View Ct
Berkhamsted HP4 ....135 B4
High Wycombe HP12 .....172 D8
[4] Leighton Buzzard LU7 ..80 E7
Park View Rd
Berkhamsted HP4 ....135 B4
Maidenhead SL6 ....195 D8
Parker Cl MK13 ....34 A6
Parker Knoll Way HP13 ...173 A7
Parker Wlk HP19 ....101 D3
Parkfield WD3 ....167 F5
Parkfield Ave MK6 ......154 D2
Parkgate SL1 ....197 C1
Parkhouse Bsns Ctr
HP12 ....172 E8
Parkland Ave SL3 ....206 D2
Parklands MK14 ....21 D1
Parkminster MK10 ....36 A1
Parkside
Gerrards Cross SL9 ......188 F7
Henley-on-T RG9 ....191 C2
Maidenhead SL6 ....195 D1
Milton Keynes MK4 ....46 A8
Naphill HP14 ....150 B1
Parkside Wlk SL1 ....206 A3
Parkstone Lodge SL6 ....196 A3
Parkview
Flackwell Heath HP10 ....185 B7
Maidenhead SL6 ....202 F7

Parkview Chase SL1 .....204 E7
Parkway
Bow Brickhill MK17 ....48 D2
Marlow SL7 ....184 A3
Woburn Sands MK17 ....49 A6
Parkway The SL0 ....200 C4
Parkwood HP14 ....150 A2
Parlaunt Park Prim Sch
SL3 ....207 B3
Parlaunt Rd SL3 ....207 B2
Parliament Cl HP16 .....151 B7
Parliament La SL6,SL1 ..196 F5
Parliament Rd OX9 .....125 F1
Parmiter Pl HP15 ....115 B8
Parmoor La RG9 ....170 E1
Parneleys MK10 ....35 F2
Parrish Piece HP22 ......87 B3
Parrock La MK10 ....36 A2
Parrot Cl HP21 ....115 B6
Parrott's La HP23 ......133 A4
Parrs Rd HP14 ....158 E4
Parry Cotts SL9 ....177 E6
Parry Gn S SL3 ....207 A2
Parry Green N SL3 ......206 F2
Parsley Cl
Aston Clinton HP22 ......117 C5
Walton MK7 ....48 B5
Parslow Cl HP21 ....115 D3
Parslow Ct HP11 ....115 D3
Parson Cl MK18 ....65 F4
Parson's Fee HP20 ......115 D8
Parson's Wood La SL2 ..198 D5
Parsonage Cl
High Wycombe HP13 .....173 C6
Tring HP23 ....119 A4
Parsonage Ct [1] HP23 ..119 A3
Parsonage Farm HP21 ....89 B3
Parsonage Gdns SL7 ....183 E1
Parsonage La
Farnham Common SL2 ....198 D5
Windsor SL4 ....210 A6
Parsonage Pl HP7 ......165 C8
Parsonage Rd HP8 ......177 B7
Parsons Cl LU7 ....78 E8
Parsons Cres MK5 ....46 C5
Parsons La HP22 ....102 B3
Parsons Rd SL3 ....206 F1
Parsons Wlk HP15 ......163 C6
Parton Cl HP22 ....131 A5
Parton Rd HP20 ....116 B8
Partridge Cl
Buckingham MK18 ....52 F7
Chesham HP5 ....144 E3
Partridge Mead SL6 ....195 F2
Partridge Piece MK43 ....25 C3
Partridge Way
[7] Aylesbury HP19 .....101 F3
High Wycombe HP13 .....161 C2
Pascal Dr MK5 ....45 E5
Pascomb Rd LU6 ....93 F8
Passalewe La MK7 ....48 D7
Passmore MK6 ....47 D6
Pastern Pl MK14 ....35 A5
Pastures The
Aylesbury HP20 ....102 B2
Edlesborough LU6 ....92 F3
High Wycombe HP13 .....161 E1
Patch Cl UB10 ....201 F4
Patches Field SL7 ......183 E5
Pateman Cl MK18 ....41 C1
Paterson Rd HP21 ......115 C6
Patricia Cl SL1 ....204 E6
Patrick Haugh Rd OX25 ..94 F7
Patrick Way HP21 ....116 A4
Patricks La MK19 ....31 F4
Patrington Cl UB8 ......201 C2
Patriot Dr MK13 ....34 B2
Patrons Dr UB9 ....189 F5
Patterson Ct HP10 .....185 E7
Patterson Rd HP5 ......144 B3
Pattison La MK15 ....35 C5
Paul's Row HP11 ....173 B6
Paulersperry CE Prim Sch
NN12 ....17 B8
Pauls Hill HP10 ....174 F6
Pavers Ct HP21 ....115 D3
Pavilion Cl HP20 ....116 A8
Pavilion Way HP16 ......166 C8
Pavilions The UB8 ....201 D5
Paxton Ave SL1 ....205 C3
Paxton Cl MK46 ....6 F3
Paxton Cres MK5 ....46 B5
Paxton Rd HP4 ....135 D4
Paynes Dr MK18 ....41 D1
Paynes Dr MK5 ....46 A8
Paynes Field Cl HP4 ....134 D7
Paynes Hos SL6 ....195 E6
Pea La HP4 ....134 D7
Peace La SL6 ....195 F6
Peace Rd SL0,SL3 ......200 A3
Peach Tree Ave UB7 .....208 F7
Peachey Cl UB8 ....208 D7
Peachey La UB8 ....208 D8
Peacock Hay MK4 ....46 C2
Peacock Rd SL7 ....183 E5
Peacocks Cl HP4 ....134 F6
Pear Tree Ave LU7 ......208 F7
Pear Tree Cl
Amersham HP7 ....165 F8
Seer Green HP9 ....176 C4
Pear Tree Ct HP15 ......163 C6
Pearce Cl
Aylesbury HP21 ....115 E4
Maidenhead SL6 ....195 F1
Pearce Dr SL6 ....195 F7
Pearce Rd Chesham HP5 .144 B2
Maidenhead SL6 ....195 F1
Pearce's Orch RG9 ......191 D3

Pearl Gdns SL1 ....205 B5
Pearse Gr MK7 ....48 A4
Pearson Cl HP19 ....115 B6
Peartree Cl SL1 ....204 F5
Peartrees UB7 ....208 D6
Peascod Pl [12] SL4 ....210 D6
Peascod St SL4 ....210 D6
Peascroft HP18 ....125 D6
Peatey Ct HP13 ....173 D6
Pebble Brook Sch HP21 .115 C7
Pebble La
Aylesbury HP20 ....115 D8
Brackley NN13 ....38 A7
Pebblemoor LU6 ....92 F3
Peckover Ct [8] MK6 ....33 F1
Pecks Farm Cl HP22 ....102 C4
Peddle Ct HP11 ....172 F7
Pednor Bottom HP5 ....143 B3
Pednor Rd HP5 ....143 E2
Pednormead End HP5 ...154 B7
Peebles Pl MK3 ....46 F3
Peel Cl SL4 ....210 B4
Peel Ct
Monks Risborough HP27 .139 B4
Slough SL1 ....205 B8
Peel Rd MK12 ....33 C6
Peel Way UB8 ....208 E8
Peerless Dr HP22 .....190 C7
Peers Dr MK17 ....49 E3
Peers La MK5 ....46 B6
Peggs La HP22 ....117 F5
Pelham Cl SL6 ....202 E7
Pelham Pl MK14 ......34 F5
Pelham Rd OX9 ......126 B1
Pelton Ct MK5 ....46 C5
Pemberley Lodge SL4 ..210 A4
Pemberton Cl HP21 ....115 F5
Pemberton Rd SL2 .....197 E1
Pembridge Chase [4]
HP3 ....146 A3
Pembridge Cl [3] HP3 ..146 A3
Pembridge Gr MK4 .....45 E1
Pembridge Rd HP3 .....146 A3
Pembroke Ho
[2] Milton Keynes MK3 ..46 F1
Olney MK46 ....6 F3
Pembroke Rd HP20 ....101 F1
Pencarrow Pl MK6 .....35 A1
Pendeen Ct SL1 ....205 A5
Pendennis Ct MK4 .....57 A8
Pendles Paddocks HP14 .158 F2
Pendrill Ho [2] HP12 ..172 E7
Penfold HP22 ....116 F2
Penfold Cotts HP15 ...163 D7
Penfold La
Holmer Green HP15 ....163 E8
Hyde Heath HP7,HP15 ..152 F1
Pengelly Ct MK6 ......35 A1
Penhale Cl MK4 ....57 B8
Penhow Rise MK4 .....45 E1
Penina Cl MK3 ....46 D1
Penington Rd HP9 ....186 B8
Penlee Rise MK4 .....57 A8
Penley Cl OX39 ......147 B6
Penling Cl SL6 ....195 E6
Penmon Cl MK10 .....35 F1
Penmoor Cl HP12 .....172 C8
Penn Ave HP5 ....144 A1
Penn Bottom HP10 ...163 E1
Penn Cl
Chorleywood WD3 ....167 D3
Uxbridge UB8 ....201 D1
Penn Ct [8] Marlow SL7 .183 E2
Tylers Green HP10 ....174 B8
Penn Dr UB9 ....189 F5
Penn Gn HP9 ....175 D4
Penn Gaskell La SL9 ..177 F5
Penn Haven SL9 .....188 F6
Penn Mdw SL2 ......198 F4
Penn Mead HP10 ....174 F7
Penn Rd Aylesbury HP21 .115 F5
Beaconsfield HP9 .....175 C5
Chalfont St Peter SL9 .177 D2
Chorleywood WD3 ....167 F1
Datchet SL3 ....211 D6
Hazlemere HP15 .....163 B3
Milton Keynes MK2 ....58 B8
Penn Sch HP10 ......174 D7
Penn Street Works Ind Est
HP7 ....164 A4
Penn Way WD3 ......167 D3
Penn Wood View HP7 ..164 A4
Pennefather Ct [3] HP21 .115 E7
Pennine Rd SL2 .....205 A8
Pennings The HP22 ..131 B5
Pennington Pl OX9 ...126 B1
Pennington Rd
Chalfont St Peter SL9 .177 D3
High Wycombe HP13 ...173 F6
Penningtons The HP6 .154 E2
Pennycress Way MK16 .21 F4
Pennycuik MK17 .....59 C1
Pennylets Gn SL2 ...199 A5
Pennyroyal MK7 .....48 B7
Penrith Cl UB8 .....201 D5
Penrith Way HP21 ...116 B7
Penryn Ave MK6 ....35 A2
Penshurst Cl SL9 ...188 E7
Penshurst Rd SL6 ...202 D5
Pentewan Gate MK6 ..34 F2
Pentland Rd
Aylesbury HP21 ......115 F6
Slough SL2 ....205 A8
Pentlands MK11 .....32 F4
Pentlands Ct HP13 ..174 B4
Pentlands The HP13 .174 B4
Penwith Fst Sch MK6 .34 F1

Penwood Ct SL6 ......202 B7
Penwood La SL7 .....183 C1
Penyston Rd SL6 ....202 C7
Penzance Spur SL2 ..198 B1
Peplar Way SL1 .....197 B2
Peplow Cl UB7 ......208 D5
Peppard Mdw HP16 ..151 D5
Pepper Hill Fst Sch
MK13 ....34 A7
Peppett's Gn HP5 ....143 D8
Peppiatts The LU6 ...92 B5
Pepys Cl SL3 ....212 B8
Pepys Dr HP16 .....151 C6
Perch Cl SL7 ....194 C8
Perch Mews HP22 ...131 B8
Percheron Pl MK14 ..34 F5
Percy Bush Rd UB7 ..208 F3
Percy Pl SL3 ....211 A6
Percy Terr HP8 .....177 A7
Peregrine HP19 .....101 E3
Peregrine Bsns Pk
HP13 ....174 A5
Peregrine Cl MK6 ...47 B8
Perivale MK10 ......35 E1
Perks La HP16 .....151 C3
Permayne MK13 ....34 A7
Perracombe MK4 ....46 E3
Perran Ave MK6 ....35 A1
Perrin Springs La RG9 .170 F1
Perry Hill HP18 ....173 A3
Perry Ho SL1 ......197 B2
Perry La Bledlow HP27 .138 C2
Sherington MK16 ....14 B2
Perry Mead LU6 ....92 E6
Perry St HP22 .....131 A5
Perrycroft SL4 ....209 F4
Perryfields Way SL1 .197 B1
Perryman Way SL2 ..197 F2
Perrys The HP22 ...131 B5
Pershore Croft [1] MK10 .36 A1
Perth Ave SL1 .....205 B7
Perth Cl MK3 ......46 F2
Perth Rd HP13 ....173 D8
Perth Trad Est SL1 .205 B8
Peter's Cl HP16 ...151 C6
Peter's Pl HP4 ....134 E6
Peterborough Ave [2]
HP13 ....173 C7
Peterborough Gate
MK15 ....35 C6
Peterhead Mews SL1 .207 A1
Peterhill Cl SL9 ...177 E5
Peterley Ave HP15,HP16 .151 E3
Peterley La HP16 ..151 E3
Peters La HP27 ...139 E4
Petersfield HP22 ..116 C3
Petersfield Ave SL2 .206 A5
Petersham Cl MK16 .22 C2
Pettifer Way HP12 .172 D6
Pettingrew Cl MK7 ..48 B6
Petty Cross SL1 ...204 E7
Petworth MK8 .....33 E1
Petworth Ct SL4 ..210 E6
Petworth Ho [2] MK8 .33 F1
Pevensey Cl
Aylesbury HP21 ....116 B5
Milton Keynes MK3 ..57 E7
Pevensey Rd SL2 ..205 A8
Peverel Dr MK1 ...47 B3
Peveril Cl HP21 ...116 B5
Pevers La MK46 ...6 A1
Pheasant Cl
Berkhamsted HP4 ...135 C3
Tring HP23 ....119 B6
Pheasant Dr HP13 .161 C1
Pheasant Hill HP8 .177 C8
Pheasant Rise HP5 .154 D6
Pheasant Wlk SL9 .177 E6
Pheasants Croft SL6 .202 A4
Pheasants Dr HP15 .163 B5
Pheasants Ridge SL7 .183 C7
Philbye Mews SL1 ..204 F4
Philip Cotts SL8 ..185 C3
Philip Dr HP10 ....185 C2
Philip Rd HP13 ...173 D7
Philips Rd HP14 ..171 C4
Philipshill Wood Nature
Reserve* WD3 ....167 A2
Phillip Ct MK5 ...46 B6
Philpots Cl UB7 ..208 D6
Phipps Cl
Aylesbury HP20 ....102 A2
Maidenhead SL6 ...202 A2
Phipps Rd SL1 ....204 E8
Phoebe's Orch MK17 .69 E7
Phoenix Bsns Ctr [3]
HP5 ....144 B1
Phoenix Ct SL6 ...202 D4
Phoenix Dr MK6 ...46 E6
Phoenix Ho [7] HP19 .115 A8
Phygtle The SL9 ..177 E4
Phyllis Court Dr RG9 .191 E3
Picasso Pl HP21 ..100 F2
Pickering Dr MK4 .46 B2
Pickford Dr SL3 ..207 A5
Pickfords Gdns SL1 .205 E5
Pickins Piece SL3 .212 A5
Pickwick Terr SL2 .206 B6
Picton St MK4 ....45 E1
Picton Terr LU7 ..139 A2
Piddington La HP14 .171 B8
Piddington Rd HP18 .196 A4
Pield Heath House Sch
UB8 ....201 F1
Pield Heath Rd UB8 .201 F1

Pierson Rd SL4 . . . . . . .209 D6
Pigeon Farm Rd HP14 . .158 E5
Piggott's Hill HP14 . . . .150 E1
Piggotts End **6** HP7 . . .165 B7
Piggotts Orch HP7 . . . . .165 B7
Pightle Cres MK18 . . . . . .41 D2
Pightle The
  Buckingham MK18 . . . . . . .41 D1
  Maids Moreton MK18 . . . .41 F4
  Oving HP22 . . . . .86 D7
  Pitstone LU7 . . . . .105 D3
Pigott Dr MK5 . . . . .46 A5
Pigott Orch HP22 . . . . . . .85 A5
Pike Cl Marlow SL7 . . . . .194 C8
  Uxbridge UB10 . . . . .201 F4
Pike Cnr HP21 . . . . .116 C5
Pilch La MK17 . . . . .54 D4
Pilgrim St MK15 . . . . .35 A4
Pilgrims Cl HP13 . . . . . .179 B5
Pilot Trad Est HP12 . . . .172 E8
Pimms Cl HP13 . . . . .174 A6
Pimms Gr HP13 . . . . .174 A5
Pimpernel Gr MK7 . . . . . .48 B6
Pinchfield WD3 . . . . .178 D5
Pinders Croft MK12 . . . . . .33 B5
Pine Chase HP12 . . . . . . .172 B3
Pine Cl Berkhamsted HP4 .135 B4
  Hazlemere HP15 . . . . . .163 B3
  Maidenhead SL6 . . . . . . .202 B7
Pine Crest Mews LU7 . . . .80 E6
Pine Ct HP5 . . . . .154 C8
Pine Gr MK17 . . . . .49 A4
Pine Hill HP15 . . . . .162 F3
Pine Rd UL6 . . . . .106 F8
Pine Trees Dr UB10 . . . . .201 E8
Pine Wlk
  Berkhamsted HP4 . . . . . .134 D7
  Hazlemere HP15 . . . . . .163 B3
Pineapple Rd HP7 . . . . . .165 F8
Pinecroft SL7 . . . . .183 D4
Pineham Rdbt MK15 . . . . .35 E5
Pinels Way HP11 . . . . . . .172 E3
Piner Cotts SL4 . . . . .209 E4
Pines The Felden HP3 . . .146 F7
  Slough SL3 . . . . .206 F5
  Tylers Green HP10 . . . . .163 B1
Pinetree Cl SL9 . . . . .177 C3
Pinewood Ave UB8 . . . . .208 F7
Pinewood Cl
  Gerrards Cross SL9 . . . . .188 E4
  Iver Heath SL0 . . . . .200 C5
Pinewood Dr MK2 . . . . . . .58 E7
Pinewood Film Studios
  SL0 . . . . .200 B5
Pinewood Gn SL0 . . . . . .200 C5
Pinewood Mews TW19 . .213 D1
Pinewood Rd
  High Wycombe HP12 . . . .172 C7
  Iver Heath SL0 . . . . .200 B4
Pinfold MK7 . . . . .48 B6
Pinfold Yd MK18 . . . . .51 B6
Pinglestone Cl UB7 . . . . .213 E7
Pinions Rd HP13 . . . . . . .173 E5
Pink Hill HP27 . . . . .149 E8
Pink La SL1 . . . . .197 B3
Pink Rd HP27 . . . . .149 E7
Pinkard Ct MK6 . . . . .47 C8
Pinkneys Dr SL6 . . . . . . .195 A1
Pinkneys Rd SL6 . . . . . . .202 A8
Pinks Cl MK5 . . . . .46 C8
Pinkworthy MK4 . . . . .46 D4
Pinn Cl UB8 . . . . .208 D7
Pinstone Way SL9 . . . . . .189 B2
Pintail Cl HP19 . . . . .101 E4
Pipard MK14 . . . . .34 E7
Pipers Cl SL1 . . . . .197 C2
Pipers Corner Sch
  HP15 . . . . .162 B7
Pipers Croft LU6 . . . . .93 F7
Pipers Ct SL1 . . . . .197 C2
Pipers La HP15 . . . . .162 C8
Pipers Wood Cotts HP7 .153 C2
Pipit Gdns **7** HP21 . . . .101 E4
Pipit Wlk **6** HP19 . . . . .101 E4
Pippin Cl MK16 . . . . .22 B3
Pippins Cl UB7 . . . . .208 D3
Pippins Sch SL3 . . . . . . .212 F6
Pippins The SL3 . . . . . . .206 F5
Pipston Gn MK7 . . . . .48 B7
Pistone Windmill* LU7 . .105 F4
Pitch Pond Cl HP9 . . . . . .175 C5
Pitch The HP14 . . . . .159 D3
Pitchcott Rd HP22 . . . . . . .86 B6
Pitcher La MK5 . . . . .46 B8
Pitcher Wlk HP19 . . . . . .115 A7
Pitchford Ave MK18 . . . . .41 E2
Pitchford Wlk MK16 . . . . .22 B3
Pitfield MK11 . . . . .33 B3
Pitstone Common Forest
  Trails* HP4 . . . . .120 E7
Pitstone Green Farm Mus*
  LU7 . . . . .105 D4
Pitt Gn MK18 . . . . .41 F1
Pitters Piece HP18 . . . . .125 B7
Pitts Rd SL1 . . . . .205 C5
Place Farm Ho HP27 . . . .139 B8
Place Farm Way HP27 . .139 B5
Plackett Way SL1 . . . . . .204 D5
Plaines Cl SL1 . . . . .204 F5
Plaiters Cl HP23 . . . . . . .119 B4
Plantain Ct MK7 . . . . .48 B6
Plantation Pl MK5 . . . . . . .46 A4
Plantation Rd
  Amersham HP6 . . . . .154 E2
  High Wycombe HP13 . . . .174 A7
  Leighton Buzzard LU7 . . . .70 F3

Plantation Way HP6 . . . .154 E2
Platt The HP7 . . . . .165 B7
Playing Field Rd NN13 . . .39 A4
Pleasant Cotts SL0 . . . . .200 B2
Pleasant Pl WD3 . . . . . . .178 E3
Pleasaunce The HP22 . . .117 C5
Pleshey Cl MK5 . . . . .46 B6
Plested Ct HP22 . . . . . . .116 C2
Plomer Green Ave
  HP13 . . . . .161 D2
Plomer Green La HP13 . .161 D3
Plomer Hill HP13 . . . . . .161 D3
Plough Cl HP21 . . . . .115 E3
Plough La Sarratt WD4 . .156 F6
  Wexham Street SL2 . . . . .199 B4
Ploughlees La SL1 . . . . .205 E6
Ploughley Rd OX25 . . . . .94 E8
Plover Cl
  1 Berkhamsted HP4 . . . .135 C3
  Buckingham MK18 . . . . . . .52 E7
  Newport Pagnell MK16 . . .22 F3
Plover The **4** HP19 . . . .101 E4
Plover Wlk **3** HP19 . . .101 E4
Plowman Cl MK12 . . . . . . .33 B5
Plum Park La NN12 . . . . . .17 D8
Plumer Rd HP11 . . . . . . .172 E2
Plumstead Ave MK13 . . . .34 D3
Pluto Cl SL1 . . . . .204 E4
Plym Cl HP21 . . . . .115 C5
Plymouth Gr MK4 . . . . . . .46 B1
Plymouth Rd SL1 . . . . . .204 E8
Pocketts Yd SL6 . . . . . . .196 B7
Pocock Ave UB7 . . . . . . .208 F3
Pococks La SL4 . . . . .205 E1
Poets Chase HP21 . . . . .115 F6
Points The SL6 . . . . .202 B3
Poles Hill Chesham HP5 .144 A2
  Sarratt WD4 . . . . .156 E6
Police Hos SL9 . . . . .189 B3
Polidoris La HP15 . . . . . .163 C7
Polish Ave HP22 . . . . . . .131 E8
Pollard Ave UB9 . . . . . . .189 F5
Pollard Cl SL4 . . . . .211 B2
Pollards WD3 . . . . .178 D5
Pollys Yd MK14 . . . . .22 D5
Pollywick Rd HP23 . . . . .119 D1
Polmartin Ct MK6 . . . . . . .35 A1
Polruan Pl
  Fishermead MK6 . . . . . . .47 A8
  Milton Keynes MK6 . . . . . .35 A1
Polygon Bsns Ctr SL3 . .212 F5
Pomander Cres MK7 . . . . .48 B7
Pomeroy Cl HP27 . . . . . .165 D7
Pond App HP15 . . . . .163 C7
Pond Cl
  Newton Longville MK17 . . .57 C2
  Tring HP23 . . . . .119 A4
  Winchmore Hill HP7 . . . .164 C3
Pond Cotts HP14 . . . . . . .171 B4
Pond La
  Chalfont St Peter SL9 . . .177 C2
  Little Gaddesden HP4 . . .121 E7
Pond Park Rd HP5 . . . . .144 B2
Ponderosa Cvn Site
  TW19 . . . . .212 F3
Pondgate MK7 . . . . .48 B8
Pondwicks HP7 . . . . .165 B8
Pool La SL1 . . . . .205 E6
Poolmans Rd SL4 . . . . . .209 D4
Pope Ct HP23 . . . . .118 F3
Pope Way HP21 . . . . .115 E4
Popes Acre HP22 . . . . . .131 B6
Popes Cl Amersham HP6 .154 F2
  Colnbrook SL3 . . . . .212 C7
Popes La SL6 . . . . .195 C7
Poplar Ave
  Amersham HP7 . . . . .165 F8
  West Drayton UB7 . . . . . .208 F6
Poplar Cl Aylesbury HP20 .102 A2
  Chesham HP5 . . . . .144 C3
  Milton Keynes MK6 . . . . . .47 E5
  Poyle SL3 . . . . .212 E6
Poplar Ho SL3 . . . . .206 F1
Poplar Rd
  Aylesbury HP20 . . . . . . .102 A2
  New Denham UB9 . . . . . .201 C6
  Wooburn Green HP10 . . .185 E7
Poplars Cl HP17 . . . . . . .114 C5
Poplars Gr SL6 . . . . .196 B2
Poplars Rd MK18 . . . . . . .52 D8
Poplars The HP22 . . . . . .131 C5
Poppy Rd HP27 . . . . .139 A2
Porlock La SL4 . . . . .46 C4
Port Field Farm MK16 . . .21 F5
Portal Cl UB10 . . . . .201 F5
Portal Rd MK12 . . . . .131 D6
Portchester Ct **1** MK8 . .33 F1
Porter's Cl MK19 . . . . . . .31 E4
Porters Way UB7 . . . . . .208 F4
Portfield Cl MK18 . . . . . . .52 E8
Portfield Way MK18 . . . . .52 E8
Portfields Comb Sch
  MK16 . . . . .22 A5
Portfields Rd MK16 . . . . . .22 A5
Porthcawl Rd MK4 . . . . . .57 C8
Porthleven Pl MK6 . . . . . .35 A2
Porthmellin Cl MK4 . . . . .57 B8
Portishead Dr MK4 . . . . . .56 F8
Portland Bsns Ctr SL3 . .211 B6
Portland Cl SL2 . . . . .197 D1
Portland Dr MK15 . . . . . . .35 C7
Portland Gdns MK15 . . . .183 D1
Portland Ho HP10 . . . . . .185 D8
Portland Pk SL9 . . . . . . .188 D5
Portlands Alley SL7 . . . . .183 D2
Portlands Mews **1** SL7 .183 D1
Portlock Rd SL6 . . . . .195 C7
Portmarnock Cl MK3 . . . .57 D8

Portnall Pl MK43 . . . . . . .25 B2
Portobello Cl HP5 . . . . . .144 A2
Portobello Cotts
  Lacey Green HP27 . . . . . .149 E5
  Lewknor OX49 . . . . .157 C2
Portrush Cl MK3 . . . . .57 D8
Portsmouth Ct SL1 . . . . .205 E6
Portway
  Milton Keynes,Bradwell Common
  MK5,MK9,MK13,MK14,
  MK15 . . . . .34 D2
  Milton Keynes,Shenley Church End
  MK8,MK5 . . . . .46 F3
  North Marston MK18 . . . . .76 B1
  Stone HP17 . . . . .114 C4
Portway Dr HP12 . . . . . . .161 B1
Portway Rd Stone HP17 .114 C4
  Twyford MK18 . . . . .62 D1
Portway Rdbt MK5 . . . . . .34 B1
Post Mdw SL0 . . . . .200 D2
Post Office Cotts SL2 . .199 A5
Post Office La
  Beaconsfield HP9 . . . . . .175 D3
  Slough SL3 . . . . .206 D7
  Whitchurch HP22 . . . . . . .87 A6
Posting Ho HP23 . . . . . . .120 A5
Potash La HP23 . . . . .104 A5
Potkiln La HP9 . . . . .175 A6
Potter Row HP16 . . . . . . .142 C1
Potters Cl HP16 . . . . . . .151 B7
Potters Cross SL0 . . . . .200 C2
Potters Cross Cres
  HP15 . . . . .162 E2
Potters Glen MK18 . . . . . .53 B1
Potters La MK11 . . . . .33 B4
Potterspury Lodge Sch
  NN12 . . . . .18 B6
Pottery Cl HP21 . . . . . . .115 A7
Pottery La HP21 . . . . . . .115 A7
Potts Pl **8** SL7 . . . . . . .183 D2
Poulcott TW19 . . . . .211 E1
Pound Cl
  Steeple Claydon MK18 . . .63 D3
  Wendover HP22 . . . . . . .131 A4
Pound Cres SL7 . . . . . . .183 C1
Pound Hill MK17 . . . . .59 C1
Pound La Heath End HP5 .134 A1
  Little Marlow SL7 . . . . . .184 C4
  Marlow SL7 . . . . .183 D1
  North Crawley MK16 . . . . .24 B7
  Preston Bissett MK18 . . . .51 C1
Pound St HP22 . . . . .131 B8
Pound The Cookham SL6 .196 A7
  Cookham Rise SL6 . . . . .195 F7
  Slough SL3 . . . . .197 D1
  Syresham NN13 . . . . .27 B7
Poundfield La SL6 . . . . . .195 F7
Poundfield Rd NN12 . . . . .18 E2
Pounds Cl MK43 . . . . .25 B1
Powell Haven MK10 . . . . .35 E3
Powis Cl SL6 . . . . .202 B4
Powis La MK4 . . . . .45 F2
Powney Rd SL6 . . . . .202 C7
Poyle 14 Trad Est SL3 . .212 E4
Poyle La SL1 . . . . .197 B3
Poyle New Cotts SL3 . . .212 F5
Poyle Pk SL3 . . . . .212 E4
Poyle Rd SL3 . . . . .212 E5
Poyle Tech Ctr The SL3 .212 E5
Poynings The SL0 . . . . . .207 F2
Pratt Ho HP6 . . . . .154 F1
Prebendal Ave HP21 . . . .115 D7
Prebendal Cl **11** HP20 . .115 D8
Prebendal Ct **1** HP20 . .115 D8
Precedent Dr MK13 . . . . .34 B3
Precincts The SL1 . . . . . .197 C1
Prentice Gr MK5 . . . . .46 C2
Prescott Rd SL3 . . . . . . .212 E5
Prescotts The SL9 . . . . .189 F3
Presley Way MK8 . . . . . . .45 E7
Press Rd UB8 . . . . .201 D6
Preston Ct MK15 . . . . . . .35 B7
Preston Hill HP5 . . . . . . .144 D2
Prestwich Cl MK3 . . . . . . .57 D7
Prestwold Ho HP19 . . . . .115 A7
Prestwold Way HP19 . . .115 A7
Prestwood SL2 . . . . .206 B7
Prestwood Cl HP12 . . . . .172 D8
Prestwood Inf Sch
  HP16 . . . . .151 C7
Prestwood Jun Sch
  HP16 . . . . .151 C6
Prestwood Lodge Sch
  HP16 . . . . .151 C6
Pretoria Rd HP13 . . . . . .173 C8
Priestend OX9 . . . . .125 E1
Priestfield Gdns HP4 . . .135 E6
Priestley Ctr HP13 . . . . .173 E8
Priests Paddock HP9 . . .175 B5
Primatt Cres MK5 . . . . . . .46 B6
Primrose Cotts HP14 . . .150 E1
Primrose Ct HP21 . . . . . .115 B6
Primrose Dr
  Aylesbury HP21 . . . . . . .115 B5
  West Drayton UB7 . . . . . .208 D2
Primrose Gn HP15 . . . . .162 F6
Primrose Hill HP15 . . . . .162 F7
Primrose Lea SL7 . . . . . .183 D2
Primrose Rd MK13 . . . . . .34 A4
Primrose Terr HP18 . . . . .110 A8
Primrose Way MK18 . . . . .52 E7
Prince Albert's Wlk
  SL3,SL4 . . . . .211 B5
Prince Andrew Cl SL6 . .203 B8
Prince Andrew Rd SL6 . .196 B1

Prince Consort Cotts
  SL4 . . . . .210 D5
Prince Consort's Dr SL4 .210 B2
Prince Edward St HP4 . .135 C4
Prince Philip Ave MK43 . .24 D2
Prince's La HP16 . . . . . . .142 D5
Prince's Rd HP21 . . . . . .115 E8
Princes Cl
  Berkhamsted HP4 . . . . . .135 A6
  Chilton HP18 . . . . .111 B3
  Eton Wick SL4 . . . . .204 F1
Princes Ct
  Bourne End SL8 . . . . . . .185 C3
  Leighton Buzzard LU7 . . . .80 F8
Princes Gate HP13 . . . . .173 D6
Princes Gdns HP27 . . . . .139 B3
Princes Pl HP27 . . . . . . .139 B2
Princes Rd SL8 . . . . .185 C3
Princes Risborough Prim Sch
  HP27 . . . . .139 B5
Princes Risborough Sch
  HP27 . . . . .139 C2
Princes Risborough Sta
  HP27 . . . . .138 F2
Princes St
  Piddington HP14 . . . . . . .160 B1
  2 Slough HP14 . . . . . . .206 B4
Princes Terr SL6 . . . . . . .185 C3
Princes Way SL6 . . . . . . .58 C8
Princes Way Rdbt SL6 . . .58 B8
Princess Ave SL4 . . . . . .210 D4
Princess Margaret Hospl The
  SL4 . . . . .210 D5
Princess St SL6 . . . . .202 F6
Printers End HP19 . . . . . .101 B1
Prior Gr HP5 . . . . .144 C1
Priors Cl Maidenhead SL6 .203 B2
  8 Slough SL3 . . . . . . .206 A3
Priors Pk MK4 . . . . .46 D2
Priors Rd SL4 . . . . .209 D4
Priors Way SL6 . . . . .203 B2
Priors Way Ind Est SL6 .203 B2
Priory Ave
  High Wycombe HP13 . . . .173 B7
  South Harefield UB9 . . . .190 C7
Priory Cl Aylesbury HP19 .101 C2
  Denham UB9 . . . . .190 A1
  Horton-cum-S OX33 . . . .108 B5
  Newport Pagnell MK16 . .22 C4
  South Harefield UB9 . . . .190 C7
Priory Common Fst Sch
  MK13 . . . . .34 B6
Priory Cres HP19 . . . . . . .101 C2
Priory Cres HP19 . . . . . .101 C2
Priory Ct **2** HP4 . . . . . . .135 C4
Priory Farm Cotts OX27 . .71 C2
Priory Gdns
  Berkhamsted HP4 . . . . . .135 C4
  South Harefield UB9 . . . .190 C7
Priory Ho
  Gerrards Cross SL9 . . . . .188 D8
  High Wycombe HP13 . . . .173 B7
  Slough SL1 . . . . .204 C8
Priory St MK16 . . . . .22 E4
Priory Way
  Datchet SL3 . . . . .211 B7
  Gerrards Cross SL9 . . . . .188 D8
  Harmondsworth UB7 . . .213 D2
Pritchard Ct MK4 . . . . . . .34 E8
Proctor Rise MK8 . . . . . . .45 D6
Progress Bsns Ctr SL1 . .204 D7
Progress Rd HP12 . . . . . .172 B7
Promenade SL4 . . . . .210 C7
Prospect Cl MK17 . . . . . . .68 D6
Prospect Cotts HP14 . . .161 D6
Prospect Ct
  Lane End HP14 . . . . .171 B5
  Yardley Gobion NN12 . . . . .18 F6
Prospect Pl
  Castlethorpe MK19 . . . . . .19 F5
  Hurley SL6 . . . . .193 F3
  3 Windsor SL4 . . . . . . .210 D4
  Wing LU7 . . . . .79 E2
Prospect Rd Marlow SL7 .183 D2
  Milton Keynes MK12 . . . . .32 C5
Protheroe Field MK7 . . . .48 D4
Providence Pl
  9 Maidenhead SL6 . . . .202 F7
  Milton Keynes MK13 . . . . .34 A4
Providence Rd UB7 . . . . .208 F5
Prudential Bldgs **1** SL5 .204 F4
Pudseys Cl SL6 . . . . .195 F6
Puers Field HP9 . . . . .176 E4
Puers La HP9 . . . . .176 E4
Puffin Way HP19 . . . . . . .101 F3
Pulborough Cl MK3 . . . . .46 D1
Pulford Rd LU7 . . . . .80 F6
Pulfields HP5 . . . . .144 A1
Pulpit Cl HP5 . . . . .144 A2
Pulpit La HP22 . . . . .76 D1
Pursers Ct SL2 . . . . .205 E7
Pursell Cl SL6 . . . . .202 A3
Pursell Pl HP27 . . . . .139 B5
Pursells Mdw HP14 . . . . .161 C2
Purton Ct SL2 . . . . .198 C5
Purton La SL2 . . . . .198 C5
Pury Rd Alderton NN12 . .17 B2
  Paulerspury NN12 . . . . . .17 D8

Pusey Way HP14 . . . . . . .171 C5
Putlowes Dr HP18 . . . . . .100 C3
Putman Ho MK5 . . . . .46 C5
Putman Pl RG9 . . . . .191 E1
Putnams Dr HP22 . . . . . .117 D5
Puttenham Ct HP23 . . . .103 F2
Puxley Rd MK19 . . . . .31 D5
Pyebush La HP9 . . . . . . .187 A8
Pyghtle The Olney MK46 . . .6 F3
  Wendover HP22 . . . . .8 E6
Pyghtles The HP22 . . . . . .85 B5
Pyke Hayes MK8 . . . . .33 D3
Pym Wlk OX9 . . . . .125 F1
Pymcombe Cl HP27 . . . .139 B5
Pynefield Ho WD3 . . . . . .167 F2
Pyxe Cl MK7 . . . . .48 A4

Q

Quadrangle The HP13 . .173 E7
Quadrans Cl MK15 . . . . . .35 A7
Quadrant The
  High Wycombe HP13 . . . .162 E1
  Maidenhead SL6 . . . . . . .203 A6
Quainton CE Comb Sch
  HP22 . . . . .85 A5
Quainton Rd
  North Marston MK18 . . . . .76 A2
  Waddesdon HP18 . . . . . . .99 A7
Quainton Road Sta*
  HP22 . . . . .84 F2
Quaker's Mead HP22 . . .116 F3
Quakers Mede HP17 . . . .127 A6
Quantock Cl SL3 . . . . . . .207 A1
Quantock Cres MK4 . . . . .46 D2
Quarrendon Ave HP19 . .101 B2
Quarrendon Rd HP7 . . . .165 E7
Quarrendon Upper Sch
  HP19 . . . . .101 C2
Quarry Cl HP15 . . . . .125 C7
Quarry Ct LU7 . . . . .105 D2
Quarry Green Cl MK19 . . .31 B3
Quarry Rd LU7 . . . . .105 D2
Quarry Wood Rd SL6,
  SL7 . . . . .195 A8
Quarrydale Dr SL7 . . . . .183 F2
Quaves Rd SL3 . . . . .206 C3
Quebec Rd HP13 . . . . . . .173 E6
Queen Alexandra Rd
  HP11 . . . . .173 A6
Queen Anne Royal Free CE
  Fst Sch The SL4 . . . . . . .210 D4
Queen Anne St MK13 . . . .33 F7
Queen Anne's Cl **10** SL4 .210 C6
Queen Anne's Rd SL4 . .210 C6
Queen Catherine Rd
  MK18 . . . . .63 E2
Queen Charlotte St **10**
  SL4 . . . . .210 D6
Queen Cl RG9 . . . . .191 E1
Queen Eleanor Combined
  Sch MK11 . . . . .32 F4
Queen Eleanor St MK11 . .32 E6
Queen Elizabeth's Wlk
  SL4 . . . . .210 F5
Queen Mother's Dr UB9 .189 F5
Queen Sq **8** HP11 . . . . .173 A7
Queen St Aylesbury HP20 .116 A8
  Henley-on-T RG9 . . . . . .191 E1
  High Wycombe HP13 . . . .173 C7
  Leighton Buzzard LU7 . . . .80 F8
  Maidenhead SL6 . . . . . . .202 F6
  Milton Keynes MK11 . . . . .32 E6
  Piddington HP14 . . . . . . .160 B1
  Pitstone LU7 . . . . .105 D4
  Tring HP23 . . . . .119 A3
  Waddesdon HP18 . . . . . . .98 F6
Queen Victoria Rd
  HP11 . . . . .173 B6
Queen Victoria's Wlk
  SL4 . . . . .210 F6
Queen's Acre SL4 . . . . . .210 D3
Queen's Cl SL4 . . . . .211 A2
Queen's Ct SL1 . . . . .205 E6
Queen's Dr SL3 . . . . .199 F4
Queen's Dr The WD3 . . .167 F2
Queen's Gate SL4 . . . . . .211 B2
Queen's Pk HP21 . . . . . .115 F8
Queen's Rd Datchet SL3 .211 B7
  Marlow SL7 . . . . .183 D2
  Uxbridge UB8 . . . . .201 C2
  Windsor SL4 . . . . .210 C5
Queen's Terr **8** SL4 . . . .210 D4
Queens Acre
  Berkhamsted HP4 . . . . . .135 A5
  1 Chesham HP5 . . . . . .144 C1
  Eton Wick SL4 . . . . .204 F1
  High Wycombe HP13 . . . .173 C6
  Princes Risborough HP27 .139 C4
  Slough SL1 . . . . .205 F6
  West Drayton UB7 . . . . . .208 F4
Queensbury La MK10 . . . .35 E1
Queensgate HP19 . . . . . .115 A8
Queensmead SL3 . . . . . .211 B6
Queensmead Ho HP10 . .174 C2

Queensmead Rd HP10 . . . . . . .174 C2
Queensmere SL1 . . . . .205 F4
Queensmere Rd SL1 . . . . .205 F4
Queensway Bletchley MK2 . . . .58 C8
  Hazelmere HP15 . . . . .163 A4
  Maidenhead SL6 . . . . .195 E2
  Milton Keynes MK2 . . . . .58 D8
Queensway The SL9 . . . . .188 D7
Quickberry Pl HP7 . . . . .165 C8
Quickley La WD3 . . . . .167 C3
Quickley Rise WD3 . . . . .167 B3
Quickly Brow WD3 . . . . .167 B3
Quill Hall La HP6 . . . . .154 F2
Quilter Mdw MK7 . . . . .48 D5
Quilters Way HP22 . . . . .130 D8
Quinbrookes SL2 . . . . .206 C7
Quince Cl MK7 . . . . .48 B5
Quinton Dr MK13 . . . . .34 B3
Quoiting Sq SL7 . . . . .183 D2
Quoitings Dr SL7 . . . . .183 C2
Quoitings Gdns SL7 . . . . .183 C2

R

Raans Rd HP6 . . . . .154 F1
Rabans Cl HP19 . . . . .100 E1
Rabans La HP19 . . . . .100 E1
Rabbs Mill Ho UB8 . . . . .201 D3
Rabbsfarm Prim Sch
  UB7 . . . . .208 E6
Rachels Way HP5 . . . . .154 D5
Rackstraw Gr MK7 . . . . .48 D5
Radcliffe Sch The MK12 . . . . .33 B6
Radcliffe St MK12 . . . . .33 D6
Radclive Rd MK18 . . . . .51 F7
Radcot Ave SL3 . . . . .207 B3
Radcot Cl SL6 . . . . .195 E3
Radcote Lodge MK8 . . . . .33 E1
Radian Ct MK5 . . . . .46 C7
Radman Gr MK12 . . . . .33 B5
Radnage CE Inf Sch
  HP14 . . . . .159 D6
Radnage Common Rd
  HP14 . . . . .159 D5
Radnage La HP14 . . . . .148 C2
Radnor End HP20 . . . . .101 E2
Radnor Way SL3 . . . . .206 E2
Radworthy MK4 . . . . .46 C3
Raeside Cl HP9 . . . . .176 C5
Raglan Dr MK4 . . . . .45 E1
Ragmans Cl SL7 . . . . .183 C8
Ragmans La HP10,SL7 . . . . . .172 D1
Ragnall's La OX33 . . . . .108 A6
Ragstone Rd SL1 . . . . .205 E3
Ragstones HP10 . . . . .174 A1
Railway Cotts
  Steeple Claydon MK18 . . . . . .64 A1
  Wigginton HP23 . . . . .119 F5
Railway St ⬛ HP20 . . . . .115 E8
Railway Terr SL2 . . . . .205 F5
Rainborough Gdns
  HP20 . . . . .101 E2
Rainbow Dr MK6 . . . . .46 F7
Rainbow Ind Est UB7 . . . . . . .208 D6
Rainsborough MK14 . . . . .35 A8
Rainsborough Chase
  SL6 . . . . .202 B3
Rake Way HP21 . . . . .115 D5
Raleigh Cl SL1 . . . . .205 A5
Ralphs Retreat HP15 . . . . . . .162 F4
Ralston Ct ⬛ SL4 . . . . .210 D6
Ram Alley MK16 . . . . .12 B6
Rambler Cl SL6 . . . . .204 B7
Rambler La SL3 . . . . .204 C3
Ramsay Cl MK13 . . . . .34 B3
Ramsay View HP15 . . . . .163 A3
Ramscote La HP5 . . . . .143 F7
Ramsey Ct SL2 . . . . .197 D1
Ramsgill Ct MK3 . . . . .34 C5
Ramsons Ave MK14 . . . . .34 E4
Ramsthorn Gr MK7 . . . . .48 B6
Ramworth Way HP21 . . . . . . .116 A6
Randall Cl SL3 . . . . .206 F1
Randall Ct SL4 . . . . .211 A1
Randolph Cl MK13 . . . . .34 A6
Randolph Rd SL3 . . . . .206 E3
Ranelagh Gdns MK16 . . . . . . .22 C2
Rangers Ct MK4 . . . . .33 F1
Rannal Dr OX39 . . . . .147 C6
Rannoch Cl MK2 . . . . .58 D5
Rannock Gdns LU7 . . . . .80 C7
Ranston Cl UB9 . . . . .189 F5
Rashleigh Pl MK6 . . . . .46 E7
Ratcliffe Cl UB8 . . . . .201 D2
Rathbone Cl MK8 . . . . .45 E7
Ravel Cl MK7 . . . . .48 D6
Raven Cl ⬛ HP19 . . . . .101 E3
Raven Cres HP18 . . . . .98 C6
Raven Rd HP14 . . . . .158 F4
Ravens Ct
  Berkhamsted HP4 . . . . .135 E6
  High Wycombe HP13 . . . . . . .161 E3
Ravens Field SL3 . . . . .206 D4
Ravens La HP4 . . . . .135 D4
Ravens Wharf HP4 . . . . .135 D4
Ravensbourne Pl MK6 . . . . . . .35 B2
Ravensbourne Rd HP21 . .115 D4
Ravenscar Ct MK4 . . . . .46 C2
Ravenscourt SL7 . . . . .184 A3
Ravenscroft Rd RG9 . . . . .191 D2
Ravensglass Croft MK10 . .36 B3
Ravenshoe Cl SL8 . . . . .185 A3

Ravensmead
  Chalfont St Peter SL9 . . . . . .177 F5
  Chinnor OX39 . . . . .147 C6
Ravenstone Mill Rd
  MK46 . . . . .12 E7
Ravensworth Rd SL2 . . . . . . .198 A2
Ravigill Pl MK12 . . . . .33 D4
Rawcliffe Ho SL16 . . . . .203 A6
Rawlings La HP9 . . . . .176 D7
Rawlins Rd MK13 . . . . .34 A4
Ray Dr SL6 . . . . .203 B7
Ray Ho ⬛ SL8 . . . . .185 A4
Ray Lea Cl SL6 . . . . .203 B8
Ray Lea Rd SL6 . . . . .203 B8
Ray Lodge SL6 . . . . .203 B7
Ray Lodge Mews SL6 . . . . . .203 B7
Ray Mead Ct SL6 . . . . .196 C1
Ray Mead Rd SL6 . . . . .203 C8
Ray Mill Rd E SL6 . . . . .196 B1
Ray Mill Rd W SL6 . . . . .203 A8
Ray Park Ave SL6 . . . . .203 B8
Ray Park La SL6 . . . . .203 B7
Ray Park Rd SL6 . . . . .203 B8
Ray St SL6 . . . . .203 B7
Ray's Hill HP5 . . . . .133 C2
Rayfield SL6 . . . . .203 B8
Raylands Mead SL3 . . . . .188 C6
Rayleigh Cl MK5 . . . . .46 B6
Raylens HP12 . . . . .172 B5
Raymond Cl SL3 . . . . .212 C6
Raymond Rd
  Maidenhead SL6 . . . . .202 D7
  Slough SL3 . . . . .207 A3
Rayners Ave HP10 . . . . .174 B3
Rayners Cl Colnbrook SL3 . . .212 C7
  Loudwater HP10 . . . . .174 C3
Rayners La MK9 . . . . .35 C1
Rays Ave SL4 . . . . .209 F7
Rays La HP10 . . . . .163 C1
Razzaq Pl HP12 . . . . .172 E7
Read Dr HP22 . . . . .102 C4
Read Ho HP19 . . . . .115 A7
Read La HP5 . . . . .154 C7
Reade Ct SL2 . . . . .198 C6
Reading Cl HP19 . . . . .101 A3
Reading Rd RG9 . . . . .191 E1
Readings The WD3 . . . . .167 F6
Reads La LU7 . . . . .78 D1
Recreation Rd SL8 . . . . .185 B3
Rectory Ave HP13 . . . . .173 C7
Rectory Cl
  Farnham Royal SL2 . . . . .198 C2
  Marsh Gibbon OX27 . . . . .71 F3
  Slapton LU7 . . . . .91 D6
  Windsor SL4 . . . . .210 A6
Rectory Ct
  ⬛ Amersham HP7 . . . . .165 B7
  ⬛ High Wycombe HP13 . . . .173 F5
  Lewknor OX49 . . . . .157 B8
  West Drayton UB7 . . . . .208 E4
Rectory Dr HP18 . . . . .99 A6
Rectory Fields MK15 . . . . .35 D3
Rectory Gdns HP8 . . . . .177 B7
Rectory Hill HP7 . . . . .165 B8
Rectory La
  Amersham HP7 . . . . .165 B7
  Berkhamsted HP4 . . . . .135 C4
  Bix RG9 . . . . .179 D1
  Yardley Hastings NN7 . . . . . . .1 A7
Rectory Mdw OX39 . . . . .147 D6
Rectory Orch MK46 . . . . .7 F8
Rectory Rd SL6 . . . . .196 E1
Rectory Terr SL2 . . . . .198 C3
Red Cottage HP23 . . . . .119 D1
Red Cottage Mews ⬛
  SL3 . . . . .206 C3
Red Ct SL1 . . . . .205 E5
Red House Cl
  Beaconsfield HP9 . . . . .175 B4
  Newton Longville MK17 . . . . . .57 D4
Red Leaf Cl SL3 . . . . .206 F5
Red Leys UB10 . . . . .201 E5
Red Lion Cl MK46 . . . . .25 B1
Red Lion Cotts SL2 . . . . .199 B1
Red Lion Dr HP14 . . . . .158 D5
Red Lion St HP5 . . . . .154 B7
Red Lion Way HP10 . . . . .185 C6
Red Lodge Gdns HP4 . . . . . .135 A3
Red Roofs SL6 . . . . .203 C7
Red Wing HP10 . . . . .101 E3
Redbourne Ct MK11 . . . . .32 F5
Redbridge MK14 . . . . .34 D7
Redcliffe Wlk HP19 . . . . .101 B2
Redcote Manor MK7 . . . . .48 A4
Redding Dr HP6 . . . . .154 A2
Redding Gr MK8 . . . . .45 E6
Reddings Cl HP22 . . . . .131 B6
Reddington Dr SL3 . . . . .206 E2
Redfern Cl UB8 . . . . .201 C4
Redfield Cl LU6 . . . . .93 E8
Redford Rd SL4 . . . . .209 D6
Redford Way UB8 . . . . .201 D5
Redgrave Pl SL7 . . . . .183 F3
Redhill UB9 . . . . .189 D2
Redhouse Ct HP11 . . . . .172 E3
Redhuish Cl MK4 . . . . .46 D3
Redland Cl MK18 . . . . .63 D2
Redland Dr MK5 . . . . .46 C7
Redland Way HP21 . . . . .116 A5
Redman Rd HP22 . . . . .172 B3
Redpitch Pk HP10 . . . . .185 F6
Redriff Cl SL6 . . . . .202 D6
Redshaw Cl MK18 . . . . .41 E1
Redshots Cl SL7 . . . . .183 E4
Redvers Gate HP15 . . . . .35 B7
Redway Sch The MK6 . . . . . . .47 C6
Redwood SL1 . . . . .197 B3

Redwood Cl
  Hazelmere HP15 . . . . .163 B3
  Wing LU7 . . . . .79 E2
Redwood Dr
  Aylesbury HP21 . . . . .115 C7
  Wing LU7 . . . . .79 E2
Redwood Gate MK5 . . . . .46 C4
Redwood Gdns SL1 . . . . .205 D6
Redwood Glade LU7 . . . . .70 F3
Redwood Pl HP9 . . . . .175 D1
Reed Cl SL0 . . . . .207 E7
Reeves Croft MK12 . . . . .33 C4
Reform Rd SL6 . . . . .203 B7
Regal Ct Maidenhead SL6 . . .203 B2
  ⬛ Tring HP23 . . . . .119 A3
Regency Ct HP21 . . . . .116 B7
Regent Ct
  ⬛ Maidenhead SL6 . . . . . . .202 F7
  Slough SL1 . . . . .205 E7
Regent Ho HP27 . . . . .139 B4
Regent Rd HP21 . . . . .116 B7
Regent St MK2 . . . . .58 C8
Regents Hall MK11 . . . . .32 E5
Regents Pl SL6 . . . . .202 D6
Regius Ct HP10 . . . . .174 D8
Reid Ave SL6 . . . . .202 E5
Reliance La MK9 . . . . .35 B3
Rembrandt End HP19 . . . . . . .100 F2
Remenham Church La
  RG9 . . . . .192 A4
Remenham La
  Remenham RG9 . . . . .192 B5
  Remenham Hill RG9 . . . . . . .191 F3
Remenham Row RG9 . . . . . . .191 F2
Remenham Terr RG9 . . . . . . .192 C2
Remus Gate MK13 . . . . .38 A6
Rendlesham MK15 . . . . .35 C3
Rendlesham Way WD3 . . . . . .167 C3
Renfrew Way MK3 . . . . .46 F3
Rennie Cl HP13 . . . . .161 F1
Repton Cl SL6 . . . . .202 C3
Repton Pl HP7 . . . . .166 A8
Ringstead Way HP21 . . . . . . .116 A5
Retreat La HP14 . . . . .148 D2
Retreat The
  Little Chalfont HP6 . . . . .166 E8
  Milton Keynes MK11 . . . . .32 D5
  Princes Risborough HP27 . . .139 B4
Revel Rd HP10 . . . . .185 D8
Revesby Cl SL6 . . . . .202 D3
Reyners Gn HP16 . . . . .152 B4
Reynold Dr HP20 . . . . .102 A2
Reynolds Cl
  Cranfield MK43 . . . . .24 E2
  High Wycombe HP13 . . . . . . .173 E8
Reynolds Pl MK8 . . . . .45 D6
Reynolds Rd HP9 . . . . .175 D3
Reynolds Wlk HP5 . . . . .144 A4
Rhodes Pl MK6 . . . . .46 E7
Rhondda Cl MK1 . . . . .47 F8
Rhondda Dr MK3 . . . . .57 C8
Rhuddlan Cl MK5 . . . . .45 F7
Rhymer Cl MK19 . . . . .10 F4
Ribble Cl MK16 . . . . .22 C4
Ribble Cres MK3 . . . . .57 D8
Ribstone Rd SL6 . . . . .202 B3
Ricardo Rd SL4 . . . . .211 B1
Richard Gdns HP13 . . . . .173 E8
Richards Way SL1 . . . . .204 F5
Richardson Pl ⬛ MK4 . . . . . .34 E1
Richborough MK13 . . . . .34 A6
Richings Way SL0 . . . . .207 F3
Richmond Cl
  Amersham HP6 . . . . .154 F1
  Milton Keynes MK3 . . . . .46 D1
Richmond Cres SL1 . . . . .206 A5
Richmond Ct HP13 . . . . .173 C7
Richmond Rd HP10 . . . . .116 C2
Richmond Way MK16 . . . . .22 D3
Rick Yd The MK16 . . . . .13 F1
Rickard Cl
  Aylesbury HP21 . . . . .115 D3
  West Drayton UB7 . . . . .208 D3
Rickford's Hill HP20 . . . . .115 D8
Rickley La MK3 . . . . .58 A8
Rickley Mid Sch MK3 . . . . . . .57 F8
Rickman Wlk HP19 . . . . .115 A7
Rickman's La SL2 . . . . .198 E6
Rickmansworth La SL9 . . . . .177 B4
Rickmansworth Rd
  Amersham HP6 . . . . .154 C2
  Chorleywood WD3 . . . . .167 F6
Rickyard Cl
  Milton Keynes MK13 . . . . .34 A4
  Whitchurch HP22 . . . . .87 A7
Rickyard Gr HP18 . . . . .83 B5
Rickyard The MK46 . . . . .7 C3
Ride The LU6 . . . . .93 B6
Riders Way OX39 . . . . .147 C6
Ridge Cl Aylesbury HP21 . . . .115 F6
  Lane End HP14 . . . . .171 C4
Ridge Ct SL4 . . . . .210 C4
Ridge Side HP14 . . . . .160 A8
Ridge View HP14 . . . . .119 C5
Ridge Way
  High Wycombe HP13 . . . . . . .162 C1
  Iver SL0 . . . . .207 C7
  Long Crendon HP18 . . . . . . .125 F4
Ridgebank SL1 . . . . .204 F6
Ridgemount End SL9 . . . . . . .177 E5
Ridgeway
  Berkhamsted HP4 . . . . .134 F4
  ⬛ High Wycombe HP11 . . . .173 A6
  Milton Keynes,Stony Stratford
    MK11 . . . . .32 F4
  Milton Keynes,Wolverton Mill
    MK12 . . . . .33 A5

Ridgeway continued
  Wing LU7 . . . . .79 E3
Ridgeway Cl
  Chesham HP5 . . . . .144 B3
Ridgeway Ct SL7 . . . . .183 E4
Ridgeway Cl ⬛ HP20 . . . . . .101 E1
Ridgeway Meads HP27 . . . . . .138 B2
Ridgeway Rd HP5 . . . . .144 B3
Ridgeway The
  Amersham HP7 . . . . .165 E7
  Gerrards Cross SL9 . . . . . . .188 D8
  Marlow SL7 . . . . .183 E4
Ridgeway Trad Est The
  SL0 . . . . .207 E6
Ridgewood RG9 . . . . .181 C1
Ridgmont MK19 . . . . .31 E5
Ridgmont Cl MK19 . . . . .31 E5
Ridgway MK17 . . . . .49 B6
Riding Court Rd SL3 . . . . .211 D7
Riding Ct SL3 . . . . .211 C8
Riding La HP9,HP10 . . . . .174 F3
Riding The MK19 . . . . .31 E5
Ridings Cotts HP15 . . . . .163 D6
Ridings The
  Amersham HP6 . . . . .154 D4
  Iver SL0 . . . . .207 F2
  Latimer HP5 . . . . .155 D3
  Maidenhead SL6 . . . . .202 A7
Ridings Way LU7 . . . . .78 B1
Rigby Lodge SL1 . . . . .205 E7
Rignall Rd HP16 . . . . .151 E8
Riley Cl HP20 . . . . .115 C8
Riley Rd SL7 . . . . .183 D2
Rillington Gdns MK14 . . . . . . .46 B5
Rimmington Way HP19 . . . . . .101 B1
Rimsdale Cl MK2 . . . . .58 D3
Ring Rd HP10 . . . . .173 F2
Ring Rd E MK7 . . . . .47 F7
Ring Rd N MK7 . . . . .47 F7
Ring Rd W MK7 . . . . .47 E7
Ringshall Dr HP4 . . . . .121 C8
Ringshall Rd HP4 . . . . .107 B3
Ripon Ho HP21 . . . . .115 F6
Ripon St ⬛ HP20 . . . . .101 D1
Risborough Rd
  Great Kimble HP17,HP27 . . . .139 E8
  Maidenhead SL6 . . . . .202 E8
  Stoke Mandeville HP17 . . . . .130 B7
Rise Hag Hill SL6 . . . . .204 A7
Rise The Amersham HP7 . . . .165 C8
  Gawcott MK18 . . . . .51 F4
  Hazelmere HP15 . . . . .163 A5
  Loudwater HP13 . . . . .174 B4
  Uxbridge UB10 . . . . .201 F3
Riseley Rd SL6 . . . . .202 D7
Risings The HP13 . . . . .162 B1
River & Rowing Mus*
  RG9 . . . . .191 F1
River Cl MK16 . . . . .22 C4
River Ct SL6 . . . . .203 C7
River Gdns SL6 . . . . .203 D4
River Park Ind Est HP4 . . . . .135 A5
River Rd SL6 . . . . .203 C6
River Side MK16 . . . . .22 D4
River St SL4 . . . . .210 D7
River View HP10 . . . . .185 B7
River Wlk UB9 . . . . .201 C6
Riverbank Point UB8 . . . . . . .201 C6
Riverbank The SL4 . . . . .210 B7
Rivercrest Rd MK19 . . . . .32 B6
Rivermead Ct SL7 . . . . .194 E8
Riverpark Dr SL7 . . . . .183 F1
Rivers Edge HP11 . . . . .174 A3
Rivers First Sch MK3 . . . . . . .46 E1
Riverdale SL8 . . . . .185 B1
Riverdale Cotts SL8 . . . . .185 B1
Riverdale Ct SL8 . . . . .185 A1
Riverside SL7 . . . . .183 D1
Riverside Bsns Ctr
  HP11 . . . . .172 F7
Riverside Cotts
  West Drayton UB7 . . . . .208 C1
  Wooburn Green HP10 . . . . . .185 E8
Riverside Cvn Pk UB7 . . .208 C3
Riverside First Sch MK16 . .22 C3
Riverside Gdns HP4 . . . . .135 A5
Riverside Mews MK18 . . . . . . .52 D8
Riverside Pk SL3 . . . . .212 E5
Riverside Pl TW19 . . . . .213 E1
Riverside Way UB8 . . . . .201 B4
Riverside Wlk SL4 . . . . .210 D7
Riverswood Gdns HP11 . . . . .174 B3
Riverway SL4 . . . . .184 A1
Riverwood Ave SL7 . . . . .184 A1
Riverwoods Dr SL7 . . . . .184 A1
Rivets Cl HP21 . . . . .115 E6
Rivetts Cl MK17 . . . . .6 E4
Rixband Cl MK7 . . . . .48 B4
Rixman Cl SL6 . . . . .202 D5
Rixon Cl SL3 . . . . .206 F7
Rixons Mdw HP19 . . . . .115 B7
Roade Hill NN7 . . . . .9 F8
Robert Rd SL2 . . . . .187 D2
Robert's Dr HP19 . . . . .101 D2
Roberts Cl
  Deanshanger MK19 . . . . .31 E4
  Stanwell TW19 . . . . .213 C1
  West Drayton UB7 . . . . .208 D3
Roberts La SL9 . . . . .178 B5
Roberts Rd
  Haddenham HP17 . . . . .127 B6

Roberts Rd continued
  High Wycombe HP13 . . . . . . .173 B8
Roberts Ride HP15 . . . . .163 A5
Roberts Wood Dr SL9 . . . . . .177 F5
Robertson Cl MK5 . . . . .45 F7
Robertson Cnr LU6 . . . . .93 F4
Robertson Rd ⬛ HP4 . . . . . .135 D4
Robertswood Comb Sch
  SL9 . . . . .177 F3
Robeson Pl MK8 . . . . .45 E8
Robin Cl Aylesbury HP19 . . . .101 F3
  Buckingham MK18 . . . . .52 F7
  Great Kingshill HP15 . . . . . . .151 D1
Robin Hill HP4 . . . . .135 C3
Robin Ho HP11 . . . . .174 A4
Robin Hood Cl SL1 . . . . .204 F5
Robin Par ⬛ SL2 . . . . .198 C7
Robin Willis Way SL4 . . . . . . .211 A1
Robins Cl
  High Wycombe HP12 . . . . . . .172 D3
  Uxbridge UB8 . . . . .208 C8
Robins Hill MK6 . . . . .47 A6
Robins Orch SL9 . . . . .177 E4
Robins Platt OX39 . . . . .147 B6
Robinson Cl HP19 . . . . .100 F3
Robinson Ct SL6 . . . . .202 E4
Robinson Rd HP13 . . . . .174 B4
Robinswood Cl
  Beaconsfield HP9 . . . . .175 C5
  Leighton Buzzard LU7 . . . . . .70 F2
Robinwood Gr UB8 . . . . .201 F1
Roblin Cl HP21 . . . . .115 E4
Robson Cl SL9 . . . . .177 E5
Robson Ct ⬛ HP14 . . . . .152 A8
Roche Gdns MK3 . . . . .58 A8
Rochester Ct MK5 . . . . .46 A5
Rochester Mews LU7 . . . . . . .80 E6
Rochester Pl HP19 . . . . .115 B8
Rochford Way SL6 . . . . .204 A7
Rochfords MK6 . . . . .46 F6
Rochfords Gdns SL2 . . . . . . .206 C5
Rock Cl LU7 . . . . .80 D6
Rock La LU7 . . . . .80 D7
Rockall Ct SL3 . . . . .207 B3
Rockingham Cl
  Pitstone LU7 . . . . .105 D3
  Uxbridge UB8 . . . . .201 C4
Rockingham Dr MK14 . . . . . . .34 E6
Rockingham Par UB8 . . . . . . .201 C4
Rockingham Pl HP9 . . . . .175 F1
Rockingham Rd UB8 . . . . . . .201 C4
Rockingham Wharf UB8 . . . . .201 B4
Rocklane Farm LU7 . . . . .79 F7
Rockleigh Ct ⬛ LU7 . . . . . . .80 E7
Rockspray Gr MK7 . . . . .48 B5
Rodney Way SL3 . . . . .212 E6
Rodwell Gdns MK7 . . . . .48 D4
Rodwell Yd ⬛ HP23 . . . . . . .119 A3
Roebuck Ave HP13 . . . . .173 F6
Roebuck Gn SL1 . . . . .204 E5
Roebuck Way MK5 . . . . .46 C6
Roeburn Cres MK4 . . . . .46 C1
Rogers Croft MK6 . . . . .47 D7
Rogers La SL2 . . . . .199 E4
Roker Park Ave UB10 . . . . . .201 E8
Rokesby Rd SL2 . . . . .197 F2
Rolfe Cl HP9 . . . . .175 E1
Rolvenden Gr MK7 . . . . .48 B7
Roman Lea SL6 . . . . .195 F7
Roman Pl SL6 . . . . .202 C6
Roman Way
  Aylesbury HP19 . . . . .115 B8
  Bourne End SL8 . . . . .185 B4
  Brackley NN13 . . . . .38 A7
Romans Field Sch MK3 . . . . . .46 E1
Rombold Ct MK1 . . . . .47 C2
Romney Ct ⬛ SL7 . . . . .183 F3
Romney Lock Rd SL4 . . . . . . .210 D7
Romney Rd HP21 . . . . .115 E4
Romsey Cl SL3 . . . . .206 F3
Romsey Dr SL2 . . . . .187 D3
Romsey Way HP11 . . . . .173 B4
Romulus Way NN13 . . . . .38 A6
Ronald Rd HP9 . . . . .175 F2
Ronaldsay Spur SL1 . . . . .205 E8
Rook Rd HP10 . . . . .185 D4
Rook Tree Farm Ind Est
  MK17 . . . . .37 F3
Rook Wood Way HP16 . . . . . .152 B5
Rookery Ct SL7 . . . . .183 D2
Rookery Mdw HP15 . . . . .163 C7
Rookery Way MK18 . . . . .63 F3
Rooks Terr UB7 . . . . .208 E4
Rooksley Rdbt MK13 . . . . .34 B3
Ropa Ct ⬛ LU7 . . . . .80 F7
Rosamund's Cotts HP18 . . . . .83 B2
Rosary The HP15 . . . . .163 C7
Rose Ave Aylesbury HP19 . . .101 E2
  Hazelmere HP15 . . . . .163 B2
Rose Bsns Est SL7 . . . . .183 D5
Rose Cnr HP14 . . . . .158 E5
Rose Cotts SL6 . . . . .202 C3
Rose Ct Amersham HP6 . . . . .154 D2
  Chesham HP5 . . . . .154 C6
  Eaton Bray LU6 . . . . .92 D6
  Olney MK46 . . . . .6 F3
Rose Dr SL7 . . . . .154 D2
Rose Hill SL1 . . . . .197 A5
Rose La RG9 . . . . .193 A1
Rose Terr HP18 . . . . .99 A6
Rose Wlk SL2 . . . . .205 B8
Roseary Cl UB7 . . . . .208 D2
Rosebank Cl SL6 . . . . .195 E7
Rosebank Cotts HP10 . . . . . .174 B3
Rosebarn La HP23 . . . . .104 D1
Rosebay Cl MK7 . . . . .48 B5

Ros – St P 243

Rosebery Ave
High Wycombe HP13 .....173 E5
Leighton Buzzard LU7 .....80 E7
Rosebery Cl MK18 .....77 B7
Rosebery Ct 4 LU7 .....87 B1
Rosebery Mews LU7 .....90 D4
Rosecomb Pl MK5 .....46 A4
Rosehill HP4 .....135 B4
Rosehill Cres MK18 .....62 D1
Rosehill Ct SL1 .....206 A3
Roseleigh Cl SL6 .....202 A7
Rosemary Cl HP22 .....161 B1
Rosemary Ct
High Wycombe HP12 .....161 B1
Walton MK7 .....48 A5
Rosemary Rd HP22 .....127 A7
Rosemead HP22 .....117 C8
Rosemoor Mews HP19 .....114 F8
Rosemullion Ave MK4 .....57 B8
Rosery The 5 SL8 .....185 A3
Roses Cl LU7 .....78 B1
Roses La SL4 .....209 D5
Rosetree Cl HP16 .....151 C6
Rosewood Gdns HP12 .....172 C4
Rosewood Way SL2 .....198 C2
Rosken Gr SL2 .....198 B3
Roslyn Ct MK15 .....35 D7
Ross Rd
Aston Abbotts HP22 .....88 D5
Maidenhead SL6 .....202 E4
Ross Way MK3 .....46 F2
Rossal Pl MK12 .....33 D4
Rossendale MK14 .....34 D7
Rossetti Pl HP15 .....163 C7
Rossini Pl MK7 .....48 D5
Rossiter Cl SL3 .....206 D1
Rossway La HP4 .....134 A7
Rostrevor Gdns SL0 .....200 D3
Rothersthorpe MK14 .....35 A8
Rothesay Cl HP20 .....101 E1
Rothesay Ct HP4 .....135 A4
Rothschild Ave HP22 .....117 E5
Rothschild Rd
Leighton Buzzard LU7 .....80 F8
Wing LU7 .....79 E2
Rotten Row MK17 .....59 C2
Roughwood La HP8 .....166 E3
Round Hill HP17 .....114 D5
Round Wood Rd HP6 .....125 F1
Roundhead Dr OX9 .....125 F5
Roundheads End HP9 .....175 B4
Roundhill Ct HP17 .....126 E8
Roundlands HP27 .....149 E6
Roundwood Rd HP12 .....172 C7
Rouse Ct SL9 .....188 F6
Routs Gn HP14 .....148 D2
Roveley Ct MK11 .....32 F5
Row The Chicheley HP5 .....133 D2
Cold Brayfield MK46 .....8 B6
Lane End HP14 .....171 B4
Newton Blossomville MK43 .....8 B3
Winchmore Hill HP7 .....164 C3
Rowan Ave HP13 .....173 D8
Rowan Cl Aylesbury HP21 .....115 E4
Beaconsfield HP9 .....175 B1
Hazlemere HP15 .....163 A3
Rowan Ho 1 SL8 .....185 A4
Rowan Gdns SL0 .....200 C3
Rowan Pl HP6 .....154 F1
Rowan Rd SL7 .....208 E2
Rowan Way SL2 .....205 B8
Rowan Wlk HP5 .....144 B1
Rowanhurst Dr SL2 .....198 C7
Rowans The SL9 .....188 D8
Rowborough Rd HP22 .....131 D7
Rowland Cl SL4 .....209 D4
Rowland Ho HP9 .....175 F1
Rowland Way HP19 .....115 B7
Rowlands Cl MK2 .....58 E8
Rowle Cl MK14 .....34 E7
Rowley Furrows LU7 .....80 D8
Rowley La SL3 .....199 D4
Rowlheys Pl UB7 .....208 E3
Rowliff Rd HP12 .....172 C6
Rowsham Dell MK14 .....21 F2
Rowsham Rd HP22 .....102 C5
Rowom Heath MK5 .....45 C5
Roxburgh Way MK3 .....46 F3
Roxhill Rd MK43 .....25 F3
Roxwell Cl SL1 .....204 E5
Roxwell Path 5 HP20 .....101 F2
Royal Buckinghamshire
Hospl HP19 .....101 D1
Royal Cl UB7,UB8 .....208 F7
Royal Cotts
Cookham Dean SL6 .....195 C7
Winchmore Hill HP7 .....164 C2
Royal Ct HP23 .....119 C5
Royal Free Ct 18 SL4 .....210 D6
Royal Gram Sch The
HP13 .....162 C1
Royal La UB8 .....201 F1
Royal Latin Sch MK18 .....52 D7
Royal Mans RG9 .....191 E1
Royal Mead HP17 .....130 C5
Royal Windsor Race Course
SL4 .....209 E7
Royce Cl LU6 .....93 F7
Royce Rd MK43 .....24 D3
Royston Way SL1 .....177 F3
Royston Way SL1 .....204 D8
Rubbra Cl MK7 .....48 C8
Rubens Cl HP19 .....100 F2
Ruby Cl SL1 .....205 A4
Ruckles Way HP7 .....165 C7

Rudchesters MK13 .....33 F5
Rudd's La HP17 .....127 A7
Ruddlesway SL4 .....209 D6
Rudds Cl MK18 .....66 A5
Rudsworth Cl SL3 .....212 D7
Ruffle Cl UB7 .....208 E4
Rugby Rise HP11 .....174 A3
Rugwood Rd HP10 .....173 F2
Rumptons Paddock HP18 .....82 F6
Run Furrow HP17 .....127 A7
Runford Ct MK5 .....46 C5
Runnymede MK14 .....21 F2
Runrig Hill HP6 .....154 E4
Rupert Ave HP12 .....172 E4
Rupert Cl RG9 .....191 E3
Rupert House Sch RG9 .....191 E2
Rupert's La HP13 .....191 E3
Rupert Way OX9 .....126 A1
Ruscombe Gdns SL3 .....211 A7
Ruscote HP4 .....135 A3
Rushall Rd OX9 .....126 A1
Rushbeds Wood Nature
Reserve* MK18 .....96 C4
Rushbrooke Cl HP13 .....162 F2
Rushburn HP10 .....185 F6
Rushendon Furlong
LU7 .....105 E5
Rushes Mead UB8 .....201 C4
Rushes The
Maidenhead SL6 .....203 C6
Marlow SL7 .....194 C8
Rushfields Cl MK4 .....45 F1
Rushington Ave SL6 .....202 F5
Rushleys Cl MK5 .....46 A8
Rushmere Cl MK17 .....48 D2
Rushmere La HP5 .....145 B3
Rushmere Ret Pk MK1 .....47 D2
Rushmoor Ave HP15 .....163 B3
Rushton Ct 5 MK8 .....45 F8
Ruskin Ct MK16 .....22 C2
Ruskin Way HP20 .....101 D2
Rusland Cir MK4 .....46 C2
Russel Ct HP14 .....161 C8
Russell Ave HP11 .....115 C6
Russell Cl
Little Chalfont HP6 .....166 D8
Tylers Green HP10 .....163 B1
Russell Ct
Aylesbury HP21 .....115 E6
Chesham HP5 .....144 D2
Maidenhead SL6 .....202 F7
Wendover HP22 .....131 B5
Russell Dr TW19 .....213 D1
Russell Fst Sch MK11 .....32 D5
Russell Ho 4 SL8 .....185 A4
Russell Sch The WD3 .....167 B5
Russell St
Milton Keynes MK11 .....32 D5
Windsor SL4 .....210 D6
Woburn Sands MK17 .....49 B4
Russet Cl TW19 .....212 F1
Russet Rd SL6 .....202 C3
Russets The SL9 .....177 D1
Russett Hill SL9 .....188 E8
Russwell La MK17 .....59 C6
Rustics Cl MK18 .....73 B5
Rustlings Gate HP14 .....171 C5
Rutherford Cl
Uxbridge UB8 .....201 F1
Windsor SL4 .....209 F6
Rutherford Gate MK5 .....46 C5
Rutherford Rd HP21 .....115 E4
Ruthven Cl MK4 .....58 C4
Rutland Ave
High Wycombe HP12 .....172 D6
Slough SL1 .....205 C8
Rutland Ct 2 HP11 .....173 A6
Rutland Gate SL6 .....202 C6
Rutland Ho 3 MK3 .....46 F1
Rutland Pl SL6 .....202 C6
Rutland Rd SL6 .....202 D6
Rutland St HP11 .....173 A6
Ryans Mount SL7 .....183 C2
Rycote La OX9 .....136 D5
Rycote Lane Ind Est
OX9 .....136 C4
Rycroft Milton Keynes MK4 .....46 B3
Windsor SL4 .....209 F4
Rydal Way
High Wycombe HP12 .....172 B5
Milton Keynes MK2 .....58 D5
Ryder Cl HP3 .....146 A4
Ryding The MK5 .....46 A4
Rydings SL4 .....209 F4
Rye Cl Aylesbury HP21 .....115 D4
Rye Rd SL6 .....202 A4
Rye Ct SL1 .....206 A4
Rye The LU6,LU7 .....92 B8
Rye View HP13 .....173 A4
Ryecote Chapel* OX9 .....136 D6
Ryecroft Rd HP5 .....154 A7
Ryefield Terr SL3 .....212 D7
Ryeland MK11 .....32 E6
Ryeland UB7 .....208 E7
Ryemead Way HP11 .....173 F4
Rylstone Cl
Maidenhead SL6 .....202 C3
Milton Keynes MK13 .....34 B3
Ryman Cl WD3 .....167 C3
Rymill Cl HP3 .....146 A3
Ryton Pl MK4 .....46 C3
Ryvers End SL3 .....206 F3
Ryvers Prim Sch SL3 .....206 D3
Ryvers Rd SL3 .....206 F3

S

Sabina Cl HP12 .....172 E6
Sacred Heart RC Prim Sch
The RG9 .....191 D1
Saddington MK6 .....47 D6
Saddlers Cl MK4 .....35 A5
Sadleirs Gn MK17 .....49 B5
Sadlers Mews SL6 .....203 B7
Saffron Cl SL3 .....211 B6
Saffron Ct HP13 .....173 C6
Saffron Rd HP13 .....173 C6
Saffron Rise LU6 .....92 E6
Saffron St MK2 .....58 D7
Saham Croft Cl MK18 .....65 E4
Sailing Club Rd SL8 .....185 A3
Saint-Cloud Way SL6 .....203 A7
St Abbs Ct MK4 .....56 F8
St Adrian's Cl SL6 .....202 B4
St Agnes Gate
Wendover HP22 .....131 A5
Wendover HP22 .....131 A5
St Aidan's Cl MK3 .....57 E6
St Alban's Rd MK18 .....65 F4
St Alban's St 7 SL4 .....210 D6
St Albans Ct 6 SL4 .....210 D6
St Andrew's Ave SL4 .....209 F5
St Andrew's CE Fst Sch
MK14 .....34 E8
St Andrew's CE Prim Sch
Chinnor OX39 .....147 C7
Uxbridge UB8 .....201 D4
St Andrew's Cl
High Wycombe HP13 .....162 F1
Old Windsor SL4 .....211 A1
Wraysbury TW19 .....211 E1
St Andrew's Cres SL4 .....209 F5
St Andrew's Rd
Chinnor OX39 .....147 C5
Milton Keynes MK3 .....57 E7
Uxbridge UB10 .....201 E5
St Andrews Cotts 1
SL4 .....210 A5
St Andrews Ct
Colnbrook SL3 .....212 D7
2 Slough SL1 .....205 E3
St Andrews Ho OX39 .....147 C6
St Andrews Way SL1 .....204 D6
St Andrews Way Ind Est
HP19 .....101 C1
St Ann's Cl HP10 .....174 C2
St Ann's Ct HP10 .....174 C2
St Anne's Cl
Henley-on-T RG9 .....191 D1
Wendover HP22 .....131 B5
St Anthony's Cl HP19 .....115 B8
St Anthony's Cl HP9 .....186 C8
St Anthony's Pl MK4 .....57 B8
St Anthony's RC Prim Sch
SL2 .....198 C1
St Augustine's RC Prim Sch
HP11 .....173 A4
St Bartholomew's CE Sch
HP23 .....119 D1
St Bartholomews MK10 .....36 A1
St Bees MK10 .....36 B1
St Bernard's Convent Sch
SL3 .....206 C4
St Bernard's Prep Sch
SL1 .....206 B4
St Bernard's RC Sch
HP11 .....173 A4
St Bernards Rd HP13 .....173 C6
St Bernards Rd SL3 .....206 C3
St Birinus HP10 .....174 A2
St Botolphs 2 MK10 .....36 B1
St Brides Cl MK12 .....35 C2
St Catherine RC Prim Sch
UB7 .....208 E3
St Catherine's Ave MK3 .....57 D6
St Catherine's Ct 1 SL4 .....210 A5
St Catherines Ct 3 SL4 .....210 A5
St Chad's Rd SL6 .....202 B4
St Christopher Rd UB8 .....208 D8
St Christopher's Cl
HP16 .....152 B3
St Christophers Ct WD3 .....167 D5
St Clement Cl UB8 .....208 D7
St Clement Danes Sch
WD3 .....167 D7
St Clement's Dr MK3 .....57 D6
St Columba's Cl SL6 .....202 B4
St David's Cl UB8 .....208 D8
St David's Cl
Iver Heath SL0 .....200 D4
Maidenhead SL6 .....202 A4
St David's St NN13 .....38 A8
St David's Par SL0 .....200 D4
St David's Rd MK3 .....57 D6
St Dunstans MK6 .....47 A6
St Edmund Campion RC Prim
Sch SL6 .....202 B5
St Edmund's Cl HP19 .....115 B8
St Edmunds MK6 .....135 C3
St Edward's RC Fst Sch
SL4 .....210 A6
St Edward's RC Jun Sch
HP21 .....116 A7
St Edward's Royal Free
Ecumenical Mid Sch
SL4 .....210 A6
St Edwards Ct MK14 .....34 F7
St Elmo Cl SL2 .....198 D1
St Elmo Cres SL2 .....198 D1

St Ethelbert's RC Prim Sch
SL2 .....206 A7
St Faith's Cl MK17 .....57 D3
St Francis de Sales High Sch
HP23 .....118 F3
St Francis Rd
Beacon's Bottom HP14 .....159 D3
Denham Green UB9 .....189 F5
St George's CE Inf Sch
HP7 .....165 E8
St George's Cl
High Wycombe HP13 .....173 D7
Windsor SL4 .....209 E6
St George's Dr UB10 .....190 F1
St George's Rd MK3 .....57 E6
St George's Sch SL4 .....210 D7
St Georges Cres SL1 .....204 D6
St Georges Cl HP12 .....172 D8
St Georges Ind Est HP7 .....165 F8
St Georges Lodge SL6 .....196 B7
St Georges Way 33 D7
St Giles Mews MK11 .....32 D6
St Giles St MK13 .....33 F7
St Govans Cl MK4 .....57 B8
St Helen Cl UB9 .....208 D8
St Helens Gr MK10 .....47 F8
St Hilda's Cl HP19 .....115 B8
St Hilda's Way HP20 .....174 A2
St Huberts Cl SL9 .....188 E2
St Huberts Cotts SL9 .....188 E4
St Huberts La SL9 .....188 F2
St Hugh's Ave HP13 .....173 F6
St Hugh's Cl HP14 .....158 F4
St Hugh's Pl HP14 .....158 F4
St Ives Cres MK4 .....57 B8
St Ives Rd SL6 .....203 A7
St James CE Sch, Akeley
MK18 .....41 F8
St James Cl MK19 .....11 A2
St James Ctyd 8 SL7 .....183 E2
St James Pl SL1 .....204 C7
St James St MK13 .....33 F7
St James Way HP22 .....102 B3
St James Wlk SL0 .....207 E4
St John Rd MK16 .....22 D4
St John's Ave HP10 .....174 B8
St John's CE Comb Sch
HP27 .....149 F4
St John's Cl UB8 .....201 B4
St John's Cres MK12 .....33 D5
St John's La MK19 .....31 A4
St John's Manor Ho
HP15 .....162 E2
St John's Rd
4 Aylesbury HP20 .....101 E1
Hazlemere HP15 .....162 F2
Milton Keynes MK3 .....57 E6
Uxbridge UB8 .....201 B4
St John's St HP20 .....101 E1
St John's Terr MK11 .....22 D4
St John's Well Ct HP4 .....135 B5
St John's Well La HP4 .....135 B5
St Johns Cl HP10 .....163 B1
St Johns Dr Stone HP17 .....114 B5
Windsor SL4 .....210 A5
St Johns La MK18 .....75 F2
St Johns Rd Slough SL2 .....206 A6
Tylers Green HP10 .....163 B1
Windsor SL4 .....210 A5
St Joseph's RC Comb Sch
SL9 .....188 C8
St Joseph's RC High Sch
SL4 .....206 A7
St Joseph's RC Inf Sch
HP21 .....116 A7
St Josephs Cl Aylesbury HP20 .....6 F4
St Josephs Mews HP9 .....175 F2
St Katherine's Way HP4 .....134 F7
St Laurence CE Jun Sch
UB8 .....208 D8
St Laurence Cl UB8 .....208 C8
St Laurence Rd MK18 .....65 F4
St Laurence Way SL1 .....206 A3
St Lawrence Cl HP3 .....146 A4
St Lawrence Way MK13 .....34 A4
St Leger Ct MK14 .....34 E8
St Leger Dr MK14 .....34 E7
St Leonard's Ave 2 SL4 .....210 C5
St Leonard's Hill SL4 .....209 E4
St Leonard's Rd
Oakley Green SL4 .....209 D1
Windsor SL4 .....210 C4
St Leonard's Way LU6 .....92 E1
St Leonards Rd HP6 .....154 E4
St Leonards Wlk SL0 .....207 F3
St Louis RC Comb Sch
HP20 .....101 F2
St Luke Cl UB8 .....208 D7
St Luke's CE Prim Sch
SL6 .....202 C6
St Luke's Rd
Maidenhead SL6 .....202 F8
Old Windsor SL4 .....211 A1
Uxbridge UB10 .....201 E5
St Margaret's Cl UB8 .....200 D3
St Margaret's Gate SL0 .....200 D3
St Margaret's Rd SL6 .....202 F8
St Margaretts Cl MK16 .....22 E4
St Margarets Gr HP15 .....151 E1
St Mark's Cres SL6 .....202 B7
St Mark's Hospl SL6 .....202 C7
St Mark's Pl SL6 .....210 C5

St Mark's Rd
Aylesbury HP21 .....115 C7
Henley-on-T RG9 .....191 E1
Maidenhead SL6 .....202 D7
Windsor SL4 .....210 C5
St Martin Cl UB8 .....208 D7
St Martin's Cl UB7 .....208 D3
St Martin's Rd UB7 .....208 D3
St Martin's St MK2 .....58 C8
St Mary & All Saints CE Prim
Sch HP9 .....175 E3
St Mary & St Giles CE Mid
Sch MK11 .....32 E6
St Mary Magdalene RC Comb
Sch MK12 .....33 A5
St Mary St
High Wycombe HP11 .....173 B6
Milton Keynes MK13 .....33 F7
St Mary's Ave
Berkhamsted HP4 .....134 D6
Milton Keynes MK3 .....57 D7
Milton Keynes,Stony Stratford
MK11 .....32 E6
St Mary's CE Comb Sch
HP7 .....165 D8
St Mary's CE Prim Sch
SL1 .....206 A3
St Mary's CE Sch HP19 .....115 A8
St Mary's Cl
Lee Common HP16 .....142 D5
Maidenhead SL6 .....203 A7
South Harefield UB9 .....190 B8
Wavendon MK17 .....48 E7
St Mary's Glebe LU6 .....92 E4
St Mary's RC Prim Sch
Maidenhead SL6 .....195 F2
Uxbridge UB8 .....201 C4
St Mary's Rd
Denham Green UB9 .....189 F5
Slough SL3 .....206 E4
South Harefield UB9 .....190 B8
St Mary's Row 7 .....115 D8
St Mary's Sch MK2 .....58 D8
St Mary's Sq 3 HP20 .....115 D8
St Mary's Way
Chalfont St Peter SL9 .....177 D1
Chesham HP5 .....154 B8
Leighton Buzzard LU7 .....80 D7
St Mary's Wlk 10 SL6 .....202 F7
St Marys Ct
East Claydon MK18 .....74 F8
Mursley MK17 .....67 D6
St Marys Cl MK18 .....51 B7
St Marys Rd MK18 .....74 F7
St Matthew's CE Prim Sch
UB7 .....208 E5
St Matthews Ct MK3 .....57 E6
St Michael's CE Comb Sch
LU7 .....68 E1
St Michael's Cl HP22 .....117 C1
St Michael's Cl Ashton NN7 .....9 F8
Slough SL2 .....197 D1
St Michael's Gn HP9 .....175 E3
St Michaels Cl
Edgcott HP18 .....72 F2
Halton HP22 .....131 C8
Stewkley LU7 .....68 E1
St Michaels Dr
Milton Keynes MK7 .....47 F6
Walton MK7 .....47 F6
St Michaels Way MK18 .....63 E3
St Monica's RC Comb Sch
MK14 .....34 F6
St Nicholas CE Comb Sch
SL6 .....196 E1
St Nicholas Cl
Cublington LU7 .....78 B1
Little Chalfont HP7 .....166 B8
Uxbridge UB8 .....208 D7
St Patrick's Cl SL6 .....202 B4
St Patrick's Way MK3 .....57 E6
St Paul Cl UB8 .....208 D7
St Paul's CE Comb Sch
SL6 .....185 D4
St Pauls Cl SL6 .....202 F6
St Paul's Rd MK3 .....57 E6
St Pauls Ave SL2 .....206 A5
St Pauls Ct MK11 .....32 D6
St Pauls Rd MK6 .....46 F7
St Pauls Yd MK16 .....22 E4
St Peter St SL7 .....183 E1
St Peter's Ave HP19 .....101 C1
St Peter's CE Comb Sch
SL1 .....197 B2
St Peter's CE Mid Sch
SL4 .....210 F1
St Peter's Cl
Burnham SL1 .....197 B1
Old Windsor SL4 .....211 A2
St Peter's St SL1 .....177 E2
St Peter's RC Prim Sch
SL7 .....183 D7
St Peter's Rd
Brackley NN13 .....38 A8
Maidenhead SL6 .....195 D2
Uxbridge UB8 .....208 D8
St Peters Cl
Loudwater HP11 .....174 B1
Speen HP27 .....150 C4
St Peters Hill HP23 .....119 A4
St Peters Way
Chorleywood WD3 .....167 B5
Milton Keynes MK13 .....34 A8

St Pirans Sch SL6 ....195 E1
St Rumbold's La MK18 ....52 C8
St Stephen's Rd UB7 ....208 D8
St Stephens Dr MK15 ......35 B7
St Teresa's Cl HP27 ....139 B4
St Teresa's La HP27 ....139 B4
St Thomas Aquinas RC Comb Sch MK3 ....57 E7
St Thomas Ct MK4 ....45 E1
St Thomas More RC Prim Sch HP4 ....135 A4
St Thomas Wlk SL3 ....212 D7
St Tiggywinkles Wildlife Hospl* HP17 ....127 A4
St Vincents MK17 ....49 C4
Salcey Forest Trail (Rose Copse)* MK16 ....4 C2
Salden Cl
  Drayton Parslow MK17 .....68 C6
  Milton Keynes MK5 ....46 B6
Salford Rd MK17 ....49 D7
Salisbury Ave SL2 ....205 C8
Salisbury Cl
  Amersham HP7 ....165 E8
  Princes Risborough HP27 .139 C3
Salisbury Ct SL6 ....202 E5
Salisbury Gr MK14 ....21 F2
Salisbury Mews SL2 ....198 C1
Salisbury Rd
  High Wycombe HP13 ....162 D1
  Uxbridge UB8 ....201 B3
Sallowsprings LU6 ....93 F2
Salmons La HP16 ....151 D6
Salop Ho MK3 ....46 F2
Salt Hill Ave SL1 ....205 C5
Salt Hill Cl UB8 ....201 E7
Salt Hill Dr SL1 ....205 C5
Salt Hill Mans SL1 ....205 C5
Salt Hill Way SL1 ....205 C5
Saltash Ct HP13 ....174 B4
Salter's Cl HP4 ....134 F6
Salters Cl
  Ludgershall MK18 ....96 C8
  Maidenhead SL6 ....203 A7
Salters La HP18 ....96 C8
Salters Mews MK14 ....34 F6
Salters Rd SL6 ....203 B7
Salters Row HP10 ....186 A4
Salton Link MK4 ....46 B2
Saltwood Ave MK4 ....45 E1
Samphire Ct MK7 ....48 A6
Sampsons Gn SL2 ....197 F2
Sampsons Hill HP7 ....164 E2
Samuel Cl MK16 ....22 F3
San Remo Rd MK17 ....49 F4
Sanctuary Rd HP15 ....163 B5
Sandage Rd HP14 ....171 B5
Sandal Ct MK5 ....46 A5
Sandbrier Cl MK7 ....48 B6
Sandbrook La HP23 ....104 C1
Sandells Way HP9 ....175 D4
Sandelswood End HP9 ....175 D5
Sanders La NN12 ....18 D3
Sanderson Rd UB8 ....201 C6
Sandford Gdns HP11 ......173 B4
Sandhill Rd MK18 ....74 F8
Sandhill Way HP19 ....115 A8
Sandholme MK18 ....63 F2
Sandhurst Dr MK18 ....52 C7
Sandisplait Rd SL6 ....202 A6
Sandlers End SL2 ....198 B1
Sandles The SL4 ....205 B1
Sandleswood Cl HP9 .....175 D4
Sandon Cl HP23 ....118 F4
Sandown Ct
  High Wycombe HP12 ......172 E7
  Milton Keynes MK3 ....57 D6
Sandown Rd SL2 ....204 F8
Sandpiper HP19 ....101 E4
Sandpit Hill MK18 ....50 F6
Sandpit Hill Cotts HP23 ..133 B2
Sandpit La HP27 ....138 B4
Sandpits La HP10 ....174 C7
Sandringham Ct
  High Wycombe HP13 ......173 B7
  Newport Pagnell MK16 .....22 B3
  Slough SL1 ....204 D7
Sandringham Pl MK2 ....58 C8
Sandringham Rd
  Maidenhead SL6 ....195 E2
  Stanwell TW6 ....213 C2
Sands Farm Dr SL1 ....197 C1
Sands Ind Est HP12 ....172 B7
Sandstone Cl MK18 ....73 B5
Sandwell Ct MK8 ....33 C2
Sandy Cl
  Buckingham MK18 ....52 F8
  Milton Keynes MK14 ....34 D8
Sandy La
  Aspley Heath MK17 ....49 B2
  Leighton Buzzard LU7 ......70 F3
  Long Crendon HP18 ....125 B6
Sandy Mead SL6 ....203 C1
Sandy Rd MK18 ....73 B5
Sandy Rise SL7 ....177 E2
Sandycroft Rd HP6 ....155 C1
Sandygate Cl SL7 ....183 D3
Sandygate Rd SL3 ....183 D3
Sandywell Dr MK15 ....35 A6
Santen Gr MK2 ....58 D4
Saracens' Wharf MK7 ......47 E1
Sargeant Cl UB8 ....201 B2
Sarum Complex UB8 ....201 B3
Satis Ho SL3 ....211 C7
Saunders Cl MK7 ....48 D6

Saunders Ct **1** HP13 ....173 F6
Saunders End HP6 ....153 C5
Saunders Pl HP19 ....115 A7
Saunders Rd UB10 ....201 F4
Saunders Wood Copse HP14 ....158 F4
Saunderton Sta HP14 ....149 C1
Saunderton Vale HP14 ...149 C1
Savage Croft MK10 ....35 E3
Savay Cl SL0 ....190 A4
Savay La UB9 ....190 A5
Savernake Rd HP19 ....101 D3
Savill La MK4,MK5 ....45 F2
Savill Way SL7 ....183 F2
Savoy Cres MK9 ....34 F3
Savoy Cl SL6 ....195 F1
Sawley Ho **5** MK4 ....46 F1
Sawmill Cotts SL3 ....199 F2
Sawmill Rd HP27 ....138 D7
Sawpit Hill HP15 ....163 B5
Sawyer's Cl SL4 ....209 E7
Sawyers Cl SL4 ....202 A2
Sawyers Cres SL6 ....202 A2
Saxeways Bsns Ctr HP5 ..143 E3
Saxborn Rd HP14 ....171 C4
Saxon Cl Amersham HP6 ..154 D1
  Dunstable LU6 ....93 E8
  Slough SL3 ....206 F4
  Uxbridge UB8 ....208 E8
Saxon Ct
  High Wycombe HP12 ......172 D8
  Stanwell TW19 ....213 A2
Saxon Gate MK9 ....34 E2
Saxon Gdns SL6 ....196 D1
Saxon Lodge SL1 ....204 F5
Saxon St
  Milton Keynes MK2 ....58 C8
  Milton Keynes,Ashland MK1, MK6 ....47 C4
  Milton Keynes,Heelands MK6,MK13,MK14 ....34 C5
Saxon Way
  Harmondsworth UB7 ......213 C8
  Old Windsor SL4 ....211 B1
Saxon Way Trad Ctr UB7 ....213 C8
Saye & Sele Cl HP18 ......92 F4
Sayers Gdns HP14 ....135 A6
Sayward Cl HP5 ....144 D2
Scafell Rd SL2 ....204 F8
Scarborough Way SL1 ....205 B4
Scardale MK13 ....34 C5
Scarlett Ave HP22 ....131 E6
Scatterdells La WD4 ......146 F1
Scatterill Cl MK13 ....34 A4
Scholars Way HP4 ....154 F1
Scholars Wlk
  Chalfont St Peter SL9 .....177 E4
  Slough SL3 ....207 A4
School Cl Asheridge HP5 .143 E5
  Cryers Hill HP15 ....162 C6
  High Wycombe HP11 ......173 A4
School Dr MK17 ....57 C3
School End
  Chetwode MK18 ....61 D8
  Great Horwood MK17 ....55 A3
School Hill
  Charndon OX27 ....73 A6
  North Marston MK18 ....76 B2
School Ho TW19 ....213 C1
School La
  Amersham HP7 ....165 A8
  Buckingham MK18 ....52 C8
  Castlethorpe MK19 ....19 F5
  Chalfont St Giles HP8 .....177 D7
  Chalfont St Peter SL9 .....177 D1
  Chearsley HP18 ....112 B2
  Cookham SL6 ....196 B7
  Cookham Dean SL6 ....195 B7
  Dinton HP17 ....113 F2
  Eaton Bray LU6 ....92 F6
  Little Marlow SL7 ....184 C5
  Maidenhead SL6 ....195 E1
  Medmenham SL7 ....183 D4
  Milton Keynes MK5 ....46 B8
  Oakley HP18 ....109 D5
  Penn Street HP7 ....164 B5
  Preston Bissett MK18 ......62 B8
  Seer Green HP9 ....176 D4
  Shabbington HP18 ....124 D3
  Sherington MK16 ....14 A2
  Slough SL2 ....205 F6
  Turville RG9 ....169 F3
  Twyford MK18 ....62 D2
  Upper Winchendon HP18 ...99 A1
  Waddesdon HP18 ....99 A6
  Weston Turville HP22 .....116 F1
  Wexham Street SL3 ....199 B5
  Yardley Gobion NN12 .....18 E6
School Rd
  Harmondsworth UB7 ......213 D8
  Tylers Green HP10 ....174 D8
  Wooburn Green HP10 .....185 E6
School St MK13 ....33 F7
School The HP23 ....118 C8
School Way HP11 ....174 B2
Schorne La MK18 ....76 B2
Schumann Cl MK7 ....48 C8
Scotch Firs MK7 ....48 C6
Scotlands Dr SL2 ....198 B6
Scotney Gdns MK3 ....57 D6
Scotsgrove Cotts OX9 ....126 A4
Scotsgrove Hill OX9 ......126 A3
Scotswood Cl HP9 ....175 D5

Scott Cl
  Farnham Common SL2 ....198 C7
  West Drayton UB7 ....208 F2
Scott Dr MK16 ....22 A5
Scott End HP19 ....100 F2
Scott Evans Ct MK18 ....66 A5
Scotts Cl
  Marsh Gibbon OX27 ....72 A3
  Stoke Hammond MK17 ......69 E8
  Stoke Hammond MK17 ......69 E8
Scotts Cnr NN13 ....39 A4
Scotts Farm Cl MK18 ......41 E4
Scotts La Adstock MK18 ...53 F1
  Buckingham MK18 ....41 E3
  Marsh Gibbon OX27 ....41 F3
Scriven Ct MK15 ....35 C7
Scriveners La MK12 ....17 A8
Scrubb's La HP14 ....160 B7
Seabrooke Ct MK8 ....45 D6
Seacourt Rd SL3 ....207 B2
Seaford Rd TW6 ....213 D2
Seagrave Ct MK7 ....48 A4
Seagrave Rd MK9 ....175 C4
Sears The LU6 ....92 B5
Seaton Dr HP21 ....115 D4
Seckloe Gate MK9 ....34 F3
Second Ave MK1 ....47 C2
Second Cres SL1 ....205 C8
Second St HP11 ....173 C4
Sedgemere MK8 ....33 D2
Sedgemoor Dr OX9 ....126 A1
Sedgemoor Gdns HP10 ...185 A8
Sedgemoor Gdns HP11 ...185 A8
Sedgemoor La HP10 ......185 B7
Sedgemoor Rd HP10 .....185 A8
Sedley Gr UB9 ....190 C7
Sedrup La HP17 ....114 F4
Seeleys Cl HP9 ....175 C4
Seeleys Cl HP9 ....175 D3
Seeleys La HP9 ....175 C4
Seeleys Rd HP9 ....175 C4
Seer Green & Jordans Sta HP9 ....176 C3
Seer Green CE Comb Sch HP9 ....176 C4
Seer Green La HP9 ....176 E3
Seer Mead HP9 ....176 D4
Sefton Cl SL2 ....198 C8
Sefton Paddock SL2 ......199 A5
Sefton Park Cotts SL2 ...199 A4
Sefton Way UB8 ....208 C7
Selbourne Ave MK3 ....57 F7
Selbourne Ho **10** SL8 ...185 A4
Selby Gr MK5 ....46 B5
Selim Ct **4** SL1 ....205 F4
Selkirk Ave HP19 ....101 D2
Selkirk Gr MK3 ....46 F2
Selwood Cl TW19 ....213 C1
Selwood Gdns TW19 .....213 C1
Selwood Way HP13 ....161 E2
Selworthy MK4 ....46 D3
Selwyn Cl SL4 ....209 E5
Selwyn Ct MK16 ....116 B6
Selwyn Pl SL1 ....204 F6
September Ct UB10 ....201 D3
Serjeants Gn MK14 ....34 F6
Serles Cl MK6 ....47 A6
Sermed Ct SL2 ....206 C5
Serpentine Ct MK2 ....58 D5
Servite Ho SL6 ....203 B8
Seven Acre Ho HP10 .....174 C2
Seven Acres HP18 ....125 B7
Seven Gables MK18 ....65 D6
Sevenhills Rd SL0 ....200 C6
Severalls Ave HP5 ....144 C2
Severn Cres SL3 ....207 B1
Severn Dr MK16 ....22 E4
Severn Ho HP13 ....173 F7
Severn Way MK3 ....57 D8
Severn Cl HP19 ....100 F2
Seymour Ct
  Flackwell Heath HP10 .....173 F2
  Maidenhead SL6 ....202 B3
Seymour Court La SL7 ....183 B5
Seymour Court Rd SL7 ...183 C4
Seymour Ct
  Berkhamsted HP4 ....134 E6
  Tring HP23 ....119 A4
Seymour Ho
  High Wycombe HP12 ......172 E4
  Slough SL1 ....206 E4
Seymour Park Rd SL7 ....183 D3
Seymour Plain SL7 ....183 C5
Seymour Rd
  Berkhamsted HP4 ....134 E6
  Chalfont St Giles HP8 .....177 C6
  Slough SL1 ....205 D4
Shackleton Cl **1** TW19 ..213 E1
Shackleton Rd
  High Wycombe HP12 ......172 E5
  Slough SL1 ....205 F6
Shaftesbury Cres MK3 .....47 A1
Shaftesbury Ct
  Maidenhead SL6 ....202 E5
  Slough SL1 ....205 E4
  Winslow MK18 ....65 F5
Shaftesbury Ho HP21 ....116 C7
Shaftesbury St HP11 .....172 F8
Shaggy Calf La SL2 ....206 A6
Shakespeare Cl MK3 ....47 A2
Shakespeare Lodge SL1 ..204 F5
Shakespeare Orch HP18 ...82 F6
Shakespeare Way HP21 ..116 A8
Shallowford Gr MK4 ....46 D4
Shamaa Ho **6** SL1 ....205 F4
Shamrock Cl MK7 ....48 B6

Shannon Ct
  Chesham HP5 ....144 C1
  Milton Keynes MK14 ....35 A6
Shantock Hall La HP3 ....145 E1
Shantock La HP3 ....145 E1
Shantung Pl HP5 ....154 C6
Shardeloes HP7 ....164 D8
Sharkham Ct MK4 ....46 B8
Sharman Row **8** SL3 ....206 F1
Sharman Wlk MK13 ....34 A3
Sharney Ave SL3 ....207 B3
Sharp Cl HP21 ....115 E5
Sharp's Cl HP18 ....99 B6
Sharrow Vale HP12 ....172 E7
Shaw Cl Aylesbury HP20 .116 A8
  Newport Pagnell MK16 .....22 A5
Shaw Ct Aylesbury HP21 .115 E3
  Old Windsor SL4 ....211 A2
Shaw The SL6 ....195 E6
Shawfield Ct UB7 ....208 E3
Shaws Cl HP16 ....151 D5
Shearmans MK11 ....33 A4
Sheehy Way SL2 ....206 B6
Sheehin Gr MK2 ....58 C8
Sheep St MK18 ....66 A4
Sheepcoat Cl MK5 ....46 A5
Sheepcote Cl HP9 ....175 C4
Sheepcote Dell Rd HP15 ......163 E7
Sheepcote Gdns HP9 ....190 A5
Sheepcote La HP10,SL1 ..186 A2
Sheepcote Rd
  Eton Wick SL4 ....205 A1
  Windsor SL4 ....209 E5
Sheepfold La HP7 ....165 D7
Sheephouse Rd SL6 .....196 B2
Sheeplane MK17 ....60 C2
Sheepridge La SL7,SL8 ..184 E7
Sheering Gr MK13 ....33 F5
Sheerness Ct MK4 ....57 A8
Sheerstock HP17 ....126 E5
Sheerwater HP19 ....101 E4
Sheet St SL4 ....210 D6
Sheet Street Rd SL4 .....210 C2
Sheffield Dr HP21 ....115 E6
Sheffield Rd SL1 ....205 C7
Shelburne Ct HP12 ....172 E4
Shelburne Rd HP12 ......172 E4
Sheldon Ct MK4 ....33 F1
Sheldon Rd HP18 ....124 A3
Shelduck Cl **3** HP20 ....101 E3
Shelley Cl
  Medmenham SL7 ....193 D7
  Newport Pagnell MK16 .....22 B4
  Slough SL3 ....206 F1
  Wooburn Green HP10 .....185 E8
Shelley Dr MK3 ....57 F7
Shelley Rd Chesham HP5 .144 B2
  High Wycombe HP11 ......172 F5
  12 Marlow SL7 ....183 F3
Shellfield Ct TW19 ....213 A2
Shelsmore MK14 ....35 A8
Shelton Ct Slough SL3 ...206 C3
  Wolverton SL4 ....49 B4
Shenley Brook End Sch MK5 ....46 A2
Shenley Rd
  Milton Keynes,Bletchley MK3 ....46 E1
  Milton Keynes,Bletchley MK3 ....57 F8
  Milton Keynes,Loughton MK5 ....46 A7
  Whaddon MK17 ....56 C8
Shenstone Ct **15** SL4 ...210 C6
Shenstone Dr SL1 ....197 D1
Shenstone Hill HP4 ....135 E5
Shepherd Cl HP20 ....102 A2
Shepherd's La WD3 ....167 E2
Shepherds MK11 ....33 A4
Shepherds Cl
  Beaconsfield HP9 ....175 F1
  Hurley SL6 ....193 F3
  Uxbridge UB8 ....201 D7
Shepherds Ct SL4 ....209 E5
Shepherds Fold HP15 ....163 D8
Shepherds Gate HP16 ...152 A2
Shepherds La
  Beaconsfield HP9 ....175 F1
  Hazlemere HP15 ....162 F5
  Hurley SL6 ....193 E4
Shepherds Row MK18 .....66 A4
Shepherds Way HP5 .....154 D6
Shepherdswell Fst Sch MK6 ....35 B2
Sheppards Cl MK16 ....22 C4
Shepperds Cl MK18 ....76 A2
Shepperds Gn MK5 ....45 F6
Shepperton Cl MK19 ....19 F5
Sheraton Dr HP13 ....162 D1
Sheraton Ho WD3 ....167 C5
Sherborne Cl SL3 ....212 E6
Sherborne Ct SL6 ....202 A5
Sherbourne Dr
  Bow Brickhill MK7 ....48 B4
  Maidenhead SL6 ....202 C3
  Windsor SL4 ....209 D3
Sherbourne Wlk SL2 .....198 C8
Shereway HP19 ....115 B8
Shergold Way SL6 ....195 F6
Sheridan Ct HP13 ....115 D3
Sheridan Ct
  Maidenhead SL6 ....203 B8
  Slough SL1 ....204 E6
Sheriff Cl HP19 ....115 B8
Sheringham Ct SL6 ......202 E7

Sherington CE Fst Sch MK16 ....14 A2
Sherington Rd MK16 ....22 E7
Sherman Rd SL1 ....205 E8
Shernfold MK7 ....48 B7
Sherriff Cotts HP18 ....99 A7
Sherwood Cl SL3 ....206 E3
Sherwood Ct
  Colnbrook SL3 ....212 D7
  10 Slough SL1 ....206 F1
Sherwood Dr
  Maidenhead SL6 ....202 A6
  Milton Keynes MK1,MK2, MK3 ....47 B1
Shields Ct HP10 ....163 B1
Shifford Cres SL6 ....195 E3
Shilling Cl MK15 ....35 A7
Shillingridge Pk SL7 .....182 E5
Shinfield Cl MK18 ....63 D2
Ship Hill SL1 ....186 A4
Ship La LU7 ....105 D3
Ship Rd LU7 ....80 E6
Ship St HP11 ....173 A7
Shiplake Ho SL8 ....185 B4
Shipley Rd MK16 ....22 B4
Shipman Ct MK15 ....35 B7
Shipton MK18 ....66 B3
Shipton Hill MK13 ....34 B6
Shipton Rd UB10 ....201 F8
Shire Ct MK14 ....45 A4
Shire La
  Chalfont St Peter HP8,SL9 .178 B6
  Cholesbury HP23 ....133 B4
  Chorleywood WD3 ....167 C4
  North Crawley MK16 ....24 E4
Shires Bsns Pk The NN13 ....38 A6
Shires Rd NN13 ....38 A6
Shirley Ave SL4 ....209 F6
Shirley Moor MK7 ....48 B8
Shirley Rd SL6 ....202 C5
Shirwell Cres MK4 ....46 D5
Shogmoor La RG9 ....170 C1
Shootacre Cnr HP27 .....149 A8
Shootacre La HP27 ....149 A8
Shootersway HP4 ....134 E4
Shootersway La HP4 .....134 F4
Shootersway Pk HP4 ....134 F3
Shop La NN7 ....1 B6
Shoppenhanger's Rd SL6 ....202 A4
Shoreditch Cl UB10 ......190 F1
Shoreham Rd (E) TW6 ...213 E2
Shoreham Rd (W) TW6 ..213 E2
Shoreham Rise SL7 ......197 D1
Short Ditch HP17 ....127 A7
Short Hale LU7 ....105 D3
Short Massey MK46 ....6 E5
Short Rd TW6 ....213 E1
Short St HP11 ....172 F7
Shortborough Ave HP27 ......139 B5
Shortfern SL2 ....206 C7
Shortway Amersham HP6 .154 D2
  Chesham HP5 ....144 B2
Shotfield Rd HP14 ....111 C4
Shothanger Way HP3 ....146 B6
Shouler Cl MK5 ....46 A6
Shrewsbury Cl MK10 ....36 A2
Shrimpton Cl HP9 ....175 D6
Shrimpton Rd
  Beaconsfield HP9 ....175 D6
  High Wycombe HP12 .....172 B3
Shropshire Ct MK3 ....46 E1
Shrubbery Cl HP13 ....173 B8
Shrubbery Rd HP13 ......173 B8
Shrublands Ave HP4 .....135 A5
Shrublands Rd HP4 ......135 A5
Shucklow Hill MK17 ....55 E3
Shugars Gn HP23 ....119 B5
Shupp's La HP18 ....112 B1
Shutlanger Rd NN12 ....9 A8
Shuttleworth Gr MK7 ....48 D6
Sibleys Rise HP16 ....152 D8
Side Rd UB9 ....189 D4
Sidings Ind Est The HP13 ....38 A8
Sidings The HP11 ....174 B3
Sidlow Ct MK11 ....32 F4
Sidney Cl UB8 ....201 C5
Sidney Ho HP14 ....111 B4
Sidney Rd SL4 ....209 C4
Sidney Terr HP22 ....131 B5
Silbury Arc MK9 ....34 E2
Silbury Bvd MK9 ....34 D2
Silbury Rbt MK9 ....34 C1
Silchester Ho SL6 ....203 B8
Silchester House Sch SL6 ....203 D3
Silco Dr SL6 ....202 E6
Silicon Ct MK5 ....46 C5
Silk Mill Way HP23 ....119 A5
Silk St HP18 ....99 A6
Silkwood Ct SL2 ....206 C5
Sillswood MK46 ....6 E4
Silsden Cres HP17 ....177 D7
Silver Birch Cl UB10 .....201 E4
Silver Birch Cvn Site HP14 ......150 B1
Silver Birch Dr HP27 .....149 C5
Silver Cl SL6 ....202 A5
Silver End MK46 ....7 A3
Silver Hill HP18 ....177 B8
Silver St
  20 Aylesbury HP20 ......115 D8
  Cublington LU7 ....78 B1
  Milton Keynes MK11 ....32 D5

Silver St continued
Newport Pagnell MK16 .....22 D4
Silverbeck Way TW19 ....213 A2
Silverbirches La MK17 ....49 A2
Silverdale Cl
4 Aylesbury HP20 ......101 D1
Tylers Green HP10 ......163 A1
Silvermead HP18 ....123 D5
Silverstone Mews SL6 ..202 C4
Silverstone Motor Racing
  Circuit* MK18 ....28 F8
Silvertrees Dr SL6 ......202 A5
Silverweed Ct MK7 ....48 B5
Simatt Ho HP10 ....174 C2
Simdims MK43 ....25 A1
Simmons Cl SL3 ....207 A2
Simmons Ct
  Aylesbury HP21 ....115 C4
  High Wycombe HP12 .....172 E7
Simmons Rd RG9 ....191 D3
Simmons Way
  Lane End HP14 ....171 C4
  Thame OX9 ....125 F1
Simms Croft MK10 ....36 A2
Simmi MK6 ....47 B6
Simon Dean HP13 ......146 A4
Simon's Way MK18 ......39 E7
Simons Lea MK13 ....34 B4
Simonsbath MK4 ....46 D2
Simpson Cl SL6 ....203 B8
Simpson Dr MK6 ....47 E5
Simpson Pr HP21 ......115 F5
Simpson Rd MK1,MK2,
  MK6 ....47 E3
Simpson Rdbt MK6 ....47 D5
Simpsons Way SL1 ......205 E5
Sinclair Cl MK4 ....47 B3
Sinclair Rd SL4 ....210 C4
Singleborough La MK17 ..54 F3
Singleton Dr MK8 ....45 D6
Singleton Way 8 HP19 ..115 A8
Singret Pl UB8 ....201 C1
Sion Terr MK18 ....51 B6
Sipson Rd UB7 ....208 F3
Sipthorp Cl MK7 ....48 C6
Sir Frank Markham Com Coll
  MK6 ....46 F7
Sir Frank Markham Com Sch
  MK6 ....47 A7
Sir Henry Floyd Gram Sch
  HP21 ....115 C7
Sir Henry Peakes Dr
  SL2 ....198 A6
Sir Peter's Way HP14 ...107 E6
Sir Sydney Camm Ho
  SL4 ....210 B4
Sir William Borlase's Gram
  Sch SL7 ....183 C1
Sir William Ramsay Sch
  HP15 ....163 A3
Sissinghurst Dr MK4 ....45 E2
Sitwell Cl MK16 ....21 C5
Six Cotts MK18 ....29 E5
Sixth St HP11 ....173 C4
Sixty Acres Rd HP16 ...151 C6
Skeats Wharf MK15 .....35 A7
Skeldon Gate MK14 .....35 A4
Skeldon Rdbt MK9 ......35 A4
Skelton Cl HP9 ....186 A8
Skene Cl MK2 ....58 C4
Skerries Ct SL3 ....207 A2
Skimmers Cl HP15 ......163 C6
Skimmers End HP15 .....163 C6
Skimmers Field HP15 ...163 C6
Skip La UB9 ....190 E3
Skippon Way OX9 ....125 F2
Skipton Cl MK15 ....35 C6
Skittle Gn HP27 ....138 A2
Skydmore Path SL2 .....197 F1
Skye Lodge SL1 ....205 E5
Skylark Rd UB9 ....189 C3
Skyport Dr UB7 ....213 D7
Skyway 14 Trad Est SL3 212 F4
Slad La Lacey Green HP27 149 F4
  Lacey Green HP22 .....149 F4
Slade Hill
  Aylesbury HP19 ....115 A7
  Mixbury NN13 ....38 D1
Slade La MK11 ....33 A4
Slade Oak La UB9 ......189 C5
Slade Rd HP14 ....158 E4
Slade The MK17 ....57 D3
Slapton La LU6 ....91 F6
Slated Row MK12 ....33 B7
Slated Row Sch MK12 ...33 A7
Slater St HP13 ....173 C6
Slattenham Cl HP19 ....115 B7
Slave Hill HP17 ....126 F5
Slayter Rd HP14 ......171 C4
Slickett's La LU6 ......92 F3
Slipe The LU7 ....105 A7
Slough & Eton CE Sch
  SL1 ....205 D3
Slough Gram Sch SL2 ..206 B3
Slough Interchange Ind Est
  SL2 ....206 A3
Slough La HP14 ....160 C6
Slough Mus* SL1 ......206 A4
Slough Rd Datchet SL3 ..211 B7
  Iver Heath SL0 ......200 E3
  Slough SL1 ....205 E2
  Slough SL3 ....205 E2
Slough Trad Est SL1 ...205 B7
Sly Cnr HP16 ....142 E4
Smabridge Wlk MK15 ...35 D7
Small Cres MK18 ....52 F8
Smalldean La HP27 ....149 E2

Smarden Bell MK7 ....48 B8
Smeaton Cl
  Aylesbury HP19 ....101 A1
  Blakelands MK14 ....22 A2
Smewin Ct HP11 ....172 E7
Smith Cl HP20 ....116 B7
Smith Ctr The RG9 .....191 B5
Smith's La
  Waterperry Common OX33 122 F7
  Windsor SL4 ....209 E6
Smithergill Ct MK13 ....34 C5
Smithfield End MK17 ....66 F4
Smithfield Rd SL6 .....202 A3
Smithsons Pl MK9 ....35 B3
Snaith Cres MK5 ....46 B7
Snakeley Cl HP10 ......174 C1
Snape Spur SL1 ....205 E7
Snells La HP7 ....166 C7
Snells Wood Ct HP7 ...166 C7
Snelshall St MK4 ....56 F8
Snowball Hill SL6 ......202 A1
Snowberry Cl MK12 .....33 D5
Snowden Cl SL4 ....209 D3
Snowdon Dr MK6 ....46 D7
Snowdrop Way HP15 ...162 F7
Snowhill Cotts HP5 ....144 F7
Snowshill Ct MK14 ......21 F2
Soames Ct MK46 ....7 F7
Soane Wlk HP13 ....173 A8
Soho Cres HP10 ....185 D4
Soho Mills Ind Est
  HP10 ....185 D4
Sokeman Cl MK14 ....33 A5
Solar Ct MK14 ....21 E1
Solesbridge Cl WD3 ...167 F6
Solesbridge La WD3 ..167 F6
Somerford Cl SL6 ......203 B8
Somerford Pl HP9 .....175 C1
Somerlea SL6 ....196 C3
Somers Lees 18 HP19 ..115 A8
Somersby Cres SL6 ....202 E3
Somerset Cl MK3 ....46 F1
Somerset Lodge 3 SL6 202 F6
Somerset Rd SL4 ......205 C1
Somerville Way HP19 ..115 B8
Sophie Gdns SL3 .....206 D4
Sorensen Ct MK5 ....45 E4
Sorrell Dr MK16 ....21 F4
Soskin Dr MK14 ....34 D6
Sospel Ct SL2 ....198 C3
Soulbury Rd Burcott LU7 .79 D4
  Leighton Buzzard LU7 ...80 D7
  Stewkley LU7 ....68 F1
Southall Bank NN13 ....38 B7
South Bank Rd MK4 ...134 F6
South Cl
  Medmenham SL7 ......193 D7
  Slough SL1 ....204 D6
  West Drayton UB7 ....208 F3
South Common Rd UB8 201 E6
South Cottage Dr WD3 167 F4
South Cottage Gdns
  WD3 ....167 F4
South Dr
  Beaconsfield HP9 ....186 B8
  High Wycombe HP13 ..173 D8
South Eighth St MK9 ...34 E2
South End HP17 ....126 F5
South End La LU6 ......91 A7
South Enmore Rdbt MK6 35 B3
South Field Cl SL4 ....204 C3
South Fifth St MK9 .....34 E1
South Fourth St MK9 ...34 D1
South Gn SL1 ....205 E6
South Hall MK18 ....41 E3
South Hills HP18 ....96 A1
South Ho MK1 ....47 D2
South La LU7 ....78 E7
South Lawne MK3 ....57 F8
South Maundin HP14 ...162 A7
South Meadow La SL4 ..210 C8
South Ninth St MK9 ....34 F2
South Overgate End
  MK6 ....35 B3
South Park Ave WD3 ..167 F4
South Park Cres SL9 ..188 F7
South Park Ct SL9 ....188 G6
South Park Dr SL9 ....188 E7
South Park Gdns HP4 .135 B5
South Park View SL9 ..188 F7
South Path SL4 ....210 C5
South Pk SL9 ....188 F6
South Pl SL7 ....183 E2
South Rd Amersham HP6 154 C3
  Chorleywood WD3 ....167 C4
  Maidenhead SL6 .....202 E6
  West Drayton UB7 ....208 F3
South Row Fulmer SL3 199 E8
  Milton Keynes MK9 ....34 E1
  Milton Keynes MK9 ....34 F1
South Saxon Rdbt MK9 34 F1
South Secklow St MK9 .34 F1
South Second St MK9 ..34 D1
South Seventh St MK9 .34 E1
South Side SL8 ....188 D8
South Sixth St MK9 ....34 E1
South St
  Castlethorpe MK19 .....19 F5
  Wendover HP22 ......131 B4
South Tenth St MK9 ...34 F2
South Terr
  Milton Keynes MK2 ....58 C8
  Windsor SL4 ....210 C6
South Vale NN7 ....1 A5
South View
  Cookham Rise SL6 ....195 E7

South View continued
  Eton SL4 ....205 B1
  High Wycombe HP13 ...161 D2
  Wooburn Green HP10 ..185 D8
South View Rd SL4 .....188 A2
South Way HP9 ....186 A8
South Witan Rdbt MK6 ..34 E1
Southampton Rd TW6 ..213 F1
Southbourne 1 HP11 ...173 C7
Southbourne Dr SL8 ...185 A3
Southbridge Gr MK7 ....48 A7
Southcliffe Dr SL7 ....177 E5
Southcote Way HP10 ..163 B1
Southcott Lower Sch
  LU7 ....80 D8
Southcott Village LU7 ..80 D6
Southcourt Ave LU7 ....80 D6
Southcourt Ho LU7 .....80 D7
Southcourt Rd LU7 .....80 D7
Southcroft SL2 ....198 B1
Southern Cotts TW19 ..213 A2
Southern Perimeter Rd
  TW6,TW19 ....213 D2
Southern Rd
  Aylesbury HP19 ....101 C1
  Thame OX9 ....125 F1
Southern Way MK12 ....33 D5
Southfield Cl MK15 ....35 E7
Southfield Cotts HP17 .130 C3
Southfield Dr HP15 ....163 A6
Southfield Gdns SL1 ..204 B8
Southfield Rd
  Aylesbury HP20 ......116 B7
  Flackwell Heath HP10 .174 A1
  High Wycombe HP11 ..161 D1
  Princes Risborough HP27 139 C3
Southgate Ho SL6 .....202 F6
Southlands Rd UB9 ...189 F1
Southlea Rd SL3,SL4 ..211 B5
Southview Rd SL7 .....183 E4
Southwick Ct MK4 ....45 F8
Southwold Cl HP21 ....116 A6
Southwold Spur SL3 ..207 C4
Southwood Gdns SL6 ..195 E5
Southwood Mid Sch
  MK4 ....34 E5
Sovereign Cl SL6 .....195 E5
Sovereign Beeches SL2 198 B6
Sovereign Ct MK18 .....75 F7
Sovereign Ct
  Aylesbury HP19 ......101 D1
  High Wycombe HP13 ..173 D6
Sovereign Dr MK15 .....35 A7
Sovereign Hts SL3 ....212 A8
Sovereign Lodge MK15 .35 A7
Spa Cl HP18 ....110 B8
Spackmans Way SL1 ..205 D3
Spade Oak Farm SL8 ..184 E3
Spade Oak Mdw SL8 ..184 E4
Spark Way MK16 ....21 F5
Sparrow Ct HP19 ......101 F3
Sparrow Hall Bsns Pk
  LU6 ....92 D3
Sparrow Hall Farm LU6 92 D3
Spearing Rd HP22 .....172 C7
Spearmant Ind Est HP22 172 B6
Spearmint Cl MK7 ......48 B5
Specklands MK5 ....46 A8
Speedbird Way UB7 ...213 B7
Speedwell Pl MK14 .....34 E2
Speen Cl Sch HP27 ...150 B4
Speen Rd HP14,HP16,
  HP27 ....150 D2
Speldhurst Ct MK7 .....48 B7
Spencer MK14 ....34 C8
Spencer Cl UB8 ....201 C2
Spencer Gdns OX27 ....72 E5
Spencer Rd SL3 ....206 F3
Spencer St MK13 ....33 F7
Spencer Villas SL1 ...204 F5
Spencers Cl SL6 ......202 D8
Spencers La MK5 ......195 E6
Spencers Rd SL6 ......202 D8
Spenlows Rd MK3 ......47 A3
Spens SL6 ....202 F8
Spenser Ho HP21 .....115 F6
Spenser Rd HP21 .....115 F6
Sperling Rd SL6 ......195 F1
Spickett's La HP18 ....113 A3
Spier's La OX27 ....71 F2
Spiert The HP17 ......114 D5
Spindle Cl HP15 ......163 A3
Spindle La MK7 ....183 B2
Spinfield La W SL7 ...183 B1
Spinfield Mount SL7 ..183 B1
Spinfield Pk SL7 ......183 B1
Spinfield Sch SL7 ....183 B2
Spinners Wlk
  Marlow SL7 ....183 C1
  Windsor SL4 ....210 C6
Spinney SL1 ....205 B5
Spinney Bglws LU7 ....91 C6
Spinney Cl
  Steeple Claydon MK18 ..63 E2
  West Drayton UB7 ...208 E6
Spinney Cotts OX33 ...123 B1
Spinney La LU6 ....93 F8
Spinney Hill Rd MK46 ...6 E3
Spinney La MK17 ....49 F4
Spinney The
  Beaconsfield HP9 ....175 E1
  Berkhamsted HP4 ....134 F3
  Chesham HP5 ....144 D2
  Gerrards Cross SL9 ..188 D3
  High Wycombe HP11 ..173 A4
  Holmer Green HP15 ..163 D7

Spinney The continued
  Milton Keynes MK13 ...34 A4
  Winslow MK18 ....66 A6
Spire View TW19 ......213 D1
Spitfire Cl SL3 ....207 A2
Spittal St SL7 ....183 D2
Spoondell LU6 ....93 F7
Spoonley Wood MK13 ..33 E5
Sportsman Cl MK18 ....63 D3
Spout La TW19 ....213 A3
Spout La N TW19 .....213 B3
Sprigs Holly La HP14 ..159 B8
Spring Cl
  High Wycombe HP13 ..173 F7
  Latimer HP5 ....155 C3
  Maidenhead SL6 .....195 F2
Spring Coppice HP14 ..171 F5
Spring Coppice La
  HP27 ....183 A3
Spring Field Rd HP4 ...135 A6
Spring Gardens Rd
  HP13 ....173 E5
Spring Gdns
  Bourne End SL8 .....185 A4
  Marlow SL7 ....183 E3
  Newport Pagnell MK16 ..22 C4
  Wooburn Green HP10 .185 E8
Spring Gr MK17 ....49 B5
Spring Hill SL6 ....202 E3
Spring Hill Sch SL2 ..183 E3
Spring La Alderton NN12 ..9 A2
  Clifton Reynes MK46 ....7 C3
  Cookham Dean SL6 ..195 C5
  Farnham Common SL2 198 C5
  Flackwell Heath HP10 .159 B8
  Great Horwood MK17 ..55 A2
  Olney MK46 ....6 F4
  Slough SL1 ....204 F1
Spring Mdw HP18 ......97 A1
Spring Valley Dr HP14 162 A7
Springate Field SL3 ..206 E4
Springbank Ct MK16 ...22 E3
Springdale Cotts SL8 ..185 B2
Springett Pl HP6 ......154 F2
Springfield SL1 ....206 A3
Springfield Bvd MK6 ..35 D2
Springfield Cl
  Aylesbury HP19 ......115 C8
  Chesham HP5 ....154 C2
  Windsor SL4 ....210 B5
Springfield Gdns
  Chinnor OX39 ....147 C2
  Deanshanger MK19 ....31 E4
Springfield Hollow
  HP14 ....158 E5
Springfield Mid Sch MK6 35 D2
Springfield Pk SL6 ....203 C1
Springfield Rd
  Chesham HP5 ....154 C2
  Dunstable LU6 ....93 D5
  Leighton Buzzard LU7 ..80 E7
  Olney MK46 ....6 F4
  Slough SL3 ....212 B7
  Stokenchurch HP14 ..158 F4
  Windsor SL4 ....210 B5
Springfield Rdbt MK6 ..35 A2
Springfield Way MK43 ..25 C2
Springfields
  Amersham HP6 ....154 C2
  Padbury MK18 ....53 C1
Springfields Cl MK18 ...53 C1
Springfields Rd MK18 ..53 C1
Springhill (HM Prison)
  HP18 ....73 A1
Springhill Rd HP20 ....83 A8
Springs Cl HP17 ......130 B2
Springs La HP17 ......130 B3
Springside 2 LU7 ......80 F7
Springwater Mill HP11 .173 E4
Springwood HP27 .....150 C4
Sprucedale Gdns
  Chorleywood WD3 ..167 D5
  Denham UB9 ....189 D4
Spruce Dene HP15 ...162 F2
Spruce Rd HP19 ......116 A4
Spur The SL1 ....204 D8
Spurgrove La RG9 ....170 D2
Spurlands End Rd HP15 163 A8
Spurt St HP18 ....112 F3
Square Close Cotts RG9 169 F3
Square The Aylesbury HP20 116 A6
  Aspley Guise MK17 ....49 A6
  Brill HP18 ....110 A8
  Great Missenden HP16 152 B7
  Harmondsworth UB7 .213 B6
  Long Crendon HP18 ..125 C6
  Milton Keynes MK12 ...33 D6
  Preston Bissett MK18 ..62 B8
  Waddesdon HP18 .....99 A6
  Yardley Hastings NN7 ...1 A6
Squires Cl MK6 ....47 A6
Squirrel La HP12 ......172 C5
Squirrel Rise SL7 ....183 D6
Squirrels Way HP12 ..172 C5
Stable Cl MK18 ....50 C7
Stable Cotts SL7 .....194 C5
Stable La HP9 ....176 C4
Stable Rd HP22 ......102 B1
Stablebridge Rd HP22 117 F3
Stables Cl SL7 ....183 B1
Stables The MK19 .....20 D3
Stacey Ave MK12 ....33 D6
Stacey Bushes Trad Ctr
  MK12 ....33 D6
Stacey Ho HP12 ......172 E4

Stacey's Ct HP8 ......177 C8
Staddle Stones HP27 .139 B4
Stafford Ave SL2 .....203 A6
Stafford Ave SL2 .....198 C1
Stafford Cl SL3 ....204 B7
Stafford Gr MK5 ......46 B6
Stafford Keep HP19 ..115 A8
Stag Ct WD3 ....167 C5
Stag La Berkhamsted HP4 135 B5
  Chorleywood WD3 ....167 C3
  Great Kingshill HP15 .151 D1
Stagshaw Gr 5 MK4 ..46 B2
Stainby Cl UB7 ....208 E3
Stainton Dr MK13 .....34 C4
Stamford Ave MK6 .....35 B2
Stamford Rd SL6 .....202 C6
Stanbridge Cl HP17 ..127 A4
Stanbridge Ct MK11 ...32 F5
Stanbridge Rd HP17 ..127 B6
Stanbrook HP14 ......36 A1
Standfield Cl HP19 ...115 A8
Standing Way
  Milton Keynes,Coldharbour
  Spinney MK3,MK4 .....46 E3
  Milton Keynes,Kingston
  MK10 ....36 C1
Standring Pl HP20 ...101 C2
Stanhope Heath TW19 213 C1
Stanhope Rd
  Milton Keynes MK42 ..131 B7
  Slough SL1 ....204 D7
Stanhope Way TW19 .213 C1
Stanier Rise HP4 ....134 F7
Stanier Sq 5 MK2 .....58 C8
Stanley Ave HP5 .....154 B8
Stanley Cl Marlow SL7 183 F3
  Uxbridge UB8 ....201 D3
Stanley Cotts SL2 ...205 F5
Stanley Ct MK46 ....6 E5
Stanley Gdns HP23 ..118 F3
Stanley Green E SL3 ..206 F2
Stanley Green W SL3 .206 F2
Stanley Hill HP7 ......165 E7
Stanley Hill Ave HP7 .165 E8
Stanley Ho SL4 ......211 A2
Stanley Spencer Art Gall &
  Mus* SL6 ....196 B7
Stanmore Gdns MK16 ..22 B2
Stanstead Pl HP7 ....165 C8
Stansted Rd TW6 .....213 F1
Stanton Ave MK13 .....34 A6
Stanton Gate MK14 ...34 D8
Stanton Mid Sch MK13 .34 B7
Stanton Way SL3 .....206 E2
Stanton Wood Rdbt
  MK14 ....34 D4
Stantonbury Campus
  MK14 ....34 C7
Stantonbury Cl MK13 ..34 A8
Stanway Cl MK15 .....35 B6
Stanwell Cl TW19 ....213 F1
Stanwell Fields CE Prim Sch
  TW19 ....213 E1
Stanwell Gdns TW19 .213 D1
Stanwell Moor Rd TW6,
  TW19,UB7 ....213 B4
Stanwell Rd SL3 .....212 C4
Stapeley Ct MK4 ......45 F2
Staple Hall Rd MK1 ...47 E1
Stapleton Cl SL7 .....183 F4
Stars La HP17 ....113 E2
Startins La SL6 ......195 C8
Starveall Cl UB7 .....208 F3
Starwood Cl 1 SL3 ..206 C3
Staters Pound MK15 ..35 A7
Station App
  Amersham HP6 ....154 C1
  Chorleywood WD3 ...167 D5
  Denham UB9 ....189 D4
  Gerrards Cross SL9 ..188 E6
  Great Missenden HP16 152 A7
  Little Chalfont HP7 ..166 D8
  Maidenhead SL6 .....202 F6
  Marlow SL7 ....183 E2
  Wendover HP22 ....131 B4
  West Drayton UB7 ...208 E5
Station Cotts
  Denham UB9 ....190 A4
  Winslow MK18 ....66 A5
Station Hill SL6 .....195 F7
Station Par
  Beaconsfield HP9 ....175 D3
  Cookham Rise SL8 ...195 F6
Station Rd Aldbury HP23 120 B5
  Amersham HP6 ....154 B7
  Beaconsfield HP9 ....175 D3
  Berkhamsted HP4 ....135 D4
  Blackthorn OX25 ......81 A4
  Bourne End SL8 .....185 A3
  Bow Brickhill MK17 ...48 C2
  Buckingham MK18 ....52 C7
  Castlethorpe MK19 ....19 F5
  Cheddington LU7 ......91 A1
  Chesham HP5 ....154 C6
  Chinnor OX39 ....147 C6
  Cookham Rise SL6 ...195 F6
  Gerrards Cross SL9 ..188 E6

Station Rd continued
Haddenham HP17 ....126 E5
Henley-on-T RG9 ....191 E1
High Wycombe HP13 ......173 C6
Ivinghoe LU7 ....105 E5
Leighton Buzzard LU7 ......80 E7
Little Kimble HP17 ....129 E2
Long Marston HP23 ....104 B4
Loudwater HP10 ....174 C2
Marlow SL7 ....183 E1
Marsh Gibbon OX27 ....71 F3
Mursley MK17 ....67 B7
Newport Pagnell MK16 .....22 C4
Padbury MK18 ....53 B1
Princes Risborough HP27 .139 A2
Quainton HP22 ....85 A4
Slough SL1 ....204 E7
Slough,Langley SL3 ....207 A4
Stoke Mandeville HP22 ...116 B2
Swanbourne MK17 ....67 A4
Taplow SL6 ....203 F7
Tring HP23 ....119 D4
Uxbridge UB8 ....201 D1
West Drayton UB7 ....208 E4
Winslow MK18 ....66 A5
Woburn Sands MK17 ....49 B5
Wraysbury TW19 ....212 A1
Station Rd Ind Est MK18 ..66 A5
Station Rise SL7 ....183 E2
Station Sq MK9 ....34 C1
Station Terr
Buckingham MK18 ....52 C7
Milton Keynes MK14 ....21 E2
Station Way HP20 ....115 D7
Staunton Ho MK17 ....60 F7
Staunton Rd SL2 ....205 D8
Staveley CI HP21 ....116 C6
Stavordale 🔢 MK10 ....36 A1
Stayning La MK14 ....34 F6
Steeple CI MK4 ....57 A8
Steeple Claydon Sch
MK18 ....63 B3
Steinbeck Cres MK4 ......56 F7
Stephenson CI
Aylesbury HP19 ....115 B7
High Wycombe HP13 ....161 F1
Leighton Buzzard LU7 ......80 E6
Stephenson Ct 🔢 SL1 ....205 F4
Stephenson Dr SL4 ....210 B7
Stepnells HP23 ....105 A1
Steppingstones LU6 ....93 F8
Stevens CI
Holmer Green HP15 ....163 B7
Prestwood HP16 ....151 D6
Stevens Field MK7 ....48 D6
Stevens Ho 🔢 HP7 ....165 B7
Stevenson Rd SL2 ....187 D2
Stewart Ave SL1 ....205 F8
Stewarts Dr SL2 ....198 B7
Stewarts Way SL7 ....183 D7
Stewkley La MK17 ....67 E4
Stewkley Rd
Cublington LU7 ....78 C1
Hollingdon LU7 ....69 C2
Wing LU7 ....79 B3
Stile Mdw HP9 ....175 E3
Stile Rd SL3 ....206 D3
Stilebrook Rd MK46 ....6 F6
Stilwell Dr UB8 ....201 F1
Stirling Ave HP20 ....101 E1
Stirling CI
Milton Keynes MK15 ....35 A6
Uxbridge UB8 ....201 C2
Windsor SL4 ....209 D5
Stirling Gr SL6 ....202 A8
Stirling Ho
🔢 High Wycombe HP13 ...173 F7
Milton Keynes MK3 ....57 D7
Stirling Rd
High Wycombe HP12 ....172 D5
Slough SL1 ....205 A8
Stanwell TW6 ....213 F1
Stock Field CI HP15 ......163 B3
Stock La MK17 ....45 B1
Stockaway HP22 ....87 C1
Stockdale MK13 ....34 C5
Stockdales Rd SL4 ....204 F2
Stocken CI MK46 ....4 D5
Stockgrove Ctry Pk*
LU7 ....70 F7
Stockgrove Park Ho LU7 .70 F8
Stockhall Cres LU7 ....68 D2
Stocking Green CE MK19 .11 A3
Stocking La HP14 ....161 E7
Stockdale HP20 ....101 F1
Stocklands Way HP15 ....151 D5
Stockley Acad UB8 ....208 F7
Stockleys La MK18 ....51 B6
Stockport Rd WD3 ....167 C2
Stocks CI MK18 ....65 F4
Stocks Rd HP23 ....120 C7
Stocks The MK19 ....19 E2
Stockwell HP17 ....127 A6
Stockwell Furlong
HP17 ....127 A6
Stockwell La
Longwick HP17 ....139 A8
Wavendon MK17 ....48 D7
Stockwells SL0 ....196 D1
Stoke Bruerne CE Prim Sch
NN12 ....9 A8
Stoke Common Rd SL2,
SL3 ....199 B8
Stoke Court Dr SL2 ....198 F4
Stoke Farm La HP21 ......115 E3

Stoke Gdns SL1 ....205 F5
Stoke Gn SL2 ....199 A1
Stoke Goldington CE Fst Sch
MK16 ....12 B6
Stoke Ho 🔢 SL1 ....205 F3
Stoke La MK17 ....59 C1
Stoke Leys Sch HP21 ....115 E3
Stoke Mandeville Comb Sch
HP22 ....116 A1
Stoke Mandeville Hospl
HP21 ....115 F4
Stoke Mandeville Sta
HP22 ....116 B2
Stoke Park Ave SL2 ......198 C2
Stoke Poges La SL1 ......205 E7
Stoke Poges Sch
Stoke Poges SL2 ....198 F5
Stoke Poges SL2 ....199 B5
Stoke Rd Ashton NN7 .....9 E8
Aylesbury HP21 ....115 E6
Leighton Buzzard LU7 ......70 D1
Milton Keynes MK2 ....58 E5
Newton Longville MK17 .....57 F3
Slough SL2 ....205 F7
Stoke View SL1 ....205 F5
Stoke Wood SL2 ....198 F8
Stokenchurch Cty Fst Sch
HP14 ....158 E4
Stokenchurch PI MK13 ....34 C3
Stokenchurch Prim Sch
HP14 ....158 E5
Stokes Croft
Haddenham HP17 ....127 A6
Haddenham HP17 ....127 A7
Stokes End HP17 ....127 A7
Stokes La HP17 ....127 A7
Stokesay SL2 ....205 F6
Stokesay Ct MK4 ....45 C2
Stokesley Rise HP10 .....185 E8
Stolford Rise MK4 ....46 B1
Stone CI MK17 ....204 B8
Stompits Rd SL6 ....203 C1
Stone CE Comb Sch
HP17 ....114 D5
Stone CI UB7 ....208 F5
Stone Croft HP17 ....114 D5
Stone CI MK46 ....13 E8
Stone Hill MK8 ....33 D1
Stone House La SL6 ......184 C1
Stone Pit CI MK46 ....6 E3
Stone View HP22 ....86 D7
Stonebridge Field SL4 ...205 B1
Stonebridge Rd HP19 ....101 B3
Stonebridge Rdbt MK13 ...33 E8
Stonechat HP19 ....101 E3
Stonecroft HP6 ....153 C4
Stonecroft Ave SL0 ....207 E7
Stonecrop PI MK14 ....34 E4
Stonefield Rd HP14 ....161 C8
Stonegate MK13 ....34 A5
Stonehaven Rd HP19 ....101 B2
Stoneleigh Ct MK4 ....45 E1
Stonepitts Pk HP18 ......111 B3
Stones Row HP11 ....173 F4
Stones Way MK17 ....68 C6
Stoney CI HP4 ....134 F6
Stoney Dean Sch HP7 ...165 F8
Stoney Gr Chesham HP5 .144 C1
Chesham HP5 ....144 D1
Stoney La
Berkhamsted HP1 ....146 B8
Bovingdon HP3 ....146 C5
Chipperfield WD4 ....146 C1
Cholesbury HP5 ....133 F1
East Burnham SL2 ....198 A4
Stoney Meade SL1 ....205 B5
Stoney Ware SL7 ....194 E8
Stoneycroft HP23 ....120 C5
Stoneyfield SL9 ....188 C3
Stonor RG9 ....179 F6
Stonor Ct MK8 ....33 D1
Stonor Ho* RG9 ....180 A7
Stony Hill NN12 ....17 C8
Stony La
Little Chalfont HP6 ....155 F1
Little Kingshill HP16 ....152 C3
Stony Stratford Nature
Reserve* MK11,MK19 ....32 D7
Stokeslade HP22 ....89 A3
Stopps Orch HP17 ....139 C5
Stork CI 🔢 HP19 ....101 F3
Stornaway Rd SL3 ....207 C2
Stotfold Ct MK11 ....32 E4
Stour CI Aylesbury HP21 ..115 C4
Milton Keynes MK3 ....57 E8
Newport Pagnell MK16 .....22 E3
Slough SL1 ....205 B3
Stourhead Gate MK4 ....45 E2
Stovell Rd SL4 ....210 B7
Stowe CI MK18 ....41 B3
Stowe CI MK18 ....41 C1
Stowe Ct MK14 ....34 C4
Stowe Landscape Gdns*
MK18 ....40 F7
Stowe Rd SL1 ....204 E6
Stowe Rise MK18 ....41 C1
Stowe Sch MK18 ....40 F7
Stowe View MK18 ....51 A7
Straight Bit HP10 ....185 B8
Straight Rd SL4 ....211 B1
Strand The HP22 ....85 B5
Strande La SL6 ....195 F5
Strande Pk SL6 ....195 F5
Strande View Wlk SL6 ...195 F5
Strangers La MK18 ....51 A6
Strangford Dr MK2 ....58 C4
Stranraer Gdns SL1 ......205 E5

Stranraer Rd TW19 ....213 E1
Stranraer Way 🔢 TW6 ...213 E1
Stratfield Ct
Maidenhead SL6 ....203 B8
Milton Keynes MK8 ....33 F1
Stratfield Rd SL1 ....206 A4
Stratford Arc MK11 ....32 D6
Stratford Ave UB10 ....201 F3
Stratford CI SL2 ....197 D1
Stratford Dr
Aylesbury HP21 ....115 B6
Wooburn HP10 ....185 D4
Stratford Gdns SL6 ....202 C4
Stratford Rd
Buckingham MK18 ....41 E1
Cosgrove MK19 ....19 D1
Deanshanger MK19 ....31 F4
Maids Moreton MK18 ....42 C2
Milton Keynes MK12 ....33 C7
Nash MK17 ....44 C1
Old Stratford MK19 ....32 B5
Whaddon MK17 ....45 A2
Stratfords Way HP21 .....127 A6
Strathcona CI HP10 ....185 C7
Strathcona Way HP10 ....185 C7
Strathnaver PI MK12 ....33 D4
Stratton Chase Dr
Chalfont St Giles HP8 .....177 B8
Chalfont St Peter HP8 .....177 A8
Stratton Gn HP21 ....116 B6
Stratton Rd
Beaconsfield HP9 ....175 B2
Princes Risborough HP27 .139 A3
Strauss Gr MK7 ....48 C4
Strawberry CI HP16 ....151 D5
Straws Hadley Ct HP22 ...89 B2
Streamside SL1 ....204 F5
Streamside Wlk HP21 ....115 C6
Streatham PI MK13 ....34 C2
Stretton CI HP10 ....174 C8
Stretton PI HP6 ....154 F1
Stringers Cotts 🔢 SL9 ..177 D2
Stringfellow CI MK43 ......24 E2
Stroma Ct SL1 ....204 D6
Stroud CI SL4 ....209 D4
Strudwick Dr MK46 ....46 F8
Stuart CI
Milton Keynes MK2 ....47 D1
Windsor SL4 ....209 F5
Stuart Ct HP6 ....154 D1
Stuart Rd HP13 ....173 C6
Stuart Way Thame OX9 ..126 A1
Windsor SL4 ....209 F5
Stubble Hill HP19 ....115 A8
Stubbles La SL6 ....195 B6
Stubbs End CI HP6 ....154 E2
Stubbs Field MK6 ....46 A3
Stubbs Wood HP6 ....153 C2
Stuchbury CI HP19 ....115 A8
Studdridge Ct HP14 ......158 C4
Studham La HP4 ....107 D4
Studland CI MK21 ....116 B5
Studley Knapp MK7 ....48 B7
Studridge La HP27 ....150 B4
Sturges CI MK7 ....48 A5
Sturman Ho HP6 ....154 C2
Stylecroft Rd HP8 ....177 D8
Styles CI OX27 ....71 E2
Styles Ct HP18 ....99 A7
Sudgrove Ho MK15 ....35 A6
Suffield Rd HP11 ....172 F6
Suffolk CI
Milton Keynes MK3 ....46 F1
Slough SL1 ....204 E7
Suffolk Ct
Maidenhead SL6 ....202 F8
Marsh Gibbon OX27 ....71 F3
Suffolk Ho HP13 ....185 E6
Suffolk Rd SL6 ....202 D4
Sulby CI HP21 ....115 C5
Sulgrave Cres HP23 .....119 C5
Sulgrave Ct 🔢 MK8 ....45 F8
Sullivan Cres MK7 ....48 C5
Sultan Croft MK5 ....46 A4
Sumburgh Way SL1 ....205 E8
Summerfield Comb Sch
MK13 ....34 C3
Summergill Ct MK13 ....34 C5
Summerhayes MK14 ....34 F8
Summerhouse La UB7 ...213 D8
Summerhouse SL3 ....205 B5
Summerleaze Rd SL6 ....196 B1
Summers CI SL1 ....197 C2
Summerson Ct MK6 ....46 F5
Summerson Rd
Bleak Hall MK6 ....47 A5
Milton Keynes MK6 ....46 F5
Summit Ctr UB7 ....213 D7
Sumner Ct MK5 ....46 A8
Sun CI SL4 ....210 D8
Sun Cres HP18 ....109 D5
Sun La SL6 ....202 F7
Sun Pas 🔟 SL4 ....210 D6
Sunbury CI MK13 ....34 A6
Sunbury Ct SL4 ....210 D8
Sunbury Rd SL4 ....210 D8
Sunderland Ct
Milton Keynes MK4 ....45 F1
🔢 **Stanwell** TW19 ....213 E1
Sunderland Rd SL6 ....202 B8
Sunningdale CI HP12 ....172 B5
Sunningdale Way MK3 .....57 D8
Sunny Bank HP15 ....162 F6
Sunny Brook CI HP22 ....117 D6
Sunny Croft HP13 ....161 C2
Sunny View NN7 ....1 B6

Sunnybank
Cheddington LU7 ....104 F7
Marlow SL7 ....183 D4
Sunnyhill Rd WD3 ....178 D4
Sunnymeads Sta TW19 ..211 E4
Sunnymede Ave HP5 .....144 E3
Sunnymede Cotts SL6 ...196 B1
Sunnyside Cotts HP5 ....145 A5
Sunnyside Rd HP5 ....144 C1
Sunray Ave UB7 ....208 D4
Sunridge CI MK16 ....22 C3
Sunrise Parkway MK14 ...34 E6
Sunset CI MK2 ....58 C7
Sunset Wlk MK9 ....34 E2
Sunters End HP12 ....172 A7
Sunters Wood CI HP12 ..172 B5
Surly Hall Wlk SL4 ....209 F6
Surrey Ave SL2 ....198 C1
Surrey PI
Milton Keynes MK3 ....46 F2
Tring HP23 ....119 A3
Surrey Rd MK3 ....46 F2
Sussex CI
Aylesbury HP19 ....101 A3
Chalfont St Giles HP8 .....177 B8
High Wycombe HP13 ....162 D1
Slough SL1 ....206 A4
Sussex Ho SL2 ....206 A4
Sussex Keep 🔢 SL1 ......206 B4
Sussex Lodge 🔢 SL6 ....202 F6
Sussex PI SL1 ....206 B4
Sussex Rd MK3 ....46 F1
Sussex Way UB9 ....189 F6
Sutcliffe Ave MK6 ....34 E1
Sutherland Gr MK3 ....46 F3
Sutherland Grange SL4 ..209 D7
Sutherland Wlk HP21 ....115 F5
Sutleye Ct MK5 ....46 A4
Sutton Ave SL3 ....206 C4
Sutton CI Cookham SL6 ..196 B7
Maidenhead SL6 ....202 C5
Tring HP23 ....119 B6
Sutton La Slough SL3 ....207 B1
Slough SL3 ....207 C2
Sutton PI SL3 ....212 B8
Sutton Rd SL6 ....196 B6
Swabey Rd SL3 ....207 A2
Swains CI UB7 ....208 E4
Swains La HP10 ....174 B1
Swains Mkt HP10 ....174 A1
Swakeleys Dr UB10 ....201 F8
Swakeleys Rd UB10 ......201 E8
Swale Rd HP21 ....115 C5
Swallow CI MK18 ....52 E7
Swallow Dr HP15 ....163 B5
Swallow Ho SL7 ....184 A2
Swallow La
Milton Keynes MK10 ....114 F8
Stoke Mandeville HP22 ...116 A1
Iver Heath SL0 ....207 D8
Swallowdale SL0 ....200 D2
Swallowfield MK8 ....33 E1
Swallowfield Lower Sch
MK7 ....49 B5
Swan CI Aylesbury HP19 .101 F3
Blackthorn OX25 ....81 A3
Buckingham MK18 ....52 E7
Chesham HP5 ....144 B4
Ivinghoe Aston LU7 ....92 A1
Whitchurch HP22 ....87 B5
Swan Cotts HP17 ....129 D1
Swan Ct
Chorleywood WD3 ....167 C5
Datchet SL3 ....211 B6
Leighton Buzzard LU7 ......80 E6
Olney MK46 ....7 A4
West Drayton UB7 ....208 D4
Swan Hill HP18 ....112 F3
Swan Hill Cotts HP18 ....112 F3
Swan La Lee Gate HP16 ..142 C8
Marsh Gibbon OX6 ....72 A3
Swan Mews HP22 ....131 B5
Swan Rd Iver SL0 ....207 F7
West Drayton UB7 ....208 D4
Swan Terr
Milton Keynes MK13 ....32 D5
Windsor SL4 ....210 A7
Swan Wharf Bsns Ctr
UB8 ....201 C3
Swanbourne CE Sch
MK17 ....67 A3
Swanbourne House Sch
MK17 ....66 F3
Swanbourne Rd MK17 .....67 D4
Swanbrook Ct SL6 ....203 A7
Swandon Ct MK18 ....42 C2
Swanns CI LU6 ....92 F3
Swanwick La MK10 ....36 B3
Swayne Rise MK10 ....36 A2
Sweetcroft La UB10 ......201 F6
Sweetlands Cnr MK7 ......48 B6
Swift CI Aylesbury HP19 ..101 F3
Newport Pagnell MK16 .....22 A5
Swift Ho SL7 ....184 A2
Swimbridge La MK4 ....46 D4
Swinden CI MK13 ....34 B4
Swing Gate La HP4 ....135 D2
Swing Gate Sch HP4 .....135 D1
Swinnerton Ho RG9 ....191 E3
Switchback CI SL6 ....195 D3
Switchback Rd N SL6 ....195 D3
Switchback Rd S SL6 ....195 D2
Switchback The SL6 ......195 D2
Sycamore Ave MK2 ....158 B8
Sycamore CI
Amersham HP6 ....154 D2

Sycamore CI continued
🔢 **Bourne End** SL8 ....185 B3
Buckingham MK18 ....52 F7
Chalfont St Giles HP8 .....177 A7
Long Crendon HP18 ....125 C6
Maidenhead SL6 ....202 C3
Stewkley LU7 ....68 D2
West Drayton UB7 ....208 F6
Sycamore Cnr HP6 ....154 D2
Sycamore Ct
Aylesbury HP19 ....101 D1
High Wycombe HP12 ....172 C4
Windsor SL4 ....210 C4
Sycamore Dene HP5 .....144 D3
Sycamore Dr
Marlow Bottom SL7 ....183 D5
Tring HP23 ....119 B4
Sycamore Ho
Amersham HP6 ....154 D2
Princes Risborough HP27 .139 B3
Sycamore Leys MK18 .....63 E3
Sycamore PI HP6 ....154 C1
Sycamore Rd
Amersham HP6 ....154 D2
Chalfont St Giles HP8 .....177 A7
High Wycombe HP12 ....172 C4
Sycamore Rise
Berkhamsted HP4 ....135 D3
Chalfont St Giles HP8 .....177 A7
Sycamore Way HP15 ....163 A3
Sycamore Wlk SL3 ....206 F2
Sycamores The HP3 .....146 F8
Sydney Gr SL1 ....205 C7
Sygnus Ct 🔢 SL6 ....202 F7
Syke Cluan SL0 ....207 E4
Syke Ings SL0 ....207 E4
Sykes Croft MK4 ....46 C1
Sykes Rd SL1 ....205 B8
Sylvana CI UB10 ....201 F4
Sylvester Rd SL6 ....195 E2
Sylvia CI HP16 ....152 B4
Symington Ct MK5 ....46 B5
Syon Gdns MK16 ....22 C2
Syresham St James CE Prim
NN13 ....27 C7

T

Tabard Gdns MK16 ....22 C2
Tachbrook Rd UB8 ....201 C3
Tacknell Dr MK5 ....46 A4
Tacks La HP17 ....126 F6
Tadmarton MK15 ....35 A6
Tadmere MK8 ....33 D1
Talbot Ave
High Wycombe HP13 ....161 D2
Slough SL3 ....206 F4
Talbot CI
Milton Keynes MK15 ....35 C1
Windsor SL4 ....210 B4
Talbot PI SL3 ....211 C6
Talbot Rd HP22 ....117 C5
Talbots Dr SL6 ....202 B6
Talbots Hyde MK46 ....6 A5
Tall Oaks HP6 ....154 D2
Tall Pines LU7 ....70 F2
Tall Trees SL3 ....212 E6
Talland Ave MK6 ....34 F1
Tallis La MK7 ....48 C5
Tamar CI Aylesbury HP21 .115 C4
Loudwater HP11 ....174 B4
Tamar Ho
High Wycombe HP13 ....173 F7
Milton Keynes MK3 ....46 E1
Tamar Way SL3 ....207 B2
Tamarisk Ct MK7 ....48 B5
Tamarisk Way SL1 ....205 B5
Tancred Rd HP13 ....162 A1
Tandra MK6 ....47 B5
Tandys CI MK43 ....8 E5
Tanfield La MK10 ....36 A3
Tangier CI SL4 ....210 D8
Tangier La SL4 ....210 D8
Tank House Rd MK18 ......66 B6
Tanners Dr MK14 ....22 A2
Tannery Rd HP13 ....174 A4
Tannery Road Ind Est
HP13 ....174 A4
Tansman La MK7 ....48 C5
Tanton Ho HP16 ....151 F8
Tapestries Hall SL4 ......211 A4
Tapestries The SL4 ......211 A2
Taplin Way HP10 ....163 C1
Taplow Common Rd
SL1 ....197 A3
Taplow Rd SL6 ....204 A7
Taplow Sta SL6 ....203 D7
Tapping Rd HP14 ....171 C5
Taranis CI MK7 ....48 C7
Tarbay La SL4 ....209 B5
Tarbert CI MK2 ....58 C5
Tarmac Way UB7 ....213 D7
Tarnbrook CI 🔢 MK4 ......46 B2
Tarragon CI MK7 ....48 A6
Taskers Ho LU6 ....92 F4
Taskers Row Cotts LU6 ...92 F4
Tatchbrook CI SL6 ....203 A8
Tate Rd SL9 ....177 F5
Tatling Gr MK7 ....48 A6
Tattam CI MK15 ....35 C2
Tattams La MK17 ....67 B3
Tattenhoe La MK3 ....57 D8
Tattenhoe St MK5 ....45 F4
Tattershall CI MK5 ....46 A4
Tattlers Hill HP22 ....89 B3

Taunton Deane MK4 .....46 D2
Taurus Cl MK18 .....63 D2
Tavelhurst MK8 .....33 E1
Taverner Cl MK7 .....48 C5
Tavistock Cl
　Maidenhead SL6 .....202 A8
　Woburn Sands MK17 .....49 B6
Tavistock Mews HP12 .....172 E7
Tavistock Rd SL8 .....208 D5
Tavistock St MK2 .....47 D1
Tavistock Wlk HP20 .....101 E2
Tay Rd MK3 .....46 E1
Taylor Rd HP21 .....115 D5
Taylor's Ride LU7 .....70 F2
Taylors Cl SL7 .....183 F2
Taylors Ct SL6 .....202 B8
Taylors La
　Little Missenden HP7 .....153 A3
　St Leonards HP23 .....132 C3
　Stewkley LU7 .....78 E7
Taylors Mews MK14 .....34 F6
Taylors Rd HP5 .....144 D2
Taylors Turn HP13 .....161 D3
Taymouth Pl MK9 .....35 B3
Teal Ho HP11 .....173 C6
Teale Cl OX25 .....94 E7
Teasel Ave MK14 .....34 E5
Tedder Cl UB10 .....201 F5
Tedder Rd HP22 .....131 D5
Tees Rd HP21 .....115 C5
Tees Way MK3 .....46 D1
Teesdale Rd SL2 .....204 F8
Teign Cl MK16 .....22 D4
Teikyo Sch (UK) SL2 .....199 D5
Telford Cl HP19 .....100 F1
Telford Dr SL1 .....205 A4
Telford Way
　High Wycombe HP13 .....162 A1
　Milton Keynes MK14 .....22 B1
Telston Cl SL8 .....185 A5
Temperance Terr MK11 .....32 C6
Templars Pl ② SL7 .....183 E1
Temple MK14 .....34 C7
Temple Cl
　Buckingham MK18 .....41 E2
　Milton Keynes MK3 .....57 D7
Temple End HP13 .....173 A8
Temple Gate HP13 .....173 A7
Temple Ho RG9 .....191 E3
Temple La SL7 .....194 D6
Temple Mill Cotts SL7 .....194 C5
Temple Mill Island SL7 .....194 C5
Temple Orch HP13 .....173 B7
Temple Pk SL6 .....193 F3
Temple Rd SL4 .....210 D5
Temple Sq ☷ HP20 .....115 D8
Temple St
　Aylesbury HP20 .....115 D8
　Brill HP18 .....96 B1
　High Wycombe HP11 .....173 A7
Temple Way SL2 .....198 C7
Templecroft Terr HP17 .....114 A4
Templewood HP14 .....150 B1
Templewood Gate SL2 .....198 C2
Templewood La SL2 .....198 E8
Tenby Gr MK4 .....45 D1
Tene Acres MK5 .....45 F6
Tennant Cl MK8 .....45 D6
Tennis La MK18 .....66 A3
Tennyson Dr HP16 .....22 A4
Tennyson Gr MK3 .....57 F7
Tennyson Rd
　Aylesbury HP21 .....115 F6
　High Wycombe HP11 .....173 A5
Tennyson Way SL2 .....197 E1
Tenterden Cres MK7 .....48 B7
Tenzing Dr HP13 .....173 E6
Terrace The
　Aspley Guise MK17 .....49 E5
　Bray SL6 .....203 C3
　☷ Tring HP23 .....119 A3
Terrent Ct SL4 .....210 A5
Terrick Row HP17 .....114 B5
Terrington Hill SL7 .....183 B2
Terry Dr HP19 .....101 C3
Terry Orch HP13 .....173 C8
Terry Pl UB8 .....208 C8
Terry Rd HP13 .....173 C8
Terry's La SL6 .....195 F8
Terryfield Rd HP13 .....173 E6
Testwood Rd SL4 .....209 D6
Tetherdown HP16 .....151 C5
Tewkesbury La MK10 .....35 F1
Tews End La NN12 .....17 B8
Thackeray End HP19 .....100 F2
Thame Ho ⑤ HP13 .....173 B7
Thame Rd
　Aylesbury HP21 .....115 D7
　Blackthorn OX25 .....81 A3
　Brill HP18 .....110 B7
　Chilton HP18 .....111 B3
　Chinnor OX39 .....147 B8
　Haddenham HP17 .....126 D5
　Long Crendon HP18,OX9 .....125 D7
　Longwick HP27 .....138 C6
　Piddington OX25 .....95 D6
Thame Rd S HP21 .....115 B6
Thame Valley Falconry &
　Conservation Ctr* 184 A4
Thames Ave SL4 .....210 D7
Thames Bank SL6 .....203 C7
Thames Cl
　Bourne End SL8 .....185 A4
　Milton Keynes MK3 .....57 E8
Thames Cres MK6 .....196 B2
Thames Dr MK16 .....22 E3
Thames Ho Datchet SL3 .....211 B6

Thames Ho continued
　Henley-on-T RG9 .....191 E3
Thames Ind Est SL2 .....183 F2
Thames Mead SL4 .....209 E6
Thames Rd SL3 .....207 B3
Thames Reach SL7 .....193 D6
Thames Side
　Henley-On-T RG9 .....191 E2
　Windsor SL4 .....210 D7
Thames St SL4 .....210 D7
Thames Valley Nuffield Hospl
　The SL3 .....199 C4
Thames Valley University (Slough
　Campus) SL1 .....205 E5
Thamesbourne Mews ☷
　SL8 .....185 A3
Thamesfield Gdns SL7 .....183 E1
Thane Ct MK14 .....34 C7
Thanestead Copse
　HP10 .....174 C2
Thanestead Ct HP10 .....174 C2
Thatcher Cl UB7 .....208 E4
Thatchers Dr SL6 .....202 A5
Theatre Wlk MK9 .....34 F3
Thellusson Way WD3 .....167 F2
Theydon Ave MK17 .....49 B4
Thicket The
　Tylers Green HP10 .....163 A1
　West Drayton UB7 .....208 E7
Third Ave Marlow SL7 .....183 F7
　Milton Keynes MK1 .....47 B2
Third Cres SL1 .....205 C8
Third St HP11 .....173 B4
Thirkleby Cl SL1 .....205 C5
Thirlby La MK5 .....46 A6
Thirlmere Ave
　Milton Keynes MK2 .....58 D6
　Slough SL1 .....204 C8
Thirsk Gdns MK3 .....57 C6
Thistle Ct HP21 .....115 C5
Thomas Bourne Ho ■
　HP4 .....135 D4
Thomas Coram Sch The
　HP4 .....135 D2
Thomas Ct
　Berkhamsted HP4 .....134 E6
　Maidenhead SL6 .....202 A2
Thomas Dr MK16 .....22 A6
Thomas Harding Jun Sch
　HP5 .....154 B7
Thomas Hickman Sch
　HP19 .....101 A3
Thomas Rd HP10 .....185 D4
Thomas Valentine Ho
　HP8 .....177 B7
Thompkins La SL2 .....198 A5
Thompson Cl SL3 .....207 A2
Thompson Dr HP18 .....100 E5
Thompson St MK13 .....34 A7
Thomson Cl HP21 .....115 B6
Thomson Wlk HP21 .....115 B6
Thorn Dr SL3 .....206 F7
Thornaby Pl HP10 .....185 E8
Thornbank Cl TW19 .....213 A2
Thornborough Inf Sch
　MK18 .....54 A8
Thornborough Rd MK18 .....55 B8
Thornbridge Rd SL0 .....200 C4
Thorncliffe MK8 .....33 D1
Thorndike SL2 .....205 B8
Thorne Rd HP14 .....171 C4
Thorne Way
　Aston Clinton HP22 .....118 A4
　Wingrave HP22 .....89 B3
Thorney Lane N SL0 .....207 F6
Thorney Lane S SL0 .....207 F5
Thorney Mill Rd SL0,
　UB7 .....208 B3
Thorneycroft La MK15 .....35 B5
Thornhill MK18 .....54 B8
Thornhill Cl HP7 .....165 B7
Thornhill Rd UB10 .....201 F8
Thornlea Croft MK6 .....47 D4
Thornley Croft MK4 .....46 C2
Thorns Cl HP27 .....139 D5
Thorns Cl HP27 .....139 E5
Thornton Ave UB7 .....208 F3
Thornton Cl UB7 .....208 F3
Thornton Coll Convent of
　Jesus & Mary MK17 .....43 C5
Thornton Cres HP22 .....131 A5
Thornton Rd MK17 .....44 A1
Thorntree Dr HP23 .....118 F4
Thorpe Cl HP21 .....116 A4
Thorpe House Sch SL9 .....188 E7
Thorpeness Croft MK4 .....56 F8
Thorwold Pl MK5 .....46 B6
Thrasher Rd HP21 .....115 D5
Three Close La HP4 .....135 C4
Three Gables HP9 .....175 E2
Three Households HP8 .....176 F6
Three Oaks Cl UB10 .....190 F1
Three Points La MK18 .....74 A6
Thresher Gr MK12 .....33 A5
Thrift La SL6 .....202 D1
Thrift View MK43 .....25 C2
Thrupp Cl MK19 .....20 A6
Thrush Cl
　⑥ Aylesbury HP19 .....101 F3
　High Wycombe HP12 .....172 C4
Thurlby Way SL6 .....202 D3
Thurley Cotts SL6 .....199 B3
Thurne Cl MK16 .....22 E3
Thurston Rd SL1 .....205 E7
Thyme Cl MK16 .....21 F5
Tibbys La HP18 .....112 F3
Ticehurst Cl MK7 .....48 B7

Ticehurst Cl MK7 .....48 B7
Tichborne WD3 .....178 D5
Tickford Arc MK16 .....22 D4
Tickford St MK16 .....22 C4
Tidbury Cl MK17 .....49 A4
Tiddenfoot Waterside Pk*
　LU7 .....91 A5
Tierney St ☷ SL7 .....183 E1
Tiffany Cl MK7 .....58 D6
Tilbrook Ind Est MK7 .....48 B3
Tilbrook Rdbt MK7 .....48 B2
Tilbury Wlk SL3 .....207 B3
Tilburywood Cl HP13 .....161 C2
Tilebarn Cl RG9 .....191 C1
Tilecotes Cl SL7 .....183 D2
Tilehouse Comb Sch
　UB9 .....189 F5
Tilehouse La UB9 .....189 E6
Tilehouse Way UB9 .....189 F4
Tilers Rd MK11 .....33 B2
Tilling Cres HP13 .....174 A7
Tillman Cl MK12 .....33 C5
Tilstone Ave SL4 .....204 E2
Tilstone Cl SL4 .....204 E1
Tilsworth Rd HP9 .....175 C1
Timber La MK17 .....60 F7
Timber Way OX39 .....147 C6
Timberley La HP16 .....142 A8
Timbers Wlk SL6 .....202 B5
Timberscombe MK4 .....46 D3
Timberwood SL2 .....187 D1
Timbold Dr MK7 .....48 A7
Timor Ct MK1 .....32 C6
Timpson La MK46 .....7 C3
Timpsons Row MK46 .....7 A3
Tindal Rd HP20 .....115 E8
Tingewick Inf Sch MK18 .....51 B6
Tingewick Rd
　Buckingham MK18 .....52 B8
　Radclive MK18 .....51 F7
Tingewick Road Ind Est
　MK18 .....52 B8
Tinkers Dr MK18 .....65 F3
Tinkers La
　Berkhamsted HP23 .....134 A6
　Windsor SL4 .....209 D5
Tinkers Wood Rd HP13 .....161 E1
Tintagel Ct MK6 .....47 A8
Tintagel Ho SL1 .....205 C3
Tintern Cl SL1 .....205 D3
Tinterne Cl HP21 .....116 C6
Tippet Cl MK7 .....205 B8
Tiree Ho SL2 .....205 B8
Titchmarsh Ct MK6 .....46 E8
Tithe Barn Dr SL6 .....203 E1
Tithe Cl SL6 .....203 C1
Tithe Ct SL3 .....207 A2
Tithe La TW19 .....212 A1
Titmus Rd HP27 .....131 E7
Tiverton Cres
　Aylesbury HP19 .....101 C3
　Milton Keynes MK4 .....45 E1
Tockley Rd SL1 .....197 B2
Todd Cl Aylesbury HP21 .....115 B6
　Holmer Green HP15 .....163 B6
Toddbury Farm Cvn Pk
　LU7 .....91 D8
Tolcarne Ave MK6 .....35 A1
Toll Bar Cnr HP27 .....138 D7
Tollgate SL6 .....202 A6
Tollgate Cl WD3 .....167 F5
Tolman Ct HP21 .....115 B6
Tom Scott Ho HP5 .....144 B2
Tomlin Rd SL2 .....197 E1
Tompion Rd HP19 .....100 F1
Tompkins Cl
　Aston Clinton HP22 .....117 F4
　Milton Keynes MK5 .....46 B3
Tompkins La OX27 .....71 E2
Toms Hill Cl HP23 .....133 B5
Toms Hill Rd HP23 .....133 B5
Toms Turn HP15 .....162 F5
Tongwell La MK15,MK16 .....22 C2
Tongwell Rdbt MK15 .....35 D8
Tongwell St
　Milton Keynes,Broughton
　MK10 .....36 A3
　Milton Keynes,Northfield
　MK15 .....35 F5
　Milton Keynes,Pineham
　MK15 .....35 E7
　Walnut Tree MK7 .....48 C6
Toot Hill Cl MK5 .....46 A4
Top Angel MK18 .....52 D5
Top Farm Cl HP9 .....175 A1
Top Mdw MK7 .....48 B3
Top Pk SL9 .....188 C5
Top Station Rd NN13 .....38 A7
Top Station Road Ind Est
　NN13 .....38 A8
Topaz Cl SL1 .....205 B5
Topland Rd SL9 .....177 D3
Topping La UB8 .....201 D2
Torbay HP22 .....85 B4
Tornay Ct LU7 .....90 F6
Torquay Spur SL2 .....198 B2
Torre Cl MK3 .....47 A2
Torridge Rd
　Aylesbury HP21 .....115 D4
　Slough SL3 .....212 B4
Torridon Ct MK2 .....58 D4
Torrington Rd HP4 .....135 B4
Tortoiseshell Way HP19 .....101 F4
Torwood Cl HP4 .....134 F4
Totteridge Ave HP13 .....173 D6
Totteridge Common Cotts
　HP13 .....173 F8
Totteridge Dr HP13 .....162 E1

Totteridge Ho HP13 .....173 E8
Totteridge La HP13 .....162 E1
Totteridge Par HP13 .....173 E8
Totteridge Rd HP13 .....173 D7
Totternhoe Knolls Nature
　Reserve* LU6 .....93 B7
Totternhoe Lower Sch
　LU6 .....93 B7
Totternhoe Rd
　Dunstable LU6 .....93 E7
　Eaton Bray LU6 .....92 D7
Towan Ave
　Fishermead MK6 .....47 A8
　Milton Keynes MK6 .....35 A1
Towcester Dr NN12 .....18 B3
Towcester Rd
　Buckingham MK18 .....41 E4
　Old Stratford MK19 .....32 B7
Tower Cl
　Berkhamsted HP4 .....135 A3
　Emberton MK16 .....13 C5
　Flackwell Heath HP10 .....185 C7
Tower Cres MK14 .....34 F6
Tower Ct HP27 .....139 B3
Tower Dr MK13 .....34 C7
Tower Hill WD4 .....146 F1
Tower Ho Iver SL0 .....207 E7
Tower Rd HP4 .....135 A3
Tower St HP13 .....162 D2
Towergate Cl UB8 .....201 E7
Toweridge La
　High Wycombe HP12 .....172 C8
　West Wycombe HP14 .....160 F1
Towers Lea HP13 .....173 C7
Towersey Way HP21 .....115 B7
Town Bridge Ct HP5 .....154 B7
Town La TW19 .....50 D6
Town End Cres MK16 .....12 B5
Town End Rd HP14 .....159 D5
Town Farm LU7 .....105 A7
Town Farm Barns HP27 .....139 B3
Town Farm Cl OX49 .....157 B8
Town Field La HP4 .....177 C7
Town La Stanwell TW19 .....213 D1
　Wooburn HP10 .....185 D4
Town Sq ☷ SL1 .....205 F4
Townfield HP5 .....154 C7
Townfield Rd HP5 .....173 C7
Townlands Hospl RG9 .....191 D2
Townsend
　Haddenham HP17 .....127 A7
　Marsh Gibbon OX27 .....71 E2
　Quainton HP22 .....85 A5
Townsend Cl MK43 .....37 F8
Townsend Cotts
　Great Horwood MK17 .....55 B3
　Middle Claydon MK18 .....74 C8
Townsend Gr MK13 .....34 B8
Townsend La OX27 .....71 E2
Townsend Piece HP5 .....101 C1
Townsend Rd HP5 .....144 C1
Townside
　Edlesborough LU6 .....92 F3
　Haddenham HP17 .....126 F5
Tozer Wlk SL4 .....209 D4
Trafalgar Ave MK3 .....46 E2
Trafford Cl HP16 .....152 A6
Trafford Rd HP16 .....152 A7
Tram Hill HP18 .....96 B2
Tranlands Brigg MK13 .....34 B4
Transcend SL4 .....210 D5
Tranter Cl HP23 .....119 B4
Trapp's Ct HP5 .....154 C6
Trapp's La HP5 .....154 C6
Travell Ct MK13 .....34 B3
Travic Rd SL2 .....197 F2
Travis Ct SL2 .....198 B2
Travis Gr MK3 .....58 A8
Treacher's Cl HP5 .....144 C1
Treadaway Bsns Ctr
　HP10 .....174 C1
Treadaway Hill HP10 .....174 B1
Treadaway Rd HP10 .....174 B1
Trebah Sq HP19 .....114 F8
Treborough MK4 .....46 D2
Tredington Gr MK7 .....48 B4
Treefields MK18 .....52 C8
Trehanger Cl HP23 .....119 B4
Trees Rd Bourne End SL8 .....185 B3
　Hughenden Valley HP14 .....162 A4
Treeside HP13 .....208 D2
Tresham Rd SL6 .....202 C3
Trelawney Ave SL3 .....206 E3
Tremayne Ct MK6 .....47 A6
Trenchard Ave HP22 .....131 C6
Trenchard St HP19 .....115 A8
Trenches La SL3 .....207 A6
Trengothal Ct NN13 .....26 D4
Trent Dr MK16 .....22 E3
Trent Rd
　Milton Keynes MK3 .....46 E1
　Slough SL3 .....212 B8
Trent Villas Est SL3 .....211 B6
Trentishoe Cres MK4 .....46 D2
Tresco Rd HP4 .....134 F5
Tresham Ct MK5 .....46 A7
Tressell The SL6 .....202 D6
Trevelyan Mid Sch SL4 .....210 C3
Trevelyan Way HP4 .....135 B6
Treves Gn HP21 .....115 E5
Trevithick La MK5 .....46 B5
Trevone Ct MK6 .....47 A6
Trevor Cl TW19 .....213 C1
Trevose Ho SL2 .....198 B1
Trewarden Ave SL0 .....200 D3
Triangle Bsns Pk HP22 .....130 D8
Trident Ind Est SL3 .....212 E4

Tring Bsns Ctr HP23 .....118 E4
Tring Ford Rd HP23 .....119 A7
Tring Hill HP23 .....118 C3
Tring Rd Aylesbury HP21 .....116 B7
　Berkhamsted HP4 .....135 A5
　Dunstable LU6 .....93 E7
　Edlesborough LU6 .....106 E8
　Long Marston HP23 .....104 C3
　Wendover HP22 .....131 C5
　Wilstone HP23 .....104 C1
　Wingrave HP22 .....89 C1
Tring Sta HP23 .....119 B4
Tring Sta SL7 .....120 A5
Trinity Ave SL7 .....183 D3
Trinity CE Prim Sch
　RG9 .....191 D1
Trinity Cl
　Old Stratford MK19 .....32 B7
　Stanwell TW19 .....213 C1
Trinity Ct Aylesbury HP19 .....101 D1
　Chesham HP5 .....154 C7
　Marlow SL7 .....183 D3
Trinity Ho SL8 .....195 F6
Trinity Pl SL4 .....210 C5
Trinity Rd
　Hazlemere HP15 .....162 F3
　Marlow SL7 .....183 D2
　Milton Keynes SL7 .....58 C6
Trinity St Stephens CE Fst
　Sch SL4 .....210 B6
Tripps Hill Cl HP8 .....177 A7
Trispen Ct MK6 .....47 A8
Trooper Rd HP23 .....120 C5
Trout Cl SL7 .....194 C8
Trout Hollow HP27 .....148 E8
Trout La UB7 .....208 C5
Trout Rd UB7 .....208 B5
Troutbeck Cl MK6 .....47 C8
Troutbeck Cl SL2 .....206 A6
Trubys Gdn MK6 .....47 A7
Trueman Pl MK6 .....46 F8
Truesdale Dr UB9 .....190 C2
Trumper Way Slough SL1 .....204 F5
　Uxbridge UB8 .....201 C4
Trumpton La MK7 .....48 C7
Trunk Furlong MK17 .....49 D6
Truro Cl SL6 .....202 A7
Trust Cotts HP4 .....107 A1
Trustees Way UB9 .....189 F6
Tubwell Rd SL2 .....199 B4
Tucker Cl HP21 .....173 C8
Tuckers Dr HP15 .....163 C7
Tuckey Hale MK7 .....48 B8
Tudor Ct Amersham HP6 .....154 D1
　⑤ Leighton Buzzard LU7 .....80 F7
　Maidenhead SL6 .....196 C2
　Piddington HP14 .....160 C1
　⑤ Stanwell TW19 .....213 E1
Tudor Dr HP10 .....185 D7
Tudor Gdns
　Milton Keynes MK11 .....32 E4
　Slough SL1 .....204 C8
　Steeple Claydon MK18 .....63 D3
Tudor Mill HP10 .....185 E6
Tudor Orch HP4 .....134 E6
Tudor Rd HP15 .....163 C3
Tudor Way SL4 .....210 C3
Tudors Cl MK18 .....73 B4
Tuffnell Cl MK15 .....35 E7
Tulip Way UB7 .....208 D2
Tulkers Cl HP6 .....151 D5
Tulla Ct MK2 .....58 C4
Tummell Way MK4 .....58 C6
Tunbridge Gr MK7 .....48 B8
Tunmers Ct SL9 .....177 C2
Tunmers End SL9 .....177 C2
Tunmers Ms SL9 .....177 C2
Tunnel Way LU7 .....91 C6
Tuns La Henley-on-T RG9 .....191 E2
　Slough SL1 .....205 C4
Turks Head Ct SL4 .....210 C2
Turnberry Cl MK3 .....57 D7
Turner Cl HP20 .....101 F3
Turner Rd SL3 .....206 C4
Turner Wlk HP20 .....101 F3
Turner's Mdw HP22 .....117 B6
Turners Dr HP13 .....173 E8
Turners Field HP13 .....161 E3
Turners Mews MK14 .....34 F6
Turners Pl HP15 .....163 C6
Turners Wlk ☷ HP5 .....154 C7
Turners Wood Dr HP8 .....177 D7
Turneys Ct LU7 .....33 A6
Turneys Orch WD3 .....167 D4
Turnfields HP18 .....124 A3
Turnfurlong HP21 .....115 F7
Turnfurlong Inf Sch
　HP21 .....116 A6
Turnfurlong Jun Sch
　HP21 .....116 A6
Turnfurlong La HP21 .....116 A6
Turnfurlong Row HP21 .....116 A6
Turnip Cl HP18 .....125 F3
Turnip Cl HP18 .....112 B2
Turnmill Ave MK6 .....35 B2
Turnmill Cl MK6 .....35 B2
Turnoak Pk SL4 .....209 C3
Turnpike Cl HP21 .....115 F6
Turnpike End HP21 .....115 F6
Turnpike La UB10 .....201 E3
Turnpike Rd HP12 .....172 D4
Turnpike The HP18 .....109 D5
Turnpike Way HP12 .....172 C4
Turnstone Way HP19 .....101 E3

Turpins Gn SL6 ....202 A5
Turpyn Ct MK6 ....47 D8
Turton Way SL1 ....205 D3
Turvey Cl HP22 ....117 E5
Turvey Lower Sch MK43 ...8 E6
Turvey Mill MK43 ....8 D5
Turvey Rd Astwood MK16 ..15 F5
  Turvey MK43 ....3 E2
Turvill End MK5 ....34 C3
Turville Rd HP22 ....116 C6
Turweston Rd NN13 ......26 A1
Tuscans Cl MK18 ....73 B5
Tweed Cl HP4 ....135 B5
Tweed Dr MK3 ....46 D1
Tweed Rd SL3 ....212 B8
Tweedale Cl MK17 ....67 C7
Tweenways HP5 ....144 E1
Twelve Leys HP22 ....99 B3
Twinches La SL1 ....205 B5
Twinflower MK7 ....48 B6
Twist The HP23 ....119 D2
Twitchell La HP22 .....117 E5
Twitchell Rd HP16 .....152 A7
Twitchell's La HP9 ....176 F5
Twitchen La MK4 ....46 D3
Two Dells La HP5 ......145 A4
Two Gates La HP5 .....143 D7
Two Mile Ash Mid Sch
  MK8 ....33 E1
Two Mile Dr SL1 ....204 E4
Twyford CE Sch MK18 ...62 C2
Twyford La MK7 ....48 C5
Twynham Rd SL6 ....202 B7
Tyburn Ave MK6 ....35 B2
Tyle Pl SL4 ....211 A2
Tyler Wlk ﬁ SL3 ....206 F1
Tylers Cres HP15 ......163 B2
Tylers Gn SL3 ....34 D3
Tylers Green Fst Sch
  HP10 ....174 D8
Tylers Green Mid Sch
  HP10 ....174 B8
Tylers Hill Rd HP5 ....154 F8
Tylers Rd HP15 ....163 B2
Tylsworth Cl HP6 ......154 D1
Tyne Rd HP21 ....115 D4
Tyne Sq MK3 ....46 D1
Tyneham Cl HP21 ......116 B4
Tynemouth Rise ﬂ MK10 .36 A1
Tyrell Cl MK18 ....52 C7
Tyrell Gdns SL4 ....209 F4
Tyrells Gdns MK17 .....69 E8
Tyrells Rd MK17 ....69 E8
Tyrill MK14 ....34 C7
Tyson Pl MK6 ....46 E8
Tythe Cl LU7 ....78 E8
Tythe Gdns LU7 ....78 E8
Tythe Mews LU6 ....92 E3
Tyzack Rd HP13 ....162 F1

U

Ufton Court Yd SL8 ...185 A4
Ufton Ct SL8 ....185 B4
Ullswater Cl SL1 ......204 C8
Ullswater Dr LU7 ....80 C7
Ulverscroft MK10 ....36 B2
Ulyett Pl MK6 ....46 E8
Umberville Way SL2 ...197 F2
Underhill Cl SL6 ......202 E6
Underwood Cotts HP7 ..164 C2
Underwood Pl MK6 ......46 E8
Underwood Rd HP13 ...173 D8
Union Bldgs UB8 ......201 B2
Union Bsns Pk UB8 ....201 B5
Union Ct ﬂﬂ HP4 ....135 D4
Union Ind Est HP12 ...172 A7
Union St
  High Wycombe HP11 ...173 A7
  Newport Pagnell MK16 ..22 D5
Univ of Buckingham
  Buckingham MK18 ......52 C7
  Buckingham MK18 ......52 C8
Univ of Buckingham (Verney
  Pk) MK18 ....52 E7
University Way MK43 ...24 D1
Up Cnr HP8 ....177 C8
Up Corner Cl HP8 .....177 B8
Upcroft SL4 ....210 B4
Upland Ave HP5 ....144 B3
Uplands SL7 ....183 D6
Uplands Cl
  Gerrards Cross SL9 ...188 E3
  High Wycombe HP13 ...173 E8
Uplands Cl SL5 ....144 C1
Uplands The SL9 ......188 E2
Upper Abbotts Hill
  HP19 ....115 A7
Upper Ashlyns Rd HP4 .135 B3
Upper Barn Farm HP18 ..84 B1
Upper Belmont Rd HP5 .144 B3
Upper Bourne End La
  HP11 ....146 B7
Upper Bray Rd SL6 ....203 C3
Upper Church St HP18 .112 F3
Upper Coombe LU7 .....80 E8
Upper Dr HP9 ....175 D5
Upper Fifth St MK9 ....34 D2
Upper Fourth St MK9 ..34 D2
Upper George St HP5 ..144 C1
Upper Gladstone Rd ﬂ
  HP5 ....144 C1
Upper Green St HP11 ..172 E7

Upper Hartwell HP17 ..114 E5
Upper Hollis HP16 ....151 F7
Upper Hundreds Way
  HP20 ....115 E8
Upper Icknield Way
  Askett HP27 ....139 E7
  Halton HP22 ....117 F2
  Monks Risborough HP27 .139 D6
  Pitstone HP23,LU7 ....105 E1
  Princes Risborough HP27 .139 B2
  Saunderton HP27 ......148 F7
Upper Lees Rd SL2 ....198 B2
Upper Lodge La HP15 ..162 F6
Upper Mdw ﬂ HP5 .....144 B1
Upper Rd UB9 ....189 D4
Upper Riding HP9 .....175 B2
Upper Second St MK9 ..34 D1
Upper St Quainton HP22 ..85 A5
  Tingewick MK18 ....51 B6
Upper Stonehayes MK14 .34 F8
Upper Third St MK9 ....34 D1
Upper Ventnor Cotts
  SL6 ....195 C8
Upper Way MK17 ....59 C2
Upper Weald MK19 .....45 A8
Upper Wood Cl
  Milton Keynes MK5 .....45 F3
  ﬂ Shenley Brook End MK5 .46 A3
Upton Cl Henley-on-T RG9 .191 E1
  ﬂ Slough SL1 ....205 F3
Upton Court Rd SL3 ...206 B2
Upton Gr MK5 ....46 C4
Upton Hospl SL1 ......205 F4
Upton House Sch SL4 ..210 C5
Upton Lea Par SL2 ....206 B6
Upton Pk SL1 ....205 F3
Upton Rd Dinton HP17 .114 A3
  Slough SL1 ....206 A3
Upton Terr HP17 ......114 A3
Upway SL9 ....177 F2
Uxbridge Coll UB8 ....201 E6
Uxbridge High Sch UB8 .201 D3
Uxbridge Ind Est UB8 .201 B3
Uxbridge Rd
  Iver Heath SL0,SL3 ...200 B2
  Rickmansworth WD3 ...178 F7
  Slough SL1,SL3 ....206 C7
  Uxbridge UB10 ....201 F2
Uxbridge Sta UB8 .....201 D5

V

Vache La
  Chalfont St Giles HP8 .177 C8
  Milton Keynes MK5 .....45 F6
Vale Cl SL1 ....177 D2
Vale Ct MK43 ....25 D2
Vale Gr SL1 ....205 E3
Vale Ho HP19 ....115 C8
Vale Ind Ctr The HP19 .101 C1
Vale Park Dr HP20 ....115 E8
Vale Rd Aylesbury HP20 .101 E2
  Chesham HP5 ....144 C4
  Windsor SL4 ....209 F6
Vale Ret Pk HP20 .....115 E8
Vale Rise HP5 ....144 C3
Vale The SL9 ....177 D2
Valens Cl MK8 ....45 F2
Valentine Ct MK6 ......45 E7
Valentine Way HP8 ....177 D7
Valerian Pl MK6 ....21 F4
Valley Cl Brackley NN13 ..38 A8
  Whipsnade HP4 ....107 E7
Valley Ctr The HP13 ..173 C6
Valley End SL3 ....199 C1
Valley Rd
  Berkhamsted HP4 .....134 F6
  Brackley NN13 ....38 A8
  Buckingham MK18 ......52 F8
  Finmere MK18 ....50 D6
  Henley-on-T RG9 .....191 C1
  Hughenden Valley HP14 .162 A5
  Uxbridge UB10 ....201 E3
Valley Rise HP13 ......38 A8
Valley View HP5 ......144 B2
Valley Way SL9 ....188 D5
Valpy Cl HP23 ....119 D1
Van Der Bilt Ct MK13 ..33 F6
Van Diemens Ct OX39 ..147 C7
Vandyke Cl MK17 ....49 B6
Vane Rd OX9 ....126 B1
Vanguard Cl HP12 .....172 D7
Vanguard Ho ﬁ TW19 ..213 E1
Vansittart Ct SL4 ....210 C6
Vansittart Rd
  Bisham SL7 ....194 E7
  Windsor SL4 ....210 B6
Vantage Ct MK14 ......34 C7
Vantage Rd SL1 ....205 B5
Vanwall Bsns Pk SL6 ..202 C5
Vanwall Rd SL6 ....202 C4
Varnell Terr HP21 ....181 C2
Vaughan Copse SL4 ...205 D2
Vaughan Gdns SL4 ....204 F2
Vaughan Way SL2 .....197 E1
Vauxhall MK13 ....33 F6
Vellan Ave MK6 ....35 B1
Venables La MK15 .....35 B7
Venetian Ct MK7 ....48 C7
Ventfield Cl OX33 ....108 A5
Venus Hill HP3 ....156 A8
Verbena Cl UB7 ......208 D1
Verdi Cl MK7 ....48 C5
Verdon Ct SL2 ....198 B2
Verdon Dr SL1 ....35 B7
Verity Pl MK6 ....34 F1

Verley Cl MK6 ....47 C8
Vermont Pl MK15 ....22 C1
Vermont Rd SL2 ....197 F1
Verney Ave HP12 ......172 D4
Verney Cl
  Berkhamsted HP4 .....134 F5
  Buckingham MK18 ......41 D1
  Marlow SL7 ....183 D2
  Tring HP23 ....119 C5
Verney Farm Cl MK18 ..74 F8
Verney Rd Slough SL3 ..207 A2
  Winslow MK18 ....65 E4
Verney Wlk HP21 ......115 D6
Vernier Cres MK5 ......45 E5
Vernon Bldg ﬂ HP11 ..172 F7
Verona Cl HP18 ....208 C7
Verwood Rd HP20 .....101 E2
Veryan Pl MK6 ....35 B1
Vicarage Cl Cookham SL6 .196 B7
  Seer Green HP9 ....176 D3
  Steeple Claydon MK18 ..63 D2
  Wendover HP22 ....131 B5
  Yardley Gobion NN12 ...18 E6
Vicarage Ct
  Hanslope MK19 ....11 B2
  Steeple Claydon MK18 ..63 D3
Vicarage Dr SL6 ......203 C4
Vicarage Flats SL4 ...210 D8
Vicarage Gdns
  Leighton Buzzard LU7 ..80 E6
  Marsworth HP23 ......105 A2
  Milton Keynes MK13 ...34 A4
Vicarage La
  Bovingdon HP3 ....146 B4
  Ivinghoe LU7 ....105 F5
  Piddington OX25 ....95 E6
  Steeple Claydon MK18 ..63 D2
  Wing LU7 ....79 E2
Vicarage Rd
  Aylesbury HP21 ....115 D5
  Henley-on-T RG9 .....191 E1
  Leighton Buzzard LU7 ..80 E6
  Maidenhead SL6 ......202 F8
  Milton Keynes,Bradwell
    MK13 ....34 A4
  Milton Keynes,Fenny Stratford
    MK2 ....58 E8
  Milton Keynes,Stony Stratford
    MK13 ....32 D6
  Pitstone LU7 ....105 D2
  Whaddon MK17 ....56 B8
  Wigginton HP23 ......119 D1
  Winslow MK18 ....65 F4
Vicarage St MK17 ......49 C4
Vicarage Way
  Colnbrook SL3 ....212 D7
  Gerrards Cross SL9 ...188 F5
Vicarage Wlk MK11 ....32 D6
Vickers Ct ﬂ TW19 ...213 E1
Vickery Cl HP21 ......115 E5
Vickery Way HP21 ....115 E5
Victor Cl SL6 ....202 B8
Victor Rd SL4 ....210 C4
Victoria CE Fst Sch
  Berkhamsted HP4 .....135 C4
Victoria Cotts SL4 ...195 C8
Victoria Cres SL0 ....208 A6
Victoria Ct
  Henley-on-T RG9 .....191 E1
  High Wycombe HP11 ..172 F8
  ﬂ Marlow SL7 ....183 E2
  Slough SL1 ....205 E5
  ﬂﬂ Windsor SL4 .....210 D6
Victoria Dr SL1,SL2 ..197 F6
Victoria Gdns
  High Wycombe HP11 ..172 F4
  Marlow SL7 ....183 E2
Victoria Ho HP11 .....211 A2
Victoria Rd
  Berkhamsted HP4 .....135 C4
  Chesham HP5 ....144 C1
  Eton Wick SL4 ....204 F1
  Farnham Common SL2 .198 C6
  Leighton Buzzard LU7 ..80 E6
  Marlow SL7 ....183 E2
  Milton Keynes MK2 .....47 E1
  Slough SL2 ....206 B5
  Uxbridge UB8 ....201 C5
Victoria Row MK18 .....52 D8
Victoria St
  Aylesbury HP20 ....115 F8
  High Wycombe HP11 ..172 F7
  Milton Keynes MK12 ...33 B7
  ﬂ Slough SL1 ....205 F4
  Windsor SL4 ....210 D6
Victory Ct MK1 ....47 B2
Victory Rd
  Berkhamsted HP4 .....135 A5
  Steeple Claydon MK18 ..63 D2
  Wendover HP22 ....131 B5
Vienna Gr MK13 ....33 E6
Villa Park (Mobile Home Pk)
  MK43 ....37 F7
Village Cl MK16 ....13 F2
Village Ct LU7 ....80 D6
Village La SL2 ....187 D4
Village Mews HP3 .....146 A4
Village Rd Coleshill HP7 .164 F3
  Denham UB9 ....190 A2
  Dorney SL4 ....204 D2
Village Sh Ctr The ﬂ
  SL1 ....205 F4
Village Way HP7 ......166 D7
Villier St UB8 ....201 D3
Villiers Bldgs ﬂ HP20 .115 E8
Villiers Cl LU6 ....41 E2
Villiers Ct SL4 ....205 D2
Villiers Rd SL2 ....205 D8

Vimy Ct LU7 ....80 F7
Vimy Rd LU7 ....80 F7
Vincent Ave MK8 ....45 F8
Vincent Dr UB10 ......201 F4
Vincent Rd HP19 .....101 A3
Vincents Way HP14 ...161 D6
Vine Cl Hazelmere HP15 .163 A3
  Stanwell TW19 ....213 A2
Vine Ct SL2 ....199 A6
Vine Gr UB10 ....201 F5
Vine La UB10 ....201 F4
Vine Rd SL2 ....199 A6
Vine Row MK43 ....8 E6
Vine St Uxbridge UB8 ..201 C4
  Uxbridge UB8 ....201 C4
Vine The HP18 ....124 D3
Vinetrees HP22 ......131 B4
Viney La HP19 ....114 F8
Vineyard Dr SL8 ......185 A5
Vineyards The HP27 ..138 A2
Violet Ave UB10 ......190 F1
Vintners Mews MK14 ...34 F6
Violet Ave UB8 ......208 F8
Violet Cl HP27 ....149 D6
Virage HP22 ....117 F4
Virginia MK6 ....47 A7
Virginia Gdns HP14 ..159 F8
Viscount Cl ﬂ UB10 ..101 F2
Viscount Ind Est SL1 ..212 E4
Viscount Way MK2 .....47 C1
Vivien Cl SL6 ....195 F6
Volta Rise MK5 ....46 C4
Vyne Cres MK4 ....33 F1
Vyners Sch UB10 .....201 F8

W

Waborne Rd SL6 ......185 B4
Waddesdon CE Sch HP18 .99 A6
Waddesdon Cl ﬂ MK8 ..45 F8
Waddesdon Gn HP21 ..115 C4
Waddesdon Hill HP18 ..99 C3
Waddesdon Manor (NT)*
  HP18 ....98 E5
Waddesdon Manor Flats
  HP18 ....99 A6
Wade Dr SL1 ....205 A5
Wadesmill La MK7 ......48 A4
Wadhurst La MK10 .....36 A1
Wadworth Holme MK10 ..35 E3
Wagner Cl MK7 ....48 C4
Waine Cl HP18 ....52 D7
Wainers Croft MK12 ...33 A4
Wainwrights HP18 ...125 D6
Waivers Way HP21 ....116 A5
Wakefield Cl MK14 ....34 F7
Wakefield Cres SL2 ..199 F6
Wakelins End SL6 ....195 E7
Wakeman Rd SL8 .....185 A3
Walbank Gr MK5 ....46 A3
Walbrook Ave MK6 .....35 B3
Waldeck Ho SL6 ......203 A7
Waldeck Rd SL6 ......203 A7
Walden St SL6 ....185 A3
Walducks Cl LU7 ......78 E8
Walford Rd UB8 ......201 D3
Walgrave Dr MK13 .....34 B4
Walk House Cl MK43 ...25 B1
Walk The Eton Wick SL4 .205 A1
  Winslow MK18 ....65 E4
Walker Ave MK12 ......33 A6
Walker Cl SL6 ....202 D7
Walker Rd SL6 ....203 A4
Walkers Rd HP27 ....138 D7
Walkham Cl HP11 ....174 B4
Walkhampton Ave MK13 ..34 C3
Walkwood End HP9 ...175 C1
Walkwood Rise HP9 ..186 C8
Wallace Cl Marlow SL7 .183 F4
  Marlow SL7 ....183 E2
Wallace Dr LU7 ....80 E8
Wallace End HP21 ....116 A6
Wallace Mews LU6 .....92 E6
Wallace St MK13 ....33 E7
Wallace Wlk SL4 .....210 B6
Wallbridge Cl HP19 ..115 B7
Waller Rd HP9 ....175 F2
Wallinger Dr MK5 ......46 A3
Wallingford Cl MK13 ..34 B5
Wallingford Gdns HP11 .173 A4
Wallingford Rd UB8 ..201 B2
Wallington Rd HP5 ...144 B1
Wallis Ct SL1 ....206 A3
Wallmead Gdns MK5 ...46 B2
Walney Pl MK4 ....45 F1
Walnut Cl
  Great Missenden HP16 ..152 F2
  Long Crendon HP18 ..125 C7
  Newport Pagnell MK16 ..22 A3
  Stoke Mandeville HP22 .116 C2
Walnut Cres HP27 ...138 D7
Walnut Dr
  Maids Moreton MK18 ...41 F4
  Milton Keynes MK2 .....58 E8
  Newport Pagnell MK16 .131 B6
Walnut Gr HP10 ......165 E6
Walnut Lodge SL1 ...205 D4
Walnut Tree Cl
  Bourne End SL8 ......185 B2
  High Wycombe HP13 ..172 C8
Walnut Tree Ct HP22 ..116 C3
Walnut Tree Ho HP11 ..174 B3
Walnut Tree La HP27 .138 C6

Walnut Tree Rdbt MK7 ..48 C7
Walnut Way
  Bourne End SL8 ......185 B2
  Hyde Heath HP6 .....153 C4
  Walnuts Sch The MK6 ..47 E5
Walpole Rd SL1 ......204 D7
Walsh's Manor MK14 ...34 D7
Walsingham Gate HP21 .173 A4
Walter Rothschild Zoological
  Mus The* HP23 ......119 A3
Waltham Cl MK10 ....36 A1
Waltham Ho ﬁ MK3 .....46 F1
Walton Cl HP13 ......162 E1
Walton Court Ctr HP21 .115 C5
Walton Dene HP21 ...115 C7
Walton Dr
  High Wycombe HP13 ..162 E1
  Walton MK7 ....47 F6
Walton End MK7 ....48 C6
Walton Gn HP21 ......115 C7
Walton Gr HP21 ......115 C7
Walton Heath MK7 .....57 D7
Walton High Sch MK7 ..48 C6
Walton La SL2 ....197 F3
Walton Park Rdbt MK7 ..48 B4
Walton Pl HP21 ......116 F3
Walton Rd
  Aylesbury HP21 ....115 C5
  Caldecotte MK7 ....48 B3
  Milton Keynes MK10,MK7 ..36 A2
  Walton MK7 ....48 D6
  Wavendon MK10,MK17 ..48 D7
Walton St HP21 ......115 C7
Walton Terr HP21 ....115 C7
Walton Way HP21 ....116 A7
Wandlebury MK14 ......35 A3
Wandsworth Pl MK13 ..34 D3
Wannions Cl MK5 .....145 A1
Wantage Cl LU7 ....79 E3
Wantage Cres LU7 ....79 E3
Wappenham Rd NN13 ...27 B8
Wapping HP18 ....125 D6
Wapseys La SL2 .....187 F4
Warbler Cl HP19 .....114 F8
Warburg Nature Reserve*
  RG9 ....179 B5
Ward Cl SL0 ....207 F7
Ward Gdns SL1 ......204 E5
Ward Pl HP7 ....165 B7
Ward Rd Brackley NN13 ..38 A5
  Milton Keynes MK1 .....47 E3
Ward Royal ﬁ SL4 ...210 C6
Ward Royal Par ﬂ SL4 .210 C6
Wardes Cl HP10 ......151 C5
Wardle Pl MK6 ....46 E8
Wardrobes La HP27 ..149 D8
Wardstone End MK4 ...46 B2
Ware Leys Cl OX27 ....71 E3
Wargrave Rd RG9 ....191 F1
Warmington Gdns MK15 ..35 B5
Warmstone Cl HP18 ...99 B6
Warmstone La HP18 ...99 B6
Warneford Ave HP22 .131 D5
Warner Cl SL1 ....204 E5
Warners Cl MK17 ......59 D1
Warners Hill SL6 ....195 D8
Warners Rd MK17 ......57 D3
Warren Bank MK6 ......47 C5
Warren Cl
  Buckingham MK18 ......52 E7
  Slough SL3 ....206 E3
  Stone HP17 ....114 B5
Warren Ct
  Farnham Common SL2 .198 C2
  Little Horwood MK17 ...55 E5
Warren Farm Cotts
  MK18 ....50 A7
Warren Field SL0 ....200 C3
Warren Ho HP19 .....101 B1
Warren Par SL2 .....206 C5
Warren The
  Ickenham UB10 ......201 F8
  Little Horwood MK17 ...55 F5
  Yardley Gobion NN12 ...18 F6
Warren The
  Chalfont St Peter SL9 .177 F3
  Chartridge HP5 ......143 E3
  Hazelmere HP15 .....163 A5
Warren Wood Dr HP11 .173 C5
Warren Yd MK12 ....33 A6
Warrendene Rd HP14 .162 A8
Warrender Rd HP15 ..144 E2
Warrington Ave SL1 ..205 C2
Warrington Rd MK46 ...7 F8
Warwick Ave
  High Wycombe HP13 ..172 B6
  Slough SL2 ....198 C1
Warwick Cl
  Aston Clinton HP22 ...117 C5
  Maidenhead SL6 ......202 B4
Warwick Ct
  Beaconsfield HP9 .....175 D3
  Chorleywood WD3 ....167 F6
  ﬁ Windsor SL4 ....210 C5
Warwick Dr LU7 ....79 E2
Warwick Ho ﬁ HP13 ..173 F7
Warwick Pl
  Milton Keynes MK3 .....57 E7
  Uxbridge UB8 ....201 C5
Warwick Row HP20 ...102 A1
Wash Hill SL0 ....185 E3
Wash Hill Lea HP10 ..185 E4

Wash Hill Mobile Home Pk HP10 185 E3
Washfield MK4 46 D3
Washingleys MK43 25 C2
Washington Ct SL7 184 A3
Washington Dr
Slough SL1 204 D6
Windsor SL4 209 E4
Washington Row HP7 165 C7
Wastel MK6 47 B5
Watchcroft Dr MK18 41 E2
Watchet Ct MK4 46 D3
Watchet La
Holmer Green HP15 163 B7
Little Kingshill HP16 152 C1
Water Cl MK19 32 B7
Water Eaton Rd MK2,MK3 58 C7
Water End Rd
Beacon's Bottom HP14 159 D3
Beacon's Bottom,Waterend HP14 159 C5
Water Gdns The HP15 162 E2
Water La
Berkhamsted HP4 135 C4
Bovingdon HP3 146 B1
Ford HP17 128 B7
Leighton Buzzard LU7 80 F7
Sherington MK16 13 E1
Speen HP27 150 C4
Water Mdw HP5 154 B7
Water Meadow Way HP22 131 B6
Water Stratford Rd MK18 51 A7
Waterbeach Cl SL1 205 D7
Waterbeach Rd SL1 205 D7
Waterborne Wlk LU7 80 F7
Waterfield WD3 167 C2
Waterford Cl MK3 46 E1
Waterford Ho UB7 208 C3
Waterglades The HP9 175 C6
Waterhall Comb Sch MK2 58 D4
Waterhouse Cl MK16 22 D4
Waterlily 5 HP19 101 E4
Waterloo Ct MK3 46 E2
Waterloo Rd
Leighton Buzzard LU7 80 E6
Uxbridge UB8 201 C4
Waterlow Cl MK16 22 C2
Waterman Ct SL1 204 E5
Watermead HP19 101 E4
Watermead Slopes & Sails* HP19 101 D4
Watermeadow HP19 101 F3
Watermill Way HP22 116 F2
Waterperry OX33 123 B1
Waterperry Gdns* OX33 123 B1
Waterperry Mews HP19 114 F8
Waterperry Rd HP18 123 D5
Waters Reach SL6 196 A1
Waterside
Berkhamsted HP4 135 D4
Chesham HP5 154 D6
Edlesborough LU6 92 F4
Milton Keynes MK6 47 C8
Uxbridge UB8 208 C8
Wooburn Green HP10 185 E7
Waterside Comb Sch HP5 154 D6
Waterside Ct HP5 154 C7
Waterside Dr SL3 207 A4
Waterside Lodge SL6 203 C8
Waterside Pk MK12 33 C7
Waterslade Pens HP17 126 F6
Watersmeet Cl MK4 46 D4
Watery La
Beachampton MK19 44 B6
Brackley NN13 38 A7
Marsworth HP23 104 F1
Wooburn Green HP10 185 E8
Watling St Bletchley MK2 47 D1
Bow Brickhill MK17 58 F8
Granby MK6 47 A3
Milton Keynes,Kiln Farm MK8,MK11 33 B2
Milton Keynes,Shenley Lodge MK6 46 C6
Potterspury NN12 18 C3
Watling Terr MK2 47 E1
Watlington Ct HP16 152 A8
Watlington Rd OX49 157 A7
Watlow Gdns MK18 41 E2
Watson Cl MK8 45 D6
Watten Ct MK2 58 E4
Wattleton Rd HP9 175 E1
Watts Cl MK19 11 A3
Watts Gn HP18 112 B2
Wavell Ct MK15 35 B7
Wavell Gdns SL2 197 F2
Wavell Rd
Beaconsfield HP9 176 B1
Maidenhead SL6 202 B6
Wavendon CE Fst Sch MK17 48 E7
Wavendon Fields MK17 48 F6
Wavendon Gate Comb Sch MK7 48 D6
Wavendon House Dr MK17 49 B8
Wavendon Rd MK17 37 C2
Waveney Cl MK16 22 E3
Waverley Croft MK10 36 A1
Waverley Rd SL1 205 C8
Waverley Wlk HP20 101 D2
Waxwing Cl HP19 101 E3
Wayfarers Pk HP4 134 F4
Waylands TW19 211 E1
Wayside
High Wycombe HP13 173 D7
Speen HP27 150 C4
Wayside Ct HP6 154 C1
Wayside Gdns SL9 188 D4
Wayside Mews SL6 202 F8
Wealdstone Pl MK6 35 A2
Weasel La MK3 57 C6
Weatherby LU6 93 E8
Weathercock Cl MK17 49 B5
Weathercock Gdns HP15 163 C7
Weathercock La MK17 49 C4
Weavers End MK19 11 B2
Weavers Hill MK11 33 A4
Weavers Rd HP23 118 E4
Webb Cl Chesham HP5 144 B1
Slough SL3 206 D2
Webber Heath MK7 48 D4
Webbs Home Cl MK10 36 A2
Webbs Mdw HP19 115 A8
Webster Cl
Maidenhead SL6 202 A5
Thame OX9 125 F1
Webster Rd HP21 116 A6
Websters Mdw MK4 46 C1
Wedgewood St HP19 115 A8
Wedgwood Ave MK14 22 A1
Wedgwood Dr HP14 162 A6
Weedon Cl SL9 177 B2
Weedon Hill HP6 153 D4
Weedon La HP6 154 A3
Weedon Rd HP19 101 C2
Weekes Dr SL1 205 B4
Weill Rd HP21 116 A4
Weir La Blackthorn OX25 81 A4
East Claydon MK18 74 E5
Whitchurch HP22 86 F6
Weirside Gdns UB7 208 D5
Welbeck Ave HP21 116 C6
Welbeck Cl MK10 35 F1
Welbeck Rd SL6 202 D5
Welburn Gr MK4 46 B2
Welby Cl SL6 202 A4
Welden SL2 206 C7
Welders La
Chalfont St Giles SL9 177 A3
Seer Green SL9 177 B3
Weldon Rise MK5 46 B8
Welford Way HP18 112 F3
Well End Cotts SL8 184 F5
Well Head Rd LU6 93 C6
Well La LU7 80 A1
Well St MK18 52 D8
Welland Cl SL3 212 B8
Welland Dr MK16 22 E3
Welland Ho MK3 57 E8
Welland Rd HP21 115 C5
Wellbank SL6 196 E1
Wellbrook Mews HP23 119 B4
Wellcroft LU7 105 F5
Wellcroft Rd SL1 205 B5
Weller Cl HP6 154 E2
Weller Ct LU6 93 C7
Weller Rd HP6 154 E2
Welles Rd HP13 173 F7
Wellesbourne Gdns HP13 162 D2
Wellesley Ave SL0 207 F4
Wellesley Ct SL0 207 F4
Wellesley Ho SL4 210 B6
Wellesley Path SL1 206 A4
Wellesley Rd SL1 206 A4
Welley Ave TW19 211 E3
Welley Rd SL3,TW19 211 E3
Wellfield HP15 163 B3
Wellfield Ct MK15 35 D8
Wellfield Rd HP14 171 B8
Wellhayes MK14 34 F8
Wellhouse Rd SL6 195 E2
Wellhouse Way HP14 161 E6
Wellingborough Rd MK46 6 F5
Wellington Ave HP27 139 B4
Wellington Cl SL6 202 B8
Wellington Pl
Aylesbury HP21 115 E4
Milton Keynes MK3 58 B7
Wellington Rd
Aylesbury HP21 115 E4
High Wycombe HP12 172 E4
Maidenhead SL6 202 D7
Uxbridge UB8 201 C4
Wellington St SL1 206 A4
Wells Cl SL4 210 A7
Wellsmead Fst Sch MK3 46 F1
Wellsmead Mid Sch MK3 46 E2
Welsh La MK18 40 C5
Welsummer Gr MK5 46 A3
Welton Rd HP21 116 B7
Wendover CE Jun Sch HP22 131 B6
Wendover House Sch HP22 131 C3
Wendover Hts HP22 131 C6
Wendover Rd
Bourne End SL8 185 A5
Burnham SL1 204 B8
Ellesborough HP17 130 D3
Wendover St HP11 172 F7
Wendover Sta HP22 131 B4
Wendover Way
Aylesbury HP21 115 F6
High Wycombe HP11 173 B6
Wendover Wood Forest Wlks* HP23 131 F6
Wenlack Cl UB9 190 A1
Wenning La MK4 46 B2
Wentworth Ave SL2 198 A2
Wentworth Cl HP13 173 C8
Wentworth Cres SL6 202 C6
Wentworth Way MK3 57 C7
Wenwell Cl HP22 118 A3
Werner Ct HP21 115 E4
Werner Terr MK18 73 B6
Werth Dr MK17 49 B2
Wescott Way UB8 201 C3
Wesley Cl HP20 102 A2
Wesley Dene 4 HP13 173 B7
Wesley Hill 1 HP5 144 B1
Wessex Ct
4 Stanwell TW19 213 E1
11 Windsor SL4 210 C6
Wessex Inf Sch SL6 202 B4
Wessex Jun Sch SL6 202 B4
Wessex Rd SL8 185 B2
Wessex Road Ind Est SL8 185 B2
Wessex Way SL6 202 B4
Wessons Hill SL6 195 C7
West Acres HP7 165 D7
West Ave HP10 163 C1
West Cl SL7 193 D7
West Comm SL9 188 D6
West Common Cl SL9 188 E6
West Common Rd UB8 201 D6
West Cres SL4 209 F6
West Ct Bray SL6 203 C4
High Wycombe HP13 161 D3
West Dales MK13 34 C5
West Dean SL6 202 F8
West Dr HP13 173 D8
West Drayton Park Ave UB7 208 E3
West Drayton Prim Sch UB7 208 E4
West Drayton Sta UB7 208 E5
West Edge OX27 71 E2
West End HP22 116 E2
West End Cl MK18 63 C2
West End Ct SL2 198 F4
West End La SL2 198 E4
West End Pl HP22 116 E2
West End Rd
Cheddington LU7 104 F7
High Wycombe HP11 172 F7
West End St HP11 172 F7
West Farm Way MK46 13 E8
West Furlong MK18 53 A1
West Hill MK17 49 D4
West Hyde La SL9 178 A4
West La Bledlow HP27 138 B1
Emberton MK46 13 E8
Henley-on-T RG9 191 D2
West Leith HP23 118 F1
West Mead SL6 195 F2
West Pas 11 HP23 119 A3
West Point SL1 204 D5
West Rd
Berkhamsted HP4 135 A5
Cranfield MK43 24 D2
Maidenhead SL6 202 E7
West Drayton UB7 208 F3
Woburn Sands MK17 49 B5
West Richardson St 2 HP11 172 F7
West Ridge SL8 185 B4
West Side Rise MK46 6 F4
West Spur Rd UB8 201 D2
West Sq SL0 207 F7
West St Adstock MK18 53 F1
Aylesbury HP19 101 C1
Buckingham MK18 41 C1
Dunstable LU6 93 F7
Henley-on-T RG9 191 D2
Leighton Buzzard LU7 80 F7
Maidenhead SL6 202 F7
Marlow SL7 183 D1
Olney MK46 6 F4
Steeple Claydon MK18 63 D2
West View Chesham HP5 144 D2
Hardwick HP22 87 B3
High Wycombe HP13 173 B8
West Way HP9 174 F1
West Waye HP13 162 C2
West Well Cl MK18 51 A6
West Well La MK18 51 A6
West Wlk MK9 34 E2
West Wycombe Comb Sch HP14 160 F2
West Wycombe Hill Rd HP14 160 F2
West Wycombe Pk* HP14 160 F1
West Wycombe Rd HP12 161 C1
West Yard Ind Est HP14 160 C8
Westanley Ave HP7 165 D8
Westborne Ct MK13 34 A6
Westborough Ct SL6 202 C6
Westborough Rd SL6 202 C6
Westbourne St 6 HP11 172 F7
Westbrook End MK17 57 C3
Westbrook Hay Prep Sch HP1 146 D7
Westbury Cl MK16 22 B4
Westbury Court Bsns Ctr OX27 71 C4
Westbury Ho 3 HP20 101 D1
Westbury La MK16 22 A5
Westbury Mill NN13 38 F4
Westbury Terr OX27 71 F2
Westcliffe MK8 33 C2
Westcoign Ho SL6 203 B8
Westcott CE Sch HP18 98 A7
Westcott Venture Pk HP18 98 A6
Westcroft Slough SL2 198 B1
Tring HP23 119 A3
Westcroft Rdbt MK4 46 A2
Westcroft Stables* HP27 150 B3
Westdean La HP5 143 C3
Westdown Gdns LU6 93 F7
Western Ave
Buckingham MK18 41 C1
New Denham UB9 201 D8
Western Dene HP15 163 A5
Western Dr
Hanslope MK19 11 A3
Wooburn Green HP10 185 E5
Western House Inf Sch SL1 204 F6
Western La MK18 65 F3
Western Perimeter Rd TW6 213 B5
Western Perimeter Road Rdbt TW19 213 C2
Western Rd
Great Horwood MK17 55 A3
Milton Keynes,Fenny Stratford MK2 47 D1
Milton Keynes,Wolverton MK12 33 C6
Tring HP23 118 F3
Westfield Aylesbury HP21 115 E3
Hyde Heath HP6 153 C4
Westfield Ave MK19 31 D5
Westfield Bglws SL7 192 F6
Westfield Cotts SL7 192 F5
Westfield Fst Sch HP4 134 F5
Westfield Rd
Beaconsfield HP9 175 C1
Berkhamsted HP4 134 E6
Dunstable LU6 93 F8
Maidenhead SL6 202 B7
Milton Keynes MK2 58 C7
Pitstone LU7 105 C3
Slough SL2 198 B1
Wheatley OX33 122 A1
Westfield Sch SL8 185 A3
Westfield Wlk HP12 172 D6
Westfields
Buckingham MK18 52 C8
Princes Risborough HP27 139 D4
Westgate Cres SL1 204 F6
Westgate Ct HP13 174 A4
Westgate Sch The SL1 205 A5
Westhill MK14 34 D8
Westhorpe Park Cvn Site SL7 184 B3
Westhorpe Rd SL7 183 F3
Westland Cl TW19 213 E1
Westlands Ave SL1 204 C7
Westlands Cl SL1 204 C7
Westlands Rd HP27 149 E5
Westlington La HP17 113 E1
Westlington Lea HP17 113 E2
Westmead
Monks Risborough HP27 139 B5
Windsor SL4 210 B4
Westminster Cl
Brackley NN13 38 A7
High Wycombe HP11 173 B4
Westminster Cres NN13 38 A7
Westminster Dr
Aylesbury HP21 115 F6
Milton Keynes MK3 47 A2
Westmorland Ave HP21 116 B6
Westmorland Ho MK3 46 F2
Westmorland Rd SL6 202 D6
Westmount Ave HP7 165 C8
Weston Ct HP22 117 C5
Weston La OX9 136 F8
Weston Rd
Aston Clinton HP22 117 C5
Lewknor OX49 157 A8
Olney MK46 6 E3
Ravenstone MK46 5 E2
Slough SL1 204 F8
Weston Turville CE Sch HP22 116 E3
Weston Way HP22 116 A2
Westover Ct HP13 161 D1
Westover Rd HP13 161 D2
Westpits MK46 13 E8
Westrick Wlk HP16 151 C5
Westron Gdns HP23 119 B4
Westside La MK16 12 B6
Westwood HP12 172 B3
Westwood Cl
Little Chalfont HP6 166 D8
Milton Keynes MK8 45 F8
Westwood Dr HP6 166 D8
Westwood Gn SL6 195 F6
Westwood Rd SL7 183 C1
Westwood Wlk 6 HP20 101 F2
Wetherby Gdns MK3 57 D6
Wethered Pk SL7 183 D1
Wethered Rd
Burnham SL1 204 B8
Marlow SL7 183 D2
Wexford Ct SL6 203 B7
Wexham Court Prim Sch SL3 206 C8
Wexham Park Hospl SL3 199 C1
Wexham Park La SL3 199 C1
Wexham Pl SL2 199 D6
Wexham Rd SL1,SL2 206 B6
Wexham Sch SL2 206 C8
Wexham St SL3 199 B3
Wexham Woods SL3 206 C8
Wey La HP5 154 B7
Whaddon CE Fst Sch MK17 56 B8
Whaddon Chase HP19 101 D2
Whaddon Hall MK17 45 B2
Whaddon Rd
Milton Keynes,Shenley Brook End MK5 46 A3
Milton Keynes,Westcroft MK4 45 F2
Mursley MK17 56 C3
Nash MK17 44 D2
Newport Pagnell MK16 22 B3
Newton Longville MK17 57 D3
Whaddon Way MK3 46 F2
Whales La OX27 71 E2
Whalley Dr MK3 47 A2
Wharf Cl
Old Stratford MK19 32 B7
Wendover HP22 131 B5
Wharf Ct UB8 201 C1
Wharf La
Berkhamsted HP4 134 C8
Bourne End SL8 185 A3
Old Stratford MK19 32 C7
Wharf Rd HP22 131 B5
Wharf Row HP22 118 B4
Wharf The
Milton Keynes MK2 58 E6
Milton Keynes,Giffard Park MK14 21 E2
Wharf View MK18 41 E1
Wharfe La RG9 191 E2
Wharfside MK2 47 E1
Wharfside Pl MK18 41 E1
Wharton Ho 2 HP20 101 D1
Whatmore Cl TW19 213 A1
Wheat Cl HP21 115 E3
Wheatbutts The SL4 204 F2
Wheatcroft Cl MK6 47 A5
Wheatfield Cl SL6 202 A4
Wheathouse Copse MK17 55 A3
Wheatlands Rd SL3 206 C3
Wheatley Campus (Brookes Univ) OX33 122 C1
Wheatley Cl MK4 46 C2
Wheatley Park Sch OX33 122 B2
Wheatley Way SL9 177 E4
Wheatsheaf Ho HP10 185 E7
Wheatsheaf Par SL4 211 A2
Wheatstone Cl SL3 206 A3
Wheeler Ave HP10 174 C8
Wheeler Cl HP20 116 B8
Wheelers End OX39 147 C6
Wheelers Flats HP10 174 D8
Wheelers La MK13 34 A6
Wheelers Orch SL9 177 E4
Wheelers Pk HP13 173 D7
Wheelers Yd HP16 152 A7
Wheelwright Mews MK14 34 F6
Wheelwright Rd HP27 138 D7
Wheelwrights HP22 116 F2
Wheelwrights Pl SL3 212 C7
Wheelwrights Way MK19 32 C7
Wheelwrights Yd HP22 85 A5
Whelpley Hill Pk HP5 145 D5
Whet Stone Cl MK13 34 B4
Whichcote Gdns HP5 154 D6
Whichert Cl HP9 175 C6
Whichford MK14 22 A1
Whielden Cl HP7 165 B7
Whielden Gate HP7 164 E4
Whielden Gn HP7 165 B7
Whielden Hts HP7 165 A7
Whielden La
Coleshill HP7 164 E5
Winchmore Hill HP7 164 D3
Whielden St HP7 165 B7
Whinchat HP19 101 E3
Whincup Cl HP11 172 F4
Whinneys Rd HP10 174 C3
Whipass Hill HP9 176 A5
Whipsnade Park Homes LU6 93 F1
Whipsnade Rd LU6 93 F6
Whipsnade Tree Cathedral* LU6 93 F1
Whipsnade Wild Animal Pk* HP4 107 E8
Whitby Cl MK3 47 A2
Whitby Rd SL1 205 C6
Whitchurch Cl
Maidenhead SL6 195 E3
Westcott HP18 98 B7
Whitchurch Comb Sch HP22 86 E7
Whitchurch Ho 5 SL6 202 F7
Whitchurch La HP22 86 D8
Whitchurch Rd LU7 78 B1
White Alder MK12 33 E5
White Cl
High Wycombe HP13 161 D1
Slough SL1 205 D5
White Cotts MK18 29 D4
White Cres HP22 131 D7
White Hart Cl
Chalfont St Giles HP8 177 A7
Ludgershall HP18 96 B8
White Hart Field HP22 85 B4
White Hart La HP17 127 A5
White Hart Mdw HP9 175 E1
White Hart Rd
1 Maidenhead SL6 202 F7
Slough SL1 205 D3

White Hart St 🟫 HP11 . . . . . .173 A7
White Hermitage SL4 . . . . . .211 C2
White Hill
  Ashley Green HP4 . . . . . . .145 C2
  Beaconsfield HP9,HP10 . . . .185 F8
  Chesham HP5 . . . . .144 D1
  High Wycombe HP13 . . . . .162 B2
  Remenham Hill RG9 . . . . . .192 A2
White Hill Cl
  Chesham HP5 . . . . .144 D1
  Marlow Bottom SL7 . . . . . .183 C6
White Hill La LU7 . . . . . . .105 D3
White Horse Dr MK4 . . . . . .46 C2
White Horse La HP22 . . . . . .87 A6
White Horse Rd SL4 . . . . . .209 D5
White Hos MK18 . . . . .50 D6
White House Cl SL9 . . . . . .177 E3
White Lilies Island SL4 . . . .210 B7
White Lion Cl HP7 . . . . . . .166 A8
White Lion Rd HP7 . . . . . . .166 B8
White Lodge SL12 . . . . . . .183 C6
White Paddock SL6 . . . . . .202 A2
White Rock SL6 . . . . .196 B1
White Spire Sch MK3 . . . . . .46 F1
White View 🟦 HP20 . . . . .101 F3
Whiteacres Dr SL4 . . . . . . .203 B1
Whitebaker Ct MK14 . . . . . .34 F6
Whitebrook Pk SL6 . . . . . . .196 C4
Whitecross Rd HP17 . . . . . .126 F5
Whitefield La HP16 . . . . . .152 A6
Whiteford Rd SL12 . . . . . . .205 E8
Whitegate Ct MK6 . . . . .47 B6
Whitehall SL6 . . . . .196 B1
Whitehall Ave MK10 . . . . . .36 D1
Whitehall Cl UB8 . . . . .201 D4
Whitehall Inf Sch UB8 . . . . .201 C4
Whitehall Jun Sch UB8 . . . .201 C4
Whitehall La TW19 . . . . . . .212 A1
Whitehall St 🟫 HP20 . . . . .101 D1
Whitehaven SL1 . . . . .205 F6
Whitehead Way HP21 . . . . .115 E6
Whitehill
  Berkhamsted HP4 . . . . . . .135 D5
  Olney MK46 . . . . .6 F3
Whitehill Cl MK4 . . . . .135 D5
Whitehorse Yd MK11 . . . . . . .32 D5
Whitehouse Cl HP10 . . . . . .174 E1
Whitehouse La HP10 . . . . . .174 E2
Whitehouse Way
  Iver Heath SL0 . . . . .200 C2
  Slough SL3 . . . . .206 D3
Whitelands Ave WD3 . . . . . .167 E5
Whitelands Rd HP12 . . . . . .172 D7
Whitelands Way HP12 . . . . .172 D7
Whiteleaf Way HP27 . . . . . .139 D5
Whiteley SL4 . . . . .209 E7
Whiteley Cres MK5 . . . . .57 F6
Whitepit La HP10 . . . . .185 D7
Whites Cl MK18 . . . . .63 D3
Whites La SL3 . . . . .211 B8
Whitethorn Ave UB7 . . . . . .208 F6
Whitethorn Cl HP22 . . . . . .130 A8
Whitethorn Pl UB7 . . . . . . .208 F5
Whitethorns MK16 . . . . .22 B3
Whitewood Rd HP4 . . . . . . .135 A4
Whitfield Rd HP14 . . . . . . .162 A6
Whitfield Way MK13 . . . . . .167 F1
Whitley Ct TW19 . . . . .213 E1
Whitley Ct HP21 . . . . .115 E4
Whitmees Cl MK46 . . . . .6 E4
Whitney Rdbt MK4 . . . . .45 E2
Whitsun Pasture MK15 . . . . .35 B7
Whittenham Cl SL2 . . . . . . .197 E1
Whittenham Cl SL2 . . . . . . .206 A5
Whittington Chase MK4 . . . . .45 E1
Whitte Parkway SL2 . . . . . .204 D7
Whitton Way MK16 . . . . .22 C3
Whitworth La MK5 . . . . .46 B7
Whurley Way SL6 . . . . .195 E2
Whybrow Gdns HP4 . . . . . .135 C6
Whyteladyes La SL6 . . . . . .195 E6
Whytingham Rd HP23 . . . . .119 C4
Wick Rd HP23 . . . . .133 B8
Wicken Park Rd MK19 . . . . . .31 B2
Wicken Rd SL1 . . . . .30 E1
Wicket The SL1 . . . . .205 E3
Wickets The SL6 . . . . .202 C7
Wickstead Ave MK8 . . . . . . .45 D6
Widbrook Rd SL6 . . . . .196 B3
Widdenton View HP14 . . . . .171 C5
Widecroft Rd SL0 . . . . .200 C3
Widewater Pl UB9 . . . . . . .190 C6
Widgeon Ho HP11 . . . . .173 C6
Widmer End Comb Sch
  HP15 . . . . .162 F6
Widmere Field HP16 . . . . . .151 C5
Widmere La SL7 . . . . .183 A6
Widmore Cl HP5 . . . . .143 E5
Widnell La OX9 . . . . .55 C7
Wigan's La HP14 . . . . .148 C6
Wiggington Ho SL4 . . . . . . .210 D7
Wigginton Bottom
  HP23 . . . . .133 B8
Wiggles La HP23 . . . . .118 F7
Wigmore Ct HP19 . . . . .101 A2
Wigmore Rd HP19 . . . . .101 A2
Wigwell Gdns MK17 . . . . . . .55 A2
Wilberforce Mews 🟫
  SL6 . . . . .202 F7
Wildacre Rd MK5 . . . . .46 A4
Wilderness The HP4 . . . . . .135 C4
Wildgreen N SL3 . . . . .207 A2
Wildgreen S SL3 . . . . .207 A2

Wildwood Ct WD3 . . . . . . .167 F5
Wilford Cl MK15 . . . . .35 C2
Wilford Rd SL3 . . . . .206 F2
Wilfrids Wood Cl HP10 . . . .185 B6
Wilks Croft MK5 . . . . .45 F7
Willen Comb Sch MK15 . . . . .35 C7
Willen La MK14 . . . . .34 F8
Willen Park Ave MK15 . . . . .35 B6
Willen Rd
  Milton Keynes MK10 . . . . . .35 F3
  Newport Pagnell MK16 . . . . .22 D3
Willets Rise MK5 . . . . .46 A5
Willetts La UB9 . . . . .200 F7
Willey Ct MK11 . . . . .32 F4
William Bandy Cl LU7 . . . . . .79 F3
William Burt Cl HP22 . . . . .116 F1
William Ellis Cl SL4 . . . . . .211 A1
William Fiske Ho 🟦
  HP4 . . . . .135 C4
William Harding Cl
  HP21 . . . . .115 E7
William Harding Comb Sch
  HP21 . . . . .116 A5
William Hartley Yd SL3 . . . .199 B1
William Ho HP22 . . . . .102 C4
William Ho 🟦 HP13 . . . . . .173 F5
William Moulder Ct
  HP5 . . . . .144 B3
William Penn Sch The
  SL2 . . . . .198 D1
William Shakman Ho
  MK6 . . . . .177 B8
William Smith Cl MK15 . . . . .35 C3
William St
  Berkhamsted HP4 . . . . . . .135 D4
  Slough SL1 . . . . .205 F5
  Windsor SL4 . . . . .210 D6
William Sutton Ho MK5 . . . . .46 A6
Williams Circ MK7 . . . . .48 A4
Williams Cl
  Aylesbury HP19 . . . . .101 D1
  Hanslope MK19 . . . . .10 F3
Williams Way HP27 . . . . . . .138 D6
Willis Rd HP17 . . . . .127 A6
Willoners SL2 . . . . .205 A8
Willoughby Rd SL3 . . . . . . .207 B3
Willoughby's Wlk HP13 . . . .161 D2
Willow Ave
  High Wycombe HP12 . . . . .172 B4
  New Denham UB9 . . . . . . .201 C6
  West Drayton UB7 . . . . . . .208 F6
Willow Bank SL7 . . . . .183 D5
Willow Chase
  Chesham HP5 . . . . .144 B1
  Hazlemere HP15 . . . . .162 E3
Willow Cl
  Chalfont St Peter SL9 . . . . .177 E1
  Colnbrook SL3 . . . . .212 C7
  Flackwell Heath HP10 . . . . .185 C6
  Moulsoe MK16 . . . . .36 E8
Willow Cres 🟦 UB9 . . . . . .201 C7
Willow Cres W UB9 . . . . . .201 C7
Willow Ct
  Aylesbury,Quarrendon
  HP19 . . . . .101 A2
  Aylesbury,Walton Ct HP21 . . .115 C6
  High Wycombe HP11 . . . . .173 E4
  Walter's Ash HP14 . . . . . . .161 C8
Willow Dr
  Buckingham MK18 . . . . .52 F7
  Maidenhead SL6 . . . . .203 B2
Willow End HP22 . . . . .116 F2
Willow Gate HP18 . . . . .112 B2
Willow Gr MK19 . . . . .32 B6
Willow Herb HP15 . . . . . . .101 E4
Willow Ho LU7 . . . . .80 E7
Willow La Amersham HP7 . .165 F6
  Milton Keynes MK11 . . . . . .32 C5
Willow Par SL3 . . . . .207 A3
Willow Pk SL2 . . . . .199 A5
Willow Pl SL4 . . . . .210 C8
Willow Rd
  Aylesbury HP19 . . . . .101 D1
  Brackley NN13 . . . . .38 A6
  Chinnor OX39 . . . . .147 C6
  Great Horwood MK17 . . . . . .55 A3
  Poyle SL3 . . . . .212 E5
  Thame OX9 . . . . .125 F1
Willow Rise HP17 . . . . .127 A7
Willow Way
  Loudwater HP11 . . . . .174 B2
  Milton Keynes MK2 . . . . . . .58 C7
  Princes Risborough HP27 . . .139 A3
  Wing LU7 . . . . .79 E3
Willow Wlk HP15 . . . . .163 A3
Willow Wren MK14 . . . . .21 F2
Willowbank Terr 🟦
  HP21 . . . . .115 E8
Willowbrook Slough SL2 . . .205 D2
  Wendover HP22 . . . . .131 B7
Willowford MK13 . . . . .33 E5
Willowmead HP17 . . . . .114 F5
Willowmead Cl 🟦 SL6 . . . .183 F3
Willowmead Gdns SL7 . . . .183 F3
Willowmead Rd 🟦 SL7 . . . .183 F3
Willowmead Sq 🟦 SL7 . . . .183 F3
Willows First Sch The
  MK6 . . . . .35 A2
Willows Rd SL8 . . . . .185 B4
Willows Riverside Pk The
  SL4 . . . . .209 C7
Willows The
  Amersham HP6 . . . . .154 B4
  🟦 Bourne End SL8 . . . . . . .185 B3
  Edlesborough LU6 . . . . .92 F3
  High Wycombe HP12 . . . . .172 E8
  Longwick HP27 . . . . .138 E6

Willows The *continued*
  Windsor SL4 . . . . .209 D7
Wilmar Cl UB8 . . . . .201 D5
Wilmin Gr MK5 . . . . .46 B7
Wilmot Rd SL1 . . . . .197 B2
Wilsley Pound MK7 . . . . . . .48 B8
Wilson Cl MK8 . . . . .45 E7
Wilstone Resr Nature
  Reserve* HP22,HP23 . . . . .118 C7
Wilton Ave MK3 . . . . .58 A8
Wilton Cl UB7 . . . . .213 D8
Wilton Cres
  Beaconsfield HP9 . . . . .175 C3
  Windsor SL4 . . . . .209 D4
Wilton Hollow HP9 . . . . . . .175 F3
Wilton La HP9 . . . . .176 E4
Wilton Rd Cublington LU7 . .176 A4
Wiltshire Ave SL2 . . . . .198 C1
Wiltshire Lodge 🟦 SL6 . . .202 F6
Wiltshire Rd 🟫 SL7 . . . . . .183 F4
Wimbledon Pl MK13 . . . . . . .34 D3
Wimblington Dr MK6 . . . . . . .47 A4
Wimborne Cres MK4 . . . . . . .45 F2
Wimpole Rd UB7 . . . . .208 D5
Winbury Cl SL6 . . . . .202 E7
Winbury Sch SL6 . . . . .203 B4
Wincanton Hill MK3 . . . . . . .57 C6
Winch Terr SL4 . . . . .209 D5
Winchbottom La
  High Wycombe HP10 . . . . .173 B1
  Little Marlow SL7,HP10 . . . .184 B7
Winchendon Rd HP18 . . . . .112 B2
Winchester Circ MK10 . . . . . .36 B1
Winchester Cl
  Amersham HP7 . . . . .165 E8
  Poyle SL3 . . . . .212 E6
Winchester Cl SL1 . . . . . . .205 C4
Winchester Dr SL6 . . . . . . .202 B3
Winchester Ho HP21 . . . . . .115 F6
Windermere Cl
  Aylesbury HP21 . . . . .116 B6
  Chorleywood WD3 . . . . . . .167 D4
Windermere Dr MK2 . . . . . . .58 D5
Windermere Gdns LU7 . . . . .80 C7
Windermere Way
  Slough SL1 . . . . .204 C7
  West Drayton UB7 . . . . . . .208 E5
Windmill Cl
  Aylesbury HP19 . . . . .115 B8
  Buckingham MK18 . . . . .41 F1
  Ivinghoe LU7 . . . . .105 C5
  Windsor SL4 . . . . .210 B5
Windmill Dr HP15 . . . . .162 F6
Windmill Hill
  Chipperfield WD4 . . . . .156 F7
  Coleshill HP7 . . . . .164 F2
  Princes Risborough HP27 . . .139 B2
Windmill Hill Dr MK3 . . . . . .57 D7
Windmill Hill Rdbt MK4 . . . .46 C1
Windmill La HP15 . . . . .162 F6
Windmill Par HP15 . . . . . . .162 F6
Windmill Rd
  Chalfont St Peter SL9 . . . . .177 D3
  Cookham Rise SL6 . . . . . . .195 E6
  Fulmer SL3 . . . . .199 D7
  Haddenham HP17 . . . . . . .127 A6
  Slough SL1 . . . . .205 D5
  Thame OX9 . . . . .126 E1
Windmill St HP18 . . . . .96 A1
Windmill Way
  Cranfield MK43 . . . . .25 C3
  Tring HP23 . . . . .119 A6
Windmill Wood HP6 . . . . . .154 A2
Windrush Ave SL3 . . . . . . .207 B3
Windrush Cl
  Ickenham UB10 . . . . .201 F8
  Milton Keynes MK15 . . . . . .35 A6
Windrush Ct
  Aylesbury HP21 . . . . .115 D4
  High Wycombe HP13 . . . . .173 F6
Windrush Ho SL8 . . . . .185 B4
Windrush Way
  Maidenhead SL6 . . . . .202 F8
  Maidenhead SL6 . . . . .203 A8
Windsor & Eton Central Sta
  SL4 . . . . .210 D6
Windsor & Eton Riverside Sta
  SL4 . . . . .210 D7
Windsor Ave
  Leighton Buzzard LU7 . . . . . .80 F7
  Newport Pagnell MK16 . . . . .22 C4
Windsor Boys' Sch The
  SL4 . . . . .210 B5
Windsor Bsns Ctr The
  SL4 . . . . .210 C7
Windsor Castle SL4 . . . . . .210 D7
Windsor Cl
  Bovingdon HP3 . . . . .146 A3
  Burnham SL1 . . . . .197 C1
Windsor Cres HP10 . . . . . . .174 D1
Windsor Ct HP6 . . . . .154 D1
Windsor Dr HP13 . . . . .162 D1
Windsor End HP9 . . . . .186 F8
Windsor Girls' Sch SL4 . . . .210 A4
Windsor Hall SL4 . . . . .210 F4
Windsor Hill
  Monks Risborough HP27 . . .139 C5
  Wooburn Green HP10 . . . . .185 F5
Windsor Ho 🟫 SL1 . . . . . . .205 F3
Windsor La Burnham SL1 . . .197 C1
  Little Kingshill HP16 . . . . . .152 C3
Windsor Rd
  Aylesbury HP21 . . . . .116 A2
  Chesham HP5 . . . . .144 B1
  Datchet SL3 . . . . .211 A7
  Gerrards Cross SL9 . . . . . . .188 C3

Windsor Rd *continued*
  Maidenhead SL6 . . . . .203 C2
  Oakley Green SL4 . . . . .209 A7
  Pitstone LU7 . . . . .105 C3
  Slough SL1 . . . . .205 E4
  Wraysbury TW19 . . . . .211 E1
Windsor Royal Sta 🟫
  SL4 . . . . .210 D6
Windsor St
  Milton Keynes MK2 . . . . . . .58 C7
  Milton Keynes,Wolverton
  MK12 . . . . .33 C6
  Uxbridge UB8 . . . . .201 D5
Winemar Cl MK19 . . . . .11 A3
Winfold La MK4 . . . . .46 B1
Wing Cl SL7 . . . . .183 C1
Wing Rd Cublington LU7 . . . .78 C1
  Leighton Buzzard LU7 . . . . . .80 D5
Stewkley LU7 . . . . .78 F6
Wingate Ave HP13 . . . . . . .173 E7
Wingate Circ MK7 . . . . .48 A4
Wingate Cl HP13 . . . . .173 E7
Wingate Wlk HP20 . . . . . . .116 A7
Wingfield Gr MK10 . . . . .36 A2
Wingrave CE Comb Sch
  HP22 . . . . .88 F4
Wingrave Cross Rds
  HP22 . . . . .88 F4
Wingrave Rd
  Aston Abbotts HP22 . . . . . . .88 E4
  Long Marston HP23 . . . . . .104 D1
  Tring HP23 . . . . .119 B5
Winkers Cl SL9 . . . . .177 F2
Winkers La SL9 . . . . .177 F3
Winkfield La SL4 . . . . .209 A1
Winkfield Rd SL4 . . . . .209 E2
Winnock Rd UB7 . . . . .208 D5
Winsford Hill MK4 . . . . .46 A3
Winslow CE Comb Sch
  MK18 . . . . .66 A5
Winslow Field HP16 . . . . . .151 F8
Winslow Gdns HP13 . . . . . .174 A7
Winslow Rd
  Granborough MK18 . . . . . . .75 F7
  Great Horwood MK17 . . . . . .54 F1
  Little Horwood MK17 . . . . . .55 D1
  Nash MK17 . . . . .55 C8
  Swanbourne MK17 . . . . .66 F3
  Winslow HP22 . . . . .89 B3
Winston Cl SL6 . . . . .202 A8
Winston Gdns HP4 . . . . . . .134 F4
Winston Ho HP11 . . . . .174 A4
Winstone Cl HP6 . . . . .154 B5
Winter Cl 🟫 SL7 . . . . .183 E2
Winter Hill SL6 . . . . .184 C1
Winter Hill Rd SL6 . . . . . . .195 A4
Winterburn MK13 . . . . .34 B5
Winters Way HP15 . . . . . . .163 B7
Winterton Dr HP21 . . . . . . .115 E4
Wintoun Path SL2 . . . . .197 E1
Winvale SL1 . . . . .205 E3
Winwood Slough SL2 . . . . . .206 C2
  Windsor SL4 . . . . .209 F6
Winwood Cl MK19 . . . . .31 E5
Winwood Dr HP22 . . . . .85 A5
Wise La UB7 . . . . .208 F4
Wisewood Rd MK4,MK5 . . . . .45 E4
Wishart Gn MK7 . . . . .48 E5
Wisley Ave MK13 . . . . .34 D3
Wistmans MK6 . . . . .46 A4
Witan Cl HP21 . . . . .115 D3
Witan Gate MK9 . . . . .34 D1
Witchell HP22 . . . . .131 B4
Witham Cl MK3 . . . . .46 D1
Witham Way HP21 . . . . . . .115 C4
Witheridge La HP9,HP10 . . .175 E7
Withey Cl SL4 . . . . .209 E6
Withington MK10 . . . . .34 A5
Withycombe MK4 . . . . .46 E3
Withycroft SL3 . . . . .206 F7
Wittington Cotts SL7 . . . . .193 D6
Wittmills Oak MK18 . . . . . . .41 E1
Witton Ho WD3 . . . . .167 D4
Wivelsfield LU6 . . . . .92 E6
Wixon Path HP19 . . . . .115 A8
Woad La MK14 . . . . .34 E8
Woburn Ave SL6 . . . . .33 C6
Woburn Cl LU7 . . . . .80 E6
Woburn La MK17 . . . . .49 E4
Woburn Lower Sch MK17 . . . .60 F7
Woburn Rd
  Aspley Heath MK17 . . . . . . .49 C2
  Little Brickhill MK17 . . . . . . .59 E6
  Sheeplane MK17,LU7 . . . . . .60 C1
Woburn Sands Rd MK17 . . . .48 D3
Woburn Sands Sta MK17 . . . .49 A5
Wodehouse Wlk MK16 . . . . . .22 A5
Wolf La SL4 . . . . .209 E4
Wolfscote La MK4 . . . . .46 B3
Wolsey Gdns MK13 . . . . .34 A4
Wolstan Cl UB9 . . . . .190 A1
Wolston Mdw MK10 . . . . . . .35 E1
Wolverton Rd
  Castlethorpe MK19 . . . . . . .20 B5
  Milton Keynes,Gifford Park
  MK16 . . . . .21 E2
  Milton Keynes,Stony Stratford
  MK11 . . . . .32 E6
  Milton Keynes,Wolverton
  MK12,MK19 . . . . .33 B8
  Newport Pagnell MK16 . . . . .21 F2
  Sherington MK19 . . . . .33 B7
Wooburn Common Rd
  HP10,SL1 . . . . .186 A4
Wooburn Grange HP10 . . . .185 D3
Wooburn Green La HP9 . . . .186 A8

Wooburn Manor Pk
  HP10 . . . . .185 E5
Wooburn Mead HP10 . . . . . .185 E6
Wooburn Mews HP10 . . . . . .185 E5
Wooburn Town HP10 . . . . . .185 D4
Wood Cl SL4 . . . . .210 C3
Wood End
  Little Horwood MK17 . . . . . .55 E2
  Nash MK17 . . . . .55 C8
Wood End Cl SL2 . . . . .187 D1
Wood End Fst Sch MK17 . . . .34 D8
Wood End La MK16 . . . . .23 E1
Wood La
  Aspley Guise MK17 . . . . . . .49 D4
  Iver SL0 . . . . .207 C8
  Milton Keynes MK14 . . . . . .34 E8
  Slough SL1 . . . . .205 A4
  South Heath HP16 . . . . . . .152 E8
  Tingewick MK18 . . . . .51 B6
  Weston Underwood MK46 . . . .6 A2
Wood Land Cl
  Flackwell Heath HP10 . . . . .173 F1
  Iver Heath SL0 . . . . .200 B2
Wood Pond Cl HP9 . . . . . . .176 C4
Wood Rd MK43 . . . . .3 F7
Wood St
  Milton Keynes MK13 . . . . . .33 F7
  Waddesdon HP18 . . . . .99 A7
  Woburn Sands MK17 . . . . . .49 B4
Wood View Cotts HP5 . . . . .144 A3
Wood Way HP10 . . . . .174 F1
Woodall Cl MK10 . . . . .35 E3
Woodbank HP27 . . . . .149 C5
Woodbank Ave SL9 . . . . . . .188 D5
Woodbank Dr HP8 . . . . .177 D7
Woodbine Cl HP27 . . . . . . .138 E5
Woodbine Cotts SL3 . . . . . .188 D8
Woodbridge Ho UB8 . . . . . .201 C5
Woodbridge 🟦 SL8 . . . . . . .185 C3
Woodchester Pk HP9 . . . . . .175 C6
Woodcock Ave HP14 . . . . . .161 B8
Woodcote SL6 . . . . .202 D6
Woodcote Cl HP13 . . . . .161 D2
Woodcote Lawns HP5 . . . . .144 A4
Woodcroft Rd HP5 . . . . . . .144 D3
Woodfield HP27 . . . . .149 D6
Woodfield Dr SL6 . . . . .202 A6
Woodfield Pk HP6 . . . . .154 B3
Woodfield Rd HP27 . . . . . . .139 C4
Woodford Cl HP19 . . . . .115 B7
Woodford Way SL2 . . . . . . .198 A2
Woodhall Cl UB8 . . . . .201 D7
Woodhill Ave SL9 . . . . .189 A5
Woodhill Ct
  Amersham HP6 . . . . .154 D4
  Gerrards Cross SL9 . . . . . . .188 E4
Woodhouse Ct MK14 . . . . . . .34 D6
Woodhurst Dr UB9 . . . . . . .189 F6
Woodhurst Rd SL6 . . . . . . .196 B1
Woodhurst S SL6 . . . . .196 C1
Woodland Ave
  Leighton Buzzard LU7 . . . . . .70 F2
  Slough SL3 . . . . .205 D6
  Windsor SL4 . . . . .209 F3
Woodland Cl
  High Wycombe HP12 . . . . .172 C6
  Maidenhead SL6 . . . . .183 E4
  Tring HP23 . . . . .118 F2
Woodland Glade SL2 . . . . . .187 D1
Woodland La WD3 . . . . .167 D6
Woodland Pl WD3 . . . . .167 F5
Woodland Rd WD3 . . . . .178 D5
Woodland View
  Chesham HP5 . . . . .154 D6
  Milton Keynes MK12 . . . . . .33 D5
Woodland Way
  Marlow SL7 . . . . .183 E4
  Woburn Sands MK17 . . . . . .49 B4
Woodlands SL6 . . . . .188 F5
Woodlands Ave HP4 . . . . . .135 C3
Woodlands Bsns Pk
  SL6 . . . . .202 A2
Woodlands Cl
  Buckingham MK18 . . . . .41 E2
  Gerrards Cross SL9 . . . . . . .189 A5
  Holmer Green HP15 . . . . . .163 C6
Woodlands Cotts 🟫
  SL6 . . . . .198 C2
Woodlands Cres MK18 . . . . .41 D2
Woodlands Dr
  Beaconsfield HP9 . . . . .175 C4
  Walter's Ash HP14 . . . . . . .161 C8
Woodlands Farm SL6 . . . . . .195 C6
Woodlands Glade HP9 . . . . .175 C4
Woodlands Hill HP9 . . . . . . .186 E5
Woodlands Park Ave
  SL6 . . . . .202 A2
Woodlands Park Prim Sch
  SL6 . . . . .202 A1
Woodlands Park Rd
  SL6 . . . . .202 A3
Woodlands The
  Amersham HP6 . . . . .154 C4
  Tylers Green HP10 . . . . . . .162 F3
Woodlands View HP13 . . . . .174 A7
Woodlane Cl HP10 . . . . .173 F1
Woodlane Gdns HP10 . . . . . .174 A2
Woodley Ct HP7 . . . . .165 D8
Woodley Headland MK6 . . . .47 C2
Woodley Hill HP5 . . . . .154 D5
Woodman Cl LU7 . . . . .79 F3
Woodmans Cl MK19 . . . . . . .31 E4
Woodmans Croft HP19 . . . . .115 A8
Woodmoor End SL6 . . . . . . .196 B7
Woodpecker Rd OX25 . . . . . .94 F2
Woodruff Cl MK14 . . . . .34 E4
Woodrush Cl MK6 . . . . .47 B4
Woods La NN12 . . . . .18 E3

Woods Pl [IC] Tring HP23 ..119 A3
Wendover HP22 ....131 B4
Woodside
 Aspley Guise MK17 ......49 D3
 Eaton Bray LU6 ....92 E6
 Flackwell Heath HP10 ..185 C6
 Milton Keynes MK11 ....32 E6
Woodside Ave
 Amersham HP6 ....154 D3
 Beaconsfield HP9 ......175 C4
 Flackwell Heath HP10 ..185 C7
Woodside Cl
 Amersham HP6 ....154 D1
 Beaconsfield HP9 ......175 C3
 Chalfont St Peter SL9 ..177 E1
 Loudwater HP11 ....174 B2
Woodside Hill SL9 .....177 E1
Woodside Jun Sch HP6 .154 E1
Woodside Rd
 Amersham HP6 ....154 D1
 Beaconsfield HP9 ......175 C3
 High Wycombe HP13 ....174 A8
Woodside Way
 Leighton Buzzard LU7 ...80 D6
 Tylers Green HP10 .....174 C8
Woodspring Ct MK10 ....35 F1
Woodstock Ave SL3 ....206 D2
Woodstock Cl
 Aylesbury HP21 ....116 B6
 Maidenhead SL6 ....195 F1
Woodstock Ct MK13 .....34 B7
Woodstock Dr UB10 ....201 F8
Woodview Cl HP12 .....161 B2
Woodview Dr HP16 .....150 C5
Woodville OX39 ....147 C5
Woodville Cres NN12 ...18 E6
Woodward Ho [4] MK2 ..58 C8
Woodward Pl MK8 ......34 A1
Woodway HP27 ....149 D6
Woodways HP17 ....127 A6
Woodwicks WD3 ....178 D5
Woollerton Cres HP22 .131 D5
Woollerton Ct HP27 ....139 B4
Woolmans
 Fulliers Slade MK11 .....33 A4
 Milton Keynes MK11 ....33 A4
Woolrich Gdns MK11 ....32 E5
Wooster Rd HP9 ....175 D4

Wootton Dr HP10 ....185 E8
Wootton Gn OX27 ....72 E6
Wootton La HP17 ....113 E1
Wootton Way SL6 ......202 C6
Worcester Cl
 Maidenhead SL6 ....202 D3
 Newport Pagnell MK16 ...22 A3
Worcester Gdns SL1 ...205 D4
Worcester Ho MK3 ......46 F2
Worcester Rd UB8 .....208 D8
Wordsworth Ave MK16 ...22 A4
Wordsworth Dr MK3 ....58 A7
Wordsworth Rd
 High Wycombe HP11 ....173 A5
 Slough SL2 ....197 D1
Wordsworth Way UB7 ..208 E2
World's End La HP22 ...130 F8
Worminghall Rd
 Ickford HP18 ....123 F4
 Oakley HP18 ....109 D4
Wormsley Cres HP14 ..158 C4
Wornal Pk HP18 ....123 C8
Worple The TW19 ......211 F1
Worrelle Ave MK10 ......36 A3
Worster Rd SL6 ....195 E6
Worthies The HP7 .....165 B7
Worthington Rd LU6 ....93 F8
Wotton End HP18 ....96 C7
Wotton Path HP21 .....115 E3
Wotton Rd HP18 ....97 E1
Wr Twr Cl UB8 ....201 E7
Wray Ct MK4 ....46 A2
Wraysbury Prim Sch
 TW19 ....211 E1
Wraysbury Sta TW19 ..212 A1
Wren Cl MK18 ....52 F7
Wren Ct SL3 ....207 A3
Wren Dr UB7 ....208 D3
Wren Path HP19 ....114 F8
Wren Rd HP16 ....151 C5
Wren Vale HP13 ....173 A8
Wren Wlk LU6 ....92 E4
Wrens Pk MK10 ....36 B2
Wrensfield SL7 ....183 C2
Wright SL4 ....209 C4
Wright Sq SL4 ....209 C4
Wright Way SL4 ....209 C4
Wright's La HP16 .....151 C5

Wrights Cl HP14 ....171 B5
Wrights Yd HP16 ....152 A7
Wroxton Ct MK4 ....45 F2
Wyatt Cl HP13 ....172 F8
Wyatt Rd SL4 ....209 D4
Wyatt's Covert Cvn Site
 UB9 ....189 F7
Wyatt's Rd WD3 ....167 F5
Wychwood HP16 ....152 B4
Wychwood Gdns HP12 .172 C6
Wychwood Rise HP16 ..152 B4
Wyclands Ho HP12 ....161 B2
Wycombe Abbey Sch
 HP11 ....173 A6
Wycombe Cl HP21 .....116 B4
Wycombe End HP9 .....175 E1
Wycombe General Hospl
 HP11 ....173 A6
Wycombe High Sch
 HP11 ....172 F4
Wycombe Ind Mall
 HP11 ....172 F7
Wycombe La HP10 .....185 E7
Wycombe Mus* HP13 ..173 B7
Wycombe Rd
 Beacon's Bottom HP14 ..159 D3
 Holmer Green HP15 ...163 B6
 Lacey Green HP14 .....149 B4
 Marlow SL7 ....183 E4
 Marlow Bottom SL7 ...183 E6
 Prestwood HP15 ......151 C5
Wycombe Ret Pk HP11 .173 F4
Wycombe View HP10 ...174 A2
Wye Cl Aylesbury HP21 .115 C5
 Milton Keynes MK3 .....46 E1
Wye Ct [2] SL8 ....185 A3
Wye Est HP11 ....173 E5
Wye Gdns HP21 ....172 D8
Wye Rd HP10 ....185 D8
Wye Valley Sch The
 SL8 ....185 B4
Wykeham Gate HP17 ..126 F5
Wykeham Rise OX39 ..147 D6
Wykeham Way HP17 ...126 F6
Wykeridge Cl HP5 .....144 B4
Wylands Rd SL3 ......207 A4
Wylie End MK13 ....34 A7
Wymering Rd HP21 ...116 C6

Wymers Cl SL1 ....197 B3
Wymers Wood Rd SL1 .197 A3
Wymondham MK10 ......36 B1
Wynbury Dr HP13 .....162 E1
Wyndale Cl RG9 ....191 E1
Wyndham Ave MK13 ...161 F2
Wyndham Cres SL1 ...197 B3
Wyness Ave MK17 ......59 E5
Wynford Gn HP21 .....115 F6
Wyngates LU7 ....80 E5
Wyngrave Pl HP9 .....175 C5
Wynn Gr HP15 ....163 B3
Wynne-Jones Ctr HP21 .115 F8
Wynnstay Gdns SL7 ...183 E5
Wynnswick Rd HP9 ...176 C5
Wynyard Ct MK6 ....46 E7
Wyre Cl HP17 ....127 A5
Wyvern Fst Sch MK12 ...33 C6
Wyvern Way UB8 ......201 C4

Y

Yalts Brow MK4 ....46 B2
Yardley Ave LU7 ......105 D4
Yardley Gn HP20 ......101 F2
Yardley Gobion CE Prim Sch
 NN12 ....18 E6
Yardley Hastings Prim Sch
 NN7 ....1 A7
Yardley Rd
 Cosgrove MK19 ....19 D2
 Olney MK46 ....6 E6
 Potterspury NN12 ......18 F4
Yarmouth Rd SL1 .....205 C6
Yarrow Pl MK14 ....34 E4
Yarrowside HP7 ....166 B7
Ye Meads SL6 ....203 E5
Ye Meads Cotts SL6 ..203 E5
Ye Meads Ho SL6 .....203 E5
Yeates Cl Thame OX9 .125 F1
 Winslow MK18 ....65 F4
Yeats Cl MK16 ....21 F5
Yeomans Cl NN13 ......38 A8
Yeomans Dr MK14 ......22 B1
Yeovil Ent Ctr SL1 ....204 F8
Yeovil Rd SL1 ....204 E8
Yew Ave UB7 ....208 E6

Yew Tree Cl
 Beaconsfield HP9 ......175 F1
 Botley HP5 ....145 A1
 Eaton Bray LU6 ....92 F5
 Maidenhead SL6 ......202 E8
 Newton Longville MK17 ...57 C3
 Stoke Mandeville HP22 .116 A1
Yew Tree Dr
 Bovingdon HP3 ....146 B3
 Hazlemere HP15 ......162 F6
Yew Tree Rd Slough SL1 .206 A3
 Uxbridge UB10 ....201 F4
Yew Wlk HP15 ....163 A3
Yewtree Cl LU7 ....105 E5
Yiewsley Ct UB7 ......208 E5
Yolsum Cl HP17 ......126 E6
Yonder Slade MK18 ....52 D6
York Ave Slough SL1 ..205 C7
 Windsor SL4 ....210 B5
York Cl HP7 ....165 F8
York Ct [3] LU7 ....80 F7
York Ho
 High Wycombe HP13 ...173 F8
 Milton Keynes MK3 .....57 E7
York Pl HP21 ....115 D7
York Rd Henley-on-T RG9 .191 D2
 Maidenhead SL6 ......203 A7
 Marlow SL7 ....183 D2
 Milton Keynes MK11 ....32 D5
 Uxbridge UB8 ....201 D5
 Windsor SL4 ....210 B5
York Way HP12 ....172 E4
Yorke Cl HP22 ....117 E5
Youens Rd HP12 .....172 C5
Young Cl HP21 ....116 A6

Z

Zealand Ave UB7 .....213 E7
Zetland Ct SL6 ....203 B8
Zodiac Bsns Pk UB8 ..208 D7

Addresses

Name and Address	Telephone	Page	Grid reference

Name and Address	Telephone	Page	Grid reference

NG	NH	NJ	NK
NM	NN	NO	NP
NR	NS	NT	NU
NX	NY	NZ	
SC	SD	SE	TA
SH	SJ	SK	TF	TG
SM	SN	SO	SP	TL	TM
SR	SS	ST	SU	TQ	TR
SW	SX	SY	SZ	TV

Any feature in this atlas can be given a unique reference to help you find the same feature on other Ordnance Survey maps of the area, or to help someone else locate you if they do not have a Street Atlas.

The grid squares in this atlas match the Ordnance Survey National Grid and are at 500 metre intervals. The small figures at the bottom and sides of every other grid line are the National Grid kilometre values (**00** to **99** km) and are repeated across the country every 100 km (see left).

To give a unique National Grid reference you need to locate where in the country you are. The country is divided into 100 km squares with each square given a unique two-letter reference. Use the administrative map to determine in which 100 km square a particular page of this atlas falls.

The bold letters and numbers between each grid line (**A** to **F**, **1** to **8**) are for use within a specific Street Atlas only, and when used with the page number, are a convenient way of referencing these grid squares.

Example *The railway bridge over DARLEY GREEN RD in grid square B1*

Step 1: Identify the two-letter reference, in this example the page is in **SP**

Step 2: Identify the 1 km square in which the railway bridge falls. Use the figures in the southwest corner of this square: Eastings **17**, Northings **74**. This gives a unique reference: **SP 17 74**, accurate to 1 km.

Step 3: To give a more precise reference accurate to 100 m you need to estimate how many tenths along and how many tenths up this 1 km square the feature is (to help with this the 1 km square is divided into four 500 m squares). This makes the bridge about **8** tenths along and about **1** tenth up from the southwest corner.

This gives a unique reference: **SP 178 741**, accurate to 100 m.

Eastings (read from left to right along the bottom) come before Northings (read from bottom to top). If you have trouble remembering say to yourself "Along the hall, THEN up the stairs"!

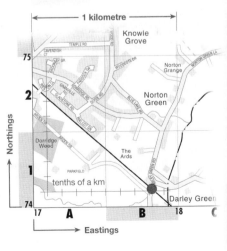

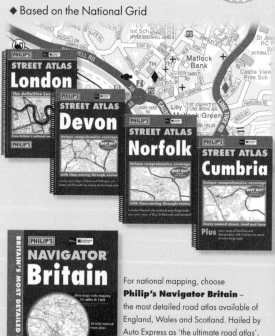